FOUNDATIONS OF CULTURE

RELIGIOUS CONSCIOUSNESS

By the same author

Caste, Class and Occupation
(4th Ed.)

The Scheduled Tribes
(3rd Ed.)

Culture And Society
(Out of print)

Occidental Civilization

Indian Costume
(Out of print)

Race Relations in Negro Africa
(Out of print)

Indian Sadhus
(2nd Ed.)

Family and Kin in Indo-European Culture
(2nd Ed.)

Bharatanatya and Its Costume

Vidyas
(Out of print)

The Mahadev Kolis
(2nd impression)

Sexual Behaviour of the American Female

After a Century and a Quarter

Gods and Men

Anthropo-Sociological Papers

Cities and Civilization

Anatomy of a Rururban Community

FOUNDATIONS OF CULTURE

RELIGIOUS CONSCIOUSNESS

G. S. GHURYE

POPULAR PRAKASHAN
BOMBAY : 1965

First Published June 1965
Jesta Saka 1887

Printed by D. D. Karkaria at Leaders Press Pvt. Ltd., 108, Motisha Lane, Mazagon, Bombay 10 and published by G. R. Bhatkal for Popular Prakashan, 35-C, Tardeo Road, Bombay 34

PREFACE

The genesis of this book lies in my duties as a lecturer to the students preparing for their M.A. examination of Bombay University with Sociology as their subject between 1924 and 1951. Study of civilization and of the principal specimens of civilization formed a part of the syllabus prescribed for that examination; and I used to cover that in my lectures every alternate year. My lectures were accompanied by illustrations with the help of pictures from various books appropriately chosen. They were much liked by many students. Some of the subject-matter of the lectures, including the few generalizations, like acceleration of the civilizational process during the course of civilization or the cumulative nature of culture, which can be illustrated only with the help of a large number of books at a time, had to be dealt without the aid of illustrations. On the cumulative nature of culture, however, once or twice I lectured to a select audience. One such occasion, in 1944 I think, was when I illustrated the generalization to the members of the Silver Fish Club at one of the more famous of Bombay's booksellers.

When the Indian Institute for Educational and Cultural Cooperation was started in Bombay, I presented to its management my ideas of illustrating the course of civilization and the principal civilizations by means of either three-dimensional or flat-pictorial representations. As the latter course was very much the cheaper one, I was asked to prepare a sketch of the scheme. The outline scheme having been approved, the Institute published it in 1947 as a pamphlet entitled *Museum, Illustrating Cultural History of Mankind.* It failed to elicit any response from or to make any appeal to educational authorities.

In 1954 or 1955, the University authorities asked the Heads of their Post-graduate Departments to submit schemes for immediate intensification and expansion of the studies under their charge. As the then Head of the Department of Sociology I submitted my scheme of a museum of cultural history, in a very brief sketch, along with my recommendation for the addition of one member to the Department to be styled Reader in Anthropology. The University approved of the whole scheme and forwarded it, as a part of its expansional programme to the University Grants Commission for approval and for the grant of the requisite funds. I heard nothing further in the matter till I retired in March, 1959.

The sketch of the proposal for a museum of cultural history did not indicate the themes, which were to form the centre of the whole plan. They have to be twofold, bio-physical and socio-cultural. The bio-physical part, evolution of man and his differentiation in the various ethnic stocks, is there in various books in photographs and pictures and also in representations and models in many of the famous museums of the world. The socio-cultural part is bound to be much more subjective and is likely to differ in particulars according to the author's equipment and attitude. My ideas on the subject of the central facts, or the foundations, of culture have centred round five categories. They are : (1) Religious Consciousness ; (2) Conscience ; (3) Justice ; (4) Free Pursuit of Knowledge and Free Expression ; and (5) Toleration.

On my retirement from the University Department of Sociology I had decided to write a book or books embodying my findings on these foundations of culture. So far, owing to other commitments, I have been able to complete only this book on Religious Consciousness. I have dealt with the three oldest and the longest specimens of religious consciousness : Mesopotamian, Egyptian, and Indian (Hindu).

University Campus
Bombay
3*rd March*, 1965

G. S. GHURYE

CONTENTS

		Page
	Preface	v
I	Mesopotamian	1
II	Egyptian–I	20
III	Egyptian–II	49
IV	Egyptian–III	69
V	Hindu Cosmology and Cosmography	98
VI	Hindu View of Human Personality	129
VII	Hindu View of Life After Death	161
VIII	Hindu View of the Godhead (First Phase)	191
IX	Hindu View of the Godhead (Second Phase)	218
X	Hindu View of the Godhead (Third Phase)	245
XI	Hindu Religious Living and its Goal	257
XII	The Mesopotamian Shrine	291
XIII	The Egyptian Shrine	296
XIV	The Hindu Shrine	312
	References	357
	Index	375

CHAPTER I

MESOPOTAMIAN

RELIGIOUS consciousness manifested itself in the work of man almost at the dawn of history, on the threshold of civilization. Death confronting him, and he seeing his dear and near ones no longer alive, conspired to urge man to invent and promulgate some techniques of the disposal of the dead. And they reveal, however constructionally, that man as early as 30,000 years ago conceived of death as ushering in another state or mode of human or spirit existence. Whether he postulated or formed the concept of some entity endowed with supreme power to intervene either in the procedure of life beyond death or in the affairs of the mundane live existence at that time is, from the nature of the evidence, not ascertainable. But the urges of civilization and the response to them made by Mesopotamian man in prehistoric times and the modern archaeologist's spade working in their remains have revealed that man must have formed the notion of such an entity at least by 4000 B.C. By 3500 B.C. Mesopotamian man would seem to have begun to put up structures either to accommodate the images of his gods and to pray in or simply to offer his prayers from them.

The building at Erech (Uruk), designated by scholars as the 'White Temple', and the earliest ziggurat at Ur with the temple on the high platform, go back to before 3000 B.C. And the plan of the 'White Temple' remains the persistent form of Mesopotamian temples for a long long time. At Ubaid, the suburb of Ur, existed, in the reign of a named monarch of the First Dynasty of Ur, a superb ziggurat temple which has been almost fully reconstructed by Woolley and Gadd. The king must have lived about 2800 B.C.[1] We do not know the names of the gods in whose dedication the earlier temples at Erech and even at Eridu were raised. But in the case of the Ubaid temple, which is a little later than these, we know from the contemporary inscription that it was consecrated to the goddess Ninkhursag.[2]

Ninkhursag does not figure in Mesopotamian mythology as the supreme god, nor, even though a major deity, as controlling a significant field of activity. She is, however, under the name of Ki, a member of the early triad of deities. S. N. Kramer thinks that in an earlier day this goddess was of even higher rank.[3] The same deity Ki or mother-earth becomes in her male aspect the male deity Enki or later Ea, and turns the Mesopotamian triad into a tetrad.[4] As Stephen Langdon[5] stated years ago four deities were, from the earliest times, at the head of the Sumerian pantheon which at its maximum was four thousand strong. Three of them, Anu or An, Enlil or Bel, and Ea or Enki, had each one associated with him a female companion. Enlil had his consort Ninlil and Enki his Ninki or Ninkhursag or Damkina. The female deity closely associated with Anu is, however, the "virgin goddess" Innini or Inanna, better known in her Semitic garb of Ishtar. "On the theory that every deity must have a female associate," Anu was given a consort known either as Antum or Anatum. But as Antum she is a shadowy figure and in actuality passed her designation to Ishtar to be her title as the "lady of battle".[6]

The "unmarried mother goddess" Nintud, known later as *Belit ilani*, "Queen of the Gods", or Nintu, meaning "the lady who gives birth", reliefs showing her as a woman suckling a child, "other children tucked away in her dress" peeping on, formed the fourth member of the tetrad. She is also called Ninmah "the exalted queen" or simply Makh, "the Supreme goddess". Ninkhursag is one of the fortyone names assigned to her in the theological lists and means "queen of the mountain" or "queen of the earth".

Anu was specifically worshipped at Erech where Innini as his consort had her shrine too. And in later times Innini-Inanna-Ishtar completely overshadowed her consort Anu. It was, however, as Ninkhursag, whose unique temple of very early date starts our series of shrines, that independent worship of mother-goddess appears to have begun in Mesopotamia, which, in the present state of our knowledge, forms the starting centre of the cult of mother-cum-lover-cum-martial goddess.[7]

As Ninkhursag, and therefore in the earliest representation, she is the giver of life and of milk as the source of life. The procession of fine cattle, and the milking dairying scene picturesquely fixed on the exterior wall of her Ubaid temple, emphasized her role as the giver of milk. And hardly any of the early rulers of southern Mesopotamia failed to include among his titles "fed with the holy milk of Ninkhursag".[8] A temple dedicated to this goddess under this particular name is also attested from Nippur which for long remained the most sacred city of Mesopotamia.[9]

In mythology she is represented in an ambivalent attitude and relation towards Enki. She refuses his advances at first but afterwards accepts him as her mate and the consequence is a daughter, born to her, known as the goddess Ninsar or Ninmu. Enki soon leaves Ninkhursag and wanders forth. Later finding Ninsar in her youth and attracted by her he mates with her and leaves her. She gives birth to a daughter named Ninkurra. He apparently repeats his performance with her, too, and another goddess by name Uttu is the consequence. Ninkhursag now warns her great-grand-daughter against Enki so that when the latter desires to mate with Uttu, she demands of him nothing short of marriage. The wily god agrees and brings the presents which are preliminaries of marriage but manages to get Uttu thoroughly drunk before the marriage rites are gone through and cohabits with her in that condition. Ninkhursag burning with hatred curses Enki but relenting afterwards goes through the pangs of delivery seven or eight times to create creatures that could take away the evil effects of her curse. In another tale she, under her title of Ninmah, is shown to be drunk along with Enki.[10]

The creator-goddess, either as Ninkhursag, Aruru or Mama or Mami, tended to be associated with Enlil, too, as her husband. Enlil is said to have raped Ninlil, who is then partnered with him as his consort. But the association of the creator-goddess with Enlil is consistently carried out, keeping her virginal character unimpaired. The cult of virgin wife or virgin mistress was principally centred near Erech, which was itself first the centre of Anu-worship and later of Innini-Ishtar.

The goddess as Ninkhursag is stated to have helped the trio of the major gods of Mesopotamia, viz., Anu, Enlil and Enki, in the creation of mankind at the beginning of the world.[11] As already mentioned, in this name scenes of milking and dairy-plenty were associated with her ; and in another name, Nintu or Nintud, she was represented as suckling a child with other children peeping through and embryos surrounding her.[12] About five hundred years later, on seals of Sargonid era, she figures as Ishtar, in the company of Shamash, the sun-god, in her martial aspect and is shown in the act of trampling on fallen enemies. About the same time or perhaps a century or so earlier, she appears in this form in a sculpture on the rocks in the Zagros range of mountains in her full martial dress dragging and trampling the enemies of the king favoured by her.

In Assyrian times she was believed to be marching before the Assyrian armies and on one occasion she is said to have "granted a theophany of herself to the whole army". A little earlier, between about 1400 B.C. and 1300 B.C., Ishtar of the Assyrian city of Nineveh, having had a high reputation for conferring favours, was twice sent to Egypt by a friendly king.[13]

The third aspect of the original mother-goddess is her role as the goddess of sexual love in which aspect her derivation from or her identification with Venus comes out the most.[14] Woolley, who describes Ishtar as the goddess of love, mentions Erech as "the seat of the licentious worship of Ishtar" and refers to the lower grades of temple-prostitutes specifically associated with it.[15]

The mother-goddess was worshipped also under other names as Anuit, Inanna, Nina and Nana.[16] The last name is the most interesting item for students of Indian religious and social history. I may take this opportunity to draw the attention of Indologists and anthropologists to the recurrence of the mother-goddess under this name. That Nana had a temple to herself at Erech is clear from a reference to her statue, said to have been carried away by the Elamites, perhaps about 2000 B.C., met with in an inscription of the Assyrian king Ashurbanipal. About 640 B.C. he is recorded to have brought back the statue from Susa and reinstalled it in her city, Erech. According to Morris Jastrow, it is in connection with her cult that obscene rites are known to have been a part of the worship. Nana, thereafter, does not figure anywhere in the known records.[17]

Eduard Meyer concluded that the pure Zoroastrianism of the Iranians was reacted upon by "the gorgeous cult of the gods of civilization (especially of Babylon)" bringing back into popular focus "the old figures of the Aryan folk-religion". In particular "the goddess of springs and streams (of the Oxus in particular) and of all fertility—*Ardvisura Anahita, Anaitis*" was "endowed with the form of the Babylonian Ishtar and Belit". She was "depicted as a beautiful and strong woman, with prominent breasts, a golden crown of stars and golden raiment". She was "worshipped as the goddess of generation and all sexual life ; and religious prostitution is transferred to her service." The cult of the goddess culminated in the reign of Artaxerxes II, 404 to 359 B.C., who "first erected statues to Anaitis" in many of the great cities. He and his son and successor both invoked her along with Mithra in their inscriptions.

It is far and distant place and time that next impress us with her presence. On the coins of the Indo-Scythians, Kushan, kings of the Panjab and Sindh of the first century before and after Christ, one of the deities mentioned and stamped is Nana.[18] The implications of this fact for the history or genesis of the esoteric and decidedly orgiastic sect called Śāktas in India in the mediaeval and post-mediaeval times—a sect which even now may not be extinct—are evident.

Inspite of the composite nature of the mother-goddess or rather the later goddess Ishtar and the licentiousness associated with her cult, one of the prayers addressed to her perhaps gives us the finest and highest religious flowering of the Mesopotamian mind. She is identified with Anu as the leader-god and is said to rule the heavens and control mankind with Enlil as her counsellor. Not only are well-being and peace associated with her but even justice and goodness are hers. The suppliant finally asks for her pity on him and for the acceptance of his prayer. According to S. Langdon, in the religious scenes depicted on seals "in all periods", she is represented as "standing in prayer beside humans and interceding with a god on their behalf". She "consistently" represented "divine mercy and compassion".[19]

To take up the threads of the story of religious consciousness in ancient Mesopotamia it is necessary to mention the fact that of the four leader-gods, Ea or Enki of Eridu and Enlil, the god of Nippur, are both represented in mythology as the sons of Anu.[20] There were two other gods, who, though not as important as the four mentioned so far, were the gods of two powerful cities. Sin or Nannar ruled at the famous centre of Ur, and Babbar, Utu or Shamash was worshipped at Larsa and Sippar. The former is the moon-god and the latter the sun-god. In later times the complete supersession of the moon-god by the sun-god under the name of Marduk, who in mythology appears as the son of Ea, reflects the change in social values and organization, which the highest of commercial civilizations that flourished before the modern era had called forth. Shamash, the sun-god, was pre-eminently associated with the institution of justice. And appropriately the greatest of ancient lawgivers, Hammurabi, the Semite, portrayed himself as receiving his famous code of laws from the sun-god.[21] Post-Hammurabi Mesopotamian civilization had so much of the complex machinery necessary for international commerce and Babylon was so much a world's emporium that it can without any exaggeration be described as the highest commercial civilization before the modern era.[22]

I may support this appraisal of the changing godhead with the considered opinion of Thorkild Jacobsen regarding the rise of the idea "that justice was something to which man had a right", that it "began slowly to take form", and that "in the second millennium—appropriately the millennium of the famous Code of Hammurabi—justice as right rather than justice as favour seems to have become the general conception".[23]

The six Mesopotamian gods were anthropomorphic and their statues do not appear to have borne any feature offending or distorting their human aspect. Among the lesser numerous gods, of course, there were some at least who were theriomorphic. Only three of these gods are known to have had special insignia showing their leader-status. And they were Anu, Enlil and Shamash, the sun-god, but not Enki, the third member of the early triad. Whereas Anu had the sceptre, the ring, the crown, the head-band and the shepherd's staff, manifest emblems of royalty and ruling power, Enlil and Shamash carry in their hand the rod and ring.[24] Later supremacy of the sun-god under the name and form of Marduk was thus inherent in his earlier counterpart Shamash and was transferred to him as the supreme ruler.

At this stage two features of theological theorizing and of divine and/or human religious expression have to be noted not only because of their importance for a complete understanding of the religious consciousness and experience of the Mesopotamians but also because of their analogues in a not very distant future nor a very distant land but in an utterly different racial and linguistic stock, among the Vedic Aryans of India between about 1800 to 1200 B.C. First, epithets like "ruler of gods", "father", are applied both to Anu and Enlil, sometimes even to Enki, and Nannar and later to Marduk in full measure.[25] Second, one god could have partial identity with many other gods and share in their natures and abilities. One form of this partial identity is that a particular god, especially Marduk, could be conceived as, say, Enlil when the question was of ruling, and simultaneously could be called Sin, the moon-god, in the act of illumining the night. Marduk, in particular, after Hammurabi's time became the object of such assimilation deliberately carried out by the theologians or rather theo-politicians. Saggs commenting on this deliberate assimilation of Marduk with many of the other gods of the pantheon does not see any force in the contention of the earlier scholars that it indicated a monotheistic tendency. He is convinced that a henotheistic tendency is the most that should be postulated.[26]

Almost a century ago, early in the history of the modern study of the 'Vedas' of India, Max Müller came to the conclusion that the religion of the Vedic Aryans had to be described as henotheism or kathenotheism. The essential trait of this complex of religion was according to him the fact that polytheism was mixed with another attitude towards the many gods, ascribing to many, single one at a time, the attributes of the overlord of them all or of the supreme godhead. A. B. Keith, half a century after Max Müller, at a time when the modern study of the 'Vedas' was at its culmination, more or less endorsed the same view of the religion of the Vedic Aryans.[27] Thus in India the Aryans would have to be considered as having arrived at a complex of religious beliefs and attitude towards godhead more or less similar to that of the Mesopotamians, about a century or two later than the latter.

But this deduction I think is not correct. For I see great difference in the actually worded attitudes and beliefs of the people and the postulated attributes of the deity in the two sets of texts.

Jastrow[28] describes the hymns in honour of the sub-god Shamash as being "among the finest specimens of Babylonian and Assyrian literature". They speak of him as "the benefactor of mankind", shedding light and warmth everywhere. His rays ripen the produce of the fields. He is said to be the source of all blessings and prosperity. He presides over the dispensation of justice and as such is the judge, the "giver of all decisions", rewarding the virtuous and punishing the wicked. He is also spoken of as the mighty warrior who overthrows his favourite's enemy on the battle-field. He is a merciful god "raising the humble" and "protecting the weak". Jastrow has reproduced a translation of what he calls "a particularly impressive hymn to Marduk" which describes Marduk as not only the strongest of the gods but also as the sole supreme god and ends in "a direct appeal for divine grace and long life".

Nebuchadnezzar, in the first half of the 6th century B.C., on his ascending the throne of his father, in an address to Marduk, whose wording Jastrow declares to be "eloquent and impassioned", entreats that he who owes his all to the great and merciful god Marduk may be led on the right path by Marduk. He implores that the fear of Marduk may be implanted in his heart, evidently for good private and public conduct. It must be mentioned for correct appraisal of the expressions used and attributes predicated of Marduk that neither in the hymns addressed to Enlil or to Enki, nor in the fine prayer of great religious fervour made to the newer goddess of great emotional appeal and perhaps of esoteric cults, Ishtar, do all of them occur together in respect of the god or goddess addressed.[29]

In the syncretism of the post-Hammurabi period, the great national festival called *akitu* was, as the specialist student S. A. Pallis[30] points out, most magnificently, perhaps solely outside Assyria, celebrated at Babylon and was centred round Marduk and no other god. It fell in the month of Nishan, which was from early times associated with the earlier leaders of Mesopotamian gods, Anu and Enlil. Its continuous celebration from about the middle of the 17th century B.C. to 537 B.C., when even the Persian emperor of Babylonia had it performed for him, is attested. The only lacunae occurred for four years during the reign of the moon-god-zealot, neo-Babylonian and antiquarian Nabonidus. As Pallis observes: "The new lords of Babylon, the Persians, celebrated the annual festival like true Babylonians". An annual festival which conferred the right to rule over Babylonia to the king who officiated at it, justifying him in the eyes of the people of that civilization as their rightful ruler deriving his authority from its god as a divine gift, must be interpreted to imply the general acceptance by the people of that god as the supreme ruler among their gods.

And the god of the *akitu* festival was none other than Marduk. Eduard Meyer informs us that Xerxes I after quelling the revolt in Egypt renounced his title of "King of Babel" and removed the golden statue of Bel-Marduk, known later as Merodach, from his temple at Babylon.[31]

This position of Marduk among Mesopotamian gods from about the 17th century to the beginning of the 5th century B.C. cannot, I think, be properly indicated by the term henotheism applied to it. For as must be apparent from what I have stated above regarding the circumstances under which Max Müller used that term to characterize the religious attitude of Vedic Aryans, that henotheism is, in the exact words of A. S. Geden[32], "the worship of one god at a time, who for the time is regarded as supreme, to the exclusive subordination of all others". The Mesopotamian theologians, however, were in the habit of ascribing the roles and attributes of one of the greater gods to another as in the case of Enlil and Shamash ; the procedure was carried a stage or two further in the case of Marduk. The ascription of the roles and attributes of one god to another is not the same as the synthesis of the Ancient Egyptians of their three principal gods, Amen, Ra, Ptah, identifying the one with the other and speaking of them in one moment as one and again as three, as if they were three separate entities. Frankfort was inclined to pass this attitude as monotheism but Wilson insists on distinguishing it as monophysitism.[33]

There is another feature of the Egyptian god-assimilation, not present in the Mesopotamian theological literature or lore about the gods of Mesopotamia or in their known iconography. And that is that one and the same god, Amen, for example, may be represented in a stone statue of human form or "in a specially selected ram, or in a specially selected gander". Gods could assume different forms for different purposes. This feature again must be clearly distinguished from the Hindu theory of incarnations of God Viṣṇu.

Both the aspects of the Egyptian religious attitude are explained by recourse to the doctrine of consubstantiality current among the ancient Egyptians, justifying Wilson's characterization of the complex as monophysitism in preference to its description as henotheistic made by H. R. Hall and H. Frankfort.[34]

Neither the developed attitude of Mesopotamians showing syncretic assimilation of powers and functions of the previous great gods in Marduk, nor the double-sided god-assimilation of either the Old Empire or the New Empire Egyptians, can be equated with the Vedic declaration of the fundamental oneness of the god-head though described under various names. In a late hymn of the earliest of the Indo-European records, the *Ṛgveda* of the Indian Aryans, it is declared that 'wise men' [35] give 'the one' many a name ; they call 'him' Indra, Mitra, Varuṇa, Agni, Mātariśvan, etc. The attitude enshrined in this passage is entirely different from those of the Mesopotamians and of the Egyptians.

There is present another strain in Mesopotamian religious consciousness expressed in records which now calls for notice. And that is the tendency for men to try to acquire superior and superhuman powers and traits by establishing one's identity, by the recitation of appropriate incantations, with the various gods known for their specific powers and functions.[36] This is clearly an appanage of the animistic stage of religious consciousness and is not met with either in Ancient Egyptian culture or in that of ancient Indo-Aryan. Vāmadeva's expression of his identity with some gods of a still later yet Vedic age commented on in the Indian section radically differs from this animistic belief and desire.

The gods mentioned above were all of them the national gods, who, with the exception of Marduk[37], appear to have had temples consecrated to them in more than one city and were worshipped or rather prayed to for succour or gifts. Yet these great and high gods it was that had engendered the attitude clothed in the ancient Mesopotamian expression "God-head awesome as the faraway heavens, as the broad sea".[38] Woolley[39] expresses the Sumerian's relation to his gods somewhat differently as "the greater gods were some thing more than symbols, but they touched his life very lightly".

The great temple complexes were so designed and the principal shrine of the deity so planned that the statue of the god was not visible from the outside. And none but the priests or the kings could go inside the shrine. The populace in fact could not enter further than the first open court-yard, wherefrom it could view the great rituals and festivals performed and celebrated, and cast longing eyes on the statue of the deity "richly clad and borne in honour on the shoulders of the priests to be displayed to the adorants".[40]

Whatever religious practice associated with these gods and their temples was all carried out by the priests as worship on behalf of the whole community. The individual's part in it was not even that of a passive participant, he having the right to be present only on certain public occasions, when processions of the gods was one of the items in the programme of celebration.

The ritual of worship of these gods as conducted by the priests may be treated under four heads, one of them coming into evidence only on occasions of the festivals and on those when the priests acted on behalf of specific individuals on their paying the requisite fee. The three items of the ritual complex, evidently practised daily, for the welfare of the community and the State as a whole were[41]: (1) libation; (2) offerings and sacrifice; and (3) liturgies. The fourth item, very much more to the fore on festivals and the only one in combination with the second item on occasions of worship on behalf of private citizens, was that of incantations, divination, penitentials and sooth-saying, which were "interspersed by prayers said by the layman in his own Accadian language" in the post-Sargonid age.

Libation, as distinct from drinks provided for the gods with their daily meals, were poured from early Sumerian times and were of "water, beer or wine, oil, or the blood of a sacrificial animal". A stone-relief from Ur of the early Sumerian period, reproduced as picture 2 in pl. II opposite page 845 of the 2nd volume of the *Encyclopaedia Britannica* (14th ed.), portrays a man pouring the libation before the image of the god, with another man behind him carrying a goat in his hands, which was the common sacrifice of those times. A record of about 2240 B.C. mentions huge and munificent grants and donations by a king of the Agade dynasty made to the sun-god Shamash. Gudea of Lagash, about half a century later, immortalizing himself with eighteen statues placed in the temples of his god, has left a record of his votive presents to his god, which is less forbiddingly huge.[42]

Two sub-items, connected with and even essential, it would appear, in worship, deserve mention here ; and specially so because they do not get a prominent notice in many accounts of ancient Mesopotamian worship, though they are intrinsically significant as they have formed part of the complex of worship of two different contemporary religions, and were a component, perhaps in a much more elaborate form, in the slightly junior religious complex of Ancient Egypt. They are anointing of the image of the god and ablutions of the god and the human participant. Both Pallis and Saggs have noted the existence of the special priests, appropriately named, whose function was anointing and ablutions. Evidently it meant that the image of the god was daily anointed with oil and washed. It is not stated anywhere if the god was daily robed with freshly washed cloth. It is noteworthy that the quarter of the temple where the washing ritual was carried out was specifically named "Ablution house".[43]

The sacrifices were of either slaughtered animals or of burnt offering and were offered either on the altar, which it appears stood in front in the temple courtyard, or on the roofs of the ziggurat temples.

The long liturgies invariably were in Sumerian, even throughout the Semitic ascendancy in Mesopotamia, and were sung by a group of appropriate priests. There were provided in the written records of later ages translations in Accadian for the use of the Babylo-Assyrian laymen. Musical accompaniment of the singing of the liturgies and litanies was such a universal feature that certain songs were named with reference to the musical instrument accompanying its singing. Thus there were "songs to the flute". Certain others, particularly the litanies, were sung to the accompaniment of an instrument called *balag*, which is believed by some to be a kind of lyre or harp and by others to be tambour or drum. A finely sculptured religious scene on a stone-vase of the 2nd half of the 3rd millenium B.C., in which two drummers are intently engaged in beating a double-sided huge drum (the Indian 'ḍhol') while a noble personage with his back turned to the drummers is making obeisance, is reproduced by S. N. Kramer in his book *History Begins at Sumer*, pl. 52. That drums were donated to temples is attested by some documents of the age (see f.n. at p. 57 of Saggs' book). A song accompanying a prostration was known by a special name which meant "song of prostration". A litany naming all the major deities of the pantheon, also necessarily to be recited by priests as part of daily worship, was called *Titular Litany*.

Psalms of private penance grew during the Accadian Semitic period, though some hymns in Sumerian of "praise", "confession", and "intercession" were recited and continued to be so recited by priests for a penitent on being commissioned to do so.[44]

Occasional, i.e., on specially appointed days, monthly and annually, religious functions were almost of the type of festivals, offering opportunities for the lay-citizens to participate in the religious experience on the communal plane but evidently of the magical and showy variety. Whatever *éclat* such experience might produce could hardly have been of the deeply religious type experienced by individuals offering their prayers, whether laudatory, propitiatory, petitionary or penitential, either as a member of a praying group or by himself. The function served by such festivals is integrative. The images of the national or communal gods came before the public gaze, reminding the citizens of the nature and lineaments of the god, who was, in daily life and living, above and beyond their ken and too high for their near approach, physical or mental.[45]

The procession within the temple precincts, the requirements of a processional path necessitating the enlargement of the precincts, leading to the extension of the temple-complex into very impressive dimensions, is a phenomenon which deserves specially to be noted.

A feature of the Mesopotamian religious complex, which is even more distinctive of it than any one of its traits so far described and one which neither the Egyptian nor the Hindu religion has possessed but is very prominent in—one may even say that it is the central doctrine of—Christianity, is that of an intercessor between frail and puny man and the mighty and awesome god. The concept of intercessor gods leading their protégés into the presence of great gods is very old in the Sumero-Babylonian religious system. On a seal of Ur-Engur of the 3rd dynasty of Ur, the king is shown as being led into the presence of the moon-god Sin—he was not one of the four great ones but one of the six only—by two goddesses, one preceding him and the other following. On a seal of Gudea of Lagash, about half a century or so later, the king is being presented to Ea, one of the four great gods, by a god and is followed by a goddess. On a seal of the Babylonian period nearing the Assyrian age, ascribed to the first millenium B.C., it is the high priest, evidently of the Sun-god, who is represented as escorting the king to that god with a goddess following him.[46] Instead of the two gods or deities of the earlier era here, about 1000 B.C., we have a priest as one of the intercessors, a remarkable development which culminates in the Christian doctrine, Semitic one in origin, of the Saviour.

The need for a less awesome and more familiar god to intercede on one's behalf before the great gods and also to serve the daily needs for lesser services was satisfied by the cult of the tutelary deity or, in Woolley's terms, by the 'domestic religion' as opposed to the state religion centred round the great gods. The tutelary god or the god of the household chapel—houses unearthed at Ur clearly prove its existence—or the personal god as we may say, according to Woolley, "had no name other than that of the family he represented". Jacobsen opines that the personal god "was usually some minor deity in the pantheon who took a special interest in a man's family or had taken fancy to the man himself" and that in origin it was the idea of luck and fortune which got focussed in the concept of the personal god. The role assigned to the god and believed in by his protégé, no doubt sincerely, was so comprehensive and complete that a Mesopotamian of the 3rd or the 2nd millenium B.C. could not think of himself as, nor could he afford to permit himself to be, one without a personal god. A saying translated by Jacobsen records that a man could not "move his arm heroically in battle" nor even could "make his living" without a personal god.[47] The personal gods of the population at large were nameless but those of great personages and kings quite often bore names, and were invoked by their names. Thus the personal god of the great victor from Umma, who supplanted the famous reformer Urukogina of Lagash, Lugal-zaggisi, was the goddess Nisaba or Nidaba and that of the even more well-known figure, Gudea of Lagash, was the god Nin-gish-zida.[48]

A man's relations with his personal god were so intimate that he could be conceived as talking to his god, pleading with him, entreating him, playing on his guarantee of pity similar to the ways of a child with its parents, or even cajoling him. A man could naturally be sulking in appropriate circumstances and express his hurt feelings and expect the god to comply with his wishes. He could do all this by writing a letter to his god urging relevant considerations.

Thorkild Jacobsen's farseeing vision has kindly provided us with an excerpt from such a letter written by one Apiladad, date not given, to his god, describing himself as the servant of his god. The 'servant' begins by questioning his so-called master, the god, why he has neglected Apiladad. Apiladad having wife and children says that he deserves mercy and requires his god's help, and calls upon him to plead his case with the great god Marduk. Apiladad, though he describes himself as his god's servant, yet puts before him his special, nay compulsive, claim on his asking him to consider who will take Apiladad's place in the matter of devoted offerings to the god, if Apiladad should cease to bring them. In essence, it is a threat that Apiladad will have to discontinue his devotion to and worship of the god, if his condition does not improve. On the other hand, Apiladad offers a bait to his god by promising to "see his face" and "kiss his feet" if he grants his appeal. But the personal god could not be a direct source of help. He was too petty for that, and had to get another and a greater god to intercede on his behalf to obtain favours for his protégé. The Babylonians were even bolder and were supremely unique in so far as they had tablets of prayers described as "incantations to cause god and goddess to repent".[49]

It is this personal god who was the source of moral behaviour in an individual. For he was to be kept in good mood through obedience of his commands and through avoidance of offences and sins which would anger him. And they included "almost all serious lapses from ethical and moral standards".[50]

Intermediate between the state religion of formalized cults and its great shrines on the one hand and the more intimate domestic religion, with its small tabernacle for the tutelary deity but supposedly greater spiritual appeal and response, stood the worship of the wayside gods and their shrines. These were structures of minor deities, at least one of whom is known by its name, an anthropomorphic goddess named Pa-sag, constructed at the initiative of a private citizen but serving a public end. Passers by could do their informal worship and obeisance there to secure protection on the way or in the activity undertaken.[51]

It will be realized that the religious complex of the Sumerians and early Babylonians in the matter of the three-fold structure of the worship and the cult, the three types of shrines particularly, much resembled the contemporary Hindu religious complex. There is the great, more or less publicly endowed, temple ; then there are the private and wayside shrines ; and lastly we have the 'devaghar', 'god's house', the apartment specially meant for keeping the household deities with its specific tabernacle of varying dignity and beauty known as the 'devhārā', 'god's room'. In the matter of the number of deities claiming and receiving attention and in the nature of these deities the Hindu complex is even more developed. There is the 'Grāmadevatā', 'village or town god', then there is the 'Kuladevatā', 'the family god', and lastly the 'Iṣṭa-devatā', 'the desired or adopted god', who is the special object of devotion to an individual and may be either one of the family deities or may be an entirely different one. There is still another deity, the god of the wayside shrine, the deity known as 'Sthala-devatā', 'the god of the place', whether of the square or of the mountain-pass or of the river-crossing, which claims and receives worship on appropriate occasions. The auspicious manes and the deities invoked at the beginning of any important ritual occasion in an élite household are still another group of gods that have to be offered their worship. The household deity itself is quite often a group of five gods, the pentad as it is called.[52]

To resume the Mesopotamian story, the special region of god Anu and of many other gods was heaven, which was conceived as being very high up, to reach which none was "tall enough". The theologians divided the pantheon into two great groups, that of the upper world being named Igigi ; and that of the lower or nether world or of the land of the dead, "the land from which there is no return", was called Annunaki. The latter were not under the power or control of the former.[53]

Death to Mesopotamian theologian as also to the common man was no more cessation of consciousness than to the ancient Egyptian. Their funerary practice, however, shows that unlike the latter their ideas of life beyond death did not entail any care on the disposal of the dead body calculated to preserve it. They held the belief that the dead led a kind of life in the underworld or the nether world named *Aralu*. The life there was believed to be one of unrelieved gloom, and suffering and misery. The offerings made to the dead by the living were meant as some kind of help to keep them as best as they could where they were. Nothing one can and may do while alive, nor the intercession of gods invoked by the living on behalf of the dead, could affect the fundamental nature of the gloomy existence. Even the famous epic of

Gilgamesh, an early attempt at snatching away eternal pleasant living, ends on a note of despair with the objective unattained. It is clear, therefore, that religious consciousness and practice, whatever its nature, however earnest and sincere it might be, had no influence on one's life beyond death. The favours that gods could shower, that one's righteous and sinless living might engender, were all confined to the removal of worldly ills and the grant of mundane good. As Woolley observes: "For them there was no Hell and no Paradise. . . In this after-life the gods played no part; man's devotion, and his prayers, aimed at temporal and material rewards."[54]

To achieve the ends of securing mundane peace, ease and pleasures individuals could not entirely depend on good conduct or devotion to the gods and prayers offered to them but sought the services of the priests to perform various magical rites for their achievement. In the ritual of the priests undertaken on behalf of the cult of the temples or on behalf of private citizens, among the articles of offerings to gods I have not seen flowers either mentioned in the list of provisions for festivals or in the description of the ritual or in any of the sculptures of gods and goddesses and their protégés approaching them for intercession. We must take it then that flowers were not an item in the ritual of worship of the Mesopotamian culture. They must be even more conspicuous by their absence in the complex of worship employed by a private citizen, though we don't have either a description of this complex or any remains bearing on it.

If one part of the complex of worship consists of what is done to the statue or idol or any representation of the deity, the other part consists of the recitation of the prayer and the attitude, gesture and posture of the worshipper, symbolism of worship in physical terms. Thus among the followers of the four great religions to-day closing of the suppliant's eyes at some stage of the complete activity is almost universal. We do not know if the Mesopotamian too closed his eyes or not at any stage of or throughout the whole procedure. Some form of salutation or bowing, showing respect and veneration, involving either the whole body or at least the hands, is also universal particularly on solemn occasions of prayerful meetings. I propose to call these attitudes, gestures and/or postures of the body symbology of worship, adoration and/or supplication, distinguishing *inter alia* the varieties according to the parts and limbs of the body brought into action.[55]

Morris Jastrow[56] commenting on the scene portrayed on an early Sumerian cylinder seal, that of king Ur-Engur of a dynasty of Ur, described one of the two goddesses appearing in it as "with uplifted hands, the gesture of intercession". The seal is figured in pl. LXXVII (opp. page 426). The same seal is pictured in pl. II in the *Encyclopaedia Britannica*, volume 2, p. 845, where the dynasty is specified as the third without the name of the king. It is seen from the picture that the seated god, the goddess leading the king, and the king himself have one of their hands in the 'raised' posture, that of the seated god to whom the king is being presented being at a much lower level of raising than those of the others in the picture. The goddess at the back, the fourth figure in the picture and the one described in the above quotation from Jastrow, has both her hands "raised" or "uplifted". The goddess leading has her left hand uplifted, the right being engaged in holding the king by his left hand. The suppliant, the king to be introduced, has his right hand uplifted. All these three hold their uplifted or raised hands in more or less the position of the upper arm making an angle of about 45 degrees with the plane of the shoulder-line and the forearm making an angle of about 70 degrees with the upper arm. The palms of the hands all face inwards, with the fingers and the thumb more or less in their natural position, so that when both the hands are raised, as is done by the goddess that is behind the king, they face each other.

S. Langdon[57] has called attention to the serene, solemn and fervent nature of certain hymns, describing them within inverted commas, and thereby indicating their designation to have been that in Sumerian language, as "Prayers of the Lifting of the Hand".

Saggs[58] has quoted the instruction which occurs at the end of a prayer hymn of great spiritual content addressed to the goddess Ishtar. It begins with the expression, "*Wording of the 'hand-raising to Ishtar'* ", and proceeds : "Before Ishtar you shall set a censer with juniper wood ; you shall pour a gruel-libation, you shall recite the 'hand-raising' three times, you shall do obeisance". It is clear that the original Sumero-Babylonian term for the symbolic act of obeisance was a word or words which meant 'hand-raising' or hand-lifting—and that the act of obeisance was symbolised by doing it thrice at least to the goddess Ishtar. It is implied that the number of times a Mesopotamian had to raise his hands for obeisance to a deity depended on the particular deity he was worshipping. Further the complete process of obeisance required the burning of incense before the god, which might have differed with the god to be attended upon, and also the pouring of a libation, which too must have been different for different gods, each being specific perhaps to only one god.

That the hand-raising as a component of the complete act of obeisance to a god was of the particular variety described above in the case of the presentation of king En-Engur but done with both hands, as the goddess in the picture standing behind the king is depicted as doing, may be assumed as the proper mode of obeisance. Another seal, that of the famous governor of Lagash, Gudea, almost equally ancient is reproduced by Woolley.[59] It shows Gudea being presented by a god to the god Ea. Both the seated god Ea and the god leading Gudea have both their hands occupied. Gudea's left hand being taken by the presenting god as in the other seal, Gudea has raised his right one as in the case of the other picture. The goddess behind Gudea is doing the obeisance and the intercession on behalf of him. She has, as in the other seal, raised both her hands. They appear, as near as possible, in the same pose, posture and angle as those of the goddess in the other seal.

Earlier in date than this seal of Gudea is the fine Stela[60] of Ur Nammu, the great builder of the famous ziggurat of Ur, commemorating his commission to build it received by him from Nannar, the moon-god of Ur. In the scene there is fully dressed Ur Nammu, who pours libation on one side to the seated god Nannar, while on the other side he is engaged in offering libation to Nin-Gal, the consort of Nannar, seated opposite to Nannar, with one hand. Behind him in each of the scenes there is a figure whose head is cut off, with both hands raised in adoration or intercession, exactly in the same manner as the gods in the scenes of the two seals described above as standing behind the kings. Nin-Gal, too, has her right hand raised and held in the same pose, while in her left one she holds some implement or insignia.

A scene on a seal about twelve hundred years later than Ur Nammu's stela, i.e., of the 1st millennium B.C. according to Saggs[61], and "probably copied from a more ancient monument", shows the fully dressed king, who is being presented to the Sun-god, sitting in his shrine, by the high-priest with his right hand held in the same position as the hand of the two kings in the two seals above described. The goddess standing behind the king and evidently interceding on his behalf has both her hands raised and held in as near as possible the same posture and angle as those of the goddesses of all the three scenes, those of the seals and the stela, described above.

Hammurabi's stella, portraying him as receiving the Code of laws at the hands of the Sun-god Shamash about 1900 B.C. is much older, of course, than the above one. The reproduction in Saggs' book (pl. 21B) is fine and clearly shows the king holding his hand in the posture stated above by me as the normal gesture of adoration or supplication. As the king is standing sideways to the observer the back of his right hand faces the observer or the reader. The palm is quite clearly turned away from the observer and not toward the king's face. Another sculpture reproduced by Saggs as plate 31 in his book shows an unnamed Assyrian king engaged in a religious ceremony. It is dated "the first millenium B.C." The right hand raised by the king in adoration has the palm turned towards the observer as the king stands sideways with his left side turned to the observer. The picture is so decisive that no magnifier is needed to show up the lines on the palm. The large picture of Hammurabi reproduced by Gadd in plate XXVI highlights that appearing in the stela as it is in the same position. In all these the fingers are far from the mouth or lips and they are sideways, the palm not being turned towards the subject's face. A Sumerian deity leading a worshipper figured in picture 2 on plate XIV of H. R. Hall's book *The Ancient History of the Near East,* presents the same gesture of adoration or intercession. To these religious scenes I may add, in further substantiation of my interpretation, the civil scene depicted in plate XXIX of Gadd's book, where an officer of Merodach-Baladin, king of Babylon about the end of the 8th century B.C., presents himself before him with a salute. The officer's right hand is precisely in the posture stated above as the common one for adoration.

In one of Gudea's prayers, seeking guidance for interpreting the command of his god, the adoration and supplication offered by him is described as the ritual gesture of "hand to the face". And Apiladad in his letter of entreaty to his god promises not only "to see his god's face" but also "to kiss his feet". Kissing the feet was thus a symbolic act of total submission or surrender or the highest adoration.[62]

Kneeling and prostration do not appear anywhere and are considered by Langdon not to have been admitted in the Sumerian form of Mesopotamian religion. He thinks that they were acts of worship resorted to at certain stages in the recitation of prayers and penitential psalms among the Semites and "were in use among the Babylonians and Assyrians". I have not come across them represented in the sculptures or the seal-scenes. The only mention of "prostration", other than Langdon's in describing certain songs as "songs of prostration" noted earlier, I have met with occurs in the Poem of the Righteous Sufferer or *Ludlul bel Nemeqi*. It reads, "who has not bowed his face, is not seen to prostrate himself, from whose mouth prayer and supplication are barred" and describes an ungodly or impious man. It would thus appear that at some time, rather late because the poem written in Accadian is assigned by Saggs to a period after the Kassite conquest of Babylonia, both bowing with face lowered and prostration were forms of adoration and supplication sometimes resorted to, perhaps by persons who were in uttermost misery. Saggs mentions a cuneiform inscription recording the prostration of a person before a god in a temple at Tirqa in Mari, a Semitic district, during the reign of the local king who was Hammurabi's contemporary.[63] Prostration must be considered to be exotic in Mesopotamia and a very rare, though a fairly early, trait of Semitic origin.

According to Stephen Langdon kneeling was generally employed in the private prayers of "the lifting of the hand". He quotes two statements recorded by the Assyrian king Asurbanipal, the one that he knelt before his god Nabu and the other that he did the same before Ishtar as the goddess of war for her help in battle. He further suggests that the position was perhaps accepted for formal prayer too. I have not come across, nor has Langdon produced any, scene portraying this gesture. He points out that Solomon of the Hebrews not only knelt before the altar but also spread out his hands to heaven as Asurbanipal must have done.[64] It is possible that kneeling was a Semitic gesture of supplication. The other part of Solomon's gesture is perhaps a common heritage of the Aryan and the Semite from of old. Anyway the composite gesture has remained the current orthodox one both among the Hebrews, the Christians and also the Muslims.

The image of the deity placed in the holy of holies appears to have been made out of wood, or perhaps also of stone like the small statue from a wayside shrine of Pa-sag, discovered by Woolley and mentioned above, was and must have been of diminutive size, at least till the time the Babylonians raised their Marduk above all. A wooden image would have been ornamented with the help of metals and precious stones at least in Babylonian times. In these latter times we are assured the idol had to be treated with some recitations and herbs to endow it with divine quality or to induce the deity to take its abode therein before it could be installed in the holy of holies. First came the ritual of the 'opening of the mouth'. Later, a ram was sacrificed and finally the priest 'opened the eyes of the God' by "touching them with a twig of the magical tamarish". Only thereafter was the idol led by the hand into the shrine. After placing on the platform or throne, a further mouth-washing of the image was done. And only at night the insignia of divinity were placed on it.[65]

There is no material either literary or archaeological which in the present state of our knowledge can shed light on the progress of domestic religion and its state in the Neo-Babylonian period of the Mesopotamian culture. But the aggrandisement of the temples of the state religion and the enormous growth of magical features lead one to think that it was smothered under their burden.

There was never an idea of soul and never did it arise among the practical, matter-of-fact commercial people. The state religion with its establishment, running like an administrative and economic unit, provided a technique as far as it could go, which the prestige and the mysteries of priestcraft conspired to magnify. And the attested fact of Nebuchadnezzar II in his reconstruction of the ziggurat of Ur having introduced a number of innovations in the total plan supports the interpretation.

Nebuchadnezzar's innovations imply certain changes introduced in the worship of the god, "tending to give it a more public character". Whereas formerly "everything had been secret, now a numerous public could watch the priest making his offerings on the open air altar" and "could see through the dim sanctuary's open door the image of the god". Nebuchadnezzar is credited with having set up an image of the god in gold and issued a peremptory "command for general worship by the public". What he was doing was, as Woolley points out, "substituting a form of congregational worship for a ritual performed by priests" which "all his subjects" were "obliged to attend" thus appearing to be an Ikhnaten living about seven centuries after him and an Aśoka living about three centuries before him. One has to interpret such a step as not merely the whim or even the newly formulated doctrine of a king but the social fact of the waning of religious consciousness, whatever it was in the past.

Nabonidus who came to power after Nebuchadnezzar was by nature a revivalist with a reverence for the traditional past. He undid what Nebuchadnezzar had done for introducing public worship. Nabonidus was a moon-god enthusiast. He did not realize that in the rise and stabilization of Marduk worship at Babylon, where he was himself ruling, during the course of about 1400 years, the days of the moon-god were numbered and those of the sun-god had dawned.[66] The Aryan tribes which had penetrated to Mesopotamia about 1600 B.C. and the others remaining behind in Iran had the worship of both Mitra and Sūrya, the sun-gods, among them. Soon after Nabonidus' departure from the scene, the Persian monarchs of Babylon brushed aside the Mesopotamian deities. Only the worship of the mother-goddess, Nana, under many names like Anaitas, etc., with an occult and sensual cult seems to have taken deeper roots.

N.B.

Langdon has interpreted the scenes on the seals—he has not taken into account, at least not mentioned, the few scenes on the sculptured stelas—to yield the gesture, which he designates as "the kiss-throwing hand posture", in which the worshipper stands with one hand "raised parallel to the breast, palm inward and fingers touching the lips" (*R.E.E.*, 12, p. 757). In none of the pictures on the seals or the stelas I have referred to in my discussion of this topic in the text have I seen the fingers even near the lips. There are one or two in Langdon's illustrations which appear to fit this description. Excepting in two or three reproductions in Langdon's illustrations all, either those on seals or on stelas, can be seen to answer my description of the gesture if a small magnifying glass is used. The Assyrian king in a religious scene with his raised hand, seen in plate 31 in Saggs' book which I have already mentioned in the text, finally clenches the issue even without the medium of a magnifier. So also does the procession of gods figured by Jastrow in plate XXVIII. Langdon's contention about the Sumero-Babylonian adoration gesture of the hand is thus erroneous and must be discarded. His statement of the gesture in later Assyrian times too falls to the ground with this. For it is essentially based on his theory of the kiss-throwing hand gesture of earlier times, this new gesture being described as "the kiss-throwing hand arrested in the last stage of the act" (*J.R.A.S.*, 1919, p. 546). Saggs has reproduced a sculpture which he lists as king Ashur-nasirpal II (2nd quarter of the 9th century B.C.) but which is really Ashur-nasirpal III and is figured in plate XXVI of Jastrow's book, without specifying the act in which he is engaged (plate 29). But it would appear that it is some act of adoration that he is occupied with. His right hand is held in the new pose. It is quite clear that the palm does not face the front of the king ; it faces to his left side. Three fingers are closed on the palm, the thumb is straight laid on the fingers with the end resting on the inward turn of the third finger. The fourth, the index finger, is lying straight by the side of the thumb and points straight away from the face of the king.

That this gesture was also probably an ancient one becomes plausible as it occurs in a religious scene sculptured on a stone-vase of the 2nd half of the third millennium B.C. (S. N. Kramer, *op. cit.*, pl. 52).

Langdon has stated that there was a second gesture used in worship or adoration by the Mesopotamians and that it consisted in folding the hands at the waist in a peculiar manner in a position naturally almost impossible.

He has witnessed Gudea's pose in his statues (*E.R.E.*, 12, p. 757). I have omitted it from the list of adoration gestures as I am convinced that it was a pose of dignity, often seen in sculptures in the round or in terracotta figures and on the persons of kings, queens, officials, and gods and goddesses. I have therefore taken it as more a pose of dignity than a posture of adoration. For in a purely religious scene it does not occur. The nearest approach to a semi-religious setting in which such posture is seen is the one of the activity of Ur Nina (*c.* 2500 B.C.) undertaken for the construction of a temple (pl. 18 in Woolley's *Sumerians*; pl. XLVI in Jastrow's book). Gudea's statues, pl. XIII, in Jastrow's book, Gudea's son Ur Ningarsu's statue, pl. 21 in Woolley's book, picture of a Sumerian official, pl. 20 in Saggs' book, picture of a diorite statue of a woman, pl. LI in Jastrow's book, picture of the mother-goddess Ishtar and that of the god Nabu, pl. XXLX in Jastrow's book and that of the latter on pl. 30 in Saggs' book all testify to my submission.

CHAPTER II

EGYPTIAN-I

It is an accident no doubt that in Egypt, where so much has been destroyed and yet so much has been left in some condition of ruin, where the national and justly famous shrines have been almost endlessly and hopelessly added to during as many as six to eighteen centuries, there is a temple at Abydos, which has been very well preserved and severely left in its original plan without additions by later generations. The state of its preservation and the compactness of the plan, and the whole structure, have evoked more than warm appreciation from western observers and writers of the twentieth century. The contributor of the note on Abydos in the fourteenth edition of the *Encyclopaedia Britannica* described it as "nearly complete and an impressive sight". D. T. Fyfe, the architect, professional and academic, in his note, in the same well-known encyclopaedia, on Egyptian architecture, not only saw deeper but also went much further in his appreciation of the structure, both from the aesthetic and the functional aspect. He observes : "Taken as a whole" it is "perhaps the most impressive building in Egypt at the present day . . . It is a lesson in the use of form and in the richness that can be obtained by an all-over method of decorating with delicate relief and colour controlled by simple lines."[1] H. R. Hall, a profound student of both Egyptian and Mesopotamian civilizations, whose famous book entitled *The Ancient History of the Near East*, written in 1913, having gone through many editions during his lifetime and some thereafter with the addition of notes by C. J. Gadd, is still in demand, while looking upon the architectural plan as "not of great beauty"characterizes the reliefs sculptured on the walls for decoration as "of the greatest beauty and delicacy" and as marking "the zenith of Egyptian art in this type of work".[2]

Abydos is a city which lies almost midway between Memphis in the north and Abu Simbel in the south. During the Hyksos conquest of Northern Egypt, Abydos was the chief necropolis of the national kingdom, and by the time of the XVIIIth Dynasty it had attained the status of the metropolis of the Egyptians who were dead. "Even if an Egyptian could not be himself interred here, he might at least have some memorial of himself set up upon the holy soil."[3] The builder of the temple was the second king of the XIVth Dynasty, Seti or Sethos I, who with his march against and the defeat of the Hittites laid the foundation of the Second Egyptian Empire, came a little later than the middle of the long national history of the Egyptians, if we begin with the IVth Dynasty about 2600 B.C.[4] Seti I ruled from about 1320 to 1300 B.C. On the walls of the temple, the reliefs, so eulogized by Fyfe and Hall both, included scenes of Seti and his very famous son Rameses II, engaged in making offerings to "the name-cartouches of the imperial ancestors back to the legendary Mena, the supposed founder of the monarchy". The list of names has proved to be an "important document for the historian of Egypt".[5]

It is a temple in which the king got his statue alongside of the great gods and thus deified, instead of following the previous practice of having the statue put up in the pyramid or tomb or, as it is generally called, funerary temple. This feature in itself is an interesting development within the complex of Egyptian religion. There are in Seti's temple seven chapels or shrines in a row arranged at right angles to the main axis of the temple. Beginning with Seti's at the left of the observer, the chapels in order are those of (1) Ptah, (2) Re-Harakhte, (3) Amen-Ra, (4) Osiris, (5) Isis and (6) Horus. At the front of Seti's chapel on the observer's left there is the hall of Nefertem and Ptah-Soker, through which at the back opened two chapels side by side, being thus in the same position as the chapels mentioned but further back, their fronts lining up with the back wall of the other chapels.

Thus there were nine gods and their chapels among whom Seti was classed but placed with the major seven. The chapel of Osiris has a door in the rear wall leading into a hall which spread along those of the front chapels, those of Re-Harakhte, Amen-Ra and Osiris. To the observer's right as he enters the hall of Osiris three doors lead to three chapels arranged in a row. The chapel behind that of the front one for Isis, is for Horus, whose front chapel naturally is next to that of Isis and the last one in frontal series. Next to this inner chapel of Horus stands that of Osiris, a door leading into another hall of Osiris. In making up the number of nine gods by adding a particular form of Ptah and the son of Ptah, mythology making Nefertem his son, Seti perhaps desired to conform the pantheon, of which he had put himself up as a member, to the accepted Egyptian notion as expressed in the postulation of the Ennead.[6]

Seti's pantheon, exclusive of him, confronts the reader with the important gods of Egypt. I should have even described it as the national pantheon if it had included the deities Thoth and Hathor. As it is, it presents to the reader the most salient features of the Egyptian pantheon. The student of the development of religious consciousness must keep in view the whole of this complex pantheon including Seti. For Seti lived more than fifty years after the headstrong reformist king Ikhnaten, who is best described as the worshipper of the Sun's Rayed Disc than as a monotheist. Ikhnaten was followed by the young and extra-ordinarily dazzling king Tutankhamen who almost silently brought back Amen worship.[7]

Seti's chapel arrangement brought out the central and the dominant position of Amen who, having been identified with or rather having absorbed the traits of Re or Ra of Heliopolis, who was the principal deity of early Dynastic Egypt, had come to be named Amen or Amen-Ra since the time of Senusret I (1971-1928 B.C.), who built great temples for Ra and Amen. The great 'pharaoh' Thothmes III, who died at the early age of thirty, in his famous hymn of victory attributed his military and other success to Amen-Ra, who by then had become the lord of Karnak. He had named his son, who later, as Amenhotep III (1408-1372 B.C.) was to further stabilize the worship of Amenra and who and his architect have left us one of the loftiest of Egyptian religious hymns, as Neb-matt-Ra. The last member of the name of Amenhotep III is the designation of the Heliopolitan god.[8]

Seti placed Amen-Ra in the centre and thus vindicated the pre-eminence that the composite Sun-Warrior-god had come to possess. Re-Harakhte's chapel, coming before, emphasizes the significance for this king, and perhaps for the generality of the Egyptians, of the old god of Heliopolis in one aspect. The Memphite god Ptah starts the series of the gods' chapels. It should be borne in mind that it was in Ptah's service under his patronage, and as one should say inspiration, too, that the Memphite theologians made the boldest religious speculation and framed ideas of the divine, which were very far indeed not only of the contemporary Egyptian mind but also of the whole humanity as we know its history. And that is as it should be, showing as it does the peculiar position Ptah as the architect-god occupied in the Egyptian religious consciousness.

The chapel of Osiris succeeding that of Amen-Ra is, however, not a singleton. The other chapel and the two inner halls of Osiris emphasize the great significance of that god. Seti, however confident he might have showed himself to have been about his future by deifying himself in the ranks of the old gods, could not have forgotten that after all the Hereafter was the sole domain of Osiris. He must have thought it but proper and wise to please the Supreme Lord of the Hereafter to make his destiny doubly secure. The Horus of the front line chapel may be the older Horus[9] who was only later confused with Horus the son of Osiris and Isis. The double chapel, front-line one and the back-side one, for Isis, and the back-one for Horus, underscore Seti's concern and his careful attention. For Isis is the consort of Osiris and Horus is their child. Thus is the Osirid triad complete, "the family triad beloved of the peoples" as Hall put it.[10]

Seti's preoccupation with his fate in the Hereafter is further indicated by his providing chapels, though side-line ones, and also a hall to both Nefer-Tem and Ptah-Soker. Ptah-Soker or Ptah-Seker is Ptah of Memphis in his aspect of the lord of its necropolis, which is modern Sakkarah.[11] Nefer-Tem was Ptah's son by Sekhmet and was thus the third member of the Memphite triad of Ptah, his consort and their son. Im-Hotep, the great architect, physician, and a wise scholar, the Vizier of the first king of the IIIrd Dynasty, was deified and substituted for Nefer-Tem, as the third member of the Memphite triad, only later in the XXVIth Dynasty.[12] Seti's non-inclusion of Sekhmet in his chapels must be attributed to the fact that he was pre-occupied with his fate after death which led him to put up Ptah-Soker. And Nefer-Tem, the youthful god with his intimate connection with solar deities, as strengthener of royalty, was to be preferred to Ptah's consort, the lioness-headed deity Sekhmet, the cruel goddess.[13]

Seti's concern with his fate in the Hereafter is further emphasized by the painting in the Osiris chapel—I take it to be inside one, though Lange and Hirmer who have obliged students of Egyptian civilization by reproducing some of the sculptured and painted scenes on the walls of the chapels, have not stated it to be so—which represents Seti as Osiris. In that pose there is an offering of seven standing lotuses artistically arranged before Seti-Osiris. And Thoth is brought to play his role here. Ibis-headed Thoth puts forward the sign of 'life' with his right hand to be pushed into the mouth of Seti-Osiris.[14]

Seti's temple, a composite one accommodating most of the major deities, the four national gods, Ptah, Ra, Amen and Osiris, and emphasizing the rising significance of the fifth, Isis, appearing in Egyptian mythology as the consort of two of the national gods, Ra and Osiris, bespeaks a complex of religious consciousness which has close affinities with that of India—Hindu—as represented in the 'Pañcāyatana' temples and in pentadic worship.[15] It is, of course, a typical representative of the complex Egyptian religious consciousness not only in the pantheonic aspect but also that of the double main concern of religions, viz., the view of death, and of life after it, which colours so much of religious belief and directs so much of the religious practice of a people.

The main features of the Egyptian pantheon are : First, there stand out four principal gods and one or two goddesses. Though there are constant references to the Ennead, nine gods, there were apparently many such groups, so that the total number of deities, major and minor, national or state and local, is not precisely known. I am sure that it was nowhere near the large number of gods known to the Mesopotamians, but there were many more than the orthodox and old number of gods recognized by the Indians, Hindus, which was thirty-three.[16] In increasing the numerical count later to thirty-three crores, i.e., three hundred and thirty millions, the Hindus appear to have surpassed the limits of imagination. I say 'numerical count' because I am sure that all the gods actually mentioned in all the religious texts of all the ages so far known counted together will not give to us anything like that number !

Second, almost all gods were in origin local, i.e., every one was the god of a particular city, town or village and of the local area. But while the functions of some were of a general nature, those of most of them were specific and particular.

Third, of these gods, two main ones of later days, Ra and Horus, were solar deities. Ra was the deity of Heliopolis the northern city of Egypt, which came into prominence first and was the principal seat of power of Northern Egypt. Amen, or Amon, came into prominence later, with the rise to power of Theban princes, whose capital was at Thebes, especially with the great resurgence forward in the time of Thothmes III in the XVIIIth Dynasty.[17] And then Ra was merged into him giving us the deity named Amenra. Ptah, the third important and national god, the creator-god, the god of architects and artisans, was a local deity of the city of Memphis and began to come into prominence with the dominance of Memphite Dynasties as the rulers of the two Egypts, Northern and Southern.[18]

The fourth national god, and he was truly national at least from the XIIth Dynasty onward having been universally recognized by both the élite and the non-élite[19], was Osiris, who though complex in origin and nature, may be said to be the central pivot of the whole religious complex of the Egyptians. With solar affinities and alignment, he figures as the supreme lord of the land of the dead "wherefrom no one returns so that he might . . . . still our hearts until we (too) shall go to the place where they have gone", and where continued existence either in the company of Osiris and consequently blissful, or in the presence of his agents and consequently one of untold suffering and torture, was the only Hereafter in perpetuity for every Egyptian born.[20]

The cult of Isis is inextricably mixed with that of Osiris. Yet she is older than the standard Osiris mythology for she figures in Ra mythology as having worsted the god and wormed out his secret name gaining thereby power over him. And she became the first royal wife of Ra and possessed many names, one of them being 'Her father's wife'. Mythology of the Dynastic period represented her "as the faithful and devoted wife who was made a widow by the murder of her husband, and was then persecuted, by her brother-in-law, who wanted to possess both her person and her kingdom. She is represented as having successfully escaped from his clutches and managed with the help of her magic to get impregnated by her deceased husband and thus to procure a lawful heir to the throne, her son Horus. The last part of the myth lent itself to the elaboration of mysteries associated with her. Two chapels for her, as in Seti's temple, clearly demonstrate her rise in the pantheonic scale, for till late only a place in some part of the temple was her reserved share. Wallis Budge informs us that "the first great temples dedicated to Isis were built under the XXXth dynasty". The greatest of her temples was built by the Egyptianized Hellenistic later Ptolemies, where the triad of Osiris-Isis-Horus continued to be worshipped till the sixth century of the Christian era.[21]

Fourth, the great god Amen or Amon of Thebes, having absorbed in himself the local ithyphallic deity Min, was provided with a consort in the person of another local goddess, Mut. In conformity with the complete triadic religious scheme, the couple has a son, in the form of the moon-god Chons or Khonsu. The young god is represented as a mummy, as are both Osiris and Ptah, with unseparated legs, and endowed with the symbols of both Osiris and Isis.[22]

This identification, assimilation or unification is briefly discussed in its theoretical aspect in the first chapter. And the chapter on Egyptian religious consciousness is begun with the description of a temple where it is demonstrated in practice. The circumstances under which it occurred and the process or processes by which it was achieved may now be appraised for their likely contribution to the sociology of religion.

Amen means 'hidden' and was originally perhaps a wind-god. He was worshipped at Karnak, the northern part of Thebes, from very early times. In the sourthern part another deity had that honour. He was the ithyphallic god Min. The animal sacred to Amen was ram, typifying pugnacity and virility. There was another god of early Egypt named Mentu, the war-god of Hermonthis. Perhaps his early form was that of a bull; and he was later transformed into a war-god. And the princes of Thebes showed their respect for him by incorporating his name as the first member of their personal names, e.g., Mentu-hotep, as we have later Amenemhat and Amenhotep named after Amen. Beginning with this first Mentuhotep the XIth Dynasty took up the Egyptian helm with vigour beginning that renaissance which a little later flowered full-blown in the XIIth Dynasty. This local prince rising to power, evidently must have had Mentu as his personal god. Success like his could not fail to be commemorated and the last two monarchs of the Dynasty, too, had Mentu as the first member of their names. It is significant for a student of the sociology of religion to note that a war-like prince who succeeded in establishing himself as the ruler of Egypt, after it was torn by dissensions, adopts a war-god as his patron-deity. It is a phenomenon which cannot fail to excite particular interest in an Indian who can remember analogous phenomena from his country's history of much later date.

The founder of the XIIth Dynasty, who, as his *Instruction* narrates, was a victim of a sinister conspiracy, in spite of the fact of his valorous deeds for the country having been recognized by the people by offering his "images" worship, and who was a native of Thebes, is the first monarch known to history to have a name framed after the name of the Theban God Amen. It must be borne in mind that his pharaonic name made him "the pacifier of the heart" of the northern Heliopolitan god, Ra. He describes himself as the son of Ra. His southern and northern campaigns, bringing under his rule the whole of Egypt, of course, came later and cannot explain his name. We should infer that the family in which Amenemhat I was born had Amen of Thebes as its tutelary deity. The priests or theologians by identifying Mentu with, or rather by incorporating him into, Amen brilliantly achieved the double feat of justifying their god Amen as a god that leads men successfully in wars and of ingratiating themselves with the king.

The ithyphallic god, Min of Koptos, north of Thebes, by his very form proclaims himself to be a god of vital generative force. The earliest statues of this god represent him as a man standing upright and holding his huge phallus in his left hand and a whip in his right. Another form of his, it is thought, may represent the union of the male and female organs of generation. The cult of the god "in his special character as the god of virility and generation was wide-spread" and important in Egypt. Statues of the god were carried in processions in towns at his festivals which offered occasions of orgastic gratification and of unbridled lust. The priests of the god condoned sexual excesses and "appear to have made prostitution a religious profession". Later,

Min came to be represented as a mummy with the legs joined together. The Bull Bukha, black in colour, and "famed for his strength, violence and pugnacity", was "the incarnation of Mentu, the war-god of the town". The Bull of Min was white. Amen was called the strong Bull. Sekhmet, the lioness-headed goddess was the female counterpart of Min.[23]

By the time of the Middle Kingdom not only had Min's speciality of the straight huge phallus been ignored or passed over but also had he come to be identified with Horus, son of Osiris. Instead of being designated "he of the uplifted phallus" as he should have been from his original nature, he came, as Horus, to be described as one "that lifteth up his arm" and to be represented "with his right arm uplifted".[24] Being identified with Horus, the son of Osiris and Isis, he became a fighter-god. For Horus it was that fought with the murderer of Osiris, Set, and subdued him.

A hymn addressed to him as 'Horus with the uplifted arm' written on a tombstone of the Middle Kingdom has provided this very valuable information. It furnishes us with the rationale for Min's assimilation with or incorporation in Amen, at about the beginning of the Middle Kingdom or rather towards the end of the Intermediate Period before it. Pritchard has reproduced a statue of a god with the Egyptian crown on his head and the fisted right hand fully raised as if for striking. The left hand also is firmly fisted. The letterpress under it reads : "Bronze god over-laid with gold and silver, from Minet-el-Beida [not shown on the map given at the end, but appears to have been a city or town of Palestine] 1500-1300 B.C."[25] I presume it is Min or Horus with the uplifted arm. It is full of life and vigour.

One other event that contributed to the rise of Min in the estimation of the Kings of Upper Egypt and of the Egyptians is recorded to have occurred in the reign of King Mentuhotep of the XIth Dynasty. The great stone quarry, so necessary for Egypt's spiritual and aesthetic needs, lay on the desert route between Koptos north of Thebes and the Red Sea. In the reign of Mentuhotep a big well or rather pond full of water was discovered in the midst of the mountains, the quarry of stones. The discovery was somehow attributed to the favour of god Min "the protector of desert paths".[26] The find of the large supply of pure water naturally opened up the quarry for use, bringing great jubilation to the Pharaoh and his subjects. The chance incident must have added to the prestige of Min in the national mind.

Erman was of the opinion that Amen was originally "only a variant form of the ithyphallic god Min" of Koptos. And we do find actually the two mentioned together, as if they were equivalents, in the Great Hymn to Amen, which must have been composed after the comeback of Amen was effected by Tutankhamen.[27] The Identification of Min, a god definitely figuring in the names of the princes of the IVth and Vth Dynasties, was, according to H. Frankfort, already completed in the Middle Kingdom and in the birth-tale of Hatshepsut, Min was one with Amen who as Thothmes I was concerned in her conception.[28]

Mut, the vulture-goddess of Thebes, had her sanctuary at Karnak, where she was worshipped under "the form of a woman with the whole body of vulture for her head". She was treated as the mother, wife and daughter of Amen, the strangest of combination even for Ancient Egypt, which looked upon brother and sister marriage as the most desirable form of mating. She is conceived of as self-produced. The vulture by herself as Nekhebt, was the goddess of the south and was considered to be the protector of the Pharaoh, for her outspread wings, seen covering her nestlings, gave a surer sense of being sheltered than the wings of any other Egyptian bird. She was shown from the earliest time onwards as sheltering the Pharaoh with her outspread wings. Her fully human representations with only the spreadout vulture as part of the head-dress surmounted by the double crown are known from the temple of Amen. She was, with natural ease, incorporated as the consort of Amen, adding to the vigour, virility, and pugnacity of bull and oversized human phallus the protective and destructive power of vulture. Her wifely status was so thoroughly accepted that in the famous temple of Der el-Bahri, erected by the extra-ordinary woman-ruler Hatshepsut, Aahmes, the wife of Thothmes I, who was believed to have been impregnated by Amen himself, is depicted as being with her, in her enceinte condition, wearing as the hood over her head the vulture-body dress of Mut. And the child was Hatshepsut herself.

Between the end of the XIIth Dynasty and the beginning of the New Empire, Egypt experienced her first foreign domination and had to go through a baptism of political tyranny and suppression of national gods. The noble house that steadily raised the banner of revolt had kings and queens whose names bore the stamp of Moon-god, Aah. Thoth, too, was an aspect of Moon-god. The god's name begins those of four Pharaohs of the XVIIIth Dynasty who came after Amenhotep I. The greatest of the Egyptian Pharaohs, Thothmes III, is one of them.

Khons, the son of Amen and Mut and the third member of the Theban triad, was conceived also as a kind of Moon-god. Actually in both forms, in which he was represented, the moon stood on his head, in one it being the full moon and in the other the crescent. The temple in Luxor near Karnak at Thebes appears to have been the first to be dedicated to this triad. It was begun by Amenhotep III, who lived a hundred years after Thothmes III, and built the temple of Mut at Karnak. Previously it appears that the triad had only a small chapel with three shrines, as, for example, the chapel built by Thothmes III which got enclosed within the later large complex of the Luxor temple.

The association of Khons with Amen was only an intensification of Amen's identity with Ra. For according to one piece of mythology Khons was Ra, born of Ra's daughter Mut, who as "the resplendent serpent wound herself round her father and gave birth to him as Khonsu". Khonsu's association with Amenra as his son must have raised his reputation, as we find his image having been sent to Palestine to cure a princess of her possession by a devil. Amen, on the other hand, being the father of this mummiform god Khonsu and being identified with another mummiform god Min, tended to be represented in that manner too.[29]

The noble house of the XIth Dynasty re-establishing the independence of the country must have adopted the moon-beginning names, according to Hall, in commemoration of their victory over the hated Hyksos. The obligation of the nation to the favour of the moon-god who was the tutelary deity of the XIth dynasty was so deeply felt that, as Hall has stated it, the names of the later Pharaohs beginning with Thoth, another moon-god, were probably inspired by that feeling.[30]

The kings of the XIth Dynasty might have patronized the god of Thebes, Amen; but their names indicate that they still had allegiance to and faith in their special tutelary deity Mentu. With the first king of the XIIth Dynasty we find ourselves confronted with Amen-allegiance in a pronounced form. Amenemhat I, the first Pharaoh to lead the arms of Egypt outside her old boundaries to complete success, must have begun the temple of Amen at Karnak, which, being tended by Pharaoh after Pharaoh, remained the nation's premier temple-complex for more than a thousand to twelve hundred years. And though the second Pharaoh, Senusret I, was even a greater conqueror and though he and Senusret III took the worship of Amen to Nubia, the great Pharaohs were still officially the sons of Ra.

Hall informs us that the records make it evident that it was in the reign of Senusret I that Amen was first mentioned in combination with Ra as Amen-Ra. He further states that "in his fully developed form" of Amen-Ra, the god first appears "on a monument of Senusret III". Hall thinks that this feat of combining the two deities into one was accomplished by the Pharaoh, Senusret I, himself.

The theologians it seems took up the idea and later philosophized about it in the Leyden Papyrus which according to Blackman[31] hails from the time of Rameses II. Wallis Budge described the work as "more or less, a philosophical treatise on the origin, nature, and powers of the god, showing that he is the source of all life, animate and inanimate". The other gods are declared to be "merely forms of" Amen so that as Wilson's quotation from the text has it: "All gods are three—Amen, Re, and Ptah—and they have no second." The one god is named Amen, his head being Ra and body Ptah. A hymn, described by Wallis Budge as 'famous' and by Erman and Breasted as "Great Hymn to Amen", addressed to Amen-Ra, or Amon-Re, forms part of a Cairo museum papyrus. It was written about the time of Amenhotep II, i.e., about 1450 B.C.

Its contents, being very important, may be briefly mentioned in this context. The importance of the contents lies in the fact that the hymn, having been "undoubtedly sung by men and women to the accompaniment of music in the temple", represents the popular notions current about Amen-ra about the time when the priests and the Pharaohs philosophized about him in their endeavour of lauding Amen into the position of the Supreme God of martial spirit and national aggrandisement. He is described not only as the "dispenser of destinies or plans more than any other god" but also as "casting down his enemy into the flame" and as making "the serpent fiend Nak vomit what he hath swallowed". Even more significant is the fact that he is said to have a spear and his eye is credited with 'overthrowing' "the Seban fiends". We see that popularly he had come to be looked upon as the god of national martial vigour, the smiter of the nation's human enemies and the wielder of the weapon, 'Spear'.[32]

Apropos of this ascription of a weapon to Amen-ra it should be noted that hardly any representation of any god of Ancient Egypt is ever seen with a weapon in hand. None of the reproductions in the two books of Wallis Budge, *Tutankhamen* and *From Fetish to God in Ancient Egypt*, contains such a one. Two gods or goddesses of war represented in the illustrations in Gardner Wilkinson's book *Manners and Customs of the Ancient Egyptians* hold a spear in their hands. Wilkinson's illustrations of war weapons contain that of a knife and of a sickle-shaped or curved small sword which he has called falchion.[33] Erman in his *Life in Ancient Egypt* has illustrated the same weapon but has called it "sickle-shaped sword". A fine bas-relief at Thebes depicts Seti I charging his enemies at close quarters, riding in his war-chariot. He is seen holding his bow unstrung in his left hand, and ready to hack his enemies with his sickle-shaped small sword, held firmly in his raised right hand.[34]

The special interest of this object, which is quite clearly an effective weapon of war in close fray, is that in at least three representations of Amen-ra, an object, which appears to be this weapon, is seen in his right hand. All of them are in connection with three of the martial Pharaohs. One is the beautiful gold statue[35] of Amen in the features of the greatest campaigner of Ancient Egypt and perhaps of antiquity, Thothmes III. The second, the most decisive, is the representation of Seti I, receiving that weapon, along with a mace, from the hands of Amen, before whom he is kneeling, wearing the attributes of Osiris. The third is on a stela of the 13th century B.C. found at Bethshan in Palestine. Slender and finely-shaped Rameses II is represented with his unstrung bow in his left hand and with his right hand raised either in adoration or to receive the weapon which Amenra confronting him is holding in his right hand, as if for handing it over to the king.[36]

On the inside of the war-chariot of Thothmes IV we find the very interesting picture of the war-god Mentu in his full panoply of the striking head-dress with two cobras peeping out and of the outspread hawk wings about the shoulders. His left hand is raised over the king, who in his sphinx form is majestically prodding over his enemies, as in protection, and his right hand holds not only the symbol of life and the staff but also the sickle-shaped small sword. Rameses II, both at Karnak and at Abu Simbel, is pictured in his war-chariot with his unstrung bow in his left hand and the sickle-shaped small sword and whip in his right.[37]

Amen or Amenra thus appears to have been not only conceived as a war-god but actually represented so. Neither Ra nor Ptah appears ever to have been represented with a weapon in his hand. Amen-ra emerged, with the exploits of Thothmes III, not only as the supreme God but also as the war-god of Egypt striking terror in the hearts of Egypt's enemies.

We shall now see how the great Pharaohs looked upon Amen-ra. The greatest campaigner whose tremendous success brought untold credit to his god Amen-ra, Thothmes III, carries the credit for having given the first historically known account of a campaign and of an actual battle, that of Megiddo, which is one of the earliest of such to be a decisive political event. The event was an incident of Thothmes' first campaign about 1468 B.C. The king in his acknowledgement of the victory as a gift from his god Amen-ra had it carved on the walls of the temple of the deity at Karnak, to which he made significant additions to show his devotion and gratitude to the god. Wilson's[38] translation of it fills seven pages. It states that it was at the command of Amen-ra that the king undertook the campaign. In the van of the attack he felt that his arm was strengthened by his "father Amen". Later in the campaign again he describes his arms as "made strong" by his "father" Amen and likens himself in his martial dress with god Horus, "the mighty of arm", and calls himself "a lord of action like" god Mentu, the war-god. The foreign princes were subdued, and came down "on their bellies" "because the power of Amen was (so) great (over every foreign country)". Then follows a list of the great booty the king brought.

On a stela was inscribed what is described by Hall as "the splendid Hymn of Victory" composed by some poet. While lauding Amen-ra for his favours showered on the Pharaoh the poet, in his preamble or dedication to the Pharaoh, has uttered ideas and sentiments which support the viewpoint attempted to be stressed in this study as a peculiar Egyptian feature of the religious consciousness of its people. It runs as quoted by Hall[39]: "Saith Amen-Ra, lord of Karnak: Thou comest to me, though rejoicest ... *I shine because of thy love;* my heart expandeth at *thy beautiful comings* to my temple; my two hands make thy limbs to have protection and life. *Doubly sweet is thy might to my bodily form.* I have established thee in my dwelling place. I have done wondrous things for thee.... I have magnified the dread of thee in all creatures, ... The chiefs of all lands are gathered in thy grasp; I myself have stretched forth my two hands and bound them for thee." In similar strain the various ethnic groups subdued by the king one by one are stated to have been made captive or smitten by Amen-ra. Amenra thus was the inspirer of the campaigns of Thothmes; Amenra was the source of his sustained effort, indomitable courage and smashing valour. Amenra was further the god that was acceptable to the Egyptians' international society. Verily can such a god be declared to be the national war-god, the god of warrior sovereigns who attributed their martial deeds entirely to his favour. And this in spite of the fact that in the rather flamboyant description of their exploits they portrayed themselves as the war-god Mentu or Montu or Month, who was the lord of Thebes before Amenra, or/and as the lioness-headed war-goddess Sekhmet.

That Amenra was a national war-god was further demonstrated by the powerfully built son and successor of Thothmes III, Amenhotep II, who wielded a mighty bow, still to be seen in the Cairo Museum, which no contemporary soldier could draw. He may very legitimately be called Egyptian Rāma. He had to lead only one campaign and that was in Palestine, whereby he succeeded, as a side result of it, in getting willing alliance of the Mitannis of north-eastern Mesopotamia. In his successful fighting in Palestine he captured seven chiefs whom he brought to Thebes and himself sacrificed them before Amen! So blood-thirsty could the war-god be within a generation, as it befitted the temperament of an individual Pharaoh, his servant in theory!

It is noteworthy that the young Pharaoh Tutankhamen in his restoration of the old gods of the country, ousted or humiliated by the wilful reformist Ikhnaten, should have dedicated in the god's temple at Karnak the only extant statue of Khons and that apparently in the king's boyish features. Even more significant is the fact that the over-life-size statue of the goddess Mut, the wife of "the king of the gods, Amen", which, too, is perhaps the only extant statue of the goddess, is thought to be "inspired by" the features of Queen Mut-nodjmet—note the name with Mut as its first part—, wife of Haremhab, who was the commander-in-chief of the army and also the first official scribe of the realm, and who secured the crown of Egypt after the premature death of Tutankhamen. Lange and Hirmer[40] vouchsafe the further information that there were three more such statues. We may conclude that a soldier of the first rank was instrumental in putting Mut on to her proper pedestal, her stature being made to reflect her pantheonic position! Haremhab, the general, himself, evidently, had the image of Amen tattooed (?) on his right forearm. Firmly was Amenra established as the god of warriors and soldiers! Seti I, Rameses II and Rameses III too have left on record their homage to Amenra as the grantor of success in war, which breathes more or less the same spirit, sometimes buttressing their own claims to martial process with the help of their likening themselves with the war-god, Mentu or Mont, and the war-goddess, Sekhmet.[41]

Beginning as Amen and supplanting Mentu or Mont and Min of Thebes and Koptos the god soon appeared in the form of Amenra as the pharaonic deity. Theologians attempted to exalt the god above others to uphold his dignity but were content more to less with placing him as an equal with the older pharaonic gods, Ra and Ptah. Slowly but surely with the success of Egyptian arms and Egyptian imperial domination under the Pharaohs, who proclaimed in more ways than one that they had the special protection of Amenra, the god came to be raised to the position of the Supreme God.

The god could not but get a lift over his erstwhile superiors according to mythology as the Pharaohs gained in mundane significance and as both the external manifestations, the temple and the rituals, of the god became more and more imposing and his possessions, both in material goods and in human servants, increased beyond all proportions. As for possessions we are informed that Amen possessed under Rameses III "five times as much land as the gods of Heliopolis [the city of Ra], and eighty-five times as much as those of Memphis [the city of Ptah]".[42] Not only was the extent of the temple area of Amen increasing by leaps and bounds, not only were imposingly huge pylons being added, not only was the most stupendous hypostyle hall, the present wonder of the world, put up in Amen's temple but also were the image and the shrine of the god made of gold, and precious stones set in the sides and the door jambs which glittered against the sun. And the god, whose nod came to decide many a plan for the Pharaoh and many a litigatious case for the élite appeared only in the court whose pavement was of silver, shining bright in the morning.[43] And it is in the memorial tablet of King Merenptah, who succeeded Rameses II, that we find the statement that the "Lord of All", i.e., Ra, ordering the same god, who is depicted in the scene, to give the scimitar, "the old sickle-shaped sword", "to my son, the upright of heart, the kindly, the gentle Merenptah", with which evidently the king must be supposed to have rid northern Egypt of the pest of the Lybian raids.[44]

A local god became a great god, a national and an international one, when kings whose tutelary deity he was went on martial exploits of self-protection or of expansion. He even became almost a war-god as far as the Pharaohs at least were concerned. I have elsewhere[45] dealt with almost analogous phenomena noticed in far-off India in very much later times. It is an aspect of the sociology of religion.

The Pharaoh was not only the son of god, would not only be himself god after death, to provide for which he used to have what is aptly called the Pyramid or funerary temple, not only was he the high priest of the gods of Egypt, but was also himself god. The peculiar position in the Egyptian religious consciousness of the Pharaoh put him on an entirely different level from ordinary Egyptians. The one difference that existed between the living Pharaoh and the national gods Amen, Ra or Osiris was that whereas the latter were called *the great gods*, the former could be designated only as the *good god.* His divinity evoked so much awe that a circumlocution was used to name him. This having been in Egyptian *per-ra*, 'the Great House' has given us the characteristic name of an ancient Egyptian king, Pharaoh. When the Pharaoh proceeded on a tour in the city, he was carried in full pomp and dignity on a sedan chair on the shoulders of eight distinguished courtiers. There were fan-bearers before and behind fanning him on the way and waving bouquets of flowers to fill the good god with sweet perfume.[46]

In spite of the great and magnificent temples, however, it is a pyramid which is the typical symbol of Ancient Egypt. It calls to the minds of all educated humanity the glorious achievements of the long departed Egyptians. The Egyptian sage Ipuwar, pondering over the conditions of his people in the period of confusion and unburdening his mind about 2100 to 2000 B.C., said : "It is good when the hands of men build pyramids and dig ponds, and make for the gods plantations with trees."[47]

(The far more travelled and also in pristine form a more commonly accepted cultic symbol and consequently a very much better known object, called an obelisk, is but only a tall square shaft of stone with its head capped by a miniature pyramid. The national symbol, a pyramid, stands for the whole complex of the ideas about death and individual's fate after death if he were the king of Egypt between about 3000 B.C. and 2500 B.C. This period of Egyptian history is known as the Pyramid Age because every king constructed a pyramid for the resting of his dead body, with its external temple at the ground level for services being rendered to his statue or, as the Egyptians thought, to him. This temple is known as the funerary or mortuary temple.)

The pyramid continued to be the resting place of the Egyptians even in the Middle kingdom period or the Feudal Age. Quite clearly it was a provision only made by the kings for themselves. No non-king could be conceived as a god in any condition and there was no question of there being such a temple for him.

The first and the most significant item of belief in the mortuary complex was that the conditions prevailing in the lifetime of the king, his court, his daily routine, were to continue after he ceased to live in the ordinary way. All the paraphernalia of mundane life, therefore, must be provided in as realistic a manner as possible in death. The king's courtiers, officials, physicians, artisans, etc. were therefore buried, after their death, round about the king's resting place, his tomb, the pyramid. But naturally the structures that housed their bodies had to be different, not only because of the current notions of social precedence and the condition of finances but also because the pyramid was a religious symbol which could be associated only with the king, the pharaoh as he was later known. Breasted has remarked on the significance of the pyramids as an index of the belief about life after death thus : "The pyramids of Egypt represent the culmination of the belief in *material equipment* as completely efficacious in securing felicity for the dead."[48] The structures that housed the officialdom and aristocracy were much smaller and truncated buildings known as "mastabas".

The common people were buried in the sand without any surface mark of their resting or rather their decomposition centres. Thus the mundane distinctions of material wealth and social status inhered in death too, leading to consequent significant differences in the states of the deceased in the Hereafter. And in so far as the complex of beliefs, whether completely integrated or loosely syncretic, required the body of the deceased person to be intact, and necessitated the erection of a statue of the deceased, in order that postmortem felicity may ensue, these common people, i.e., perhaps more than 70 to 80 per cent of the Ancient Egyptians, were in their lives throughout faced with the stark picture of a bleak future. (Even if they had loving relatives, who, after their death, would bring them food and drink, if not quite regularly, at least on the main festive days, the large bulk of the Egyptian people, the workers, the peasants and the artisans, could not look upon their condition after death as anything but dreary.) If there was a non-élite complex of beliefs regarding death and life thereafter it is not known. And it appears to me to be almost sure that even if such a system existed, it could not be vital in face of the stupendous and gorgeous monuments depicting the scenes in the form of the pyramids or the later rock-cut tombs advertising the imperative need of a long and costly ritual and a solid and intricate structure for securing the desired post-mortem felicity.

The anonymous tract known as 'The Instructions for King Merikere or Merikara', which is assigned to some time in the latter half of the 3rd millennium B.C. during the period of great confusion and social upheaval, actually advises on this point thus : "The soul goeth to the place it knoweth, and strayeth not from its paths of yesterday. (Wherefore) make fair thine house of the West, and stately thy place in the necropolis, even as one that is just, as one that hath done right. That it is, whereon their heart reposeth."

It is well known to students of Ancient History that for the first time in the recorded history of about 5000 years of human culture and social organization, it was in Egypt that an upheaval occurred convulsing the whole social order. It occurred about 2300 B.C. and left very clear marks and distinct echoes in the Egyptian utterances and writings of about two to three centuries later. The most important of these, besides the *Instructions for King Merikare*, referred to above, are the tracts known as the *Admonitions of a Prophet* and the *Prophecy of Neferrohu*.[49]

The prophet who admonished must have lived before king Amenemhat I of the XIIth Dynasty and may therefore be assigned to between 2100 and 2000 B.C. His name is Ipuwer. A. H. Gardiner, to whom goes the credit of having given the world a clear and intelligible rendering of the difficult piece of writing, in which Ipuwer's utterances were clothed in a mutilated text, refers to him as an Egyptian Sage. Ipuwer tells us that things had come to such a pass that foreigners easily posed as good Egyptians, while virtuous men went "in mourning because of what had happened in the land". There were plunderers everywhere so that even when the bounteous Nile was in flood none cared or dared to plough the land saying : "We know what hath happened throughout the land."

Social and economic phenomena of the land had got topsyturvy. Not only were "the high-born full of lamentation and the poor full of joy", not only was "the son of a man of rank no more distinguished from him that hath no such father", not only are "gold and lapis lazuli, silver and turquoise, carnelian and bronze . . . hung about the necks of slave girls", not only were the "limbs" of ladies "in sad plight because of their rags", not only did the "hearts" of these ladies "shudder when greeted" owing to their having been recognized in their miserable plight, but also were "boxes of ebony broken up" and "precious wood cut in pieces for beds" instead of, as it would appear, being kept for making the coffins so necessary for the funerary ritual of the nobility and the upper classes.

He that slept "unwed through want" found "ladies" ; he that had "nothing" possessed "wealth" ; he that had "no bread" owned "a barn" ; "the bald head that used no oil" possessed "jars of pleasant myrrh" ; he that had "no yoke of oxen" owned "droves" ; she that had "no box" owned "a coffer" and she that looked at her face in the water possessed "a mirror", of course a rarity in those times.

Persons who were architects in the social order which was thus being uprooted had to turn themselves into field labourers, so had the erstwhile commanders of the royal ships. Door-keepers started plundering, washermen refused to carry their loads, persons carrying on such peaceful occupations as confectionery and brewing were up in revolt and "the rabble" occupied "the positions of the upper classes". Records, whether of the court of Justice or of the treasury or granary, were destroyed. Ladies of the harem that should have been singing and playing music were engaged at the grinding mills. Former messengers had become masters summoning others as their messengers.

The most significant upset from our present viewpoint, the development of religious consciousness, and more particularly here that of the mortuary complex of beliefs and practices, are the following facts brought out by Ipuwer, so obligingly, for us : "The mummy cloth speaketh (although) not drawn nigh unto [?]. Nay, many dead men are buried in the river. The stream is a sepulchre, and the Pure Place (the place of embalmment) is become a stream", meaning that the corpses were too numerous to be buried and were being thrown into the stream like dead cattle. The mummies of the great ones that had rested in their tombs (Pure Place) were strewn on the high ground. And the secret of the embalmer's art had thus become exposed and known.* The "magic spells are divulged *and are now ineffectual* (?), for the people have them in mind". He "that was buried as a hawk (the king) lieth on a bier". "What the pyramid hid (the sarcophagus) will become empty" ; naturally as it would be plundered. The whole statement, delivered as a future contingency, has to be understood as a statement of actual occurrence. On the other hand, "He that could make himself no sarcophagus now possesseth a tomb"†, a rifled one of course.[50]

Incidentally in Ipuwer's statements we get references to some of the elements, forming part of the mortuary complex other than the tomb, the pyramid with which I started my account of it. Of these items and some others, not mentioned by Ipuwer, nonetheless invariable components, I shall treat in

* Note that this statement occurs thrice in "The Admonitions".

† This statement occurs twice.

due course. Here I want to emphasize the coincidence, if it was nothing more than that, between the occurrence of the catastrophe, of which Ipuwer so feelingly and eloquently had left a short-hand account, and the important changes in mortuary rites-complex that became manifest between the VIth and the XI dynasties, between 2200 B.C. and 2000 B.C.

The kings raised pyramids as their resting places but they were brick structures and the rock-cut tomb with the funerary temple abutting made its appearance. The local grandees, the landed gentry, and high officials began to have their final resting places in such tombs in their own districts or near their estates, and the halls of these structures began to be gaily painted with the scenes of their owners' doings while alive. The funerary texts of the earlier period are known as the Pyramid Texts and those of this Intermediate Period as Coffin Texts because the coffins now became a very widely prevalent feature of the mortuary equipment and they bore these texts, whose purpose was magical. Though Ipuwer thought that their formulae having been known would be ineffectual, the nobles, the landed gentry and the officials who lived and died during this period were not of Ipuwer's opinion. On the other hand, they now claimed a right to enter heaven which in the earlier period was the sole preserve of the kings. Thus we see that instead of decrease in faith in magic, magic was made a handmaid of the first stage of democratization of the mortuary-belief-complex. The Coffin Texts clearly show that in the hereafter the deceased could have his family with him and need not be a solitary figure. They also contain the beginnings of that complex which painted the grave and numerous dangers on the way to and in the hereafter, which a deceased person had to pass through.[51]

We shall study the other constituents that formed part of the total mortuary complex which posited that physical death was but an appearance, the deceased person continuing his existence somewhere and in some form, which, not clear to any one perhaps of the Egyptians and their theologians, is not yet clear to us in spite of the selfless efforts of a galaxy of scholars toiling away at an explanation. However, one thing is clear and that is that in spite of their over-confident belief in the continuation of existence after death, the theologians desired, and the mortuary complex was moulded accordingly by them, to keep the dead body in the grave free from decomposition and intact, and in as lively and life-like a condition as possible.

To this end, the viscera were removed from the dead body, separately treated, and placed in receptacles, one in each. In much later times they came to be replaced in the body. The body was embalmed and swathed in various wrappings and was thus mummified. This practice of mummification was a progressive growth, responding to the challenges made to the desired end of perfectly preserving the body with as life-like an appearance as possible and was not fully developed till the XVIIIth Dynasty, i.e., till about 1600 B.C. It reached its perfection in the XXIst and XXIInd Dynasties. Mummification was practised till late, i.e., till about the 8th century B.C., only by the royalty, the upper classes and some of the middle classes. The common people gained the privilege only at about the beginning of the Saite period, i.e., from about 700 B.C.[52] The mummified body was placed in a sarcophagus, which in the earlier period was of stone but in later ages, particularly in the case of people other than the royalty, was of wood. The sarcophagus, which in the earlier period was almost plain inside, in the later period bore various texts, which were nothing but magical formulae, and was very carefully closed and sealed so that no air should enter to help the desiccation of the body. These texts are referred to as Coffin Texts, having been written and having been required to be written on the coffins.

With the sarcophagus were laid all kinds of articles of food and other necessaries, quite often in permanent representations, and also various figures meant to be servants or rather persons who would attend when the deceased would be called for work by the Lord of the Hereafter. They were, therefore, appropriately named 'answerers', i.e., those who answer the call for service on behalf of their master, the deceased person. In the opinion of Flinders Petrie these figures began to appear about the time of the XVIIIth Dynasty. But Hall says that they could be traced to the XIIth Dynasty.[53] Evidently they must have grown larger in number in the later ages. They highlight one of the items of change in the religious and mortuary complex that came in after the second resurgence of Egypt.

The food and other necessaries thus provided were not thought to be adequate. Periodical replenishing by newer offerings by the living were necessary to keep the deceased from hunger. It was believed that the deceased could and should enjoy usual festive occasions as he used to do while alive. On both considerations, festive days of the calendar were occasions for such celebration at an appropriate spot, near or in the sepulchre of the deceased. For all these needs and contingencies priests were contracted and varying endowments made by the persons before their death, just as most often the tomb, the resting place after one's death, was constructed.

The difference between the courtiers and others whose tombs were formed by the truncated structures called *mastabas* and the kings in these behalfs was only of degree though vast, the latter quite often making all the provisions for the life hereafter of courtiers and officials in their own endowments. But just as the pyramid, the national symbol, was the tomb reserved for the king, and no amount of wealth of a courtier or a landed magnate, a governor of a district or province could entitle him during the Old Kingdom to raise a pyramid for his resting place, so too there were other very marked and even more intimate and fundamental differences in the requirements and accompaniments, of the two types of tombs, i.e., between those of the kingly order and of the world of the aristocratic officialdom.

The last noted differences cannot be grasped without as clear an understanding as is possible to have of some concepts which are the *sine qua non* of most developed religions as central notions and in relation to which the mortuary-rites-complex is commonly shaped. The concepts refer to the non-material element of human personality.

We have seen that the Mesopotamians, in their long and in some ways very glorious history of about 2500 years, did not evolve any such concept as soul. The Indians, who have proved themselves to be so fruitful and creative in the realm of philosophical and religious thought and systems, had not arrived at their analogous notion of 'ātman' of an individual till about 1200 B.C.

The Ancient Egyptians on the other hand, enigmatically enough, had early postulated more than one element in human personality which was non-material. There are at least three concepts appearing in the religious texts, two of which are represented in the mortuary-rites-complex, and all the three appear to be implicit and, moulding or distorting as the case may be, the current view regarding the precise manner of existence after death. They are *ka*, *ba* and *akh* : These are the spellings which Wilson and also Frankfort give. Erman speaks of *ka* but does not refer to the other two concepts. H. R. Hall in E.B. VIII mentions all the three with different spellings for the last two as *bai* and *ikh*. Wallis Budge (*From Fetish etc.*) quotes a Pyramid Text in which, while the first two are spelled as in the text above, the last is given as *akhu*. J. H. Breasted (*Dawn etc.*) speaks of and deals with both *ka* and *ba* but does not mention the third. From a footnote (p. 231), however, it would appear that the last concept is rendered by him as "glorious one", when the deceased is transformed. M. Murray (*Splendour etc.*) lists all the three concepts, spelling the third as 'Yakhu' and translating it as "shining one" ; but she does not deal with it at all.

Of the three[54], the concept of 'ka' appears to have been fairly well known from the earliest times. At least it is mentioned in a unique piece of Egyptian literature, fortunately preserved through a copy made in 700 B.C. The original document is now assigned to the very beginning of the history of the Union of the two Lands of Egypt, North and South, i.e., to about 3000 to 2700 B.C. It is known as the Memphite Theology, the Memphite Drama as J. H. Breasted christened it. It states that Ptah transmitted life to all gods "as well as (to) their *ka*'s" and that "all the gods, as well as their *ka*'s gathered themselves to him, content and associated with the Lord of the Two Lands", this latter statement glorifying the deification of the king of the Union of the Two Lands of Egypt so freshly formed. In another passage *kas* are mentioned as *ka*-spirits and were made, as earlier stated, by Ptah by his speech, together with another variety of spirits called *hemsut*-spirits who in contradistinction to *ka*-spirits were merely "appointed" by Ptah. It appears that both the sets of spirits together made "all provisions and all nourishment". Thus the gods had *kas*, they were created along with them, i.e., even the gods could not be conceived except as coeval with their *kas*. And the function of god's *ka* was to make all provisions and nourishment, in which important function another set of spirits, who do not figure in any of the writings of the various authorities I have drawn upon for my connected account, were also concerned. In connection with one individual, the Pharaoh Unas of the Vth Dynasty, *hemsut* is mentioned immediately after his *kau* (*ka*) as the female counterpart. The *kau* of Unas are said, in the text, to be behind him, in this account of Unas' life beyond the grave narrated in the Pyramid Texts, while his *hemsut* are "under his feet". I shall leave this *hemsut* out as the spirit is never mentioned in connection with the mortuary rites as requiring some performance or the other, drawing attention to the fact that an individual, a male here, had not only a male spirit as *ka*, commonly understood to have been a guardian but also a female one, *hemsut*, who remained utterly in the background.

Frankfort has discussed the concept of Akh at some length along with the concepts *ka* and *ba* in unravelling the significance of Ptah-hotep's maxims and to uphold his contention that from the earliest times the Egyptians conceived the destiny of the dead as an eternal "cosmic circuit".[55]

The word *akh* occurs in relation to *maat*, righteousness, where it is stated by Ptah-hotep that 'maat' "is good" or "is advantageous". Frankfort contends that it must mean in the context either "is effective" or "splendid" or "sacred" or "transfigured". Rendering the word "akhu" by "transfigured spirits" he observes : "The dead were transfigured spirits. As such they were never depicted for they existed in a sphere well beyond the ken of man. . . . they were seen at night as stars in the sky especially in the northern part." He further states that the word *akh* occurs in inscriptions of the First Dynasty, and that the shafts of the tombs of the Old Kingdom are on the north side to enable the dead to join their companions, 'the venerable ones', clustered around the heavenly pole." He quotes a Pyramid Text which reads : "Spirit (Akh) to the sky, and corpse into the earth" and remarks : "It is, then, a mistake to consider the notions of Ba and Akh incompatible ; the dead could be manifest upon earth as Ba's but they were Akhu in their own peculiar and exalted form of existence."

I have mentioned at length the fresh views of an eminent student of Early Near East and its culture in all its complexities regarding this very elusive concept of *akh*, indeed much more elusive than *ba* and even *ka*, though hardly touched upon except by Wallis Budge and Gardiner among the scholars whose authoritative works I have consulted. As a Hindu and a student of Hindu religion from Vedic times down to the contemporary age I feel there is here much that is intriguingly near to certain Hindu notions about the manes and tantalizingly shrouded in mystery in view of Frankfort's explanation of *akh* in relation to the Egyptian dead.

It is necessary therefore to see what light, if any, other scholars have shed on the illusive concept. Unlike Frankfort, Wilson[56], it appears, even after Frankfort's strong plea in favour of his thesis regarding destiny of the Egyptian dead, identified the 'Field of Rushes' and the 'Field of Offerings' where the dead were said, in the old texts, to dwell with Elysian Fields stating that the dead would live there as an *akh*, an "effective spirit". He still held that "the goal of the deceased was the region of Dat* in the northern part of heaven, where he would join the circumpolar stars 'which know no destruction' and thus live for ever himself". And a deceased person, according to him, became an *akh* after joining his *ka* in the Hereafter. This was the destiny of the common man (?) of the Old Kingdom, "to continue with his *ka,* and to become an *akh,* an 'effective' personality". The Pharaoh was, of course, to become a god residing in the realm of the gods.

Wallis Budge[57] states that there are several passages in the Pyramid Texts in which the deceased is mentioned with groups of beings who are called *Sekhemu, Sahu* and *Akhu* and that at one time they were thought to be the "members of the mental or spiritual parts of a man", *Akhu* being "held to be a sort of ethereal, translucent, and transparent spirit soul akin to, but somewhat different from, the *Ba*". But that view had proved itself to be wrong. The view current, when Budge wrote the book in 1934, was that all the three were "Bau or 'Souls' who had attained to a high degree of power, glory, and knowledge" or that they were "different orders of spirits, similar to the orders of Angels, Thrones etc. which are enumerated by St. Paul". He quotes in full a text from the Pyramid of Unas of the Vth Dynasty, and commenting on it states that "in the earliest times kings and others [as in the case of Unas] were believed to enjoy their life of immortality in the form of stars and to join the company of the 'imperishable' stars of heaven".

In the very first line of the text Unas' *ka, Ba* and *Sekhem,* each one separately, are declared to be pure. In the next two lines his *ka* is thrice mentioned. The next three texts are devoted to *ba,* one, (a) declaring it to be "equipped like the star Sirius", another, (b) stating that Unas had "become a *ba* being made a *ba*", and the third, (c) asserting that Unas' *ba* "is a star, behold it is the foremost of its brethren". The next text asserts that Unas' "*Sekhem* cometh" to him "among the *Aakhu*". In the next two texts first his *sekhem* is asked to be "set among the gods" and then his *akhu* "among the *Aakhu*". The next two texts are devoted to *akhu.* The first declares: "Behold, Unas cometh forth on this day in the true form of a living *Aakhu*" and the second insists on Unas: "Behold, thou art an *Aakhu;* Thou art an *Aakhu* with all the *Aakhu*". Then comes the double mention of *Sāh,* firstly as "thou hast received thy *Sāh*"; and secondly, in the final pronouncement of the successful magical operation and as the triumph of the endeavour that "The life of Unas is everlasting, his limit is eternity in this his *Sāh*".

In the papyrus of Ani belonging to the XVIIIth Dynasty, about 1600 B.C., a portion of a section of the region known as the "Field of Offerings", i.e., the Hereafter, is described as the "Seat of the *Akhu,* a group of the beatified, who are said to be seven cubits (i.e. between 11 and 12 feet) in length (i.e. height), and the grain, which is three cubits in height, is reaped by the honourable *Sahu,* another class of beatified beings."

---

* This word is also spelled as Duat and Dewat and even as Tuat.

Frankfort has not mentioned either the *sekhem* or the *sahu*, though as is quite plain they are some kind of allied concepts, the three together *akh*, *sekhem* and *sahu*, offering very tantalizing analogy to the Hindu *pitṛs* who even in the *Ṛgveda* are mentioned as of three stages or states and also the other categories of beatified beings like *sādhyas* and even *devas*.[58] But it is not possible to venture further in this field without a close study of the original texts of the Egyptians, most of which are not available here. I shall therefore return to the two of the three concepts, with the mention of which I started our study of the mortuary practices of the Egyptians.

As it happens, one of these two concepts is the most important for the immediate topic in hand, i.e., the mortuary rites and practices. Though the other concept is not less important it has close connection with the belief system, not only mortuary and religious but also ethical. The first concept, which is almost peculiarly Egyptian, almost without any parallel unless the so-called guardian angel of Christian faith complex can be likened to it, is that of the *ka*. The second, that of the *ba*, the soul, is a concept which, in some form or another, is common to many religions though its actual form may differ.

To begin with the concept of *ka*[59], as we have seen, the *kau* of gods were created along with them. Similarly the *ka* of any human being is created when he is born. The *ka* of the born human being, got joined to him at some stage and must have left him at some stage of the death phenomenon, so that "to go to one's *ka* was a euphemism for dying". The *ka* of an individual was "his guide and protector in heaven", it lived in the individual's tomb near his body and was required to be fed very regularly and sumptuously. To this end the tombs of the higher and middle class people were so constructed, in the ages before the New Empire, that a small chamber, called 'serdab', near the chapel, where the food and other things were to be offered, and having some connection however tenuous and concealed with it, was provided in the tomb. In this 'serdab', except for the small opening for the tenuous connection completely closed, was placed a life-like statue of the deceased to enable, as most of the authorities consulted maintain, the *ka* of the deceased to know its owner or its ward and to return to him to receive the regular nourishment through the small opening and to smell the incense which was absolutely necessary for continuance of blissful existence in the Hereafter. Not far from this 'serdab' lay the close opening of the shaft at the bottom of which down under lay the sarcophagus with its mummy. During the New Empire, particularly its latter part, the belief in *ka* as the sole guardian angel seems to have suffered a partial eclipse, at least with the coming into prominence of both magic, personal god, and fate. Any way the common tombs of the middle classes of these ages were not constructed with 'serdab' attached. And the belief in the need for a deceased person's *ka* to repair to the tomb and its mummy was fulfilled through the device of the upper side of the lid of the sarcophagus itself having the representation of the deceased lying at full length, face uppermost.[60]

The royal tombs since the IVth Dynasty, the pyramids and even the later ones, the rock-cut ones, did not have the 'serdab'. But the chamber near the offering hall and other part of the vast tomb housed more than one statue of the king. In addition, there was the funerary temple, which in the Pyramid Age abutted from the east face of the pyramid but in the later age was constructed in the necropolis separately, where the king in his statue was regularly served by his priests. Further there was the more or less magnificent valley temple, a free standing temple, where, in the earlier period, only the deceased king whose statue was placed was worshipped. In the later ages, as we have seen in the case of the temple of Seti I with which we started our study of the Egyptian complex of religious consciousness, the representations of the great national gods occupied the central place. Not infrequently the statues of the great gods must have been in the image of the deceased king himself as in the case of the gold statue of Amen in the likeness of Thothmes III.[61]

If the concept of *ka* was dimmed and pushed in the background to some extent at least in the Egyptian resurgence after the domination of the foreign and hated Hyksos, that of *ba* was polished and brought forward. We meet this concept, from of old, i.e., from the time of the Vth Dynasty at least, which has provided us the earliest of the representations of *ba*. *Ba* appears as a bird in the earlier period and as a human-headed hawk later, pert but intelligent and eager-looking. In this form we see *ba* in the pictures of the scene of the Hall of Judgment in the Court of Osiris in the Hereafter. And these scenes are known to occur only from the XVIIIth Dynasty onwards. The concept of *ba*, which, all authorities agree, means 'soul', was slowly but surely gaining in importance during some centuries before it actually came to discharge a very important function of being present at the weighing of the heart —mark, it was not the soul that was to be weighed and judged—in order to decide whether the deceased shall be admitted as pure into the Court of Osiris, to stand witness for the deceased.[62]

Frankfort looks upon *ba* as "not a part of a living person but the whole of a person as he appears after death", i.e., *ba* represents "the dead man conceived as living an animated existence after death". This was also the view of Breasted expressed by him half a century ago. Wallis Budge, who takes another view of *ba*, asserts that *ba* "acted as a kind of conscience", and comments on the speech of Thoth after weighing of the heart of the deceased: "This suggests that the *Ba* of the deceased watched carefully the doings of the man *in whose body it lived* because any evil deeds committed by the man would endanger his success in the Judgment Hall, and destroy its own chance of a renewed life in the Kingdom of Osiris."[63]

Further corroboration that *ba* was an entity, however elusive, separate from, though of the essence of, the personality of a person, comes from a wonderful specimen of literature[64], a solo performance of question and answer, which Frankfort designates as the "Dialogue of a man Weary of Life with His Soul" and which Breasted termed "The Dialogue of a Misanthrope with his Own Soul". The very fact that a living person thinks of his *ba* in such a manner as to call 'him' up to hold a converse or a consultation suggests that *ba* was looked upon as a distinct though non-material entity, whether within the body of a person or outside but always available for guidance, encouragement and help of a kind. The end of the whole episode further highlights the effectiveness of the 'opinion' of a person's *ba*. It was only when the 'weary man's' *ba* declined to have to do anything with his outrageous plan to end his life that the weary man probed further into the pros and cons of his misery and suffering. He finally concluded that it was much better to suffer in the present mundane life and hope for and get proper justice in the Hereafter after his death.

This unique piece of moralization and evidence of the sovereignty of the soul over an individual is believed to be dated about 2000 B.C. Thus it antedates the much cruder discussion of the Mesopotamian pessimist who held such a converse with his slave, there having been no concept of soul, though the dialogue is ascribable only to about 1000 B.C., i.e., about a thousand years later than its Egyptian prototype mentioned here!

With all this which appears to raise the presumption in favour of considering *ba* as an entity existing in a living individual, it must be pointed out that the great Egyptologists quoted or referred to in our discussion have not presented any text other than that of the Misanthrope's Dialogue with his Soul, *ba*, which suggests directly or indirectly the existence of *ba* in the living, much less testifies to its activity during the individual's life. Going through the texts, whose translations are provided by Erman and Blackman in *The Literature of the Ancient Egyptians* and by Wilson in Pritchard's book *The Ancient Near East*, I find that, except for the few references to *ba* already mentioned in this discussion, there are only four other places where 'soul' or 'souls' occur and I presume that these are the places where the Egyptian word used must be *ba*. Two of them occur in the *Instructions to Merikare*[65]. In one of them, as the quotation already made shows, the soul is said to go to the place it knows best and the assertion is used as an argument supporting the advice that one should have built one's tomb well in time during one's life implying that the soul, *ba* (?), can have no difficulty after one's death in finding the tomb, and hence the dead body, to enter in or to take the nourishment and to carry it to the man or the *ka* or the *ba* (?) in the Hereafter. The footnote running "Souls require a good tomb, in which they may find food and lodging, when they come on earth to enjoy the light" apparently does not uphold the above interpretation, but seems to suggest some special occasions as the implication. However, as no such special occasions of visits are mentioned by these authorities as a routine of life after death, I submit that the straightforward interpretation offered above must hold true.

The other reference is much more important as it appears to envisage the soul as an operative non-material element of the human personality. It runs: "A men should do that which profiteth his soul: in that he performeth the monthly service of priest, putteth on white sandals, frequenteth the temple, uncovereth the mysteries, entereth the sanctuary and eateth bread in the temple. It should be borne in mind, while appraising the contents of this piece of advice, that it was meant for an Egyptian King and not for an ordinary or even aristocratic citizen. Kings were priests of temples but had come to do their service very irregularly or even not at all, leaving it to the priest. Merikare is advised to discharge his erstwhile priestly and spiritual functions properly and thus to gain merit, and to profit his soul after death. If this is correct, then again the soul (*ba* ?) can hardly be said to be a really operative element in the living human personality. It is not the conscience with its discerning and dictating function. It is the non-material element that endures after death whose fate in life after death depends on what one does during life.

A papyrus of the reign of Rameses III, about 1164 B.C., mentions "all the souls of Egypt" thus: "Said King User-matt-Re Meri-Amon-life, prosperity, health! the great god [the dead king], to the officials and leaders of the land, the infantry, the chariotry, the Sherden [mercenary troops], the many bowmen, and all the souls of Egypt." It is clear that 'souls' here means persons and nothing more, as the address precedes the description of the king's benefactions. In a temple inscription of the same king, boasting that he had successfully checkmated the efforts of foreigners to cross into Egypt in force, he proclaims: "those who reached my frontier, their seed is not, their heart and their soul are finished for ever and ever." In this context soul can mean life or vitality.[66]

I should point out that what is predicated of the soul in the first of these four references is also said about heart in one place at least, i.e., that "it hasteneth to a place that it knoweth".[67] *Ba* or soul thus does not appear to be an operative element of personality but a non-material, spiritual if one likes it, entity that can be and has to be evoked after death of a person, being very significant for his continued existence in the Hereafter.

Compared with the paucity of references to *ba* or to *ka* in the literature the references to heart strike one as very numerous and frequent. Wherever desires, ideas, thoughts, intentions, purity, delight, joy, fear, courage, are mentioned, heart is the organ that is spoken of as their seat. Even understanding is sometimes attributed to heart. Not infrequently belly[68] is mentioned as the seat of desires, thoughts or intentions. This preponderance of the significant role of heart in the description of human attitudes, feelings, capacities, and thoughts must explain the weighing of the heart in the Court of Osiris to adjudge the dead person's "justification" or otherwise. Neither the *ka*, the so-called double or guardian angel, nor even the *ba*, the so-called soul, is ever shown as being judged in the Judgment scene, which came to the fore, and that in this particular form, only in and after the XVIIIth Dynasty.

Before passing on to see what light, if any, the literature used in the foregoing discussion sheds on the nature and function of the concept of *ka*, I shall dwell a little on a curious piece which is entitled *The Quarrel of the Body and the Head* found on a writing-board of a school boy of the XXIInd Dynasty, 950-730 B.C., to get some idea of the Egyptian notions of the inter-relations and functions of the different limbs and organs of the body. It is the belly, sometimes figuring as stated above as the receptacle of ideas, thoughts and desires, which disputed with the head and argued out the dispute before the usual council of the Thirty. The head answered back proclaiming its supremacy with a statement how the various limbs of the body stood and functioned under its position and command. If the belly was silenced by this, we have to understand, because of the entry of the mouth claimed to be its subordinate by the head, that the mouth finally asserted its superiority over others.[69]

There are three references to *ka* in the Instructions of Ptahotep, who lived in the reign of the Pharaoh Izezi of the Vth Dynasty about 2400 B.C., which are in a different key from the rest of such references which only occur in connection with either birth-origin or death. Ptahotep observes[70]: "If thou art one of those sitting at the table of one greater than thyself. . . . Do not pierce him with many stares, (for such) an aggression against him is an abomination to the *ka*." Wilson's comment that "the *ka* was the protecting and guiding vital force of a man and thus his social mentor", harmonizes with the next two mentions of *ka* in Ptahotep's instructions. Observes Ptahotep: "A great man, a little man—it is the *ka*'s abomination . . . ." It is a sentence which as Wilson himself points out may mean "Do not draw invidious distinctions" but was understood by Erman and Blackman to forbid the use of "ordinary expressions to replace the choice language" of one's employer. Another wise observation of Ptahotep runs: "As for the great man when he is at meals, his purposes conform to the dictates of his *ka*. . . . . The great man gives to *the man whom he can reach*, (but) it is the *ka* that lengthens out his arms". In both these contexts *ka* may mean the inner voice, the inner man or the soul and thus the moral mentor. But it can as well mean merely "mind", the motivating element of the human personality, even if one calls it the vital force. Erman and Blackman have commented in an illuminating manner thus: "Upon this vital force in a man also depended, according to the view here [in the Instructions of Ptahotep] held, his disposition and therewith his whole conduct."

Thus on a comparison between the use of the terms *ba* and *ka* in the literature, non-mortuary and non-priestly, one cannot but conclude that between the two concepts *ka* has the greater claim to being looked upon as the equivalent of 'conscience' and to the extent that conscience and soul can be equated, that of 'soul' too. J. H. Breasted, a great and unprejudiced student of the development of thought, religion and morality in Ancient Egypt, in his most mature pronouncement on the subject only speaks of the 'heart' which implied 'understanding' and was considered to be "the seat of responsibility and guidance". The word 'heart' came to have "a meaning which made it more fully equivalent of our word *conscience* than it had been in the Pyramid Age". Here and there individuals went even further and asserted that "the heart of a man is his own god".[71] Neither *ba* nor *ka* figures in the masterly presentation of Breasted's views on the religio-ethical complex of the Ancient Egyptians.

Before leaving this topic of the specification of the content of the concepts *ba*, *ka* and heart in this more or less nebulous condition, for no fault of mine nor any disinclination to probe further, I shall present here one use each of the concepts "heart' and *ka* from popular literature of Ancient Egypt, which will bring to my readers a realization of the hopeless task. In the *Tale of the Two Brothers*, a piognant story of a man's wife's sexual approach to her husband's younger brother, his repudiation of her in righteous indignation, her revengeful, malicious and cowardly poisoning the ears of her apparently hen-pecked husband, the latter's cruel and mean attempt to murder the younger brother and the latter's providential escape. A conversation followed between the two brothers who were by then on opposite sides of a stream infested with crocodiles. The younger brother cut off his phallus with his own hands and fainted. At this the "heart" of the elder brother is said to have been "smitten with great grief". The younger brother divining the future told the other that he would be going to a valley known fabulously as the Valley of the Cedar and asked him to take care of him when he heard any mishap happening to him and do certain things whereby he would be revived and the brothers could talk and he would "make answer to the attack" made on him.

In this connection again it is the 'heart' that comes in the picture. The younger brother says that when any mishap would have happened to him he would enchant his "heart" and "place it on the flower of the cedar". When the cedar would be cut down the elder brother was to seek for the "heart" of the younger brother without allowing his "heart" to be dismayed even if he had to conduct the search for seven long years. On finding the "heart" he was to place it in a vessel of cold water whereby he would be revived. The elder brother was to know the occurrence of a mishap to the speaker when a vessel of beer put into the hands of the former "frotheth over the sides". Pronouncing this prophesy and the elder brother's duty in the future the younger brother left for the Valley of the Cedar. The elder brother returned to his home in utter distress and burning rage. He killed his wife and threw her body to the dogs.

Bata, as the younger brother was named, through the favour of the Nine Gods (Ennead) or, as the text has it, with "the hearts of the Nine Gods inclined to him", had a beautiful woman as a help-mate. And "every god was contained in her". Miraculous happenings led the Pharaoh of Egypt to send his emissaries to the Valley of the Cedar in search of that woman and to bring her to his harem. There she revealed to the Pharaoh that her husband would die if the Cedar was cut. Pharaoh's servants cut down the Cedar and also the flower "whereon lay the heart of Bata". Next day when Bata's brother, Anpu, had his bowl of beer placed in his hand it frothed over. Immediately Anpu set out on his quest to the Valley of the Cedar and found his brother Bata lying dead. He spent three years in searching for the "heart" of Bata. At the onset of the fourth year Anpu's "heart desired to go forth to Egypt". Yet he spent a day or two in searching for his brother's "heart" which he found in the form of a berry. The "heart" of Bata having laid in cold water for a day absorbed the water. In the evening Bata began to quiver and looked at Anpu. Anpu on his part brought the bowl of water in which Bata's "heart" lay immersed and gave the water to Bata to drink. When Bata had drunk the water his "heart" resumed its proper place and Bata was revived. The brothers embraced each other. Further miracles are narrated in the story which need not detain us as there is nothing of special interest from the viewpoint from which this story has been summarized so far.[72]

In the colophon of the same story, mentioning the names of the scribes who wrote it and the name of the copyist-scribe, it is stated that it was "through the Ka of Kagabu" that the copy was made for the text written. Budge comments on this : "By the 'Ka of Kagabu' may be meant his genius or his love of or interest in literature." So nebulous was the concept of *Ka* to the Egyptian scribes and has been to great Egyptologists, while that of the "heart" was so general and such a pet with the common man of Ancient Egypt !

The *ba* was supposed to be provided with food and other things when the deceased was justified in the realm of Osiris and his companion gods. Yet it is said that the *ba* visited the tomb to take nourishment. *Ka* too is stated to be doing so. And it was the desire to make continuous provision of food in the Hereafter to the deceased that in the later ages articles representing food but made of some permanent material were placed in abundance in the tomb. It is very interesting to find that both *ba* and *ka* are shown by the side of the figure of the famous Tutankhamen in a fine wooden carving of his as Osiris.[73]

The Pharaohs and the noblemen and such other wealthy people as could afford it, as already stated, made endowments and contracted priests to carry on the periodical celebrations at their tombs and to provide food regularly. Worship for the Pharaoh was provided in their temples, both the mortuary and the valley ones, whether their statues in the latter case were placed by themselves or along with those of the great gods of Egypt. In the case of nobles and other grandees, worship had come to be provided by getting their statues placed in the temples of the local gods, of course with the permission or as a favour of the Pharaoh. Such contracts written on the papyrus or actually graven on the walls of the tombs showing their number and the vast extent of the endowments testify to the anxiety of the Ancient Egyptians about their life after death and to the intensity of their belief in the need for continuous supply of the material things of this world for their welfare in the Hereafter.[74]

With all the complex of belief and practice about death and provision for life after death which is so distinctive, unique and in marked contrast with the current and recent mortuary complex of the Hindus, it is very intriguing that the Ancient Egyptians considered a libation of water at their tombs poured by anyone as a means of happiness in the life hereafter and were happy to be assured of it. Poet-prophet Neferrohu, "The wiseman of the East", who lived about the time of Amenemhat I, i.e., 1990 B.C., ends his popular exercise on the confident personal note that his prophecy would come true and that "A man of learning shall pour out water for me (in my tomb)".

Another wiseman by name Anii, who lived in the late XXIInd Dynasty, about 950-730 B.C., advised his generation in even a more Hindu-wise manner thus: "Offer water to thy father and thy mother, who rest in the desert valley . . . Omit not to do it, that thy son may do the like for thee". Further quaint similarity which must sound familiar to a Hindu is recorded in an old account of an exile who was permitted to return to Egypt by Senusret I, about 1950 B.C. Sinuhe, the exile, in referring to the Pharaoh's deceased father says: "King Amenemhat flew away to heaven and was united with the sun and the god's body was merged with his creator."[75] !

CHAPTER III

EGYPTIAN-II

THE Ancient Egyptians' view of life after death and their notion of death being only a temporary suspension of life, which can go on, and must be made to continue indefinitely in another world, were ingrained in them. The complex that appeared in its full form later in their civilization was a growth of centuries, in which their theological speculations and the nature of the gods brought to the forefront by them and frequently embraced by the people had their share. However, the basic complex was strong and basically identical enough to give the world the first and the most ponderous endeavour of man towards securing immortality through material appurtenances. A people who valued the supposed life-after-death so much and who were evidently so seriously concerned about it, may be expected to enthrone a divinity presiding over the Hereafter with its troupe of gods, or angels if one likes it that way, and cling to it. And the Egyptians certainly did so. For whatever may be said about the glory and greatness of the three gods of the three cities that came into prominence and were accepted by the people as the supreme ones, one at a time, in the different periods of Egyptian history the one god who kept on receiving their unstinted allegiance is Osiris. Breasted[1] has appropriately named the Osiris cult as the "folk-religion" of Ancient Egypt!

I shall waive the question of the origin of Osiris, whether he was a nature- or a hero-god, and proceed with his acceptance as some form of the solar deity when he came to be a generally accepted divinity, not later than the XIIth Dynasty. I have mentioned his consort Isis and their son Horus and also, in the barest outline, the very romantic myth about the murder of Osiris and the exploits in securing Isis and her husband's possessions and future. Mythology says that the murdered Osiris was cut up into fourteen, sixteen or even eighteen parts according to different texts.[2] Whatever the number of the parts into which Osiris was said to have been cut up, only sixteen are known to have been buried at as many different places in Egypt, and as many sanctuaries raised over them. The Osiris mythology, which in a connected form is known only from very late sources, is, as Frankfort (*Ancient Egyptian Religion*, p. 126) states, mentioned in parts in religious literature of the third millennium B.C. Breasted, too, held the same opinion (*The Dawn of Conscience*, pp. 99-104). Though the dismemberment of Osiris is not mentioned in the hymns addressed to him, hailing from the middle kingdom (2000 B.C.) and the XVIIIth Dynasty, yet shrines of and worship to him in a number of places are referred to (Erman and Blackman, pp. 140-5).

This part of the myth, the dismemberment and the holiness of the places where the various limbs of Osiris came to be buried has analogy with the legends connected with *Śaktitīrthas* or the holy places of Śakti and Śāktism, Śaivism and even Hinduism in general.

Budge informs us that in Graeco-Roman times the sanctuaries of Osiris had risen to be fortytwo and each nome (district) came to possess a "central shrine of Osiris" known as "Serapeum" as by then the identification of Apis[3], the bull of Memphite Ptah, had come to be ascribed to it many of the attributes of Osiris. The temple of Abydos became and remained the principal shrine of Osiris where he received worship in seven partially different forms. This part of the Osiris cult may be compared with Śaivism in which Śiva is credited with "eight" forms or "majesties".

In the temple of Seti I, with which we started our quest of the elucidation of the Egyptian complex of religious consciousness, in the Osiris chapel a fine painting shows Thoth, the writer-god, presenting to the seated Seti-Osiris the symbol of life.[4] This is clearly the illustration of that part of the Osiris myth which deals with the resurrection of Osiris by Horus[5], which in the present context also assures Seti I of his resurrection in the Hereafter presided over by Osiris.

A much more important deity, one of the rare ones in the pantheon of Ancient Egypt, being an anthropomorphic representation of the abstract concept of order, truth, law, righteousness, is the goddess Maat. As will be presently clear, she is much more important than Thoth because she plays a major role in the development of not only the religious consciousness of Ancient Egyptians but also of their conscience and the system of justice. The concept of *Maat* can be compared with that of *ṛta* in the *Rgveda* of India. Here I shall confine myself to the role of Maat, the goddess and the concept in the field of religious consciousness.

At the outset it should be noted that her symbol, which, whenever she is represented in the human form, she bears erect in her slight headdress, is feather, an object which is proverbial for lightness.[6]

Perhaps her earliest human representation is that which we get in the papyrus of Nebseni, which according to Budge is the oldest so far, being dated as "much older" than that of the scribe Ani, which was written in the XIXth Dynasty[7], i.e. about 1300 B.C. Nebseni's papyrus may be taken to be dated about 1600 B.C. But the concept and also the representation was much older, coming from the Pyramid Age about 1200 years earlier. In the Pyramid Texts "Maat, or truth, is closely associated with Ra, and each of his two boats was called *Maat*". The goddess Maat was "the daughter of Ra".[8] In all her representations she holds in her right hand the symbol of life, an attribute of god-head. The weighing of the heart of Nebseni is being done in the presence of the standing Osiris, Nebseni eagerly watching his heart in the scale ; the god Thoth, in the form of a baboon perched on a stool, looks at the scales intently and by his side stands Maat who too appears equally concerned. This anthropomorphic presence of Maat occurs also in a late papyrus, that of Nekht of about 1000 B.C.[9] The papyrus depicts a scene from the life of Nekht in the realm of Osiris. Nekht and his wife are shown as adoring Osiris who is seated in his dignity by the side of a lake in the garden of Nekht's house. Behind him stands Maat with her left hand placed on the shoulder of Osiris. Maat's association with Osiris, outside the weighing scene and without Thoth, underscores her wider significance in the religio-ethical system of the Ancient Egyptians.

The weighing of the heart of the deceased makes a very impressive scene as in the painting on the papyrus of Ani of the XIXth Dynasty. But the scene of the weighing gets illustrated in the mortuary appurtenances from the XVIIIth Dynasty onward. The earlier period of the Egyptian history has not produced any such illustration. The Pyramid Texts, however, raise a presumption that the deceased Pharaoh, before being admitted into the Osirian company, had to pass some test. And the *Instruction for King Merikare* of the IXth or the Xth Dynasty, which, as Erman and Blackman have observed, contains "religious conceptions that are practically non-existent in the other works of the same class", has this to say about the judgment of the deceased in the Hall of Osiris: "The judges who judge are not lenient on the day of judging.... A man remaineth over after death and his deeds are placed beside him in heaps. But it is for eternity that one is there, and he is a fool that maketh light of them. But he that cometh unto them without wrong-doing, he shall continue yonder like a god, stepping boldly forward like the Lords of Eternity."

Almost all writers[10] on the subject of Egyptian religion are agreed that the scene of the Judgment after death as depicted in the papyrus of Ani forms one of the impressive scenes of anxious waiting for a favourable judgment on self after death and creates solemn atmosphere for those who see it. It hovers in one's imagination for long. The whole set-up is such as cannot but drive home to any one the solemnity of the occasion, the arbiter of one's eternal bliss or perpetual suffering and misery. Every single element in it contributes its quota to the total effect. In this scene the goddess Maat is absent. The weigher is the jackal-headed god Anubis. Anubis, who may be described as the apothecary of the gods, is said to have helped Isis and Horus in mummifying the body of Osiris, and was the *de facto* arbiter of the scales. Though Thoth as the writer is present to record the result of the weighing it is the word of Anubis that is recorded. The heart of the deceased is very significantly represented by a small jar, a container but a small one. It is no accident, as the voice of the heart is declared to be "small" and "still" by later humanity. The Hindus, as will be evident later, very early, about 800 B.C. at the latest, too, had settled the size of the individual soul as of the measure of one's thumb! It was weighed against a feather, a light object and the symbol of Maat, or righteousness, among the Ancient Egyptians. The heart to be pronounced worthy, as one that has passed the test, must keep level with the feather, so light it must be. Here, too, how significant that later humanity should also think of a pure heart as light, as one not heavy with the load of bad actions!

Just beyond Thoth couches the ugly devourer of the dead, ready to pounce upon the deceased whose heart is adjudged unworthy. It was well with Ani that his heart was righteous. The favourable result of the weighing having been announced, Ani, relieved and pleased, is led by Horus, who, with his left hand raised as in adoration and holding Ani with his right, addresses the majestically seated Osiris: "I come before thee, Un-Nefer [Good Being]. I bring unto thee Osiris Ani. His heart is righteous (having) come forth from the Scales. He is not evil before any god (and) any goddess. Thoth hath him in accordance to the written orders which the Company of the Gods uttered in respect of him. . . . I pray thee that there may be given unto him bread, cakes, (and) beer, (and) a coming forth (appearance) in the presence of Osiris. Let him be like the Followers of Horus."[11]

In the final section of the scene, Ani, arrayed in feastal attire, in which a sort of a small cap perched on the crown of the head is the most distinguishing addition, and surrounded with various kinds of offerings, is shown adoring Osiris. He kneels with his right knee and the lower leg bent back under the thigh and the buttock and the left foot resting on the ground with the knee bent forward. With his right hand raised, Ani poses the Egyptian attitude of adoration.

For the role of the judgment scene in the religious consciousness of the Egyptians, Budge's very balanced appraisal deserves to be quoted. Says Budge[12]: "The large size of the picture and its prominent place in all the great funerary papyri clearly indicate the predominance which the Judgment of Osiris occupied in the minds of his votaries. For the man who was cast out of the Hall of Maat condemned could have no lot or portion in the kingdom of Osiris with the beatified."

Since very early, it appears, the Osiris cult had been associated with some esoteric rituals and had been having one of the most exciting annual festivals at Abydos, in which the main feature was the drama of the death and resurrection of Osiris.[13] The festival was known under the Middle Empire, i.e., about 2000 B.C. Women took the part of the two consorts of Osiris, i.e., Isis and Nephthys. The search for Osiris lasted for three days during which "loud cries of lamentation resounded throughout the town, for crowds of weeping women who beat their faces and breasts, bewailed the loss of Osiris, and also the wounds and other injuries" received by their husbands and sons who were supposed to have joined in the fight. Budge tells us that the Osiris Drama was performed in the capitals of many of the nomes and that probably at least some scenes of the drama were enacted in every shrine of Osiris. He further assures us that the Osirian festival was almost "the most popular form of amusement for the people". Breasted adds his weighty observation that it "gained a great place in the affections of the people", and the significant information that "over and over again, on their Abydos tablets, the pilgrims pray that after death they may be privileged to participate in this celebration".

The Osiris hall behind the principal chapels in the temple of Seti I, described in the previous chapter, to which access was had only through a door in the back wall of the Osiris chapel, and the small chapels attached to it lying at right angles to the main axis of the temple, bear concrete evidence for the assertion that the Osiris cult had some esoteric rites and rituals which were naturally to be conducted in secrecy and under mystery-creating circumstances. The scenes on the walls actually depict "the celebration of some of the mysteries".[14]

What was the kind of perpetual living the "justified" or the beatified dead were to have and what was to happen to those whose hearts failed to justify their owners are the next important questions in our quest of the Egyptian religious consciousness.

The usual term for the Egyptian Hereafter is *Dat*, *Duat*, *Dewat* or even *Tuat*.[15] Wilson has used the word *Dat*, Elysian Fields, nether world and underworld, in expanding his views on aspects of mortuary belief and practice, whenever he has an occasion to deal with them, his principal task not being concerned with the exposition of Egyptian religious consciousness and practice. Dat is, according to him, "the area between earth and the counter heaven" and was "the realm of the immortal dead".[16] According to Budge, however, Tuat was the name which "the Egyptians gave to the abode of the spirits and souls of the dead" and was commonly rendered "Other World" or "Under World" but was translated by some by "Hades" or "Hell". Margaret Murray uses the word *Duat* and tells us that it was divided into "twelve sections or countries, each section having its own name" being separated from the next by a gate guarded by a warden. Budge states the total number of states to be *twentyone* out of which seven were "the special domain of Osiris".*

Tuat was a place full of dangers to all souls and all "had to traverse it in order to reach the abode of the gods and the beatified souls". Each section of it contained special types of fields, devils, monsters, most of whom were known to the priests by their names even in the old period, and such torture-agencies as boiling water or blazing fire. But, as Budge assures his readers, no illustration or picture of any part of the *Tuat* before the XIth or XIIth Dynasty, i.e., before about 2000 B.C., is known.

Under the New Empire the illustrations on the coffins abound indicating that the practice of painting these scenes had become general among the élite. The fact that the priests had by then "compiled a sort of Guide to the *Tuat*" containing detailed description of its "inhabitants and such life-like pictures of the foes which the deceased would meet there, together with lists of their names and magical formulae, that he would find it impossible to lose his way, or be overcome by any monster".[17]

There were two versions of the nature of the *Tuat* and the journey of the deceased through it, one of them based on Amen-Ra and the other on Osiris. Budge thinks that the former view was favoured by the Court, nobles and high officials, while the other received the allegiance of the common people.

* Italics mine. They are intended to invite attention to Indian analogy, Hinduism recognising twentyone hells very early in its history before A.D. 200.

According to the former only those persons who were able to secure a place in the Boat of Amen-Ra, in which the journey through the under-world was made, could emerge at day-break as living beings. On the other hand, in the latter view the state of beatification was enjoyed by only those who had worshipped Osiris on earth, turning aside from other "wretched little gods", and lived a righteous life on earth. They were given estates, farms, homesteads in the kingdom of Osiris where they cultivated the "plant of truth" and daily fed on it. On the relative strength of the appeals of both these views Budge asserts: "As a whole the peoples of Egypt in every period of their long history preferred the reward of Osiris to that of Amen-Ra."[18]

A very late papyrus giving the miraculous story of Khamuas and his son records the scenes of many of the halls of the Kingdom of Osiris purporting to have been personally seen by Khamuas and his son, having miraculously got admission into it. In one hall they saw famishing men lying about, though asses nearby them were feeding themselves; there were others over whose head hung food and water in plenty but which they could not reach as they were digging away the ground from under their feet. In another hall were standing a number of good spirits while at the door were standing evil-doers praying to these spirits for help. In the Hall of Judgment Khamuas and his son saw a marvel. They recognised a person present there. He was a poor man from Memphis, whose funeral and mortuary rites were of the most rudimentary kind. However, it having turned out on the scales that his good deeds had outnumbered his bad ones he was clothed in a gorgeous garb which they recognised as the one which was sported by a rich man on earth at his burial. As the latter's bad deeds outnumbered his good ones on the scales he was stripped of his raiment. It was then presented to the righteous poor man of Memphis whom they saw draped with it. Some of these and other scenes of torture and suffering are illustrated just as are the "fields of Peace and Offerings" where lived the "justified", which was known as Iaru[19].

There are evident similarities in the much later—these Egyptian ideas are all early and illustrated, too, on documents or objects of before 1000 B.C., later by about five to six hundred years—musings and the theorizings of the Hindus.

None of the other three Great Gods, Ra, Ptah and Amen, appears to have had as many shrines, in so many cities other than the one with which he was associated as its principal deity, as Osiris had. Amen's temple at Karnak had shrines for both his consort Mut and their son Chons. Ra's temple at Helipolis and Ptah's at Memphis would appear to have enshrined only them. In many other cities the principal god was one of the many therianthropic functional deities postulated in the Egyptian pantheon. Hathor the cow-goddess, the least therianthropic, was a deity, who in one or other of her various forms, was worshipped in her shrines in all the great towns of Egypt, though her own city was Denderah. Bast, the cat-headed goddess, was a local deity of the deltaic city Bubastis. She rose to be an all-Egypt deity only later, when in the XXIInd Dynasty the local prince became the Pharaoh of Egypt. Thoth, the ibis-headed writer-god, so important in his functions, was the local god of Hermophilis. Min, the ithyphallic deity, had his temple at Koptos. Khnemu, the ram-headed potter-god, was worshipped in the Island of Elephantine.[20]

The position of the formal or the state religion may be stated as one in which the three great gods Ra, Ptah and Amen had attained all-Egypt status, the last having done so the latest, i.e., after the Middle Empire. The spread of Osiris shrines was also all-Egypt as already mentioned. Apart from these gods, every district, whether it had or had not a shrine of one of them, had its own god and "every town of any size had a temple to the local deity", its size and splendour varying with the wealth of the city. This layer of the Egyptian religious complex was public contribution. It was so prominent and ubiquitous that Erman, impressed with the excessive concern of the kings for the gods particularly under the New Empire, considered "the state as really maintaining the religion of the country".

Besides these shrines and their deities was the second layer of the religious complex, formed by subordinate deities like Renutet, the goddess of harvest, Bas, the dwarf god of joviality and love, Ta-urt or Apet, the hippopotamus goddess of the birth-chamber, which were offered worship either in the house or in the fields, occasionally in a shrine.[21]

The third layer, which, it appears, is not quite distinct from the second, was formed by domestic chapels and worship. Erman wrote as if every house of Ancient Egypt had a room which was "a little chapel". Flinders Petrie is much more specific and in his specification corrects the view that one gets from Erman's statement. The permanent place in an Egyptian house for worship was a small "recess in the main hall, about two feet wide, coloured red", the particular colour having been regarded as "a spiritual passage". Petrie found the recesses in the houses of Tell Amarna "thrice on the west wall, twice on the south, once on the east, but never on the north".[22] This orientation must remind one of the Hindu ideas and practice in the temple orientation.

Wilson[23] is of the opinion that domestic worship represents a later development in the religious consciousness and practice of the Ancient Egyptians. He thinks that in the Old Kingdom "the gods of the pantheon were more remote from common man" and his *ka* formed the intermediary. I have not seen any support for this opinion in the writings of the other celebrated Egyptologists whose works I have consulted and so largely drawn upon. Wallis Budge[24] has observed just the contrary: "Viewing such evidence as we have it seems that the Egyptian at this period possessed a feeling, which was born with him and was an integral part of his spiritual nature, of reverence or even fear, of a great unknown God whom he felt it his natural duty to worship." Wilson further states that "a close personal relation to a specifically named god, who was his protector and controller" came to be entertained by

Egyptians of the latter part of the Empire and that the "town god", "the equivalent of the local saint", might have been the precurser of the personal god. He has, however, not instanced any specific god as having been mentioned as his god by any Egyptian of the latter part of the Empire. Nor have I come across such a mention in the works of the other authorities, nor with the exception, which I shall presently state, of one such reference, have I chanced upon any in the literary pieces presented in Erman's book *The Literature of the Ancient Egyptians*.

The reference to what is quite clearly the personal god of an individual occurs in *Papyrus Anastasi*, which Hall[25] assigns to the XVIIIth Dynasty. A scribe having set up "a small statue of Thoth, the patron divinity of the learned, in his house", greets the image, portrayed as "a squatting ape". Both the form and the content, greeting and prayer combined in one, are very interesting and instructive to students of later religions whether of Semitic or Indo-European origin. I shall therefore quote Blackman's translation of the text, except the last sentence, whose meaning, according to Blackman, is that the image of Thoth will "surely" protect the owner, the installer scribe, from the evil eye. It runs: "Praise to thee, thou lord of the house! Ape with white hair and pleasant form, with friendly nature, beloved of all men. He is of sehret-stone, he, even Thoth, that he may illumine the earth with his beauty. That which is upon his head [the moon's disk] is of red jasper, and his phallus is of quartz. His love leapeth (?) on his eyebrows, and he openeth his mouth to bestow life. Mine house is happy since the god entered it; it flourisheth and is (richly) furnished, since my lord did tread it. Be happy, ye people of my quarter, and rejoice, all my kindred. Behold, my lord it is that maketh me (gives me prosperity and advancement); yea, mine heart longeth after him."[26]

There is some evidence from artefacts and objects of art which Flinders Petrie thinks supports the prevalence of household worship. Many bronze figures of various gods upto eight or ten inches high, which were found not in the vicinity of temples, might have been in his opinion intended for such worship.[27] Perrot and Chipiez[28] have reproduced a number of bronze images which though they might actually be very late, i.e., of the Ptolemaic epoch, are thought to represent the practice of an older age. There are figured the cat-headed goddess Bast, the cow-headed goddess Isis-Hathor and the ibis-headed Thoth, the first two were cast in bronze and the third in enamelled clay. They measure between five and six inches in total height.

The images of god installed in a temple, Erman tells us, must have also always been small, i.e., about two feet high. Perrot and Chipiez assert that no statue of a god can be confidently ascribed to the first six Dynasties. Petrie goes further and states that there are very few examples of the great temple statues before the XIXth Dynasty, about 1300 to 1200 B.C.[29] Perhaps the earliest of such statues is that of Amen seated, protecting Heremhab, about 1340 B.C. It is "rather over life size" and "carved in hard white limestone". Rameses II, 1301-1235 B.C., dedicated two statues of Ptah at Memphis, one of which was over ten feet in height. The statues placed in processional temples, which were open shrines, were meant for being carried in procession on stated occasions and were made of wood in a portable size.

The processions of gods, and the different and more costly materials out of which evidently even images meant for procession were made at least in the earlier period, about the XIth Dynasty, i.e., about 2050 B.C., are mentioned in *The Instruction for King Merikare* left by his father. The father asks his son to "reverence God upon his road (i.e., in a procession ?), even him that is fashioned of precious stones and formed of copper . . . There is no river that suffereth itself to be concealed; it destroyeth the dam(?) with which it was hidden (i.e., God is only seemingly hidden)."[30] Tutankhamen, who, coming after the reformist Pharaoh Ikhnaten, zealously reinstated the previously current religious complex of the land, is well known as one whose rich furniture and gold coffin dazzled the world with the brilliance that he had attempted and achieved while he lived, 1358-1349 B.C. He it was who had got made the "handsome" silver figure of Aman-Ra "plated with gold" which is preserved in the British Museum. Budge thinks that it must come from a shrine of the god. In other statues he caused to be used lapis lazuli and other varieties of precious stones. A figure of Ptah was decorated partly in silver gold or gold, lapis lazuli, turquoise and other such stones. He got made "sacred images of all the gods of real *teham* metal".[31] The boat or the barge in which the great gods of Egypt were placed and carried, too, was quite often made of such costly and dazzling material. It sometimes served the purpose of a shrine, the image of the god being placed inside the boat-cabin.[32]

Images or statues of gods placed in temples are calculated to inspire awe by the suggestion of god's ever-presence and also by accustoming the people to thinking of their forms and associated qualities and traits. The divine presence, and transcendent guidance and assurance of help, are conducive both to steady and straight action of man in society, to his individual peace of mind and some kind of contentment. They form, under appropriate mythology and teaching, a powerful incentive to striving and law-abiding. In view of this function of the statues of gods in their shrines, both the material of which they are made and their size are important. Their forms are even more significant but they are given by the current mythology. It is noteworthy that the sizes of statues of the gods of Ancient Egypt were rather small and grew to greater proportions only in the latter part of the Empire period as already stated on the authority of Flinders Petrie. Their material was quite often of the costliest. We are told that the image of Amen at Karnak was either of Gold or of gilded wood. Its impressive speciality appears to have been moveable head, arms and legs.[33]

In a country and a civilization where the king of the people was a veritable god in life and was regularly worshipped as such in an imposing structure to the accompaniment of a pompous and appealing ritual after his death, the statues of the kings stationed in the chapels of sanctuaries or even in the surrounding courtyards, passages and halls, pillared or small, acquire a relevance in the perspective of the functions of statues of gods mentioned above. The case must be appreciated as very different from that of the Mesopotamian religious complex. There the king was not only a servant of god in theory but was often actually represented in the act of digging or carrying material intended for the construction of a shrine of god. Gudea's twelve or fourteen statues, whatever their size, however big relative to the size of the statues of Enlil or Nannar, could not raise his stature above that of god in the eyes of the Mesopotamians. In Egypt, however, with the background mentioned above, the situation was bound to be different. This background was further deepened for the peculiar situation by the practice of artistic representation of closest friendship and perfect equality between the king and gods. Thus, we have, fortunately restored for posterity by Reisner, at least three portraits in the round of King Mycerinus or Menkaura of the IVth Dynasty, who succeeded King Chephren or Khafra about 2600 B.C., which once graced his non-funerary temple at Gizeh.[34] In one portrait the king and his queen appear in standing pose, the height of the king being four feet and eight inches, rather short. His queen is only a little shorter so that the couple sppear well matched. She is portrayed with her right hand round her husband's back and right side, with its palm resting on his abdomen and the left palm resting on his left upper arm. Altogether the position may be described as one of affectionate public embrace. In the other two sculptures, the king, in his more formal dress with the high crown on his head, is depicted standing between two goddesses. In one of them which is three feet and two and a half inches high the goddesses are, Hathor on the king's right, and a local deity on his left. All of them hold their hands straight down, the left of Hathor's holding the right palm of the king. In the other, which is only three feet and one inch high, the two goddesses are, Hathor on the right, and a different local deity on the left. Hathor's left arm lies round the back of the king, the palm clutching the left upper arm of the king, while the right arm of the other goddess entwines round the king's back and rests its palm on the right upper arm of the king, exactly paralleling Hathor's on his left. The pose may be described as mutual affectionate embrace for public avowal of friendship and equality.

About six hundred and fifty years later in the pillared temple of King Senusret or Senusert I, 1971-1928 B.C., sculptured on the pillars can be seen king Senusret or Senusert I, wearing his crown and holding the symbol of life in his left hand, being led by his right hand into the presence of the ithyphallic god of Thebes by the great god Atum of Heliopolis. The king is as tall and as sprightly and lively as the god himself, though the latter is conferring on him his favour by presenting the symbol of life before him.

On another column, whose total height is twelve feet, again there is a sculpture of King Senusret I and the great god Atum. The height of the sculpture itself is not given; but one can well imagine it to be a lifesize one at least, as it stands on such a big pillar. In it the king is dressed exactly like the god, even their crowns being identical, the only distinction being the cobra-hood on the forehead of the king and the peculiar beard on the chin of the god. Atum is shown as holding with his left hand the king's left upper arm and drawing him close with his right, which he has passed behind the king's head, the intention evidently being to join the head with his and thus share with him the breath of life. The king holds his staff and sceptre and stands stiff and proud. In a third sculpture figure another great god, Ptah, and the king, both having identical faces. In this panel, Ptah has embraced the king by putting both his hands round his waist and the king grasps the god's head evidently to share with him the breath of life. Lange and Hirmer[35] characterize the latter scene as "silent, proud companionship of god and king" with "a noteworthy dignity".

To add to the complete deification of the king and to contribute to the consequent eclipse and stultification of gods, the proper attire of the kings in religious functions was, from the Vth Dynasty onwards, the same as that of the gods. The inscriptions, whether charms, incantations, or invocations in the pyramids, such as those in the pyramid of Unas, were such as to exalt the dead king over the gods. As Hall aptly puts the situation, "The arrival of the dead ruler [in the Hereafter] is to be the signal for general commotion and fear on the part of the denizens of the other world."[36] The Pharaoh was not only the god-king of the Egyptians but was to be the terror-inspiring king of the gods of the Hereafter!

Now we shall note the kind of statues the kings put for themselves, particularly in their valley or non-funerary temples, where they received regular and impressive worship long after they had died. We find that Chefren or Khafra, the 4th Pharaoh of the IVth Dynasty, the predecessor of Menkaura, almost wholly pre-stalled Gudea of Mesopotamia more than five hundred years before him in that he had made at least nine, more or less complete, statues of himself, which evidently were placed originally in his valley temple. The seated portrait in diorite figured by Lange and Hirmer[37], a powerful one, measures five feet and six inches in height. The fine life-size statue, total height being five feet and ten inches, hewn out of copper plate, of King Phiops of Pepi I of the VIth Dynasty, about 2400 B.C., is not ascertained to have been a temple installation. Semusert I of the XIIth Dynasty about 1950 B.C. vied with Chefren or Khafra of the IVth Dynasty, in having put up ten seated statues of himself, though only in his burial chamber. The height of the statue is great, being six feet and six and a half inches. King Amenemhat III, about hundred and twenty years later, whom Hall[38] describes as "a monarch of original and powerful mind", "of whom we would fain to know more than we do", is represented, besides the sphinxes with his face, in a life-size statue, which, in the words of Lange and Hirmer, having "refined, quietly severe solemnity", was meant for his funerary temple. Its height is five feet and three inches. His previous monarch, Senusret III, is shown in the picturesque temple at Der-el-Bahri "at different periods of his life, from a young to an old man", the heads discovered at Abydos and Karnak confirming the portraiture of the monarch in his old age.

It is seen that the life-size and even over-life-size portraits of kings went on being made from the IVth Dynasty to the end of the XIIth, and were being placed either in their non-funerary temples or funerary ones. In the Middle Kingdom, the XIth and XIIth Dynasties, they appear to have been placed in a number of ordinary temples in different cities. It was also during this period that the powerful and majestic sphinxes, in the mein and with the head of the reigning monarch[39], came to be made and placed in prominent passages in temple premises. Even the reformist king Amenophis IV, before his conversion into Ikhnaten, had a huge statue of himself placed in his Aten temple. In its height of thirteen feet it foreshadowed the stupendous sizes that were to be in vogue with Rameses II and some of his successors. The young Tutankhamen satisfied himself with a statue which is only "almost life-size". One of the almost innumerable statues which Rameses II had put up of himself in one or the other place and form is fortytwo feet in height, while his four seated colossi stationed at the entrance to his rock-cut temple at Abu Simbel rise sixtyfive feet high.[40]

Perrot and Chipiez appropriately summed up the situation for the Egyptian religious consciousness years ago, when they remarked that the statues of gods must have attracted much less attention than those of kings. The place occupied by the king's huge statues in the temple-complex under the New Empire is thus described by them : "The Pharaoh who built a temple fitted it with his own effigies. His colossi sat before the gate, they helped to form those structural units which we call Osiride piers, and figures of smaller size were ranged under the porticos. In that part of the Great Temple at Karnak, which dates from the XVIIIth dynasty, statues of Thothmes III alone have been found to the number of several dozens."[41]

The process of making of the reigning king a god, who was even from the earliest looked upon as the son of god or god on earth but became a god to be capable of receiving divine worship only after death, appears to have grown apace with the political phenomenon of the appropriation of the land of other peoples, particularly that of the barbaric people of the south, i.e., Nubia or Sudan. The importance of Nubia for the national welfare was early realized by the Pharaohs. The waters of the Nile could be properly controlled if they were handled higher up in Nubia. The gold of Nubia was a great lure and a certain gain. Raids and invasions on Nubia came to be carried out in the reign of Senusret or Senusert I, Sesostris as he is often called in foreigners' records, about 1950 B.C.

But it was Senusret III who created permanent fortresses there about eighty or ninety years thereafter. And it was he who first utilized religious complex as a missionary and an emissary of international aggrandizement, and also as an agency for incorporation of foreigners as docile nationals. Taking advantage of the religious backwardness of the Nubians and of the elements common to the religious complexes of Egyptians and Nubians, he built a temple at one of the two fortresses which he put up and installed therein a Nubian deity named Dedun or Didun (the Tithonos of the Greeks). The ritual of worship, however, was enjoined to be purely Egyptian. In the other fortress opposite, he built a temple of the Egyptian divinity Khnumer Chnum, the god of the cataracts, in which he also installed himself alongside of Khnum. Senusret by the act of putting up the conqueror's or the reigning monarch's statue as the image of god to be offered worship to by the new subjects of the national state of Egypt began an additional ground for treating the Pharaoh as living god. The national pride of the Egyptians in the event of the territorial acquisition and of the deification of the Pharaoh among their new compatriots must have made the acceptance of the king as god quite easy for them.

Amenhotep or Amenophis III, about 1390 B.C., penetrating further south into Nubia, erected south of the Second Cataract "sanctuaries on a scale of imperial magnificence". At Sulb or Soleb he built a great and splendid temple to Amen and to "his own Image living upon earth, *Neb-Maāt Rā*". Hall gives the name of the temple as called after the king as *Kha-m-maat*, "He who appears as Maat (the goddess of Right and Law)". And he went a step further in erecting a temple to his queen at Sedeinga, a few miles to the north, as a goddess of the Sudan, and in showing himself on a stela as worshipping himself. Hall thinks that it was this Amenhotep that "developed" a contemporary worship of himself as the personification of the Empire". In the perspective, however, it is clear that he was not the originator of the idea.[42]

I should close this discussion of the development in the process of the deification and magnification of the reigning Pharaoh and its significance for a proper understanding of the religious consciousness and practice of the Ancient Egyptians with what Margaret Murray[43] calls "an interesting suggestion of a change in the attitude of the Pharaoh towards the deity", in about five and a half centuries that elapsed between Thothmes III and Sheshenk I. Thothmes, after his great Syrian conquests about 1480 B.C., presented the huge booty to Amen "as a freewill offering". Sheshenk I, on the other hand, about 930 B.C., pictured Amen on the walls of the Karnak temple, to which his projected addition remained unfinished, as leading the many towns of Palestine, which were reduced by his expedition, and presenting them to the Pharaoh. The roles of the deity and its votary the Pharaoh are thus seen to have been exchanged to the tremendous aggrandizement of the latter. The change recorded by Murray, however, must have occurred not between Thothmes III's time and that of Sheshenk I but between that of Rameses III, 1198-1166 B.C., and Sheshenk I. As she herself[44] has noted Rameses III, in some of the scenes in the great temple at Medinet Habu built by him, is depicted as presenting the plundered treasures of the Amorites as tribute to Amen. This accords very much more fittingly with the suggestion made in the discussion that the huge statues of reigning kings and in large numbers figuring in the temples and their corridors and passages strengthened the process of making a god of a reigning king as a component of the religious complex of Ancient Egypt. The Rameseses were almost the last word in the matter of size and number of the statues of the Pharaoh !

Statues of gods, as we saw in the Mesopotamian civilization, before being installed as images representing them in their temples and treated as such with worship, were ritually treated in order to invoke and establish in them the spirits of the appropriate gods. In India in the Hindu religious complex a whole group of rituals known as "prāṇapratiṣṭhā", 'establishment of the spirit or soul', has to be performed on the image, whether intended for installation for temple worship or for domestic worship, before worship can be offered. In view of this, one's curiosity naturally seeks enlightenment on the kind of practice current in Ancient Egypt in this matter. I have been able to get very little ; but that little it appears to me to render it certain that the statue of a god could not be treated as its representation entitled to worship and as consecrated, unless some ritual to endow it with the spirit, 'breath' or 'life' as the Egyptians would rather have called it, had been performed over it.

In that unique piece of theological speculation, which the priests of ancient Memphis produced about 2900 B.C., known as the Memphite Theology, we are told that it was the creator-god Ptah of Memphis who made the gods and the whole religious complex along with other creations of it. But Ptah's creation of gods went further than naming them. He placed them in their shrines, after of course framing their bodies to their satisfaction. Yet the gods have "to enter their bodies which are [made of] various kinds of wood, and various kinds of stones, and various kinds of earth (i.e. clay, lime, etc.) and other substances in which they have taken their forms".[45] This assertion can only mean that the spirit of the god whose image is made to its satisfaction, i.e., in conformity with its standard form, has to be invoked in it to turn it into the representation of that god. Wallis Budge[46] has recorded the fact that in the complex of Ra-worship prevalent in the Vth Dynasty, about 2560-2420 B.C., the worshippers of the Sun believed that "their god dwelt in a particular stone of pyramidal shape" known as the *benben*, and that their priests used to "induce the Spirit of the Sun to inhabit the stone". After the priests had induced the Spirit, the god was supposed to be present and gifts were then offered.

The Memphite Theology takes the shrines of gods for granted when it states that Ptah "placeth the gods on their shrines". It further asserts that he "foundeth their sanctuaries"[47].

And it is in keeping with this theoretical view that the temples of Ancient Egypt were generally built by the Pharaohs. This fact by itself can set its seal of state religion on the pantheon and the worship prevalent in Ancient Egypt.[48] Even the structures housing the pantheon and the feasts associated with them, though they have been described by two of the most eminent of modern Egyptologists, Flinders Petrie and J. H. Breasted, as either "the externals of religion" or "the outward and official manifestations of religion",[49] reflected the Pharaonic inclinations much more than regional or individual or even sectarian. The names of many of the principal temples since the Middle Kingdom illustrate this, meaning as they do that they were the imperishable glory of the particular Pharaohs in the house of the particular god, whose temple the specific Pharaoh had built.

A development, which serves both as an indication and a consequence of the public, Pharaonic, nature of Egyptian religious complex is the use of the Egyptian temple and its religious complex as an advance guard, ambassador or missionary of the Egyptian State and as an agent of ethnic and territorial incorporation in the body politic of Egypt. The first two Pharaohs of the XIIth Dynasty, i.e., the kings that came to the throne of Egypt after she had emerged through the baptism of social and political confusion of about two centuries, Amenemhat I and Senusret I, were great builders of temples. And characteristically enough the former appears to have built a temple not only at Karnak to enshrine the Theban god, Amen or Amon, after whom he was named, but also at Shedit, near Begig, to mark or protect the great reclamation work that later yielded a large piece of fertile land.[50]

Senusret I has left us an inscription, recording how he undertook the building of a fresh temple to Ra or Atum at Heliopolis and also why, which sheds direct light on the purpose of building a temple. He says : "I establish the food-offerings of the gods, and do a work for my father Atum in the great hall. (I) cause him to have (by my work on this temple) it as broad as he hath caused me to conquer. I victual his altar on earth. I build mine house in (his) vicinity (a second new temple in the vicinity of the older one). *Thus my beauty will be remembered in his house, my name will be the ben-ben stone, and my memorial the lake.* It is to gain eternity, if one doeth for him that which is good, and no king dieth that is mentioned because of his (god's) possessions.... A name that standeth thereupon is.... mentioned and perisheth not in eternity. What I do is what will be, and what I seek is what is excellent."[51]

Earlier in another connection, I have mentioned the later exploitation of this medium by the Pharaohs Senusret III and Amenhotep III to assist in their process of incorporation of the Negro ethnic group and of its Nubian territory.

As if to impress this feature of the Egyptian religious complex, e.g., that it was rather a royal and a state business and not so much a matter of religious consciousness of the Egyptians at large, time and circumstances conspired to leave to posterity the imposing and stupendous tombs, called the pyramids, of the early Pharaohs with their funerary temples, the temples purely for the worship of the deceased Pharaoh by his endowed priests and his successors, and to obliterate even their valley-temples where they were gods, after their death, even to their subjects, the Egyptians at large.

As will be seen later the temple proper of Dynastic or Old Empire Egypt was a small structure compared with the tomb, the pyramid, which the Pharaohs built for themselves. The Egyptian monarchs and by implication the Egyptians as a whole, in those ages, before the middle Kingdom or rather the New Empire, were primarily concerned with securing their life in the Hereafter, which was expected to be eternal and for which their religious consciousness and practice other than centring round disposal of the dead, can hardly be said to have provided a complex of belief and ritual, and only secondarily attended to the provision of facilities for the purely religious complex and its practice. Their temples may be said to have been inconspicuous and their funerary monuments stupendous and domineering. Religious consciousness and its practice were subordinated to the theory of death and life after death. In one way, therefore, the Ancient Egyptians can be declared to have been other-worldly like the later Hindus, though the fundamental systems of belief leading to the result, and the endeavour to put them into practice, differed very much.

We shall see later that this situation, the relative significance of the tomb and the shrine, changed, almost turning a full circle, so that the shrine became by far the more imposing and beautiful structure and the tomb a fairly moderate to insignificant feature. Without any fundamental change in the doctrine of death and life after it the religious belief-complex changed so that god and even Supreme God became a considerable force in the theory and practice of living. Worship to him and to others, too, of the old pantheon appears to have become a more regular feature, at least more organized and institutionalized.

As a matter of fact, most of what we know to-day regarding the ritual of worship in Ancient Egypt is what came to be practised in the New Empire.[52] The ritual of worship resembles markedly the later complex current among the Hindus, particularly those of the Vaiṣṇavite sects, except in one main particular. That main particular is the attitude symbolic of adoration, worship or veneration. The attitude of adoration seen depicted on the monuments of Ancient Egypt, whether of the Pharaohs or of the Queens or of the gods or of common men, in the presence of any deity, is one, which is symbolic among most other civilized peoples of just the opposite of adoration or supplication. It is one commonly employed in giving assurance, granting protection or blessing and not in supplicating or adoring. The portrayals show the adorant with both his hands raised, palms forward and pointing towards the deity adored, the fingers being slightly bent forward.[53] Literary references to this form of adoration appear to be very rare. I have come across one in the *Story of the Shipwrecked Sailor*, which contains at least two references to another mode of supplication. When the sailor was asked by the serpent all about him he tells the readers that he "raised his hands in supplication to" the serpent and then began the narration.[54] Strangely enough the same gesture is shown as having been adopted by gods when blessing the Pharaohs or by one god towards another god.[55]

Another posture of adoration or supplication portrayed in the scenes is that of the adorant or worshipper kneeling before the god or gods and raising his both hands or one hand, if the other is engaged in making an offering or in any other item of worship.[56] The kneeling, too, appears in two varieties : (1) that of both the knees in unison resting on the ground and (2) that of one knee, right or left, resting on the ground in a forward thrust and the other in a deep backward thrust. In the former attitude the buttocks naturally rest on the heels, as in the beautiful representation of young Thothmes III, and in the latter the whole figure makes a fine curve of the backside with the chest beautifully thrust forward, a pose which in Indian terminology may be described as 'vīrāsana', 'warrior's pose' or simply 'brave pose', as in the case of the representation of Rameses II. One important variation of this posture[57], as in the case of Amenhotep III adoring Amenra, is that the Pharaoh kneels and touches with his right hand the feet of the image, while his left hand holds one of his royal insignia.

In a relief[58] which portrays people paying homage to this Pharaoh we find them standing with both hands raised in adoration as above, some kneeling in the standard position and holding their raised hands as above, while still others have knelt and placed their palms down and bent their hands low as if to kiss the ground. And kissing the ground, whether on one's knees or flat on one's belly, appears to have been a fairly common mode of supplication by ordinary people before gods, kings or even other superiors. In the Sailor's story he is described as having fallen on his belly before the serpent at least twice.[59] In a hymn to Osiris his subordinate gods in the underworld are said "to kiss the ground", evidently in adoration to Osiris, while those in the necropolis or earth are said to "make an obeisance".[60] There is no indication of the actual distinction and I take it that making obeisance meant only raising the hands in adoration as described above. While the gods of Babylon near Cairo are said to be "in jubilation", those of another city are said to be "kissing the earth" evidently in exultation at the same event of Amen, Atum, Ra having been reinstated in their place after their eclipse in the reign of Ikhnaten. When the goddess Astarte of Palestine arrived in Egypt in the XIXth Dynasty "the great gods stood up before her. The lesser ones laid them on their bellies." In the myth of "the Deliverance of Mankind", it is stated that when the gods were summoned in the presence of Ra they came "nigh unto him and touched the ground with their foreheads".[61] According to the ritual of worship at the Thebes temples the priest, as soon as he opened the shrine of the god and saw him, had to throw himself down on his face and kiss the ground.[62]

The daily ritual of worship[63], which appears to have been more or less the same in all temples, was standardized at Thebes under the masterful influence of Thothmes III. The god was roused in the morning by the singing of a hymn of praise, a most marked similarity with the much later Vaiṣṇavite practice of Hindu India. Then followed his toilet which was effected by sprinkling water twice over the statue and by clothing it with linen bands, white, green, red and brown. The statue was then anointed with perfumes and painted with green paint under the eyes and black on the eyelids. Incense was burnt in good quantities. Though offering of flowers is not mentioned in the accounts on which I have drawn for this résumé, there is evidence that, perhaps unlike their contemporary Mesopotamians, the Ancient Egyptians offered flowers to their gods.[64] During the reign of Rameses III, in thirtyone years that is, more than one crore and ninety lakhs, i.e., nineteen millions, of bouquets of flowers were issued to the temples on behalf of the royal treasury. Temples generally used to have gardens within their premises as also a lake. Rameses II, offering flowers to the lioness-headed goddess Sekhmet, or Seti I, pouring libation of water with right hand over the bunch of flowers already placed on the offerings stand and holding the incensor with fuming incense in it in his left hand, before the god Ptah-Soker, in his temple at Abydos, are scenes enough to justify my statement. Ornaments were put on the image.

When the Pharaoh himself attended to the worship he would, after opening the door of the shrine and purifying it, embrace the deity. Having gone through the other acts as above he would make the offering of a figure of *Maat*, the goddess of truth and justice. At some stage of the ritual the god laid—the statue had some moving and movable parts, as it could nod, as we know, by way of giving an oracular decision—his hands on the body of the king in order to transmit to him the fluid of life and lengthen the king's life.

After the completion of anointing etc. food was placed before the statue. The clothes and the food could next day be offered to the statues of the dead persons privileged to keep them in the temple. This practice was doubled-blessed in the eyes of the Egyptians. For a man could guarantee his receiving food and raiment for eternity by making an endowment to the god. Thereby he could insure his future doubly as he would have done a good deed which would be a passport for him in the Hall of Judgment, and he would have got his supplies regularly and thereby kept himself happy in the Hereafter. The temple and the priests would have benefited by the endowment as the pre-requisites could be actually utilized by the temple priests and servants. Such endowments having been irrevocable there was no fear of lapse or stoppage.

It is worthwhile noting that the live coals needed to be put in the incensor had to be ignited with fire kindled with the help of a bow-drill, and that the priest, after washing his feet at the lake or pond within the temple precincts, had to carry the incensor with fuming incense in his hand while breaking open the lock of the shrine door.

At every stage of the ritual some formulae had to be uttered. As musician-priestesses were attached to every temple it is possible they kept company with their musical implements like the sistrum[65], a shaking rattle. Male musicians and dancers, too, might have taken part in the temple services.

The first meal over, the god was brought out with chants and hymns into the main court "to give audience" and "to transact business" brought before him and also to receive offerings. It appears that, besides the processions on festive and regular occasions, it was at this part of the temple ritual that common men could "see" their god. Otherwise the shrine being situated beyond the court and partitioned off from profane view the statue of the god was beyond their ken. In the Old Kingdom period we are told the laity was actively associated with the daily worship but under the New Empire dispensation the lay element was "jealously excluded".

In the afternoon the god retired to other rooms which were his private apartments to rest and was entertained with music and dance, for besides sistrum-shaking musician-priestesses there were human concubines attached to several deities. In the evening again a meal was offered after which the robes were removed, incense was burnt before the statue and the evening hymn was sung. The shrine doors were then made fast with a lock.

The ritual which was followed in domestic worship is not described by the writers on the subject evidently because the scenes depicted or the literary records preserved are silent on the point. The receptacle housing the statue of the domestic deity was so small, being almost a niche in the wall, there could not be any elaborate ritual of worship even in the élite households. This situation, if it is correctly inferred, would stand in marked contrast with that in India. The Hindu élite, the Brahmins, have had an elaborate worship ritual since a long time. Since how long we cannot exactly state ; but the mention by the seventh century romance-writer Bāṇa[66] of as highly developed a ritual of worshipping Śiva in domestic worship as at any time later, raises the presumption of the currency of an elaborate ritual of domestic worship perhaps from about the heyday of the Gupta Empire in the fourth century after Christ.

Festivals and processions in connection with them appear to be a recurrent and standard procedure of all great religions. The Mesopotamian religion had perhaps only one such which was the national event. Religions putting up statues of gods, anthropomorphic or theri-anthropic, would naturally make them the central objects of such events and processions connected with them. And we found that the Mesopotamian religion included the statues of its gods in the procession and they were the most important forces of attraction for the generality of Mesopotamians.

In Egyptian religion[67], the role of festivals and statue-gods-processions in all pomp and state was even more important and integrative, so that far from being "the externals" of religion they were the magnetic cores not only for the national state and culture but also for individual religious consciousness, its satisfaction and consequent feeling of peace and happiness. They had also a more immediate and practical function to discharge, viz., that of an oracle. The god of the festival and the procession could and did "express his will oracularly by being heavy on his bearers at a particular spot". The pomp and the impressive paraphernalia of these occasions, as we find them depicted on the monuments later on in the New Empire, might have been the additions or innovations to be credited to the easy Pharaonic wealth gained in foreign booty, tribute and exactions, but the events and occasions themselves, placing the statues of gods in the truest centre of the whole complex, certainly date back to the time before the XIth Dynasty.

In the record known as "The Instruction for King Merikare" ascribed to about 2100 B.C. the instructor enjoins[68]: "Reverence the God upon his road (in a procession?), even him that is fashioned of precious stones and formed of copper, even as water that is replaced by water (His image which is His substitute, God keeping Himself hidden)". The purely religious significance of such occasions is demonstrated by the fact that even the reformist and heretic king Ikhnaten indulged in them with all the pompous paraphernalia. The general who secured the Egyptian throne after the short reign of Tutankhamen who followed Ikhnaten, Haremhab, too, is portrayed in similar surroundings in the celebration of the main festival. And the magnificence-and-pleasure-loving Pharaoh, Rameses III, is depicted[69] on the temple at Medinet-Habu as conducting a fully equipped and a purely religious procession, which offers, even in its bare outline through the pictures, interesting and even intriguing analogues with religious processions conducted in the temples south of the Narmada in contemporary India.

The great thing on a festive day was for the people to "behold the beauty of their lord". Petrie describes the procedure of a religious procession thus : "The portable shrine was carried round, with priests bearing symbols [standards and banners] and then placed on a stand on various sites for admiration and adoration. Incense was burnt and offerings made before it."

The polylatrous, and non-congregational religious, festivals at regular intervals tend to serve the same purpose that regular and almost compulsory attendance at congregations in the local shrines of monolatrous or monotheistic religions fulfil. The case of the Hindus is in point in the contemporary scene.[70] In Ancient Egypt we have the high authority of Flinders Petrie to assert that the festivals formed a bond of union for the peoples and fostered "a corporate religious sense" for the whole country.

Votive offerings to certain gods on these occasions formed a prominent feature of the popular religion of Egypt, just as a long narration of the alternative titles and attributes of the great gods was an element of the élite practice of religion.[71]

CHAPTER IV

EGYPTIAN III

RELIGIOUS consciousness and practice can be shown to have fulfilled three needs of man in society. They are : First, a preparation for death, providing an adequate theory of the condition after death, an assurance of moral support, and a guarantee of happiness therein ; Second, some feeling of security through the vicissitudes of mundane living, to which so much suffering and so many trials are incidental, some incentive from supernatural or divine source to practise moral and social virtues, and some assurance of protection and help from the same source in distress through sustained hope ; and Third, a theory about the supernatural and the divine vis-à-vis nature and man.

Not all the three needs are always satisfied in all the known complexes. We have already seen that in the Mesopotamian complex there was hardly anything which could fulfil the first need. The Mesopotamian man's view of death and life after it was so bleak that he could not devise a system of belief and practice which could be a source of assurance and hope. Nor had he derived from his cogitation on nature and man any notion of an element of human personality which is non-material, any idea of soul, in short. Mythology having impressed upon him the impossibility of any immortality, the great hero Gilgamesh having failed at securing it, the Mesopotamian rested content with this world itself and his life in it as the whole universe of living and action. His "divine", therefore, was such as may be described as mundanely competent. His pantheon reflects the political situation of the Mesopotamian culture. There were many important and great cities. They had their gods. Their political vicissitudes decided the currently Supreme God, meaning by supremacy the overlordship of all in the same manner as the erstwhile governor of the city had become the sovereign lord by his conquests. The Mesopotamian man could not develop any philosophy which looked beyond this world ; and his God, however powerful and great, never became omnipotent and omniscient. The god-assimilation which is seen in his religious complex is the counterpart of the justification of the transference of political authority from one city to another. Appropriately, the Mesopotamian temple, the external and concrete symbol of a people's religious consciousness and practice, was not merely a religious institution but also an economic and social security one. In this connection the following observation of H. Frankfort[1] is worthwhile noting : "The accounts of the temple do not differentiate between its role as central store of the community and its religious function ; goods withdrawn for sacrifices are treated exactly like those serving for rations. . . . The temple community was a religious institution regulating the social life of the community, and the two aspects which we distinguish were apparently experienced as one and indivisible."

In the Egyptian complex, on the other hand, the theory of death and the conviction of indefinite continuation of life after it, the need for and the endeavour of making adequate provision for it, created a whole complex of religious consciousness and practice, which, though intertwined and interrelated with the other complex of religious belief and practice, appears so far complete and distinct in itself that one may speak of the Egyptian religious consciousness and practice as composed of two religious complexes : One centred round Osiris, the god of the dead, and the other round the triad, Ra, Ptah and Amen, with Thoth, as the indispensable member, though not independent, making up the tetrad. I have already dealt with this aspect of the Egyptian complex.

The second need is seen to have been attempted to be fulfilled in both the Mesopotamian and Egyptian complexes; and as much of it as is concerned with purely individual needs—leaving out the part that is mainly concerned with ethics or justice which must belong to the categories of Conscience and Justice—has to be studied in this part of the work. Accordingly, in the Mesopotamian subsection I have briefly expounded the theory and practice which buttressed up the Ancient Mesopotamians in their daily life. As for the Egyptians I have done this so far only partially or indirectly, and I propose to start with it and lead on to their views of and practice in the third field of human needs of religious complex, the former being almost dependent upon the latter.

What did the Egyptians provide for in their complex of religious belief and practice as far as this world and their mundane living were concerned ? At the very outset it must be mentioned that as the account of the other parts of the complex shows there was a development achieved and recorded in the Egyptian history of about 2500 years. In the earlier part of the Egyptian history it was the king, the Pharaoh, who, though himself almost a god, was principally thought of in the official or state religion. The reliefs on various structures of the early period suggest that the whole object of worship was to obtain the favour of gods for the Pharaoh, in return for the offerings made to them. There was an idea of a covenant, though not expressed, present in the belief system, whether it was the offerings of or on behalf of the Pharaoh or private men. For the Pharaoh the god or gods, in return for his great benefactions to and gorgeous worship of them, were to grant "victory, gladness, life, stability, health, good fortune, abundance, millions of years, an eternity of jubilees etc."[2] The common man spoke in terms of prosperity on earth. Even in the preponderatingly pietistic Instruction to Merikare we read : "Do something (i.e. make offering) for God, that He may do the like for thee . . . God is cognizant of him that doeth something for Him."[3] This is from the XIth Dynasty time, i.e., about 2000 B.C. In the "Wisdom of Anii" of the XXIInd Dynasty, i.e., about 850 B.C., occur the following injunctions : "Celebrate the feast of thy God. . . . God is wroth with him that disregardeth it. . . . make offerings to thy god and keep thyself from trespassing against him."[4]

In the spiritualization of the religious complex that took place after the social catastrophe, the common men including courtiers cultivated a purely religious attitude in their approach to the deity or gods. Thus Sinuhe, the exile, addressing Senusret I, about 1970 B.C., a letter of thanks, after recounting the varied titles of the Pharaoh showing him to be the favoured one of many a god of Egypt, expresses his prayerful wish or beseeches them : "may they all give life and happiness to thy nose, may they endue thee with their gifts, may they give thee eternity without limit, everlastingness without end" without any stipulation or even suggestion that he will make any offering to them for the conferment of these boons on his beloved king.

In the reign of Rameses II, about 1300 B.C., a memorial tablet was put up by one Nebre in homage and thanksgiving to the god Amen. Finding his son very ill and dying, Nebre prayed to Amen or "composed adorations to him and addressed prayers to him". He found that the god heard his prayers and changed the conditions so that his dying son revived and recovered from his illness. The stela put up is described as a memorial in the name of Amen. The inscription on it, however, makes it clear that the hymn of praise was a votive offering, Nebre having evidently in his mind stipulated to put up the memorial and the hymn if Amen saved his son.

In the "Tale of the Two Brothers" datable towards the end of the XIXth Dynasty, about 1200 B.C., we are informed that the younger brother fleeing away from the impious and unprovoked wrath of his elder brother prayed to Ra-Harakhti to save him when it was becoming clear that the elder brother would succeed in reaching him and that the god listened to his prayer and created an artificial lake full of crocodiles in between the two brothers. The younger brother, on the other bank of the lake, could successfully defy the impious elder brother who wanted to kill him unjustly. In the tomb of Rameses IX, about 1110 B.C., were discovered a number of poems which Erman describes as "charming hymns". Beginning with the laudation of the God Horus they end with an entreaty to the God to help the poet "against a powerful enemy who has maliciously deprived the writer of his post". Almost ultimately, i.e., about the 7th century B.C., the "Instruction of Amenemopet" advises a person to make a prayer to the Sun-god on his rise, saying "Give me prosperity and health", and asserts : "He will give thee thy needs for this life, and thou wilt be safe from terror."[5]

At this stage we must turn to the third need fulfilled by all great religions, viz., a theory about the nature of the divine, and the relation between the divine and nature on the one hand, and man on the other, presenting inter alia the pantheon of the people whose religious consciousness and practice is the focus of attention. In the case of the Mesopotamian religious complex we could almost start with it because this aspect was so rudimentary, and it showed hardly any development during about two thousand and five hundred years. In the case of Egyptian religious consciousness and practice we come up with an altogether different pattern.

A whole half century has elapsed since one of the greatest of Egyptologists on the literary side of the subject, J. H. Breasted[6], gave to the world in English language a clear account—which was perhaps the first illustration of the history of a religious complex other than the Hebrew, over a period of more than two thousand years, and that too, from about 3200 years before Christ —of the development of religious thought and practice in Ancient Egypt. Since then the important discovery and its general acceptance by the world of scholars that the tract, now commonly known as Memphite Theology, was first written almost at its beginning, i.e., about 3000 B.C. as the accepted chronology of Ancient Egypt to-day makes it, has greatly changed the perspective. Discovery of some Papyri, particularly the Chester Beatty Papyrus No. 1 of about 1160 B.C., still further amplified the material for the study of the development of the religion of the Ancient Egyptians. E. A. Wallis Budge, an equally renowned Egyptologist, could go a step further in 1934 and name his book, which he wrote as a substitute for his older book on Egyptian Gods which had gone out of print about thirty years before, *From Fetish to God in Ancient Egypt*. He thus made specific the nature of the development of the Egyptian religion in terms of the nature of the divine postulated in it. Breasted, too, followed his own earlier trail and published. not much after Budge's book, his own, naming it by a much more general title, *The Dawn of Conscience.* Though the book dealt only with the development of religious thought and practice of Egypt, the particular development, that of conscience and piety, being the earliest specimen of human endeavour in this line, Breasted thought it but appropriate to name the book with the general title. The material made available during the interval of a quarter of a century was so much and so crucial that Breasted could preface his book with six Egyptian quotations, ranging in accepted dates from about the 27th to the 7th century B.C.

The *Memphite Theology*, the earliest available document, not containing any idea of the kind from which viewpoint Breasted presented his thesis, does not figure in Breasted's quotations. But from our point of view in this section, the nature of religious consciousness and practice, the theory of the nature of the divine, the kind and extent of the pantheon, the tract is not only the earliest fixed point but, from the nature of its contents, also becomes the pivot, as I do not propose to dive into the earlier fetishistic stage, if there was one. Both Breasted and Budge in the early thirties of the 20th century were agreed that the aim of the theological exposition contained in the document was not merely the assertion of the greatness and superiority of Ptah, the creator- or artizan-god of Memphis, the city which was chosen by Menes as his capital for the United Two Lands of Egypt, but also contained the presentation of an entirely new approach to the theory of creation.

To Breasted[7], "it discloses the old nature god, the Sun-god Re [Ra] completely transformed into an arbiter of human affairs, already viewed from a moral angle", reveals "the prehistoric background of the Logos doctrine of

New Testament days" and introduces "abruptly, and without any gradual transition stages . . . the world of nature gods" transformed into "a ripe and developed civilization, in which the organisers of religion and government are producing mature abstract thinking". Budge's[8] appraisal which is made purely from the religious point of view, without any reference to the moral aspect, is equally or perhaps even more laudatory. Budge is convinced that the document "removes once and for all from the religion of ancient Egypt the stigma of gross materialism. The doctrines of the priests of Memphis under the Old Kingdom were of an almost unbelievable spiritual and philosophical character. And they had a broadness and boldness never attained by the religious theories and conjectures of any other of the great priesthoods of Egypt."

J. A. Wilson[9], writing in the forties of the twentieth century, is more subdued in his appreciation of *Memphite Theology*. To him the text appears to have "brought together into a broad philosophical system" the elements which were "present in other Egyptian texts in isolated instances". He views it, therefore, as a great essay and achievement in synthesis rather than a new departure in thinking of and viewing the universe. However, his endorsement of Breasted's valuation of the document in respect of the role it ascribes to Speech or Logos in creation must contradict some aspect of his subdued valuation, unless it can be shown that other Egyptian texts, dating from before the document, which, according to Wilson himself, "comes from the very beginning of Egyptian history", contain a doctrine like this. To my knowledge Wilson has not produced any such instance.

For a correct appraisal of the religious scene in the long history of Ancient Egypt from about 3500 B.C. to about 700 B.C. it is essential to be clear about the status of the tract known as *Memphite Theology*. To me it appears that in the present state of our knowledge there is no doubt that it represents a unique and supreme effort of the Ancient Egyptians made under the first really political upsurge and in the earliest flowering of the national energy. It is generally accredited to be the work of the priests of Ptah, the God of Memphis, who were, it is suggested, commissioned by Menes to devise a theology stabilizing Memphis as capital of the New Union of the Two Lands of Egypt. The Memphite priests did not stop with claiming Ptah, the god of Memphis, a higher status than that of the great god of Heliopolis, Ra, who till then was the overlord of all.

In this important religious document, the priests declared Ptah to be the head of the Ennead of Memphis, just as Ra or Temu was that of the Ennead of Heliopolis. They postulated eight forms of Ptah. Four of them, which are specifically mentioned, represented him as "the father and mother of Temu" or Atum or Ra and proclaimed him to be the heart and tongue of a Company of gods. The eight forms taken together represented the Eight Primeval Gods of Hermopolis, another very ancient Egyptian city. Ptah was probably conceived of "as a predecessor or prototype of Thoth" for Thoth was always regarded as the head of the Ogdoad of Hermopolis. Thus the priests established their Company of Gods as the oldest in Egypt.

The gods mentioned by name in the document as the first creations of Ptah are Atum or Temu (Ra), Horus and Thoth. Ptah "thought of and created by speech the creator-god Atum", while Horus and Thoth were his "heart and tongue" respectively. Thus all the major gods of Egypt, then recognized as such, were accounted for as the creation or organs of Ptah. But the creation being a mental one, and the organs of Ptah which formed Horus and Thoth being of thought and speech, the whole pantheon of three gods is by one stroke turned into spiritual entities in place of their earlier material selves. Further exercise of his speech by Ptah produced the two other gods, Shu and Tefnut, who in the current mythology were, and it appears ever after remained, the couple that created other gods, all of them being gods of nature. In the Pyramid Texts, wherein this myth of the creation of the Ennead of Heliopolis occurs, Shu and Tefnut are described as having been the result of masturbation by Atum in Heliopolis. In the *Memphite Theology* that physical image has been replaced by the mental or spiritual. Both Shu and Tefnut were not the products of a physical process but of a mental or a spiritual one. Hence the whole pantheon was the result of a spiritual act or process and Ptah was the one whose activity was that process. Ptah thus is at once conceived of as a Spiritual Force. As such it would have been anathema merely to identify him with Ra, the material god of nature, the Sun-god. Ra was equal with others, i.e., even those who were in the current mythology produced from his masturbation, the mental creation of Ptah. Everything else including not only the spirits of gods, not only their images of varied material but also their shrines, of course in Egypt, and their offerings too, was made by Ptah. The moral order whereby 'good is given to the good' and 'evil for the evil' too was his work ; and "life was given to him who has peace and death was given to him who has sin". Thus it was discovered and understood that Ptah's power was greater than that of any other god. And so Ptah rested.[10]

The tract further makes Memphis "the granary of the god" and introduces Osiris in the sacred drama on account for Memphis being the granary on the ground of Osiris having been drowned in the water there.[11] This mention of Osiris is quite clearly meant to justify Menes' selection of Memphis as his capital. Ptah's glorification and enthronement over the gods, too, is quite clearly motivated by the urge to justify the same action. If Ptah, the god of Memphis, were left in the status of the craftsman-god that he was, the premier position ascribed to Memphis could not be established in the minds of the Egyptians. Ptah, though considered to be a craftsman-god was also some kind of earth-god in the aspect of vegetative fertility,[12] and thus had a dual nature, that of a nature-god and of an anthropo-mummiform god. The latter form, according to Sethe, might have been given him to make him resemble Osiris, the god of Abydos from which city Menes came.[13]

Temu or Atum was always represented as a full-fledged man, his special animal not being used to turn him into a therioanthropic deity. Horus was the Hawk-god and thus theriomorphic, whose cult, older than that of Ra of Heliopolis, was "essentially materialistic" and whom Budge describes as "the oldest Sky-god in Egypt". Thoth was manifest in moon and also in two animals, the baboon and the ibis, and was represented as a therioanthropic deity in the form of an ibis-headed man. According to an ancient legend Thoth was the son of Horus. He was credited with the invention of writing and the science of numbers. In mythology, the greatest feat of Thoth was bringing back the missing eye of Ra and restoring it to its proper place. His special place of worship was the city named Khemenu, which his priests asserted was the piece of ground on which the Sun-god first stood. The Greeks popularized the name of the city in the form in which it generally appears, i.e., Hermopolis. It is worthwhile noting that in the dogmas of the priests of Hermopolis, Thoth was "the mind and intelligence and reasoning power of the self-created, self-subsistent god"; and Budge categorically states that "the theology of Thoth was of a highly spiritual character" and was "diametrically opposed" to that of the priests of Heliopolis, i.e., of the great god Ra. The role as a god of creation assigned to Thoth by his priests is stated to have become obscured only later, when his special work came to be specified as the invention of writing. In the Pyramid Texts the great respect in which the gods held the word of Thoth is explicitly mentioned.[14]

Competent Egyptologists have stated that in the texts which are later than about 3000 B.C. there are two characteristics of the Sun-god, which evidently were persistently attributed to him to such an extent that they were often personified as deities. And they were "Command" and "Understanding". That these qualities of the Sun-god were made over to Ptah who became the successor of the Sun-god by the act of the Pharaoh of making Memphis his capital was a suggestion of Alan Gardiner which is accepted by Breasted.[15] Both of them further agree that the phraseology of the solar theology was changed by the Memphite theologians, the organ of understanding, heart, being substituted for its function, and the organ of command, i.e., speech, tongue, for its function of speech or word. Ptah was thus conceived of as both heart and tongue or understanding or intelligence of mind and command or speech or word.

Ptah thought, to speak in familiar Indian terminology of the *Upaniṣads*, that there should be Atum; Ptah gave vent to his thought and Atum was produced. That Atum in the tract is said to be both heart and tongue must be stressed here. It marks him out, as the creator of other gods and of the whole creation, which are ascribed to him in his role of the creator god in the earlier Heliopolitan theology. Ptah having been asserted as the creator, and his nature having been specified as heart or mind and tongue or speech, all creative power is automatically equated with the duality, mind and speech. Thoth being Ptah, tongue comes naturally from the nature of Thoth's function and work, but Horus being his heart remains to me enigmatic. Whatever the justification for it, considering the status of Horus in the then Egyptian religion and his acceptance by the contemporary Egyptians, the derivation assigned to him by the Memphite theologians is not such as was likely to affect the acceptance of their religious speculation. The crux of the situation must have lain in the subordination of Atum and of Thoth. Thoth's case as argued above is explained. In the case of Atum, the ascription of the two main characteristics of the Sun-god to Ptah could put the latter on the same plane as Atum. It appears to me that one element in the mythology about Atum which Breasted[16] has drawn attention to as current in one temple, viz., that "Ptah had shaped an egg out of which the Sun-god had issued", provides the bridge. The status of artizan god which Ptah enjoyed in the mythology of the Egyptians facilitated the ascription of the shaping of an egg to him. If Atum came out of an egg shaped by Ptah*, the latter could be presented as not only earlier than Atum but as in the position of his creator. With the attributes of the Sun-god transferred to him Ptah could thus be presented as the god earlier and greater than Atum.

To make this valuation acceptable to the Egyptians in general the Memphite priests took the help of two other devices. First, they transformed the atributes of the Sun-god into categories more acceptable to the Egyptians, whose whole process of thought and culture shows them to be appreciative of the concrete and the material. The tradition of pictographic writing had not merely left its traces on the Egyptian mind but was ingrained in it, so that concrete heart and tongue were more readily acceptable as the attributes than the abstract 'understanding' and 'command'. Second, they made their Ptah score over Atum by postulating the existence of both Shu and Tefnut as Ptah's teeth and lips, i.e., as brought into existence by Ptah's words, whereas Atum could create them only by masturbating. Masturbation, as we know from the *Book of the Dead*, was one of the 42 sins from which a man must be free to get clearance, "to be justified", in the Hall of Judgment in the Hereafter.[17] Ptah was thus physically and morally superior to Atum. This superiority of Ptah is further demonstrated by attributing to him the creation not only of the gods and the heavenly order but also of the coveted institutions of the Egyptians like their state and the shrines along with the offerings for the gods, which latter the pious Egyptian was wont to make to his gods.

So far, the process of raising the status of Ptah can be seen to be an essay in the synthesis of the psychological and sociological factors that can be utilized from the current material for the formulation of a modified religion. The urge for undertaking the venture, we know, was specifically political. And we have reason to believe that in the socio-economic conditions of the time there were no special factors calling for it or engendering it. The favour-

---

* Hindu cosmology with Hiraṇyagarbha, the golden embryo or egg, as the origin suggested in the *Rgveda* and developed later may be noted for comparison. The Hindu notions are later by about 12 centuries.

able circumstance for such an endeavour in the social organization was the existence of the priesthood of the god to be taken up for substituting the older god. But then the older and other gods, too, one or two at least, had their priesthoods, which naturally must have countered the efforts as best as they could. And this factor continued for a long time in Egyptian history. The great difference between the priesthoods of the Old Kingdom and of the New Empire was that, among the priesthoods of the latter age, that of Amen of Thebes was so wealthy and powerful that even if all the other priesthoods of the land were to combine against it they would have been powerless to counter its work of promulgation of the theology of Amen.

It will be seen that the religious remoulding that was undertaken in Egypt about 3000 B.C. affords not only the earliest but also one of the very best examples of religion in the making. As such it deserves special attention of the students of the sociology of religion. And that is why I have discussed the genesis of the particular form, powers, and work of Ptah, the god who was the focus of the new remoulding of religion. The procedure has been fairly simple, one of utilizing the notions existing in a scattered way by bringing them together. The nature predicated of Ptah, that of spiritual entity, intelligence and speech, is a reflection of the burst of mental energy which is manifest in the stupendous pyramids, reverberant in the life and doings of the fabulous-sounding Imhotep and pulsating in the scientific achievements and spirit illustrated by medical literature of the age. Imhotep himself, who came to be deified as the third member of the Memphite triad along with Ptah in later ages, was not only an architect but also a physician. The curiously scientific text on surgery known as the Edwin Smith Papyrus hails from that age.[18] Breasted[19], who produced the first complete edition of the treatise in two volumes, remarks on its significance in the process of the "great transformation", to use his own words, that was going on in the approach of man to nature and to the supernatural: "The domain of natural causes in the economy of the human body is here distinguished from the realm of good- or ill-fortune controlled by the gods—a profound observation occurring, in so far as I know, for the first time in the surviving records of human thought."

The intrepid and brilliant author of the surgical treatise was the first man, as we can say on the basis of existing data, to understand the importance of the contents of the human skull and to coin a name for it, viz., "mass of the skull" or "marrow of the skull", brain as we call it. Though this word and the unique organ denoted by it did not supplant the earlier word and organ, heart, as the seat of intelligence, its recognition underscores the rising tide of understanding and intelligence in human affairs and in human approach to all problems.

This upsurge of intelligence as the controlling agency and its significance for all behaviour stands recorded and stabilized for Ancient Egyptians in the tract known as "The Instruction of Ptahotep".[20] The importance or the focal position of heart is insisted in the words: "It is the heart that maketh its owner into one that heareth or one that heareth not. His heart is a man's fortune . . . As for the fool that heareth not, he can do nothing at all. He regardeth knowledge as ignorance and good as bad." And the need for balance between heart and tongue is emphasized : "Then men see how admirable he is : his heart is evenly balanced (?) to his tongue, and his lips are exact when he speaketh."

There is one more element in this spiritualization of religion through upgrading of the deity Ptah to the position not only of the Supreme God, not only as the creator of Horus and Thoth and of Atum, but also as the Eternal Mind, operating as spiritual force, which strikes me as particularly interesting to Indians and Hindus in particular. And that is the pantheistic statement that Ptah exists in every god, man and object as heart and tongue.

This aspect of the philosophization of the *Memphite Theology* does not appear to have been explicitly mentioned by any of the three or four leading authorities on the religion of Ancient Egypt ; and one of the most recent and original contributors, H. Frankfort[21], has actually countered any such interpretation of the statement with the affirmation that "Ptah as creator appears as a transcendent, not an immanent, power." The straight interpretations of the statement as given by expert students are necessary to decide the issue. Wallis Budge[22] has rendered it thus : "It happened that the heart and the tongue acquired power over all (the other) members, teaching that he (Ptah) lived as the governor in every body, and as the tongue in every mouth, of all the gods, all cattle, all reptiles, and everything else—at the same time Ptah (as heart) thinks, and (as tongue) commands as he wishes." It is clear that Ptah is asserted to be both transcendent and immanent like the Brahman of the Vedānta philosophy of the Hindus. Pantheistic approach is thus seen to be the oldest of civilized man's spiritual attitudes and has a venerable antiquity.

Pantheism has been so much identified with India and the Hindus and is the prevailing attitude of such a large number of the élite of India that it would be amiss if I do not briefly mention its early occurrence and its nature in this context. Pantheistic attitude and imagery are attested in the oldest literature of India, viz., the *Ṛgveda*, though only, perhaps, in the latest sections*. There appear some very close similarities between them and those in the *Memphite Theology*. There is, however, a fundamental dissimilarity in the fact that the Ṛgvedic imagery is in two minds : one of lower rank is on the physical plane and the other busy on the mental plane is very sublime but snaps abruptly. It is to be presumed that the effort on that plane was too much for the poet-philosopher to sustain to the end. It was about 1200 B.C., or a century or two earlier, that the Ṛgvedic poets sang on the banks of Sutlej, perhaps, that the Primaeval Being, from the sacrifice of Whom the whole creation resulted, having enveloped the whole universe outreached it by "ten fingers". He is described as having eyes all over, mouths all over, hands all over and feet all over to indicate His limitlessness, omnipotence, omni-

* Even these cannot be later than 1200 B.C.

presence and omniscience. No wonder at all that all the worlds are asserted to be not only His creation but also as resting in Him.[23]

It is said of Ptah that his Ennead, the Company of Nine gods, "is the teeth and lips in his mouth, which pronounced the name of everything, from which Shu and Tefnut came forth, and which was the fashioner of the Ennead". Knowing the names was the power of Ptah which enabled Him to create the creators of the Ennead. The Ṛgvedic poet[24] in his own way also thought of the power, the knowledge of the names of things and persons beforehand gave the Supreme Being. This our Father, our Creator, our Fashioner, who knows all the worlds and its creatures framed the names and their possessor-gods like Indra, Vāyu, etc. Curiously, though it is not this Supreme Being or the Primaeval Being, of whom anything about the food eaten etc., which is mentioned in the text-quotation below, is predicated, the deity to whom these things are said to be owing is Vāk, Speech or Logos, one of the twin characteristics of Memphite theologians' Ptah.

Vāk, Speech or Logos, first declares herself not to be the same as a number of Vedic gods, those named being Rudras, Ādityas, Viśvedevas, Mitrāvaruṇau, Indrāgnī, Aśvinau, Soma, Tvaṣṭṛ, Pūṣan and Bhaga but as the one who either supports them or helps them to go on with their functions. Ptah, too, is asserted to be more or less in the same position or perhaps even a slightly higher one by the Memphite theologians. Vāk, Logos, further asserts: "Through me alone all eat the food that feeds them—each man who sees, breathes, hears the word outspoken. They know it not, but they dwell beside me. Hear one and all, the truth as I declare it."[25]

In another place where we find the origin of all creation traced or ascribed to the Supreme Being's "desire", which is, of course, the same as "thought" or "heart" of the Memphite theologians, the Ṛgvedic poet soars into a higher plane. The hymn (*RV.*, X, 129) has been known for ages as the hymn that speaks of the creation which was neither "Being" nor "Not-being" in origin. There was all chaos when "rose Desire in the beginning [of course it is Desire of the Supreme Being who is often referred to as 'Aja' or unborn and sometimes as "Hiraṇyagarbha", golden embryo]—Desire, the primal seed and germ of Spirit. Sages who searched with their hearts discovered the existent's kinship in the non-existent".[26] The deeper probing by the Ṛgvedic poets is indicated in the last expression. There is that problem to be faced by all cosmological theories, the relation between the deity, existence and non-existence, spirit and matter. And the Ṛgvedic sages provided their own poetic answer to it, but the description of the process of creation is left off abruptly!

At this stage I should profitably enter into a discussion of another feature prominently appearing in the long history of the Egyptian religion. And that is the assimilation of or equating one god with another, which recurs more often than the assertion or acceptance of the superiority of one over another, as a general theory and not as an individual choice. In an earlier chapter I have dealt with, at length, the assimilation of the more or less regional or local gods, Min and Mentu or Month with, and their incorporatiion in, another distinctly local god Amen, which took place according to the dating of the leading Egyptologists about 2200 B.C. and was completely established by about 2000 B.C.

About 1971 B.C., when Senusret I ascended the throne of Egypt, the process of identifying Amen with the pre-eminent deity of the land, Ra, was begun and the first actual mention of the result as recorded in the name of the deity, Amen, occurred in the reign of Senusret III a century later. Amen emerged as Amen-Ra or Amenra. As pointed out in that discussion it was the political aspect of the societal complex that predominated in this process. In the light of our discussion about Ptah and the assertion and establishment of his superiority over Atum or Ra, however shortlived, this jointure of two separate deities into a single compound one must be counted as the second illustration in the lifetime of the single nation of Ancient Egypt.

The first occurred about 3000 B.C. as a consequence of the unification of the two regions, northern and southern, of the country. And that cosmological and cosmogonic adjustment, using the word appropriate from the purely societal viewpoint and not also from the intrinsic religious one, asserted the superiority of the new god adopted by the unifier of the two lands over the old god of the earlier kingdom, though he was accepted as the god by the Egyptians as a whole. The political nature of the situation appears to have been the deciding factor, though there was a purely religious or pantheonic one and also a purely socio-cultural one involved as pointed out. Acceptance by the populace as a whole, i.e., a purely social factor, does not appear to have weighed much !

The second pantheonic adjustment was much more motivated by social factors. First, there were at least three local gods, perhaps of more or less equality, and one goddess who claimed the allegiance of the people. And there was another important, though not included among the three major national gods, god, Thoth, in the vicinity. Three of these deities were distinctly associated with virility, fecundity, and martial prowess ; and the fourth, who was the chosen deity, Amen, in his mythology and iconography, did not reflect these qualities. The patrons of that god could raise his status easily by incorporating the qualities of the others in their god, Amen, wherever possible. In the case of the goddess, the better way, that of making her the consort of the tutelary deity, being feasible under Egyptian pantheonic notions, was the one adopted ; and Mut, the vulture-goddess, was made Amen's consort. This integration got started as we know after the first chaotic period which was ushered in and characterized by social upheaval and disorder. The new era was naturally one of political cohesion and social integration. Its motive force came from Theban noble families. Theban gods naturally became prominent. The religious development of the earlier period had carried the Egyptians fairway towards monolatry at least as far as the State religion was concerned. The mental climate of the new age was conducive to integration. The many local gods, or at least as many as were prominent in the nearby localities, were assimilated, and incorporated, and one Amen was the result.

The integration of Amen with Ra was complete by the time of Senusret III, on whose stela Amenra is portrayed for the first time. But soon after, towards the end of the XIIIth Dynasty, some people whom the Egyptians hated and who must have reciprocated the sentiment in a much stronger force, the Hyksos, overran the country and ruled it for about a century and a half, till at last some noble family from the south, whose tutelary deity was the moon-god, started "the war of liberation". It was again a moon-god-named Pharaoh who founded the XVIIIth Dynasty, which was not only the starter of the national regime but proved in its later members to be the extender of domains and glory of Egypt into far-off lands.

The Hyksos are said to have "demolished the temples of the gods" of the Egyptians.[27] A southern king, perhaps the most persistent and consistent opponent of the extension of the Hyksos dominion, about the end of the XVth Dynasty, has left an inscription on a gateway of Senusret I in the temple of Min at Koptos, which is one of the most interesting documents of antiquity and is even unique amongst such. It illustrates the close relation between religion and politics that was evident in the earlier history and has been known to have prevailed almost till modern times or the 20th century. It is his decree of excommunication, perhaps the first case of excommunication, which has been so favourite a tool of social cohesion and a weapon of social tyranny in Indian society through the ages. Thereby the king summarily dismissed and excommunicated an official by name Teta for having received the Hyksos emissaries in the temple of Min. The Hyksos are referred to in it as "the Enemy of the God".[28] The destructive work of the Hyksos must have conceivably affected the pantheonic aspect of the Egyptian religious complex after their overthrow. As the princes who led "the war of liberation" to final success came from Thebes, the god, who had already been made the focus of the pantheon by the Pharaohs of the Middle Kingdom and was presented in the joint form of Amenra, was bound to revert to the position with a stronger rebound.

It was from the resurgent XVIIIth Dynasty onwards that Amen came to be represented in human form, though usually with the curving horns of the ram which was the animal sacred to him.[29] And the great Amen temple at Karnak was begun in this Dynasty on the site of the shrine, raised there by the Pharaohs of the XIIth Dynasty and fallen into decay. In the sanctuary for the bark of Amen, Amenhotep I, the second Pharaoh of the Dynasty, is portrayed, in the mural relief in the interior, as standing before Amen, "who bestows everlasting life upon him with a sceptre". This portrayal may not unreasonably be contrasted with the sculptured scenes in the temple at Karnak raised to Amen-Min by Senusret I of the Middle Kingdom, about 1970 B.C., where Atum is shown as playing more or less the same role as Amen in this

Amenhotep's sanctuary. In the hymn to Amenra which is perhaps the oldest of its kind, the age of the papyrus on which it is found being the reign of Amenhotep II, his two horns are mentioned in the expression "established with two horns, beautiful in appearance, lord of the Uraeus Crown, exalted of plumes, beautiful of tiara, exalted one of the White Crown".[30]

Destructive work was only one aspect of the Hyksos in Egypt. Though that was the one that was identified with them in the minds and traditions of the Egyptians, there was another, which worked slowly and steadily and achieved what must be considered to be almost a religious revolution in the Delta of Lower Egypt, and later affected Upper Egypt, at least its royal personnel. Some king of the Hyksos, who must have had a streak of genius in him, saw fair similarity between one of the gods, to whom the Hyksos were accustomed or devoted, and the Egyptian god Set, who was originally a god of Upper Egypt. He adopted Set as his god who came to be known in the Delta as also Sutekh and Nubti. Already in the Pyramid Texts Set was represented as the twin brother of Osiris who not only had murdered his brother Osiris but had attempted persistently to dispose of Osiris' son, Horus, and had contended against his right to succeed to his father's estate. He was thus looked upon as an evil god and was disliked and hated by Egyptians. But when he was patronized by the powerful Hyksos he came to be looked upon almost as a war-god and though we have only scraps of information left here and there through the later patronage of Set by Rameses II, we can, from that information, conclude that Set must have very much risen in the esteem of the Deltaic Egyptians during the Hyksos period.[31]

As for Set's coming back into favour with Egyptians and my referring to the feature as almost a religious revolution, I should dwell on what little we know about it from the scenes depicted in the famous temple of Der-el-bahri, built by the extraordinary Queen Hatshepsut, the fifth monarch of the XVIIIth Dynasty. They depict the ceremonies at the coronation of Hatshepsut as Pharaoh. She is shown "between two priests representing Horus and Set, who place the crowns of Upper and Lower Egypt on her head".[32] Set in this situation, taken as a cooperator and complement of his arch enemy Horus, so beloved of the Egyptians whose monarch, the Pharaoh, was de facto and living Horus, is a revolution in pantheonic valuation. And that was the consequence of foreign patronage of the god and his acceptance as representative of the region of Egypt, where the strongly entrenched foreigners had adopted this god as their own and had succeeded in popularizing him as more or less a war-god! Once before, and that in the hoary past at the end of the IInd Dynasty, a powerful southerner uniting the two regions under him by his conquest and founding the IIIrd Dynasty had thought of this combination of the two irreconcilables. To stress the union and the significance of his exploit he had added to his name the titulary phrase "He hath opened peace to Horus and Set".[33]

The separation of the region of Lower Egypt and the rehabilitation of a hated god there must have dictated the need for specifically integrating the region with its old religious centre of Heliopolis and its god Ra, that god having been the patron deity of the Vth and VIth Dynasties and of the whole land of United Egypt under them. The new device of combining the name of the god, whose characteristics were to be ascribed to another god, Amen, must have been appreciated as the best under the circumstances. And this Amenra, and not simply Amen, went on his imperial career, reminding the Egyptians and the world that the two lands of Egypt were one and that the two gods of the two lands were now a conjoint one. Politico-social circumstances thus are seen to have conditioned the new pantheonic aspect of the Egyptian religious complex of about 1550 B.C.

Leaving the consideration of this pantheonic religious development, we should be well advised to look more closely at the success or failure of the theological philosophy and the theogonic modification, which the Memphite theologians had sought to introduce and effect through the *Memphite Theology*. Sympathetic students of Egyptian religion like Wallis Budge of the past generation and H. Frankfort of the later, have uttered their disappointment, and the former even chagrin, at the failure or overthrow of the Memphite speculative thought, it having failed to get established in the Egyptian mind and religious consciousness.[34]

Two main ideas characterize the speculative theology put forward by the priests of Memphis in response to Menes' choice of the city as the capital of the two lands of Egypt in the eyes of the Egyptians. First, the Ptah of Memphis, the artificer-god as till then characterized and valued, was the uncreated Supreme Being; Second, that Ptah was a Spiritual Force, the Eternal mind; and the whole creation was a mental act of volition of His. The latter notion with its abstract concepts of name and speech, mind and idea, though lofty, could be seen by any rational individual to have been too abstract but for the best minds only of any group of mankind till very recently, and must have been certainly so to the Proto-Dynastic and early Dynastic Egyptians. Their whole religious complex was made up of concrete material gods and goddesses, animals and birds of various kinds being included among them. To popularize the highly spiritual notions a concerted effort was necessary. There is not the slightest evidence that any effort was made in that direction. The literature produced soon after, like the very practical advice of Ptahotep, is singularly devoid of any spiritual concepts, except the one whose practical significance was patent. And that, as was pointed above, concerned the correspondence or balance between heart and tongue for exact speech. The life experiences and wisdom gathered therefrom by another equally old sage and high official, known as *The Instruction for Kagemni*, though its incompleteness and the fact of its having been transcribed during the Hyksos period might be a valid justification of such omission, too, moves on the ordinary plane, advising against pride in one's strength because "one knoweth not what may chance, what God doeth when He punisheth".[35]

We shall see later that the powerful priesthood of the national god Amenra of the Imperial Pharaohs showed not only willingness for but insight in using some of the imagery and basic ideas of this spiritual and abstract portion of the *Memphite Theology*. But it appears never to have been sufficiently associated with Ptah of whom it was first predicated. For in the hymn to Ptah made in honour of Ptah by the theologians of the XIXth or XXth Dynasty they are conspicuous by their absence.[36] He is spoken in high terms no doubt, but they are all those that became current in the highly developed religious consciousness about the Personal though Supreme God. He is uncreated ; he illumines the earth, creates the gods, begets men and fashions their lives ; he is everlasting, and makes the earth fruitful. He is further the creator of all lands and countries [not only of Egypt]. Two of the great feats of Ptah, one specifically mentioned and another implied in the *Memphite Theology*, are credited to him in this hymn and to that extent the speculative thought of the Memphite theologians of about seventeen to eighteen hundred years before had taken root in the minds of Egyptians.

The two exploits and traits which are here credited to Ptah by the hymners of the XIXth Dynasty clearly establish the unwillingness or rather the inability of the Egyptians to rise to superior flights of thought in religious matters. They could not accept and work out the implications of Ptah being equated with Eternal mind working in the mental and spiritual way in the matter of creation and upholding of it. The only aspect of this abstract concept persisting in this hymn is the statement that words come forth from Ptah's nostrils. But then it is also asserted that waters flow from Ptah's mouth and grain grows on his back. It is the compound concept of the air-god or wind-god, water-god and earth-god that must have suggested this phraseology which is material enough. One exploit, which it is clear became Ptah's own, is that of uniting the Two Lands. As the text has it : "thou didst find thyself in the condition of the One who made his seat, and who moulded the Two Lands". This admission and conviction highlight the Ancient Egyptians' love of their country and the focussing of their patriotic sentiment around the Union of the Two Lands and underscore their historical sense.

The second exploit is his having had Ra, who is "aged", as his son. The *Memphite Theology* asserted that Ptah created Atum, the Sun-god [Ra]. The hymn asserts that Ra was the older god and hence "aged" and also that he is the son, i.e., a creation, of Ptah. But then the admission cannot be wholehearted or is not completely worked out in its implications. For when it is said "Thou art the Babe born daily" and also "When thou restest darkness cometh ; and when thou openest thy two eyes beams of light are produced", Ptah is quite evidently thought of as and identified with the Sun-god, Ra. The fact appears to be that monotheistic attitude having been developed in the interval and recorded in the Amenra hymns as will be seen later, the prevailing concept of assimilation of the major gods with one another and the evolving notion of Trinity again asserted itself in the Amenra hymn ; and the remnants of the older speculative thought about Ptah were syncretized, no comprehensive theological or philosophical basis having been attempted to accommodate the compound notions in a harmonious whole.

And now a word about the rather high-sounding and spiritual-looking epithet applied to Ptah in this hymn. Ptah is declared to be the "Lord of the Hidden Throne, himself being hidden, Hidden One whose form is unknown, . . ." This is an old idea about God, having been expressed in the Middle Kingdom instruction for King Merikare.[37]

The IIIrd and IVth Dynasties were Memphite; and many, perhaps most of the Pharaohs of the IInd Dynasty, too, ruled from Memphis. It is one of the Pharaohs of the IInd Dynasty who is credited with having instituted the worship of the Apis-bull there, whose festival continued to be a great annual event at Memphis till late in the Ptolemaic period of Egyptian history. The same Pharaoh, however, is believed to have established the cult of Ra's bull at Heliopolis.[38] The majestic individuals, who employed their great energy, the developed knowledge and great skill of their officers and people, and the enormous wealth of their country to raise resting places, monuments and abodes to guarantee everlasting bliss to them when dead, and put up the gigantic pyramids near Memphis, are not known to have raised any temple to Ptah, which surviving them could convey to posterity their special veneration of that Spiritualized deity. On the other hand, as Hall assures his readers, during the rule of these Dynasties, Horus was "the supreme deity of Egypt, if supreme deity there was".[39]

On the other hand, there is some evidence incidentally occurring in a narrative, purporting to give magicians' tales, recounted to the Pharaoh Khufu of the IVth Dynasty, to suggest that the revolution in speculative thought and the theogonic adjustment of the Egyptian consciousness by the Memphite theologicians was looked upon as impious. The prophecy part of the narration, predicting the onset of the Vth Dynasty from outside the progeny of the Pharaohs of the IVth Dynasty, implies that the kings of the Vth Dynasty were "pious kings, according to the popular view, in contrast with those of the fourth". It is well known that the Pharaohs of the Vth Dynasty were not only of Heliopolitan origin but were also devoted to Ra. And the special devotion shown by the monarchs of this Dynasty to Ra makes it clear that they were bent on rehabilitating their deity to the high position of the national god, and also demonstrates the manner in which theogonic adjustment could be stabilized. Every one of them, we are told, built for himself a special shrine of the Sun-god, represented by a short obelisk. And specially honoured noblemen alone were appointed to their priesthoods.[40]

Small wonder that Ptah receded into the background for a long time. The *Memphite Theology*, however, as pointed out earlier, did not entirely prove a futile adventure in ideas. This is then the sociology of a religious movement, of an attempted advance in spiritualizing religion and a proposed adjustment in its theogonic aspect, in a polylatrous society engendered and conditioned by the political events of the early Egyptian history.

We may now study the religious consciousness of the freed, regenerated and conquering Egypt of the New Empire period.

Amen's glorification and raising to the position of the Supreme God of the Egyptian pantheon after his successful absorption of two local deities and his subordination of another, as goddess, was fairly easy. First, the earlier gods or rather the previous god who was the major national deity, Ra, to some extent at least must have suffered eclipse. In the delta, Ra's own home region, a foreign enemy had lodged himself comfortably. He had further raised Set, against whom mythology declared that Ra had delivered his judgment and who was the arch enemy of Horus, almost a national or supreme god, to the Egyptians whose monarchs used to have Horus-names and were considered to be living Horuses. This situation itself must have given rude shock to the prestige of Ra and made many an Egyptian sceptic about Ra's Supreme godhood. Added to this situation pregnant with loss of prestige of Ra, his priesthood too must have suffered double setback. Its endowments could not have remained as large as before the Hyksos kings and its influence, too, in matters, religious, legal, and intellectual, must have dwindled. Ra was thus in a way humbled and his priesthood must have become more sobered and accommodative.

Ptah's claims to Supreme godhood were so radical and were so unsupported, as we have seen, both by the people and also by the monarchs, that they could have worked only as a leaven to any religious foment that might occur. Ptah, a non-martial god, was one whose spiritualization and fatherhood of Ra was a fact; and the great cultural achievements of the ancient and cherished Egyptians of long ages past hailing from Ptah's city of Memphis could not have failed to associate him with them. The combined circumstances must have placed Ptah above the multitude of other gods. And the god who was claimed as the creator of Atum could not be neglected. That he was actually not completely neglected is clear from the relief sculptures in the temple of Senusret I, the second monarch of the Middle Kingdom about 1970 B.C. If in one scene Senusret is shown in the friendly embrace of Atum, in another he appears in even a closer one of Ptah.[41] The great Pharaoh, Thothmes III, built or perhaps rebuilt the small temple of Ptah, which lay as a separate unit in the great complex of Amen temple at Karnak and in which "stands" a damaged statue of that god. The reliefs on the walls of the temple portray Thothmes in the act of worshipping Ptah and also Hathor.[42]

It was this great Pharaoh who added a number of structures to the great temple of Amen; and it was he who is believed to have established the elaborate temple ritual for Amenra at Karnak, which was followed elsewhere. It was during the performance of this ritual that the various hymns to Amenra which have been recovered from the records were recited.[43]

I shall briefly summarize the contents of the oldest of these hymns which as Erman and Blackman state hails from a record made in the reign of Amenhotep II, who succeeded Thothmes III in 1450 B.C. It is this hymn that is earlier mentioned as the Great Hymn to Amen.[44] 1), Adoration to Amenra is first addressed to him as "Bull of Heliopolis", i.e., as Ra ; and praise is paid him as "lord of Karnak, who presideth in Thebes". And many times he is spoken of as if he was Ra and addressed by Ra's other names and forms, too, as Atum, Harakhti, Atum-Khepre. Once he is spoken of as Min, Amen, his identification with or absorption of Min being presumed. The one reference to Thoth in it is not understood. It is to be noted that the only mention of Ptah in the hymn ascribes the creation of the "beauteous form" of Amenra to Ptah. Ptah is thus clearly not absorbed in Amenra but is looked upon as his creator ! 2), Yet Amenra is not only "unique in his nature, . . . among the gods", not only the "chiefest of all gods" but also their "father", and gods "fawn at his feet, when they know his majesty to be their lord", "Father of the fathers of all gods". And he is the "Sole One", "The One and Only", "Sole One and Only without peer", "Sole One and Only with the many hands". 3), In regard to the actual specification of Amenra's traits and powers, besides his beauty "over which the gods rejoice", it is asserted that "Authority" rests in his mouth ; he created mankind and assigned their natures to them, he made all sustenance and everything, and that the Nile worketh for his love. His name is hidden and his chapel, too, is hidden, this latter specification evidently being influenced by his identity with Ra. 4), In his majesty Amenra is "the fearful, the terrible, great of will and mighty in appearance". Otherwise he is "kindly of heart when one calleth to him", "rescueth the fearful [fearing] from the oppressor", "judgeth between the miserable and the strong", and "giveth his hand to him whom he loveth" and "*assigneth* his foe to the fire", "suffereth mankind to come out to him". He "passeth the night wakeful, when all men sleep, seeking the best for his cattle (as a good herdsman)". 5), And now for the reactions of his creatures towards him we have : "Homage to thee in all they say" ; "Jubilation to thee, because thou weariest thyself with us !" ; "Reverence to thee, because thou didst create us !" ; "*We shout for joy to thee,* because thou fashionedst us. We offer thee praise, because thou weariedst thyself with us."

I have quoted above the description of Amenra as beauteous form. This description of Amenra has struck me as worth being looked into at greater detail. On viewing it closely I have discovered that the evident joy of the worshipper at the beauty, real or only discovered or realized by him, is much more insistently and with great elaboration stated in this hymn than is to be met with in other descriptions, hymnal or routine, of other gods. Thus a scribe who set up an image of his tutelary deity, Thoth, in his house has not hesitated to speak of "pleasant form" of his god, though he has prefaced that expression with the description of him as "Ape with white hair" and has afterwards mentioned the precious stones used in the make-up of the image, including "his phallus of quartz". But that is all and done once. There are two other prayer-pieces addressed to Thoth, and they contain nothing about his supposed beauty of form.[45] In a poem addressed to Min-Horus similarly, reference to beauty of the deity is absent. Nor do the two songs in the *Book of the Dead* addressed to Ra contain one. The hymn to Osiris, too, is conspicuous for the absence of any reference to the beauty of Osiris.[46]

In the hymn to Amenra under study, however, we come across the following references: "More eminent of nature than any god, over whose beauty the gods rejoice"; "Firm of horns [the ram horns which form part of Amenra's head-dress as already stated], fair of face. Lord of the crown and lofty of plumes, with beauteous diadem and tall white crown .... Fair of face, when he taketh the atef-crown"; "The prince, beauteously crowned with the white crown"; "The Gods rejoice in his beauty"; "Lord of the crown, lofty of feathers; with beauteous diadem and tall white crown"; "The gods love to gaze at thee, when the double crown resteth on thy brow"; "Thy beauty captivateth the hearts, and the love of thee maketh languid the arms. Thy fair form maketh feeble the hands; the heart forgetteth when one looketh upon thee"; "Amen, bull of goodly countenance, darling in Karnak, great of appearing in the House of the Benben [the short pyramidal stone representing the Sun-god in the early temples], crowned again in Heliopolis [referring to Amen's identification with or his absorption of Ra, the god of Heliopolis]"; "The gods rejoice over his beauty, and the betel-apes (which greet the Sun at his rising) extol him"; "Fair of face, who maketh festive the breast. With pleasing form and tall plumes, ... the two serpents on his brow".

It is seen from the number of expressions used how it is the worshipper's heart's desire to dwell on the appearance, at times of the health- and joy-bringing rays of the morning sun, at others of the human face and the whole head-dress of national significance, the stereotype of political health for the Ancient Egyptian élite at least. The various items of the head-dress evoking the worshipper's aesthetic sense have of course their political significance and are not items striking purely religious chords of the mind. These references tend to further support the thesis maintained earlier that Amenra, the god of Egypt of upsurging nationalism and of expanding colonialism, was a martial god of United Egypt, fully endowed with great striking power, though he is at the same time, for internal affairs, a just and kindly god ready to succour the poor. Pantheonic adjustment in a polylatrous society is once again seen to be conditioned by politico-social needs. This aspect of the sociology of religion, thrice illustrated in the history of Ancient Egypt, is, as elsewhere[47] maintained by me, amply demonstrated in the history of India in a modified manner befitting the different nature of the Indian religious thought and of the pantheonic set-up of about sixteen to eighteen hundred years later than the Egyptian milieu in which Amenra was conceived.

These "beauty" references, too, have a distant echo in India. When I first read the Amenra hymn and was struck by the many and varied references to the "beauty" of the face and the head-dress of the god occurring in it, I was reminded of certain popular and favourite songs and chants about Lord

Kṛṣṇa and more specifically of the chant, which I have been hearing, and off and on repeating, during about fifty years, and which embodies the heart-pouring of Tukārāma, the famous saint-poet of Maharashtra, whose activity lay in the second quarter of the 17th century. It runs : "Beautiful is the Vision standing on a brick with hands placed akimbo, with necklace of 'tulasī'-beads round the neck, with a yellow-golden garment covering the lower part of the body, and a golden scarf over the upper part, with sandalwood and 'kasturī'-paste on the forehead, with a crown having flanking pendants heightening the beauty of the auspicious face, with shining ear-ornaments and brilliant neck-ornaments flashing ! Blue like the cloud, this royal and handsome statue of veritable Cupid, eclipsing both the sun and the moon, is bliss incarnate. All my happiness is concentrated in it. I will stand gazing with love at the auspicious face! " The two chants whose substance I have translated in the above passage stand at the beginning of the book of Tukārāma's chants known as the *Gāthā*. And these are only the two most often repeated verses from among the many which that famous devotee, who is believed, by many a pious and devout soul, to have achieved salvation while still living, a most difficult achievement but one which almost every Hindu believes is the be-all and end-all of all human existence, addressed to his "beloved" representation of God, Viṭhobā of Pandharpur.

This tradition may be traced further back in the classical age to the great poet Kālidāsa. Kālidāsa has put some elegant and pregnant praise in the mouth of the leader of the gods, when they approached the Supreme God, prepared to incarnate Himself to save the good and destroy the evil in this world, Viṣṇu reclining on the Great Cobra. And it must be regarded as more or less a routine of ordinary life which necessitated a request to be preceded by praise or prayer. But when he devotes some beautiful poetry, sixteen lines to be exact, to describe the God as the Gods saw Him, it is another thing. It must be considered to be a practice in the religious complex of Kālidāsa's time, to extol the appearance of the representation of the deity on viewing it. Its purpose quite clearly was to lift oneself into the emotional stage of preparedness for communion with God.

Kālidāsa gives a minute description of the posture, surroundings, accompaniments, ornaments, in loving terms as did Tukārāma later of his favourite God. The one or two special features stressed in Kālidāsa's description of Viṣṇu, not appearing in Tukārāma's outpourings, underscore the thesis put forward earlier regarding the social conditioning of pantheonic approach in a polylatrous society. Kālidāsa mentions the presence of both the cobra and Viṣṇu's ever-ready servant eagle in close proximity, stressing the natural opposition and enmity between the two and its cessation in the calming presence and blissful environment of Viṣṇu. The other feature described by Kālidāsa is a marked speciality of Hindu pantheonic and theological mythology. And it is that the Gods have special weapons, characteristic of the major ones ; and that the weapons, too, can be conceived in anthropomorphic terms and described as 'present' in actual form, ready to be 'ordered' to 'do' their task. In the case of Viṣṇu, as Kālidāsa describes it, His special weapons, the unfailing discus, "Sudarśana" by name, along with others not named by him, but known from mythology to be the mace, were in readiness there awaiting "orders".[48] The whole description strikes one as intended to assure oneself, through raising the emotional tone, of the certainty of achieving the goal of one's religious effort.

Still further back, about 700 to 800 B.C., we have an Upaniṣadic authority for the use of expressions describing the beauty of the object of worship. In the oldest Upaniṣad the *Bṛhadāraṇyaka* (V, 15, 1) the Ṛgvedic prayer address to god Pūṣan is repeated so as to be directed to the Supreme soul. The deity is entreated to withhold the rays so that the worshipper "may behold" him "of loveliest form". In the *Śvetāśvatara Upaniṣad* (IV, 21) a glorification of Rudra, the fear-inspiring god, ends thus : "O Rudra, may your face which is gracious protect me for ever."

To return to the identification process in the Egyptian theological speculation and practice, we see that in this "Great Hymn to Amenra", Amen is identified with Ra completely, so much so that as Erman and Blackman have noted "on the whole Amunre [Amenra] is actually nothing more than the old powerful sun-god".[49] It must also be noted that though Amenra is asserted to be not only the father but also the father's father of all gods, yet the Egyptian theologian and the Egyptians did not think it amiss to state in the same breath that Amenra's "beauteous" form was fashioned by Ptah. This is syncretism still at work showing that the speculative process had not proceeded far enough. The fact of Amen's being identified with Ra is also a departure from the technique of the Memphite theologians of fifteen hundred years earlier. They had humbled Atum (Ra) by making him the creation of Ptah. The New Empire theologians discarded that language of subordination and used one of greater equality and emphasized the equality by combining the names into one.

Identification of this nature it appears to me does not involve any difficulty. It can be explained without any special elaboration as the pantheonic accommodation in a polylatrous society conditioned by political circumstances for which there was no serious impediment of a religious nature.

In the reign of the Pharaoh in which the papyrus recording the abovementioned hymn was written the Egyptians reached the furthest north and east into western Asia. Their military advance brought them the friendship or overtures of the Mitannis, whose royal and noble families were Aryan, and also of the Hittites of Cappadocia who, too, appear to have been Indo-Europeans.[50] Soon marriage-alliances began to be sought and entered into between the Mitannis first, and then the Hittites, on the one hand and the Egyptian royal house on the other, so that from the reign of the next Pharaoh, Thothmes IV, there came into Egypt knowledge of the Indo-European pantheon and its influence. Also the Assyrian Goddess Ishtar made her appearance more than once and must have strengthened the esoteric and orgiastic cult of Isis.[51]

And it happened that the second monarch after Thothmes IV to ascend the throne of Egypt in sole charge in 1372 B.C. soon discarded the old gods of Egypt for a modified form of Sun-god worship. Discarding first Amen, the god of Theban empire, he changed his name to announce the fact, from Amenhotep to Ikhnaten. He displaced the god of his forefathers, Amen, by his adopted god whom he named Aten, his representation having been the Sun-disc with spreading rays. Ikhnaten's sponsoring of Aten as the One god and his founding of a new city to be presided over by Him was a greater cataclysm in Egyptian religious history than anyone before it. On the whole, it appears to have benefited Egyptian religious development not less momentously than the much earlier revolution in favour of Spiritualized Ptah attempted by the theologians of Memphis. But it adversely affected the national life of Egypt, upsetting both its political and economic balance at a time when internal solidarity and economic stability were much more needed than at any time before. For it happened to be the era when a strong and ruthless power arising in Northern Mesopotamia, the Assyrians, had started on a career of international aggrandizement.

Ikhnaten was so much busy nursing his pet worship-complex—the new complex was really not so new as it is tried to be made out but was tried to be promulgated it appears in a spiteful and revengeful manner against the strongly entrenched priesthood of Thebes—that he turned a pure introvert, to such an extent that some writers on Ancient Egypt have declared him to have been a maniac, and shut himself up from active political life. The future strong enemies of Egypt got splendid opportunity to consolidate their power by reducing her erstwhile allies and subordinate confederates to be their vassals or by keeping them at their mercy by show of prowess.[52]

More than forty years ago Wallis Budge wrote to suggest that there was a good deal of influence of the Mitannian religion on the religion of Aten which Ikhnaten promulgated. And in particular he maintained that the insistence in the hymns to Aten on the beauty and power of light showed this at its best. He went further to contend that the certain traits emphasized in some of the Ṛgvedic hymns addressed to gods Sūrya and Varuṇa by the Indo-Aryans of the Panjab are parallel to those used in the Aten hymns. Comparing the two sets of hymns, those of Aten on the one hand, and those to Sūrya and Varuṇa of the *Rgveda* on the other, he very properly exposed the limitations of the moral and religious content of the Aten hymns vis-à-vis the Indo-Aryan ones. He says: "Varuṇa possessed one attribute, which, so far as we know, was wanting in Aten; he spied out sin and judged the sinner . . . And Varuṇa was a constant witness of men's truth and falsehood." As for the Sūrya hymns he presented a translation of the famous "Gāyatrī", the verse known as "Gāyatrī Mantra" or simply "Gāyatrī" or "Sāvitrī", from the *Rgveda* with its "petition for spiritual enlightenment, understanding or wisdom" and pointed out that the Aten hymns did not contain any such petition! It is not that one suggests direct Indo-Aryan influence much less any haphazard borrowing from it but one emphasizes in this contrast the difference in the national attitudes towards religion and its content, national aspirations and culture. The Indo-Aryans of the Panjab who chanted these prayers to Sūrya and Varuṇa, must have been later than the Egyptians of Ikhnaten by not more than a century. A few centuries later, not later than 1000 B.C., in the texts of the *Yajurveda* Sāvitrī is ascribed the function of controlling mind and thought in the service of truth and is specially praised for this function. The texts are bodily embodied in the doctrine-complex of the theistic Upaniṣad, *Śvetāśvatara*. The finale is provided by a new text calling upon all to delight in the ancient prayer to Sāvitrī, the inspirer. The national mind of India yearned for intellectual and spiritual inspiration and urge from divine source as typified by the Sun. And this yearning for intellectual and spiritual inspiration from the Sun has, ever since till to-day, remained a characteristic of élite Indians, the descendants of the Ṛgvedic Indo-Aryans.[53]

Whatever the originality of Ikhnaten and his theologian-courtiers, whatever the traits attributed to Aten, the Egyptians did not take to Aten-religion kindly. The next monarch, a young boy, who was named Tutankhaten, on ascending the throne after Ikhnaten, changed his name to Tutankhamen, substituting Amen in place of Aten, and thus proclaimed that the new-fangled religion of Aten was superseded by the earlier national one of Amen. Thus the religion centred round Amenra came back and that with added vigour. For as Tutankhamen has himself recorded : "He made to flourish again the monuments .... which had fallen into ruin. He had put an end to rebellion and disaffection ..... *He sought after the welfare of father Amen.*"* He cast a figure of his "August emanation" in gold or 'silver-gold' and also "fashioned a figure of 'Father Amen' on thirteen staves .... formerly the figure of Amen only possessed eleven (?) staves".[54]

The epithets that this renovator or revivalist monarch, nurtured in the school of the so-called monotheistic father, Ikhnaten, uses and the proclamation of his governing policy he makes are characteristic of the Egyptian religious consciousness and representative of polylatrous societies, which have not developed a unifying philosophy like that of the Hindu society. They also support my frequent statement about the Egyptian pantheon being a triad or better yet a tetrad. Of course Amenra comes first, the king having been "beloved of" him ; but the king was also beloved of Temu or Atum, and of Ra-Harakhti, and of Ptah. Even Thoth, the wisdom-god, was not forgotten as the king was beloved of Thoth. But Amen's superior position again leads to the assertion that the king was the son of Amen, a fiction which had become a fixed convention from the birth-story of Hatshepsut.

Ptah's getting status by the side of Ra or Atum and later of Amen I have already mentioned. Now came another occasion when Ptah's acquired status is tested and proved. Tutankhamen also made a figure of Ptah and had it

* Italics mine. They are intended to draw attention to the king's egotistic attitude of patronage towards the Supreme God,

decorated with precious metal and stones almost as in the case of Amen's statue. He, it appears, even had got additional staves into the original statue of Ptah in the Memphis shrine.[55] There were only six, the number of the additional ones not being given. This lower number of staves in Ptah statue may be noted, as also the undeclared addition which may or may not have made up the deficit. In all probability their number must have been brought up very near to that of the staves of Amen, thus equalizing the two gods. Anyway in the hymn to Amen recorded in the reign of Rameses II, which claims our attention next, about sixty years later, it is declared with great emphasis that Amen, Ra and Ptah, the three are One.

The hymn is really a song forming part of a work known as *Poems on Thebes* and its God contained in the Leyden Papyrus.[56] That the songs were written after Ikhnaten's reign is clear from the opening of its seventh chapter which reads: "The wicked are cast off from Thebes" which now is the strongest city and "the Mistress of Cities . . . Every city extolleth (herself) in her name." Then again in a later section it is said: "Thou triumphest, O Amenre [Amen-ra]! The caitiffs are overthrown, repelled by the spear."

As for the status of the god, who is, in the above quotation, called by his XVIIIth Dynasty name, it is to be noted that in this work he is mentioned as Amen only. And that is proper because the new technique of identification, significantly adopted here to suit the identification of three gods and not two, makes the three originally separate gods into a triadic unity. In a way both Ptah and Ra have thus appreciated in their status as a consequence of the confusion produced by Ikhnaten's persecution of the other sects. It must have been considered politically very desirable to combine all the three gods and their chief cities to forge national solidarity. The superior position of Amen is stressed by making him self-created. The device used to state Ptah's relationship to Amen renders my suggestion that the newer technique of assimilation through equal status, and turning it into integration, was the consequence of the political and social situation emerging out of the utter neglect of the secular affairs of the State in the reign of Ikhnaten. Tenen, i.e., Ptah, though earlier than Amen, was only a form or manifestation of Amen. This device reminds me of a well-known occasion during the dialogue of Kṛṣṇa and Arjuna, that is recorded as having taken place on the battle-field of Kurukṣetra near Delhi and recorded in the famous philosophical Hindu book called the *Bhagavadgītā*, the Lord's Song. Kṛṣṇa in the process of persuading Arjuna to join battle said that He had expounded a particular doctrine to Vivasvat i.e. the Sun. Arjuna promptly asked Kṛṣṇa how it was that Kṛṣṇa, the mortal man of the Vṛṣṇi race and a contemporary of Arjuna, could have taught a doctrine to one, Vivasvat, who lived ages earlier. And Kṛṣṇa, the mortal man, effectively answers him by asserting that he had many many births before, and as the Supreme God He remembered them. So the theologians or the intellectuals of Ramessid Egypt asserted that Ptah was the early form of Amen, and that Amen had taken that form for the purpose of fashioning the Primordial

Gods. It appears to me that the argument or rather the theory comes very near the *Gītā*-doctrine of God's incarnations, discontinuous as writers on comparative religion specify them, owing to their occurring only at intervals !

Though Amen's form is declared to be mysterious and his image "not spread out in books" this self-created god, who came out of an egg which he himself had shaped, is said to have shone so at the first occasion that "all that existed was dumbfounded at his glory", and his "shape" is described as "gleaming". He is "the wondrous god with many forms. All gods make their boast in him, in order to magnify themselves with his beauty, for he is so divine." As Erman tells his readers the last sentence means that all the other gods are "proud of being a part of him", i.e., as I should put it they have their being and their glory through Amen.

Here again, in the ascription of many forms, mysterious and wondrous to Amen and in the attitude of other gods and their nature, we come very near the doctrine of the *Bhagavadgītā* known as the "Vibhūtiyoga", "manifestatory Aspect" of the Supreme God, which will be described in its proper place in the Indian Hindu section of this work.

Amen's form is not known nor is his name. His image is "not spread out in books". Though he is said to have fashioned Ra, the third god of the trinity, he is said in the same breath to have "completed himself" as Atum, a form of Ra. It is clear the theologians intended to apply their new technique of assimilation even to Ra. They completed this speculation about Amen's priority or juniority in the new strain by making him the Hidden Core and making Ra the face and Ptah the body of Amen. They felt fully satisfied with their performance and declared in the end : "Three are all gods—Amun [Amen], Re (Ra), and Ptah—and there is none like them . . . Only he is . . . Amun and Re and Ptah, together three."

Amen or Amenra was thus put up as the God by about 1200 B.C. ; and we find the warrior-king Rameses II mentioning in his hour of dire need the fact, to him patent and significantly entitling him to special consideration, that the Asiatics, "wretches" as he calls them, did "not know God", and questioning Amen what they should hence mean to him, thereby suggesting that they had no claim on Amen's help or favour and therefore should be forsaken by Amen.[57]

However, the self-same Rameses signing his treaty with the Asiatics, the Hittites, named, as being worshipped by him, the gods Amenra, Harakhti, Atum, Amen, Ptah and Sutekh. In the swearing clause, however, at the end he names Amenra, Sutekh, "the gods male and gods female of the hills and of the rivers of Egypt".[58] He thereby illustrates and underscores the irony of polylatrous society imperfectly attempting to rise to monolatry and perhaps also monotheism without the conceptual basis, the philosophical background or the religious synthesis as opposed to mere syncretism sweetened with a few nice-sounding terms !

The Hittites, another polylatrous people but of Indo-European culture, some of whose deities are common to the Indian Vedic pantheon, were quite clearly eclectic and accepted gods of the peoples with whom they came into close contact.[59]

The Mitannis further east with an Indo-European, nay an Indo-Iranian, royalty and nobility at their head, an equally polylatrous society, in their treaty swore by the four gods, quite Vedic in their names, Mitra, Indra, Varuṇa and Nāsatya.[60] The form in which the name of the last deity—a double or twin deity in the Ṛgveda and as such its name occurs always in the dual number—occurs quite definitely excludes Iranian element.

The pantheonic aspect of the religious complex having been thus dealt with in its development, it is desirable to make a brief but connected statement about the content, the attitude and the spirit, the religious complex enshrined and the nature of the influence the pantheonic aspect exercised on the people.

Earlier Egyptologists[61] had concluded that the Egyptian religion "had essentially the same character in all after ages" since the Pyramid-age with mythology getting more confused as time went on. They pointed out the extraordinary growth of the priesthood and its baneful influence in making religion a lifeless matter of ritual technique and drew attention to the institution of temple-dancing women and prostitutes. But they admitted that in one direction, however, in that amalgamation of the divinities into one type there was progress. "This course" Erman opined "would gradually lead to the abolition of polytheism and in fact this tendency is very apparent." Evidently the undiminished and ever-vigilant efforts of the priests of the numerous sanctuaries of different gods all over the country prevented the culmination. Drawing on the saying of one of the wise-men of Ancient Egypt, Erman even admitted that private piety for "the serious-minded" at least was "not a mere show" though it was eclipsed by "the pious offerings of the state".

Breasted[62] advanced the view that there was development and growth not only of moral sense but also of religious content in the long history of Egypt till about 700 B.C. Over and above the approach to a sort of monotheism through the glorification of one of the major gods of Egypt there was first of all, as mentioned in this discussion in an earlier chapter, the democratization of the Egyptian Hereafter which must have necessarily affected the nature and extent of the religious consciousness and practice of the common men. Further, with the resurgence of Amen after his temporary eclipse by Aten, the older and scattered doctrines about God, His relations with man and the latter's attitude towards Him "culminated in the profoundest expression or revelation of the devotional religious spirit ever attained by the men of Egypt". Further, he was convinced, and he demonstrated his view, that the belief "in an intimate and personal relation between the worshipper and his god had . . . . become widespread among the people". So much was this the case in his view that he summed up the new situation in the words : "An age of personal piety and inner aspiration to God now dawned among the masses." It was the decline of the Empire in the 12th century that brought in its wake a halt in the process of the vitalizing of religion that had brought about the advance to the age of personal piety. With the priesthood's mastery of Egypt about 1100 B.C. the stage was set for entire attention to be turned to the grandeur of the external and official manifestations of religion, producing "those forms of dignity and splendor" which "no Oriental religion had before displayed", and giving us the sanctuaries which "will always form one of the most imposing survivals from the ancient world". The decadence of spirit proceeded apace till about 700 B.C., when "the creative age of inner development was forever past".

Writing more than twenty years after Breasted made his above-quoted appraisal of Egyptian religious history, Wallis Budge[63] pondering over the whole complex asserted that the Egyptian Religion stood "alone; nothing exactly like it is known". And he evaluated the evidence of the period of high achievement thus: "... many of the scribes were truly religious men and had truly spiritual aspirations and yearnings. They were conscious of their sins and longed to be free from guilt before their god, even after they had offered up the statutory sacrifices and oblations .... But their highest and best spiritual ideas and conceptions were overshadowed by their *ineradicable belief in magic*". As he further points out, the Egyptians "*from first to last believed that the performance of ritual ceremonies, coupled with ceremonial personal cleanliness, produced holiness*".

The development of magic to smother the still small voice of conscience, as noted already, was an accompaniment of the glorious advance in the line of the judgment of the dead. Special charms were prepared to guarantee that the heart of the dead man did not give him away in the Judgment Hall. Breasted[64] himself first remarked on this development which he described in detail as "it had become a positive force for evil". We have no evidence to show that magic got less important as the age of piety dawned. In this connection the succint description of the evidence from the tomb of a vizier of the Late Period, of about 600 B.C., given by J. A. Wilson is not only instructive but almost decisive. The walls of the tomb are covered with "ritual and magic texts ... The life of this world is completely lacking; the funeral services and the world of the dead are the only concerns of this man ... His good consists in magic, ritual, and the favour of his god".[65]

Wilson's position regarding the religious development of Egypt and particularly regarding the age of piety appears to me to be the correct one. And it is, the age of piety was also the era of "deterministic philosophy ... stated in terms of the will of god, placed over against man's helplessness". It naturally showed a strong sense of fate as the external determining force. I have, in another connection, drawn attention to the fact that the god of Fate, Shay, made his first appearance in the papyrus of Ani as standing by the scales in the Judgment Hall. Amenemopet about the 7th century B.C. advises his reader not to ignore both Fate and Fortune, i.e., the god Shay and the goddess Renenut. Wilson has remarked on it that the "two deified concepts" had "particularly strong governing role" at that time.[66]

Here then we have piety which is likely to be the reflex of the socially depressed and rather insecure tenure of life. The god himself round whom the piety was centred was not known to be distinctly and unreservedly above magic and fate. As a matter of fact in the XIXth Dynasty book of songs, as if to assure the doubting folks, it is stated that Fate and the Harvest goddess are "with Amen for all people",[67] and not that they do not count where Amen is favourable, nor again that they take to flight before Amen. Ceremonial purity, magic, Fate and anxiety about earthly security and other-worldly existence combining with personal piety give us something like the picture of Hindu society of about the 18th century without its redeeming high philosophy. It is the concourse of these attitudes and practices, in the promulgation of which the self-interest of the priesthood is to be blamed not a little, that prevented the emergence of a true monotheism in Egypt about 1000 B.C. That the Egyptian endeavour, which proved inadequate to evolve a true monotheism, was, however, not totally lost is the burden of the message of both Breasted and Budge. The Hebrews profited by it and appear to have utilized the Egyptian thought for their own religious set-up.

CHAPTER V

HINDU COSMOLOGY AND COSMOGRAPHY

In the beginning, opines a sage of the *Bṛhadāraṇyaka Upaniṣad* (I, 4, 1-7), was only the self in the form of a person. He looked round and said "I am" ; and that was the beginning of the concept named 'I'. Since then one begins distinguishing by first separating oneself as 'I' from others as 'thou' or 'they'. He got frightened owing to his loneliness but dispelled his fear by pondering that there was nothing besides himself of which he should have to be careful. Yet he could not rejoice, because one cannot rejoice all alone. He therefore desired to have a second or a companion ; and with one-half of himself he produced a woman, who became his wife ; the husband and wife together produced human beings. The woman got shocked at being treated as a wife though she was produced from the person of the "self" himself and then followed a game of hide and seek between the two, giving the world the various kinds of animals of both sexes. Then the 'self' rubbed his palm of the hand on the inside of his mouth and produced fire. Moisture and 'soma', the drink, were produced from his semen. Because fire was produced from his mouth people offered and offer sacrifices to 'self'. He created the gods, who are immortal.

In another mood immediately after the above account occurs one with Brahman, the Universal Being, as the Origin (*BrU*, I, 4, 9). Being the only one and not flourishing, Brahman went into creative activity. And curiously, it began with the Kṣatriya class and then with the other two, viz., the common people, and the servant class. Along with each of these three classes certain of the Vedic gods were associated. Even then Brahman did not flourish or rather did not think that 'It' flourished. It then created an "excellent form" known as 'Dharma'. It is the power of the Kṣatriya class. And it is through 'Dharma' that a weak man hopes to stand up against a powerful one, as in current affairs one does through the king and his officers. Dharma is truth itself and therefore a man who speaks, or does justice, is said to speak or follow truth, 'Satya'. Later the same *Upaniṣad* (I, 5, 23) declares, quoting an ancient authority, that the gods made breath (prāṇa) the "law" (dharma). So much so was this the case that if one practises control of breath one wins complete union [sāyujya] with that divinity and residence in the same world with him [salokatā].

The self alone verily was in the beginning is the assertion of a sage in the *Aitareya Upaniṣad* (I ; II ; III, 1-2). Nothing else then winked. The self thought to himself : "let me now create the worlds". He created the worlds, i.e., water, light-rays, death and the waters. Water is above the heaven and the waters are down below. The light-rays are atmosphere and death is the earth. He then thought of creating the guardians of the world (lokapālas). For this purpose he drew forth a person from the waters and gave him a shape.

He brooded over him, whereupon his mouth opened out like an egg ; and from it issued forth speech, and from the latter fire. Then the nostrils were separated and from them issued breath from which came air. On the eyes being separated out there was sight from which issued the sun. The ears were then separated out [?] and from them came hearing. From the hearing came the quarters of space. The skin being separated out there came hairs and from them plants and trees.

Next the heart was separated out. From it came the mind and it brought out the moon. The navel when separated out produced the outbreath (apāna) and from the latter death (mṛtyu). The penis being separated out gave out semen and from the semen came waters. He also created hunger and thirst in them. These divinities, i.e., fire, air, the sun, space or atmosphere (ākāśa), plants and trees, the moon, death (mṛtyu) and water, cried for appropriate abodes and food. The self brought them a person (man) well-formed and shaped and asked them to resort to him for their abode and food. Then fire in the form of speech entered the person's mouth ; the sun becoming sight entered the eyes ; the quarters of space becoming hearing entered the ears ; plants and trees becoming hairs entered the skin ; the moon becoming the mind entered the heart ; death becoming outbreath entered the navel ; and water becoming semen entered the penis. Hunger and thirst were assigned a place in the divinities and thus in the person as sharers with them. The self then brooded over the waters, the last item in the worlds created by the self, from which issued forth food.

The *Taittirīya Upaniṣad* (II, 1 ; II, 6) records only one account of creation as from Brahman, Ātman. From Brahman, the Self, arose ether ; from ether air ; from air fire ; from fire water ; from water the earth ; from the earth herbs ; from herbs food and from food the man (person - pūruṣa). It must be assumed from the second reference that Brahman first desired "let me be many" and practised austerities to achieve the purpose. It should be noted that this account accords primacy and priority to ether among Brahman's creations. In the *Chāndogya* account of creation from Sat it is 'tejas', light-heat, which receives this priority ; and ether does not figure at all.

The *Chāndogya Upaniṣad* (VI, 2-7) prefers 'Sat', simple Being, as the Origin of the Cosmos. In the beginning there was only Being without a second. Some people say that it was non-being alone that was in the beginning. But their opinion is wrong ; for how could being be produced from non-being ? Therefore it was only being that was there in the beginning without a second. It thought : "Let me be many ; let me create." It created light-heat (tejas). That light-heat thought "let me be many" and it brought forth water (āpaḥ). That water again desired to be many and brought forth food (anna), standing as usual symbolically for earth (pṛthivī). All living things were produced from this last, with only three origins, i.e., either from an egg, from a living being [elsewhere more appropriately described as from the placenta] or from sprout [evidently for the sake of analogy and symmetry of the design of creation and growth adopted in this passage, the fourth origin already mentioned in the *Atharvaveda* I, 12, 1, i.e., from moist heat (sveda - sweat), being omitted]. Entering into light-heat (tejas), water (āpaḥ) and food-earth (pṛthivī), termed divinities, the Being produced everything else using the finer elements of these three in the process. Fire, the sun, the moon and lightning each have three colours, i.e., red, white and black, mixed in their forms. These are derived from light-heat (tejas), water and food. Food eaten, water drunk and heat, i.e., fat, eaten, each is reduced into three densities and parts. The coarsest parts of the three forms the faeces, the urine and bone respectively; the middling density portions are turned into flesh, blood and marrow; the finest or the subtlest portions become mind, breath and speech respectively. So mind is food-made, breath is water-made and speech is light or heat-made.

There are at least two Upaniṣadic accounts of creation which eschew Brahman, Ātman or Sat as the origin of the cosmos. In one it is water and in the other a spontaneous egg which begins the work of creation.

In the beginning this universe was all water. Water produced the true (satya). And Brahman is that 'true'. Brahman produced Prajāpati who produced the gods. The gods meditated on the real (true), which consists of three syllables, two of which completely enclose the third, which stands for untruth and death. Therefore it is that the true or real (satya) is free from death and this knowledge makes its possessor free from injury or death [?] (*BrU*, V, 5).

In the beginning this world was non-existent (asat) and later it became existent (sat). It grew and became an egg which lay for a year. At the end of a year it burst open. The two shell-pieces became golden and silvern. The latter is the earth and the former, the golden half, is the sky (dyauḥ). The outer membrane is the mountains; the inner membrane is the mist with the clouds. What were the veins (dhamanyaḥ) are the rivers. What was the fluid inside is the ocean. And what was born from it [?] is the sun (*ChU*, III, 19, 1-2).

Two accounts of creation, in both of which Prajāpati figures as the creator and may therefore refer to secondary creation rather than to the first one of the cosmos as a whole, may now be presented. There was nothing whatever in the beginning. 'Mṛtyu, or Death, desiring to have a self (ātman) for himself created the mind (manas). He then moved about offering worship (arcana), i.e., he resorted to worship evidently to get further impulse or energy or power. While he was engaged in the act of worship water (ka) appeared. That is why water is called *arka* which means fire. Water is verily fire (arka). The froth (śara) [e.g., Mālvaṇī 'śirān'] of the water got solidified and that was the earth (pṛthivī). He rested on the earth and got heated (through the performance of austerity). From this condition of his issued forth fire (agni). He now divided himself into three parts, as fire, sun and air (vāyu). He thus stands firm in waters. He then desired that another form be born of him. Thus the union of speech with mind was caused. With speech he produced the Vedas. But he desired again. And this time it was the older form of worship in its newer garb he adopted to materialize his desire to create. He sacrificed and that too with a 'greater' sacrifice, i.e., austerities. In this performance his breaths got exhausted and his body swelled but the *mind within held on.* And he went on desiring, now, that his body should be fit for sacrifice, evidently with the intention of sacrificing it for further creation. But, perchance (?), or rather because he thought of the object fit for sacrifice, a horse was produced, that being the most coveted object for sacrifice in that age, as 'aśvamedha', horse-sacrifice, was the greatest of sacrifices. Letting it to roam about for a year as in the Vedic 'aśvamedha', he sacrificed it for himself after the end of the year. Hence, as the text has it, is a horse-sacrifice offered to Prajāpati, thus giving us both the new theory for spiritualization of the horse-sacrifice through this allegory and also the identification of 'mṛtyu' with Prajāpati. Of course the account of creation from 'mṛtyu' by 'mṛtyu' ceases to be a logical one. It has to be counted as creation by 'Prajāpati' with the help of 'desire', 'worship', 'sacrifice' and 'tapas' (*BrU*, I, 2).

The other account which is from the *ChU* runs thus: Prajāpati brooded over the worlds, and extracted their essences. He extracted fire from the earth, air from the atmosphere and the sun from the sky (dyauḥ). He then brooded over these three deities. As they were being brooded upon there issued forth from them the *Ṛgveda*, the *Yajurveda* and the *Sāmaveda* respectively. He further brooded over the three-fold knowledge and extracted their essences in the form of the three syllables, 'bhūr', 'bhuvas' and 'svaḥ', respectively (*ChU*, IV, 17, 1-3).

Before passing on to the cosmography in the Upaniṣads, it is necessary to call attention to the cosmological views expressed in the *Śvetāśvatara Upaniṣad* which, in one or two respects, takes up the threads of the Ṛgvedic views on the subject and carries forward the Vedic view of One God, not the impersonal Brahman or Sat but evidently a personal god, being the Creator of the cosmos. Whereas the Ṛgvedic view must be understood to have named this personal God, the Origin of the cosmos, as Hiraṇyagarbha, the view propounded in the *Śvetāsvatara Upaniṣad* makes Rudra the Creator and the Origin of the world, and states that He, Rudra-Śiva, created Hiraṇyagarbha (III, 4; IV, 12), and both together, with the instrumentality of matter, called Prakṛti or even Māyā of God Rudra-Śiva (IV, 9-13; VI, 3, 9-13), produced the cosmos (III, 3; IV, 4-5; VI, 3-4, 18). The abode of Rudra-Śiva is evidently described in VI, 14. It is noteworthy that it is said to be beyond the reach of the rays of the luminaries, the stars, the sun and the moon or fire. I should stress this because in the next phase of the development of the Hindu religious complex, though not comprehensively represented in the *Bhagavadgītā*, as the Vaiṣṇava deity Lord Kṛṣṇa used almost the same phraseology to characterize His abode (*BhG*, XV, 6).

Turning to the cosmography of the Upaniṣads we meet with the mention of a number of worlds other than this world of men. In general terms it asserts the existence of worlds other than this one of men (*BrU*, IX, 3, 9). The god of

Death himself is made to declare: "To the childish the shining 'beyond' does not present itself, as they are careless and deluded by the glamour of wealth. They think that this is the only world and that there is no other. Thus do they fall again and again in my power" (*KaU*, 1, 2, 6). The universe having only two worlds, this world of men and the other world, which was conceived of as having more than one sub-world, is the concept the Upaniṣadic era carried forward from the earlier Ṛgvedic era. But it could not and did not rest with the complete acceptance of it as final. The growth of certain ascetic techniques and the speculative boldness which led the Upaniṣadic thinkers to the grand postulation of the Universal Being as the source and end of the universe and to the even bolder assertion, backed by realized experience of some extra-ordinary individuals like Yājñavalkya, of the unity of the Universal Being and the non-material element, the individual self or the embodied soul, in man, almost automatically forced upon the thinkers the postulation of many worlds, outside the ken of the ordinary senses of man.

The *Chāndogya Upaniṣad* (VIII, 2) went so far as to speak of not only the standard worlds, as will be presently seen, of the Fathers but also of the world of Mothers, of Brothers, of Sisters, of Friends, of Women and even of Food and Drink, of Fragrant Unguents and Flowers, and also of Song and Music. Leaving these wish-fulfilling worlds, which might have been the creation of the over-developed minds, we have in the *Bṛhadāraṇyaka Upaniṣad* a whole section (III, 6), a serious reply of the great Yājñavalkya to the earnest questioning of the most intelligent and argumentative member of the deliberative assembly, shot through and through with keen rivalry, of which this portion formed a part of the dialogue. And the questioner, moreover, was a lady not to be easily put down, as a further question by her in the progress of the debate shows. Yājñavalkya maintaining that wind is accommodated in the world of space proceeds to specify the various worlds which establish the whole universe in the world of Brahman or in Brahman, the Absolute Universal Being. And they are in the ascending order: the world of Gandharvas (mythical fairy-like beings), of the Sun, of the Moon—this specification is rather anomalous; for it is seen in almost all passages, in the Upaniṣads and in other texts of sacred or mythological nature that the sun is the more important, the greater and the nearer to the Supreme Deity god than the moon—, the world of Stars, that of the Gods, that of Indra—this also appears to be a solecism as Indra even by the time of this Upaniṣad was enthroned as the king of the gods and could not have had a world of his own different from that of the gods. As a matter of fact in the *Kauṣītakibrāhmaṇa Upaniṣad* (III, 1) we are told that the great king Pratardana, the son of Divodāsa, went to the abode of Indra—mark that it is not the world of Indra through his valour and effort. Then follows the world of Prajāpati, and finally the world of Brahman. Thus according to Yājñavalkya's enumeration of the worlds constituting the universe of which the world of Brahman is the final rest and source, there are eight worlds besides the world of men, which stretch between it and the final world of Brahman or Brahmaloka. In the account of the cosmic position of the Brahmaloka given in the *Kauṣītakibrāhmaṇa Upaniṣad* (I, 1, 1-3), there intervene seven worlds between this of ours and the final one of Brahman. They are those of the Moon, of Agni, of Vāyu, of Varuṇa, of the Sun, of Indra and of Prajāpati.

Apropos of the number of the worlds postulated in the cosmographic section of the *Bṛhadāraṇayaka Upaniṣad* I may venture the suggestion that the number so posited may not be utterly arbitrary. In the *Bhagavadgītā*, a book which has drawn upon the Upaniṣads extensively for its doctrines, Lord Kṛṣṇa declares (VII, 4-5) that He as the Supreme Soul has an eightfold nature which is His lower aspect. The eightfold nature is formed by the five great elements of nature, known in Indian philosophy and to most Hindus of some pretension to the knowledge of Hinduism as the five "great beings" or "Mahābhūtas", and mind, intelligence and ego-sense. The Upaniṣads apparently do not speak of this aspect of the cosmos as constituting the lower nature of Brahman or Puruṣa. But at least one of them, the *Kaṭha Upaniṣad* (I, 3, 10-11) specifies the hierarchy of senses, sense-objects, mind, intellect, with "mahān ātmā", "great self" and 'avyakta', undeveloped root-matter in between them and the self or Puruṣa in the case of an individual personality.

Whether or not the postulation of eight worlds between this world of mortals and that of Brahman, the Universal Being, was a more or less cogent development of the speculative thought, which is a specific conclusion in the matter of cosmology, it stands by itself and in its complete form is hardly ever depended upon for either explanation of life after death or for any other religio-philosophical purpose. The same *Bṛhadāraṇyaka Upaniṣad* (IV, 3, 32-33) narrating the relative value of the worlds, or the conditions attained by persons after their death, is content with drawing upon five worlds, only three of which are identical with the three of the eight in the other list, i.e., that of the Gandharvas, that of Prajāpati, and that of the gods. Though I have spoken of all the five as worlds, I have done so by construing the context. In actual specification only two of the conditions are spoken of as worlds or "lokas", viz., that of the Gandharvas and that of Prajāpati.

The first grade of enjoyment over that of mortal men in the world of mortal men is that of the Fathers, who have won the worlds, and it is one-hundred-fold that of mortal men. I have taken this to imply the world of Fathers as the next to that of men. The fourth category, which is in this passage specified in two stages or grades, one above the other, in the same degree and measure as the previous category, is above that which precedes it, as the enjoyments of "Karmadevas", "gods through actions", and those of "Ājānadevas", "gods by births", as meaning the same world as that specified in the other account as the world of gods. Each succeeding world or condition provides enjoyments which are one-hundred-fold those of the preceding one. Thus the world of Brahman is established to provide enjoyments which are ten billion times those of the world of mortal men.

The *Taittirīya Upaniṣad*, too (II, 8), has a similar text regarding the relative corpus of enjoyments available in the hereafter. It does not mention any world, except that of the Fathers, who are specified or qualified as those whose worlds last long. It further introduces two varieties of Gandharvas and adds Bṛhaspati enjoyment in between those of Indra and Prajāpati. It further, very illogically, interchanges the order of gods by actions and gods by birth in the grades. Needless to say not only is the number of possible worlds to be postulated for cosmography but also the size of enjoyments to be had with Brahman becomes very large. In cosmographic discussion, therefore, this text may be left out.

The worlds outside this one of ours being three in number is a notion figuring more consistently in the cosmography of the Upaniṣads. Thus in the *Kaṭha Upaniṣad* (II, 3 and 5) we have the world of Fathers, that of Gandharvas and that of Brahman. In other references to three worlds, however, we have the more standard and for all practical purposes the correct enumeration of the three worlds, as this world of mortals, the world of Fathers and the world of gods (*BrU*, I, 5, 4 ; 1, 5, 16 ; III, 1, 8). Both these accounts ultimately agree in making the number of worlds four ; for in the *Kaṭha* account there is to be added the world of mortals and in the *Bṛhadāraṇyaka* account there is finally the unending or imperishable world achieved by persons who have attained full knowledge, or, as in some other accounts, who have meditated on the syllable "Aum" in a proper manner. This imperishable world is more commonly called in the Upaniṣads "Brahmaloka" or the world of Brahma (*PrU*, V, 3-5). This Brahmaloka recurs in the account of the communication system between the world of mortals and the hereafter which conducts the dead to their destination. It is quite clear from these accounts that the world of Brahman is postulated on the analogy of the world of Fathers and that of gods to posit a world more stable than and utterly imperishable in comparison to that of gods. In strict application of the implications of the philosophy of Absolute Brahman, however, there cannot be a world of Brahman, only the individual soul becomes one with the Universal Being. How can the Universal Being have an abode or a world which by implication must be a finite, howsoever big, unit ?

The notion of three worlds is basic in Upaniṣadic cosmography ; for as will be seen later the cardinal principle of Brahmanism and Hinduism, i.e., the doctrine of transmigration and metempsychosis arose and was postulated in the Upaniṣadic era by its speculative thinkers ; and the doctrine presupposes, in terms of attainable worlds, at least two besides this mortal world. And we find in three Upaniṣads, *Chāndogya* (VIII, I, 6), *Muṇḍaka* (I, 2, 1) and *Praśna* (III, 7), the mention of a world which is either attained through or won by merit or is merely meritorious or again is one of good deeds, i.e., won by good deeds. Against this we have also the opposite world, world of demerit or one reserved for persons of evil actions. These then are the two worlds which become necessary for working out the implications of the doctrine of transmigration, the world of mortals, the third world, being always present and also necessary.

The fact that some worlds are characterized as won by meritorious living in this world, i.e., as a reward of virtuous mundane life (*ChU*, VIII, 1, 6; *MuU*, I, 2, 1; *PrU*, III, 7), while the world of mortals is either attained owing to mixture of good and bad mundane life or through one's deeds or is said to be won through progeny (*BrU*, I, 5, 16), presupposes a world which must be reserved for the out and out evil-doers, the sinful ones. As the *Praśna Upaniṣad* (III, 7) has it the "Sinful world" is attained through evil deeds and work. And though the *Chāndogya Upaniṣad* (V, 10, 7) roundly declares that those who do evil and disgraceful acts in this life are reborn either in the lowest castes or even in the lower species of animals like dogs and pigs, it asserts in the next but one sentence that the person who steals gold or drinks wine or violates his preceptor's bed or murders a Brahmin "falls", as do also the persons who associate with such a one.

In the *Atharvaveda* (II, 14, 3; XII, 4, 36) a place called 'naraka' and a world of that name 'narakaloka' are mentioned as the place to which some persons after death have to go. S. V. Ketkar[1] has brought together all the passages in the Vedic literature relating to 'naraka'. 'Naraka' has remained the only designation till today of the place where sinful people are subjected to various kinds of punishments and is supposed to be down below the earth and ruled over by Yama, the god of Death. Ketkar finds reference to a deep and dark place reserved or designed for evil-doers even in the *Ṛgveda* (*RV*, IV, 3, 5; VII, 104, 3). He finds a fairly full description of the tortures in this 'naraka' or hell in one of the passages of the *Śatapatha Brāhmaṇa* (XI, 6, 1).

In the *Taittirīya Āraṇyaka* (I, 19) at least four of these places are specifically named. The great philologist Yāska, who was probably a contemporary of the authors of the latest of the twelve Upaniṣads we have used for this résumé of evolving Brahmanism and Hinduism, derives the word "putra" meaning a son, from a hell, 'naraka', named 'put'. The idea that there was not only an evil place, a dread world, but also that it was one to which certain persons, or most persons under certain circumstances, had to repair was very firmly rooted in the eschatological beliefs of the people before 500 B.C. Further there were more such places than one, and that they were specifically named. If persons without sons had to repair to the hell named 'put' according to Yāska, a wife who behaved crookedly towards her husband had to go to another hell, which is unnamed (*Nirukta*, I, 11; II, 11). Yāska derives the word 'naraka' so as to make it a place lying below the earth or a place without the slightest joy. We thus see that the cosmography of the Upaniṣadic era must have had in view a fourth world, called 'naraka', or hell. It must be noted that no such place appears in the list of hells recorded in the Vedic literature of the age ending before about 800 B.C., i.e., the end of the *Brāhmaṇa* period and the beginning of the Upaniṣadic period.

The world of Fathers, 'pitṛloka', is conceived of as a noisy place in the

Bṛhadāraṇyaka Upaniṣad (III, 1, 8) and also as a place from which one has to pass on to another world, that of the moon, and return to the cycle of birth and death (*BrU*, VI, 2, 16 ; *ChU*, V, 10, 3-7). One wins it by means of the performance of Vedic rites (*BrU*, I, 5, 16).

We do not have any description of the world of gods. We are told, however, in the *Chāndogya Upaniṣad* (III, 7, 1) that the gods neither eat nor drink but are satisfied with looking at the nectar, which would appear to be abundant in their world, as the 'sādhyas', a variety of divine beings, are said to live on it (*BrU*, III, 10, 1, 6, 9).

The *Bṛhadāraṇyaka Upaniṣad* (I, 5, 16) pronounces it to be the highest of the worlds which is to be won only through knowledge and explains why it burns bright (III, 1, 8).

The general trend in the Upaniṣads is for the world of Brahman to be considered the highest, the one worthwhile attaining and the one which, when the world of gods is mentioned along with it, is the goal to be achieved through the latter (*BrU*, VI, 2, 2-15). So much is Brahmaloka considered to be the final goal, the place where one dwells for eternity, wherefrom there is no return to the cycle of birth and death, that sometimes (*BrU*, V, 10) it is merely mentioned as the world, i.e., "he proceeds to the world, which is free from sorrow and cold". The souls dwelling there, and they do so till the final dissolution, can assume any form at will (*MuU*, III, 2, 6). There the individual soul and the Supreme soul live as light and shadow (*KaU*, II, 3, 5). The Brahmaloka is declared to be spotless and open only to those in whom are truth, austerity and chastity established and crookedness, falsehood and trickery do not exist (*PrU*, I, 15-16).

The Brahmaloka, the world of Brahman or Brahma, which in the system of religion and philosophy propounded in the Upaniṣads is the goal of all pious and religious people, that being the place which is above the law of recurring return to the cycle of birth and death, even when the dead person is one qualified to attain it, is reached after crossing a number of obstacles, to do which he receives divine help from time to time. It appears that that world having been conceived in terms which are physical as in the case of the other worlds, which are supposed to be peopled by certain varieties of entities and personalities, was provided with a topography worthy of it, bringing out its both features, i.e., the difficulty of access and the unlimited blissfulness. The description of the heavenly world, 'svargaloka', which one comes across in the Ṛgvedic cosmology evidently formed the prototype. And the fact that in more than three or four places in the eleven Upaniṣads, omitting the *Kauṣitakibrāhmana Upaniṣad*, the heavenly world, 'svargaloka', is either referred to or actually lauded as the eternal abode of the emancipated souls, suggests that a model description of the 'svargaloka' and consequently of the 'Brahmaloka' was current among the élite at least.

Svargaloka is the world reached by those who are able to travel to the 'hereafter' by the Brahmapatha (*BrU*, IV, 4, 8) ; or is the world attained by those who have realized the Brahman in their hearts (*ChU*, III, 13, 6). One who understands the real meaning of the word 'satya' goes day by day into the heavenly world (*ChU*, VIII, 3, 2-5). Vāmadeva with the intelligent self, soared upward from this world and having enjoyed all in the heavenly world became immortal (*AiU*, III, 1, 4). It is possible that in the last passage the 'svargaloka' is mentioned only as the penultimate stage of the journey in the hereafter and the reference to Vāmadeva's immortality is meant to indicate his passage to the Brahmaloka. However it must be borne in mind that the *Kaṭha Upaniṣad* (I, 1, 12-13) speaks of the 'svargaloka' as the world of imperishable joys. In the 'svargaloka', it affirms, there is no fear whatever. One has no fear of old age and one overcoming both hunger and thirst and leaving sorrow behind rejoices in the world of heaven. Similarly in the *Kena Upaniṣad* (IV, 8) we are told that the truth-knower gets established in the "svargaloka", heaven, a world worthy to be won. Even in the *Kausitakībrāhmaṇa Upaniṣad* (I, 2) where the moon is described as the door of the heavenly world, the latter is used as synonymous with either the Brahmaloka or the route which reaches one there.

A situation like this will explain the paucity of descriptions of the highest goal in a literature whose eloquence over the newly discovered reality, the Absolute, the Supreme Being, and the identity of the individual self with this Reality, the Universal Self, is so magnificent, and to those who can read the literature in the original, with its tuneful cadence makes an irresistible appeal.

The *Chāndogya Upaniṣad* (VIII, 5, 3-4) presents a few features of the geography of the world of Brahman which are more tantalizing than satisfying. It informs us that the Brahmaloka is in the third heaven—mark the correspondence of the location of the Brahmaloka with the Ṛgvedic cosmographical data about 'svarga'—that there are two seas there by name 'Ara' and 'Ṇya'. There is also the lake *Airammadīya* and the tree exuding 'Soma', the coveted drink of the Vedic people and the indispensable accompaniment and equipment of their sacrificial rites. This specification of the drink available in the Brahmaloka, making it different from that of the gods, which is nectar as we have seen, and identifying it with the one to which the Vedic people in their life were accustomed, emphasizes the distinction of the Brahmaloka from the world of gods, as the world to be attained by knowing men through their own endeavour of realizing the Reality. It appears to me that it further brings out the inherent immortality of the place and its denizens by implying that they do not need any external aid like that of nectar to keep them immortal. In the Brahmaloka further there is the city of Brahman, which is named "Aparājitā", significantly called so; for the term means, "the undefeated one". And in the city stands the golden hall of the Lord.

The far more complete delineation of the position of the Brahmaloka in the cosmos and the detailed topographical description of the Brahmaloka itself is found in the *Kauṣitakibrāhmaṇa Upaniṣad* (I, 1, 2-7), with the lake, and not sea as in the old account of the *Chāndogya*, named 'Āra' and not 'Ara'. In allegorical symbolism 'Ara' is taken to mean, such psycho-ethical enemies as desire, wrath etc., which have to be subdued. Then there are the rather abstruse category called 'Yeṣṭiha moments' and further a river named "Virajā'*. There is also the tree but it is named 'Ilya'. The city is named 'Sālajya' and the abode is named "Aparājitā", which in the *Chāndogya*-account is the name of the city of Brahman. It is guarded by Indra and Prajāpati as door-keepers. The hall therein is named "Vibhu", the throne in it "Vicakṣana" and the court "Amitaujas". And there stand the beloved "Mānasī" and her counterpart "Cākṣuṣī". Such is fancied to be the world of Brahman in the Upaniṣadic cosmography and topography, the latter more allegorical than physical. But the description is made in purely sensuous terminology. The reason for this is, as pointed out above, the fact of the hereafter having been, in the Ṛgvedic era, pictured as the abode of all sensual pleasures and of eternal duration and occupation so that even the highly spiritual category of complete realization and final liberation had to be depicted in terms easily appreciable by the people accustomed to the physical and sensual view of the perfect hereafter. When the person reaches the Virajā river five hundred fairies attend on him, with garlands, unguents, powders, clothes and ornaments in their hands, one hundred of them with each one of the five luxuries named.

Another aspect of the description of the universe has to deal with the communicatory system which evidently will differ according to the nature of the unit of the cosmos and its denizens as well as its visitors, those who are privileged to enter or travel in that region. The journey of mortals when they have to leave this world at death is what concerns the thinkers. It must be intimately connected with or rather must form part of the whole complex of eschatological beliefs. It is possible of course to postulate condition or conditions after death without reference to any path which leads to them; but mundane morality has always tended in any developed system of religious consciousness to be based in part at least on the future life after death. If radically different conditions result from significantly different ways of living, with particular reference to morality, and they happen to be associated with or to be lived in certain specific worlds or units of location, logical thought would tend to posit specific paths leading to them, fundamentally differing from each other. The paths so postulated would tend to be influenced by the particular nature of the world to which they lead.

That the theory of paths and their ends or goals was pre-Upaniṣadic is as clear as under the circumstances of the literary scene of those times could

---

* This name is according to the text of the Nirnayasagar Press edition. Radhakrishnan's text has the reading "Vijarā", "ageless". I am convinced from the context that the correct term is the one given in the N.P. edition. In section 4 the achievement in spiritualization made by the traveller at the crossing of the river is the discarding of his good and evil deeds and these are symbolically dust or dust-particles and not 'jarā', old age. Virajā is so-called because it renders the person crossing it free from the stains or spots in the form of his deeds in the world of men.

permit is already stated. The two paths, communicatory channels, of Devayāna and Pitṛyāṇa are adapted to the newer religio-philosophical thought and practice first in the *Bṛhadāraṇyaka Upaniṣad* (VI, 2, 1-2), the text which embodies the seminal speculations of the great Yājñavalkya and Janaka who between them detail most of the new speculative thought. It is interesting and also instructive to note that the adaptation of the theory of the two paths to the new thought and practice complex is made by Pravāhaṇa Jaivali of the Pāñcālas, i.e., the people and the country where the later of the hymns of the *Ṛgveda* must have been composed. The fact that in the other old Upaniṣad, *Chāndogya* (V, 3), the doctrine of discrimination between these two paths, and hence the adaptation of the Vedic theory on the subject in even a more distinct specification, is stated as having been known to Pravāhaṇa Jaivali is proof conclusive that the adaptation of the theory of life after death and its entire dependence on the quality of mundane living while alive was made in the land of the later Vedic scene. In both places it is the same great Brahmin student and radical thinker Śvetaketu Āruṇeya, the son of the famous speculative thinker and inquisitive enquirer Uddālaka Āruṇi, who figures as the ignorant one or as the inquisitive disciple.

In three other Upaniṣads at least there is mention, and even slight elaboration, of the theory of paths, the communicatory channels, for life after death. They are *Praśna* (I, 9-10), *Muṇḍaka* (III, 1, 6) and *Kauṣītakibrāhmaṇa* (I, 2-3). In the second of these neither the questioner, if any, nor the propounder is mentioned but the doctrine in a partial form just mentioned impersonally, indicating that the theory of the two paths was by then very well known, so that only a limited reference for a specific purpose was adequate. The passage of the *Muṇḍaka*, wherein, almost at the middle of the beautifully and nobly worded outpouring of a mind which had encompassed the relation that exists between the Supreme Soul and the Individual Self, the mood passing on to dwell on the splendour and grandeur of the Supreme Soul and emphasizing the lustrous nature of the enlightened Individual Self, declares the mode of approach, the kind of living that achieves the culmination, the realization and attainment of the basic unity of the two. Finally it proclaims : "Only truth conquers and not untruth ; by truth is the "Devayāna" path laid out. It is by that path that sages having controlled all desires, travel to that place which is the final abode of Truth."

In the passage of the *Praśna Upaniṣad* it is His Holiness Pippalāda, hoary sage like Sanatkumāra, that figures as instructing and answering the queries of one Kabandhi Kātyāyana, who happens to be one of the seekers of knowledge through whose search for it the thought-wealth of the particular Upaniṣad got collected. In that text only "Pitṛyāṇa" in the masculine gender is specifically mentioned just as in the *Muṇḍaka* passage only the "Devayāna" is described. The other path is delineated only in contrast without naming it. But the Upaniṣad has another whole 'question' (V, 1-7) devoted to the answer which Satyakāma Śaibya's query brought from the same sage Pippalāda.

The query having been made regarding what happens to the individual soul at a person's death, the answer, being more or less complete, delineates both the conditions either of which can happen to one after death, depending upon one's mundane living while alive. But the paths, travel by which leads to the two conditions, are not specified by name.

The *Kauṣitakibrāhmaṇa Upaniṣad* at the outset states that some of the knowledge garnered therein was the result of the instruction which the sacrificing patron Citra Gārgyāyaṇi had to give to his chief priest who was to officiate at the sacrifice. And the Officiant was no other than the famous sage Uddālaka Āruṇi himself. Citra Gārgyāyaṇi devotes a whole section to the explanation of the "Devayāna" path, which when one is on it leads through various stages, by-ways, and proffered help to the dearly coveted goal of life after death, union with Brahman in Brahmaloka. The great significance of this passage is the geographical and spiritual details of the way which are already fully described. The sensuous world and its very enchanting description, the tree, the river and some other equally and intriguingly interesting details remind me of the description of the Egyptian Hereafter made about 1500 to 1400 B.C. and given full description of in some of the early Papyri.

Let us now return to our older sources of knowledge of this very interesting piece of cosmic geography which, from the most ancient times, has been interwoven with the sanctions for mundane right living.

Pravāhaṇa Jaivali asks Śvetaketu if he had known the saying of old sages that there are two ways or paths, 'sṛti', 'passage', apart from the way of living common to men, one of which is specific to 'Pitṛs' and the other to 'Devas'. He further questioned him whether he knew the stages of the path called 'Pitṛyāṇa' or of the other path the 'Devayāna'. Without waiting for a reply he plied the young baffled open mind of the priest with the more specific and searching enquiry if Śvetaketu had known the particular regimen of living which led one to the 'Pitṛyāṇa' or the 'Devayāna' path. Śvetaketu flatly disowned any pretension to knowledge of this apparently important yet perhaps till then esoteric section of the religio-philosophical complex. Being utterly non-plussed the young priest ran back to his father and asked him about it. Āruṇi himself did not know anything about the matter ; and the true philosopher that he was he forthwith proceeded along with his son to Pravāhaṇa Jaivali and requested him very respectfully to explain that esoteric section of the religio-philosophical complex.

During the course of Jaivali's discourse, almost at the end of it, it is that we get a statement of the doctrine in almost complete details. Without going over the ground covered in the early portion of this section on cosmography his assertions may be noted here.

A—(1) One path begins with light which is specifically styled here as 'arcis'—this may be carefully noted that in the philosophical literature of the succeeding age the path is commonly referred to as 'arcirādi', 'one which begins with "arcis", i.e., 'light' ; (2) Its final end, goal of the traveller by the path, is 'Brahmaloka', "the world of Brahman", or the abode of Brahman ; (3) those who travel by this path having necessarily reached the abode of Brahman never return to the mundane existence ; (4) This path is gained at death, or perhaps even while living (?), by those who seek knowledge and truth resorting to forest-solitude for that purpose, i.e., by those who in pursuit of knowledge of Brahman renounce the world of desires and actions ; (5) One of the stages and stops on this path is Devaloka ; and (6) It is open (?) only during the six months when the Sun is in the northern transit.

B—(1) The other path begins with smoke, 'dhūma' ; (2) Its final end is the moon-world ; (3) The world being one of enjoyment, those who reach there get varied pleasures ; but they have to return by the same path to the earth after they have exhausted the stock of enjoyment-credit earned by them ; (4) This path is gained by those who have performed sacrifices, made charities and performed austerities ; (5) One of the stages—here also there is a distinction marking this path in this that the stage is only the next preceding the final one—on the path is 'Pitṛloka', the world of 'Pitṛs' ; and (6) It is open during the six months when the Sun is in its southern transit.

The passage of the *Chāndogya* which expounds this doctrine as propounded by Pravāhaṇa Jaivali more or less tallies with the above exposition with a few additions, which, mostly referring to the doctrine of what is known now as transmigration or metempsychosis, will have to be mentioned in their proper context later. The other differences, though few, are not insignificant but are concerned with the mode of life that leads to the particular path. Thus the 'Devayāna' path is open to those who seek knowledge and not truth, 'satya', do penance, 'tapas', in forest, while 'Pitṛyāṇa' comes to the share of those, who, living in society, not only do charities and perform sacrifices but also undertake works of public utility at their own cost.

The most important difference, however, is the statement emerging in the course of the application of the paths theory to the norms of mundane living. It elaborates the two paths theory and extends it to one of three paths. The third path is not named. It is tantalizing to equate it with the way to hell or 'naraka', a world not only postulated in the Vedic cosmography but also developed enough to have been differentiated into at least four types or kinds. But the clear delineation, though in a cryptic manner, of altogether another idea precludes this identification. This leaves a small gap in the cogent presentation of a complete theory in terms of perhaps the Vedic view of this life and its connection with the attainment of particular condition of being in the life after death and quite clearly in terms of the later theory of living and the life after death. The *Chāndogya* speculation of Pravāhaṇa Jaivali in so far as it has succeeded in retaining an element of his full doctrine not envisaged in the *Bṛhadāraṇyaka* text is very valuable. It shows that Jaivali's view about the third path assumed that the existence of lower life, which goes on incessantly arising, dying and arising explains it. But then there remains the fate in life after death of the perpetrators of heinous and criminal sins. In the cosmography, which posits hells, these are the special worlds which take care of the heinous criminal sinners. In this *Chāndogya* passage these sinners are not forgotten. They are merely mentioned along with those who associate with them as people who "fall", 'patanti'.

The Upaniṣadic thinkers were primarily concerned with emphasizing the doctrine that Brahma-realizers were assured of an everlastingly safe and covetable future, and secondarily with the assertion of the evanescence of the future joys and consequent return to the trials of mundane existence as the lot of those who did not achieve Brahma-realization. From one point of view this position may strike one as sectarian, i.e., that of propounders of one view of God and spirituality. But on a closer reasoning and appraisal of the speculative thinking laid out in the two Upaniṣads *Bṛhadāraṇyaka* and *Chāndogya* as well as of the general air breathing in the other eight or nine principal ones, one gets convinced that the novel spiritual idea was a uniquely satisfying experience of some of the very great personalities of the age.

The discipline involved in the search and pursuit of Brahma-realization appears to have resulted in the case of some of the earnest spiritual practitioners, like Vāmadeva of old, in some extraordinary achievement of powers and capacities, which must have convinced them and their contemporaries of the unique nature of the personality achievement of these practitioners.

At least in two of the eleven older Upaniṣads, the *Bṛhadāraṇyaka* (I, 4, 10), and the *Aitareya* (II, 5-6), Vāmadeva and his traditionally accredited Vedic (*RV*, IV, 18) utterance of an extraordinary nature are mentioned as if they were more or less items of common knowledge among the seekers of philosophic truth and the élite of the time. In one passage Vāmadeva's bold proclamation of his perception of his former existences as Manu, the Sun, etc. on his attainment of Brahma-realization is mentioned as an illustration of the logical nature of the new philosophical doctrine of the identity of the Individual Self and the Supreme Soul. In the other text, Vāmadeva and the declaration made by him while he was still in his mother's womb that he knew all the births of all the gods and of his own, are brought in to substantiate the doctrine of varied births-sequence of the individual self.

Further information about Vāmadeva's spiritual attainment vouchsafed in the *Taittirīya Āraṇyaka* (II, 5), which is even more catching, also belongs here. The text is the earliest record of that achievement of highest spirituality, which has ever since continued to enchant our people, and to make them flock round anyone whose spirituality appears to be above the average, and has ever inclined them to believe in such stories as the one told about the ascent to heaven of Tukārāma, the Maharashtrian saint-poet of the second quarter of the 17th century. The condition and the achievement is known as "jivanmukti", liberation in life, i.e., while alive and with the earthly body itself. It is said there that Vāmadeva having attained immortality ascended the heaven.

Vāmadeva is traditionally far famed, whether or not he is the same as the one who is the author of some hymns of the *Rgveda* (IV, 46-48), whether or not it is correct to ascribe the Vedic text quoted in the *Bṛhadāraṇyaka* passage (I, 4, 10) to Vāmadeva, it is he who figures in these two Upaniṣadic passages and construably in the third, even earlier, passage of the *Taittirīya Âraṇyaka* (II, 5).

The fame of Vāmadeva as a liberated soul was so great and persistent that he, and the legendary Śuka, the supposed reciter of the eighteen *Purāṇas*, were long regarded as the only liberated souls known to sacred literature. Rāmadāsa, the ascetic-philosopher-organizer of the latter half of the 17th century Maharashtra, had to combat that opinion with his authoritative pronouncement that a dozen others, too, lived who attained liberation (*Dāsabodha*, VII, 6, 18-30).

A less known personality, too, figures in the *Taittirīya Upaniṣad* (I, 10). His name is Triśaṅku.* Triśaṅku in his developed spirituality is said, in a Vedic passage, to have proclaimed his earlier births.

The Upaniṣadic thinkers modified the meaning and content of the term Devayāṇa occurring in the *Rgveda* which was "the path by which the sacrifice of a man [offered by a man] was borne to the gods or by which they came for it, and by which on death he joined the Fathers and the gods in heaven" (Macdonell, p. 167 ; Keith, pp. 14-15, 575) and made it the path by which the adept in the newer religio-philosophic technique travelled to the abode of everlasting peace and union with the Supreme Soul. Accordingly in a passage of the *Chāndogya Upaniṣad* (IV, 15, 6) this 'Devapatha' is otherwise designated 'Brahmapatha', i.e., from the path taking the travellers to the gods it was turned into the path which leads to that condition which renders it unnecessary and impossible to return to the mundane whirlpool, as the text picturesquely puts it.

The other path which is secondarily singled out for explanation, i.e., 'Pitṛyāṇa', is also mentioned in the *Rgveda*. In one text (*RV*, X, 2, 7) Agni is said to know the 'Pitṛyāṇa' path, while in another (*RV*, X, 16, 10) it is mentioned along with Ṛta in the context of death, the hymn being one of the funeral ones. The Upaṇiṣadic thinkers, having come to the philosophical realization of the futility of all else but Brahma-realization, could look upon all the older religio-philosophical paraphernalia as but nothing, as one which could at best lead to a temporary blissfulness or rather super-enjoyment. The path naturally was reserved for those erring souls that still clung to the practice of older religion. Further as the path in its cosmographical extent ended with the moon, the blissful condition enjoyed by the denizens of that moon-world could be fairly and logically conceived as not lasting. For the moon, if it waxes,

* Mythology evidently enshrined the memory of this Triśaṅku when it preserved the greatest exploit of the sage Viśvāmitra centring round the desire of a king of that name who was a predecessor of Rāma of the Ikṣvāku dynasty to proceed to heaven in flesh and blood !

also wanes. The joys of its denizens could very properly be considered to be ephemeral. The world of change must throw its denizens into the whirlpool of change, the cycle of life and death. Per contra the other path, 'Devayāna', led to the Sun, the self-lighted luminary that does not change. Those who reach there and pass on cannot, therefore, have any change and would not return. This significance of the Sun as almost the last stage on the 'Devayāna' path is, apart from the passages quoted or referred to in the cosmographical section, stressed when the lot of those who practise austerity and pursue Brahma-knowledge in forests is mentioned in *Muṇḍaka Upaniṣad* (I, 2, 11): "They pass dustless through the Sun-gate to where the immortal and changeless Soul and Being dwells." The same purifying function is predicated of the Sun-stage in the *Praśna Upaniṣad* twice. Once in the passage about the paths referred to above (I, 10) it is stated in the regular stages-narration of the path. In the other passage (V, 5) the function of ridding the self of its sins, comparing the process to the shedding of its skin by snakes, is ascribed to the heat-light of the Sun.

It should further be noted that in all these three Upaniṣad passages, *Bṛhadāraṇyaka*, *Chāndogya* and *Praśna*, though not quite directly, these paths are designated 'Uttarāyaṇa' and 'Dakṣiṇāyana'. Yet enough direct indication in terms of the solar transit are given to warrant our assumption of the 'Devayāna' and the 'Pitṛyāṇa' being known by their later designations of 'Uttarāyaṇa' and 'Dakṣiṇāyana'. And the names may not have been exclusively tuned to the course of the apparent transit of the Sun but may have derived support from, or even perhaps may have been inspired by the early monopoly of the north by Gods. The towering Himālaya could not fail to fix the north and its own summits as the abodes of gods very early in the Aryan advance into the land, later known as that of the Kurus. When the Fathers came to be placed under the charge of one of them, viz., Yama, the god of Death, this having taken place early in the Ṛgvedic period, his path was naturally conceived to be separate from that of the gods (*RV*, X, 18, 1). The south was clearly the quarter which could be thought of as the abode of Yama, the god of Death, and his charge the Fathers. Ever since the south has remained associated with them.[2]

The next important work, the *Bhagavadgītā*, mentions the two paths of the Upaniṣadic cosmography, designating them either in the precise Upaniṣadic terminology as 'sṛti' (VIII, 27) or paraphrasing it as 'gati', motions (VIII, 26). However, it characterizes them in a new but meaningful terminology as white (śukla) and dark (kṛṣṇa) (VIII, 26), in addition to its definite specification of them in time-terms (VIII, 24-5). As a matter of fact it is the time-terms that provide this new and significant nomenclature. Lord Kṛṣṇa tells Arjuna that He will now enlighten him on the time of passing away of a 'yogin', which will secure him non-return and on that which will cause his return to this world and the mundane cycle of birth and death (VIII, 23). He then mentions "fire", light or flame, daytime, the bright half of the month (śukla) [pakṣa], and the six months of the northern transit of the Sun (uttarāyaṇa) as the time, dying at which a 'yogin' will have his soul merging with Brahman; and smoke, night, the dark half of the Sun (dakṣiṇāyana) as that when his death occurring his soul, having gone to the moon-world and enjoyed his merit, will return to the mundane cycle of birth and death. It will, later, become clear that the two conditions and the two worlds, to speak in terms of cosmography, are not the entire cosmos even in the *Bhagavadgītā*, which has not attempted to give any cosmological and cosmographical background to its doctrines.

The *BhG* view of the Upaniṣadic paths, the communicatory system conducting the souls of the dead, must be quite clearly considered to be, that they are not so much paths with stages but are the two sets of time-period, death in which meant either final liberation or return to the mundane cycle of birth and death, according as it took place in the one or the other of the two sets. That the paths and the stages of progress of the soul had come to be conceived as time-periods which determined the fate of the departing soul well before the time of the *BhG* and was current among the people as a concurrent view with that of the Upaniṣadic doctrine of paths and stages, and that it was, in essence, a rather mechanical and fatalistic determination of the fate of the departing soul is quite clear from Bādarāyaṇa's disquisition and conclusion on the subject.

In his *Brahmasūtras* the great systematizer, Bādarāyaṇa, may be said to clinch the issue of his taking up the matter with the current view of the time-periods and their significance for the departing soul with his assertion (IV, 2, 20) that the Brahma-realizer's soul departs by the 'arcirādi', light-heat, path even if the person dies during 'dakṣiṇāyana' or the transit of the Sun through the southern part of the sky. And he explains away the current view, with the help of the word 'yogin' occurring in the *BhG* passage quoted above, with the pertinent observation: "Smṛtis prescribe a particular time etc. with regard to Yogins only. Sāṁkhya and Yoga are mentioned in the Smṛtis (IV, 2, 21), and evidently they are not so mentioned in the Śruti or the Vedic Upaniṣadic texts, whose specification of paths thus having to be construed in relation to Brahma-realizers".

The life story of the great bachelor and master-archer of the Mahābhārata story, 'grandfather' Bhīṣma, has fixed the idea of the 'uttarāyaṇa' and 'dakṣiṇāyana' as the coveted and disliked periods for departure from this world in the minds of the Hindu élite. And this inspite of the fact that the Vedānta philosophy as authoritatively stated by Śaṅkarācārya has not only presented the theory as one of paths and stages, singling out only the desirable one as 'arcirādi' path, but has also explained away the incident at Bhīṣma's death. The strict adherents to this philosophy of course follow Śaṅkarācārya's lead, but the Hindu populace at large cherishes Bhīṣma's death-episode as a demonstration of the inauspicious nature of the period of the Sun's southern transit, during which to die means for the soul of the dying person great hardship. And strictly orthodox people used to, and perhaps even now some may do, perform pacifying rites, or 'śānti', as they are called.

The authorized version of the text of the *Mahābhārata* (VI Bhīṣma Parvan, 114, 85-100, B.O.R.I. ed.) has it that when the great leader of the Kaurava armies was struck by a deadly arrow on the tenth day of the battle and when he was about to fall to the earth an ethereal voice reminded him that it was the period of the sun's southern transit and that he as a Brahma-realizer must not die during it. Bhīṣma replied that he had it in his mind and that he would lie down on a bed of arrows awaiting the beginning of the northern transit, to allow his soul to depart from his body. And he is said to have done so and actually died only when the northern transit began. He could do that because he was endowed with the specially miraculous power of arranging his death at will. The clear implication of the story is that even for a highly moral and spiritually developed person like Bhīṣma it would have been impossible to get his final liberation and salvation if he had died during the inauspicious period of the southern transit of the sun.*

The over-riding control of the time-period over a person's destiny after death would be anathema to any religio-philosophical system and the ethico-spiritual living that it may enjoin. In the religio-philosophical literature and other literature of the Hindus, fortunately, there is hardly any trace of it in spite of the *BhG*. In the *Manusmṛti* (VI, 84) the two goals of life after death are mentioned as heaven (svarga) and eternity (ānantya), and no separate times or even paths are indicated. Northern transit (uttarāyaṇa) and southern transit (dakṣiṇāyana) are only referred to in connection with defining the day and night of the gods (I, 67). In the non-technical world of the élite, the semi-élite and the common folk as represented by the clientele and audience of the popular Sanskrit work of the fifth century A.D., *Pañcantantra* (I, 453), it is the stage-aspect of the so-called path, leading to final liberation, that was current. In the context we are told that one of the current beliefs was that one who died in defending a Brahmin or a cow would shoot through the sun's disc to the highest goal of eternity—mark the expression about the penetration of the Sun's disc which is almost an echo of the Upaniṣadic expression! Rāmadāsa in the 17th century A.D., who gives, as will be presently clear, a cosmology and a cosmography, which is not only very much more extended than that of the Upaniṣads but also purports to be more definitive and measured, has not a word to say about the paths much less about the time-periods for death. The Upaniṣadic communicatory system of the cosmos then drops out of the Hindu cosmology and cosmography and we may now follow the development of the latter.

* The awkwardness of this episodic anecdote comes out quite well on the background of what is described about the doings of Droṇa, the great Brahmin archer, and the venerable preceptor of the Kauravas and the Pāṇḍavas, on the battlefield, only five days after Bhīṣma fell. He is described as having given up his arms at the news of the death of his only son in utter distress and dismay and as having sat in 'yoga'-concentration to have transferred his soul in the form of purest effulgence to Brahmaloka (*Mbh*, VII, 165, 39-57).

The *Bhagavadgītā* carries forward the cosmology of the Upaniṣads, wherever its principal subject-matter permits it, in its main outline. Its chief contributions to it are four : (a) It makes the Supreme Soul or God the efficient cause of the cosmos describing Him either as the master or president (adhyakṣa) (IX, 8, 9), or as the One who sows the seed (VII, 10 ; XIV, 3-4) ; (b) The partner in the process, is matter ; i.e., the five great beings, mind (manas), understanding (buddhi), and ego-sense (ahaṁkāra) as in the Upaniṣadic cosmology. *BhG*, over and above introducing the newly developed doctrine of three qualities (guṇas) and the name of the whole matter complex (prakṛti), coins a convenient expression to epitomize the complex, which, as will be seen, has become almost a current coin, a stereotype for the non-sentient partner of the whole creative process. It is named eightfold nature (aṣṭadhā prakṛti) and is, quite logically and to the great benefit of the religio-philosophical complex, declared as the lower aspect of the Supreme Soul (VII, 4-6, 12-14 ; XIII, 19) ; (c) It accommodates the theory of recurrent creation of the cosmos with its time-cycles of 'yuga' and 'kalpa' and its dissolutionary floods (pralaya); (d) It interposes the older creator (Prajāpati) in between the creators of the secondary and other newer creators (manus), too, perhaps in the secondary or even tertiary creative operations (III, 10 ; VIII, 17-18 ; IX, 7 ; X, 6 ; XIV, 2).

As for cosmography, the *Bhagavadgītā* mentions (I, 42, 44 ; II, 32, 43 ; VI, 41 ; VII, 23 ; VIII, 16 ; IX, 20-1 ; XVI, 16, 21) Brahmaloka or Brahmabhuvana, Surendraloka, Svarga, Martyaloka (human world) and Naraka plainly, and both heaven (svarga) and hell (naraka) indirectly or impliedly as the world of gods, the world of manes (pitṛs), the world of those who have acquired merit in this world, and the dark world of those who have been under the influence of the three spiritual enemies, desire, anger and greed, in this world (IV, 31 ; VII, 23 ; IX, 20 ; IX, 25 ; XVI, 22). Perhaps another altogether new world, necessitated by the development in religio-philosophical complex of the personal god, first adumbrated in the *Śvetāśvatara Upaniṣad* (I, 10 ; III, 2-10 ; IV, 10-16 ; VI, 3, 6-11) centring round the Vedic deity Rudra-Śiva, is postulated and referred to in *BhG* (VII, 23 ; VIII, 16 and XV, 6). Lord Kṛṣṇa in the last-referred verse, speaks of His highest abode or home or world, which is beyond the reach of the rays of the sun, etc. and is imperishable and eternal. It is possible that there is a veiled reference to the Vaiṣṇava world of salvation, the abode of Viṣṇu, named later Vaikuṇṭha, in the three verses referred to above. All the same the cosmos is understood to comprise only three worlds, 'lokatraya' being the term employed (*BhG*, XI, 20) as in later literature.

The cosmology with which the current text of the *Manusmṛti* begins, though in parts it is not quite clear and seems to contain contradiction, appears to me to be the one that had come to be formulated out of the Vedic, Upaniṣadic and non-Vedāntic thought that had gone on between the time of the *Śvetāśvatara Upaniṣad* and the beginning of the Christian era. In parts it is reflected in the cosmology and cosmography of the *Bhagavadgītā*, which owing to its context is naturally partial and circumscribed. And what is significant is that the later Hindu Cosmology remains much the same, as will be seen in the sequel. It is therefore proper at this stage to describe the cosmology of the *Manusmṛti* and bring out its points of contact and identity with some of the cosmological statements, and the others that happen to be utterly fresh ones, not encountered in any of the twelve principal and old Upaniṣads which we have taken as our source for Upaniṣadic thought.

When everything was nought and dark, Lord Svayambhu, Self-existent, manifested Himself. He is beyond the ken of senses, eternal, non-manifest and incomprehensible. Manifesting Himself he desired to create the cosmos and with that end in view He created waters (ap). And therein he dropped a seed. The seed grew into a fine golden egg out of which after a whole year came Brahmā, the grandfather of the cosmos, having broken it open through His own thought. This Brahmā it is, having been produced out of the golden egg, that is known as Hiraṇyagarbha. The Self-existent is otherwise called Nara and waters being His creation are known as 'nārāḥ'. Hence it is that Brahmā, Hiraṇyagarbha, is otherwise known as Nārāyaṇa, one whose abode is waters. Out of the two halves of the egg he produced the heaven (div) above and the earth (bhūmi) below, leaving the ether (ākāśa) in between, and the eight quarters and the seas. Out of Himself He brought out mind (manas) which is of the nature of both existence and non-existence, the ego-sense, the 'mahān ātman', i.e., 'buddhi' or understanding of the other accounts, and also the five sense-organs. He also brought out of Himself all the things of the three qualities (triguṇa). With the help of the six (I, 5-26)—here is the defective and contradictory portion of the *Manusmṛti* cosmology—i.e., as is understood by tradition, the five great beings (mahābhūtas) and ego-sense (ahaṁkāra), leaving out both mind and understanding, which together as eight are mentioned in the *BhG*, as above noted, as the lower aspect of the Supreme Soul and presiding over which He is said to have created the cosmos.

In attributing the creation or rather extraction of the four classes of society (varṇas), i.e., the Brāhmaṇa, the Kṡatriya, the Vaiśya and the Sūdra, to Brahmā Hiraṇyagarbha from His mouth, arms, thighs and feet respectively, *Manusmṛti* (I, 30-1) combines the relevant section of the creation said to have been the result of the actual sacrifice of the Primordial Being in the famous Puruṣa-sūkta of the *Ṛgveda* (X, 90) with the Upaniṣadic theory of the creation of the cosmos.

Curiously enough, and here is another defect in the cosmological theory of the *Manusmṛti*, Brahmā, after having done so much of the creative process, is said to have divided Himself in two, one part being the male and the other the female. And it is at this stage that copulatory activity begins to come into the picture of the creative process. Of the female thus created, who remains unnamed, was born, through His male part, Virāj. With Virāj or Virāṭ on the scene, austerity steps into the creative process ; for Virāj, practising austerities, created Manu, the virtual or rather the immediate Creator of all this universe. Manu, too, practised severe austerities with a view to creating such of the creatures and objects and forces as were not subsumed in the earlier creative process of Brahmā Hiraṇyagarbha. And he produced ten great sages, known as Prajāpatis, because they themselves became the creators of other creatures. They are specified by their names (I, 35). Strangely, seven other great sages (I, 36) who are named later (I, 62-3) are said to have been created by the ten Prajāpatis created by Manu, along with gods, their worlds or abodes, manes, demons, Yakṣas and others. They are called Manus and not Prajāpatis in the text, though the pronominal adjective 'anyān', others, seems to imply that they, too, are Prajāpatis or Prajāpati-like. There is of course no unanimity in tradition about the number of these Prajāpatis; yet only seven, thirteen, fourteen or twentyone appear to be mentioned in the *Purāṇas* as S. Chitrav has stated (*Prācīna Caritrakośa*, p. 350).

I have characterized the separate creation of the seven great sages in the *Manusmṛti* account of the creation as strange because seventeen Prajāpatis, or secondary creators as we should call them from their functional position, generally go together in the accounts of the immediately following literature, epic and religious. Thus in the *Rāmāyaṇa* of Vālmīki (III, 14, 7-9) we are introduced to seventeen Prajāpatis, through Rāma's curiosity to know the names of all. Not more than eight out of the seventeen named occur in the list of *Manusmṛti*. The seven great sages created by the ten Prajāpatis are noted as Manus. Even on that score the *Manusmṛti* account does not harmonize with the later traditional number of Manus, which is fourteen.

The great time-period known as 'kalpa', which is a whole day of Brahmā, is divided into fourteen parts, each one of them being presided over by one specific Manu, the ruler or the president of the age, and is called the reign of that Manu, i.e., 'manvantara'. The period of a 'Manvantara' according to *Manusmṛti* (I, 79) is 71 times the number of years comprising the four 'yugas', ages of 'kṛta', 'tretā', 'dvāpara' and 'kali'. The present time falls within the reign of Manu Vaivasvata and is therefore in all declaratory formulae mentioned as such by the worshipper. The age (yuga) is Kali. Fourteen 'manvantaras' occur during one day of Brahmā which is 1,000 times the period of the four Yugas together (*Manu*, I, 72-3; *BhG*, VIII, 17). Brahmā's day is called a 'kalpa', at the end of which occurs what is known as 'mahāpralaya' or even simply as 'pralaya' or flood. Though the full traditional quota of Manus for a whole 'kalpa' is fourteen (S. Chitrav's *Prācīnacaritrakoṣa*, p. 428) it appears that in the earlier literature there is no mention of more than seven of them, of which Vaivasvata, the present one, is the last. In the *Bhagavadgītā* (X, 6) only four Manus are mentioned by Lord Kṛṣṇa as his 'mental' sons.* Jñāneśvara (X, 93) commenting on the verse takes care to state that four Manus mentioned are the elderly four out of the total number of fourteen Manus.

* This is the straightforward interpretation of the text and is the one given both by Śaṅkarācārya (?) and Jñāneśvara. Lokamanya Tilak construes it differently whereby he assumes the mention of seven Manus by the plural 'manavaḥ'.

Tradition gives a set of seven great sages to everyone of the 'manvantaras' (Chitrav, loc. cit., pp. 429-31). They have a function to discharge in the creative process and in the governance of the cosmos. *Manusmṛti* forgets them. But the earlier text (*BhG*, X, 6) asserts their existence and states that they are the "mental" sons of the Supreme Soul or of Lord Kṛṣṇa in that aspect.

The creation whose account is presented so far is the primary one, i.e., the one which occurs at the waking up of Brahmā after having been dormant during His night, which is also one 'kalpa' long, i.e., 4,320 million human years. The new creation is expected to last His day which is also 4,320 million human years in length. The present 'kalpa' is called 'Śvetavārāha' and is so announced in every declaratory formula. During this day of Brahmā at the end of everyone of the fourteen 'manvantaras', the periods of the sway of specific Manus, there is a flood which in distinction from the 'final' flood is called 'āvāntara pralaya', intermediate flood or destruction. Every time the flood occurs the three worlds are dissolved and have to be created anew at the appointed time of their manifestation. These are intermediate or subsidiary creations. They are effected by 'mind' (or, buddhi ?) through the creation of one of the five great beings, ether (ākāśa). Ether developing produces air (vāyu), the latter similarly producing light-heat, which in its turn produces waters (āpaḥ), the earth resulting from the development of the last 'great being' (*Manu*, I, 75-8).

Kālidāsa appears to have adopted in the main Manu's version of creation with mind-born Brahmā as its starting point. In the *Kumārasambhava* (II, 2-8) he has taken special care to mention its first stages by way of a hymn of praise chanted by the frightened gods to win over Brahmā to their side against a mighty demon, who had previously secured favours and boons from Him.

The notion of 'Kalpa'-period and the great-flood at the end of it destroying the whole creation is likely to give the creative process a finite appearance, and the *Manusmṛti* (I, 80) takes due care to dispel such wrong impression by asserting that innumerable such 'manvantaras' with their creations and their partial and complete destruction have gone on and will go on. The Supreme Being, so to say, carries on His playful activity in that manner.

That the notion of 'Kalpas' and 'Yugas' was firmly fixed in the Hindu mind there is clear evidence, 'kalpa' symbolizing almost endless eternity. In some of his inscriptions Aśoka[3] refers to it. Later even the term 'yuga' came to be sometimes used in the sense of 'kalpa', the much longer time-period. Thus in the Girnar inscription of the Kśatrapa king Rudradāman of about A.D. 150, in the description of the storm that broke the dam of the lake Sudarśana the speed of the wind is said to have been like that of the wind that blows at the end of a 'yuga'.[4] The nationally representative poet Kālidāsa, about the 4th century A.D., described the meditative sleep of Viṣṇu, after withdrawing Himself from the cosmos, as the one befitting the end of a 'yuga', meaning of course 'kalpa'[5]; for such sleep of the Supreme Creator occurs only at the end of a 'kalpa'. This does not mean that the notion of the four 'yugas' was obliterated. That notion is quite basic and is mentioned by Kālidāsa in another connection.[6] Kalhaṇa, the historian of Kashmir, writing his history in A.D. 1150, expressed his satisfaction and happiness at the wisdom of a Kashmirian king by wishing that it "may outlast this 'kalpa' ". The king was a contemporary of the historian.[7]

Kālidāsa (*Kumārasambhava*, II, 8) refers to the day and night of Brahmā without specifying the period in actual years but suggesting the length of it in the tacitly accepted notions which appear to have been the same as those expressed in the *Manusmṛti* and times the creation and the end of the cosmos with the waking up of Brahmā and his going to sleep.

For actual currency and the more or less specific form in which this notion of cosmological time-period occurs among the Hindus,[8] I shall draw upon the popular treatise of the Maharashtrian saint-poet-philosopher Rāmadāsa of the latter half of the 17th century.

Rāmadāsa[9] states the precise number of years over which the four 'yugas' spread, making the total as usual and as in *Manusmṛti* to be 4.32 million. As in *Manusmṛti* he equates Brahmā's one day, but omits any mention of Brahmā's night, with one thousand times that period, giving us the usual time-period of a 'kalpa' to be 4320 million years. He, however, goes further and accommodates the three other major deities that had come to occupy the central position in the Hindu pantheon. One thousand days of Brahmā make only one 'ghaṭikā', i.e., one sixtieth of the whole day, of Viṣṇu ; one thousand days of Viṣṇu make only one 'pala', i.e., a moment, of Īśvara (Śiva). And one thousand years of Īśvara (Śiva) make only half a 'pala', i.e., half a moment, of Śaktī (Devī of the pentad). Rāmadāsa's arithmetical account emphasizes the paramount importance that had come to be attached to 'Śakti', "Female Energy" as a deity. Parabrahma, Paramātman or Brahma of the philosophers, the Supreme Soul—the individual soul having been identified with Brahman of the Vedāntins, in the Indian languages of the people the Supreme Soul has come to be referred to as 'Parabrahma', Great or Superior Brahman in formal religio-philosophical discourse—persists and pervades through innumerable creations of cosmos through recurrent innumerable Śaktis. Parabrahma, the Supreme Soul, is thus permanent and incomprehensibly superior to everything, and the cosmos of anytime is mere nothing in comparison with Him or It.

The end of the present cosmos, as of other past cosmoses and future ones, is mentioned in the manner of *BhG* and *Manusmṛti* as 'pralaya' or flood and is significantly referred to as 'kalpānta', i.e., the one that occurs at the end of the cosmic time-period 'kalpa', a more or less graphic description of the expected happenings being made. The flood is alternatively known as 'Brahmapralaya', the flood of Brahmā, as it occurs at the end of Brahmā's day. Rāmadāsa speaks of five floods and expounds their occurrence and the attendant phenomena.[10]

The extension of the continuity and the past of the cosmos, present in Rāmadāsa's account, is a common heritage of the Hindus. Tulasīdāsa, the most widely read of Indian saint-poets, and a northerner, who lived in Vārāṇaśī about a century and a half before Rāmadāsa, has made a passing reference to it, which, no doubt, the expounder of his highly popular *Rāmāyaṇa*[11] must be explaining at length. He speaks of many 'Brahmāṇḍas', cosmoses, and postulates further that the three great Gods, Brahmā, Śiva and Viṣṇu as well as Manu and Guardians of the quarters are separate in each. There is also an incidental reference to hundreds of 'Kalpa'-periods.

The beginninglessness and endless extent of the cosmos are thus a common cosmological tenet of the Hindus.

The notion that every creation of the cosmos is the sport or activity of the Supreme Soul through His lower aspect, 'prakṛti', which the *Bhagavagītā* propounded in an implicit way, specifying the lower aspect as being eightfold, continues to be stated very explicitly. The lower aspect of the Supreme was logically specified as eightfold in the *BhG* and was thus stereotyped. Rāmadāsa has no alternative but to repeat the standard expression and postulate the lower aspect of the Supreme as eight-fold. But instead of the standard eight elements mentioned in the *BhG* we have, in Rāmadāsa's[12] account, only the five 'great beings' with the three 'guṇas', qualities of the Sāṁkhya system, also taken note of and applied in various ways in the *BhG* but not in the act of Creation, in place of 'manas', 'buddhi' and 'ahaṁkāra' of the *BhG*.

Without going into the detailed account of creation which postulates the ultimate source of the five 'great beings', the 'pañcamahābhūtas', in one of them, viz., ether ('ākāśa') or, sometimes, air (vāyu)[13], I must point out that the cosmos, 'Brahmāṇḍa' or 'Brahmā's egg', as it came to be and is now called, is declared to have only seven constituents. In what appears to be quite clearly a development of the Upaniṣadic speculation regarding the individual soul Rāmadāsa, in conformity evidently with the religio-philosophical view current for some centuries before him, pronounces the individual soul to be seven-cloaked or seven-sheathed in Upaniṣadic terminology ('saptakañcuka'). The cosmos, too, it is further maintained, is seven-sheathed.[14]

Tulasīdāsa[15] speaks of the cosmos as having seven coverings ('āvaraṇa'), Brahmaloka being included in the cosmos. Jwalaprasad Misra's comment, which leaves earth from amongst the 'five great beings', and takes the remaining four and makes up the number seven with 'mahat', 'ahaṁkāra' and 'prakṛti', is evidently not correct and only demonstrates that there is a discontinuity in tradition and that this new notion of seven sheaths has been a difficulty not properly explained in terms of the older notions on the subject. The commentator of Rāmadāsa's *Dāsabodha*, S. S. Dev (?), has interpreted the seven sheaths to be the five 'great beings' along with 'mahat' and 'ahaṁkāra'. This explanation appears to be in keeping with the thought and speculation on the subject. But it, too, cannot be taken to justify this description of the cosmos as having only seven sheaths or constituents. For the omission of the eighth, mind (manas), which has been found in their company in standard accounts of these notions, whether of cosmos or of human personality, is not justified. And I have no explanation to offer except that the number seven appears to have captured the minds of the speculative thinkers of India very early.

In the Vedic literature the seven rivers (sapta-sindhus) are the only well-known category of seven. The seven stars, i.e., the astronomical constellation of Ursa major, known in Indian literature and opinion as 'saptarṣis', seven sages, came to be so specified only a little later than the Ṛgvedic 'saptasindhus'. The notion of Agni, Fire, having seven tongues ('saptajihva') is Vedic, just as that of the Sun ('Sūrya', 'Savitṛ') having seven rays ('saptaraśmi') or seven horses to his chariot.[16]

The *Bhagavadgītā* (X, 6) mentions the category of seven 'maharṣis', great sages. And each Manu-period in theory has its own set of seven Maharṣis. The *Manusmṛti* (I, 19 ; 63) postulates only seven first elements used in creation, and speaks of seven Manus only, though according to the theory of Manu-periods there ought to be fourteen of them, the latter number being a multiple of seven. The influence of the number seven in cosmological speculation—astronomical knowledge having been in step with it, as there were only seven known planets and seven days to the artificial division of time known later as a week—is clearly demonstrated by Kālidāsa, the national mind, in his works which are pure literature, using the cosmological and religio-philosophical data incidentally. In his poem *Raghuvaṁśa* (X, 21) he has given his version of the prayer gods and men would have addressed to the great God Viṣṇu lying on the seven-hooded cobra. It is dominated by the number seven as the characteristic accompaniment or means to the propitiation of Viṣṇu. He is sung in seven 'sāman' hymns ; He lies over the seven oceans ; He has as his mouth the seven-rayed Fire and He is the one support of the seven worlds. It is seen that before Kālidāsa's age, the worlds were counted as seven in number and the number of oceans had come to be fixed as seven. In another context in the same work (XVIII, 78) Kālidāsa has told us that the great mountains, the 'kulaparvatas' or 'kulabhūbhṛts' or 'kulācalas', as they are known, and may be translated as the stabilizing mountains, which have become almost fabulous legends in Hindu cosmography, were already known to be seven in number. He describes the seven sages (*Kumārasambhava,* VI, 3-10, 15-19) in a glowing manner as those who are called 'upholders' (dhātāraḥ) by antiquarians and as what do not vanish even at the great destruction ('mahāpralaya') taking place at the end of a 'kalpa'. One of the worlds of the cosmos, the earth is itself a seven-islanded (saptadvīpa) unit (*Śākuntala,* VII, 33) of which Jambudvīpa, in which India (Bharatakhaṇḍa) is situated, is one.

According to the Purāṇic account of the seven islands of the earth two appear to be too shadowy. Leaving them one finds that four of the five, the fifth being 'Jambudvīpa', have each of them seven regions, seven mountains and seven rivers in it.[17] The *Purāṇas* further postulate seven nether regions in the cosmos or in the earth, each region being known as Pātāla.[18] The term 'Pātāla' is more commonly used to designate the lowest of the seven nether regions; and it is in that sense that Kālidāsa (*Raghuvaṁśa*, I, 80; XV, 84) uses the word, informing his readers that the region was very vigilantly guarded by poisonous snakes.

The influence of the number seven having been operative for centuries, *Manusmṛti* (I, 19), as pointed out above, having, too, postulated seven first elements, produced the kind of Hindu cosmology and cosmography that we get explicitly stated by Rāmadāsa in the latter half of the 17th century and implied in the very popular book Tulasīdāsa's *Rāmāyaṇa* more than a century earlier.

Rāmadāsa, though he speaks of both the cosmos and the individual person being seven-sheathed, does not clearly enumerate the seven sheaths of either, and as we shall see later in the case of the latter, he actually expounds his views on the pattern of the eightfold constitution of human personality, with the addition of a few more constituents postulated by him.

Rāmadāsa's cosmology has seven oceans, which are specifically and after the Purāṇic manner very tantalizingly named after various drinks, seven islands, seven nether regions ('pātālas'), seven great sages.[19] Though he mentions by name some of the great stabilizing mountains[20] he has not specified their number.

The number of hells is not mentioned, though some of them are specified by name.[21] Hell, or 'naraka', is a late Vedic cosmological unit, as already noted. In the *Manusmṛti* (IV, 87-90; XI, 37; XII, 75) not only is 'naraka' specified as a place of punishment in the hereafter for sinners but the specific number of 'narakas' is given as twentyone, and they are also listed by their names. And these twentyone hells, their names in a general way indicating the relative severity and type of torture employed therein, have remained the standard bugbears presented to the imagination of a Hindu. Rāmadāsa mentions (*Dāsabodha*, III, 8, 18-20; IV, 1, 24) at least two of them by name and the suffering which sinful persons are made to go through in them. The postulation of the world of 'naraka' has important bearings on earthly morality and on the view of life after death. This standard number of hells reveals another facet of the influence of the number 'seven'.

In Rāmadāsa's account of the Hindu cosmology this influence is further demonstrated by the number of heavens, 'svarga', postulated by him in his *Dāsabodha* (IV, 1, 16; VIII, 4, 51; X, 10, 21) which is like that of hell ('naraka') twentyone. He has further added one category of world or sub-world in his cosmography by postulating fourteen such units called 'bhuvana' (ibid. XX, 10-12),* which number, too, reflects the same influence.

Another support for my hypothesis about the influence of the number 'seven' on the cosmological speculation is provided by what appears to me to

* Much earlier Jñāneśvara, too, notes the number of 'bhuvanas' as fourteen: *Jñānesvarī*, XI, 183.

be the unique postulation by Rāmadāsa (loc. cit., XX, 3, 13-15; 5, 10-11) of the original matter ('mūlaprakṛti') as being fourteen-fold and of the basic nature of these fourteen units or elements. Finally it is noteworthy that he specifies fourteen (XX, 3, 13-15 ; 5, 10-11) Brahmās or their names (VII, 3, 2-10).

Rāmadāsa, to whom ether ('ākāśa') typifies the Absolute (Brahma) and is therefore the most important and the prior entity among the five great beings (pañcamahābhūtas), ascribes to it seven attributes (VIII, 5, 34-41) thus further reflecting the influence of the number seven on his cosmological speculation.

The influence of this mystic number, seven, has affected the development of cosmological notions and the actual cosmography of the Hindus and has made them, as detailed in Rāmadāsa's *Dāsabodha*, somewhat incoherent with itself and with those accepted in the past. This feature of some incoherence characterizes, as will be clear later, some other aspects of the Hindu religious consciousness and practice too. It is the consequence of the synchretic attitude which refuses to create a synthesis by leaving out the incoherent features !

Whatever synthesis the account of cosmology the *Manusmṛti* represented, it accommodated both the personal deities concerned in the creative process adumbrated in the *Ṛgveda* (X, 90), Hiraṇyagarbha and Virāj. The former is not so named in the *Manusmṛti* and is only suggested through the imagery of the golden egg in which He was in the embryo-form. He is named both Brahmā, the Grandfather of all the worlds, and Nārāyaṇa because of His intimate connection with waters (I, 9-11). Virāj was produced by Hiraṇyagarbha, Brahmā-Svayambhu or Nārāyaṇa, sexually through the union of one half of Himself as man and the other half as woman (I, 32-33).

These Creation-Deities of Ṛgvedic antiquity through the *Manusmṛti* account of creation got firmly fixed in the Hindu cosmology. Kālidāsa (*Kumārasambhava*, I, 50-7) in the fourth century mentions the waters and the seed portion of the theory of Creation and also that of the division into male and female by Brahmā for further creation. He, however, does not name the Creation Deities. Śaṅkarācārya, commenting on certain verses of the *Bhagavadgītā* (VIII, 17-18 ; XIV, 3) in the eighth century A.D., brings them in, though not expressly mentioned in the text of *BhG*. In the first passage only Prajāpati is mentioned and the unmanifest or unmodified form of the cosmos is alluded to. Śaṅkarācārya, however, renders Prajāpati by Virāj and understands the reference to unmanifest or unmodified form as the sleeping condition of Virāj. In the second passage of the *BhG* what is actually stated to be the material source of the cosmos is the 'seed' dropped by the Supreme Soul in 'Mahat Brahma' and what Śaṅkarācārya wants his readers to understand by it is the creation of Hiraṇyagarbha, who alone then proceeds as the efficient cause of the cosmos.

Rāmadāsa mentions both Hiraṇyagarbha and Virāt (Virāj) but not in connection with the creation of the cosmos and asks his disciples to transcend them to comprehend Parabrahma, Superior Brahma, by which term he likes quite often to name the Supreme Soul (Paramātmā).[22] The creation is the consequence of a desire arising in the Supreme Soul or Superior Brahma, even the non-spiritual element concerned in the act and process of creation, viz., 'prakṛti', called by Rāmadāsa 'original illusion' ('mūḷamāyā')[23] rather than eightfold 'prakṛti' (aṣṭadhā prakṛti) though identical with it, being the result of that desire or the desire itself.[24] Once this 'mūḷamāyā' appears on the scene further process appears to be automatic. In his system of cosmology, of the five 'great beings' (Pañcamahābhūtas) ether or 'ākāśa', as already mentioned, is almost equivalent to Parabrahma, Superior Brahman, and occupies the position of the prime material. It is there that air or wind (vāyu) starts which developing produces another of the five great beings and the process of creation going on apace stops with the final creation of 8.4 million breeds of creatures.[25] Original desire is called at least once[26] 'Ādi Nārāyaṇa', 'original Nārāyaṇa', thus reflecting the influence of and echoing the creation theory of the *Manusmṛti*.

The notion that there are 8.4 million breeds of creatures, or as the Indian expression goes 'cauryā-aiśī lakṣa jīva yonī', has become a basic one in Hinduism. And in the theory of transmigration, a cardinal principle of Hinduism, it figures as the central doctrine, there being the possibility of the Soul having to pass through so many births in different species and breeds.

I have not been able to trace this notion further back than Jñāneśvara who worked in the third quarter of the thirteenth century, though in *Manusmṛti* (VI, 63) we get a reference to a plurality of breeds or stocks (yoni) in indefinitely large number like thousands of crores, when it was evidently well-established. Commenting on a *BhG* passage (VII, 6) which only generally mentions 'all beings' and 'the whole world' as arising out of the activity of the Supreme Soul and His lower aspect, Jñāneśvara[27] tells us that there result in the process "eightyfour lakhs of strata".

For a long time after the Upaniṣadic cosmology, the creation of the cosmos out of the eightfold lower aspect of the Supreme Soul through His desire, till the *Manusmṛti* account introducing two creation-deities, Hiraṇyagarbha and Virāj from the Vedic heritage, there does not appear to have been any deity inserted into the account, which therefore reads as if creation was a physico-chemical process. Either from before the *Manusmṛti* age, though not included in its account of the creation of the cosmos, or soon afterwards there arose the need to accommodate the three Gods, Brahmā, Viṣṇu and Maheśa or Śiva, who had risen to be the head of the pantheon, in the creation account. The traditional and mythological function of Brahmā has been that of creation. The Brahmā of the *Manusmṛti*-account is otherwise called therein Nārāyaṇa. There is no mention of Maheśa in it. Not long afterwards, however, we find Kālidāsa[28] taking special pains not only to record all the three gods and their specifically individual functions but also their unity so that the idea of One Supreme Being or Principle may not be missed or ignored. It was a problem for the cosmology-theorists, who lived thereafter, to account for these great

Gods without violence to the old cosmological theory, which, in essence, was also their one, and has remained the only generally valid one for the Hindus as a whole.

In vernacular literature and folk-culture the earliest accommodation of these Gods is perhaps met with in *Jñāneśvarī*. Jñāneśvara, in the fourth quarter of the thirteenth century, commenting on *BhG*, XIV, 3, where the Supreme Being is stated to put His seed in the eightfold lower aspect of Himself and begin the work of creation, brings in these Gods in his account of the creation in a manner to connect them with it. After detailing the entire creation, he asserts that Brahmā is the morning, Viṣṇu the midday and Sadāśiva (Maheśa) the evening of this creation. The manner in which he further connects Śiva with the evening of creation (*Jñāneśvarī*, XIV, 111-2) suggests that it is Śiva who goes to sleep at the end of a 'kalpa' and it is He who wakes up in time! In another context, however, he appears to imply the identity of Brahmā with Viṣṇu, mentioning Brahmā and Īśa, i.e., Śiva, as the highest developmental aspects of the cosmos (XIV, 199-207 ; *BhG*, XV, 1).

Rāmadāsa places Brahmā, Viṣṇu and Maheśa together in the position of entities resulting through the operation of the activity of the three "qualities", 'sattva', 'rajas', 'tamas', evidently in the personalized aspect of the Supreme Soul engaged in the creative process (*Dāsabodha*, X, 4, 16-19 ; X, 9, 10-12 ; XI, 1, 4 ; XII, 6, 7-9).

There was a much greater elaboration of cosmography going on, to judge by the accounts in the *Purāṇas* for a long time, some of which is already mentioned above in a general manner. It is now desirable to fill in some of the details, which find their place in the complex, though brief, cosmography of Rāmadāsa's *Dāsabodha* as it has swayed and still sways the minds of the Hindus in the manifestation of their religious consciousness.

It must be stated at the outset, in view of the enumeration of a large number of worlds in this cosmography, that inspite of all the elaboration the number of worlds to be taken note of continues to be three, at least from the time of the *Bhagavadgītā* (XI, 20 ; XV, 17) to that of Tulasīdāsa's *Rāmāyaṇa* and Rāmadāsa's *Dāsabodha*, and is the only significant number in the Hindu counting of today. They are heaven ('svarga'), earth ('mṛtyu') and the nether region ('pātāla'). Kālidāsa (*Kumārasambhava*, V, 77) speaks of Śiva as the Lord of the three worlds. 'Trailokya', the complex of three worlds, or 'triloka' or 'lokatraya', the three worlds, has come to signify the entire comprehensible cosmos. Thus, for example, the poet-dramatist Bhavabhūti, in the eighth century A.D., eulogizing Rāma's young son speaks of him as one whose eyes treat the three worlds as if they are so much grass, i.e., whose brilliant eyes reflect the conviction that the entire cosmos is but a mere nothing for their possessor (*Uttararāmacarita*, VI, 19). Kālidāsa, who referred to Śiva as the Lord of the three worlds ('lokatraya') praises Viṣṇu as the source of 'trailokya', the complex of three worlds (*Raghuvaṁśa*, X, 53).

Jñāneśvara refers to three worlds as if they were the whole cosmos more often than once (*Jñāneśvarī*, II, 134 ; III, 114 ; VIII, 167 ; IX, 280 ; X, 181; XI, 165, 265, 324, 444, 516, 566). He specifies them either as 'svarga', 'saṁsāra' and 'naraka', or 'svarga', 'mṛtyuloka' and 'naraka', or again keeping the first two as before and naming the last as either 'adhodeśa', the lower region, or as 'pātāḷa', rarely changing the first into 'dyorloka', heavenly world (II, 244 ; IX, 310-30 ; XI, 315). In one of these contexts (XIV, 105) he has imagined the whole cosmos as a young woman and placed the three worlds in three parts of her person, 'svarga' being her neck, 'mṛtyuloka' being her middle part and 'adhodeśa' being her hips and loins. He has mentioned Amarāvatī as the capital of 'Svarga' and Nirayapurī as that of 'Naraka' (IX, 320 ; XVI, 431).

Rāmadāsa does not stop with the mention of the three worlds, nor even with the twentyone heavens ('svarga') and an equal number of hells ('naraka'), giving the names of some of the latter, nor with the mention of Indra's capital Amarāvatī (*Dāsabodha*, IV, 10, 13). He specifies (loc. cit., IV, 10, 11-13) three regions or abodes of the three Great Gods, with reference to whom it would appear—though actually it was and is with reference to only the two of the three, the first being absent in all counting—salvation had been, and is almost wholly, thought of in Hinduism. Their abodes or regions are situated on the fabulous mountain, the supposed centre of the cosmos, Meru, its three peaks providing the sites. The Brahma-peak is 'Satyaloka', the abode of Brahmā, and is of ordinary stone ; the Viṣṇu-peak is 'Vaikuṇṭha', the abode of Viṣṇu, and is of emerald ; the Śiva-peak is 'Kailāsa', the abode of Śiva, and is of crystal. Indra's Amarāvatī is placed lower than these peaks. The mountain on which 'Satyaloka', 'Vaikuṇṭha' and 'Kailāsa' are placed supports the earth and is called Great Meru 'Mahā Meru', its height being limitless. It is, however, imbedded in the earth to a depth of 16 thousand measures and its spread is measured by its breadth which is 84 thousand measures. The Himālaya—here we land into the domain of geography—lies on this side of Mt. Meru, beyond which lies the road to heaven, which is very difficult and blocked by great and terrific snakes. The Pāṇḍavas in their march to heaven, 'svarga', except the eldest of them, Dharma, dropped down there. Only Dharma and Śrī Kriṣṇa could go beyond (IV, 10, 5-8).* Badrikāśrama, Badrinārāyaṇa and Badrikedāra—here is a solecism for the three names connote one and the same place and not three different ones—lie on the hither side of the Himālaya.

This is the cosmology and cosmography which the Hindus believe in and to which their faith and religious practice are tuned.

* Rāmadāsa in his eagerness to find some company for Dharma has in this assertion done violence to the tradition and to the version of the *Mahābhārata* wherein Kriṣṇa is not mentioned in the company that left the country on their way to heaven.

CHAPTER VI

HINDU VIEW OF HUMAN PERSONALITY

THE nature of man as understood and believed in any society has the most intimate relationship with the development and manifestation of the complex of religious consciousness and practice prevailing in that society or in a particular age of that society. Ideas about life after death must, to some extent, depend upon the view that man takes of his nature, whether all that is known as man while in life is all earth when life ceases, or whether some of it is earth and some non-material element which is not destroyed by death, or whether some of it is non-material and some not merely earth but also other elements of nature, tangible or intangible, perceived or inferred. Both the Mesopotamian and the Egyptian data on the religious consciousness and practice have borne out this view to a greater or less extent. The Indian data, it appears to me, go much further and suggest that the view of the nature of man, the ideas about life after death and the religious consciousness of a people are intimately interrelated and influence the development of each other. If this submission comes out fully credentialled from the study that is being presented here then their partial association seen in the polylatrous societies of Mesopotamia and Egypt cannot be construed as an objection to the generalization. On the other hand it will strengthen the generalization with an extension of it in one particular.

The Indian people early in their religious and cultural history—I count not more than five centuries could have elapsed since their emergence into civilization before this happened—in their speculative adventures in the realm of religious, philosophical and ethical ideas, arrived at the view that there was One Supreme God and that man was born out of His sacrifice and that what is called man is the body which can become lifeless, and 'manas' or 'soul'—mark that the Vedic term for the non-material element in man, the element that can leave it during sleep and return there at the end of it and that leaves it for good when what is called death overcomes man, is 'manas', mind. A. A. Macdonell[1] observes: "In a whole hymn *RV*, X, 58, the soul (manas) of one who is lying apparently dead is besought to return from the distance where it is wandering." It was believed to be dwelling in the heart, "hṛd" (*RV*, VIII, 89, 5).[2]

The cosmology of the Upaniṣads briefly presented above shows that there had arisen a fairly agreed general notion that the human body was composed or made of the same five elements in their subtle aspect as those which in their gross aspects appear as the five elements of nature, i.e., earth, water, light-heat, air and ether. Though the full-fledged theory of the subtle elements, their extraction from the gross elements of nature and their combination in a specific way to produce the human being, is not stated, the few glimmerings of it we get in the Upaniṣads, not only in the form of the enumeration of the eight fundamental factors of creation, i.e., the five cosmic elements, the "great beings", mentioned above and the three mental factors of mind, intelligence and ego-sense, but also in the explicit mention of the subtle elements, in their technical designation of "mātrā", we have a reasonable guarantee that the process must have been thought of even in the Upaniṣadic era. The *Bṛhadāraṇyaka Upaniṣad* (IV, 4, 1) mentions only the 'mātrā', subtle particle or element of light-heat, "tejas" : but that is in connection with the dissolution of the body in death. And the text represents the self as gathering these particles and descending into the heart and thereafter as the "person in the eye" as turning away. The account of dreamless sleep given in the *Praśna Upaniṣad* (IV, 6-8) goes much further in this line of thought to such an extent that as S. Radhakrishnan[3] remarks about it : "We have here an enumeration of the *Sāṁkhya* principles of the five cosmic elements, the ten organs of perception and action, mind, intellect, self-sense and thought together with light and life." And it is very necessary to add that it goes beyond enumeration in specifically mentioning the elements, "mātrās", of the five cosmic elements, earth, water, "fire" (light-heat), air and ether.

The human individual as conceived by the philosophers of the Upaniṣadic era emerges out as an active configuration of sixteen or nineteen endowments. The former number of constituents of human personality as in the *Chāndogya Upaniṣad* (VI, 5-7) leaves out the controller, the ruler so to say, the self. The *Chāndogya*-account appears to contemplate the inclusion only of the five organs of action, the five organs of perception, the five life-breaths, and mind (manas). The five organs of action as the *Praśna Upaniṣad* specifies them are : (1) speech, (2) hands, (3) feet, (4) excretory organ and (5) generative organ. The five organs of sense or perception are : (1) sight, (2) hearing, (3) nose, (4) taste and (5) skin. Then there are the purely non-material and internal as well as mental and vital factors of (1) mind, (2) intellect, and (3) ego-sense. Of these the *Chāndogya*-account must be considered to include only the mind. There are recognized, in the Upaniṣads and thereafter through all Indian thought of a religio-philosophical nature, five vital breaths, though it is not only admitted but taken for granted that they are all the same vital breath classified into five categories in terms of the direction of movement of each within the body. In the *Prasna*-account of the human personality "Prāṇa" in the singular as only one vital breath is counted as its constituent. In the *Chāndogya* statement I have taken it to have been counted in its five-fold aspect. The *Praśna*-account of the human personality which so far has accounted for fourteen constituents, makes in the statement the all-important addition of the self, the active agent, the seer, the hearer, the smeller, the taster, the thinker, the doer, the knower, the clear understanding incarnate, as the text exhaustively and charmingly describes him.

So far it is a cogent account but it accounts for only fifteen constituents. But it is clear that some of the speculative thinkers of the age were not satisfied that all the features of the knowing and thoughtful aspects of human personality were fully covered by the two mental categories of mind and intelligence. They postulated a third one, called here 'citta', but elsewhere also as 'cetas' (*Muṇḍaka Upaniṣad*, II, 2, 3 ; III, 1, 9-10), the aspect of the human personality or the faculty which revolves the knowledge, thoughts and ideas and realizes them [?]. Thus the constituents of the human personality are made up. They are picturesquely but not quite appropriately described as 'mouths' in the *Māṇḍūkya Upaniṣad* (3-4) ; for at least 'citta' and even 'prāṇa', or vital breath, can hardly be conceived as receivers of any sensations or perceptions. The passage where the expression 'mouth' in respect of these constituents is used enumerates them as nineteen. S. Radhakrishnan identifies them as the five organs of "sense", five organs of action, five breaths or vital airs, mind, intelligence, "self-sense" (ego-sense) and "thought", 'citta'. In this view of the human personality as composed of nineteen constituents it is seen that the self is left out. This appears to me to be a serious omission. The account in the *Praśna Upaniṣad* including as it does the self among these constituents is taken by me in this study to be the standard Upaniṣadic view of the nature of human personality. The counting of 'prāṇa', life-breath, as one entity, and not as five separate though related entities, however, cannot be justified. The total constituents of human personality as commonly envisaged in the Upaniṣads, nevertheless, can be and I think should be taken to be nineteen, as 'citta', which is counted as a separate constituent, is mentioned in discussions of the various conditions of man only off and on.

In the *Chāndogya Upaniṣad* (VII, 1-15), in the instruction of Sanatkumāra, we are introduced to a long disquisition on the hierarchy of numerous categories, physical, mental and moral in an attempt to emphasize the primacy of self. It is in one section (5) that 'citta', rendered by S. Radhakrishnan as 'thought', figures as higher than not only speech but mind and also "will", 'saṁkalpa', but lower than contemplation ('dhyāna'), understanding ('vijñāna'), and many other not only mental and moral categories but also strength ('bala') and food ('anna'). Such an enumeration, whatever its value for an understanding of the religio-philosophical contribution of the Upaniṣads, cannot be held valid for consideration of the nature of the human personality formulated and accepted in that era. The fact of the matter is that it is only later, and that, too, in the Yoga system of thought, that 'citta' becomes a category by itself as an organ taking the place of 'manas', mind. Thus we have the famous definition of 'yoga', as the "suppression of the dispositions of 'citta' " ("yogaścittavṛttinirodhaḥ"). Otherwise 'citta', as in the few passages of the Upaniṣads where it occurs, is a mental product and not a category. It is like 'saṁkalpa', resolve, which, too, figures in the *Chāndogya* passage as another category. Besides this reference, 'saṁkalpa' is mentioned at least in three other places (*ChU*, VIII, 2, 10 ; *AiU*, III; *KeU*, IV, 5). In the first of these three, 'saṁkalpa' means desire or wish, in the second it equals understanding or 'vijñāna', while in the third it clearly means volition or will. Volition or will really speaking ought to be recognized as a separate category but evidently in the Upaniṣadic psychology it is subsumed under, I believe, "ahaṁkāra and ātman", ego-sense and self together. If thus 'saṁkalpa' is not to be counted as a distinct constituent of the human personality, 'citta' surely should not be.

Looked at from the view-point of the self, the controller, the master, or the occupier of the chariot in the form of the human personality as the *Kaṭha Upaniṣad* (I, 3, 3) tellingly puts it, the constituents, all of which serve the self, can be seen, as organized and classified in another way, as so many sheaths or coverings of the self. The outer covering or rather the grossest sheath is formed by food, i.e., all material aspect, the organs both of action and sense being together looked upon as the lowest equipment of the self. As the organs, as will be presently seen, are directly the products of the elements of the five cosmic elements, the 'great beings' (pañcamahābhūtas), the sheath formed by them can justifiably be classed as the lowest, i.e., as the biophysical one. The sheath formed by the life-breaths similarly can be appreciated to be of a higher and rarer aspect, breath being very much less material. Mind or 'manas', in the way of counting which does not enthrone 'prāṇa', is superior to breath ; and 'vijñāna' or 'buddhi', understanding, is clearly a high aspect of mind. These two being considered as two more sheaths of the self they must rank in that order. In the Upaniṣadic thought and experience 'ānanda' or bliss is the highest plane of anything because it is so pure and absorbing that all dualities and distinctions disappear or are put into the background during its currency. The sheath formed by bliss, revealing therein to the self its identity with the Supreme Being or Soul, naturally is the final culmination, the be-all and end-all of the human personality. In routine circumstances and for the generality of men, therefore, the human personality can be taken to be operative on four different levels and grades of mentality. This in effect is done in the *Taittirīya Upaniṣad* (II, 1-3 ; III, 10, 5).

Taking up the lowest of the sheaths of the self for consideration, we shall begin with the account of the various organs and their functions, or inherent natures or qualities, whether specifically described as objects or not, as laid out in the oldest of the Upaniṣads, the *Bṛhadāraṇyaka* (II, 4, 10 ; III, 2, 1-9). The redoubtable Yājñavalkya, having made up his mind to leave the home for the forest as the last stage of his fruitful and thoughtful life, asked his favourite wife Maitreyī about her wishes as to his effects which he desired to divide between her and his other wife, Kātyāyanī. Maitreyī, the Brahman-believer and-realizer that she was, desired to have fuller knowledge rather than worldly goods, and engaged him in a noble and instructive conversation leading him on to a soul-elevating and tuneful monologue on Brahman. It is at one stage of his sonorous exposition, through homely similies, bold metaphors, and poetic imagery, of the nature of Brahman that the sensory organs and their functions are brought in. Says Yājñavalkya : ". . . as the skin is (the goal) of all kinds of touch, as the nose (nostrils) is that of smell, tongue that of taste, the sight* that of form, the hearing† that of sound, the mind is the goal of all desires‡, the heart is that of all knowledge, the two hands that of all manual work, the generative organ that of all enjoyment, the excretory organ that of all evacuation, the two feet are that of movement and speech is the goal of all the Vedas", so is this Soul, the Absolute Brahman, the end and goal of all the elements.|| In the second passage of the *Chāndogya* the philosophical view that the organs of sense are all of the nature of bonds and their natural objects or functions tightness of the same, 'graha' and 'atigraha', is enunciated. There only seven out of the twelve enumerated in the previous text, which, with the addition 'prāṇa', life-breath, make up eight, and are so numbered, figure. This last feature introduces an aberration which is not explicable to me in that only one of the remaining four varieties of breath is associated with it.§

The *Chāndogya Upaniṣad* (VIII, 1, 1-3) describing the location and the nature of the individual self, starts with characterizing the human personality or rather the human body as the city of Brahman, 'Brahmapura', just as the *Kaṭha Upaniṣad* (II, 2, 1) and the *Śvetāśvatara Upaniṣad* (III, 18) describe the human body as a city with eleven or nine gates respectively. In this city of Brahman there is an abode, shaped like a small lotus flower—this refers to the physical organ known as the heart. Within it there is a small space, 'ākāśa'. And within that space dwells the one to be sought and understood. However, the space within the heart and the cosmic space are really the same, the former having within it both heaven and earth, fire and air, the sun and the moon, lightning and the stars. Here we have a straight and unambiguous statement of the doctrine, derivable from the Upaniṣadic cosmology and elaborately mentioned in some passages like that in the *Praśna Upaniṣad* (III, 5-9) which we shall have occasion to refer to later, that the individual's heart and the cosmic space are both the same in their fundamental elements. However, it will be presently seen that this view is rather unique or aberrant and seems to have been adopted by the particular speculative thinker as a short cut to the identity of the individual self with the Supreme Soul. As a matter of fact it is not consonant with the common view and the Upaniṣadic cosmology which see the counterpart of cosmic space in the organ of hearing of the individual, the quality or the inherent nature of both being sound or word. In the *Bṛhadāraṇyaka Upaniṣad* (IV, 4, 21) the space within the heart as the abode of the self, the ruler of all, the controller of all, is mentioned but without any attempt

* As the word used is 'cakṣu' and not 'akṣi', I have rendered it thus. Whereas 'akṣi' is used in this literature when the eyes are meant, 'cakṣu' is the word employed when the abstract organ behind the eyes, sight, is meant to be conveyed as in *Aitareya Up.* (I, 4).

† I have avoided the word 'ear' as the number used is singular and not dual.

‡ The word used is 'saṁkalpa' which means 'desire' or 'resolve' and I have chosen the former as in the next account the word used is 'kāma'.

|| The same occurs verbatim in the *Bṛhadāraṇyaka Upaniṣad* (IV, 5, 12).

§ The same verbatim in the *Bṛhadarāṇyaka Upaniṣad* (III, 2, 1-9).

at its identification with any cosmic element. In another passage (IV, 1, 7) it identifies the heart with Brahman. In the *Chāndogya Upaniṣad* itself in another passage where the identities of the five life-breaths are established (III, 13, 1-5), cosmic elements of air, 'vāyu', and space, 'ākāśa', find their counterpart in the upward breath, 'udāna'.

As seen in the cosmological section, it is in the *Aitareya Upaniṣad* (I ; II) that we get a clear statement of the production of the constituents of the human personality from cosmic elements, five "great beings", 'mahābhūtas', as they are called here (III, 3) and ever afterwards. In that account of creation we have the entities, mouth, nostrils, eyes, ears, skin, heart, navel and penis, evidently of the Puruṣa, known as the Golden Embryo. From these organ-entities, arose, we are told, speech, vital breath, sight, hearing, hair, mind, downward breath and semen respectively. From these again came out fire, air, the sun, space, herbs and plants, the moon, death and waters. These cosmic entities are designated deities 'devatā', and they are said to have been ordered by Puruṣa or Ātman to go to the individual plane for their sustenance. Thereupon, fire becoming speech entered the mouth of the individual human being, air becoming vital breath entered the nostrils or nose, the sun becoming sight entered the eyes, quarters or space becoming hearing entered the ears, herbs and plants becoming hair entered the skin, the moon becoming mind entered the heart, death becoming downward breath entered the navel and waters becoming semen entered the penis.

We can see that the objective of the thinker in this elaborate and what appears to us now a roundabout way, was to assert the derivation of the most important physical constituents and of the psychical elements of the human personality from certain cosmic elements and entities. The five "great beings", 'mahābhūtas', are there : fire, the sun and the moon all three representing the cosmic element of light-heat, and herbs and plants, the earth. As regards the individual there is some addition and some omission, both not being explicable except as evidence of early groping. It is that there is breath and navel and penis which do not figure among the organs in any list, while taste and its perceiver as well as smell and touch go unnoticed and unexplained.

In the *Chāndogya Upaniṣad* (III, 13, 1-5) we have in one passage a double identity and also the divinity of the cosmic elements blandly stated as connected with the human heart. The heart is said to have five openings for the gods, i.e., of course the five breaths. The organs mentioned with their identities are : sight, hearing, speech and 'manas'. Their counterparts of the higher or cosmic order are the vital breath and the sun of the first ; the diffused breath and the moon of the second ; that of the third the downward breath and fire and that of the fourth, mind, equalizing breath and rain. The fourth opening and its breath, i.e., out-breath, is both air ('vāyu') and space ('ākāśa'). Among the organs that of taste is left out. Only three of the five cosmic elements figure in the metaphorical statement. This is perhaps due to the fact that in the view of the school of thinkers represented in this Upaniṣad only three of the five cosmic elements were employed or played their parts in the creation or evolution of the human personality.

In the *Bṛhadāraṇyaka Upaniṣad* (III, 2, 13) the boldest speculative thinker Yājñavalkya coolly describes what happens when a man dies. He assures his listeners that the speech departs to fire, the breath to air, the sight to the sun, mind to the moon, hearing to space, the self to ether, the body-hair to herbs and the head-hair to plants, and blood and semen are placed in water. The enumeration more or less closely agrees with that of the account of creation met with in the *Aitareya Upaniṣad* (I ; II) already narrated at fair length.

What is stated as happening in the event of a man's death to the constituents of his personality in the *Bṛhadāraṇyaka Upaniṣad* is more or less precisely stated in the *Kauṣītakībrāhmaṇa Upaniṣad* (II, 15) in the description of what is called there the father-son ceremony or the ceremony of transmission from father to son.

It is clear from this account of creation and dissolution of a human individual that the most important constituents, almost the sole constituents of human personality, were derived from the cosmic elements and were presided over by the gods, i.e., the divinities in the cosmic elements, and that at the death of a human being they fly to or are merged into those elements and their deities.

And there is at least one reference to some of the sense-organs of a dead man having been conceived to have their proper destinations in their respective deities in the *Rgveda* (X, 16, 3) itself. S. V. Ketkar[4] drew attention to it. The eye is asked to go to the sun while the breath is told to go to air. Ketkar further remarked that the idea must have been prompted by the notion of the sun having been formed out of the eyes of the Primordial Being, whose sacrifice resulted in the great creation of the cosmos as conceived in the *Rgveda* (X, 90, 13). Thus the idea of the identity of some of the constituents of an individual personality and the cosmic elements is a very old one. It must be taken as having been current, though neither in the full form nor in the precise manner of its affiliation, in the Upaniṣadic cosmology and bio-psychology presented so far.

Complete elaboration of this identity between the cosmic and the individual, though its establishment in the case of life-breath or 'prāṇa' in its five-fold variety, which is partially stated in the *Chāndogya* text referred to above, is presented in the *Praśna Upaniṣad* (III, 5-9). It is there stated that the sun supports or favours the life-breath ('prāṇa') and the latter pervades sight, hearing, mouth and nose ; the presiding deity of the earth supports the downward breath ('apāna'), which pervades the anus and the generative organ ; space supports the equalizing breath ('samāna'), which pervades the navel; air favours the diffused breath ('vyāna'), which pervades the fine channels ('nāḍis') in the heart ; and fire supports the upward breath ('udāna'), which pervades the most important of the channels ('nāḍis') called specifically 'suṣumṇā'. It is this channel through which passing away of the self at death is most desirable. Here we find all the five cosmic elements brought into intimate affiliation with not only the organs of action and of sense but also other important bio-physical elements, the navel and the channels, especially the most important 'suṣumṇā'.

The psychic entities among the constituents of the human personality are here left out. And I think, it is perhaps due to the doctrine of subtle body of the self having been developed and its accompaniment of the departing self at death having been accepted as an article of eschatological theory. The omission is also explicable on the ground that the psychic entities are in nature the same as the entities that manifest themselves in the process of cosmic development. Thus in the *Kaṭha Upaniṣad* (I, 3, 10) it is maintained that the hierarchy in cosmic development is formed by the senses, the objects that are to be grasped by them, and mind, intelligence ('buddhi'), and the great soul ('mahat'), the unmanifest ('prakṛti' or 'pradhāna') and the Supreme Soul ('Puruṣa'). The configuration called human personality is described in the same work (I, 3, 3-4) thus : "The self is the owner-occupier of the chariot called the body ; intelligence (buddhi) is the charioteer ; mind (manas) is the rein and the organs are the horses while the objects are their fields. In the constituents of the individual personality, in the hierarchy above the objects, both mind ('manas') and intellect ('buddhi'). which is in the very next verse called 'vijñāna' or understanding, figure as lower than the self. The self on the individual plane is the counterpart of the Supreme Soul on the cosmic one. In the individual configuration both 'mahat' and 'avyakta' are naturally lacking. In the fully developed account of the human personality as well as the cosmic development we find ego-sense (ahaṁkāra) in addition to the entities mentioned. Thus 'manas', 'buddhi' and 'ahaṁkāra', i.e., mind, understanding and ego-sense, the three psychic entities in the constituents of the human personality, are the same as those that became manifest in the process of the cosmic development. Their identity is thus almost self-evident and needs no special pronouncement in the Upaniṣadic climate.

Of these categories the ego-sense, 'ahaṁkāra', is declared to have been the proximate cause of the Supreme Soul engaging in the activity of creating the cosmos (*BrU*, I, 4, 1). In the *Praśna Upaniṣad* (IV, 8) in the description of what happens to the constituents of human personality, we are informed that the ego-sense ('ahaṁkāra') along with "what can be connected with the self" rests in the Supreme Soul. Here not only is the category of 'ahaṁkāra' asserted to be the same in fundamentals as operative in the embodied soul as one of the constituents of the human personality as that working on the cosmic plane, but also that it, like other constituents, rests in the Supreme Soul during the individual's dreamless sleep. The *Śvetāśvatara Upaniṣad* (V, 8) in describing the size of the individual self endowed with thought ('saṁkalpa'), which being an activity of mind, 'manas', must be understood in the context to stand for 'manas', mind, ego-sense, and understanding ('buddhi'), goes a step further in configurating the purely mental categories as constituents of the human personality, assuring that the size of the individual self thus conditioned is the temporary distinction between him and the Supreme Soul, who is infinite and limitless.

The next higher mental category is that of 'buddhi', understanding, which is its regular designation in later literature and practice. The *Chāndogya Upaniṣad* (VII, 1-24) recounts twentythree categories, in which figure some of the cosmic elements, some physical traits, some abstract qualities and many mental and moral categories. Buddhi is conspicuous by its absence in that long list; but 'vijñāna', discrimination, is mentioned. In the *Aitareya Upaniṣad* (III, 2) we have a comprehensive list of mental functions which are pronounced by the author of the particular school of thought to be all of them only different names of intelligence, 'prajñāna'. Curiously the list starts with heart ('hṛdaya'), which is equated with mind ('manas'). Then follow consciousness, perception, "discrimination" ('vijñāna'), intelligence, wisdom, insight, steadfastness, thought, thoughtfulness, impulse ('jūti'), memory, conception, purpose, life, desire and control. It must be evident to an impartial and critical student, that, even making allowance for the nebulous state of mental analysis in the time of the thinkers who compiled the *Aitareya Upaniṣad* about 600 B.C., they are carried away into a confusion of categories and seeming distinction of mental acts by the wonderful plasticity of the language, which enabled them to form or bring together words having for the second member the word 'jñāna'. As my purpose is not to write a complete study of the psychology in the Upaniṣads, I shall content myself with the observation that whereas heart ('hṛdaya') is a physical organ, a concrete object with a location, mind ('manas') is a postulate, implying a meaning, a perceiving configuration. Heart ('hṛdaya') is mentioned a number of times in the Upaniṣads which attribute to it important place, and even functions, but they are different and are never grouped in the mental activities and categories which are configurated as the human personality. It will be dealt with after studying all the three mental categories which form part of the constituents of the human personality commonly conceived in the Upaniṣads. For the time it is necessary to emphasize the fact that 'buddhi' does not figure in the long list of mental functions and to maintain that 'vijñāna' takes its place.

That 'vijñāna', discrimination, is the equivalent of 'buddhi', understanding, in the psychological set-up of the Upaniṣads comes out very clearly from the *Kaṭha Upaniṣad* itself. In the five verses (I, 3, 5-9) next to the one which describes the relation between the individual self (ātman), understanding ('buddhi'), mind ('manas'), the organs ('indriyas') and objects ('arthas'), the place of 'buddhi' is occupied by 'vijñāna', the same functions and relations being ascribed to it as those assigned to 'buddhi' in the previous text. That 'buddhi' and 'vijñāna' are or were interchangeable is quite clear from the fact that immediately after this in the standard enumeration of the hierarchy of these categories (I, 3, 10) 'buddhi' replaces 'vijñāna'.

In the *Bṛhadāraṇyaka Upaniṣad* (IV, 3, 7) the limitation of the Supreme

Soul in the form of the embodied soul is mentioned to be 'vijñāna'. He is described as "the person here who consists of knowledge ('vijñānamaya')". In the glowing homage paid to Brahman or the Supreme Soul almost everywhere the last part either specifies Him as the 'vijñātā', the Discriminator, or asks the pre-answered question "how should one be able to know the Discriminator" (*BrU*, II, 4, 14; III, 4, 2; III. 7, 21-23; IV, 5, 15; *PrU*, IV. 9). In the *Taittirīya Upaniṣad* (V) the fourth sheath, i.e., the self short of full realization, is described as 'vijñānamaya' and is the next higher than the sheath formed by mind ('manas'). In the *Praśna Upaniṣad* (IV, 9) again it is the 'vijñānātmā', discriminating self, that is declared to be the form of the embodied soul. The *Muṇḍaka Upaniṣad* (III, 2, 7) speaks only of the same form of the embodied soul as getting liberated. And the same work graphically describing the nicely ensconced self in glowing terms mentions 'vijñāna' as the instrument with which one transcends the lower sheath of the embodied soul formed by mind (II, 2, 7-8).

The third member of the mental triad, which is a component of the human personality as conceived in the Upaniṣads and which has been more or less the same down the ages, is mind or 'manas'. It is rightly conceived in Brahmanism and Hinduism as an organ, a formless and locationless one, which has the dual nature of the organs both of action and of sense.

In considering 'manas', mind, and the nature and role ascribed to it in the Upaniṣads, it is best to begin with the more or less explicit and full statement about it we get in the *Bṛhadāraṇyaka Upaniṣad* (III, 2). It is seen from inclusion of mind among the organs of sense and of action that it was looked upon as the sixth organ of sense and of action. It is also worthy of notice that its over perceiver is declared to be desire. Mind was thus conceived of as the organ which 'perceives' or engenders desires. In one account of the creation given in the same Upaniṣad (I, 2, 1), that by Death or Hunger, which was the only existent one in the beginning, mind is said to have been the first of that creation, the first self of Death or Hunger, the creator. In another passage (I, 5, 3) we have a statement about the perceiving and recording functions of the mind. It is with the mind that one sees, that one hears. And not only is desire the creature of the mind but also are resolve ('saṁkalpa'), doubt ('vicikitsā), faith ('śraddhā') or the lack of it, steadfastness ('dhṛti') or the absence of it, "shame" ('hrī', shyness or humility?), intellection ('dhī), fear ('bhī) all mind. Touch too is mind, for one feels it even if one is touched on his back, i.e., without seeing it. It is through the mind that, according to the *Śvetāśvatara Upaniṣad* (II, 8), one has to control one's organs, by confining them within the heart. It is but a straight application and explanation of the metaphor used in the *Kaṭha Upaniṣad* (I, 3, 2-4) of the chariot, its owner and the charioteer, mind being described as the reins. The function of the reins is precisely to pull up and keep the reined ones, the organs, on straight path, preventing their going astray.

Another important constituent of the human personality is breath ('prāṇa'), a category which is physical and vital. And unlike other categories it became the centre of a whole set of practices called 'yoga' even in the Upaniṣads, which came to be considered in the Upaniṣadic era, and perhaps from much earlier times too. as a necessary adjunct to religious and philosophically right conduct and for the achievement of the goal of final liberation. It attained the distinction of being accepted as a technique, which conferred upon adepts in it miraculous powers of all kinds. And almost all this development appears to have taken place within about a century or two, between about 800 B.C. and 600 B.C. Along with the acceptance of the significance of breath and the speculative analysis of its different aspects or varieties there appears to have gone forward either speculative thinking about, during certain states of mental concentration and alertness, or such thinking aided by some more scientific exploration of, the anatomy and physiology of man. Some such concatenation of circumstances and conscious exploration of the nature of the human personality alone will explain the specific-looking knowledge embodied in the two earliest of the Upaniṣads regarding the number and size of channels ('nāḍīs') issuing from the heart and other matters.

The *Aitareya Upaniṣad* in its account of the creation (I, 4) asserts the creation of two breaths, the vital and the downward as part of it. The *Praśna Upaniṣad* (II, 1-3), however, in an inquiry about the number of gods and their functions, states 'prāṇa' to have been the only one of the breaths that contested the claim to supremacy over the five 'great beings' ('mahabhūtas'), and the four principal organs of sense, i.e., skin, mind, sight and hearing. The nine entities mentioned are said to have declared, "We sustain and support this body". 'Prāṇa', vital breath, answered back : "Do not have this delusion; I, alone, dividing myself fivefold, supporting this body sustain it." Further the supremacy is again pronounced in the next section (III) raising the question of the source of the origin of this breath ('prāṇa'), how it gets into the body, how it stations itself in its different areas, and how it departs as well as how it, which is internally located, can support the body which is external. The final question asks about the relation of this 'prāṇa' to the self. In the comprehensive reply which Pippalāda is recorded to have given, the last question is, I think purposely, answered first. Pippalāda starts by asserting that vital breath ('prāṇa') is born of the self ('ātman') and that it is related to the latter as a person's shadow to him. 'Prāṇa', further, is declared to get into the body through the action of 'mind' (manas)—this view should naturally make 'prāṇa' secondary to 'manas' and reduce its importance to that extent and contradict the assertion by 'prāṇa' of its supremacy made in the previous section, but somehow the sage, who must have been a Yoga-adept and thus a doctrinaire, glided over that difficulty ; and his questioners somehow did not realize it. Once in the body 'prāṇa' set about ordering the different breaths—this manner of speaking again presupposes the existence of all the five 'prāṇas' with one of them, the vital breath, as their lord and does not support the assertion made earlier that 'prāṇa' (vital breath) alone existed and it divided itself into five, including itself—in the various parts and areas of the body as does a ruler, no less majestic and authoritative than a sovereign monarch, his various officers in the different areas of his administrative domain.

Leaving the specification of the fivefold breath and its detailed location in the body, their affiliation or identity with the five 'great beings' ('mahābhūtas') for the time, I shall follow the train of the earlier passage from the *Praśna Upaniṣad* about the rivalry, among the various components of the human personality for the supremacy in it, mentioned above. The two oldest Upaniṣads, the *Bṛhadāraṇyaka* and the *Chāndogya*, too, have in them passages (*BrU*, VI, 1 ; *ChU*, V, 1) which speak of the rivalry among the various constituents of the human personality. And though there is a slight difference in detail between them, the two must be declared to be identical. Their beginning, their referee and their wording even are all the same. The difference in detail may be first mentioned and disposed of. It is that in the *Bṛhadāraṇyaka* text, the additional element, which is not frequent, though not altogether absent, in the accounts of creation, and one which I do not remember to have noticed as figuring in any Upaniṣadic configuration of the constituents of the human personality, is semen. Leaving out semen, the contending parties are the same four constituents of the human personality which are said to have entered into the contest with the five great beings and 'prāṇa' in the *Praśna Upaniṣad* (II, 4-13). They are : speech, sight, hearing and mind. This order, placing mind above the other sense organs, is the proper one, considering the importance of mind and the functions predicated of it. In the *Praśna Upaniṣad* it is evidently the metrical necessity that has disrupted this order, 'manas' (mind) having to be put next after 'vāk' (speech) for the sake of euphony.

In all the three contests the outcome is the complete victory of 'prāṇa'. In the two older texts, where the referee is Prajāpati Himself and not a sage like Pippalāda, 'prāṇa' is not allowed by the four constituents, speech, sight, hearing and mind, to leave the body, so convinced were they of its need for the body including themselves. They praised 'prāṇa' and may be said to have prayed to it to stay on, every one of them declaring that 'prāṇa' was the highest, the eldest or the best and that what they were severally 'prāṇa' was all singly. Everyone of the four constituents of the human personality, i.e., speech, sight, hearing and mind, is thus identified with 'prāṇa' and is to be known as 'prāṇa'.

In the *Bṛhadāraṇyaka* text the finale is very interesting as in the peculiar manner of the Upaniṣads and the Brāhmaṇas a lesson is culled out and conveyed. And the lesson refers to a Brahmanic practice which till today is scrupulously observed by the orthodox among Brahmins and similar twice-born men. It is about sipping water with the accompaniment of the recitation of some mystic syllables or some part of a Vedic text, both before beginning to eat one's meal and at its end before getting up from one's seat. It is like the thanksgiving prayer at dinner of pious Christians.

In the *Praśna Upaniṣad* passage 'prāṇa' is stated to have demonstrated this indispensability, whereupon only the four praised 'prāṇa', identifying it with a number of gods, calling it 'father'. Finally they prayed it to protect them as a mother does her sons and to grant prosperity and wisdom (II, 13). This is perhaps the earliest of prayers which speaks of the divinity prayed as mother. The Vedic prayers wherever they contain any reference to relationship speak of the divinity as father, thus asking to treat 'us' as a father does his sons.

The five 'prāṇas', whether four of them arose out of the primordial one or not—it would appear the texts are better harmonized by assuming that all the five are more or less separate entities or one entity with five separate and specific functions—in the *Praśna Upaniṣad* (III, 5-9) they are assigned five separate gods and in the *Chāndogya Upaniṣad* (III, 13, 15), too, as door-keepers of the five openings of the heart for gods are connected with the same gods. They are located in the different parts of the body thus : 'prāṇa' (vital breath) in eyes, ears, mouth and nose ; 'apāṇa' (downward breath) in the anus and the generative organ ; 'samāna' (equalizing breath) in the navel ; 'vyāna' (diffused breath) and 'udāna' (upward breath) in the heart. 'Vyāna' pervades the hundred and one channels, which are very very fine, spread about the heart ; and 'udāna' in one particular channel ('nāḍī') known as 'suṣumṇā', which goes up from the region of the heart to the suture of the skull called 'vidṛti' (*AiU*, I, 12) or described merely as the "spot where the roots of the hair of the head lie apart" (*Tait. Up.*, I, 6, 1). In later thought it is spoken of as the Brahmarandhra, 'the hole of Brahman', meaning the opening, passing through which at the death of a person, the individual self merges into the Universal Self.

It is necessary to make mention of recent and contemporary practice, current in the complex rite of the disposal of the dead as in vogue in Maharashtra at least, that it is thought highly essential that the supposed opening at the top of the skull should have occurred before the body is finally and wholly consumed by fire. I have recorded the practice of picking up a suitable piece of stone by one of the principal mourners on their way to the cremation ground carrying the corpse for cremation and with it to break the skull, if after a reasonable time from the start of the firing of the funeral pyre a loud cracking sound is not heard. The cracking sound is a guarantee that the skull has broken open. insuring thereby the escape of the spirit through its proper channel. If that does not occur normally then the stone is used to break the skull. Under all circumstances it is used first to break the pot of water which has to be carried around the pyre. And that stone, called 'aśmā', a Sanskrit word which means only a stone, is believed to contain the spirit of the dead person and has to be treated with some rites.[5]

The region of the heart plays an important role in the religious, philosophical and ethical beliefs and systems of many peoples. In Hindu thought, heart, though not figuring in any of the accounts of creation so far narrated, occupies a unique position. It is the abode of the embodied soul. Now that it has had to be mentioned in connection with the specification and distribution of 'breath' as presented in the Upaniṣads it is appropriate at this juncture to present an account of its special position and significance as envisaged in the Upaniṣadic thought.

To begin with the most developed ideas on the subject, the latest in the Upaniṣadic era I have demarcated as early, i.e., ending before 500 B.C., we shall have to take note of the contents of the *Kauṣitakībrāhmaṇa Upaniṣad.* In the dialogue between the proud Bālāki and the famous king Ajātaśatru of Kāśī (Vārāṇasī) as recorded in the Upaniṣad (IV, 18-20), when the former was humbled in the discussion, and approached the latter for being accepted as a pupil, Ajātaśatru delivering his message said, pointing out to a person lying asleep : "While asleep, (the person) not dreaming any dream, he (the self) remains in the channels called 'hitā' which are as thin as a hair divided (longitudinally) a thousandfold and are full of a thin fluid, mixed in colour with white, black, yellow and red (elements in it), and which extend from the heart to the pericardium ('purītat'). Then he (self) becomes one with vital breath. Then speech and names, sight and forms, hearing and words, and mind and thoughts all go into it. When he awakes then the vital breaths proceed to their respective stations etc." and life goes on as before sleep.

In the oldest Upaniṣad, the *Bṛhadāraṇyaka* (II, 1, 19 ; IV, 2, 3 ; IV, 3, 20 ; IV, 4, 7-9), the 'hitā' channels are mentioned precisely in the manner of the above passage, their fineness, their colour, their location. Further the additional information vouchsafed specifies their number spread around the heart exactly as seventy-two thousand and not vaguely as seventy-two thousand branches of everyone of them as in the *Praśna Upaniṣad* (III, 4-10) or as the smaller number of only hundred and one as does either the *Chāndogya Upaniṣad* quotation of an earlier verse (VIII, 6, 6) or the *Kaṭha Upaniṣad* (II, 3, 16). It is further stated that they extend to the pericardium. Further, without naming, the particular channel that leads from the heart to the opening in the skull at the top is also mentioned as the path by which the knowers of Brahman depart after death to the state of beatification. It is stated further that in deep sleep the embodied soul comes through the 'hitā' channels to the pericardium and rests there, as a youth, or a great king or a great Brahmin might lie at ease when he has attained the summit of bliss. Ordinarily too, it appears, the embodied soul resides there, eating finer food than the body, as the 'hitā' channels bring only finer food. The description of the spot where the self, "immersed in the food", dwells given in the *Muṇḍaka Upaniṣad* (II, 2, 6-9) likens it to the hub of a wheel, the channels representing the spokes.

In the *Chāndogya Upaniṣad* (VIII, 6, 1-6) the colours of the fluid are mentioned with the further elaboration that they reflect the colours of the sun and that there exists a straight connecting path between the sun and them, so that when the self departs at death he passes by them to the sun.

We may proceed with our study of the place of the heart in the religio-philosophical thought of the Upaniṣads, without any reference to the channels. In the *Bṛhadāraṇyaka Upaniṣad* there are at least four places where heart ('hṛdaya') without any mention of it as embedded in or connected with the channels, is specifically mentioned. One of them (II, 4, 11) speaks of it as the one goal of all learning or departments of knowledge. The remaining three (IV, 1, 7 ; IV, 3, 7 ; V, 3) making it either the abode of the embodied soul or identifying it with Brahman, emphasize its significance as the source of morality and the goal of religion and philosophy. The one statement which the *Chāndogya Upaniṣad* (VIII, 3, 3) makes about heart is very instructive, suggesting to us how it is sometimes the non-philosophical and purely technical and linguistic speculation that might have led the Upaniṣadic thinkers to some of the grand notions that later became the centre and compelling motives of religious consciousness and practice. 'Hṛdaya', we are told, through its etymology proclaims itself to be the seat of the embodied soul ; for it is the compound expression for the two words, which in effect, in Sanskrit, form a sentence, 'hṛdi' and 'ayam', making it mean the place where "this one", the self, of course, 'is', i.e., dwells.

In some passages there are expressions in which the word 'hṛdaya' occurs in a compound. Thus we have (*ChU*, VIII, 10, 1-2, 11, 1-2) Indra in his pursuit of true knowledge under the discipleship of Prajāpati twice described as śāntahṛdaya', meaning 'one with a tranquil heart'. In the *Kaṭha Upaniṣad* (I, 1, 10) to convey the same idea, the expression used is 'śāntasaṁkalpa', which in the context must mean 'one who has quietened or become tranquil', the two additional expressions used meaning 'one whose anger is gone' and 'one whose mind is well-disposed'.

It is in the *Chāndogya Upaniṣad* (III, 12, 2-4 ; VIII, 1, 1-3) that we get not only one of the most complete characterizations of the embodied soul but also the earliest mention of the lotus, the heart-lotus (*hṛt-puṇḍarīka*) as it later has come to be known, within which ensconced within a small space the embodied soul dwells : The *Bṛhadāraṇyaka Upaniṣad* (IV, 3, 7) speaks of the embodied soul as "the light within the heart". In the *Chāndogya* text we have the soul described as having the form of light. His resolve is truth itself and his soul is space. He does all activity, entertains all desires, smells whatever is smelt, tastes all that has taste. Speechless and unconcerned he can yet encompass the universe. He lies within the heart, being in size smaller than a grain of rice or barley or mustard seed or than the kernel of a grain of millet. Yet he is greater than the earth, the atmosphere, the sky, than all the worlds. And that Ātman in the heart is Brahman. Heart as the seat or abode of the self is mentioned in other passages too.

The thinkers represented in the *Aitareya Upaniṣad* (I, 2, 4 ; III, 2), a work next in antiquity to the above-mentioned one, made a special approach to this duality of mind ('manas') and heart ('hṛdaya') and announced that what is mind is heart. They in their effort of identification of the two categories even propounded their common association with one divinity, the moon. In most accounts such association of mind is either derived from or intimately connected with the moon. In this *Aitareya*-statement the moon is declared to have entered the heart in the garb of the mind. It is clear from the statements about these categories from the Upaniṣads and from later religio-philosophical literature that this attempt at identification of the two mental categories failed. 'Hṛdaya' and 'manas' have continued to be separate, with traits and functions which are definite enough to distinguish them. The position assigned to the heart of being the seat or abode, whether described as a lotus or not, of the self became fixed. Thus here is what the unique book known as the *Kaṭha Upaniṣad* (II, 1, 12-13 ; II, 3, 17)—almost unique in the whole literature of the world because it purports to be a dialogue between an intensely inquisitive lad by name Naciketas and no other personality than the God of death—says: "the Self (Puruṣa) who is of the size of the thumb, like a smokeless flame, stands in the middle of the ātman (body), ruler over the past and the future, unchanging from day to day" ; "The Self ('Puruṣa') of the size of the thumb is always established in the hearts of people as their inner self." This latter phraseology has become much more common than the previous one. Thus the *Śvetāśvatara Upaniṣad,* the most specifically oriented to the idea of a personal god and away from that of the absolute and formless Brahman, has (III, 13 ; IV, 17 and 20 ; V, 7 and 8) the same text with the addition of "he is the lord of the knowledge formed by the heart and the mind", which figures also in the *Kaṭha Upaniṣad* (II, 3, 9). These texts have their echoes directly in two of the oft-cited and deeply cherished verses of the *Bhagavadgītā* (XVIII, 61 ; XV, 20).

It is the heart that entertains doubt and cherishes world-binding desires and that, therefore, it is in the heart that the senses must be confined and their desires-conveying capacity immobilized for one's beatification and final liberation. This is stressed in the *Śvetāśvatara Upaniṣad* (II, 8), the *Muṇḍaka Upaniṣad* (II, 2, 9) and the *Kaṭha Upaniṣad* (II, 3, 15). But heart, somehow, does not figure in the Upaniṣadic configuration of the constituents of the human personality. Is it because it is too much identified with the individual soul ?

Human personality, the non-physical, non-material, non-concrete part of it, i.e., the essence of it, is formed by the senses of sight, hearing, smell, taste and touch and the purely internal categories of mind, intellect and ego-sense with the controller and the ruler of all, the individual self, as the central one. The individual self forms the spiritual component, the others making up the psycho-physical part.

Of these, the first five are derivable, and have been so derived in the cosmological accounts, from the five great beings, the five cosmic elements. The next three, the internal elements, similarly considered to have been the counterparts of the identical categories on the cosmic plane in the process of creation. The speculative thinkers working on these accepted hypotheses and beliefs must have tended towards appreciating or expecting an intimate connection between the individual self as the Principle or the Deity that, by that time, or rather long before it, had come to be posited and believed in as the source and maker or inspirer of the process of creation and of the whole cosmos. The accepted Vedic cosmology represented the cosmos and the individual human being as the actual parts of the sacrificed Puruṣa, the World Spirit. This cosmological belief itself should incline the speculative minds to the notion of identity of the individual soul, which as we have seen was postulated very early in the Vedic age, and the Universal Being or Puruṣa. Inspired sages, their minds being turned by the constant and long practice of some technique of Yoga, more or less completely known, practised and believed in as the unfailing and effective means of extraordinary powers and super-sensuous experience, like Vāmadeva, very famous and immortalized in Indian religio-philosophical literature from the Ṛgveda down (*RV*, IV, 18 ; *Taittirīya Āraṇyaka*, II, 5 ; *BrU*, I, 4, 10 ; *AiU*, II, 5-6), and the less illustrious Triśaṅku, in their entranced moment, having realized some extraordinary experience declaring their identity with the Supreme, must have further made the élite receptive to the notion of identity of the individual self with the Supreme Soul. In this surcharged climate the bold speculative thinker Yājñavalkya conceived the grand notion of postulating an Absolute Principle rather than a personal god as the source of the cosmos and proclaiming in tuneful peal its identity with the embodied soul. Thus we have the Upaniṣadic concept of the human personality as in essence the Universal Soul in temporary bondage and limitations.

The spiritual component of human personality, the centre of individual life, the embodied soul to whom some references have been incidentally made above, while speaking of the position of heart in the totality of human personality, must now occupy our attention. And here it is both necessary and desirable to present a composite picture of the concept of the embodied soul as seen from the Upaniṣadic thought to that of about the fifth century of the Christian era, i.e., of about a millenium. The view of the embodied soul that is current in élite Hinduism today even may be said to be more or less the same. The notion did take on some modification during the later millenium. The principal modifications, however, are mostly related to the various sectarian systems of devotion, and are largely in the vernacular literature of the different regions of India.

To follow up the Upaniṣadic trail of the nature of the embodied soul, keeping clear of the texts which evidently refer to the Supreme Soul, whose reflection, or rather the double, is the embodied soul, I may begin with the question put to the great Yājñavalkya by Jaratkārava Ārtabhāga as to the fate of his 'puruṣa', i.e., of the embodied soul, when a person dies. Yājñavalkya's answer (*BrU*, III, 2, 13) is not given in explicit terms but one infers that he informed his questioner that the soul passes on to another body according to 'his' deeds, good or bad, as the case may be. Thus one's embodied soul at one's death passes on to another body. It is clear that the embodied soul is indestructible. The soul is ensconced within the heart among the very fine channels and is fed on very special food, which is superfine and quite distinct from that by which the body is sustained (*BrU*, IV, 2, 3). His nature is that of understanding, 'vijñāna', i.e., buddhi' as later interpreted (*BrU*, IV, 3, 7). The ideas about the embodied soul and the Supreme Soul are much more mixed in this grand though the oldest Upaniṣad and, though many of them are soul-lifting, have to be passed over for more or less similar notions expressed more prosaically in the other and later ones.

Thus the *Kaṭha* speaks of Puruṣa, the embodied or inner soul, as being of the size of a thumb and lying in the heart or standing within the body (II, 1, 12 ; II, 3, 17), or again as smaller than the smallest laid in the cave (heart) of a person (I, 2, 20), or again proclaims him as the unborn one, that is not killed when the body is destroyed (I, 2, 18). The *Śvetāśvatara* (V, 8) goes a step further in enlightening us on the nature of the embodied soul and his being of the measure of a thumb and of the effulgence of the sun but actually as of the size of a one-hundreth part of the end-point of a hair, owing to being enveloped in the body and conditioned by the three mental elements of mind ('saṁkalpa'), ego-sense ('ahaṁkāra') and understanding ('buddhi'). The description given in the *Muṇḍaka Upaniṣad* (II, 2, 7-8) that the embodied soul, who is of the nature of mind, is established in the city of Brahmā, the ether of the heart, being seated in the body, controlling the heart, leads the life and body of an individual, expands the cryptic description of the *Bṛhadāraṇyaka*. In doing so it has attributed to the embodied soul a function, a moral one, which, unfortunately not quite often, nay very rarely at all, is ascribed to him. This description it is, however, which I think ought to be taken as the standard one of the role and nature of the embodied soul in Hinduism, at least in the élite form of it. In the *Kena* (I, 1-3, 5, 8) this role of a leader of the embodied soul is specified in greater detail, by mentioning the various functions of the body and life over which he presides. The *Kaṭha* (II, 1, 3 ; 2, 1 ; 2, 3-4) emphasizes the distinction of this embodied soul from the life-breaths and states categorically that it is the embodied soul through whom a person 'lives' and that the life-breaths themselves are supported by him. It is this that is left when the body is destroyed. It is this that persists during sleep and waking. It is this that knows and enjoys.

About two hundred fifty years later than the latest of the Upaniṣads on which I have drawn for the brief statement of the growth of religious consciousness and thought in early India, was compiled the *Bhagavadgītā*, the *Lord's Song*, which is one of the most-translated books of the world and the most-translated or -expounded of all the Indian books. The phraseology and the imagery, which this great book employed, much of which it borrowed, with an understanding and insight remarkable for their sureness, from the Upaniṣads, have stamped the subsequent religio-philosophical thought and literature. The *Gītā* refers to the embodied soul as either 'dehin' or 'śarīrin', the embodied one (II, 13, 18, 22, 30 ; XIII, 5-7), as 'ātman', soul (III, 42-3 ; VI, 5-8 ; X, 20), or as 'puruṣa', the man (VIII, 4 ; XIII, 22 ; XV, 16), or again as 'kṣetrajña' or 'kṣetrin', the knower or occupier of the field (XIII, 1-2 ; 33-4), the body being known as 'kṣetra' or field.

Of these terms for the embodied soul 'kṣetrajña' and even more so 'jīva' with the suffix 'ātman', thus becoming 'jīvātman', became current later as the standard terminology of Hindu religio-philosophical thought, élite or even non-élite.

The term 'jīvātman' or the 'jīva-self' for the embodied soul is to be supposed to have been popularized by the great systematizer and epitomizer Bādarāyaṇa, who must have lived at best a little before the compiler of the *Gītā*. Bādarāyaṇa's treatise is the well-known *Brahma-sūtras*. It forms the basis or supplies the authority for all the Vedāntic systems of Hindu philosophy. Bādarāyaṇa is supposed to have dealt with the problem of the origin and nature of the embodied soul in 'sūtras' 16-20 in the 3rd section of the 2nd chapter of his work. And all the great systematizers, Śaṅkara, Rāmānuja, Nimbārka, Madhva and Vallabha, have taken 'jīvātman' to be the term used by him for the embodied soul and they themselves adopted it. The relation of 'jīvātman' to the body is expounded by Bādarāyaṇa in 'sūtras' 19-36 of the same section of his work. Bādarāyaṇa concludes the discussion with the assertion that the embodied soul, 'jīvātman', is an agent.

Bādarāyaṇa of course derived his thought-material for the nomenclature of 'jīvātman', and also largely for his characterization of it, from the Upaniṣads, but the selection of and preference for this term was his, which was the result of his systematic and cogent philosophic analysis of the nature of the universe and God-head. In the *Chāndogya Upaniṣad* at least twice (VI, 3, 2 ; VI, 11, 3) and in the *Śvetāśvatara Upaniṣad* at least once (V, 9) the embodied soul is specifically and explicitly called either 'jīva' or jīvātman', and in the *Praśna Upaniṣad* once (V, 5) we have it mentioned as 'jīvaghana', 'jīva-substance'. That it was Bādarāyaṇa's clear insight that selected and stabilized the particular term becomes very clear from the fact that there are at least five, perhaps seven or eight, passages in the Upaniṣads where the embodied soul is called 'Puruṣa'. They are : *BrU*, IV, 3, 8 and IV, 4, 5 ; *Praśna Up.*, VI, 1-2 ; *Muṇḍaka Up.*, III, 1, 2 and *Śvet. Up.*, III, 13. But the term 'Puruṣa' like 'ātman' is double-edged, being also applicable to the Supreme Soul. And Bādarāyaṇa very properly passed it by and preferred 'jīva' or 'jīvātman'. In the *Gītā* perhaps we have to see the echoes of Bādarāyaṇa's contribution in the expression 'jīvabhūtā prakṛti' (VII, 5) of the Supreme Soul, as also in the statement that in the world of mortals the 'jīva' is a portion of the Supreme Soul enveloped by the subtle body (XV, 7).

Very briefly stated the relation of the embodied soul to the body according to the *Gītā*, which I adopt as the one which finds acceptance with most people is: (1) The body is like a suit of clothes of the soul and can be and is changed from time to time (II, 13, 18, 22) ; (2) the burning of or the destruction of, the body in any other manner, or any other state of the body, does not affect the embodied soul (II, 20, 30 ; XIII, 31-2) ; (3) It is the ego-sense-component of human personality that makes the embodied soul think of himself as the actor, though in reality activity is the functioning of the body through the impulse of matter and its properties (III, 27 ; XIII, 29 ; XIII, 5-7 ; XVIII, 15-17) ; (4) Organs, particularly the sense-organs, are finer than and superior to their objects which are all gross ; mind is superior to these organs ; 'buddhi' or understanding, the faculty by which or the capacity through which one is able to make a distinction and select among contending events or factors, is superior to mind which receives and conceives but does not discriminate. The one greater than and superior to 'buddhi' is 'he', i.e., the embodied soul (III, 42 ; XIII, 31-33). The embodied soul is thus superior to the other constituents of the human personality, his function of being the agent and the enjoyer being its conditioned reflex in the embodied state (XIII, 22 ; XV, 9).

Another and even more influential treatise, for the purely religious side of the complex, the *Manusmṛti*, which may be considered to have been compiled about the first or the second century of the Christian era, evidently attempted a synthesis of views and terminology. The book has been looked upon for ages as the most authoritative text for conduct of life, particularly the religious component of it. And unlike most books on sacred law it begins with a full view of cosmology and ends with a brief disquisition on philosophy, the nature and goal of human life, with a concise statement of the nature of the Supreme Soul, of the individual soul, of the human personality, of the life hereafter and of the attainment of salvation (XII, 3-23, 24-26; 39-50; 54-74, 75-81; 83-88; 90 ; 91-102).

Manusmṛti refers to the embodied soul both as 'antarātman' (VI, 63 ; VI, 73), 'inner soul', and as 'jīva', the term being used once in that behalf (XII, 13 ; XII, 23). It is this 'antarātman' or 'jīva' that gets subjected to the cycle of births and deaths (VI, 63 ; XII, 23). The observance of rules of conduct and injunctions of sacred law is presented as having a sanction in this aspect of human personality and its eternal good. Religio-philosophical sanction for morality, injunctions of sacred law and social behaviour are thus based on the abiding good of the human personality in addition to the divine origin of law and morality.

It must be pointed out that the term 'antarātman', as also 'ātman', stands in the *Bhagavadgītā* for 'mind' or 'internal mental organ', i.e., 'manas' or 'antaḥkaraṇa', in a number of passages (VI, 47 ; XI, 28 ; II, 64 ; V, 7, 11, 17, 21 ; VI, 7, 14, 29, 36 ; IX, 26 ; XIII, 7 ; XVIII, 49, 54).

The view of human personality in action, apart from the role of the embodied soul and also of the Supreme Soul, who, as 'antaryāmin' or 'inner controller', is believed to 'reside' in the heart of man, propounded in the *Bhagavadgītā* may be said to have held the field with slight modification, if any, over the centuries and in the sectarian ramifications. It may now be presented in brief as it is only in continuation of that gathered from the Upaniṣadic texts and stated above.

In the Upaniṣadic view of human personality qualities, traits, mental or moral, as pertaining to aspects of personality are only rarely mentioned. I have already noted the degrees and varieties of perception and knowledge, which are mentioned in one account, and pointed out how it is more linguistic plurality rather than difference of function or product that appears to have determined the terminology. Leaving out these and other mental states, which are more or less mere equivalents, like 'prajñā', 'medhā', 'dhī', either 'buddhi' or 'vijñāna', only few other mental states, like 'bhī', fear, or 'dhṛti', steadfastness, 'śraddhā', faith, 'hrī', humility, 'vicikitsā', doubt or curiosity, and 'saṁkalpa', decision or desire, are predicated of mind, 'manas', in the *Bṛhadāraṇyaka Upaniṣad* (I, 5, 3; III, 2). Other mental states or moral qualities, mentioned in these works but not necessarily in respect of the human personality and its constituents, number altogether about forty and they are: 'asat', untruth; 'ānanda', delight; 'anṛta', untruth; 'ārjava', straightforwardness; 'aśanā', desire to eat; 'āśā', desire; 'bhūti', prosperity; 'brahmacarya', chastity; 'carita' and 'sucarita', good practice; 'cetanā', conation; 'dama', control; 'dayā', compassion; 'dāna', charity; 'dharma', righteous conduct; 'duḥkha', unhappiness; 'harṣa', joy; 'hrī', modesty or humility; 'jūti', impulse; 'kāma', desire; 'kīrti', fame; 'kratu' purpose or desire; 'mahas', greatness; 'manīṣā', intention; 'moda', joy; 'nirveda', distaste or dislike; 'niṣṭhā', steadiness or concentration; 'ojas', lustre or power; 'pāpman', sin; 'pipāsā', desire to drink; 'pramoda', jubilation; 'pratīkṣā', expectation; 'ṛta', truth or straightforwardness; 'saṁvid', sympathy (?); 'saṅga', attachment; 'saṅgata', companionship; 'saṅkalpa', desire or urge; 'sat', truth; 'sattva', essence; 'satya', truth; 'śama; calmness; 'śānti', tranquillity; 'śoka', sorrow; 'śraddhā', faith or inquisitiveness; 'śrī', glory; 'smṛti', memory; 'sukha', happiness or pleasure; 'sūnṛta', courtesy; 'tapas', austerity; 'vṛtta', conduct; 'yaśas', success or fame.

The *Bhagavadgītā* makes up for the omission, met with in the Upaniṣadic speculation, of an operative view of human personality. One important development in metaphysical thought that had taken place, since the Upaniṣadic sages had speculated on the nature of man, the world and the Supreme Soul, was the postulation of three dispositions, possessed by the original material substance or by the lower aspect of the Supreme Soul, out of which the man and the whole universe were developed. And as such the three dispositions *ipso facto* are taken as constituents of the human personality diversifying its mental, moral and active sides. The *Bhagavadgītā* (XIII, 5) incorporating this doctrine and working it out fully does so by including 'avyakta', or 'prakṛti', i.e., primordial matter, out of which the five great elements, 'pañcamahābhūtas', got developed and which along with them and the mental categories of 'manas', 'buddhi' and 'ahaṁkāra' it speaks of as the eightfold but lower aspect of the Supreme Soul (VII, 4). In the case of the embodied soul the configuration of these eight with the addition of 'avyakta', i.e., the three dispositions of 'goodness', 'dustiness' and 'darkness', in balanced composition, along with the ten organs and the five objects of the five sense-organs, thus forming a group of twentyfour items, is the field or the domain over which it presides. This field, ordinarily called body, is augmented in the text of the

Gītā with the significant addition of certain mental and moral traits which a human personality shows in its routine operation. The whole complex is therefore in the tenor of the field-terminology. The field in manifestation or operation is 'savikāram', which literally means 'inclusive of changes' (XIII, 6). These traits, whose enumeration must be understood to be only indicative and not exhaustive, are : 'desire', 'hate', 'pleasure', 'pain', 'steadfastness' ('dhṛti') and 'conation' ('cetanā'). There is one more item in the list of the text which is rather problematic and is clearly tautologous. It is 'saṁghāta', i.e., the combination of the items or the total whole.

The incongruity hinted at above regarding the listing of 'avyakta' among the constituents of human personality, though it is absent in the enumeration of the eightfold lower nature of the Supreme Soul, was fully realized by Śaṅkarācārya, who in his commentary on *BhG*, VII, 5 included 'avyakta' in 'ahaṁkāra', with the explanation that 'ahaṁkāra' meant 'avyakta' endowed with desire ('vāsanā'). He had thus no difficulty in identifying the set of items enumerated in the first half of *BhG*, XIII, 5 with the eightfold lower aspect of *BhG*, VII, 5.

Expounding human personality in operation the *BhG* does not reiterate the Upaniṣadic ideas on the subject of the identity in essence between the five cosmic elements and the five sense-organs on the one hand and the five organs of action on the other, with which the individual operates. Nor does it mention this aspect of cosmic and individual identity in its cosmology which is given in the briefest outline. The organs are thus placed under the charge of the mind though their objects in the external or material world form their immediate excitants (*BhG*, II, 67 ; III, 6-7 ; III, 41 ; VI, 24). It is this fact that leads to their description as 'erring' (*BhG*, II, 60).

In conformity with the importance of the mind as the agency of control over organs, its fickle and wayward nature itself has to be appreciated. For after all mind, 'manas', is not an entity with a concrete structure and a more or less regulated function, but a construct, a complex, which is a postulate necessitated by the facts of functioning of the organs of life. It is the receptive or the perceptive side of the human personality, a capability of it, which enables the sensations as they occur being recorded and perceived. As such it is likely to be in tune with the functioning of the organs and therefore their boon-companion rather than their master and controller. The fickleness of mind, 'manas', is therefore stressed ; the need to bring it under control is urged ; and a simplified technique selected out of the completely developed complex of 'Yoga', calculated to calm the mind and tranquillize and fit it for controlling the powerful organs is recommended in the *Bhagavadgītā* (VI, 10-14, 18, 19, 26, 27, 34, 35).

The structure and physiology of the human breath ('prāṇa'), and heart ('hṛd'), have been mentioned, however briefly, in the earlier paragraphs, as they figure in the Upaniṣads without going into the technique based on them and the use, if any, made of them in religio-philosophical practice in those times. This is the proper place for a short statement on that aspect of the achievement of the Upaniṣadic age. The numerous channels, 'nāḍīs', their spread round the heart etc. are already mentioned. Here I shall speak of the use to which that knowledge was put. The *Kaṭha Upaniṣad* (II, 3, 10-11) asserts that when the five sense-organs together with mind ('manas'), stand unmoved and steady, and when understanding ('buddhi') does not function, one attains the highest mental state, evidently for spiritual living: "That condition of steady control of the senses" they call Yoga, on attainment of which one keeps non-distracted. In the same text (II, 3, 18) we are informed that the God of Death expounded to the inquisitive and intrepid lad Naciketas not only the highest philosophical knowledge but also "the whole of the Yoga-technique". We thus are assured that quite early in the Upaniṣadic age the knowledge of human physiology, however arrived at, was put to the very significant and practical use of formulating a technique for tranquillizing the mind, and even the higher mental function of understanding or 'buddhi'.

In the *Śvetāśvatara Upaniṣad,* where (II, 2-3), as in the *Kaṭha* (I, 3, 4-5), controlled mind is praised and is asserted to be the proper prerequisite for praying, we are presented with a brief description of how to attempt the control of mind and almost a full statement of the miraculous results of the attainment of the complete and the final stage of the Yoga-attitudes (I, 14; II, 8-14). In the first passage the imagery used is the familiar one of the daily routine of fire-kindling. It is stated that of the two sticks, which when rubbed properly against each other give out the spark of fire, one's body is the lower stick in the practice of Yoga for concentration. The upper stick is the mystic syllable 'aum'. And meditation is the technique which produces the necessary friction, the fire in this case being the vision of God. In plain language it means that meditating on the mystic syllable 'aum' in a concentrated manner, blocking out all external thoughts, ideas or even objects, reveals the vision of God to the concentrated mind. In the latter passage the prescription enjoins that sitting on a fairly raised seat, keeping the body straight—the spinal cord has to remain quite vertically straight—the organs have to be confined, with the help of the mind, within the heart. The spot to be chosen for the seat is further specified. In that state, the mind, which is as it were being carried by unruly horses in the form of the organs, has to be kept steady. An adept in the technique by its practices is guaranteed a lustrous body and a number of other miraculous or extraordinary attainments. Whether those powers are desired or not, whether they are made use of or not, the ulterior result of the attainment is the glorious vision of God and final beatitude.

The *Bhagavadgītā* does not allude to any powers as the result of the 'yoga' technique laid down in it. The technique is fairly simple; and it is doubtful if it is intended to lead to the acquisition of the last two stages of the complete system, i.e., 'dhāraṇā' and 'samādhi', in ordinary daily life. Its main purpose is to stabilize the mind and to enable it to control the organs (VI, 11-15).

However 'dhāraṇā' with breath confined in the head, accompanied by the muttering of the mystic syllable 'aum', is mentioned as a sure way of final release (*BhG*, VIII, 12-3). The main difference, however, between the view-point of the *Upaniṣads* and the *Bhagavadgītā* in the matter of human personality in operation is that the latter enthrones 'buddhi', understanding or reason, assuming its primacy over mind, 'manas', which is after all a double-faced organ and as such more or less one of them. 'Buddhi', on the other hand, is an independent mental capacity, which, in modern terminology, may be identified with the functions of the cerebral cortex. The *BhG* characterizes 'buddhi' as 'vyavasāyātmikā', i.e., as leading to or consisting in decision (II, 41), or as Śaṅkarācārya, in his commentary on II, 41 ; III 42 ; VII, 10 ; VII, 24 ; X, 4 ; XII, 14 ; XVIII, 51, put it, is either of the nature of decision or of the essence of discrimination or subtle distinction.

In keeping with this view of the relations between mind ('manas'), and reason ('buddhi'), the *BhG* (XVIII, 30-32) distinguishes the latter in three degrees and kinds according as it is conditioned by one or the other of the three dispositions, 'sattva', 'rajas' or 'tamas', but not the mind. Similarly the Lord identifies Himself with 'buddhi' of the intelligent ones (*BhG*, VII, 10). As for the mind, the Lord says He is 'mind' among the organs (X, 22) but does not identify Himself with the mind of any one.

The importance attached to the mental capacity called 'buddhi', or reason for short, is further indicated by the number of times the category, either in combination, compound or by itself, is used in the *BhG*. I have noted at least fortythree occasions or places where the term occurs in the whole disquisition. There are at least nine other occasions, when the more or less equivalent words 'prajñā' and 'medhā' are used.

In all these contexts, wherever the two, 'manas' and 'buddhi', occur the latter is clearly the superior capacity ; elsewhere the mental complex is incomplete without the latter. I think the early passage *BhG*, II, 65 is the only one where the context suggests as if steadfastness of 'buddhi' was dependent on some mental capacity or function other than it. Otherwise 'buddhi' is the true and sure refuge of all spiritual seekers (*BhG*, II, 49 ; X, 10).

'Buddhi' is helped by 'dhṛti' (VI, 25), a moral quality, which like it can exist in three varieties being conditioned by one or the other of the three dispositions ('guṇas'), and is mentioned at least ten times in the disquisition.

Even in actual reference, mind ('manas') either as 'manas' or 'mānasa' occurs about five times less than the superior category. And there are at least twenty references to another aspect of mind under the category of 'citta' or 'cetas', which, as we saw, only very occasionally figures in the Upaniṣadic texts. Śaṅkarācārya very often renders 'citta' by 'antaḥkaraṇa', internal organ. He has rendered at times even 'ātman', especially when it occurs as the latter member of a compound word, by the same term (*BhG*, II, 64 ; VI, 14, 29, 36, 47 ; XI, 24), and twice at least 'buddhi', too, by it (*BhG*, XVIII, 7 and 49). We may conclude from this development that a new aspect of mental capacity or a fresh mental function, not clearly envisaged in the earlier analysis, was being realized and formulated into a category.

The triad of 'manas', 'buddhi' and 'ahaṁkāra' (mind, reason and ego-sense) continues to be the complex of internal organs, i.e., the mental capacities which perceive, discriminate or reason out, and appropriate. The last capacity I propose henceforward to speak of as volitional; for the individual appropriation of a certain decision is the main motive power for putting it into action. The will to do tends to be a companion and even a result of the acceptance by the ego of decisions as one's own. The integral organs or the complex of mental capacities which can normally bear training and control, of course, are the first two. With the attempt at mastery over the third, i.e., the ego-sense, one moves into the sphere of high spirituality and profound metaphysics.

In the *Bhagavadgītā*, the term 'hṛd', heart, occurs at least four times (VIII, 12 ; XIII, 17 ; XV, 15 ; XVIII, 61). In three of these it figures as the place of abode of the Supreme Soul or God. In one (VIII, 12) it is the place, rendered by Śaṅkarācārya by 'hṛt-puṇḍarīka', heart-lotus, where 'manas' (mind) is to be confined to gain complete control over the external world and to attain appropriately tuned mental condition, technically called 'dhāraṇā', steady concentration. This may be taken to imply that according to the tenets of the *Gītā* heart was also conceived as the abode of the embodied soul, 'jīva' or 'kṣetrajña'.

The placing of the mind with the nine doors of the body locked up in the heart, 'hṛd', by bringing it under complete control by means of concentration, 'samādhi', became an accepted doctrine of the Yoga-technique and was appraised as such by the later élite. Thus Kālidāsa in his *Kumārasambhava* (III, 50), describing the austerity embarked upon by God Śiva or Hara, states that the God had achieved this feat and was engaged in the act of "looking into the Absolute", which made the god of Love lose his mastery over himself and rendered him helpless to discharge his arrows. The great commentator Mallinātha, commenting on the text, has quoted an appropriate passage from Vāsiṣṭha, i.e., I take it, from the book known as *Yogavāsiṣṭha,* the Yoga as propounded by Vasiṣṭha.

Besides the psycho-ethical traits which are earlier mentioned as an additional component of the human personality as conceived in the *BhG*, there are conditions or states ('bhāva'), which, emanating ultimately from God, are the individual's endowments in varying ways, depending on the latter's stage of psycho-spiritual development. There are twenty of them enumerated (X, 4-5) out of which three are the negations or opposites of other three traits. And 'pain', or 'sorrow' (duḥkha'), though a positive category, is but the opposite of happiness (sukha). Leaving these four out, we have sixteen states or traits with which an individual human personality is intimately related. It is significant that this list should begin with 'buddhi', reason. It stresses the significant role the *BhG* attaches to reason as a component of the human personality, though its being grouped with such items as charity, pleasure, fear or austerity stfikes one as rather strange. 'Sukha' and 'duḥkha', which are said to form part of the body in XIII, 6, curiously figure among these.

There are two other categories, both mental states, to which in another context the *BhG* (III, 37-43 ; V, 23-28 ; XVI, 12, 18 ; XVII, 5 ; XVIII, 53) assigns significant roles, which, by their very nature, appear to belong to the group characterized above as states emanating from God, like fear. They are attachment (kāma), and wrath (krodha). Their force is so impetuous that they are declared to be the arch enemies of man, clouding human personality. For they occupy the organs, fill the mind and even reason and thus entice away the individual from the right path. Desire ('icchā') and hate ('dveṣa') form part of the human personality (XIII, 6) ; but attachment ('kāma') and wrath ('krodha') are not included in the psycho-ethical extension of the dimensions of human personality. We have to understand the enumeration of psycho-ethical traits as components of human personality as being merely illustrative and not exhaustive.

I have listed, omitting purely negative ones, not less than seventy-five different psycho-ethical or religio-ethical items mentioned in the whole disquisition of the *BhG*. In regard to a very large number of these, their valuation as manifestations of human personality in operation is more or less clear in the context.

For the next stage of thought on the subject, I shall pass on to Jñāneśvara's commentary on the *BhG*. Jñāneśvara to Rāmadāsa spans a period of about four centuries just as from the early *Upaniṣads* to the *BhG* covers a period of over four centuries. While the development of the latter period lay in the north and took place through the medium of Sanskrit, language of the élite, that of the other lay in Maharashtra and was effected with the help of one of the people's languages, Marathi.

Jñāneśvara's work, on which I have drawn, being the most widely read and held in the highest esteem, is known as *Jñāneśvarī** and is a commentary on the *BhG*. It is thirteen times as much in extent as its original, the *BG*. Jñāneśvara's view on human personality, apart from the few special features to be mentioned, on the whole conforming with that in the *BhG* harkens back to that of the Upaniṣads even more. Thus in the matter of the human organs of sense Jñāneśvara (XVIII, 349-51) brings in the Upaniṣadic views of their origin from and their quasi-identity with the divinities and luminaries already specified in the relevant sections above. There is no occasion for Jñāneśvara to expound the significance of this identity, in the text. He has, however, found sufficient reason to emphasize the significance of at least one of the five great elements or divinities, viz., air ('vāyu'). The opportunity is twofold.

First, in the Vedānta philosophy of Bādarāyaṇa, 'prāṇa', or life-breath, came to acquire great importance. Almost the whole of the fourth section of chapter II of Bādarāyaṇa's *Brahma-Sūtras*[6] is devoted to the discussion of life-breath,

---

* The text used by me is Balakrishna Anant Bhide's *Sartha Jñāneśvarī* (Marathi), 1928.

its significance and manifestation along with a disquisition on the importance and nature of 'air' as one of the group of the five "great beings", the only other element getting somewhat of that treatment being light, 'jyoti' as it is termed in the text. And Śaṅkarācārya commenting on the 14th aphorism affirmed that "it is determined on the authority of the scriptures, that the Prāṇas are presided over by deities".

The second ground for Jñāneśvara to bring in the view of the organs being presided over by deities or the "great beings" is provided by what appears to have been his own elaboration of the elements, making up the human body, the field ('kṣetra') of the *BhG*. Commenting on *BhG*, XIII, 5-6 which specify the *Gītā* view of the human personality as having thirtyone components in place of the earlier and the usual number of only twentyfour or twentyfive, Jñāneśvara (XIII, 149-50, 155; XU, 484) has raised them to thirtysix. The group of his thirtysix is made up by the addition of five new components to the already specified number of thirtyone. And these five are, according to Jñāneśvara (XIII, 119-20; XVIII, 334-5) the five activities associated with the five organs of action, these having been provided with something analogous to the five specific functions of the five sense-organs. He calls them 'objects', just as the specific functions of the sense-organs are called in the standard terminology. These activities in his view are further the result of a particular aspect of the "great being" air ('vāyu') presiding over them (?).

On examining the functions attributed to these organs of action one finds that they are not quite specific and exclusive to each one, nor has each one only one type of specific function. The analogy proves to be very partial. Perhaps Jñāneśvara himself might have felt so. For in his comment on *BhG*, XVIII, 14 he speaks of the human body as a "family house" of twentyfour 'elements' (XVIII, 318-9). Anyway his view does not appear to have found favour with the later thinkers. Rāmadāsa, about four centuries after Jñāneśvara, elaborating a number of the older doctrines, did not incorporate this one of Jñāneśvara's.

Two categories, heart ('hṛdaya') and reflective capacity ('citta'), become more prominent in Jñāneśvara's system. Indeed, the latter comes to be a specific aspect, or to be conceived of as a distinct organ by itself, as one of a group of four, of what is called 'antaḥkaraṇa-catuṣṭaya', "group of four internal organs". The three others are the old triad of mind ('manas'), reason ('buddhi') and volition ('ahaṁkāra') (*Jñāneśvarī*, XV, 94-7; XVIII, 498).

Calling it 'cidvṛtti', reflective urge or desire, he equates it with the 'mahat-tattva' of the Sāṁkhya system. This identification and specification occur in a context of the *BhG* where there is no direct mention of it in the text but only a general reference to the mundane world and its evolution and nature. Where the text of the *BhG* itself has 'citta' or 'cetas' Jñāneśvara generally keeps the word in his rendering, sometimes using also 'cittavṛtti' (V, 148; VIII, 81-5; XVIII, 1261, 1267-9). While explaining *BhG*, V, 11, where only 'buddhi' and 'manas' are the mental categories mentioned in the text, he brings in both the categories of 'citta' and 'ahaṁkāra' in his explanation. For the context, speaking of the cleansing power of non-attached activity, is concerned with the whole human personality in operation.

It is noteworthy, that Jñāneśvara should speak of 'citta' as if it was 'cidākāśa', 'cid-ether' (V, 153; VIII, 95), which immediately brings to mind the term 'hṛdākāśa' of the Upaniṣads and of other religio-philosophical systems. But what is clearly intended is to imply its identity with the 'brahmarandhra', 'brahma-hole', the top-suture of the skull, the most desired exit for the embodied soul, 'jīva' or 'prāṇa', to depart. However, keeping to his text and his practice, he is prone to identify both 'manas' and 'citta', the latter more than the former, with 'antaḥkaraṇa' as a whole (VI, 186; VIII, 113-4, 122; XIII, 511-512; XVI, 369; XV, 97). Even heart is once spoken of as 'antaḥkaraṇa' (X, 20). Once 'buddhi' is separately mentioned from it (XIII, 967).

Speaking about heart, as a matter of fact, Jñāneśvara, at least in one place (IX, 28), speaks of it as "hṛdaya-ākāśa", heart-ether, and at least thrice (II, 71; VI, 280, 286) he mentions it as heart-lotus. Generally, however, he leaves the word 'hṛdaya' as it is, recognizing it as a physical entity, which, in accordance with the doctrines of the *BhG*, he takes as the abode of both the Supreme Soul and the embodied soul, 'jīva' or 'kṣetrajña' (II, 317; VIII, 124; XII, 153; XIII, 939; XV, 421; XVIII, 61). The *Gītā*-view that the organs have to be controlled by the mind, 'manas', and that the latter has, for being quietened, to be confined within the heart, i.e., even mental experience of sense-objects has to be discontinued so that heart remains open and free for the pure light to shine out, is also accepted and stated more than once (II, 321, 325; VI, 188, 460; VIII, 113, 184; IX, 215; XII, 47; XIII, 130).

The great Rāma-devotee chanter of North India, Tulasīdāsa, about two and a half centuries later, often places the Supreme Soul as the controller in the heart, using the word 'ura', or 'hṛdaya', to denote this abode in the individual (*Rāmāyaṇa*, pp. 634, 799, 800, 1127, 1155).

It would have been surprising if Jñāneśvara, an adept in the Yoga-technique, perhaps the greatest known, to be bracketed with Gorakhanātha himself, had not, with so much instruction on the Yoga-technique and glowing description of some of the esoteric features of its mastery and the phased experience (VI, 54-60, 163, 390, 460-73; VIII, 92-115; IX, 212-18, 422; XII, 46-59; XVIII, 333-42; 1035-41), followed up the Upaniṣadic view about the marvellous net of channels round the heart, and the still more wonderful and rarified food they offer to the embodied soul who sits in the heart-lotus amidst their net-work. Jñāneśvara informs us that the net of channels itself is the mysterious 'kuṇḍalinī' and speaks of 'her' as "great goddess", consisting of pure light and is designed as the fine food, of course of the embodied soul (VI, 221-29, 273-4, 280-82, 299-301, XVIII, 1038-40).

Bādarāyaṇa and the Vedānta philosophy founded on his great work had resuscitated the view of the identity of the human organs with the divinities or of their being presided over by them. Just as Jñāneśvara accepted the view and referred to it, similarly Tulasīdāsa in his popular book *Rāmayaṇa* (VII, 186, 11-16, p. 1176)* gave currency to it. This is the more remarkable as evidence of the general acceptance of the view among the élite and semi-élite of the Hindu world, of the partial divinity, even in the material part of it, of the human personality.

'Buddhi', in spite of the fourth internal organ, viz. 'citta', being added to the previous triad, continues to have primacy in Jñāneśvara's view, as in that of the *BhG*, in the human personality in operation. He characterizes 'buddhi' as the faculty which "decides what is happiness, what is misery, which selects what is good from what is bad, which knows what is poison to the embodied soul, *which is the origin of the element 'light-heat' ('tejas') which develops the 'sattva' quality and effects the union of the embodied soul with Ātman*" (*XIII*, 86-88).† He conceives it metaphorically as the food of the embodied soul fed to it by the mysterious master channel, 'kuṇḍalinī' (VI, 280-2).

The spiritual component of human personality, after Bādarāyaṇa named it 'jīva', has continued to be so named, Jñāneśvara using the term almost uniformly except in a few places where he has to mention its other name 'kśetrajña', as the context referring to the metaphysical categories like 'kṣara'/'akṣara' or 'kṣetra'/'kṣetrajña' or 'brahma' (XV, 494-5 ; XIII, 7-9, 1135) requires it, or when he himself happens to explain things in purely metaphysical terms (XIV, 79-80).

The use of the term 'jiva' for the embodied soul has facilitated, perhaps with the practice initiated by Śaiva sects, the aphoristic and alliterating combination 'Jīva-Śiva', giving us a stereotype for the ordinarily incomprehensible doctrine of the identity and unity of the Supreme Soul and the individual soul. I do not know when this combination first came into use ; but I find in Jñāneśvara's work the theoretical postulation of it in the supremely enlightening experience, and its convincing expression by a great 'siddha' or "enlightened being" (*Jñāneśvarī*, VI, 273-92, 301). And if I have understood the text correctly this theoretical postulation appears to have been taken by him from a Śaivite source. Being himself, in spite of his affiliation with the Nātha sect, a great Vaiṣṇava, he corrects this one-sided identification by bringing in Mahāviṣṇu (VI, 291).

Rāmadāsa, whose activity spans the first three decades of the latter half of the 17th century, a period agog with martial spirit, guerilla activity, tremendous courage and untold self-sacrifice on the part of the people of Maharashtra, the region of Rāmadāsa's birth and activity, in spite of his activist and militant religious attitude, side by side with his politically energizing message, preached not only the cult of the deity Rāma and his factotum the monkey-God Hanuman but also a sort of monistic faith accompanied by a complete theory and a comprehensive mode of approach. He is one of the rare writers

* Shri Venkateshvara Press edition with the commentary of Pandit Jwalaprasada Mishra.

† Italics mine.

who composed an independent treatise on religio-philosophical topics in the vernacular language. And his treatise is much more independent and embodies a markedly original scheme of the nature of the universe and man, and their relation, and a more complete system of worship and daily routine than perhaps of any other vernacular writer who lived before him.

Rāmadāsa carries out the principle of quintuplication through and through and postulates human personality with twentyfive components in subtle form and twentyfive in gross form. Thus the human personality in Rāmadāsa's scheme has fifty components with the embodied soul, 'jīva' or jīvātmā', the spiritual component, as the fiftyfirst (*Dāsabodha*, XVII, 8, 3-29 ; XIII, 1, 1-25 ; XVI, 7, 14-22 ; XVII, 6, 1-4 ; XVII, 9, 11-22 ; XX, 1, 25-6 ; XX, 7, 13-15, 18 ; XX, 8, 3-10).

Rāmadāsa presents a whole theory of human personality in operation with the specific workings of the different components clearly enunciated (XVII, 8). The urge, the inspiration of life, he places at the navel and equates the capacity with the 'parā'-variety or -grade of 'speech', the highest of the four (*Dāsabodha*, XII, 5, 8) postulated in the Vedānta-cum-Yoga philosophy, though they do not appear to have any sanction in either the *Upaniṣads* or in Bādarāyaṇa's *Brahma-Sūtras*. Jñāneśvara, the supreme mystic, commenting on *BhG*, VI, 15, and developing his scheme of 'yogic'-practice for complete concentration, has mentioned at least two of these four 'vāṇīs', speech, i.e., 'paśyantī' and 'vaikharī' (VI, 303, 312) in that connection. Earlier in describing the attainment of 'success' (VI, 271) he has mentioned the third higher variety of it, i.e., 'madhyamā', the middle one, imagining it to be a sort of a staircase for this attainment to reach the heart. Again in VIII, 94 he brings in the same variety but this time in connection with the uppermost aperture, the 'brahma-hole' so-called, with the staircase metaphor again in XX, 55. The variety called 'parā' by Rāmadāsa is also called 'sūkṣmā', subtle, and is otherwise known as 'anapāyinī', firm or imperishable.

Rāmadāsa places his fifth unit of the group of five internal organs, the 'antaḥkaraṇa' par excellence, in the 'parā' speech itself at the navel. It is here and through this 'antaḥkaraṇa' that a spontaneous initiative or urge starts. The faculty or capacity that thereafter takes hold of the idea, or whatever form the urge takes, and hesitates and wavers over it is 'mana', i.e., as I understand it, properly the perceptive aspect of the whole mind in the modern sense or the purely mental component of human personality. It is 'buddhi' that makes a rational choice, reasons about the correctness or otherwise of the mental urge ; 'citta' revolves on it, and 'ahaṁkāra', ego-sense, propels to action. That is why I think we have to equate 'ahaṁkāra' of the Hindu view of human personality with volitional aspect of personality in terms of psychology. These five mental aspects together form the five-fold internal organ, 'antaḥkaraṇa'.

Five organs of action, five organs of sensation or knowledge, five objects of these sense-organs, i.e., their capacities whereby sound, touch, light, flavour and smell convey the impression of the external world to the mind and the human personality, five breaths, and five internal organs, these twentyfive items form the subtle body. Rāmadāsa goes a step further than, I think, all the previous thinkers—at least his elaboration is not found either in the *BhG* or in the *Jñāneśvarī*—and assigns to every one of the five 'great beings', viz., ether, air, light-heat, water and earth, five of these items, there being only one each in the group of five from one of the five quintets making up the twentyfive 'subtle' components. The order too of the enumeration of these five great beings, is peculiarly his, he, as is briefly mentioned in the cosmological chapter, according the greatest significance and priority to ether, next after which he places air. In this scheme while 'mana', mind, is a transformation of air, 'antaḥkaraṇa' is that of ether and 'buddhi' that of light-heat. Water contributes 'citta', and the dross earth supplies 'ahaṁkāra', so despised from the spiritual point of view (XVII, 8, 10-22).

Rāmadāsa develops, evidently out of the *BhG*-statements on 'kāma', desire, and 'krodha', wrath (III, 37-43), as also on 'icchā', wish, and other six moral and mental traits (XIII, 6) conceived as parts of human personality, a whole doctrine of a gross body composed of the 'great beings' (XVII, 8, 23-29). The five physical constituents of the body, viz., bones, flesh, epidermis, channels (nāḍīs) and hair are the transformations of the element earth. Semen, blood, saliva, urine and sweat are the contributions of the element water, and movement, bending, extension, contraction and withdrawal are the work of air. Hunger, thirst, sloth, sleep and sexual urge are the effects of the element light-heat, while the purely psycho-ethical traits of desire ('kāma'), anger ('krodha'), sorrow ('śoka'), infatuation ('moha'), and fear ('bhaya') are the effects of the most important, semi-spiritual element in Rāmadāsa's scheme, ether (IV, 9, 24 ; VIII, 5, 35-6 ; IX, 9, 21).

The dweller in and the owner of, this body, of course, is the spiritual component of human personality and is almost invariably referred to as 'jīva' or 'jīvātman' or 'jīveśvara', i.e., 'jīva-lord'. He is the experiencer, the knower and the decider (XI, 1, 34-5 ; XIII, 9, 1-38 ; XV, 1, 1-10 ; XVI, 7, 12-22, 30-33). With 'jīva' as the word for the embodied soul, the identification of the Supreme Soul with it became facilitated in alliterative and convenient mode in the duality or compound 'jīva-śiva' or 'jīvātmā-śivātmā'. And Rāmadāsa uses the alliterative combination quite often (VIII, 3, 18 ; VIII, 7, 43-50 ; IX, 6, 35 ; X, 10, 18 ; XI, 1, 38 ; XIII, 1, 24 ; XVI, 8, 6 ; XX, 1, 25).

'Viveka' is an extra category which figures very frequently in Rāmadāsa's disquisition and scheme, though it is not postulated as a component of human personality in any the widest of his schemes. It is evidently a particular aspect of or working of 'buddhi', reason, and it is necessary now to bring some evidence to establish this statement. With this identification it would be admitted that in Rāmadāsa's view of human personality the embodied soul and the component of 'buddhi', reason, occupy the central position. The embodied soul has the power to, and, therefore, is expected to, act with reason as the guide.

'Viveka', discrimination and balanced thought in combination, is the arbiter of almost everything (II, 7, 9 ; V, 10, 30 ; VI, 9, 24-25 ; VIII, 7, 64-65 ; X, 9, 25-8 ; XIII, 1, 1-2 ; XIII, 7, 27-9 ; XIII, 9, 40 ; XIV, 1, 77 ; XV, 1, 6, 10 ; XV, 3, 5; XV, 8, 36-7; XVII, 10, 2, 4, 16, 18, 27, 29 ; XVIII, 2, 27 ; XVIII, 3, 1-2 ; XVIII, 6, 21-2 ; XVIII, 7, 19-20 ; XVIII, 8, 14-17, 25 ; XVIII, 10, 17, 38-40, 46-8 ; XIX, 6, 27-30 ; XX, 5, 26-7, 30 ; XX, 7, 25, 27 ; XX, 10, 29).

In one place Rāmadāsa (XVII, 8, 7) speaks of both 'buddhi' and 'viveka' in one context in such a manner that the latter appears as if it is a superior faculty, but the insistence on 'buddhi' as the faculty by which one, the embodied soul, decides, must mean that the two go together as one, 'viveka' being only a specific aspect of the activity of 'buddhi' or reason. That is why he speaks of 'buddhi' as God's gift, without which a man is useless, an unripe fruit or an unbaked piece of clay (XV, 1, 15). In the alternative he identifies 'buddhi', the faculty of properly knowing or discriminating, with God Brahmā in the body, i.e., asserts that just as in the cosmos God Brahmā fills the role of the creator so in the individual personality 'buddhi' plays the dominant role of the creative force (IX, 5, 7 ; X, 1, 30 ; X, 4, 17-19).

CHAPTER VII

HINDU VIEW OF LIFE AFTER DEATH

A PEOPLE'S view of life after death is intimately connected with their cosmology and cosmography. But their view of the human personality may not be so connected, though their acceptance of the idea of a spiritual and imperishable element as its constituent or non-acceptance of it appears to have such a relation. The Buddhists alone, it appears to me, with their indifference about the probability of the human soul, could and can think of complete annihilation called 'Nirvāṇa' as the final condition of human beings in their endeavour of living their lives well and usefully! In the case of the Hindus whose views on human personality are conditioned by their cosmology both sets are very intimately connected with, nay may be said to determine in a large measure, the people's view of life after death.

In the earliest stage of Hinduism, as far as it can be judged from the scattered references in the hymns of the *Rgveda*, which must be dated between 1800 to 1200 B.C., we are aware of the people having belief in a spiritual or non-material element as a constituent of human personality. This element could wander away from the material body and could return to it under certain circumstances. Though it is designated as 'manas', mind, it is generally considered to be the same as 'soul' of later terminology. There is a whole hymn concerning it (*RV*, X, 58). There are a number of hymns which either are concerned with describing in some part what happens at death or refer to the conditions after death. Perhaps, the most important one from our view-point and for the subject of discussion in this chapter, is the 14th hymn of the Xth book of the *Rgveda*. The spirit or the soul of the dead is asked to proceed by the paths made by seers of old to the realm of the Fathers, where both Yama, the deified Lord of the Dead, and Varuṇa, the Law-giver, dwell. It is asked to meet Yama and the Fathers as well as the merit of the acts, ordained or/and voluntary, performed by the person while living, there in the highest heaven. In the Ṛgvedic universe three heavens, lowest, middle and highest, are postulated (*RV*, I, 35, 6; VIII, 5, 8; VIII, 41, 9; IX, 113, 9). The soul is conjured to leave sin and evil [down below ?] and seek its new dwelling, the highest heaven, the world of the Fathers and of Yama, their Lord, and of Varuṇa, the Law-giver. Perhaps this clearance from sin and evil was to be accomplished through the agency of the rays of the sun and the passage of the soul through the realm of eternal light. The Fathers are said to be connected with the rays of the sun or are united with or are said to guard the sun; and their abode is described as the highest point of the sun, or they are connected with the highest step of Viṣṇu; and pious men are said to rejoice in the highest step of Viṣṇu (*RV*, I, 109, 7; I, 154, 5; IX, 113, 7-11; X, 14, 8-10; X, 15, 3; X, 15, 14; X, 107, 2; X, 154, 4-5).

In the abode of the Fathers, the world of Yama where Varuṇa too is present, in the highest heaven, the spirit of the deceased unites with a glorious or refulgent body. The resurrected dead becomes dear and welcome to gods and enters upon a delectable life. For the Lord of the Dead and the blessed sits under a tree with fine [eternal ?] foliage (*RV*, X, 135, 1 ; *AV*, V, 4, 3) drinking with the gods in the company of Varuṇa, in a world where there is 'pasturage', which nobody can rob the dead of. There old age and other frailties and imperfections of mundane life do not exist. There the strong cannot subject the weak. In immortal life the dead, when they reach there, join Yama to delight themselves at his banquet, which is evidently imperishable and continuous. The strength of the body acquired in the resurrected form in the realm of Yama is said to vary with the faithfulness with which the rules are observed in life. With the resurrected form the dead person is believed to be able to go on without food for "thirteen days, and later four, six or twelve months or even a hundred years". Finally "they are able altogether to dispense with it". Deussen summarized the conditions of living in the world of Yama as described in this early literature, in the following felicitous verses, more than half a century ago : "The kingdom of inexhaustible light, . . . Among the holiest of the heavenly world, ... Where the third loftiest heaven spreads its vault, . . . Where resides bliss and felicity . . . . Where the craving of desire is stilled, There suffer me to dwell immortal."[1] The last line expressing the desire of a dying person pinpoints the state of the dead in the realm of the hereafter.

In more particulars, the life in the realm of the pious dead is full of music and singing, of the elevating drink 'soma', of ghee, of milk and of honey. One meets one's parents and children too, as the *Atharvaveda* states : The joys are said to be hundredfold higher and deeper than those of the earth, as the two or three centuries later work, the *Śatapathabrāhmaṇa* (XIV, 7, 1, 32-33), has it.[2]

It should be carefully noted that the body is said to be acquired in the hereafter, and that the soul is described more or less clearly as leaving the body without carrying anything with it. It is said to be united with the merit of good mundane work, no doubt ; but there is no indication of any subtle vehicle like the later subtle, or 'liṅga' body, enveloped in which the soul is conceived of as departing in the later theory. Secondly, the existence in the hereafter is very much like that of the gods, more or less independent of any needs of the kind we mortals know of and suffer from. Thirdly, the living in the company of gods, and particularly that of Yama and Varuṇa, indicates that though the possibility of weighing the merits and the demerits of the dead is there, such a test, if any, is to be supposed to have been passed. And it must be with the help of one's merit, and of prayers either offered by oneself or by others on one's behalf to such gods as Agni, Pūṣan, the path-finding deities of the Vedic age.

Pūṣan is prayed to conduct the dead to the Fathers and he sees that they go safely to their destined place (*RV*, VI, 55 and 58 ; X, 17, 4). Both Agni and Savitṛ lead the dead to the abode of the righteous (X, 16, 1-4 ; X, 17, 3).

In order to reach the world of Yama, the Soul had to pass by the two spotted four-eyed dogs of Yama that guard the entrance to it.[3]

The dead on entry into the realm of Yama meet and become one with the Fathers, 'pitṛs' or 'pitaraḥ'. The Fathers are said to be of three classes, the highest, middling and the lowest. They are conceived as sorts of gods; they partake of 'soma' and are said to deserve a share of such an offering. Agni is invoked and invited to come along with them. They are primeval God-adorers, Eaters and drinkers of oblations and travel with the Deities and Indra. They are known to Agni. They are prayed to for aid and blessings. In short, as Deussen stated more than half a century ago, the Fathers in the *Ṛgveda* figure on a footing of equality with the gods. There are more than half a dozen groups of them mentioned by name as Agniṣvāttas, Aṅgirases, Atharvans, Bhṛgus, Kāvyas, Navagvas, Vairūpas, Vasiṣṭhas, etc.[4]

One direction or request made in *RV*, IX, 90, 13, though it occurs in a different context, is noteworthy as indicating the speculative source of the cardinal ideas of the origin of the human being and his personality. And that is the direction given to the eyes and breath of a dead person to depart to the sun and the wind or air respectively. It has been stated in the previous chapter how, in one of the *Upaniṣad* texts (*BrU*, III, 2, 13) describing what happens at the death of a person, it is asserted that the eyes go to the sun, the breath to the air or wind and the other organs to various other deities. What is expressed as a desire, a wish, a request or a direction in the Ṛgvedic text became in the next three or four centuries, with the speculative development of the current ideas, a fact to be accepted as such and a basis for a whole theory. As S. V. Ketkar pointed out more than forty years ago, no doubt the idea is intimately connected with that cosmology of the Ṛgvedic age which was based on the sacrifice of the Primordial Being described in the famous Puruṣasūkta, the hymn of Puruṣa (the Primordial Being). It is said therein (*RV*, X, 90) that when the Primordial Being was cut up His eyes formed or became the sun and His breath, the wind or air. The direction for the eyes and the breath of a dead person occurs therein too. It is clear that the idea is more or less directly suggested, as Ketkar says, by the cosmological theory.

However it may be, it must be admitted that with this direction for the eyes and the breath of a deceased person, the latter's soul cannot be presumed to be enveloped in or accompanied by any of the organs of the deceased person in a subtle form as its subtle or 'liṅga' body. The notion of the subtle body could have only one of its aspects originating in this idea and had to wait till the more general theory of a subtle state of all natural elements was developed. Even then, in all probability, an intermediate stage of theoretical development, which, I believe, is preserved in the notions of the subtle body mentioned in the *Manusmṛti* (I, 56; XII, 16-22), had to be passed before the full theory could be formulated. Of this development, however, I shall speak later.

At this juncture there is another important point arising out of the description of the Fathers and their world which deserves our special attention. The

Fathers appear in the role of some kind of Divinities and not merely as manes. There are a number of different groups of them, bearing specific names, whatever might have been the principle of naming. In the next period of the development of religious thought we find the groups to be many more. Those that are named, and we are assured that they are only some of the very many such groups evidently known but not specifically mentioned by name in the time of the *Manusmṛti*, which may be ascribed to a time not later than the 2nd century A.D., are: Agnidagdhas, Agniṣvāttas, Anagnidagdhas, Ājyapas, Aṅgirases (Haviṣmantas), Barhiṣadas (Atrijas), Kāvyas (Somapās), Mārācas, Saumyas, Somapās, Vairāṭas (Somasadas), Vasiṣṭhas (Sukālins) (*Manusmṛti*, III, 195-200). It is further stated (loc. cit., I, 33 and 36; III, 194) that the Fathers ('Pitaraḥ' or 'Pitṛgaṇas') are the sons of the ten sages, who are asserted to have been the sons of Manu himself, the grandson of Hiraṇyagarbha, the Golden Embryo that began the creation of the cosmos.

In the early Vedic literature the Fathers are not represented as part of the original creation. They are, however, not only declared to be immortal (*AV*, VI, 41, 3) but are described as Gods (*RV*, X, 56, 4). In a number of texts they are said to be worshipped and prayed for both protection and succour as also for compassion and favour. They are further ascribed some work of the cosmic order.[5] In the *BhG*, about the 2nd century B.C., they figure in the company of multifarious gods as another variety of gods. And Lord Kṛṣṇa (IX, 25) tells Arjuna that the worshippers of the Fathers—an expression which testifies to the god-hood of Fathers and to their regular worship and devotion as an established practice—go after death to them. Thus the world of the Fathers, which as is amply clear from an earlier chapter, the one on cosmology, was a well-known unit in the cosmological and cosmographical notions of the later period, one which antedates the age of the *BhG* by about three to five centuries and thus is separated from and later than the Vedic age by about five to seven centuries.

The Fathers are further mentioned as seen among many Vedic gods like Aśvins, Maruts, Rudras, Ādityas, Vasus and Sādhyas, though under a name, 'uṣmapā', which is a peculiarity of the manes (*BhG*, XI, 22). The *Manusmṛti*, too, mentions them in one place (XII, 49) along with gods, Sādhyas, sages, luminaries and some other categories as the breed which is the consequence of the Sattvaguṇa, the pure quality, while in another place (III, 195) it declares that one of the above-mentioned groups of the Fathers is the manes of the Sādhyas and another of the gods. Again in another mood, the same work states (III, 201) that the Fathers were born from the sages and in turn created gods and men. Further, it declares the Fathers to be even primordial deities that are celibate, pure and un-angered (III, 192). More specifically the *Manusmṛti* (III, 284) identifies the first generation of the Fathers, the Pitṛs, with Vasus; the second, the 'Pitāmahas' (grand-fathers), with Rudras; and the third, the Prapitāmahas (great-grand-fathers), with Ādityas. These are the three main deity-categories that are mentioned along with the Sādhyas and the Fathers in the above quoted text of the *BhG* (XI, 22) together as seen in the open mouth of the Great Being.

The early Vedic literature makes the Fathers immortal like gods, and denizens of the highest heaven in perpetuity.

It becomes necessary to know what kind of a place heaven was considered to be apart from its abounding in perpetual, inexhaustible and varied joys. Was it desired as the goal to which souls of deceased should repair or not, even if we have no reference to the Fathers dwelling there or their nature ? Was it looked upon as a place of sojourn from which the soul had to go after a fixed or varying period ? If heaven was looked upon as a temporary resort, one cannot expect references to it as the goal of the soul after death as if it was the final resort to aspire for, which was the most cherished idea in the pursuit of which all manner of prescribed good living, however trying it may be, was to be attempted through mundane existence.

We have seen in an earlier chapter how some of the Upaniṣadic (cf. *Kena Upaniṣad*, IV, 9) thought represented heaven, 'svarga', as if it was the final resort of the pious and righteous dead. This view carries forward the early Vedic belief in heaven as the be-all and end-all of life after death for the pious and the righteous. The impious and the unrighteous evidently were relegated to the dark world, the nether world, called 'naraka', hell. We have studied, too, the emergence and the almost full-fledged development of the other view, best and earliest represented in the speculations of the Upaniṣadic sages, that even heaven ('svarga') and its joys are perishable. Leaving the further advance of thought and belief in that line for later consideration, I shall have to state in brief the continuities or the vestiges as the case may be of the early Vedic belief in the finality and permanence of heaven and its joys, as the condition of life after death for the pious, a future reward for good life led on this earth.

No testimony in favour of the finality and permanence of heaven and life in it as the future reward of pious and righteous living on earth can be as authoritative and compelling as the persistence of the view that heaven is the final goal of hereafter. Buddha himself always brushed aside any query about it.[6] So much is this the case that D. C. Sircar[7], finding Emperor Aśoka, the first mighty Buddhist follower, speaking of the attainment of 'svarga', heaven, and the importance of safeguarding one's living there after death as the other world to be inhabited, suggests without any authority, and therefore hesitatingly, that "a school of early Buddhists may have believed that the attainment of Svarga by lay worshippers ultimately led them to Nirvāṇa".[?]

Emperor Aśoka in his inscriptions has left to posterity not only his views of what is good, pious and righteous living on earth but also his mental processes which proceeding from and working on them dictated to him his goals, both 'mundane' and 'other-worldly'. The last two expressions, 'mundane' and 'other-worldly', are straight translations of the ones used by the extraordinary Emperor himself in three or four different Prakritic and Sanskritic versions.

For the mundane world he has the following expressions as rendered by D.C. Sircar, evidently following the standard experts on the subject: 'ihaloka', 'aihika', 'aihatya', 'aihalaukika', 'iha', 'ihatya'.[8] For the objective, the goal after death, the other world *par excellence*, he uses words whose Sanskrit equivalents are: 'paraloka', 'paratra', 'pāralaukika', 'pāratrika'.[9]

The gist of Aśoka's pronouncements on his endeavour of living righteously, expressed in the passages referred to here, is that he was convinced that the pattern of activity and living adopted by him and prescribed by him to his subjects was calculated not only to procure earthly fame and happiness but was competent to secure bliss in the hereafter, that world being nothing different from 'svarga', heaven. Actually more than once in these texts he either specifies the wooing of heaven ('svarga') as the goal to be aimed at or asserts that his prescription if followed would grant that reward, which evidently must have been to him and his society a coveted one. Once or twice he even asserts that the bargain for the practitioner of his pattern of living and activity of heaven or 'svarga', is relatively a very favourable one, 'vipula' (vast) in comparison with the endeavour of living involved. In view of this, D. C. Sircar's suggestion, whatever its plausibility in regard to the early Buddhism, that 'svarga' or heaven in Aśoka's inscriptional exhortations is to be taken to imply only an intermediate stage and not a final one of bliss, cannot apply to Aśoka and his teaching as preserved in his inscriptions. To Emperor Aśoka, in spite of his enthusiasm for his new faith, 'svarga' or heaven remained the goal of earthly living to be attained on one's death, the final blissful condition of life after death.

The ten centuries of belief in heaven as the final and blissful condition of life after death, attained by the pious and the righteous, which the Ṛgvedic poet-sages represented as the world of the Fathers, whom, because of it, they portrayed as gods of a kind, had fixed the Fathers and their varied groups or 'houses' as immortal denizens of heaven ('svarga'), so that in spite of the onslaught of the Upaniṣadic school and of the post-Upaniṣadic Buddhist sect on the impermanence of heavenly bliss and the promise and speculative substantiation of an eternally blissful condition as the ideal goal for attainment in the hereafter, the view of heaven ('svarga') as the final abode held sway for a long time.

The view peeps out as a vestige from time to time in many later speculations and deliberations on the subject of life after death. Suffice it here, in order to clinch the issue about 'svarga' and its nature, as they figure in about the 3rd century B.C. in Aśoka's thoughts, to state that the *Manusmṛti* (III, 89), which may be a century or even four centuries later than Aśoka's time, specifically asserts the possibility of life in 'svarga' or heaven being eternal ('akṣayya', inexhaustible). Anticipating a little, I may further mention as evidence of the continuity of this view the fact that on the eve of resurgence of Hinduism in A.D. 279 an inscription from a place near Bhopal, written in Sanskrit, asserts that the utility work, the tank, got executed by the donor was intended to procure for him not only pleasure, happiness and prosperity in this world but also to secure for him hereafter the attainment of eternal 'svarga' happiness ('akṣayya svarga').[10]

That the Fathers were offered some worship or oblation or libation without any reference to one's manes is a practice recorded in a side-reference in Kālidāsa's dynastic semi-epic *Raghuvaṁśa* (V, 8). And Mallinātha, the thirteenth-century learned commentator of the work, names the age-old groups or 'houses' of Fathers, i.e., 'Agniṣvāttas' and others, as the recipients of such attention. We may infer that Kālidāsa's reference was specifically to them and take it as evidence of their currency till his time.

In the *Rāmāyaṇa*, whose compilation may be dated between the 2nd century B.C. and the fourth century A.D., though the groups or 'houses' of the Fathers are not named, the Fathers figure in a number of important legends and incidents. In the potent incantation called 'ādityahṛdaya', sun-heart, the recitation of which on the battlefield was calculated to secure victory to its reciter, imparted by the hoary miracle-working sage Agastya to Rāma (VI, 105, 2-21), among the various names under which the sun is invoked occurs the Fathers ('pitaraḥ') along with Vasus, Sādhyas, Aśvins and other deities as in the earlier texts quoted or referred to above. In a legend, in which a fanciful account of the loss of Indra's testicles and of his having later grafted on him those of a ram is given, it is the Fathers who were importuned by all the gods, they being called not merely 'pitṛs' but 'pitṛdevas', Father-gods, to do the skilful operation (I, 49, 1-10).

At least four of the *Purāṇas*, dated about the 5th century to about the 9th or the 10th, mention a varying number of these groups. In three of them seven of these occurring in the list of the *Manusmṛti* figure. In one, their number is stated to be thirtyone ! The relation between gods and these Fathers is curiously stated to be that of father and son as well as that of son and father. They are stated to be of two kinds, either as embodied and disembodied or as divine and human or as 'deva-deva' and 'santānika' [?] or again as 'express-framed' and 'subtle-framed'. The seven groups are traced to the seven great sages, created with the primordial cosmos. It is also asserted that the human manes became through their own good work the divine Fathers.[11]

The notion that by good and pious living human beings and other similar creatures or their advanced representatives could attain divinity and that the first-stage divine beings could progress into a higher class of divinities, evidently by similar means is a belief implicit in the distinction between 'ājānadevas', born-gods, and 'karmadevas', work-gods, i.e., those gods who attained their divinity through good living, stated in the oldest Upaniṣad, *Bṛhadāraṇyaka* (IV, 3, 32), and referred to in an earlier chapter. In A. B. Keith's opinion the notion that the gods earned their divinity is implicit in the Ṛgvedic mythology.[12] The *Manusmṛti* (I, 22) describing the creation of the cosmos by Brahmā mentions 'Sādhyas' and 'Karmadeva', 'karmātman deva', is the expression used.

Jñāneśvara, in the fourth quarter of the thirteenth century, in his comment (XV, 195-6) on *BhG*, XV, 2, elaborating in detail the picture of the cosmic scene in the imagery of a vast banyan tree, mentions the Fathers along with sages, and Vidyādharas, another mysterious race of beings, and also the sun and the moon as side-branches of it.

Fathers, who were thus originally manes, who had attained godhood and dwelt in heaven in perpetual, ample, and varied bliss, and were in no need of being supplied with food and drink by their descendants living on earth, continued to figure in the imagination and belief of the people ages afterwards as more or less such, even when the development of another set of beliefs about the future condition of the human soul and all life had made such a situation impossible and incompatible with the fully developed theory of life and death!

I shall now review the situation as regards their erstwhile permanent abode heaven ('svarga'), and the means for its attainment and the changes, if any, in it, before examining briefly the rise and progress of the theory of life and death which turned the Fathers and their permanent bliss into a temporary and transitory phenomenon.

The *Rgveda* (X, 154, 1-3) promised heaven after death to doers of certain actions; and that attainment must have guaranteed immortality to them for that is what was desired by the Ṛgvedic poets and their patrons (*RV*, V, 55, 4; V, 63, 2). The *Bhagavadgītā* (IX, 20-21) in the same tune as that of the much earlier philosophical work, the *Chāndogya Upaniṣad* (VIII, 1, 6), asserts the impermanence of the broad and pleasant heavenly world, mentioning that pious people have in the past worked zealously through various sacrifices for its attainment. The heavenly world, blessed and divine, providing enjoyments fit for gods, is called the world of Indra or the Lord of gods.

However, in the epic and other literature and in the doings and aspirations of the heroes of both, there is very clear and outstandingly prominent evidence showing that heaven, 'svarga', or the world of Indra, had continued to be looked upon as the be-all and end-all of life, the goal that was so covetable that no effort for it was considered too heavy or costly. And whether in imitation of or out of inspiration from that assurance of salvation while still living on earth ('jīvanmukti') through a particular system of living or from the recorded examples of such individuals as Vāmadeva and some others, we have in that literature a record of the efforts at the endeavour of walking into or being transported into heaven ('svarga') with the mundane body as either a feat attempted and achieved in green old age, on the eve of the call for death, or in healthy middle age. The notion itself finds mention in the later Vedas where it is stated that by performing certain sacrifices a man could go to heaven in person.[13]

Nahuṣa, one of the far-famed legendary kings, is the most outstanding example of such men, and perhaps the earliest recorded one in traditional history. In his own person he had actually held sway over the whole of Indra's heavenly domains and was being served by all the divine damsels and even perhaps by the consorts of some of the gods. He figures in the literature from about the 3rd century B.C. onwards as having lost his heavenly acquisition and possession through misconduct while he had the sovereign command over them.[14] The famous tale of a remote ancestor of Rāma in his pursuit of this feat of going to heaven in his bodily form, that of Triśaṅku, who has remained almost a laughing stock of the people[15] as the standard example of a person who gets to neither end of an enterprise but has to be hanging in between, is told at length in the *Rāmāyaṇa* (II, 57-60), as the greatest exploit of the sage Viśvāmitra.

Indra, the natural and constitutional ruler of heaven, himself appears in literature owing to his alternate name of 'Śatakratu' (one who has performed one hundred horse-sacrifices) as being jealous of kings bent on performing one hundred horse-sacrifices and of sages practising severe austerities and thus jeopardizing his heavenly rule. Kālidāsa, the mirror of the national mind of ancient India, whose passing reference to Triśaṅku is already attended to, gives us a full description of the obstacle that Indra created in the performance of the hundredth horse-sacrifice of Dilīpa, the fourth ancestor of Rāma, and of the circumstances which procured for Dilīpa a place in heaven, in spite of the non-performance of the hundredth sacrifice, as a special case (see *Raghuvaṁśa*, III, 50-69).

The idea of walking to heaven in person as equivalent to preparing for one's death, 'mahāyātrā' or 'mahāprasthāna', the great pilgrimage or the great journey, as it came to be significantly called, is implicit in the description of Rāma's last days as described in the *Rāmāyaṇa*, though in the end Rāma, being by then looked upon as an incarnation of Viṣṇu, is shown as having disappeared into His original form. In the *Mahābhārata* there is a whole book ('parvan') entitled 'Svargārohaṇa' (XVIII), meaning ascending to the heaven, in which the progress of the Pāṇḍavas on their way to heaven is described, Yudhiṣṭhira, the eldest of them, alone being shown as reaching his destination.

In the *Rāmāyaṇa* it is stated that Rāma having assumed His original Viṣṇu form asked Brahmā to assign his associates an appropriately deserving but evidently unending world (VII, 110). Thereupon Brahmā assured Rāma that all of them would be admitted to the world known as 'Santāna' or 'Santānaka', which is only next lower than or next previous to the final abode, the most perfect world of Brahmā.

The later version of the happenings and the assignments of worlds to Rāma and his associates bear testimony to the changing notions regarding 'svarga', the final goal, and to the rise of new conceptions of salvaging activity.

Kālidāsa's version must be considered to be only a little later than that of the *Rāmāyaṇa*, though its being more or less contemporary with it is not impossible. When Rāma was admonished about his time for departure from the earth, he, with the household fire being carried before him, started northwards with all his associates. At a particular spot on the bank of the river Śarayū, known as Gopratataraṇa, which is considered by the Hindus as a holy place of pilgrimage, he received the divine air-vehicle for him to take to His abode. Boarding it he arranged that all those bathing in the river at that spot would go to heaven ('svarga'). For his intimate followers like the monkey-king Sugrīva, he had another 'svarga' made; for they were, as Mallinātha gives us the reason, only 'new gods'. 'Svarga' in this account could not have been a place from which its denizens would have to return to earth but must have been looked upon and conceived as a permanent abode of final release (*Raghuvaṁśa*, XVI, 92-102). From Tulasīdāsa's version[16] of about twelve centuries later we learn that Rāma arranged with Brahmā the entrance to the city of gods for people touching the waters of the river Śarayū in one particular month. There is no reference therein to another special world for Rāma's associates; but there is an assurance of Rāma given to Bibhīṣana, the demon-devotee of Rāma and the ruler of Laṅkā, that after he had ruled over Laṅkā for a whole 'kalpa'-period he would go to the world of gods ('svarga'?).

Rāma's injunction to Brahmā to create a special 'svarga' for his close associates and his assurance that people bathing in the Śarayū shall attain heaven, 'svarga', which were only whittled down in Tulasīdāsa's version of the story owing to the development of new thought and practice regarding life after death, must raise the presumption that not only till Kālidāsa's time but till even much later, 'svarga', the perfect and blissful world of the Ṛgvedic and the Atharvavedic poets, continued to figure and therefore to be looked upon as such, and did not get completely eclipsed as the final goal to be achieved through pious and righteous living on earth!

For ages, 'svarga' has been the reward for heroes who die on the battlefield fighting without turning their backs to their opponents. Thus Lord Kṛṣna's worldly retort to Arjuna on his declaration that he will not fight is that he would thereby be throwing away the golden opportunity of open gates to heaven ('svarga'). Arguing the matter he points out that fight at that stage was doubly advantageous to Arjuna. For if he was killed in battle he would attain heaven ('svarga') and if he succeeded he would gain sovereignty over the world (*BhG*, II, 32-33 and 37).

Perhaps this sentiment is much older than the 5th century B.C. In the *Kauṣītakībrāhmaṇa Upaniṣad* (III, 1) we are told that Pratardana, the son of Divodāsa, attained the favourite abode of Indra, i.e., heaven, through fight and manly courage. This should naturally mean that Pratardana died while fighting bravely in some cause and thereby attained heaven.

Anyway the belief and the sentiment are very well represented in the national poet's, Kālidāsa's, work, and also in the still later popular text of hortatory nature, *Pañcatantra*. In his *Raghuvaṁśa* (VII, 53) Kālidāsa makes a reference, which is quite definitive not only to show that the attainment of heaven for death in a battle was sure but also that it was instantaneous. That is why Kālidāsa represents two opponents of Aja, who succumbed to his arrows simultaneously, as quarrelling over one beautiful Apsaras, one of a class of charmingly enticing damsels who attend on persons in heaven. And the tabloid expression 'amartyabhāve'pi' (even though they had become immortals or gods), almost as an aside remark, vouchsafes to us the significant information that going to heaven, 'svarga', meant even so late as Kālidāsa's time attainment of immortality.

In the *Pañcatantra* the belief and the sentiment that a hero dying in a battle goes to heaven without any ado are repeated more than once (I, after verse 227 ; I, vv. 332, 335 ; IV, v. 69). In three other contexts at least 'svarga' (heaven) as the goal of meritorious living in this world is emphasized and recommended as an objective which is rather difficult to achieve (I, v. 276 ; II, v. 115, IV, vv. 2-5). There is one context, the most important one for our present purpose, as it widens our knowledge of the extent to which the attainment of heaven as a great prize after death and of its view as near-eternity had reached. We are told that a woman on immolating herself on her husband's funeral pyre wins the right to live in heaven ('svarga') for thirtyfive million years, thirtyfive million being the number of hair on a woman's body (II, v. 179).

Though the gods like Agni and Pūṣan are prayed to take the soul of the deceased to the world of the Fathers, yet it was described as the world of the pious only, implying, and, as mentioned earlier, even stating it in so many words sometimes, that the non-pious had no access to it (*RV*, X, 15 ; X, 154, 3). It is also mentioned that severe austerities, death in a battle on the battlefield or liberal gifts and charities in sacrifices earn the persons concerned as a reward a place in 'svarga' (heaven) (*RV*, I, 125, 5 ; X, 107, 2 ; X, 154, 2-5).[17]

It is to be presumed, though explicit mention of the belief comes later, that the impious ones and perpetrators of evil, including of course non-performers of sacrifices and non-donors, were relegated to the dark nether world known as 'naraka'.[18] This world evidently of Yama, had received a specific name some time later, as Bādarāyaṇa in his *Brahmasūtras* (III, 1, 13) calls it 'Saṁyamana', the place where appropriate torments had to be suffered by its inmates. In later literature, however, the name does not figure. Instead the specific names of many hells, as already noted in an earlier chapter, take its place.

A priori, the nature of 'svarga' and its provisions for its denizens, including the ancient Fathers and the new ones admitted to it, leave no need for any food or drink being provided to the Fathers, except perhaps what might have been thought to be necessary during their transit of the soul from this world to that of the Fathers. Accordingly we do not find any specific mention of funeral worship and oblations to the manes in the early literature, except a stray mention of Fathers-worship in its later name of Pitṛyajna (*RV*, X, 16, 10). And P. V. Kane[19] has not discovered any earlier reference to the later and the standard form of oblationary worship of the manes, 'śrāddha', than the one in the late-looking and late-breathing epilogue of the *Kaṭha Upaniṣad*, which appears at the end of the chapter (I, 3, 17), though he sees an implied reference to such a rite in *RV*, VIII, 30, 3 and VIII, 63, 1.

In this connection the tradition that is recorded in the *Āpastamba-dharmasūtra* (II, 7, 16, 1-3) is significant. It is stated there that gods and men were living together on earth. Gods went to heaven having acquired it as a reward for their sacrifice. To enable men to acquire heaven Manu promulgated the rite known as 'śrāddha'. In it, the Fathers, 'pitaraḥ', are the deities, the Brahmins invited to dinner serving the role which Agni does in a sacrifice, i.e., of the conveyer of the offerings. The rites known as 'śrāddha', whose chief function was to provide for the animal needs of the manes by offering them to Brahmins—had they come to be looked upon as gods on earth even if no such express statement is attested for that early date ?—thus providing the priestly class with an additional, or rather, as becomes probable in the light of the religio-social condition of the time between Janamejaya's death and the resurgence of Brahmanic Hinduism about the 3rd century B.C., a substitute source of livelihood.

That Parīkṣita or Janamejaya was perhaps the last great performer of the old elaborate sacrifices in which immense amount of riches, as many as two hundred thousand cows, and an amount of silver and gold, used to be distributed to Brahmins. In the *Bṛhadāraṇyaka Upaniṣad* (III, 3, 1-2) as typical of the fate of the performers of the sacrifices of the Vedic religion is mentioned the limited achievement of Pārikṣitas, the performers of horse-sacrifice. S. V. Ketkar's succinct résumé of the information about the performance of great sacrifices from the epics and the Purāṇas supports the same view.[20] The whole teaching of the speculative thinkers as preserved in the older Upaniṣads was against the performance of sacrifices as insignificant nothings in the valuation of the religio-philosophical destiny of man. In the Upaniṣadic age, the value of Brahma-knowledge as the supreme means of final bliss came to be acknowledged ; but the institution of sacrifice with the accompaniment of emoluments to participating Brahmins was not extinct. And Janaka, the king-philosopher, who, in the endeavour of arriving at philosophical truths in that age, was only second to the Brahmin-philosopher Yājñavalkya, offered such sacrifices in the hope of helping forward the cause of that endeavour with tempting emoluments as stakes. Thus we are told (*BrU*, III, 1, 1-2) that on one occasion he got together the leading Brahmins of the far-famed country of the Kuru-Pāñcālas, where the great sacrifices of old and even that by Janamejaya must have been celebrated, and offered, as the prerequisite for the one who volunteered, or dared to volunteer, to solve the riddle of the universe if asked to do so, one thousand cows, to each of whose horns twenty gold coins were tied. And Janaka was so much known as a munificent donor and liberal patron that he had excited the jealousy and the rivalry of the neighbouring king, Ajātaśatru of Kāśī (Vārāṇasī).[21] It is seen that the gifts offered by this most munificent of the donors of the new age were a mere title of the earnings Brahmins and priests, officiating and participating in a great sacrifice, would have made !

Janaka represents the generous kings of the age. Jānaśruti Pautrāyaṇa, on the other hand, represents the great merchant princes. He is described as one who was the giver of much and to many, and the feeder of innumerable, doing all that with great faith (*ChU*, IV, 1, 1). He is said to have offered to one Raikva, a reputedly competent person, six hundred cows and one gold coin, along with a chariot drawn by a mare for expert service. Raikva having declined the offer, Jānaśruti offered further to add to the corpus both his daughter for wife and the village where Raikva was residing (*ChU*, I, 2). The size of the gifts for an extraordinary expert, compared with the emoluments of the priests in the earlier religious dispensation, is so small that we may conclude that as the consequence of the speculative philosophy of the Upaniṣadic age the earnings and earning opportunities of the Brahmins, i.e., of the priestly class, the class that was educated and was both intelligent and alert, had dwindled.

The propaganda of Buddha and his followers and the rapid spread and long sway of the Buddhist doctrines over a large part of the country, and particularly over North India, must have reduced the practice of performing sacrifices with ample gifts to Brahmins almost to nothing. The priestly class must have lost one of the most lucrative of its means of earning and livelihood. How much it must have meant to that class during the four or five centuries of the utter absence of the sacrificial activity one can gauge better by a look at and appraisal of the priestly fees and gifts paid and made by Nāganikā, a Śātavāhana queen, recorded in a cave inscription, from Nānāghāṭ in Ahmednagar district, of about 50 B.C., i.e., about 2 centuries after the resurgence of Hinduism in North India had started. In all the many sacrifices taken together, she had donated 13 villages, 10 elephants, more than one thousand horses, one horse-chariot, more than 50 thousand cows, and more than 34 thousand 'kārṣāpaṇas', i.e., about one thousand gold coins.[22] In the *Rāmāyaṇa* (I, 50), which must have been put into shape at about this period, little earlier or little later, we are told that King Daśaratha, at the end of the performance of the Aśvamedha and other sacrifices, first donated his kingdom to the priests who successfully completed the great task. The priests then had it exchanged, on the plea that it was not their business to manage a kingdom, for one hundred million of silver coins. In addition the king gifted away to other Brahmins on that occasion millions of gold coins! A little later Kālidāsa in his *Raghuvaṁśa* (V, 86) represented Raghu, the grandfather of Daśaratha, as having performed a sacrifice which involved gifting away his total wealth!

It is not unlikely that with decrease of faith in sacrifices and with the rise of doubt in the permanence of 'svarga', the orthodox thinkers, those who could not see their way to agree with the philosophical radicals, the Upaniṣadic Brahma-upholders, too, began to waver in their belief in the assured destiny of the pious in their line of thinking and living. Economic interests of the class to which they belonged clearly required a substitute for the huge sacrificial fees that were becoming rare or had become practically absent. At such a time a brilliant idea like the one attributed to Manu in the *Āpastambadharmasūtra* mentioned above could be particularly susceptible of being accepted with open hands. And once the need of the Fathers for replenishment of their food was accepted, other fine distinctions and subtle theories regarding the condition of the soul of the departed could arise and weave themselves into a supremely complex web of funeral rites, punctuated with offerings and gifts, most of which, almost the entire lot, very naturally and quite logically in the Hindu religious complex, being the perquisites of the priestly class.

The *Bhagavadgītā* with its authoritative voice announced through Arjuna that the Fathers, whether in heaven ('svarga') or in their world ('pitṛloka'), would "fall", evidently towards the nether world, if oblations and libations were not offered in their names by their lineal descendants on earth (*BhG*, I, 42). Lord Kṛṣṇa's views, very clearly expounded, maintained that the worshippers of the Fathers went to their world, and that just as those who attained heaven had to descend from it to the mundane world after their merit was exhausted, the deceased, i.e., the manes, could not fall or descend because they did not receive the oblations but only when the merit accruing to them by their actions while living had got exhausted (IX, 20-1, 25). However, there is nothing in the text of the *Bhagavadgītā* which rebuts or contradicts Arjuna's bland statement about the dire need of oblations and libations being made to the manes for an indefinite period or rather perpetually! The assertion of Lord Kṛṣṇa about the perishability of 'svarga' follows the line of thought explicitly laid out in the *Bṛhadāraṇyaka Upaniṣad* (VI, 2, 16) in its own imagery but is silent about any requirements of the Fathers in the intervening period.

The *Mahābhārata*[23] appropriately contains an episode, which, though the context stamps it as an extraneous insertion with a purpose, is calculated to emphasize this point of view. The Ṛgvedic references to Agastya and his solicitation of Lopāmudrā are dressed up for a full-blooded story, though with jarring and even unintelligible elements of Agastya the bachelor being forced to seek marriage at the behest of and in commiseration for his ancestor-manes. Somehow in the midst of Agastya's exciting undertaking to subdue the demons Ilvala and his brother, he happens to come across some souls precariously hanging, head downwards, in an emaciated condition. On inquiry he finds that they are his ancestor-manes, who because of Agastya, their descendant, having remained unmarried, had not received their food through the performance of 'śrāddhas', and were emaciated through inanition and that they would fall into the abyss, if Agastya did not manage to marry and beget a son and carry on the 'śrāddhas'. Agastya struck with remorse 'creates' a fine woman as Lopāmudrā, the daughter of a Vidarbha king, and marries her. In the sequel occurs the solicitation!

The funeral-oblations-rites called 'śrāddha' proper must have been promulgated after the 8th century B.C.[24] Their introduction and vogue being rendered feasible by the previously long existent tendance and worship of some kind indicated by the terms 'pitṛyajña' and 'tarpaṇa' or libation of water which is perhaps an equally old custom.

The 'śrāddha' rite once introduced developed a tremendous complex very soon; and Pāṇini, the grammarian, who could not have been later than 300

B.C., had to explain the derivative words, 'śrāddhika' and 'śrāddhin', meaning one who has eaten a 'śrāddha' dinner.[25] The *Manusmṛti* speaks of not only the 'śrāddhas' to be performed immediately after death and during the first year till the supposed or effected unification of the deceased with the Fathers is accomplished, but three or more to be offered annually thereafter. Fearing that the heavy load of so many oblation-rites could not be willingly borne, or rather finding that the willingness to bear it had diminished, it exhorts their meticulous performance by such incentives as the expectation of prosperity and the possibility of misery as a consequence of the performance or the non-performance of the many 'śrāddhas'.[26] This situation occurring about three to five centuries after the *Dharmasūtra* of Baudhāyana, which eulogized the performance of an oblation-rite for the manes (II, 8, 1) but did not name it as 'śrāddha', is particularly indicative of the rapid development of the rites in the post-*Bhagavadgītā* century or two, which happened to record the first signs of Hindu resurgence, though in a limited area of the country, with the horse-sacrifice performed by the *Śunga* monarch, Puṣyamitra.

The plurality of the 'śrāddhas', injunctions and exhortations regarding their meticulous performance and specification of ample and abundant food at these rites lead one to the inference that the supply of food to the manes at regular intervals in a year by their earthly descendants was a dire need of theirs and that but for it they were all too frail. At the same time, their ideational persistence as some kind of gods, capable of granting boons or bestowing curses on their descendants, and the varying periods of satisfaction to the manes, particular invitee-Brahmins and/or the particular kind of food offered at the rite are asserted to cause, are clear indications that not only the divine nature of the manes, Fathers, is still remembered and believed in but also that that condition of theirs is capable of being rendered eternal. It is stated that a Brahmin of specific qualifications in Vedic lore eating the food at a 'śrāddha'-dinner can bring about a satisfaction to the manes which would last for seven generations, the unity of the domestic hearth and the earthly household.[27] It is possible that such satisfaction may even be perpetual![28]

A need which can be disposed of permanently through a specific technique cannot be considered to render the condition of the Fathers or manes a precarious and temporary one which must depend for its continuance on periodic offerings for an indefinite period! Beginning with two-months-satisfaction caused by fish, the foods, meats, end with the flesh of rhinoceros, which causes satisfaction for eternity. One could even procure the same result of providing perpetual satisfaction to the manes more cheaply and less riskily by offering something mixed in honey on one particular day of the year. In the alternative even anything given in the name of the manes with 'complete faith' is said to achieve the same end.[29] Such being the possibilities even in the heyday of the 'śrāddha'-rites one may legitimately conclude that the notion of 'śrāddha' and its complex multiplication and practice were conditioned by the newer view of the impermanence of 'svarga' and its happiness, and fostered by the economic interests of the priestly class which had come to lose one of the most lucrative of its sources that had formed an integral part of the earlier religious complex and had nearly ceased to be so in the newer dispensation. How well the purpose, if it was one as suggested here, of this near-innovation was fulfilled can be judged from an inscription of Ṛṣabhadatta, the son-in-law of the Kṣatrapa Nahapāna which he left on the Karle-cave-door in about A.D. 120. It informs us that as a dutiful son Ṛṣabhadatta fed from year to year annually one hundred thousand Brahmins to please his father who had gone to heaven, i.e., at the 'śrāddha' of his father.[30]

There was another and even more significant development in religio-philosophical thought, which had resulted in the postulation of a view of life after death, before the ferment of the speculative upsurge of the Upaniṣadic age, within the fold of strictly Vedic learning. That is the theory of transmigration or metempsychosis, which has been for ages now the most distinguishing mark and a cardinal principle of Hinduism. It is to its credit that writers time out of number have laid some of the patent national defects and shortcomings of the Hindu world. Not only is the general atmosphere of pessimism, or at least the lack of optimism, attributed to this belief but also is the tendency to inaction or at least the absence of real dynamicism laid at its door. The belief is that the soul of a human being soon after death has to take on a new birth in any of the manifold species according to the merit and demerit that its owner achieved by his living. In the intermediate period the soul has either pleasant time in 'svarga', heaven, or has to suffer varying degrees of suffering in 'naraka', hell, or both according to the stock of good deeds or bad ones. After wearing out the effects of past actions in this manner, in appropriate situations the soul has to enter a body, which is also determined by the nature of the activity in mundane living that its owner had engaged in. This cycle of birth and death, called 'saṁsāra' or rarely even 'prapañca', means, as the word regularly does later, 'worldly manifestation'.[31] It is described as ever revolving ('parivartin' or 'satatayāyin'). Only rare individuals, of course only human, can succeed in freeing their souls from it, which condition is called salvation ('mokṣa').[32] Such ones do not have to return, the state being characterized as non-return 'apunarāvṛtti'[33] or 'abhūyaḥsaṁnivṛtti'.[34]

Competent students like Macdonell and Deussen are agreed that there is no trace of the doctrine of transmigration in the Vedas.[35] S. V. Ketkar[36] too, writing more than forty years ago, like Macdonell before him, traced its mention in the *Śatapatha Brāhmaṇa*. It is said there that "those who do not perform rites with correct knowledge are born again after their decease and repeatedly become the food of death" and also that one is reborn as man as a reward for a certain esoteric knowledge but becomes one with Brahman being freed from death (and life) through a particular kind of knowledge.[37] Macdonell further observed that it is not till the period of the *Brāhmaṇas* that "the notion of future punishment appears plainly developed", the *Śatapatha Brāhmaṇa* (XI, 2, 7, 33) being the earliest text to assert that "everyone is born again after death and is weighed in a balance, receiving reward or punishment according as his works are good or bad".[38] Ketkar, who too made the same point later, added to it on the basis of two more texts of the same book. He wrote: "The views preserved in the *Brāhmaṇas* appear to maintain that after death both the good and the bad people are reborn in the other world and enjoy the fruits of their works appropriate to them."[39]

The *Kaṭha Upaniṣad*, which, though it is later than two or three other Upaniṣads, cannot be put down to a later date than 500 B.C., has preserved to us the most extraordinary episode in the history of man of a youth daring the god of Death in his den in order to know the truth about life after death and about problems connected with life both here and hereafter. In that extraordinary document, embodying the supposed dialogue between Naciketas, the youth, and Mṛtyu, the god of Death, we are told that there was a deep curiosity and a long discussion about whether there was life after death or not, and that the matter was considered so important and the difficulty of arriving at the truth was so great that even the gods apparently had not been able to decide the issue conclusively (I, 1, 19-22 and 29). One of the almost positive assertions Mṛtyu made to Naciketas in this behalf maintains by implication that this world is not an end in itself, and that there is, therefore, further life after death so that those, who rest in the cold comfort of their mistaken notion of this world of life here being the end, come under the power of Mṛtyu and are killed over and over again, i.e. of course after being reborn after death (I, 2, 6).

That this question and something like its answer must have been worked out about two to three centuries at least before the time of the *Kaṭha Upaniṣad* is clear from what has been stated above regarding the views preserved in the *Śatapatha Brāhmaṇa*. The same conclusion is further corroborated by our study of the older Upaniṣads and our knowledge of the state of the views and beliefs about them preserved in them. The next stage, chronological but not necessarily developmental, is represented by the philosophical texts. But before presenting a brief account of the views adumbrated in them it is necessary to outline the state of the notions, current in or arrived at about the time of the oldest Upaniṣads, regarding the condition of the departing soul at the juncture of its leaving the body.

We have seen above that the Ṛgvedic notions on the subject preclude the probability that the departing soul was believed to have had any envelopment or covering in which it left the body. It is stated in so many words there that the soul received a body, more or less proportionate to the worth of works of its former owner on earth, in the other world. And in this matter it is that perhaps the greatest change in the religio-philosophical complex of the Vedic-Brahmanic system of views on and beliefs about life and death took place. The approximate period of time or of the literary stage when this took place cannot be determined. But, as must be clear from the chapters on cosmology and human personality, and from the views on these subjects, which are preserved in the Upaniṣads, particularly and at fair length in the *Bṛhadā-*

raṇyaka, the *Chāndogya*, the *Kaṭha*, the *Praśna*, and the *Aitareya* Upaniṣads, the belief in transmigration and the notion of subtle body must have appeared on the scene some time before the oldest Upaniṣad, may be about 1000 B.C.

In the *Bṛhadāraṇyaka Upaniṣad* text (IV, 4, 1-6) describing what happens when death approaches, how breath leaves the body, how the soul 'leaps' on to another body, it is stated that it is 'vijñāna', or 'buddhi' in later terminology, that accompanies it as also the lore and the works, evidently the last being the same as the 'iṣṭāpūrta' of the Ṛgvedic texts. In the end a verse is quoted. Quoting a verse means using an already accepted notion contained in it. The notion in this particular verse is the significant one for the new view-point of life after death which maintains that the soul leaves the body at death accompanied by or rather enveloped in 'karma', works, and 'manas', mind, which are its 'liṅga', i.e., its mark, or characteristic, its subtle body. The subtle, 'sūkṣma', body of a soul is appropriately called 'liṅga', because it embodies the characteristic and specific mark of the person who was the owner of that soul. In the *Praśna Upaniṣad* text (III, 9) the soul is said to take on another birth with senses enveloped in mind. We have to understand from this that the subtle body, according to the school of teachers represented by this Upaniṣad, consisted of the five sense-organs and mind, of course in their subtle form. It is exactly these six in their elemental form that the *Bhagavadgītā* (XV, 7-8) asserts the Lord, in his aspect of the 'jīva' or individual self, draws with Him, whenever and wherever He takes up a new body. The imagery used is quite befitting the subtle nature of the elements forming the 'liṅga' body. It is said that 'jīva'-self draws them as wind does smell from its source.

Still there was no name given to the subtle body, enveloped in which a soul was believed to leave a body and enter another. In the *Manusmṛti* (I, 36) in the account of the creative process, the soul's departure from and entrance into a body is stated in general terms without mentioning the subtle body; but the term, 'saṁsṛṣṭa', has been understood by three great commentators on the work, and Bühler has followed them, to mean 'united with the fine body'. And what is significant is that even Medhātithi, the 9th century commentator, like the other two who are much later, states that the subtle body consists of 'puryaṣṭaka', which is apparently a technical term, though I have not been able to trace its existence anywhere else. "Puryaṣṭaka' as its etymology, owing to the latter portion of the word 'aṣṭaka' meaning eight, implies, meant the eight constituents, i.e., the rudimentary elements, 'bhūtas' [?], organs of sense (five 'indriyas'), mind ('manas'), and intelligence ('buddhi'), memory of past actions ('vāsanā'), merit or demerit ('karma'), the vital airs, i.e., their elemental origin ('vāyu'), and nescience ('avidyā'). This is how the later 13th century commentator Kullūkabhaṭṭa has rendered the text quoting for his authority one Sananda. The passage from the *Brahma-Purāṇa* which he has quoted in support of his interpretation of the term 'puryaṣṭaka' does not mention the constituents seriatum but, calling it 'liṅga', as the

Bṛhadāraṇyaka Upaniṣad does, and thus equating it with the subtle body, only states that the 'jīva'-self is united with vital airs ('prāṇa') and others.

P. V. Kane[40] has abstracted all the information available in the *Purāṇas*, the earliest of which is commonly dated in the 5th or the 6th century A. D., and the mediaeval law digests, regarding the views on what happens to his soul on a person's death. In it there is no mention of 'puryaṣṭaka'. Its counterpart is known thereir as 'ativāhika', which is clearly an etymologically proper expression for whatever envelops and carries the soul. The word in the sense of a carrier or conveyer is actually found in the *Brahmasūtras* (III, 3, 4) of Bādarāyaṇa, 2nd century B.C., in connection with his discussion of the two paths believed to be taken by souls, the one or the other being open according to their destiny determined by the actions of their owners when living.

Strangely enough these texts maintain that the 'ativāhika' body has only fire (light-heat), wind ('vāyu' or air) and ether ('ākāśa') as the three constituents.

The same texts testify to the great elaboration that had come to be woven round this central theme of the condition of a soul after it leaves the body of a person dying. They also, in so far as the many ritual performances with appropriate oblations and gifts are enjoined in that connection, emphasize the view taken above that the 'śrāddha' rites were being worked up and upon by the priestly class in deference to its economic interests.

The rites to be performed after cremation during the ten days of mourning are enjoined in order that the departed soul may acquire another body, appropriately designated 'bhogadeha', 'experiencing or enjoying body', because with it the soul has to work out the effects of the past actions. Further rites ending with what is significantly known as 'sapiṇḍīkaraṇa', because the mixing of the offered rice-balls is believed to cause the union of the departed with the manes of the family, provide the departed soul with another body, which, curiously, is not named in the sources and is said to be the one with which alone the soul reaches heaven or hell!

The germ of the theory of the second body known as 'bhogadeha' lies in an earlier elaboration of the views on life after death, fortunately preserved for us in the *Manusmṛti* (XII, 16-22). It is stated there that in the case of persons whose actions in this world were bad and sinful, a new body formed from the subtle particles of the five 'great beings', earth, water, light-heat, air, and ether, is provided in the hereafter in order that their souls may be administered appropriate punishment. When the sufferings and tortures are fully experienced by the soul, the new body, called here only by an etymologically appropriate expression as 'yātanārthīya', meant for suffering tortures or pangs, dissolves itself into the original elemental particles, which get assimilated with their source, the 'five great beings'. The soul so chastened and freed from all blemish merges with 'mahat' and the Supreme Soul, 'paramātman'. These latter weigh the merits and demerits of the soul and evidently endow it with proper amount of happiness and misery. It is then provided with a gross body. If the merit accrued by the soul in consequence of the deeds of its erstwhile possessor overweighs his demerit then in that gross body it enjoys happiness in heaven, 'svarga'. But if the demerit is greater than its merit-credit then the embodied soul is given over to the tortures of Yama. When the soul has suffered its full share of these tortures of Yama it is reborn for another life.

It is seen from this statement in the *Manusmṛti* that there is a body, other than the subtle one, which for all practical purposes must be considered to be in a gross state, though first adumbrated as being made out of subtle elements, which is provided to everyone in the hereafter. Second, the elements of that body, which as a complex is the same as the original subtle body postulated both in the *Bhagavadgītā* and in the *Manusmṛti*, leaving the soul, unite with their source and the soul goes to its source, the Supreme Soul. Third, after the appropriate sufferings have been experienced the soul regains its subtle body and is reborn in an appropriate birth. Fourth, those of the souls whose merits are greater than their demerits, however, go to heaven ('svarga') and enjoy these, evidently for eternity!

Enjoyment in 'svarga' or tortures in Yama's world, 'narakas' or hells of the twentyone-named kinds, can be had only with a kind of gross body, the original subtle body because of its nature being unfit for or incapable of such experience. Here arises the need for a body other than the natural covering of the departing soul, which is its subtle body composed of six of the constituents of the human personality. The views in the *Purāṇas* and the mediaeval digests were the outcome of the attempts to provide for this need, appropriately adjusted to the earthly needs of the normative class, the priestly class, that badly required a new source of livelihood as a substitute for one of the most lucrative of such sources which had almost dwindled away. But the complex created under these circumstances appears to me to be almost a medley, leaving a number of aspects unexplained and even contradictory. The original simple notion of a subtle body, constituted by the subtle elements of the fundamental part of the human personality, was a reasonable postulation satisfying one's rational or rather logical nature, and yet providing for the potent seeds germinating into the next birth for the soul. There would have remained the difficulty of reward or punishment, as the case may be, being carried out, as the soul by itself cannot be subjected to such experiences without the gross body. That could be explained by accepting the Vedic hypothesis that a new body is automatically provided by the governors of the hereafter to a soul that goes there. Yama was, and even now is considered to be, that governor or ruler of the nether world, the world or worlds where torture and such other punishments are meted out to the appropriate deceased persons. Yama had according to Vedic cosmology an abode of his in heaven too. It is not at all clear that later Paurāṇic mythology denies Yama an abode in heaven. True he was not the governor or ruler of heaven, 'svarga', that honour having been, and is, a preserve of Indra. However, he was along with

Indra one of the four Lokapālas, cosmos-protectors, and also along with him one of the six divinities as noted in a Nānāghāṭ-cave-inscription in Maharashtra of about 50 B.C.[41] And Yama having provided each soul as it arrives to him a body can be imagined to pass on the embodied soul to its proper destination, heaven or hell, the latter of which was under his complete control. As pointed out earlier Yama's special world was sometimes designated by an appropriately significant name, as 'saṁyamana', 'place that controls', or 'place where one suffers', as in Bādarāyaṇa's *Brahmasūtras* (III, 1, 13). In this manner the simple notion of the subtle covering of the departing soul, without further elaborations which render the complex of belief and élite practice regarding life after death a little too cumbrous and strains one's logical sense too much, can fulfil the needs of the theory of life hereafter. The elaboration as carried out, on the other hand, multiplies rites, and burdens a religion, already loaded with ritual practices, with still more, which I think form the least satisfying section of ritualism.

As we have noted above, in the *Brāhmaṇas*, where the idea of weighing the merit and demerit accruing to a deceased person's soul is adumbrated for the first time, the tortures of hell are described in fair detail.[42] The task of assessing was assigned in the *Manusmṛti* to the Supreme Soul; and it is but proper that later mythology diverted it to Yama, such work being too insignificant for, and I should think even derogatory to, the Supreme Soul to attend to. To help Yama in his work mythology and popular belief have provided him with an assistant, a cosmic accountant so to say, who is believed to keep meticulous account of the doings of mankind in his book. In the drama *Mudrārākṣasa* (I, 20), written by Viśākhadatta in the 7th or the 8th century, we have a reference to the work of this accountant who is named Citragupta. Śaṅkarācārya's comment on a text in Bādarāyaṇa's *Brahmasūtras* (III, 1, 15) which speaks of only seven hells as being postulated in the Paurāṇic cosmography, makes it clear that to him and in his time Citragupta was one of the many dignitaries with whose help Yama conducted his business of torture for the sinful in the hells, which Śaṅkarācārya, too, agrees were only seven.

The famous Tamilian temple city of Kañcī or Conjeevaram has the glorious distinction of having the only known temple dedicated to this divine personality. And Tamil almanac, it appears, shows a particular full-moon day in April-May as a day of special worship to be offered to him. The metal image, as well as the sculpture in the sanctum, shows the divine personage as standing, with a book of palmyra leaves in the left hand and a metal stylus in the right, evidently ready to write down the faults and merits of human beings.[43]

The three doctrines, that of transmigration or rebirth, the one of judgment on the soul of the deceased and appropriate award of reward or punishment, and the one of the passing out of the soul of a deceased one in the subtle body-covering, the 'liṅga-body', hang together today as one complex. The first two, as we have reason and evidence, too, to believe, appeared simultaneously as one set. Whether they were so developed or whether they happened to get a combined mention we do not know. But the third, quite clearly, came to be conceived and get formulated at least a century later than the other two.

The fourth doctrine, fraught with so much social consequence, that of the post-cremation and later periodic oblation-rites for the deceased, came to be fully formed and stated still later. The Hindu law of inheritance in one large part of the country was formulated in relation to it and in the other parts, though expressly it was centred in other principles, the law was evidently adjusted to its demands and ramifications to a large extent; the rearing of a family and much of the archaic and sometimes fantastic-looking custom about it were its almost direct outcome. Today though it may be said to have ceased to affect the law of inheritance and succession, it remains the main driving force of the desire for progeny and particularly male progeny, forming a great obstacle to the cause of control of population.[44] From the purely religious point of view it has emphasized the ritualistic content and nature of Hinduism as well as helped to continue the polylatrous view and practice. With all this, it is a doctrine which is not consistent with the older view of the Fathers having blissful existence in heaven for eternity, a view, which as already shown, peeps through the newer notion and practice in more ways than one and thus reminds one of its contradictions. Nor is it in consonance with a strict and logical view of the doctrine of transmigration as will be presently indicated.

Before entering on a discussion of how far the doctrine of the need of oblation-rites for deceased persons is in harmony with the theory of transmigration, or repeated rebirth, it is necessary to make a brief historical, or rather sequential, statement of the development of that theory.

In the earliest of the Upaniṣads, *Bṛhadāraṇyaka* (IV, 4, 4), where the theory gets its first explicit and almost full expression, it is unequivocally and quite definitively stated that the departed soul takes on [immediately] a newer, and [in some cases] a more auspicious form as that of a Father, a Gandharva, a divinity, a primordial law-giver ('prajāpati'), a creator ('Brahmā') or that of any other being. Neither is there any time-interval between death and taking of any form laid down, nor is there any limit set to the possibilities of forms. Second, it is further (IV, 4, 5) stated that the new form which the soul takes depends on the actions and conduct ('ākāra' and 'ācāra') of the deceased person, the form being good and meritorious if the actions were good and meritorious, and bad and evil if they were bad and sinful. It is the actions of the person while living that determine the form his departing soul can take.

In the almost equally old Upaniṣad, the *Chāndogya* (V, 10, 5-8), while we have a further elaboration of the theory, we have also a much more important addition to the theory which introduces a modification in the Vedic view of the world of Fathers and of the Fathers themselves, along with a clear and very positive amplification of the new birth-cycle the soul can or does take. The amplification, which rests the claim for a new form on the nature of the actions while living, introduces a new term for them leaving out the *Bṛhadāraṇyaka* ones. It is 'caraṇa' which etymologically must be the same as 'ācāra' of the older text. There is a third word for almost the same idea and derivable from the same root, i.e., 'carita', which, though not in identical context, is used in the *Taittirīya Upaniṣad* (I, 10, 2). Later, Bādarāyaṇa, the celebrated formulator of the system of philosophy known as Vedānta and the greatest authority on this subject for posterity, in his *Brahmasūtras* (III, 1, 8-11), introducing a further elaboration in the theory, discusses the term 'caraṇa', conduct. Śaṅkarācārya in his commentary on the passage observes: "Caraṇa, 'ācāra' and 'śīla' are synonymous, while 'anuśaya' [the new term and concept introduced by Bādarāyaṇa to explain the dynamics of rebirth] means a residue of actions other than those whose fruit has already been experienced". Those whose conduct has been bad are reborn in a vile stock, like that of dogs, pigs or the Cāṇḍālas [the untouchable and perhaps unapproachable class of human beings forming the outcaste members of the Upaniṣadic society]. Those whose conduct has been good are born in a handsome stock like that of a Brahmin, a Kṣatriya or a Vaiśya [the three higher castes, the twice-born ones, of the then four-fold society]. Other souls, too tarnished to be discriminatingly dealt with as the above mentioned ones, went straight into other species, the non-sentient ones or those of the vegetable kingdom.

In making this amplification, the school of teachers, whose views are embodied in the *Chāndogya Upaniṣad*, were evidently attempting to answer a possible question and explaining away a likely objection to the theory of transmigration. The possible question and the likely difficulty lies in the arithmetical aspect of the theory. If from the beginning of the cosmos—and the cosmos in the Hindu counting is hundreds of million years old—persons dead were being reborn, and as every time only a few or a small percentage could possibly have managed to free itself from the necessity to be reborn under the compelling force of the law of 'karma' and its consequences, *a priori* a very large number would be reborn. If all of them were reborn as human beings, with all the births and deaths that must have to be counted in billions of billion times, the population of the world today would have had to be stated in terms of astronomical figures! There could hardly have been enough space on this planet to provide for only standing room for all of them. The present population, which is very big, disturbingly large, for the welfare of man, is only a tiny fraction of the total that can be expected on the basis of the theory of rebirth in human species! These two arithmetical aspects present a grave difficulty in the acceptance of the theory of transmigration as confined within human species. The amplification of the theory so as to open the possibility of humans of one birth being reborn as members of non-sentient species and/or of the vegetable kingdom, where once gone there is no return to the human species, helps to obviate the difficulty. As the text has it: "Because the beings in the low species [the vegetable kingdom] go on continually revolving in the round birth and death [without any escape] in that third world, this world [the world of humans] is not filled up [with human beings]." A little deliberation can convince anyone that even this explanation is too facile to eradicate the difficulty or meet the objection, which appears to me to be, in the last resort, of an irreducible nature !

The modification introduced in the Vedic view of 'svarga' (heaven) and of the Fathers is that it is a world where souls can remain only till the fruits of the actions of their previous possessors are enjoyed, and that all those, who go to 'pitṛloka', the world of the Fathers, have to be reborn in this world of mortals, as the text of the *Bhagavadgītā* (IX, 21) maintaining the possibility and non-permanence of 'svarga' as a condition of life after death puts it. When the souls are ready for rebirth they get born in the various stocks of man or animal in accordance with the worth of the works of their former possessors. With this interpretation which is a straightforward one, one has to admit that the departed souls of even evil-actioned persons manage to go to the world of Fathers or have to go there, as they must have had some merits to their credit. One's actions in this life thus have twofold result : first, the determination of the length of stay in the world of Fathers and its adjuncts, and second, the kind of the stock in which rebirth occurs. This is the destiny of those who attempt to live according to the injunctions of the standard religious system. And those among them who have committed certain heinous offences and sins evidently go direct to hell, i.e., 'fall'. Those who follow the course of living according to the new dispensation and attain knowledge of Brahman proceed to their destination of eternal bliss by another path. There is also a third path, or rather a fourth way of life after death, for some 'others' not specified that have to proceed by a third path to another type of birth and that is of the non-sentient vegetable kingdom.

The last condition of life after death, i.e., birth in a non-sentient stock, is mentioned as a state open after death in the *Kaṭha Upaniṣad* too (II, 2, 7) depending on action and learning. The *Śvetāśvatara Upaniṣad* (V, 11-12) refers to varied forms in general, without specification, in rebirth as due to action and in conformity with its worth.

Under such an exorable law compelling rebirth for a departed soul the only possibility of its need for provisions can arise during its temporary sojourn in the world of Fathers. But by the theory itself it is put out of court. The world is gained as a reward and is so assigned to the soul because there are enjoyments available, which are a befitting return for the trouble taken by its erstwhile possessor in living a good life. Second, the periods of stay being very varied no general rule can be formulated. Third, the souls that have to go to hell cannot benefit by any such tendance. Fourth, those souls that have to travel by a third path are wholly incapable of any benefit from anything. On the whole, therefore, it is clear that with the acceptance of the theory of transmigration as a valid theory of life after death, the oblational rites have no meaning. They must be considered to be an anachronism or a hang over from the past, from the intermediate stage of the development of the views of life after death, when the Fathers and their world had ceased to be looked upon as permanent and provided with eternal supplies on the one hand, and the performance of great sacrifices was becoming rare, when the theory of transmigration was started.

That something like this was once the actual state of affairs, anyway that the promulgators of the 'śrāddha' theory and practice had an inkling of the weakness of their position in face of the theory of transmigration, must be presumed from the later postulation of certain nondescript states after the cremation of the dead body, and of the need to provide bodies for those states. The attribution of the promulgation of 'śrāddha' to Manu, too, suggests that the new-fangled notion and practice were not thought to be capable of being accepted without demur, as they were in evident contradiction of the Ṛgvedic view, persisting through later Vedic and even classical times, of the inexhaustible and imperishable provisions in the world of the Fathers. The manes, who were to be among and of the Fathers, who were to be, and even now are, on occasions as Nāndīmukha (auspicious-faced) Pitṛs (Fathers), invoked to give blessings, could not easily be put in the position of poor dependents of their earthly descendants or be made to appear in the role of semi-evil spirits capable of causing misery and suffering to their close relatives on earth! Some compelling factor or some unquestioningly acceptable authority was needed to buttress up the new notion and practice of 'śrāddha'. And what could be better authority than the fabulously omnipotent and even omniscient Manu, represented in the *Manusmṛti* itself and accepted by posterity as the grandson of the Supreme Soul engaged in the process of the creation of the cosmos?

A more direct and emphatic indication of the discomfort and discordance felt by the promulgators of śrāddhas', or their followers, is preserved in the formula[45] that is cited at the beginning of a 'śrāddha'-rite. It announces the identity of the three immediate ancestors of the ego with Vasus, Rudras and Ādityas—I have quoted above the dictum of the *Manusmṛti* on this aspect—and declares solemnly that it is meant not only to bring merit to the manes named but also to procure salvation, 'mokśa', for them! This assertion is evidently made to silence any objection that the rite cannot benefit the manes, who must have been reborn, by stating that it will eventually have stopped for them the process of rebirth!

In spite of the contradiction between the theory of transmigration and rebirth after death on the one hand, and the postulation of the Fathers, their world, the manes and their 'śrāddhas' on the other, both of them went on developing. The complexity into which the latter grew, both in the postulation of newer needs of the departed soul for post-cremation bodies, and in the multiplication of oblational rites ('śrāddhas'), have been briefly stated above. There remains to be given a short account of the development of the theory of transmigration and rebirth.

At the outset of such an account of the theory of rebirth it may be pointed out, as a notable feature of current Hinduism, that the actual practice of the day shows the complex of belief and practice about the manes and their needs to be fairly common only in the most contracted form. The belief, however, in the theory of 'karmavipāka' and 'punarjanman', to use the significant term for the theory of transmigration and rebirth, is much more common and uniform through all the classes of society and is tenaciously held. So much so is this the case that the theory is rightly considered to be a cardinal principle of Hinduism.

An account of the theory of transmigration must begin with the famous Vāmadeva, who figures through history as the unforgettable archetype of all highly developed and liberated souls, and his bold and emphatic pronouncement of his experience. Vāmadeva may or may not have been a living personality and might have been only a mythical or legendary figure. And if he actually lived as a human personality we do not know the time when he lived and we may not be able to do so either. But all that does not very much matter for the history of the theory we are considering. For we know it for a fact that the speculative thinkers, who have for the first time represented Vāmadeva as having had that experience and who have left a record of his supposedly actual pronouncement of it, cannot be dated later than 500 B.C. and may be reasonably ascribed to the 6th century B.C. In the *Aitareya Upaniṣad* (II, 1, 3-5) the pronouncement attributed to this famous sage, while still he was lying in the womb of his mother, is that he knew all the births of all the gods and that he [in one of his own births] had put down one hundred towns of iron, i.e., he was Indra. The context in which this pronouncement is brought in, the section beginning as it does with the statement that it is a man who becomes an embryo, i.e., with the acceptance of rebirth, and proceeding to the specification of the third birth which is rebirth, fits the pronouncement into a support for the theory of transmigration and rebirth.

The next important statement, compelling unwavering acceptance of the theory is that of Lord Kṛṣṇa made in the *Bhagavadgītā* (IV, 5) in response to a challenging query of Arjuna. And that is that there have been many births, before the one in which they were acting together, both of Kṛṣṇa and Arjuna ; only that Arjuna was ignorant about them and Lord Kṛṣṇa remembered all of them. Further on, Arjuna, desiring to know what happens to a practitioner of 'Yoga', who is unable to acquire complete mastery over himself and the consequent or concomitant knowledge before he dies, Lord Kṛṣṇa assures him (*BhG*, VI, 37-45 ; also VII, 19) that nothing good is ever lost and that such a soul gets reborn in such families and with such endowment that they perforce advance him on the road to complete mastery and after many such progressively higher and better births he attains salvation. The *Bhagavadgītā* (XIV, 14-5) made a further elaboration in the theory of transmigration and rebirth in terms of the three qualities, 'sattva', 'rajas' and 'tamas', which, as constituents of primordial matter, go into the make-up of human personality. It maintains that persons if they die when their 'sattva' quality is in the ascendant or predominance attain worlds fit for gods and such other personalities to live in ; if they die when 'rajas' is strong they attain the worlds of people who are attached to action, while if they die when 'tamas' is the uppermost they are born in such low and silly stocks as those of the beasts and birds.

As Jñāneśvara made it clear in his commentary on the *Bhagavadgītā* text referred to above it refers to rebirth of individuals.

The *Manusmṛti* (XII, 40 ; and also VI, 63-5) compresses the two verses of the text referred to above into one verse and straightforwardly states that the preponderance of the quality of 'sattva' gets one after death into the divinity class, that of 'rajas' into that of men, while the excess of 'tamas' leads them to the low stocks. In every one of the three classes or three stocks ('yonis') 'sāttvika', 'rājasa' and 'tāmasa', there are three grades. It is noteworthy that the lowest grade of the lowest class, 'tāmasa', includes all immobile things like rocks and trees as also all small beasts and sentient creatures. The second grade, it should be noted, which contains the large beasts, like lions, pigs, horses and elephants, includes two human groups, one formed by the hated foreigners ('mlecchas') and the other by the 'sūdras', the fourth class of Hindu society ! In the highest grade of the 'tāmasa' class fall strangely birds, demons, ghosts and two groups of humans, one formed by actors and others like them and the other by deceitful persons ! While kings and Kṣatriyas, the second class of Hindu society, as well as, strangely, royal priests, with others, form the middling grade of the 'rājasa' destiny, and Brahmins, ascetics, saints among others the lowest grade of the 'sāttvika' class, the Vaiśyas are left out ! Sages, sacrificers and the Fathers with others and gods form the highest grade of 'sāttvika' destiny.

A still further elaboration is entered into in order to bring the subject of the normative book in active relation with the philosophy of life. The topic of offences and crimes against society and its morals is an important subject-matter of the book which has been the mentor of the Hindu Society for ages. They are grouped into sins of varying intensity; the most heinous sins, forming the most highly condemned actions, are called 'mahāpātakas'. The consequences of committing them, besides earthly punishment by the king, refer to the conditions of life after death. Such consequences are twofold. The perpetrators of such sins, i.e., their souls, have, first, to undergo suffering and tortures in various hells. Secondly, after suffering such punishment for 'many many years'—according to the thirteenth century commentator, Kullūkabhaṭṭa, for many thousands of years !—they are born into various stocks including those of dogs, pigs and camels ! Other sins and offences bring on births in other specific stocks (XII, 53-81). In the end it is stated that the 'entire' "bearing of fruit by actions" is thus expounded. This subject of differential condition of life after death and later differential births as consequences of specific actions while living is called the "bearing of fruit by actions" (XII, 82) or "resulting fruit of actions" (XII, 1) or "movements caused by action" (XII, 3).

The people's reaction to the theory, if available, is bound to be an indicator of the state of life after death in their beliefs. And I shall now turn to such evidence. The first piece of information that comes to my mind is Sītā's lament over her abandonment by Rāma as narrated in the *Rāmāyaṇa* (VII, 48, 4). Perplexed by her condition she wonders what sin she must have committed formerly or who it was that she had got separated from his wife that she should, in spite of her pure and chaste conduct, have been put away by Rāma, the king. In the counting of women of that epic age such a calamity as abandonment by a woman's husband, in spite of her pure and chaste conduct, could befall a woman only if she had perpetrated some heinous sin, or had, more specifically, caused a separation between a husband and a wife. Abandonment, without adequate cause, of a woman by her husband in this life was considered to be a retribution for one's evil action, in the previous birth, of bringing about a similar situation in the life of a couple.

An ordinary character, one from among the higher grades of labouring classes, appears to, and, almost boldly, in spite of his servile position, professes to be mindful of consequences of his actions for him in the hereafter in the drama *Mṛcchakaṭika* (VIII, ll. 33 after v. 24 to v. 27). Further he explains his servile condition as the consequence of his actions in previous life, and avows that he would not 'buy' more of such low condition in the next life by doing a wicked act in this life.

A book that has been world-famous for ages and a popular hortatory text of about the same age as the above-quoted drama, *Pañcatantra* by name, in its side-references and remarks provides a view of this theory, which is almost wholly modern, and contemporary as far at least as the non-élite majority is concerned. The word "prāktana" or "purākṛta" with 'karma' appended to it, 'the effect of the actions of the past', i.e., of the past birth, is said to follow its doer and track him out as a calf does its mother among thousands of cows. It lies down when he sleeps, and walks by his side when he moves and stands when he stands. Just as light and shade are invariably associated with each other so are the doer of actions and their effect (II, vv. 132-4). The belief associated with the such acceptance of the theory of 'karma', or 'prāktana' as the later-day vernacular usage has it, in working order prompted the author of the text to make a female pigeon, that was caught in a snare, aver that the condition, which it was in, was nothing but the fetters of past actions done by it (III, vv. 153-4), and to proclaim that all the worldly shortcomings like poverty, disease and pain are the fruits of the tree in the form of one's own evil action [in the past birth]. In another context the author philosophizes more widely and generally to declare that what is to happen, either good or bad, will happen in spite of the embodied ones acting continuously with a particular end in view. There is nothing to be said or done about it. For that is the earning in this life, which is the fruit of the actions, 'karma-pāka', of the embodied ones in their previous lives (I, v. 403).

This need not be considered to be a pessimistic attitude nor one of passivism as will be made clear in a later chapter, the one on Religious Living and its Goal,

Rāmadāsa, from the author of the *Pañcatantra,* is a far cry but his is the next statement on the subject that is to be considered. For that is more or less the current view of the matter in Maharashtra at least, and, as in many other points wherever parallel literature from the North has shown to be the case, in the North too. Even Rāmadāsa offers us rather little on the specific topic over and above what information I have already placed before my readers in connection with Hindu cosmology and cosmography. He reiterates the possibility of births in lower stocks like those of various animals in which there is no possibility of acquiring any knowledge or of making any attempt to get salvation. The birth in human species is a rare acquisition which is only had if a person has acquired merit equal to his demerit. For this latter important pronunciation he vouchsafes the authority of Vyāsa who is the counterpart in philosophy of Manu in law.

Rāmadāsa states the now-accepted dogma of transmigration being a cycle of eightyfour hundred thousand (8.4 million) birth-stocks (*Dāsabodha,* VIII, 20-8). This number of total birth-stocks, 'yonis', only the last of which is the human race, must have come to be fixed early ; how early I cannot specify. Jñāneśvara in the 13th century mentions (*Jñāneśvarī,* VII, 24 ; XIV, 107 ; XV, 149) the same number. Later the great North-Indian poet-saint-philosopher, Tulasīdāsa, who lived before Rāmadāsa, too, mentions the same number (*Tulasīdāsa Rāmāyaṇa,* I, d. 11, 1-2 ; VII, d. 68, 4). Whenever this number came to be fixed, it is to be noted that it is very much smaller than was postulated in the famous *Manusmṛti,* more than a thousand years before Jñāneśvara. According to it these stocks number thousands of crores, a crore being equal to ten million (VI, 63).

Another important piece of information regarding the theory, which tends to uphold my observation that the newer bodies said to be provided through 'śrāddhas' to the soul of the deceased are a new-fangled idea concomitant with their multiplication. Rāmadāsa definitively asserts that there are enough bodies in heaven both for those who have been righteous and thus have made their souls meritorious, and for those who are sinful. It is with these bodies provided there that the souls of the deceased are given over to either heavenly happiness or to hell fires (VII, 8, 16-17).

One 'svarga', heaven, that of Indra, is described in some detail. There all the 'lokapālas', guardians of the quarters, all the 'gandharvas', mythical beings of musical propensities and charming appearance, and all the 330 million gods reside. These are provided countless cows known as 'kāmadhenu', cow that oozes milk when desired, forests of wish-fulfilling trees ('kalpataru') lakes of nectar at every turn, innumerable wish-fulfilling stones ('cintāmaṇi') and mines of diamonds and gold-turning stones ('parīsa'). The ground there is all shining gold. And there being rocks of nine jewels the whole region is most beautifully variegated. Joys and delights there have no end or intermission. Meals consist of nectar. Sweet-smelling and divine unguents and similar flowers are in plenty, and completely satisfying music goes on unintermittently. There youth is eternal and the only age, neither old age nor death disturbing its even tenor. Needless to say there is neither pain nor disease there. Naturally the bodies of the denizens are both beautiful and brilliant (IV, 10, 13-22).

Some of the twentyone hells and their tortures too are briefly described. In one there are old worms, in another all decaying filth, in a third one hot ground, in another hot pillars to which the souls are tied up. In others souls are dragged, stretched out and thrown down, in others again they are whipped without intermission. Such are the torments of the hells, each one having a special variety of it befitting its name (III, 9, 19-27).

CHAPTER VIII

HINDU VIEW OF THE GODHEAD (FIRST PHASE)

IN the Ṛgvedic age, i.e., between about 1800 B.C. and about 1200 B.C., the Aryans in India, the incoming people who with the local residents were later to be known as Hindus, adored many deities. Their way of adoration, when the literature came under the scrutiny of western scholars, who, besides their Christian affiliation and staunch faith in one God, were aware of many other forms of religious consciousness, raised a controversy as to the name their religion should be known by. More or less soon and concertedly it came to be recognized that polytheism could not be the correct description of the religious attitude and consciousness exhibited in the *Rgveda*.

The *Rgveda* is a book, no doubt, but one which is a collection made some centuries after the poems or chants were composed by individual poets and by families of such, over a period of about five to six centuries from about 1800 B.C. to 1200 B.C. The collection consists, and has consisted for years since its compilation, of ten chapters with one thousand and twentyeight hymns ('sūktas'), comprising more than ten thousand and four hundred verses. Such a store of chants or prayers or poems spread over such a long period can hardly be expected to present only one unified view of the divine, the cosmos, and its creation or even of the total religious complex at that age of human culture.

In the first chapter I have briefly mentioned the view that favours looking upon the attitude towards the divine dominating the bulk of the poetry as henotheism. I have also pointed out that I consider the attitude of the Ṛgvedic poets to be different. It appears to me that it is sufficient to name it polylatry tending towards acceptance of a Supreme ordainer, either in the personal form of Puruṣa or Hiraṇyagarbha, or even in the impersonal one of Sat or Brahman.

The standard number of gods mentioned in the *Rgveda* itself is thirtythree (*RV*, I, 139, 11). They and some others, too, were offered worship for securing some worldly benefit. And the prevailing form of worship was one which, consisting of an offering, either oblation or a libation or both, was commonly called a sacrifice. Thus sacrifice was the mode of approach to, the technique of worship of, a deity. The offering, whether an oblation or a libation, and the latter was usually that of the intoxicating drink called Soma, was made into the fire. Fire or Agni was the carrier-deity, the god that carries the worship offered by the worshipper to a god, anyone of them to whom it was appropriate for the purpose to do so.

Agni or fire, a carrier, was thus an intermediary and also an intercessor. Functional gods appear to have been an important component of the Ṛgvedic pantheon. Many of them, however, like others whose nature raises them into great gods, though not ceasing to have a functional aspect, were invoked for general blessings or succour almost like great gods. However, their functional character so far predominates in their traits and in the incidents, if any, narrated of them that they must be described primarily as functional gods.

Agni or Fire-god, as a carrier of oblations to the gods, would in any functional hierarchy tend to rank higher than other functional gods. And the fact that he did so in the *Rgveda* would lend strong support to the suggestion that functionalism was an important aspect of the Ṛgvedic view of the godhead. A. A. Macdonell[1] observes: "Next to Indra he [Agni] is the most prominent of the Vedic gods". He is called "the nearest kinsman of man" and is often described as a father, sometimes as a brother, and even as a son or mother of his worshippers.[2]

None of these epithets is applied to Bṛhaspati, another functional god primarily—he is believed by expert Vedic students to be non-Indo-European and a pure Indian product[3]—, though, as his name implies, he was the lord of prayers or incantations, 'brahman', though he it was who communicated prayers to the human priests[4], prayers without which sacrifice, i.e., worship, could not be offered. And Bṛhaspati is not a minor or an insignificant deity in the *Rgveda*. Macdonell[5] tells us that "he occupies a position of considerable prominence". He is even called the father of all gods (*RV*, II, 26, 3). And he has been identified with Agni in several passages and even brought into the Indra complex as the latter's ally.

The importance of prayer, chant, or laud, 'brahman', in the Ṛgvedic religious complex is quite clear. It is so significant a category that it is personified and its vastness and majesty dwelt upon: "The fifteen lauds are in a thousand places: that is as vast as heaven and earth in measure. A thousand spots contain the mighty thousand. Vāk spreads forth as far as Prayer extendeth" (*RV*, X. 114, 8. Griffith's version*). Brahman is a potent protective force for human beings as the famous Bharatas in their dire need discovered in the prayer of their priest Viśvāmitra (*RV*, III, 53, 12). Another poet declares without any limitation or context the power of prayer in his song thus: "Our sires with lauds burst even the firm-set fortress, yea, the Aṅgirases, with roar, the mountain. They made for us a way to reach high heaven, they found us day, light, day's sign, beams of morning." (*RV*, I, 71, 2). Appropriate prayers, 'brahmans', are said to bring down Indra from heaven to help his worshipper (*RV*, III, 53, 8).

Pūṣan is another functional deity, appropriate for the pastoral stage of culture and also for the agricultural development in the Vedic age. He is the path-finder *par excellence*, one who seeks out hidden store or lost cattle and guides on unknown or tricky paths. His special epithet, 'paśupā', protector of beasts, underscores his pastoral connections. Macdonell observes: "The welfare which he bestows results from the protection he extends to men and cattle on earth, and from high guidance of men to the abodes of bliss in the

---

* Most of the renderings of Ṛgvedic texts are from R. T. H. Griffith's "The Hymns of the Ṛgveda".

next world."[6] Yet he does not receive the terms of affectionate phraseology which Agni does.

The path-finding, uncovering and revealing function had come to be so associated with Pūṣan that in the oldest Upaniṣad the thinker, who had come to postulate the Absolute but was evidently unable to visualize it, owing of course to the great mystery, addressed a prayer to Pūṣan, imploring him to reveal the mystery for him (*BrU*, V, 15).

Aśvins or Nāsatyas—actually, the twin-deity being a pair, the Sanskrit usage shows them in the dual number as 'Aśvinau' or 'Nāsatyau'—are an even more pronouncedly functional god. They are *par excellence* the healer-gods of whom early humanity, with so little knowledge of disease and its remedies and cures, was in dire need. The dual deity is not only the physicians of the Ṛgvedic Indians but also their surgeons. The exploits of relief and cure, comfort and rehabilitation, ascribed to this twin-deity are marvellous, almost bordering on the impossible. The space having been conceived as an ocean, this deity was also ascribed the function of saving ships in distress and finding treasures from the ocean. By a natural extension the deity could be and was made the guardian of immortality and was thought to be capable of warding off death from its worshippers. As Macdonell[7] observes: "In the *RV* they [the Aśvins] have come to be typically succouring divinities. They are the speediest helpers and deliverers from distress in general . . . [They] heal diseases with their remedies, restoring sight, curing the blind, sick, and maimed. . . . . Apart from their character as helpers, healers, and wonder-workers, their general beneficence is often praised." On the statistical ground of the frequency of reference this twin-deity is considered to be the most prominent in the *RV* next after Indra, Agni and Soma. They had so far been associated and even identified with their healing and comforting function in the Ṛgvedic age that the natural phenomenon, which is believed to have been its basis, was completely obscured. The deity had become so far anthropomorphized that a consort and a sister were postulated for it.[8]

In reference to the opinion of Vedic experts mentioned above it must be pointed out that on the score of the obscurity of the original nature of the twin-deity they had inferred that the deity was pre-Vedic and belonged to the Indo-European pantheon. Its name Aśvins was taken to be purely Indian[9] and it apparently remains so in spite of the later discoveries. That the Iranian *Zend-Avesta* speaks of a being called Nahonhaithya has been known for long. It is also known that he figures as an evil spirit in that Iranian literature along with another Ṛgvedic god even greater than him, i.e., Indra.[10] Still earlier attestation of this deity and much further west was known when A. B. Keith wrote and he drew on it to make a statement which I shall pass by here. F. Hrozny[11], the talented decipherer and interpreter of the Hittite tablets, is quite definite that in the treaty of about 1380 B.C. entered into between the Hittites and the Mitannis, the deities mentioned as the guardians of the treaty and by whose name the two nations must be taken to have sworn, so to say, are the four gods, i.e., Inarash or Indra, Arunash or Varuṇa, Mitrash or Mitra and Nashattijanna or Nāsatya.[12] It is further of great interest to know that though Aknish or Agnish, Ṛgvedic and Indian Agni, was one of the gods of the Hittites, he was not prominent enough to be given the position of a guardian deity, bearing witness and protecting the terms and conditions, and that Indra was known to the Hittites in 112 forms !

It will be appreciated that even with very limited delineation of the traits of Nāsatya among the Mitannis at our disposal, we have to acknowledge that the position of that deity in the Mitanni pantheon, whatever its composition and number, was much higher than and different from that of the counterpart, Ṛgvedic Aśvin-Nāsatya. The Mitanni deity had the position of a great god, one amongst the four witnesses to and guarantors of solemn contracts. The Ṛgvedic god was predominantly a rescuer, a succourer, a healer and a finder of hidden or lost treasure ! With all their marvellous exploits, however, Aśvins have not received from the Ṛgvedic poets any of those highly endearing epithets which have been heaped on Agni or Indra.

The unquestionably greatest[13] of the Ṛgvedic gods is, of course, Indra, whom Macdonell describes as "the favourite national god of the Vedic Indians" and Keith as "the greatest god of the Ṛgveda, with the solitary exception of Varuṇa, who may be deemed to equal him in might". The latter part of Keith's estimate is, I think, not quite correct and I shall have to say something about it later. For the present I want to make the point that Indra is the warrior-god, *par excellence*, of the Ṛgvedic peoples. As such there is no compeer of his and if this point is established and put to the readers, the question of the inaccuracy or impropriety of Keith's comparison of Varuṇa with Indra can be readily acknowledged.

Indra is the warrior-god of the Vedic Indians or as Macdonell puts it "the god of battle, who aids the victorious Aryan in the conquest of the aboriginal inhabitants of India", and as I should point out his devoted worshippers under the expert care of special poet-priests to such an extent that he appears with his exploits as "primarily the thunder god", the conqueror of the demons of drought or darkness. I do not mean to suggest that in origin it was not the phenomenon of thunder that gave the basis for this god but only to stress that the phenomena of light and rain and waters might have come to be represented in the light of battles as Indra came to the fore as a fighting god. Let me enumerate a few points in the description of the god as it occurs in the *Rgveda* sustaining this characterization of the deity as the warrior-god *par excellence*.

First, Indra is the only deity whose characteristic weapon, 'vajra', the thunderbolt, is a mighty killer, a most effective, invincible and special tool. Only once has this weapon been said to be borne by any other deity. And the deity is the group-one, the Maruts, who are the only gods other than Indra to whom sometimes the great exploit of Indra, the killing of Vṛtra, is attributed. And they are even spoken of as Indra's sons or brothers.[14] Second, Indra is called 'vajrabhṛt', wielder of the bolt, just as in later mythology Śiva is 'Śūlin', wielder of the spear, and Viṣṇu is 'Cakrin', wielder of the discus. Third, he receives not only the epithet of 'maghavan', reminding his worshippers and others of his bounteous nature, but also of 'śakra', 'śacīvat' or 'śacīpati', the mighty one, which, being very rarely applied to any other deity, is almost exclusively his, and becomes one of his names in later mythology. The latter two later provided the name of his consort, Śacī. Fourth, Indra is the only Ṛgvedic god who is credited with helping named historical persons in battle against their powerful enemies and securing them victory. He is once said to have slain more than 60,000 of the enemies of Suśravas. Macdonell observes on the variation in the tales of his military succour: "This varying attitude is a tolerably sure indication of historical matter. Here the national warrior god appears as the patron of Aryan migrations."[15] Even Keith[16] has to say: "It is he on whom men call in battle, and, little as the Vedic poetry is inspired with war-like spirit, here and there it is clear that the poet has caught some of the tone of war poetry."

The preeminence of Indra as the warrior-god secured for him a plenitude of sacrifices from the Vedic Indians. And worship or appeal through sacrifice meant the offering of 'soma', the intoxicating drink. Hence it came about that the Vedic usage called Agni, Fire-god, the carrier of offerings but Indra and Indra alone 'somapā' or the drinker of 'soma'. He was portrayed or very conveniently and naturally believed as very fond of that drink, so fond indeed as to lose his self-control and get intoxicated.[17] Soma, because of its great significance in the life and ritual of the Ṛgvedic Indians, had come to be personified and deified. Being associated with Indra in his exploits against Vṛtra, as his drink before the fight and the source of his vigour for it, Soma came to be "spoken of independently as a great fighter".[18] The observations of Keith on the same point are no less pronounced and corroborative of this view. He says[19]: "The poetry of the Ṛgveda is mainly connected with the Soma sacrifice, and this fact must be borne in mind in estimating the importance of the god Soma . . . he is invoked in parts of four or five others, and also as a joint deity with Indra, Agni, Pūṣan and Rudra . . . . the deeds which are given to Soma *are simply borrowed by him from the other gods, especially Indra and Agni, with whom he is very nearly associated, since the former is the great Soma-drinker* and the latter for his part is a god of ritual like Soma."

At this stage I shall quote an observation of Macdonell which puts Keith's statement about Varuṇa's might being equal to Indra's in its proper perspective and supports my view on the basis of which I described it earlier as not correct. Observes Macdonell[20]: "Regarded as a whole the attributes of Indra are chiefly those of physical superiority and of dominion over the physical world. Energetic action is characteristic of him, while passive sway is distinctive of Varuṇa. Indra is a universal monarch, not as the applier of the eternal laws of the universe nor as a moral ruler, but as an irresistible warrior whose mighty arms win victory . . . He is not usually described as possessing the moral elevation and grandeur of Varuṇa. There are, however, several passages which ascribe to Indra actions characteristic of Varuṇa."

It is not an adventitious circumstance that Viṣṇu bears in the Ṛgvedic poetry, as "most prominent secondary characteristic", "his friendship for Indra" and frequently figures as the latter's ally in his fight with Vṛtra, the greatest single exploit of Indra. This close association in wars of national significance to the Ṛgvedic Indians is reflected specifically in the fact that in the hymns extolling Viṣṇu, Indra is the only other deity that gets an explicit or implicit mention.[21]

This early association of Viṣṇu with Indra in the activity of clearing the earth of the human opponents of the Vedic Indians and also of the demoniac enemies foreshadows Viṣṇu's role in the mythology of later times as the helper and reliever of men from their wicked and cruel tormentors.

It is Indra's supremacy, as a god of might, and the people's loyalty to him as their war-god that must be considered to be responsible for Indra's description as incomparable and unequalled. In the words of the Ṛgvedic poets, "No one like him is known among the gods ; no one born, past or present, can rival him." The endearing terms used of him are even more varied and more frequent. He is not only a brother, a friend, a father, but even a mother or rather a father and mother in one.[22]

Indra is one of the four gods mentioned as witnesses and guardians of the treaty entered into between the Mitannis and the Hittites about 1380 B.C. I have already referred to Hrozny's statement that Indra as Inar or Inarash was not only a god of the Hittites mentioned in their treaty with the Egyptians but also that he was known to them in 112 forms. We have no more information about the nature attributed to him by the Mitannis or the Hittites. But the fact that both of these war-like and militant nations had him in their pantheons and put him down in the solemn conclusions of their wars must be interpreted as proving his role of a warrior-god. That he could not have been looked upon as a demon is quite certain. This has to be emphasized in view of the fact that in the religious literature of the Iranians, which is about five centuries later than the document of the Mitanni-Hittite treaty, Indra figures only as a demon just like, as pointed out above, Nāsatya !

It would have been in the fitness of things to speak of Varuṇa immediately after Indra but I have to defer his study in preference for Maruts and Mitra. For the former as Maruttash was a deity current among the Kassites, who, as Hall[23] stated years ago, were Indo-Europeans and had gained supremacy in Mesopotamia about 1700 B.C. The latter as Mitrashshil leads the group of four gods invoked as witnesses to the Mitanni-Hittite treaty.[24]

The Maruts, the Ṛgvedic deity, not infrequently invoked conjointly with Indra and as the sons of Rudra, are sometimes described as malevolent but have warlike exploits to their credit in the company of the earlier god Indra.[25] Nothing is known about the traits of Maruttash of the Kassites.

Apropos of Mitrashshil of the Mitannis—if he was also a deity of the Hittite pantheon is not known—it must be pointed out that the chief god of the Kassites was Suryash, who, as pointed out by Hall[26], is the Indian Sūrya, the sun-god. The sun-god is represented in the Ṛgvedic pantheon not only as Sūrya but also as Savitṛ and to some extent at least as Mitra.[27] Three other gods are aspects of the same deity. One of them, Pūṣan, has already been described above as an outstanding illustration of the functional nature of the god-head as conceived by the Ṛgvedic Indians. The other two are Aryaman and Varuṇa who are described as standing "in close connection with Sūrya". There is moreover Uṣas[28], the Dawn, whose intimate association with the Sun-god is too plain to be missed, much less ignored. To this list has to be added Viṣṇu, a deity who, from being of secondary status in the *Rgveda*, rose to be the supreme one at about the end of the Brāhmaṇa period, i.e., about five centuries thereafter, who "was originally conceived as the sun . . . as the personified swiftly moving luminary, which with vast strides traverses the whole universe".[29]

Then there is the whole group of gods called Ādityas ; the name of these gods in later mythology and literature in the singular came to be appropriated by the sun. Among the six most frequently mentioned Ādityas occur Mitra, Aryaman, Bhaga and Varuṇa. In the later sections of the *Rgveda* the number of Ādityas comes to be specified as seven. It is interesting to note that one more Āditya, the eighth, who is described as having been brought in later, is Mārtaṇḍa. Mārtaṇḍa in later mythology and religion becomes a name of the sun. In some stray references both Sūrya and Savitṛ are listed among the Ādityas. The more commonly intended Ādityas are Mitra, Varuṇa and Aryaman, a deity most commonly coupled with Mitra and Varuṇa.[30]

Sūrya as a member of the Kassite pantheon lends significance to their word 'bugash' for 'god' which in the form of 'bogu' in the Old Slavonic and as 'Bagaios' in the Phrygian[31] is perfectly Indo-European. Its cognate Sanskrit is, of course, Bhaga, who is one of the deities of the solar complex in the *Rgveda*. In the Iranian form of 'bagha' meaning 'god' it occurs in the *Zenda-Avesta* as an epithet of Ahura Mazda. Yāska, the ancient Indian philologist, describes Bhaga as presiding over the forenoon. Uṣas, Dawn, is described in the *Rgveda* as Bhaga's sister.[32] In at least two verses of one hymn (VII, 38) and in one verse each of two others (V, 42, 5 ; 48, 5) he is spoken of in such context with Savitṛ that it leaves a strong impression on the readers' mind that Savitṛ is addressed as Savitṛ-Bhaga, the two being identified with each other. In the marriage hymn, Sūrya's bridal hymn, Bhaga is invoked in the company of Savitṛ and Aryaman (X, 85, 36). It is in keeping with this specification that one expert opined that Bhaga is identified with Savitṛ, or the latter with Bhaga, "in the single hymn of Savitṛ Bhaga".[33]

Another deity of the solar complex is also attested as clearly Indo-European but confined to their Asiatic branch. Mitra appropriately figuring as Mithra in the Iranian language is considered by Vedic experts as "an almost undoubted sun-god" in Iran.[34] He has been mentioned already as figuring in the Mitanni-pantheon. But Mitra is not traced in the early European Indo-Europeans.

Maruts traced among the Kassites and Hittites have not evidently been traced among the Iranians. Aryaman on the other hand is known among the Iranians[35] but so far not among the more western Indo-Europeans.

Both Savitṛ and the group of solar gods, Ādityas, are met with only among the Ṛgvedic Indo-Europeans. And it is a well-known fact that only among their descendant Hindus Savitṛ, the sun-god since the Ṛgvedic times, has kept the function ascribed to him. He is still invoked with the same prayer with which the Ṛgvedic Indians addressed him : "On the splendid brilliance of God Savitṛ do we meditate ; that He may excite our intellect" (*RV*, III, 62, 10) is the prayer repeated twice a day by twice-born Hindus, who still perform their morning and evening adoration as laid down. That this adoration was almost a universal observance among the twice-born section is capable of being attested from literature. Here I shall mention only one example of it which is undoubtedly the most significant. In the *Rāmāyaṇa* (III, 11, 68-9 ; VII, 81, 21-3) Rāma's evening adoration is specifically drawn attention to as a necessary and unavoidable observance. It is in the *Rāmāyaṇa* (VI, 105, 3 ff), too, that the great importance attached to the sun-god as a victory-grantor comes out in bold relief. Agastya is represented as having taught Rāma the great victory-procuring chant called "Āditya-hṛdaya", 'Sun-heart', whose repetition is suggested as the source of Rāma's final and complete victory over Rāvaṇa.

In the Egyptian sections of this work I have drawn attention to the observations of the great Egyptologist E. A. Wallis Budge emphasizing the very superior nature of the Ṛgvedic attitude and approach to the Sun-god as enshrined in the verse quoted above and in other texts of the *Rgveda*, compared with the almost mechanical view of the Sun-god which the hymns of the reformist pharaoh of Egypt, Ikhnaten, typifies. Ikhnaten and his theological advisers were preparing their hymns in Egypt about the same time that the Ṛgvedic poet-sages were composing and using their prayers to Savitṛ in India ! The great contrast underscores the difference in the attitude of the Indians, which is not only more intellectual but also more religious and philosophical.

The special development and emphasis on the functions ascribed to the complex of solar deities by the Ṛgvedic Indians must, to some extent at least, explain the slow but sure eclipse of the god of moral law, to a subordinate and almost nondescript place. The extraordinary importance of Indra as the warrior-god was already a potent factor in this process and the development of the solar complex, with its close connection with not only holy and eternal Law but also with Varuṇa himself, supplemented the force at work, so that, with the philosophical speculation already recorded in many hymns of the First and the Tenth books, the latest among the entire lot, at about the end of the Ṛgvedic age Varuṇa receded into the background and his ordinances ('vratas'), and his fetters ('pāśas') were supplanted by the more ancient 'ṛta', 'order', and later on by 'satya', truth.

The complex of solar deities as gods was ascribed the special functions of proclaiming the innocence of the worshippers (*RV*, I, 123, 3 ; V, 82, 6 ; VII, 60, 1 ; 62, 2 ; 66, 4 ; X, 12, 8 ; 35, 2 ; 36, 1 and 12), of exciting their intellects (III, 62, 10 ; V, 82, 2) and of maintaining or strengthening the Law (III, 59, 2 ; V, 81, 4 ; VII, 82, 10 ; 63, 3 ; VIII, 75, 5).

Leaving out Varuṇa and Uṣas all the other deities of the complex have together received about 38 hymns. The most famous expression of the second function is given above in another connection. I shall add one specimen each of the other two functions. Here is one praying to Savitṛ for proclamation of innocence : "The counsel which the Gods meet to consider their secret plan,—of that we have no knowledge. There let God Savitṛ, Aditi, and Mitra proclaim to Varuṇa that we are sinless."[36] Of the last function, that of maintaining or strengthening holy Law, the following is a good example : "May Indra, Varuṇa, Mitra and Aryaman vouchsafe us glory and great shelter spreading far. We think of the beneficent light of Aditi, and Savitṛ's song of praise, the God who strengthens Law."[37]

The god, who in later mythology got displaced, totally as I should say, for he lost not only his dominance in the awe-compelling domain of mundane life but also in the reverence-inspiring one of life hereafter, Varuṇa now claims our attention as the ordainer *par excellence* of the earlier period. As for his position in the Ṛigvedic pantheon and age Macdonell's[38] estimate that Indra and Varuṇa "tower above the rest as leading deities about equal in power, Indra as the mighty warrior and Varuṇa as the supreme moral ruler" more or less adequately sums it up for the earlier period. As against 250 hymns for Indra, 200 for Agni, 120 for Soma and 50 for Aśvins, for Varuṇa there are only about 30 hymns.[39] Varuṇa, therefore, cannot be called a popular deity of the Ṛgvedic Indians, though his greatness and even supreme eminence in the earlier period cannot be gainsaid.

Varuṇa was a god of the Mitanni-pantheon and was an important one too, as his name was mentioned along with Mitra, Indra and Nāsatya as the guarantor of their treaty with the Hittites. About three or four centuries later, i.e., about 1000 B.C., in Iranian religion as reformed by Zoroaster, Varuṇa, as Ahura Mazda, became the Supreme God of the people of Iran.[40] In the *Rgveda* not only Varuṇa but other gods, too, were often, particularly in the earlier period, called Asuras. But later throughout Hindu mythology, beginning with that of the later portions of the Ṛgveda, the term 'asura' meant a demon, and its opposite 'sura', as god, came to be in regular use, so that 'asura' appears as a negative formation from the original word 'sura' meaning 'god'. The other word for 'god' is 'deva'. It is attested in the Ṛgveda almost throughont.[41] And gods, 'devas', as a category are protectors *par excellence* (*RV*, X, 36, 2-12) but not so 'great deities' or 'asuras'. As a matter of fact I am not at all sure that the plural of the word 'asura' is used in the *Rgveda*. 'Deva' was so much of a linguistic currency that its standard negative 'adeva', meaning, either demon, man or godless man, occurs not quite infrequently (*RV*, VIII, 46, 21 ; X, 37, 3).

For whatever reason the word 'asura' came to be used to designate the human and non-human enemies of the Indo-Aryans in the literature known as the *Brāhmaṇas*[42], there is reason to believe that this use of the word, however, was much earlier though evidence of the fact is not as full and explicit as is available in the *Brāhmaṇa* literature. Thus in the *Atharvaveda* (II, 40, 8)[43] Indra's 'vajra', bolt, is called the Asura-slaying missile. That the word 'asura', at least, was an earlier formation and linguistic usage in the consciousness of the ancient Indians may be said to be preserved in the story of the earliest *Upaniṣads* (*BrU*, I, 3, 1) about the competition between Asuras and Devas in which it is stated that 'Asuras' were the elder brothers of Devas.

The word 'asura', however, is so far traced only among the Iranians besides the Indo-Aryans ; but the word 'deva' is thoroughly Indo European with its cognates in Greek, Latin and Lithuanian, with more or less the same meaning. The English word 'deity' shows it to be as alive today among a large section of the contemporary Indo-Europeans as 'deva' is among the Indo-Aryans and Hindus. In the Iranian language and literature, however, it signified the opposite of a deity, a demon.[44]

One Ṛgvedic usage appears to me as instructive and that is that whereas Varuṇa is frequently called 'asura' and Savitṛ, the sun-god in the role of an inspirer, is addressed as 'deva', the latter term is hardly ever applied to Varuṇa.[45] Macdonell[46], observing that "in nearly half its [Savitṛ's] occurrences the name [Savitṛ] is accompanied by *deva*, god", suggests that the association should be interpreted as indicating the fact that the name was still looked upon as "an epithet meaning 'the stimulator god' ". In so interpreting it Macdonell did not give due weight to the absence of the application of the term 'deva' to Varuṇa and of the word 'asura' in connection with Savitṛ. One has also to remember that another name, etymologically meaning 'god', Bhaga, though an independent deity in the *Rgveda*, is "often added to that of Savitṛ so as to form a single expression" *Bhagaḥ Savitā*[47] which parallels 'Devaḥ Savitā'.

Proper appreciation of this differential use would suggest the dichotomy of 'asura' and 'deva' being intimately associated with the postulation of the newer aspect of the Sun-god, that of a stimulator, more of intellectual than of physical energy, as against that of Varuṇa, whose sun-aspect was so pale and remote. It is very natural, too, that the term 'deva' meaning etymologically 'the shining one', should be attached to the sun rather than to any abstract or metaphorical aspect of it. I have already drawn attention to Wallis Budge's pointed remarks on the great contrast between the Ṛgvedic prayer chants addressed to Savitṛ, the Sun-god, and the famous hymn of Aten composed by Ikhnaten and his religious advisers in Egypt about the fourteenth century B.C.

To emphasize the significance of the advance made by the Vedic Indians in their approach to the Sun-god I shall mention here Gurney's estimate of the development in the Hittite religion through three centuries to about the middle of the 13th century B.C. The Sun-god appears in the mythology as the king of gods and figures in most of the lists of gods attached to the treatise as guarantors. Like his Babylonian counterpart, Shamash, he appears as the god of right and justice. The prayer addressed to the Sun-god by King Muwatallis, the one who brought about the victorious end of a long conflict with Egypt about 1285 B.C., reads: "Sun-god of heaven, my lord, shepherd of mankind! Thou risest, O Sun-god of heaven, from the sea and goest upto heaven. Oh Sun-god of heaven, my lord, daily thou sittest in judgment upon man, dog, pig, and the wild beasts of the field."[48]

The Hittites were a nation whose royalty and the topmost aristocracy must have been formed by a band of immigrant Indo-Europeans.[49] In view of this the development of the idea of the Sun-god as the stimulator of intellect among the Ṛgvedic Indians is certainly a significant one, which should explain the relative eclipse of Varuṇa. This process was helped by the common practice of attributing some of the traits of one god to another, not only those like strength, glory, generosity and wisdom in general, which are the attributes of the major gods[50], but especially some which Varuṇa is known to have had in abundance more or less as his speciality, to all sun-deities in some measure. Savitṛ, in particular, as already pointed out above, was ascribed almost all the moral traits of Varuṇa though not in as great an abundance or in as great a frequency or in even as great an earnestness.

It appears to me that there had been taking place another ideological growth in the Ṛgvedic age which helped the process of Varuṇa's eclipse through his having been associated with the Sun-god, either as plain Sūrya or as the stimulator Savitṛ. And that is the postulation and furtherance of Truth, 'satya', as an abiding principle over against Eternal Law, 'ṛta', the special field of Varuṇa among the Ṛgvedic Indians, which was an Indo-European heritage common to the Khurris, the Mitannis and the Indo-Aryans. The idea connoted by 'ṛta' had been so incorporated in the culture of the former two peoples that the word formed the first member of the names of some of their kings, the component expression meaning 'the most pious'.[51]

Before substantiating the above suggestion about the relative eclipse of Varuṇa and his special field of moral authority through the newer development of the stimulator-aspect of the Sun-god as Savitṛ and the prominence of the principle of truth, 'satya', which appears to synchronize more or less with the postulation of abstract deities, particularly like 'Śraddhā', Faith, and 'Vāk', Speech or Logos, and of the Absolute 'Sat', Being, I must briefly characterize Varuṇa as a deity of the Ṛgvedic pantheon.

Macdonell[52], appraising the relative importance and roles of the two Ṛgvedic gods, Indra and Varuṇa, the former of whom receives 250 hymns and the latter only about 30 in the whole collection of hymns called the *Rgveda*, singled them out as the "leading deities about equal in power, Indra as the mighty warrior and Varuṇa as the supreme moral ruler". Further expanding his appraisal he stated that Varuṇa with his moral attributes—we have seen that he was an Indo-European concept of wide prevalence about 1400 B.C.—developed among the Iranians into the supreme god Ahura Mazda with moral attributes and domain. Many other scholars have put forward more or less similar views and Keith in particular, reiterating Macdonell's opinion, has attempted to account for the different situation in the Indian pantheon on the ground of the importance of the warrior-god in the Indian situation, on the one hand, and of the sacrificial god, Agni, on the other, and with the additional ground of the later postulation of Prajāpati as the Supreme God. He has rightly insisted that only these three gods could be conceived as having any special connection with moral order or morality.[53]

Macdonell did not stop at the judgment recorded above but added the most proper and necessary elaboration that Varuṇa "cannot be called a popular god". I may add what I have already pointed out in proper context that Indra and Agni and some other gods, too, on the other hand, can be called 'popular' gods. Perhaps there was a rivalry between Indra and Varuṇa for this position. However, the result was ultimately in favour of Indra, in spite of the argument, as presented in the 42nd hymn of the IVth book of the *Ṛgveda*, turning in support of Varuṇa as Keith[54] has pointed out.

The two titles of royal status occurring in the *Ṛgveda* are 'svarāj', independent ruler, and 'samrāj', universal ruler. The former more precisely belongs to Indra while the latter is frequently associated with Varuṇa, who is only occasionally called 'svarāj'. The title of 'samrāj', on the other hand, which is not infrequently predicated of Indra is also given to Agni a few times. It is, however, in association with Mitra that Varuṇa and therefore Mitra-Varuṇa, receives mostly this title. It appears from the statements of both Macdonell and Keith that the epithet 'svarāj' is never, or almost never, applied to any other deity than Indra.[55] Further I should point out that in the appropriate gender form the royal title 'queen' is bestowed on the great abstract deity Speech or Logos who describes herself as 'raṣṭrī' in a hymn[56] which begins with the declaration by Vāk, Logos, that she bears up on high Varuṇa and Mitra as well as Indra and Agni and the twin-gods Aśvins.

The special features of Varuṇa are that not only has he thousand eyes but also has spies who are thousand-eyed and he is consequently omniscient in a true and verbal sense, his omniscience serving as the standard of comparison. His 'pāśas', fetters, are another distinctive trait of his. They are the most dreaded because they can bind, the word being used in connection with another deity—only one and that is Agni—only once.[57] Varuṇa's speciality of the fetters makes him much sought after for forgiveness. As Macdonell points out, there is, therefore, no hymn addressed to him which does not contain some prayer for forgiveness of guilt.

Confession of sin, pleading innocence on the plane of intention and expression of repentance even for an unintentional breach are beautifully expressed in one hymn (*RV*, VII, 86) addressed to Varuṇa, no such expression occurring in any of the prayers addressed to other deities.[58]

The concept of moral order in the universe, in the opinion of Vedic experts, was enshrined in the term 'ṛta' which meant not only straight but also correct. And as mentioned above the word goes back to Indo-European times and occurs in the records of about 1400 B.C. in such a context that its reference to righteousness is unmistakenly its early connotation. In the *Ṛgveda* 'ṛta', which is said to be under the guardianship of the highest gods—Mitra-Varuṇa, Indra-Varuṇa, Bṛhaspati, Agni, Soma, Ādityas, being mentioned in its connection in the more than one hundred references, not counting the repeated mentions in the same hymn, which occur in the *Ṛgveda*—, also designates the order of the sacrifice or rite[59] in the world of religion apart from morality.

Varuṇa by himself or more commonly in the company of Mitra and sometimes Aryaman, too, is called[60] 'ṛtapā', guardian of 'ṛta', 'ṛtasya rathyaḥ', the charioteer of 'ṛta' or 'ṛtāvan', observer of order.

Varuṇa's association with 'ṛta'—though Keith himself points out the threefold aspect of 'ṛta', eternal law or order ; and he and others have not failed to emphasize the fact of the association of 'ṛta' with other gods—has led Keith to make an observation which I think is doubly incorrect and conducive to erroneous view of the Hindu religious development, and must be contested at this stage. Keith observes[61] : "Varuṇa is essentialy connected with Ṛta whereas Indra with Satya."

Indra, however, whether in Keith's characterization of him or in the more detailed and systematic one of Macdonell, does not show any trait which speaks of his association with 'satya' as such. As a matter of fact Macdonell's[62] remark that "in the great majority of instances *satpati*, 'stronglord', is appropriated to Indra is in amplification of his observation that the epithet 'śatakratu', 'having a hundred powers', is almost wholly applied to Indra, who is thus the god of might. Thus what is associated with Indra is might and not right or truth.

'Satya', truth, on the other hand, is quite clearly and preponderantly associated with the Sun-god either as Sūrya or Savitṛ. Thus the Sun-god, Sūrya, is expected to declare the truth, 'satya', i.e., the sinlessness of the worshipper, to Varuṇa and Mitra (*RV*, VII, 60, 1) ; and 'Savitṛ' is called 'satyadharmā', one whose nature is truth (*RV*, X, 34, 8), just as Varuṇa is 'dhṛtavrata', one whose ordinances are firm. In another context yet (*RV*, X, 37, 2) truth-speech is exhorted to protect the worshipper and the exhortation is somehow connected with the rise of the Sun, 'Sūrya'. Alternatively, Savitṛ is called 'satyasava', one who produces truth (*RV*, VI, 83, 7 ; X, 36, 13). This does not mean that 'satya', truth, is not at all associated with any other god. As a matter of fact 'Mitrā-Varuṇau', Mitra and Varuṇa, are not only 'ṛtāvānau', possessed of 'ṛta', their special trait, but are also 'satyau', truthful, (*RV*, V, 67, 4), and Varuṇa in particular is known as a discriminator of 'satya', truth, and 'anṛta', falsehood (*RV*, VII, 49, 3). But then Soma, too, is said to protect the truth and to bring falsehood or the false ones to nothing (*RV*, VII, 104, 12).

The opposite of 'sat', truth, is 'asat', falsehood, and the word is used in that sense in at least two places (*RV*, VII, 104, 8 and 12). 'Sat' also came to own its etymological meaning of great philosophical significance, the kernel or the soul of Hindu philosophy, from the Upaniṣadic age, i.e., from about the 9th or the 8th century B.C., to contemporary times, at the end of the Ṛgvedic age. We have that famous hymn (*RV*, X, 129, 1) which is known in the Indian tradition as the 'Nāsadīya Sūkta' with its declaration that "Neither non-Being nor Being was there then".

The concept of 'satya' appears to have been a purely Indian invention, showing no parallel formation in the other Indo-European peoples and languages. It is, therefore, interesting to note: First, that like 'ṛta', 'satya', too, even in the *Ṛgveda* itself, has its negative 'asat'; and second, that both the words 'ṛta' and 'satya' sometimes, however infrequently, occur in the same passage implying some difference and distinction in the connotations of the two words. Thus in the 85th hymn of the Xth book of the *Ṛgveda* we read[63]: "Truth ('satya') is the base that bears the earth; by Sūrya are the heavens sustained. By Law ['ṛta'] the Ādityas stand secure, and Soma holds his place in heaven." And it is instructive to note that tradition, as represented in the interpretation of the word 'satya' in this passage by the great commentator Sāyaṇa, equated 'satya' with Brahman, which actually and factually is the case in many Upaniṣadic passages. Another Ṛgvedic poet was more specific and emphatic about the primordial state and the origin of the universe, and asserted (X, 72, 2-3), as did, later, one of the Upaniṣadic thinkers, that in the beginning there was only 'asat', non-Being, and that 'sat', Being, was produced from it.

In another text of the *Ṛgveda* (X, 190, 1) describing the creation of the universe, both 'ṛta' and 'satya' in that order are declared to have been produced from 'tapas', austerity, or fervour as Griffith tenders it. More often than not, Sāyaṇa, wherever he finds the two words 'ṛta' and 'satya' in the same passage, interprets the former as meaning mental or ideational truth and the latter as uttered truth. 'Ṛta' is the ideational truthfulness and 'satya' is the spoken counterpart, the two together meaning 'truthfulness in thought and speech'.

It may further be noted that in a number of passages, where 'ṛta' occurs by itself without the juxtaposition of 'satya', Sāyaṇa renders it by 'satya' (*RV*, IV, 5, 11; X, 35, 8; 61, 19; 62, 3; 86, 10), thus suggesting that with process of time and thought 'ṛta' and 'satya' were being assimilated to each other. However, the actual record shows that the distinction was not only fully recognized but that more or less consciously 'satya' was being pushed into the forefront and 'ṛta' into the background.

In the *Bṛhadāraṇyaka Upaniṣad*, ascribed to before the 8th century B.C., in one account of the creation wherein water is the primordial substance, the first creation from it is declared to have been 'satya'. And 'satya' is said to have created Brahman in a sense, because Brahman is itself 'satya' or rather 'satya' itself is Brahman (V, 5, 1). The text further elaborates the statement in the light of the preceding (V, 4) assertion repeated here that 'Truth' is Brahman. The way the emphasis is laid on making the word one of three syllables and the manner in which its mystic significance is elaborated in a succeeding passage quite clearly establishes the fact of 'Satya' having attained to more or less the same position as the mystic syllable 'aum', though with a different history and an actual connection with its etymology. The *Chāndogya Upaniṣad* (VIII, 3, 5), an almost equally old book, not only repeats the statement of 'satya' having three syllables but also goes a step further in its bold pronouncement (VI, 9, 4) : "That which is the subtle essence, this whole world has for its self. That is the Truth ; that is the Self and that thou art, Śvetaketu." This self-same text recurs in the *ChU* twice : once (VI, 16, 3) in the context of an ordeal which clearly establishes the recognition of the power of 'satya' to protect its practitioner, devotee or worshipper but without the preliminary reference to the subtle essence, and another time (VI, 15, 3) without that context but complete with the preliminary reference. Thus the elevation of 'Satya' into the Individual self and the Supreme Soul is complete.

The *Taittirīya Upaniṣad* (I, 12) address to Brahman and to Vāyu, the wind-god, as the manifest Brahman, in further identifying Vāyu and Brahman, as 'ṛta' and also as 'satya', carries forward the ideological achievement regarding 'satya', still keeping alive the consciousness of the earlier 'ṛta', whose place 'satya' was being made to occupy. In conformity with this attitude of the particular Upaniṣad in another passage (I, 9), where a number of moral qualities and study are enjoined as imperative accompaniment of Brahman-pursuit, the enumeration begins with 'ṛta' and passes on to 'satya', ultimately recording the opinion in favour of 'satya', austerity ('tapas'), and study and teaching, as the most acceptable one. The *Kena Upaniṣad* (IV, 8) in a straightforward manner pronounces Truth, 'satya', to be the abode of Brahman, while the *Praśna Upaniṣad* (I, 15) asserts that the world of Brahman is attained by them alone in whom austerity, chastity and truth, 'satya', are established. And the *Muṇḍaka Upaniṣad* (II, 1, 7) in its account of the creation from the Immutable, lists austerity ('tapas'), faith ('śraddhā'), chastity ('brahmacarya'), injunction ('vidhi') and 'satya', truth, dropping out 'ṛta' altogether.

Then comes the climax in the career of 'satya' as proclaimed first in the *Bṛhadāraṇyaka Upaniṣad* (I, 3, 28 ; I, 4, 14) and later in the *Muṇḍaka Upaniṣad* (III, 1, 4-5). In the first passage the prayer-formula, "From the unreal ('asat') lead me to the real ('sat'), from darkness ('tamas') lead me to light ('jyotis'), from death ('mṛtyu') lead me to immortality ('amṛta')", clearly envisages 'satya' as the Real, the Absolute. In the second passage the creation of the universe from *Brahman* is detailed, evidently with the sole purpose of tracing the origin and maintaining the identity of 'satya' and 'dharma' or Truth and Justice. For *Brahman* is described as not being content with the creation of the four classes ('varṇas') of the society and as having proceeded to create for the Kṣatriya, the ruling class, its 'real' power, viz., 'dharma'. It is further asserted without any ado that what is 'dharma' is nothing but 'satya'. Thus 'satya' is identified with the new category of 'dharma' and the latter with 'satya' in the words, "Verily, both these ('dharma' and 'satya') are the same." Here 'satya', which was previously raised in the philosophical sphere to the supreme position as being identical with *Brahman*, was further enthroned in the social sphere as not the embodiment of 'dharma', the special creation in the interests of the social order, but as 'dharma' itself, as being the other word for the same concept.

Keith[64], commenting on the use of the words 'ṛta', 'satya' and 'dharma' in the *Rgveda* and the later Vedic literature, states that 'satya' superseded 'ṛta' in the *Brāhmaṇa* literature and that 'dharma' was formally personified in the *Śatapatha Brāhmaṇa*. He has mentioned only four references to 'dharman' in the *Rgveda*. Two of them being the replica of each other, in reality they turn out to be only three. He has not given any reference to 'satya', for which about a dozen I have already mentioned. Surprisingly Keith has omitted the only one more reference to 'dharma' which is very important because in that text (*RV*, VIII, 35, 13) Dharma appears as a deity in the company of the gods, Mitra, Varuṇa, Maruts, Sūrya, Uṣas, Ādityas and Aśvins.

The relations between 'satya', 'ṛta', and 'dharma' in the masculine gender, postulated in the Upaniṣadic thought are such that 'satya' occupies the supreme position in the philosophical field, though 'ṛta' is mentioned as something very significant, and it gets identified with 'dharma' which thus has the additional accretion of significance in the social field.

It is no wonder that India (Bhārata), though a secular state in theory, has as its motto the Upaniṣadic pronouncement of the supremacy of 'satya', viz. 'Truth alone is victorious' (*Muṇḍ. Up.*, III, 1, 6). The latter portion of the Upaniṣadic text, which is omitted in the motto reads: "but not untruth. Truth opens up the Devayāna path", i.e., leads to salvation. And truth formed the supreme value in the religio-ethical thought of the Upaniṣadic age. A preceptor, giving his pupil, who was in residence with him for about twelve years, leave to depart on the completion of his studies, exhorts him to conduct himself in a specific manner. The very first exhortation reads, "speak the truth", 'satya'. It is further emphasized by the injunction not to deviate from the truth, 'satya' (*Taittirīya Up.*, XI, 1).

'Ṛta', order, though it was moral Law, was also physical and ritual order of the sacrifice. 'Satya' has no such connections with or connotation of physical order or sacrificial rite. The enthronement of 'satya' can thus be adjudged to be an advance in the philosophical orientation of Indian religion from the predominantly sacrificial one of the *Rgveda*.

I need not make an apology to draw the reader's attention to a development in regard to 'ṛta' that must have taken place in the Iranian society and religion as I have not seen any reference to it anywhere in the literature on Vedic or Hindu religion, perhaps not even in any book on comparative religion.

D. C. Sircar has obligingly provided us with a very important inscription of the great Iranian Emperor Xerxes, about 470 B.C. (*Select Inscriptions*, pp. 14-5). It informs us of the change in religious practice of the Indians of north-western India that Xerxes had brought about. He had got them to worship Ahura Mazda and to observe the 'ṛta's and the 'brahman's of his. The expression 'ṛta's and 'brahman's is rendered as "truthful words approved in the Persian religion". In the same inscription the word 'ṛtavān' is rendered as "happy". It is clear that more or less parallel development had gone on in the Iranian society in the matter of 'ṛta', with this difference that the word 'ṛta' was given the connotation of 'satya' by the Iranians without having the latter as a new concept, and also that of the general one of happiness in the life hereafter.

Sacrifice, of course, was the mode of approaching the gods with requests for worldly and other goods and freedom from distress. It consisted in making an offering in fire with the accompaniment of chants, lauds, hymns or prayers. And it is the collection of these chants, mostly to be recited at the sacrifice with the 'soma'-drink, that is known as the *Rgveda*. The 'soma'-drink was such an essential element in the total act of sacrifice that Soma as a deity receives, as already stated, a sizeable number of hymns in its praise; and pressing of soma itself implies a religious action or a pious mind which deserves, and is expected, to receive glorious rewards from the gods.[65]

Sacrifice was so important an approach to the deity, so necessary for the cosmic order that the whole creation came to be thought of as an act of sacrifice. Without sacrifice nothing could be conceived to have resulted as in the life of the people nothing could be gained without offering a sacrifice to the gods! That is how we get the famous Puruṣa-hymn (*RV*, X, 90) which chants the glory of the great sacrifice of the Primordial Being and the creation of the cosmos out of it. In two other hymns (*RV*, X, 81 and 82) at least, both addressed to Viśvakarman, the creator-god who in later mythology becomes the artisan-god or the artificer-god, the notion that sacrifice is an act of creation is suggested through the assertion that Viśvakarman was both a primeval sacrificer and a creator. In another hymn (*RV*, X, 130, 2-3 and 6-7) we are told that the great seven sages—they figure as such throughout Hindu mythology till today as secondary creators—who first offered sacrificial worship and thus may be said to have promulgated the particular mode of approach to the deity, had become by that very fact god-like. The hymn is known as the creation-hymn and deals with sacrifice, the first of its kind, suggesting that it constitutes creation. And a question is asked in regard to the specification of its various parts in terms of the creation but is left unanswered. Sāyaṇa evidently gives us the traditional view that the deity addressed in the hymn is Prajāpati, the creator-god *par excellence* as he emerges towards the end of the Ṛgvedic age and remains so throughout later mythology till displaced by Brahmā, and that the composer-sage is Yajña, Sacrifice, personified. Such was the significance of sacrifice in the religious consciousness of the Ṛgvedic people that they not only identified the sacrificial act with the act of creation but also tended to raise it into a sort of a godhead !

Almost every part of the sacrificial act, every important object, implement or accessory of it tends to be enthroned, personified and even deified in the hymns of the *Rgveda*.

To begin with the hall, in which a sacrifice used to be offered, we find its doors fancied to be the portals of the cosmos conceived as a house, or the doors of the eastern quarter, which ushers in the light of the sun, or are referred to as "the sovereign and all imperial" portals, or deified and addressed as deities (*RV*, I, 188, 5 ; II, 3, 5 ; III, 4, 5 ; V, 5, 5 ; IX, 5, 5 ; X, 110, 5). Here is the description as it occurs in the last-referred text[66] : "Let the expansive Doors be widely opened, like wives who deck their beauty for their husbands. Lofty, celestial, all-impelling Portals, admit the Gods and give them easy entrance."

Next to the hall of sacrifice, which typified to the Ṛgvedic Indian cosmos itself, comes the specific receptacle in which fire was kindled and the offerings or oblations burnt, the altar, or altars ; for there were to be three of them for the complete performance of the rite (*RV*, V, 11, 2). The hall being the cosmos, the altar, particularly the primary one, came to be either described or referred to as the earth's centre or as its extremest limit next to heaven or as its choicest or the loftiest station (*RV*, I, 164, 34-5 ; II, 3, 7 ; III, 5, 9 ; III, 23, 4 ; III, 29, 4-5 ; III, 53, 11 ; IV, 5, 7 ; V, 43, 14).

Of the goddesses, deities in their own right, Āramatī, Bhāratī, Iḷā, Mahī, Sarasvatī, Vāk, Iḷā is specially connected with the sacrificial rite and the altar is spoken of as the place where Iḷā, personified sacrificial worship (*RV*, I, 128, 1 and 7 ; III, 7, 5 ; 23, 4 ; 29, 3-4 ; V, 4, 4 ; VII, 16, 8 ; 44, 2 ; X, 70, 8 ; 91, 1 and 4), abides. In some texts Iḷā is commonly referred to in the company of Bhāratī and Sarasvatī (*RV*, II, 1, 11 ; 3, 8 ; 4, 8 ; VII, 2, 8 ; IX, 5, 8 ; X, 110, 8). In a few places she is mentioned along with Sarasvatī and Mahī instead of Bhāratī (*RV*, I, 13, 9 ; 188, 8 ; V, 5, 8) and in one place at least (*RV*, I, 143, 9) Iḷā figures in the company of Bhāratī, Mahī and Sarasvatī. Āramatī does not appear in the company of Iḷā and perhaps also of any of the other two goddesses.

Āramatī, identified by experts[67] with Devotion or Piety and treated as distinct from Śraddhā, Faith, is equated by them with her Iranian counterpart Armaiti. Macdonell is disinclined to date the personification, which is clear in the *Rgveda*, to the pre-Indian age, Keith, writing almost thirty years later, being disposed to favour it, though not unreservedly. In six separate references to this goddess she clearly figures as the personification of Devotion or Piety, being called the Holy at least once, and being asked to bring the gods for the acceptance of sacrifice another time. In one text, the first one of the above-mentioned ones, it is well to note, she appears in connection with Savitṛ, the special aspect of the Sun-god developed by the Ṛgvedic Indians!

The offering of an animal at a sacrifice required a tying pole. And animal sacrifices were almost as important in the Ṛgvedic age as non-animal ones. The far-famed and long-practised—its celebration has been attested from time to time since the Ṛgvedic age, through heroes of both the epics, the *Rāmāyaṇa* (I, 12-15) describing the horse-sacrifice performed by King Daśaratha, the father of Rāma, as a son-producing rite, to almost the 8th century of the Christian era—horse-sacrifice was resorted to in the Ṛgvedic age. There are two hymns (*RV*, I, 162 and 163) in which the sacrificial horse forms the focal point of interest. And strange as it may seem, it is clearly stated in them that the animal so sacrificed straightway went to heaven, though not for its own salvation. The sacrificial pole or post, to which the horse was tied and at which it was killed, too, has received a whole hymn to itself (*RV*, III, 8; I, 13, 11) and is evidently personified. Its knob was apparently a symbol of something and the whole carving of the wooden object was a matter of both religious and artistic concern. It is endearingly described as golden-headed and its brightly coloured aspect, evidently it was elaborately painted, formed the standard of comparison even for the hues and tints of the charmingly invoked goddess Dawn, 'Uṣas' (I, 92, 5; 162, 6; IX, 5, 10).

In later ages the sacrificial post, called 'yūpa' throughout, became a symbol of religiosity and piety. The national poet, Kālidāsa, has described with evident pride the hundreds of 'yūpas' standing planted in their altars on the banks of the Śarayū near Ayodhyā as almost the sign-posts of the large number of sacrifices which the kings of the Raghu dynasty had celebrated (*Raghuvaṁśa*, XVI, 35). This word and the object with the idea have recorded an echo and an image as far south-east as Borneo in inscriptions, attesting the fact of a sacrifice there in the 5th century A.D.[68]

Sacrifice was an important mode of approach to the deity in the Ṛgvedic age. Vedic scholars are convinced that the institution of sacrifice went on steadily developing, getting more and more elaborate. With the elaboration, helped by the worldly success of the Aryan tribes on the Indian soil, sacrifice as a form of worship acquired such prestige that in the *Yajurveda*, a collection which can hardly be two centuries later than the Ṛgveda, the whole control of the universe came to be credited to it, the renewal of the universe requiring its performance.[69] In the *Brāhmaṇas* Prajāpati came to be identified with Yajña, sacrifice, it being regarded as the soul of all gods. And Prajāpati was already declared in the *Rgveda* itself as the god of gods.[70]

The Ṛgvedic hymn was both a sincere and pious prayer and a kind of magic formula, the latter aspect being less in evidence as the sacrificial mode had not then come to be so apotheosized as to make it the mechanism for compelling acceptance of the worshippers' request by the deities. Keith says: "The Ṛgveda shows quite clearly that conception of prayer for aid to a god without the performance of any sacrifice was quite natural and intelligible . . . But the priests were, from the earliest period of the later Saṁhitās and probably earlier, ready to find formulae with which the deity should be addressed in every stage of troubles and, what was still more important, to lay down the nature of the necessary offering."[71]

Keith thus put the situation in its proper perspective about the nature of sacrifice and the role and content of Ṛgvedic prayers. He also pointed out that there are sets of hymns in the collection which are not intimately connected with sacrifice.[72] However neither in connection with these observations of his, nor in his specific treatment of the very crucial topic of the relations between the Gods and their worshippers, though he is quite eloquent about and correctly appraises the moral atmosphere pervading some of the hymns of the *Ṛgveda*, has he quoted any of the prayers where the mental aspect of the spoken word is emphasized or where mere praise of the god or gods is the central theme. On the other hand, the particular ending he has given to his otherwise fair chapter, 'The Gods and their Worshippers', leaves a rather unfavourable impression on the reader's mind about the Ṛgvedic conception of the deity. To enable the reader to gain a proper perspective I quote below in Griffith's rendering a few examples of the Ṛgvedic prayers of the abovementioned variety.

Here are texts which praise a homage to gods by itself in a hymn to Viśvedevas (*RV*, VI, 51, 8-9) : "Mighty is homage ('namas') : I adopt and use it. Homage hath held in place the earth and heaven. Homage to Gods ! Homage commands and rules them. I banish even committed sin by homage." Another text reads : "Glory to Gods, the mighty and the lesser, glory to Gods, the younger and the elder !" (I, 27, 13). Still another (X, 65, 14) runs : "With Holy thoughts and with Purandhi [Plenty or Boldness personified] may all Gods, knowing the Law immortal, Manu's Holy ones, Boon-givers, favourers, finders of light, and Heaven, with gracious love accept my songs, my prayer, my hymn". Another hymn, again addressed to Viśvedevas or All-Gods, has the following exaltation of prayer in relation to the abstract goddess Vāk, Speech : "The fifteen lauds are in a thousand places : that is as vast as heaven and earth in measure. A thousand spots contain the mighty thousand. Vāk spreadeth forth as far as Prayer extendeth." (X, 114, 8).

The hymner is sometimes in the mood of a pure artist taking delight in the chant that he has composed to sing the praises of a God, as in the following one meant for Ṛbhus, deified humans : "The holy work I wrought before is wrought again ; my sweetest hymn is sung to celebrate your praise" (I, 110, 1).

Sometimes, as in X, 85, 17, where the bride Sūryā along with other gods, and particularly Mitra and Varuṇa, are mentioned, the singer simply states the fact of his adoration and leaves it there : "To Sūryā and the Deities, to Mitra and to Varuṇa, Who know aright the thing that is, this adoration have I paid."

Agni is asked to be paid a homage as in X, 69, 12 or as in I, 27, 1. The hymner announces that he will glorify him with worship ; or as in I, 36, 1 he simply asserts that he and others supplicate Agni with holy hymns. In another mood of the hymner or in relation to another aspect or role of Agni the poet only praises (X, 122, 1) : "I praise the God of wondrous might like Indra, the lovely pleasant Guest whom all must welcome."

The praise of a god for mighty deeds, as the comparison in the last quoted text implies, comes more naturally in the case of the national war-god Indra. Thus the hymn I, 32 where the mighty deeds of Indra are recounted as a pouring of a grateful heart starts with the announcement "I will declare the manly deeds of Indra".* In similar strain and expression it is said of Viṣṇu who is sometimes Indra's helper in his mighty achievements, "I will declare the mighty deeds of Viṣṇu, of him who measured out the earthly regions" (I, 154, 1). Even Maruts, the other companion-deity of Indra, get their share of such a proclamation as in I, 166, 1 ; V, 54, 1 ; 58, 1.

It may be mentioned that in the hymn-making activity there was another disinterested source, and that was the desire to sing the god's praises so that generations of men may have knowledge of the gods. So we have in X, 72, 1, "Let us with tuneful skill proclaim these generations of the Gods that one may see them when these hymns are chanted in a future age." Hence a singer may pour out his heart as the composer of I, 159, 2 does, on Heaven and Earth : "With invocations on the gracious Father's mind, and on the Mother's great inherent power I muse. Prolific Parents, they have made the world of life, and for their brood all round wide immortality."

I have drawn attention to the distinction Sāyaṇa draws between 'ṛta' and 'satya'. It clearly implies attention being given to the mental attitude as a complement of overt behaviour, whether speech or action. In connection with prayer and worship too, we find some reference to the mental content and attitude, which is, as I pointed out above, a significant feature. In a highly mystic context, we read a statement assuring the singer's purity of mind while contemplating on the Divine : "With simple heart, 'pākena manasā', have I beheld Him from anear : his Mother kisses him and he returns the kiss" (X, 114, 4).

In another place, a singer in a distressed mood, wishing to free himself from the accusations and torments caused by false ascriptions, utters in a maledictory tone, so natural in such circumstance : "Who so accuses me with words of falsehood when I pursue my way with guileless spirit [pākena manasā], may he, the speaker of untruth, be, Indra, like water which the hollowed hand compresses. Those who destroy, as is their wont, the simple, and with their evil natures harm the righteous [pākaśaṁsa] . . ." (VII, 104, 8-9). In these three verses occurs the word 'pāka', meaning in the Ṛgvedic age 'simple' or 'guileless' or 'pure'. It later came to signify 'offering' or 'food'. In the Ṛgvedic sense the term, by a strange irony of fate, is retained to-day in the name of the Islamic State of Pakistan as its first member !

* Other similar or even identical texts are : II, 15, 1 ; III, 51, 1-2 ; IV, 17, 1-2 ; IV, 30, 1 ; VI, 17, 8 ; VI, 18, 1-3 ; VI, 22, 1 ; VII, 33, 1 ; VIII, 15, 1 ; VIII, 16, 1 ; VIII, 24, 1 ; VIII, 59, 1 ; VIII, 87, 1-2 ; X, 54, 1 ; X, 89, 1-4 ; X, 99, 1 ; X, 111, 1 ; X, 152, 1.

It may further be noted that the winning of the heart of the deity and not mere mechanical offering, whether of coveted food and drink, or of the much-prized song or of both, was considered to be the true mode of worship or as its core. In a hymn addressed to various deities (VIII, 31) the last four verses (15-18) end with the refrain: "The man who, sacrificing, strives to win the heart of Deities will conquer those who worship not." And in more positive and benign mood another singer exhorts: "When he enkindles Agni, man should with his heart attend the song", on which Griffith notes: "A devout spirit will compensate the want of milk and properly prepared food." (VIII, 91, 22).

Functional deities like Aśvins, Parjanya, and Pūṣan, and protective spirits of local existence like Vāstoṣpati, the Lord of the House, did not receive the same consideration in prayer or sacrifice as the great gods of either war, morality or worship, i.e., Indra, Varuṇa, Agni, and Soma, evoked from the worshippers. Of these last four, Indra, Agni and Varuṇa may be said to be the great triad of the Ṛgvedic pantheon, with Indra drawing with him on occasions other gods like not only Maruts but even Viṣṇu.

These gods with the possible exception of Varuṇa were not rarely called upon to cause some evil to one's opponents or enemies or bad people in general. Rudra, however, was the god *par excellence* of malevolence. Vedic religion in practice thus must have been one not only of propitiation and off and on of pure homage but also of appeasement, mollification and even vowing.

There are also a number of hymns which are quite evidently charms to procure something or to avert some evil or to remedy some disease.

On the pantheonic side there was not only the development of the solar-deity in the newer aspect of a stimulator of intellect but also of tree and animal worship to some extent. The horse-hymns have already been referred to. One cannot avoid the conclusion, though the horse was sacrificed and though it received whatever adoration it gets in the hymns because of its having been the chief object in the important sacrifice, the horse-sacrifice, there must have been associated with the animal and its sacrifice the idea of 'mana', the notion that the power of the animal was transferable to the sacrificer, to the eater of the sacrifice; and as we know from the full-fledged ritual in the slightly later literature to the queen who was enjoined to lie by the side of the sacrificed animal. This power aspect of the animal had so strongly impressed the Ṛgvedic people that their poets sang of one legendary and mythical animal of that species identifying it with the Highest Spirit as they could conceive at the time.

Dadhikrāvan or Dadhikrās claims four hymns (*RV*, IV, 38-40; VII, 44) and gets some mentions in other hymns. It is clearly an aspect of the solar deity complex that is represented through Dadhikrās. Yet the imagery is almost always that of a horse. Thus we read in IV, 38, 7 and 9: "And that strong Steed, victorious and faithful, obedient with his body in the combat, speeding straight on amid the swiftly pressing, casts over his brows the dust he tosses upward . . . The people praise the overpowering swiftness of this fleet Steed who giveth abundance. Of him they say when drawing back from battle, Dadhikrās hath sped forward with his thousands."[73]

In later religious consciousness and practice three animals get worshipful reverence. The boar incarnation of Viṣṇu in preference to the other two animal incarnations of his, i.e., the one which typifies animal power, got its sculptural embodiment in the Gupta-age and received full worship that a deity is given. In later and current Hinduism, however, it is only Viṣṇu's mount, the eagle, that gets some kind of worship and reverence, geting here and there a temple consecrated to it. The third animal is the bull, which is invariably the recipient of worship in a Śiva temple, where it is placed just before the entrance to the sanctuary. Sometimes it is installed by itself too. But it is as the mounts of these Great Gods that the animals get worship and not independently. To that extent the older notions about 'mana' and similar properties have been shed !

With tree worship, however, it is a different story. Both plants, 'oṣadhi', in general and large trees, 'vanaspati', literally 'lord of the forest', are addressed as deities in the *Rgveda*, a whole long hymn (X, 97) being devoted to the praise of plants with special reference to their therapeutic value. Naturally the people who were so much dependent upon the juice of a particular plant, 'soma', for their religious practice and their enjoyment of life would deify some other and bigger trees, that with their spreading branches afforded shelter both to men and cattle. And it is very interesting and instructive to find first, 'Aśvattha', *Ficus Religiosa*, which, through Buddhist practice in India, has come down to current Hinduism as a sacred tree, and second, 'Pana' or 'Palāśa', *Butea Fondosa*, which perhaps moret hrough the non-Aryan acceptance and practice, got into current Hinduism in a secondary position of sanctity, are the two trees getting special and specific mention in it.

Another element in the religious consciousness and practice of the Hindus which is its strongly marked feature, linking it up with the ancient Sumero-Babylonian and Egyptian religious complexes, is that all the three Supreme Gods of the theistic pantheon, Brahmā, Viṣṇu and Maheśa or Śiva, have their consorts, Śiva having a son also usually by the side of the couple. Viṣṇu's issue is not known to mythology, and Brahmā's daughter is an enigma shrouded in contradictory myths. But Brahmā having become a shadowy figure in current Hinduism[74] may be left out. The two Supreme Gods, Viṣṇu and Śiva, have their consorts and are worshipped along with them in certain forms of the Gods at least. And the Ṛgvedic religion in providing the great gods of its pantheon with consorts has proved itself to be the fountain-head of modern and current Hinduism !

The Ṛgvedic pantheon has goddesses in plenty but they are not our concern here in the main. One of them, the glorious Uṣas, Dawn, evoked some of the best poetry of that age, poetry which by any standard must rank as beautiful. But Uṣas is only the daughter of Heaven and is not germane here. Indrāṇī,

Varuṇānī, Agnāyī and Aśvinī are known as the wives of Indra, Varuṇa, Agni and Aśvins.[75] Of them only Indrāṇī is thoroughly anthropomorphized and is shown as an active wife of Indra. She "occasionally receives offerings" and "has borrowed a trait or two from Uṣas" as Keith points out. The poet prays to her and others (*RV*, V, 46, 7) : "May the Gods' spouses aid us of their own free will, aid us to offspring and the winning of the spoil."

The picture that we get from this account of the religious complex of the Ṛgvedic Indians may best be described as polylatry bordering on polytheism and is very much like that of current Hinduism in practice with two or three most notable differences.

Sacrifice as the preponderant mode of approach to the deity is the one speciality of it which later Hinduism shed and current Hinduism as a whole lacks in. The great deities of the Ṛgvedic pantheon are placed in their proper places as functional deities without any of the attributes of the Supreme Gods. They thus become minor gods or godlings. The consciousness of one Supreme God either conceived ordinarily as personal God or as the Absolute with manifestations in the personal God, giving the whole polylatry a philosophical unity and making it a kind of pantheism, is the one speciality characterizing and ennobling the atmosphere of manifestly plural god-head in current Hinduism. And that notion, the idea of One Supreme God, had not only begun to take shape in the Ṛgvedic age but had actually been formulated though the Supreme Godhead was still conceived under different names. However, it is possible to look upon that trait of the Ṛgvedic speculation, too, as a characteristic foretaste of what was to come and what is now there in current Hinduism.

Current Hinduism thinks in terms of at least two Supreme Gods, Viṣṇu and Śiva, with Brahmā in the background as the third. Ṛgvedic theistic speculation conceived Him under the name of Viśvakarman and also under that of Prajāpati with Hiraṇyagarbha in the background. This Hiraṇyagarbha, who is declared to have alone existed in the beginning (*RV*, X, 121, 1), is later identified with Prajāpati and through that identification finally the term gets to be a designation of Brahmā.[76]

This development, call it transition from polylatry to monolatry, or the philosophy of pantheism in embryo, can be studied in the hymns of the *Rgveda* itself. And I shall present a brief résumé of the process in view of its significance for comparative religion and also for the sociology of religion.

The many or thirtythree gods of the Ṛgvedic pantheon came already to be grouped into three types as Vasus or terrestrial gods, Rudras or aerial gods and Ādityas or celestial gods. The first group is associated with Indra, the second with Rudra, and the third with Varuṇa.[77] Alternatively the thirtythree gods are distributed as : "O, ye, Eleven Gods whose home is heaven, O ye Eleven who made earth your dwelling, Ye who with might, Eleven, live in waters."[78] Keith sees the germ of the later recognition of only three major deities in the above-guoted text. Reduction of the gods to an order and unearthing and establishing some interconnections among them with the possible postulation of a hierarchy lays the foundation for the superstructure of some kind of monolatry or even monotheism.

In the second place, doubts as to the god or gods to whom worship was being currently offered had begun to arise. There is a whole hymn (X, 121) the refrain of whose ten verses is the question "To what deity shall we make obeisance". posing the question about the god who was to be worshipped. And Deussen[79]. writing seventyfive years ago, commented on the answer given to the question in the hymn itself, i.e., Prajāpati, that he was gradually displaced by Brahman and that finally "the most definite expression for the object of man's search was found in the conception of the ātman". It is thus clear that the great and sympathetic interpreter of the history of religio-philosophical thought of ancient India saw in this germ, very correctly, the source of the later monistic philosophy. Macdonell[80], writing only a few years after Deussen, saw, in the last three verses of the hymn, the pantheistic view fully developed a little later in the *Atharvaveda*, as against the prevailing or the earlier Ṛgvedic attitude of what he calls "polytheistic monotheism".

This is not the only form of the query that had arisen in some of the more active minds of the Ṛgvedic people. The traditionally famous hymn, known as 'asyavāmīya' (I, 164), which is addressed characteristically to Viśvedevas is an instance. The hymn is one of the longest in the whole of the *Ṛgveda* and contains at least three very famous and oft-quoted texts in the religio-philosophical literature of later times. One of them lauding sacrifice as the first of the religious ordinances and as the source of the greatness of the gods forms part of the formal prayer which is recited in group-chorus at the conclusion of every public or semi-public worship in Maharashtra. The other two will come in at a later context where the pantheistic adumbration will be discussed.

Here I shall refer to four other verses which bespeak the spirit of doubt and inquiry. In those four verses (I, 164, 4-7) the questions asked are: (1) Who has seen the Prime Mover, the Supreme Spirit; (2) Who may approach such a knowledgeable man if there is one. The admission of the singer's limitation made is that he is both of unripe mind and indiscriminating. He asks those who are supposed or believed to know (a) the God's established places and (b) the lineaments of the Prime Mover, the Unborn One, the Controller and Lord of the universe. There is further almost a challenge to him who knows the answers to the singer's questions and his limitations to declare them.

In another hymn (X, 82) the singer asks what the primeval germ, the source of all Gods, was and in another mood adds by way of an answer, after cogitating about it a little, that one will not find that source of all creatures (vv. 5-7).

On the background of such cogitations the declaration by Indra in the 26th hymn of book four of the *Ṛgveda* attains significance for our quest. Indra announces: "I was aforetime Manu, I was Sūrya: I am the sage Kakṣivān, holy singer. Kutsa the son of Ārjunī I master. I am the sapient Uśanā: Behold me." The abstract deity Vāk, Speech, on the other hand (X, 125,

1-3), declares herself not as the self-same person as Rudras, Ādityas, Viśvedevas, Mitrā-Varuṇau, Indrā-Agnī, Aśvinau, Soma, Tvaṣṭṛ, Pūṣan and Bhaga but as the one who supports them or helps them to go on with their functions. In still another hymn (IV, 40, 5) the mythical horse Dadhikrāvan, personified as a deity, is identified not only with 'ṛta', the eternal Law, but with various forms of the Supreme Being. A text glorifying the Goddess Aditi, the mother of gods, goes even further. It (*RV*, I, 89, 10) runs : "Aditi is the sky, Aditi the air, Aditi is mother, father and son, Aditi is all the gods and the five tribes, Aditi is whatever has been and will be born."

In these texts we meet with the phenomenon of identification of one god with another and one deity announcing its supremacy over others, a situation in the pantheonic development which presages the outcome of a supreme deity, the upshot of One God as the over-lord of all deities, functional or otherwise. And we have, apart from the postulation of a Supreme Being or of One God under three names mentioned above, a fourth one which in later philosophy figures as the designation of the Absolute in the personified aspect, viz., Puruṣa. Puruṣa, through His sacrifice, is said to have fashioned the whole universe in a famous hymn (X, 90) which is known as the Puruṣa-hymn and is recited in various religious contexts throughout the history of Hinduism.

The Supreme Being when not named is simply the Unborn One, 'aja' (I, 164, 6; VIII, 41, 10; X, 82, 6). In the first text we have the famous identification of the Supreme Being with Indra, Mitra, Varuṇa, Agni and Garutman, declaring with absolute confidence that all these are but names of the same Supreme Being in the oft-repeated words: "To what is One, sages give many a title: they call it Agni, Yama and Mātariśvan." We have there also the even more well-known, and the sheet-anchor of later philosophical disquisitions, doctrine of the identity of the Individual Soul and the Supreme Soul which reads: "Two Birds [the Supreme Soul and the Individual Soul] with fair wings, knit with bonds of friendship, in the same sheltering tree have found a refuge. One of the twain eats the sweet Figtree's fruitage ; the other eating not regardeth only."

Both as Viśvakarman (X, 81, 3) and as Puruṣa (X, 90, 1) the Supreme God is described as multi-eyed, multi-armed, multi-footed, multi-headed or multi-mouthed. Viśvakarman is further described as the Sole God producing earth and heaven, while Puruṣa is described as "pervading earth and transcending it by ten fingers' width". This description is another way of asserting the transcendence of the Supreme Being, called Puruṣa here, but as Uttama Puruṣa, or Puruṣottama in the *Bhagavadgītā*. Since Lord Kṛṣṇa identified himself with that Uttama Puruṣa, Puruṣottama has been one of the names in which the Supreme God of Vaiṣṇavite Hinduism, Viṣṇu, has been most endearingly and ennoblingly chanted.

Some of the attributes of the Supreme Being of the One God, of the Unborn, may now be listed as they figure in the three hymns, X, 82 ; X, 90 and X, 121. He is mighty in mind and power, Maker, Disposer and most lofty Presence,

He is the Deities' name-giver. He made ready all these things that exist. He is the One wherein abide all existing things but He cannot be found. He is all that yet hath been and all that is to be. He is the Lord of Immortality. He is the giver of vital breath, of power and vigour. All the Gods obey his commands. He is the Sole Ruler of all the moving world that breathes or slumbers. He is the God of gods, and there is none beside him. He alone comprehends all these created things. He is, in brief, both immanent and transcendent.

Another and perhaps parallel development made as a consequence of the enquiring spirit mentioned above must have been the postulation of the impersonal First Principle. Though I find nothing in the *Rgveda* which enables me to indicate a step or two by which the notion of the Abstract Absolute can be approached yet the notion is there, almost very clearly put down in a famous humn (X, 129) which has been, in Indian tradition, looked up to as the source of the philosophical speculation, preserved in the Upaniṣads and other later literature.

It proclaims the arrival, the upspring of Being in place of the original non-Being. With the upspringing of Sat or Being there arose desire, the primal seed and germ of Spirit. Sages who searched with their hearts concentrated then discovered the Being's kinship in non-Being!

This Ṛgvedic situation, both in the matter of the pantheon and of cosmology and philosophical approach to the riddle of the universe, was very much more advanced than any society of ancient times, Sumero-Babylonian, Egyptian or Hittite, had arrived at either contemporaneously or even much later or towards its end!

CHAPTER IX

HINDU VIEW OF THE GODHEAD (SECOND PHASE)

THE two developments in the religious consciousness of the Ṛgvedic Indians' that make their appearance in literature, were : (1) Questioning the plurality of gods and tendency to postulate not only a hierarchy among them but also one Supreme God above all under three different appellations ; and (2) Postulation of an abstract First Principle, 'Sat', as the Source of all.

The mode of worship or approach to the deity, which was sacrifice, however, had got more established and proliferated so that 'Yajña', sacrifice, could be said to be another name for the Supreme God. This development, it is clear from the literature of the next two hundred years or so, is recorded as having culminated and taken its final shape by 900 B.C., as the ritualistic literature of the age, the older *Brāhmaṇas*, testifies. There is no indication in this literature of any doubts about the religious value and the efficacy of sacrifice. But the literature, which, in tradition, represents the end of the *Brāhmaṇa-literature*, the *Upaniṣads*, by the very nature of the definitiveness of its speculative statements gives clear indication that over a fairly long period before their formulation, the two developments mentioned in the previous paragraph must have progressed on lines of thought which must have questioned the efficacy of sacrifice in the religious sphere.

There three developments are represented in a highly developed form in the eleven older *Upaniṣads* on which I have drawn for elucidating the Hindu view of the God-head and of the nature of religious consciousness in Hinduism.

Already in *Bṛhadāraṇyaka Upaniṣad*, the earliest of these books, dated about the 8th century B.C., we have the far-famed speculative philosopher Yājñavalkya (III, 9, 1-7), in reply to a clever and inquisitive Brahmin named Śākalya, running through the gamut of enumeration of the gods, beginning with their number as three thousand three and ending with only two, i.e., Indra and Prajāpati. Inter alia he asserts that there are only thirtythree gods, others being only their 'manifestations' or 'glorifications', (mahimānaḥ). Soaring higher he finally (III, 9, 9) pronounces that there is only one God and that is Brahman, otherwise named 'Tyat' (that). Another passage of the same book (I, 4, 11-65), which categorically declares *Brahman* as the only One in the beginning, mentions Indra, Varuṇa, Soma, Rudra, Parjanya, Yama, Mṛtyu and Īśāna as rulers among gods. It should be noted that Rudra who came to be raised to the position of the Supreme, One and Only, God in the slightly later Upaniṣad, the *Śvetāśvatara*, finds a place among the group of ruler-gods, and that Īśāna, which in later literature became an epithet of Rudra-Śiva, also figures in it by the side of Rudra. And these gods were but the first creation of *Brahman* : "that, being one, did not flourish" and began to create for satisfaction.

The whole of the fifth chapter of the book presents a closely worked up scheme in which Indra and other gods appear as the children of Prajāpati and the latter, the Supreme God of the *Ṛgveda* and more so of the *Brāhmaṇas*, figures as the creation of Brahman, the Absolute Supreme of the cosmos. In the end the identity of the Individual Self with Brahman as (Yonder) Person is asserted.

In the sixth book of the *Bṛhadāraṇyaka Upaniṣad* some rites, which must be called magical, for gaining certain objects are rather incongruously prescribed. The deities which figure in them are some of the gods of the Vedic pantheon. The authors of the book or at least of the particular chapter thus showed their valuation of the Vedic deities as being connected with lower things of worldly life! The Vedic gods were no longer conceived as Great Gods but only as minor deities, a position which they have continued to occupy in the orthodox and élite ritual.

The *Chāndogya Upaniṣad*, only slightly later than the *BrU* (III, 6-10), uses another imagery, to drive home the inferiority of the Vedic gods and to establish their subordination to Brahman. The pairs of Vasus and Agni, of Rudras and Indra, of Ādityas and Varuṇa, of Maruts and Soma, and lastly of Sādhyas and Brahman are said to be related to one another in some way not clear. But the two components of each pair are so related that the latter one of the pair is the month by which the former one can drink nectar and attain the status of the former for as long as the sun shines. Then in the 11th section, the one which follows the abovementioned schematic representation, the reader is told that in the world of *Brahman*, evidently the latter component of the last mentioned pair, the sun ceases to shine, i.e., to set too ; and he is assured that, therefore, for the Brahman-knower the nectarine or rather supernectarine existence is unending. Verily, the supremacy of *Brahman* over the gods of the Vedic pantheon, great and small, is asserted. Further we are specifically instructed as to the origin of this knowledge. And the source is no other than Brahman in the masculine and therefore conceived as personal God. Prajāpati received it from Brahman. Prajāpati is thus, as in the *BrU* passage referred to above, subordinated to *Brahman*.

The *Chāndogya* in other passages (VIII, 7-12) has portrayed Indra as a pupil of Prajāpati for one hundred and one years seeking the knowledge of *Brahman*, which he realized at the end of that long period. What a puny intelligence and person Indra is depicted to be in relation to Prajāpati and the new but all important field of knowledge, the *Brahman*-knowledge! The mighty warrior-god of the Vedic Indians, their trusted friend and helper in their wars with their enemies, particularly the non-Aryan enemies, falls low in the newer context of spiritual search and religious consciousness!

Indra's search for and attainment of *Brahman*-knowledge evidently helped to keep up his status. For in the *Aitareya Upaniṣad* (III, 1, 3) which is next in chronological sequence, the question is asked who is the Self that one worships and the answer given accommodates Indra in the company of not only Prajāpati but also *Brahman* as that Self, 'ātman'. And finally *Brahman* is identified with intelligence, 'vijñāna'. In the slightly later work, the *Kena Upaniṣad*, in two sections (III and IV), one of them known as "the allegory of the Vedic Gods' ignorance of Brahman", Indra's supremacy over the other gods of the Vedic pantheon, Agni and Vāyu-Mātariśvan being actually mentioned, is ascribed to his acquisition of *Brahman*-knowledge. And finally the latest of the first ten works, yet old enough to be considered distinctly pre-Buddhist, the theistic *Upaniṣad* named *Śvetāśvatara*, rehabilitates (IV, 1-2) some of the Vedic gods in their appropriate status as but other forms of the Supreme One, proclaiming that Agni, Ādityas, Vāyu, Candra, Āpaḥ and Prajāpati are but *Brahman*.

The rather sceptical and highly critical attitude of the early speculative thinkers of the Upaniṣadic age did not eschew the age-old human instrument of ridicule and satire in their dealings with the Vedic gods. Jealousy of the gods is openly asserted in a passage of the *Bṛhadāraṇyaka Upaniṣad* (I, 4, 10). It is stated that one who asserts difference between himself and *Brahman* and the latter and other gods is an animal to the gods. For every man is to the gods as are animals to a man. Animals are useful to man ; so are men useful to the gods for they increase their glory! If a man should be deprived even of one animal he feels displeasure ; what to speak of if he is deprived of many or all? Gods too feel highly displeased if they are deprived of their worshippers, the men. Gods, therefore, are not happy that men should know that there is but only One Supreme, i.e., *Brahman*, and it is identical with one's Self! This ratiocination about a polylatrous religious consciousness by a speculative thinker of before 500 B.C. marking the culmination of the monistic trend of the Upaniṣadic thought is a master-piece as social psychology of religion and should prepare one for the arrival of the monolatrous pantheism or pantheistic monolatry of later and current Hinduism.

The thinkers, whose bold speculations led them not only to subordinate the gods of the Vedic pantheon, the cherished and venerated gods of their successful ancestors, but also to postulate the Absolute Principle as the beginning and the cause of the cosmos, could hardly be expected to rest content with sacrifice as a mode of worship. We find them accordingly, almost vehemently, questioning the efficacy of such ritualistic approaches to the Deity as sacrificial acts and like rites.

The inadequacy of sacrificial rites for religious ends had come to be appreciated to some extent at least even before the time of the *Śatapatha Brāhmaṇa*, i.e., by about 1000 B.C. A floating verse quoted in that book (X, 5, 4, 15) and used by Deussen[1] runs in his translation thus : "By knowledge they climb upwards, Thither, where desire is quenched, No sacrificial gift reaches thither, nor penance of the ignorant."

The general tenor and even specific prescription in the same *Brāhmaṇa*[2] (II, 6, 4, 8 ; XI, 4, 4, 1, 21 ; 6, 2, 2, 3) however are distinctly in favour of the sacrificial and other rites being considered as quite adequate even for the new *summum bonum*, identity with *Brahman*.

The earliest questioning begins with an attempt to allegorize the sacrifice, which had by then become the most important, the most majestic and colourful as well as the most cherished of the sacrifices, the 'aśvamedha', the horse-sacrifice. The *Bṛhadāraṇyaka Upaniṣad* opens with a statement of the identity of the various parts of the body of the sacrificial horse with various Vedic deities and cosmic items, spiritualizing the rite by giving it a cosmic significance. Running the allegory through full two sections the book ends the second with a justification of 'aśvamedha', horse-sacrifice. With all the spiritualization and glorification of the horse-sacrifice the attitude towards sacrifices in general recorded in this great text of Brahman-speculation is one which relegates them to the secondary and lower rank in the hierarchy of religious modes. In III, 9, 16 it is clearly announced that offerings and sacrifices can only lead the worshipper to the world of gods, which after all is perishable and as such an object of only lower desires.

Sacrifice in general is further sublimated in the *Chāndogya Upaniṣad* in two sections (16 and 17) of its third chapter. S. Radhakrishnan[3] gives them the significant headings : "The whole Life is symbolically a Sacrifice" and "Man's Life a Sacrifice". Sacrifice in these passages is the standard of comparison, but the end of life is, unlike that of sacrifice, the attainment of "higher light". Sacrifice, still, is so important that its correct performance is insisted on and the technique for correction is prescribed (IV, 17). In six sections of the fifth chapter the practice of control over breaths is described in purely sacrificial terminology, which is styled by S. Radhakrishnan[4] as "The Sacrifice to the Universal Self in One's own self". The seventh section, ending the chapter, is then devoted to draw the moral, as it were in terms of the sacrifice known as 'agnihotra', fire-sacrifice, and the superior moral worth and calibre of the performer of this newer kind of sacrifice are stressed.

On the other hand, thes ame *Upaniṣad* has a small section, twelfth section of the first chapter, which S. Radhakrishnan[5] characterizes as "a satirical protest against the exernalism of the sacrifical creed, in the interests of an inward spiritual life". The crowning piece of this attitudinal mansion is offered in the beginning of the seventh chapter. Two of the most revered ascetics—one of them, Sanatkumāra, has been a bye-word for high philosophy and religious insight, the other being Nārada—are introduced as engaged in a dialogue. The occasion is a solemn and serene one, Nārada having approached Sanatkumāra for being admitted as a pupil of that most learned sage. The would-be teacher, in the manner of a meticulous guide for Ph.D. research in a modern University of high standards, questions Nārada as to his previous attainments in the domain of learning. Nārada tells him that he has mastered all the learning that was then more or less organized, which included the entire Vedic lore with the addition of a few bizarre and practical departments of knowledge.[6] As soon as Nārada has recounted his achievements in the domain of learning he realizes that it is concerned with only those departments which have no bearing on the knowledge of Self and admits that he is like one who knows only the names of things and objects and not the things and the objects themselves. Sanatkumāra emphasizes the utter inadequacy of Nārada's learning by repeating Nārada's characterization of it as mere names. He then starts off his disquisition beginning with speech, i.e., name, as Brahman and ends with the declaration of the primacy of Self, all that being the knowledge concerned with the quest of Self, knowledge that shows up the further shore of darkness. He does not call it the Higher Learning in contrast with the Vedic lore of Nārada which is the Lower Learning.

This characterization of the two learnings is done in explicit terms in the *Muṇḍaka Upaniṣad* (I, 1, 1-5) where it is Angiras who expounds the view to one Śaunaka. The new lore itself is traced back to Brahmā, the foremost of the gods, the creator of the cosmos and the protector of the world.

The story of the lad named Naciketas, who confronted his father, who was bent on giving away all his belongings as a sacrifice, with a query which suggested the futility of such rites and the subsequent development resulting in his daring the god of death and getting from him the knowledge of Brahman, narrated in the *Kaṭha Upaniṣad* (I) is a grand condemnation of sacrificial rites for the realization of Self or as a mode of worship in the light of the newer religious horizon. The whole configuration of doubt, hesitation and inadequacy of sacrificial rites as a mode of approach to the Deity is capped by the forthright declaration made in the *Muṇḍaka Upaniṣad* (I, 2, 7) that "the floats in the form of sacrifices with their different lower acts directed or performed by eighteen persons are shaky and leaky". It is only the deluded ones who stick to them.

The Upaniṣadic attitude towards Vedic pantheon and Vedic mode of worship by means of sacrificial rites was the consequence of the realization by the speculative thinkers of the age that the ultimate source of the universe was One and only One, and that is the Reality, and further that fundamentally the spiritual element in the human personality and that Reality, the One, the Universal Self, are identical. The One is more commonly realized to be Absolute Principle, the Abstract Brahman or Ātman; but not infrequently the One was conceived as a Personal Being, as "Puruṣa", whether called "Uttama" the Ultimate or the Best, or "Para" the Higher, or not.[7] It is only in the *Śvetāśvatara Upaniṣad* that the One is propounded to be the personal God, Rudra-Śiva.

The next landmark, in the present state of our knowledge, on the path of Hindu religious consciousness, is clearly the *Bhagavadgītā* which is commonly dated about three centuries later than the *Śvetāśvatara Upaniṣad*, i.e., about 200 B.C. Every reader of that great and almost fascinating book, who has any knowledge of the contents of the *Śvetāśvatara Upaniṣad*, or has gone through excellent summaries of the two books in English presented by R.G. Bhandarkar[8] half a century ago, is bound to discover its dependence on the Upaniṣad for its thoughts and even imagery. Anyone who reads both the books in original Sanskrit will be struck very much by similarities and particularly by the recurrence in the *Bhagavadgītā* of certain verses *ad verbatim* from the *Śvetāśvatara Upaniṣad.*

As remarked already the *Upaniṣad* is theistic as contrasted with the other nine and slightly earlier Upaniṣads and the one Supreme God round whom its theism, which is more correctly described as "Śaiva mono-pantheism", is centred, is the Vedic god Rudra, singled out as one, though in the *Ṛgveda* the deity is always referred to in the plural as Rudras. He is given the new appellation Śiva meaning 'auspicious'. Thus we have Śiva as the Supreme One, Universal Soul, impersonal in the other Upaniṣads being transformed into a named personal deity. And He is one of the two Supreme Gods of current Hinduism.

The *Bhagavadgītā* may be said to be a newer *Upaniṣad*—and it should be noted that in the traditional ending of the chapters of the book it is characterized as an Upaniṣad—putting forward the claim, and also accepting it, of Kṛṣṇa-Viṣṇu to be considered not only as the Supreme God but also as the Universal Soul. One may appropriately conclude that the theism of the *Bhagavadgītā* is Vaiṣṇava mono-pantheism as that of the *Śvetāśvatara Upaniṣad* is a Śaiva one.

From the eighth or the 9th century of the Christian era, when Śaṅkarācārya wrote his commentary on the *Bhagavadgītā*, which is perhaps the earliest of its commentaries, till today the book has gone on appreciating in the public esteem as shown by the innumerable commentaries or disquisitions and translations in many languages. But the culmination of the glory and value of the book may be said to have been reached before the end of the 13th century. For the saint-poet-philosopher Jñāneśvara of Maharashtra, in his great commentary, the greatest among the commentaries on the *Bhagavadgītā*, raised the book above the so-called 'non-human' and divine Vedas, by making it the source of the Vedic thoughts and ideas. In his exposition of the sixtysixth verse of the last chapter, XVIIIth, of the book, he dilates on this estimate of his in poetic imagery and significant words, devoting ninetysix verses. And this Jñāneśvara has done almost at the end of the whole work in spite of the fact that in his commentary on *BhG*, XV, 20, where Lord Kṛṣṇa himself characterizes the book and its body of doctrines, he has followed the text and has called it the essence of the Upaniṣads and not their source.[9]

The *Bhagavadgītā* as pointed out by me[10] elsewhere had acquired the character of a sacred book and had in a way supplanted the Vedas even before the eleventh century. Evidently it is the *Bhagavadgītā* that the practical author of the *Pañcantantra*[11], a popular work of the fifth century A.D., had in mind, when he referred to Keśava, i.e., Kṛṣṇa, as 'satśāstravān', the preacher of True Science, or the preacher who expounded the nature of Being. The *Bhagavadgītā* must have been current then as the book of True Science. And this inference is strengthened by the intimate and expert use of its ideas and expressions made by the national poet Kālidāsa at least a century earlier. In the profound panegyric of God Viṣṇu which Kālidāsa left for posterity in his semi-epic poem *Raghuvaṁśa* (X, 16-32), one verse alone (27) draws upon and epitomizes in the most compressed yet felicitous manner the leading ideas and expressions of fourteen different verses from eight different chapters of the *Bhagavadgītā*.[12] In characterizing Śiva Kalidāsa uses[13] the expression 'tamaḥ pāre vyavasthitam', meaning 'existing beyond darkness', which is reminiscent of the *BhG*[14] expression 'tamasaḥ parastāt', emphasizing the luminous nature of the Supreme God. Kālidāsa thus bears indubitable testimony to the *BhG* having become a religio-philosophical book of great currency and authority among the Indian élite from before the 4th century A.D.

The *Bhagavadgītā* deals with the two developments, which I mentioned above as having taken place in the Upaniṣadic age and affected its thought differentially. The various Vedic gods are not only relegated to the secondary and even tertiary place but their world, too, is pronounced to be a lower religious goal, with further denunciation of the worshippers of such gods.[15] Even the Vedas are pronounced to be dealing with matters of a lower order and are declared to be of limited use and authority.[16]

On the other hand, the *BhG* (III, 10-16) makes an attempt at rehabilitating the institution of sacrifice by remoulding it and sublimating it. It puts forward a new theory about the inter-dependence of the welfare of this world and the institution of sacrifice and propounds the theory of the moral responsibility of man in its performance.

The nature of the Supreme God posited in the Upaniṣads has continued to form the basis of the view of the Godhead with slight modifications and variations, among the élite and semi-élite followers of the many theistic sects that mark current and recent Hinduism. The postulation of Impersonal Brahman as the Supreme Universal, which is the greatest single achievement of the Upaniṣadic sages in the domain of religious philosophy, too, has continued to be there, even though as the background, if not always as the bedrock. A brief statement of the characterization of these two aspects in which the Supreme God is conceived by the Hindus as it is found in the Upaniṣads must be our next endeavour.

The Supreme God as Impersonal Principle, i.e., as Brahman, is merely referred to as 'Tat', that, as in the famous quintessential expression 'Tat-tvam-asi', 'that thou art' (*ChU*, VI, 15, 3 ; 16, 3) or in the impersonal and more elaborate characterization of the *Kaṭha Upaniṣad* (II, 2, 8) as : "That indeed is the pure ; that is Brahman ; that alone is called immortality ; in It all the worlds rest ; none ever goes beyond It. This verily is that."[17] ; or again in the statement of the *Muṇḍaka Upaniṣad* (I, 1, 3) "the other is the higher learning through which that Immutable ('Tat Akṣaram') is attained" ; or as in the refrain of eight verses in the first section of the second chapter of the *Kaṭha Upaniṣad*, "This verily is That".

Brahman is 'Akṣara', etymologically meaning immutable (*BrU*, III, 8, 8-11 ; IV, 5, 15 ; *MuU*, I, 1, 5-7 ; II, 2, 2 and 11 ; III, 1, 7 ; *PrU*, IV, 9-10). It is otherwise 'Amṛta', meaning immortal or immortality (*BrU*, I, 3, 28 ;

II, 5 ; IV, 4, 17 ; *MuU*, II, 2, 2 and 11). Brahman is alternatively 'Satya', Truth (*BrU*, V, 5 ; *ChU*, VIII, 3, 5 ; *MuU*, II, 2, 2). The mystic syllable 'om' too, is Brahman, and contemplation on it leads to salvation (*ChU*, I, 1, 1 and 4 ; I, 4 ; *KaU*, I, 2, 15-16 ; *PrU*, V ; *MuU*, II, 2, 6).

The Supreme as Impersonal Brahman, whether called 'Tat', or 'Akṣara' (*TaU*, II, 1), in some of the most famous words is 'satyam, jñānam, anantam', i.e., Brahman is Truth, Knowledge and Infinity. Or from another angle, in a cryptic way (*ChU*, III, 14) it is 'jalān', i.e., the whole world as it emerges, as it lives, and as it gets dissolved into It. In the words of *Praśna Upaniṣad* (IV, 10), Brahman is shadowless, bodiless, colourless, pure, imperishability. As such mortal eye does not reach It, nor does speech express It ; nor even mind comprehends It. The same notion is more felicitously expressed as "Brahman is that from where speech and mind both recoil without comprehending" ; and "One knowing or realizing the bliss attendant on reaching Brahman is never afraid". (*TaU*, II, 4; 9 ; *KeU*, I, 3-4 ; *KaU*, II, 3, 9-12 ; *MuU*, III, 1, 8). Brahman is thus pure bliss or in the enquiry concerning bliss proves to be the ulterior limit of it (*MuU*, II, 8).

The Absolute, the Supreme, the Impersonal Brahman, if It is beyond comprehension, it is so in so far as It is "Unperceivable, ungraspable, nameless, casteless, eyeless, earless, hand-less, foot-less, constant, all-pervading, omnipresent, superfinely subtle and undecaying, though the source of all beings" (*MuU*, I, 1, 6). In other words, Brahman is "unmoving, swifter than mind, always ahead of and beyond the senses, and though standing still, It outstrips all the runners" (*IśU*, 5 ; cf. *MuU*, III, 1, 7 ; II, 2, 11). It is "wordless, touchless, formless, tasteless, smell-less, beginningless, end-less, undecaying, abiding and beyond the great" (*KaU*, I, 3, 15).

In one of the most majestic and serenely worded passages in the whole of Sanskrit literature Yājñavalkya characterized Brahman for the edification of one of the acutest of questioners of his time, a lady by name Gārgī Vācaknavī, thus : "That, O Gārgī, the knowers of Brahman call the Imperishable. It is neither gross nor fine, neither short nor long, neither glowing red nor adhesive ; It is shadowless, not dark; It is neither air nor space ; It is unattached, tasteless, smell-less, eyeless, earless, mouthless, voice-less and without breath, mind, measure, or radiance. It has no inside or outside. It eats nothing and no one eats it" (*BrU*, III, 8, 8; cf. *PrU*, IV, 10).

This description of the Supreme in negative terms is so characteristic of the Upaniṣadic thought and so ingrained in it and in later philosophy that I think it desirable to draw the readers' pointed attention to the fact that even when the Supreme in the Upaniṣadic texts is thought of in personal terms as Ātman, as the great Yājñavalkya does in more than one of his highly emotive discourses, the same method persists. Thus the later and popular description of the Vedāntic Supreme as 'not that', 'not that', first occurs in the text : "That Self is not this, not this. He is incomprehensible and is not comprehended ; He is indestructible and is not destroyed ; He is unattached and is not attached to; He is unbound; He does not suffer; He is not injured" (*BrU*, III, 9, 26; IV, 2, 4; IV, 4, 22; IV, 5, 15). Alternatively He is described as free from evil, free from old age, free from death, grief, hunger or thirst (*ChU*, VIII, 7, 1; cf. VIII, 1, 5). In purely psychological terms "He is not that which cognises internal objects, not that which cognises external objects, nor what cognises both, nor a mass of cognition, nor again cognitive or non-cognitive; is unseen, unreferable, ungraspable, distinction-less, unthinkable, unnameable" . . . Thus the syllable '*om*' is the very Self" (*MāU*, 5-12).

However inscrutable the speculative thinkers of the Upaniṣadic age might have thought the Ultimate Reality they had discovered to be, they had to find out ways and means of characterizing It in some positive terms for the comprehension of their students and followers. And we come across in these very *Upaniṣads* the conception of the Supreme in much more personal terms than even that of Ātman. The old Ṛgvedic word Puruṣa, standing in the Ṛgveda for the Primaeval Being, the source of all creation, is found employed in a number of texts, including some from the old and rather mystical Upaniṣad the *Chāndogya*. I shall therefore summarize the characterization of the Supreme God conceived as Puruṣa.

The individual soul on the death of a person rises up from the body and when it reaches the highest light appears in his own form, viz., that of the Supreme Person, 'Uttama Puruṣa' (*ChU*, VIII, 12, 3). The Supreme is otherwise called merely 'Para Puruṣa', 'the Higher Person', 'Parātpara Puruṣa', 'the Highest Person', or 'Divya Puruṣa', 'Luminous Person' (*KaU*, II, 3, 8; *MuU*, III, 2, 8). "The Great Person has the lustre of the sun and is beyond darkness. That Person fills everything; nothing is greater, nothing is smaller than Him" (*ŚvU*, III, 8-9).*

The two most important characteristics of the Supreme, whether as Impersonal Brahman or as Personal Ātman or Puruṣa, are infinity and limitlessness, immanence and transcendence. These characteristics are tried to be impressed upon the reader, the learner, the inquirer under different imagery, varying with the mood of the thinker and also with the aspect, impersonal or personal, in view at the time and in the context.

The one refrain of such texts, the constant element in them is that whatever object in the cosmos, whatever element of the human personality, one thinks of, the Universal, the Supreme, is not only the final cause but is also the controller from within, 'antaryāmin' as the term goes, though It or He is all the time also the controller from without being outside and beyond it.

Perhaps the most majestic and solemn of all such passages[18] is the one which is the reply of the greatest of the Upaniṣadic thinkers, Yājñavalkya, to a query of another very great contributor to the new knowledge of the age, Uddālaka Āruṇi (*BrU*, III, 7, 3-30). The words introducing the query are enough to give the import of that magnificent passage, wherein Yājñavalkya recounts

*** Portions of text under quotation marks are free renderings from the originals.**

one after another various great natural elements and individual human senses and elements and concludes his answer. The question is "What is the thread by which the world, the other world and all beings are held together"; and the reply in its concluding portion is: "It is your Self, the inner controller, the immortal. He is never seen but is the seer, never heard but is the hearer, never perceived but is the perceiver, never apprehended by thought but himself apprehends, and not known but knows. There is no other seer but He, no other hearer but He, no other perceiver but He, no other thinker but He. He is your Self, the inner controller, the Immortal one."

The *Śvetāśvatara Upaniṣad* (III, 14-21) being almost wholly theistic, presents this view of the Supreme in the personal form of Puruṣa in more physical terms. Quoting the first two verses of the famous Puruṣasūkta (*RV*, X, 90) positing for Puruṣa a thousand heads etc., it paraphrases it in its own words[19], expanding the ideas a bit to include appropriate qualities, so indispensable in a theistic system of religious consciousness. As a verse or more and a few expressions occurring in this passage recur in the *BhG* and have become the common heritage of Hinduism I shall give a free summary of it:

"It [He] has hands and feet everywhere; Its [His] face is everywhere; It [He] hears from everywhere; It [He] envelops every place. It [He] reflects the qualities of all senses, though devoid of any senses. It [He] is the lord of all and the refuge of all. The embodied soul is the Universal Soul in the city of nine gates, the human body, and is the controller of all that is stationary or moving. He knows all that is there to know, though none knows Him. They call Him the Primeval, the Great Person. The expounders of Brahman proclaim Him to be constant. I know this unageing, ancient, omnipresent and all-pervading Self."

In this characterization one sees abrupt transition from the personal to the impersonal and back again to the personal. This is a trait noticeable in Hinduism of all sects, for the postulation of the Universal Absolute, Brahman, so powerfully advocated and stabilized by the Upaniṣadic thinkers, took deep roots. The theistic systems of later times, which claim the allegiance of a very large bulk of the present day Hindus, though they propounded them on the basis of the personal God, either Śiva or Viṣṇu in one or the other forms of His, keep in their background the notion of the Absolute Brahman more or less intact. It is a well-known fact that a sectarian will quite often address his God in the words: 'Saccidānanda Prabho', 'O Lord, who You are Being, Consciousness and Bliss', or merely utter the trio 'Saccidānanda' as if it was the name of a particular God. Now 'Sat', Being, 'Cit', Consciousness, and 'Ānanda', Bliss, combined together as a trio characterize Brahman. S. Radhakrishnan[20] has told us that "the essential nature of Brahman is said to be '*sat*' or being, *cit* or consciousness and *ānanda* or bliss". He has not provided appropriate reference to any authoritative text, and it must be concluded from Śaṅkarācārya's comment on the dictum "satyam, jñānam, anantam brahma" that the expression is not his. In R. G. Bhandarkar's

"*Vaiṣṇavism, Śaivism etc.*"[21] this trio is stated to be viewed as the characteristic of "the One, Highest, Brahman" in the religio-philosophical system of Nimbārka and of the Vīraśaiva or Liṅgāyat sect. That would date the formulation rather very late, not earlier than the 12th century A.D.! Whatever the date of the formulation of the famous trio, 'sat', 'cit', 'ānanda', it has been used as a characteristic mark of Vedānta philosophy alternatively with the Upaniṣadic trio, 'satyam', 'jñānam', 'anantam', or with 'tat', 'tvam', 'asi', 'that thou art', the last being more particularly considered to belong to the Vedānta system of Śaṅkarācārya, which is popularly known as 'Māyāvāda', the doctrine of illusion.

The characteristics of the Supreme as envisaged in the Upaniṣadic thought so far dealt with and their persistence in current Hinduism, doctrinal, élite or popular, were thus summarized by R. G. Bhandarkar[22] fifty years ago in his comments on the great *Bṛhadāraṇyaka Upaniṣad* passage III, 7, 7-30, briefly epitomized above: "Herein are brought out the peculiar points of Hindu theism: God is the only seer, the only hearer, and the only knower, that is, he is all-seeing, all-hearing, and all-knowing; and nobody can see him, hear him, or know him [fully]. He is distinct from all objects, but dwells in them and controls them ... God, being thus distinct from the world, though immanent, can be the object of devoted mediation and can be attained by means of truth, knowledge and purity."

One positive feature of the Absolute in the personalized form of Ātman or Puruṣa, or even as Brahman, which the Upaniṣads over and over again harp on, may now be mentioned, as it is not only repeated and that too with added emphasis by Lord Kṛṣṇa in the *BhG* but is also supposed to have been demonstrated in a most marvellously miraculous scene, which is described in full detail in the 11th chapter of *Bhagavadgītā*. The chapter is significantly entitled "Vision of the Cosmic Form".

The Ātman, Puruṣa or Brahman is not only beyond darkness, 'tamasaḥ parastāt' (*ŚvU*, III, 8), but It or He is also 'jyoti', flame or 'suvarṇa jyoti', 'golden flame', or 'adhūmaka', smokeless like flame (*BrU*, IV, 3, 7; *ChU*, VIII, 3, 4; *TaU*, III, 10; *KaU*, II, 1, 13), or 'jyotiṣām jyoti', light of lights, i.e., the supreme lustre or luminousness (*BrU*, IV, 4, 16; *MuU*, II, 2, 9-10; III, 1, 5), or merely of the form of light, 'bhārūpa' (*ChU*, III, 14, 2), or is merely golden-coloured or golden person (*BrU*, IV, 3, 11-12; *MuU*, III, 1, 3-5), or is of the colour of the sun or the form like that of the sun (*ŚvU*, III, 3; V, 8). The Absolute, in the plainest of imagery based on lustre and colour, is at least 'śukra', pure, or 'śubhra', white (*IśU*, 8; *KaU*, II, 2, 8; *PrU*, VI, 10; *MuU*, III, 1, 5; III, 2, 1; *ŚvU*, IV, 2). This feature is predicated of even the individual Self, 'jīva-self', for after all the latter is but the Universal Soul, got temporarily confined in the human body.

Briefly speaking immanence of the Supreme in man gives us some of the famous and bold assertions of the Vedānta philosophy: 'Ahaṁ Brahmāsmi', 'I am Brahman' (*BrU*, I, 4, 10), with the glorious illustration of the legendary master of learning, the sage Vāmadeva, as having realized his unity with Brahman; 'Sohamasmi', 'That I am' (*ChU*, III, 14, 1-4; VIII, 1, 1-5; *Iśā. Up.*, 16). In theistic thought this has given us two famous formulations about the individual soul and the Supreme Soul which may be said to be at the background of the religious consciousness of the bulk of the Hindus. The first one from the *ŚvU* (III, 13, cf. V, 8) reads: "A 'person' of the measure of a thumb is ever placed in the hearts of men as the inner soul." The second is from the *BhG* (XVIII, 61; cf. XV, 15; XIII, 17; X, 20; VIII, 4) and reads: "God, O Arjuna, abides in the hearts of all beings and rotates them like creatures on a machine through His wondrous power." This formulation is in comparable terms with those of the *ŚvU* passage. But the *BhG* in another text (XIII, 22; cf. XIII, 2), whose phraseology is a much more current coin, goes forth boldly in asserting that the Great Puruṣa in the human body, the individual soul, is also known as Paramātman, the Supreme Soul.

The main current of the Upaniṣads with the exception of the *ŚvU* led to the postulation of Impersonal Brahman, not infrequently spoken in personalized terms like Ātman and Puruṣa. The stream of thought and practice, however, represented in the literature of the later *Vedas* and the *Brāhmaṇas*, which are a century or so earlier than the earliest of the *Upaniṣads*, had raised two of the Gods of the Ṛgveda, viz., Rudra and Viṣṇu, to the position of the supreme god-head.[23] That Prajāpati, the creator-god, had, in the Ṛgveda, attained the position of the Supreme God is already mentioned. During the Upaniṣadic age, side by side with the speculative philosophy of the sages and their Brahman as the Supreme Deity, the three gods, Prajāpati (Brahmā), Rudra and Viṣṇu must have claimed and received the allegiance of the people at large. About the end of the period of the very early *Upaniṣads*, before the appearance of Buddha on the Indian stage, in the *ŚvU* we have complete evidence of Rudra, with Śiva and Hara as alternative epithets, being enthroned as the Supreme God. He takes the place of supremacy among and over the numerous gods of the Vedic pantheon as their overlord and also as the personalized substitute of Absolute Brahman, the Supreme Reality of the Upaniṣadic thinkers.[24]

The concept of personal God with a name and of His relations to man and the world expounded in this *Upaniṣad*, before 500 B.C., being the earliest known so far not only in the history of Indian-Hindu religious consciousness but also of that of humanity as a whole deserves to be briefly summarized here. There are three unborn elements: one of them is unknowing, mutable and powerless, the object of enjoyment, which is Pradhāna or Prakṛti; another is knowing, immutable, unmanifest, but, being enjoyer, is bound, which is the individual soul; the third is the universal and infinite soul, immortal and imperishable, ruler over both the enjoyer and the enjoyed. He is God, Hara, Śiva, Maheśvara (I, 8-12; III, 1-4; III, 12; IV, 5; IV, 10-12; V, 7-8; VI, 10; VI, 16). This God pervades all quarters. He is the first-born but also the last one in the womb. He stands facing all quarters and has eyes, ears, hands and feet on all sides. He is the fire in the waters, He enters the whole cosmos, He is in plants and trees. God Rudra is one and there is no place for a second. He rules supreme. He is the creator and the protector. He is more minute than the minute, takes manifold forms and encompasses everything. He is fleet though without feet, sees though without eyes and hears though without ears. He reflects the qualities of all the senses though devoid of senses. His form is not to be seen, nor is He to be seen with the eye. None has grasped Him and there is no likeness of Him. He is the Lord of all gods and the master of all masters and the cause of all causes. He both encompasses everything and is within every being. Being the inner self of all creatures He is the director of their activity, its knower and also its witness. Yet he is the Only One and devoid of qualities. He lies hidden in all beings like the superfine film that rises out of clarified butter or like fire latent in its source or like oil in sesamum seeds or like water in riverbeds or again like cream in butter [milk] (II, 16-17; III, 9-12; 14-20; IV, 10-11; 14-16; V, 2; 13-4; VI, 2-4; 7-13; 16-8; IV, 16; I, 13-16).

Rudra, Śiva, Hara or Maheśvara is thus declared to be the Supreme God, the Only God, with all the attributes of such god-head, most of which are pairs of contraries, besides those of utter supremacy and of miraculous power. At the same time His identity with the Absolute, Brahman of the other Upaniṣads, is from time to time stressed in such expressions as: "Brahman, higher than Vedic gods and the world, the supreme, the great one, hidden in all creatures and enveloping the world, is the Supreme Person of sun-like colour, i.e., Rudra. He is the lord in whom the seers of Brahman and the deities are united. He is the one God who, according to his own nature, covers himself like a spider with threads produced from Pradhāna (unmanifested matter) who gives entrance into Brahman" (III, 6-7; IV, 15; 18; V, 6; VI, 14). The sage Śvetāśvatara in this discourse is said to have spoken about Brahman, the Supreme, the pure (VI, 21).

The relation between Rudra-Śiva, the Supreme God, and the individual soul is further brought out in terms of the Ṛgvedic and Upaniṣadic imagery of two birds, constant companions of each other, who cling to the same tree. One of them is the individual soul eating the sweet fruit of its activity. The other is the Universal Soul, here Rudra-Śiva, who merely looks on. The former, deluded and grieving in its helplessness, looks on the latter, the Lord, and worships Him and His greatness to free himself from sorrow (IV, 6-7). The embodied soul is described as a person of the measure of a thumb. He is the lord of knowledge, dwelling in the hearts of men and is confined by heart and mind. In the outside world, i.e., as the Universal Soul, he works as the controller of the whole world. He as the Universal Soul is called the Primeval, the Supreme Person. God, the Maker of all things, the great self, is ever seated in the hearts of creatures. Those who know Him as abiding in the heart through their heart and mind become immortal. The adorable God, Rudra-Śiva, abides in one's mind ('citta') or 'self' ('ātman') and is to be worshipped as such ; and knowing Him, the immortal, to be in one's own Self one attains Brahman (III, 13, 18-21 ; IV, 10 ; 17 ; 20 ; VI, 5-6). Finally it is clearly stated that perception of the identity of the individual soul with Him, Rudra-Śiva, leads to eternal happiness, because the truth is that the identity of the two is lost sight of in the mundane existence through ignorance (VI, 12 ; V, 1 ; IV, 5).

The Supreme God, Rudra-Śiva, brings in righteousness ('dharma'). He is the lord of prosperity ('bhageśa') ; He drives away sin and evil ('pāpanud') ; He is the giver of boons ('varada'), i.e., He is kind ; He is the refuge of all ('sarvasya śaraṇa'). It is through His favour, grace ('prasāda'), that one can speak about the Supreme, Brahman, as the sage Śvetāśvatara did to the ascetics, or can behold Him as the Lord and His majesty (III, 17, 20 ; IV, 11 ; VI, 6, 21).

Proclaiming that the kind of knowledge expounded in the text comes naturally and fructifies only in their cases who have the highest devotion ('parā bhakti') for God, and also for their teacher as for God, the sage himself offers his surrender ('śaraṇa' of the text and 'prapatti' of later theism), that he may achieve liberation (VI, 19-20 ; 23).

The other great God out of the three Supreme Gods, who has devoted to Him a whole book setting forth His attributes and depicting Him in the glory of the Supreme God, is Viṣṇu-Kṛṣṇa. The *Bhagavadgītā*, the 'Lord's song', about three centuries later than the *Śvetāśvatara Upaniṣad*, the book of the charter of Rudra-Śiva, is unlike the latter a discourse given by the person who himself is identified in it with the already accepted Supreme God, Viṣṇu. He is Kṛṣṇa-Vāsudeva of the race of the Vṛṣṇis. A human being deified and identified with a god, previously acknowledged as a Supreme God, must be considered to be a new phenomenon in the history of the religious consciousness of man, and it is quite clearly so in the religious history of the Hindus, which extends over about 1600 years before the accredited rise of this phenomenon.

We have been told by students of Vedic literature like Macdonell, Bhandarkar and Keith[25] that three or four forms of Viṣṇu, which later came to be known as 'avatāras', incarnations, of His, occur in the Vedic literature but they are not called such in that literature ; and only one of them is human, that of the dwarf, while two of the three animal ones are also ascribed to Prajāpati (Brahmā). Viṣṇu was in all probability raised to the status of the Supreme Being before the time of the *Kaṭha Upaniṣad*. i.e., a century or so even before the enthronement of Rudra-Śiva by the school of Śvetāśvatara. For as Bhandarkar pointed out, in a passage of the *KaU* (I, 3, 9) the soul's journey is said to have Viṣṇu's highest place as its goal. But actually we are not told that that was the highest end. We cannot assume that that was considered to be the abode of eternal bliss.

In the *Bhagavadgītā*, side by side with Kṛṣṇa-Vāsudeva's assertion that he is the Supreme God. and alongside of His emphasizing this aspect of his with a miraculously managed vision of the Cosmic Form, 'Viśvarūpa', of the Supreme

God in precisely the traditionally assumed form and equipment of Viṣṇu, as one of the three Supreme Gods, is adumbrated a theory of God's incarnations. He is addressed, too, as Viṣṇu.

The verses (*BhG*, IV, 5-8) in which the doctrine of incarnations is stated read: "Many are the births that I and you, Arjuna, have passed through. But while I know them all, you do not know any. I am unborn, unchanging, the lord of beings. Yet I get born through the material nature which is my power and my working material. [If you ask me the occasion and purpose of my births, because, unlike you, I am not under the law of Karma forced into repeated births, then I should tell you that] I bring myself to births, whenever there is decline of righteousness and whenever unrighteousness prospers, in order that I may protect the good and destroy the wicked and thus firmly establish righteousness from age to age."

It must be borne in mind, while appraising the value of this theorizing about God's incarnations, which are strictly occasional and conditioned by temporal and social needs, for the history of incarnations as an aspect of the sociology of religion, that Lord Kṛṣṇa was led on to its statement by Arjuna's being at a loss to understand how Kṛṣṇa could have taught certain philosophico-religious doctrines to certain sages who had lived ages before. Arjuna's doubt did not include a query about the purpose or purposes of Kṛṣṇa's rebirth. But Kṛṣṇa for two perfectly good reasons, utilized the opportunity to include in his reply the purpose for which He gets re-born. First, there is no doubt that he wanted to establish his god-head; and second, it was quite imperative that Arjuna should be made to fight with the Kaurava forces with a sound assurance of his ensuing victory. Both these purposes are served by the additional information regarding the purpose for which God incarnates Himself and in particular He had incarnated Himself as Kṛṣṇa.

The later two of the four verses have become a bye-word with agitators and leaders, rallying people against unrighteousness or oppression, as also with reformists and revivalists, to assure their hearers that they have the word of God, and therefore God, on their side. They have also served as solace to the common mass of Hindus in their hours of depression and agony through either foreign religious persecution or through rapid changes in the ethico-religious tempo of the Hindu society.

Five centuries later—it is quite clear from the work, *Buddhacarita*, of Aśvaghoṣa, who lived a century or more before Kālidāsa, that Buddha was not yet appropriated in Hinduism as an incarnation of God, much less as one of the incarnations of Viṣṇu—the national poet Kālidāsa in his felicitously worded poetry, in the context of emotionally charged atmosphere of the birth of Rāma in the family of the famous Ikṣvākus, gave proof of the complete acceptance of the theory and stabilized it even more by his weighty prestige.

Here I shall make a brief though prosaic statement of what Kālidāsa said on it in mellifluous words of a majestic language. The occasion is the gods' waiting upon Viṣṇu-Nārāyaṇa to request him to protect them and the world of righteousness from Rāvaṇa who was troubling them all, having fortified himself by a boon from Brahmā that no god could vanquish him. Almost at the end of a beautiful hymn of religious import extolling the qualities of the Supreme God, the gods proclaim that Viṣṇu-Nārāyaṇa takes birth and enters the field of activity only as a favour on the world. This implies that past births and appropriate activity of the Supreme God are taken for granted and their sole purpose is stated to have been to help the world out of a bad situation and suggests the extreme kind-heartedness of the God. Viṣṇu-Nārāyaṇa, cogitating for a second, answers the request of the gods by promising to incarnate Himself as a human being in the form of a son of king Daśaratha. In promising to take human birth Viṣṇu-Nārāyaṇa was guided by the nature of the boon granted to Rāvaṇa by Brahmā. He could not prevail against Rāvaṇa as Viṣṇu without traducing Brahmā's boon. He had therefore to incarnate Himself as a man and act like one (*Raghuvaṁśa*, X, 31, 43-4 ; cf. XI, 80-85 ; VI, 49 ; *Meghadūta*, 15 ; 57).

In two particulars Kālidāsa's presentation of and therefore his acceptance of the theory of incarnations differs from that propounded in the *Bhagavadgītā*. First, in the *BhG*, Kṛṣṇa asserts that he remembers all his previous births. He must be presumed to have fresh memories of his activity in previous births. Kālidāsa, who is quite emphatic about Rāma having been an incarnation of the Eternal Puruṣa or Viṣṇu, however, is particular to deny such memory for Rāma. He says that Rāma felt uneasy at a certain place quite unwillingly and not because he remembered his activity in his previous birth, the incarnation of Viṣṇu known as the Dwarf or Vāmana (*Raghuvaṁśa*, XI, 22). Vāmana incarnation to Kālidāsa was the next previous to Rāma because evidently he and his age did not accept Paraśurāma as an incarnation of Viṣṇu. Second, Kālidāsa looks upon Nārāyaṇa, who is generally meant by Eternal Puruṣa or Viṣṇu, and not different from Him, also as an incarnation of the Supreme Being (*Raghuvaṁśa*, XI, 80).

It is no special leaning on the theory of incarnations of Jñāneśvara that he should comment on the appropriate verses of the *BhG* in his great commentary. Not even his waxing eloquent in it on the great satisfaction that devout persons receive by way of increase of righteousness as a consequence is an indication of greater faith in it. That he should end his particular comment with the concluding remark, which adds to the connotation of the *BhG* text, that those who discern the fact of God's, Viṣṇu-Kṛṣṇa's, incarnations as being taken on behalf of righteousness are the wise people, is but natural for an expounder of his ability. But when later in the context of God's various glorious manifestations, not His incarnations, Jñāneśvara snatches the opportunity, afforded by the mention of Rāma and Kṛṣṇa's description of him as his glorious manifestation because he is the archetype of all weapon-wielders (*BhG*, X, 31), he clearly emphasizes the complete acceptance of the theory of incarnations. He devotes eight lines (X, 251-55) to explain the greatness of Rāma, the task which was accomplished by him in killing Rāvaṇa, and its consequences in the form of the freedom of the gods and the rehabilitation of righteousness in the world. He does not point out the inappropriateness of Rāma being included among others, the best and the first ones of their class or group of objects, creatures, men or gods. None of the other manifestations occurs in the standard list of ten or even more incarnations of Viṣṇu while Rāma, since before Kālidāsa's days, was quite definitely considered to be an incarnation of Viṣṇu! The fact appears to be that when Kṛṣṇa was making out a case for himself being recognized as an incarnation, or better yet when the supporters of the Lordship of Kṛṣṇa were doing it about the 3rd century B.C., Rāma had not received as much recognition as would entitle him to be classed as an incarnation. If this reasoning is correct the theory of human incarnations of Viṣṇu must be considered to have been getting formulated about the time not much earlier than the age of the *Bhagavadgītā*. That the purpose in any of God's activities is the welfare of the world is an ancient notion, the same having been mentioned in the *Brāhmaṇas*, and even in the Vedas, in respect of Viṣṇu's three steps.[26]

The times in which Rāmadāsa, in the 17th century, composed his *Dāsabodha* in Maharashtra, provided a favourable atmosphere for the reiteration, with specific emphasis, of the theory of incarnations. Shivaji, the extra-ordinary Maratha leader, against tremendous odds, had achieved such exploits that almost in any clime he could have made people wonder at them and class their owner among divinely inspired persons. In Maharashtra, where five centuries of religious literature and devotional singing had gone on on a very very large scale, the climate was particularly congenial to such a man as Shivaji being looked upon as a divinely inspired person. And Rāmadāsa was so far convinced himself that Shivaji was a kind of incarnation of God and had so much need for such a belief being widely held by the people of Maharashtra at that time, that he at least twice voiced the doctrine of incarnations (X, 4, 41-2; XVIII, 6, 20). He says: "The men who rehabilitate righteousness are the incarnations of God. They flourished in the past; and they will occur in the future. God has ordained so." And more on the lines of an exposition of the *BhG* text he says: "Viṣṇu has to take births and assume different incarnations in order to kill the wicked and establish righteousness. Therefore all those men who rehabilitate righteousness are Viṣṇu's incarnations."

We may now review the description of god-head as it is made in the *BhG* so that we have a standard Vaiṣṇava pattern to put by the side of the Śaiva one already briefly sketched from the *ŚvU*.

At the very outset I should like the reader to note that the two words most commonly used to express the Absolute God-head in élite and semi-élite Hinduism in modern and recent times are Parabrahma and Paramātmā (XIII, 22; 39; XV, 17) in place of the Upaniṣadic Brahman and Ātman. The word Parabrahma (VIII, 3; X, 12) being neuter in gender still retains the aroma of the Impersonal Absolute; but Paramātmā being masculine gender lends itself to easy and agreeable accommodation in the theistic systems of religious consciousness as they centre round a personal God. A third word of about the same import and of personalized nature is Parameśvara (XI, 3; XIII, 27), which is more current among the non-élite today than any other designation of the Supreme God. A fourth word of similar formation is 'Uttama Puruṣa' or 'Puruṣottama' (XI, 3; XV, 17-19).[27] Since its formulation in the *Bhagavadgītā* it has become one of the thousand names by which Viṣṇu is known and forms one of the twentyfour names of Viṣṇu, indeed the last in the group of twentyfour, which a twice-born person has to recite everyday in his 'sandhyā'-adoration or which any Hindu performing any religious rite has to utter at the beginning with appropriate use of water for sipping, etc.

The Supreme God as described mostly throughout the *BhG*, leaving out the special eleventh chapter named 'vision of Cosmic Form', is: He is the Lord, the supporter and the goal of all; He is the source, the rest and the deluge and end of all; He is the changeless seed of all creatures and the world; He is the witness of everything and also the friend of all (IX, 18; X, 20; VII, 6, 10; X, 39; V, 29). He is the refuge ('śaraṇa') of all and one does best to seek refuge in Him (IX, 18; XVIII, 62, 66). Yet He is non-doer, being the Master of all creatures; He is unborn and unchanging, without beginning and eternal; He is in all creatures and yet not confined therein; everything is contained in Him. Everything is threaded through Him. He knows the past, the present and the future but none knows Him completely. He is the inner soul of men. His abode is the place of eternal bliss (IV, 6, 13; VI, 31; VII, 7, 25, 26; VIII, 21; IX, 4; X, 3, 12; XV, 6, 15, 17; XVIII, 56).

These attributes of the Supreme God are such that they can be and have been, most of them at least with appropriate grammatical change only, predicated of Absolute Brahman. They figure in the description of Rudra-Śiva in the *Śvetāśvatara Upaniṣad* too. But theism has found its strength in many additional attributes of Him as personal God, which assure the worshipper of his welfare, not only in life after death but also in mundane living. As a matter of fact it appears to me that the history of the religions of mankind reveals, as the main basis of the victory of theism over philosophical religions or of one theism over another, the relative emphasis, authority, and exclusiveness with which such assurances are made.

Theism of the *Bhagavadgītā*, Vaiṣṇavism or rather Kṛṣṇaism, goes a long way in making very reassuring statements which in reality are the attributes of the Supreme God of that theism. The assurances figure, because of the nature of the text, as the word of God Incarnate, and not as postulations or formulations of the thinker, the theologian or the worshipper. To that extent, however, they gain in authority. I shall summarize them briefly in terms which will place them in their proper context as attributes of the Supreme God in the word of God Himself: "God looks after the welfare of those who think of Him and meditate on Him single-mindedly and worship Him. Though

God is fundamentally impartial, none being liked or hated by Him, yet in fact He is with them who worship Him with devotion as they are with Him in thought and practice. No devotee of God ever can come to grief. God saves his devotees from the bondage of the world, enabling them to attain complete salvation" (IX. 22, 29, 31 ; XII, 7, 8).

Thus the personalization of the Supreme is complete, even more complete than that achieved by the thinkers whose work the *Śvetāśvatara Upaniṣad* is. The God around whom they wove it, Rudra-Śiva, was not a person ever known or believed to have lived on earth and as such did not afford specially easy circumstances for personalization. The God of the *Bhagavadgītā*, on the other hand, tradition tells us, was a living human being. Further the declarations and assertions are all supposed to be made by Kṛṣṇa himself, which naturally has aided the process of personalization. With all this, however, the old attributes, or the fundamental nature, of the Absolute as the God-head, so well laid out in the Upaniṣads, the immanence and transcendence of Brahman, are still there, in more or less the same or similar imagery and even words, and are bodily attributed to personal God. This feature has continued to be a speciality of Hinduism as a theistic system. It has uplifted the ancient polylatry, facilitated it, and expanded it without any wrench or qualm being felt by the body social.

Lord Kṛṣṇa as Supreme God says about Himself: "In my non-manifest form I am spread over the whole cosmos ; I am the sustainer of all creatures ; all creatures are contained within me and yet they are not in me owing to my wondrous power. Though I reside in them I am not contained by them. For it is like air-space which is everywhere and thus contains everything. I, too, am everywhere ; all creatures are thus within me. [It is because of this immanence and transcendence of the Supreme God] that one who sees, i.e., realizes, Me as being everywhere and everything as being in Me and worships Unity never falls, never goes without My full support" (IX, 4-6 ; VI, 30-31).

Lord Kṛṣṇa not only identifies Himself with Brahman but indirectly even asserts His superiority over Brahman (XIV, 27 ; XV, 15, 17-8 ; XIII, 17 ; cf. XI, 37 ; VIII, 21 ; VIII, 3). The transcendence and immanence of Brahman is stated in the standard Upaniṣadic pattern as : "Great Brahman without beginning is described as 'Neither Being nor Non-Being' ; It has hands and feet everywhere and head, mouth, eyes and ears in all directions. It envelops everything. Without any limbs It has all the appearance of qualities and limbs. Though not attached It supports all ; and though without qualities It enjoys their fruit. It is both inside and outside beings ; and is both moving and stationary. Being subtle It is unknowable. It is near yet far off. Though Itself undivided whole, It appears in beings as if divided and disparate. It creates, sustains and destroys creatures. It is light of light and is beyond darkness. Yet It dwells in the hearts of all" (*BhG*, XIII, 12-17 ; cf. *BrU*, IV, 3, 7 ; IV, 4, 16 ; V, 6 ; *MuU*, II, 2, 9 ; *IU*, I, 5 ; *ŚvU*, V, 8, etc.).

The grip of the notion of Brahman on the thinkers of India since the Upaniṣadic age was so strong that even when Brahman was being replaced by personal God as the Supreme, whether Śiva or Viṣṇu, the curious syllable 'om' was being treated as a representation of Brahman. One of the reasons or perhaps the principal reason for the syllable being accepted was that the chief mode of approach to the deity, the method of worship for the generality of men, was coming to be conceived of in terms of some kind of concentration on some emblem or symbol, accompanied by verbal repetition of the name. The syllable—it is called a letter in *BhG* (VIII, 13)—'om' had come to acquire mystic significance and to be valued as a symbol of the quintessence of the three Vedas already in the *Brāhmaṇas* (*Ait. Br.*, V, 32).

In the *Praśna Upaniṣad* (V, 1-7) and in the *MāU* (I, 2-12) the mystic and sacred symbol, 'om', is specifically analysed into its three elements or letters, the whole being a syllable and not a single letter, one text bringing out *inter alia* its supposed extraction from the three Vedas, the *Ṛk*, the *Yajus* and the *Sāman*. One Satyakāma, 'Truth-seeker', Śaibya asked the hoary sage Pippalāda, 'Eater of the Ficus Indica fruit', what world a person who 'meditates' on the syllable-symbol 'om' to the end of his life attains. The sage after expounding the composition and formulation of the syllable-symbol concludes his answer by asserting that even with the help of the receptacle in the form of the syllable-symbol 'om', the wise man attains the 'supreme', 'param',—the same word with a noun, either 'pada', meaning 'place', or 'dhāma', meaning abode, occurs in the *BhG* in its description of the final beatitude—that is tranquil, unageing, immortal and free from fear. The *KaU* (I, 2, 15-6) goes even further and states that the word 'pada',—mark the word used—which is proclaimed in all the Vedas evidently as the goal of meditation and of religious living is 'om'. That it should identify it with everlasting Brahman is but a paraphrase of the previous statement. Alternatively the syllable is identified with Ātman (*MuU*, II, 2, 6 ; *MāU*, I, 12).[28]

Two other Upaniṣadic texts (*MuU*, II, 2, 4 and *ŚvU*, I, 14) are particularly of interest. In both, the sacred symbol is called 'praṇava', a word which the *BhG* also uses (VII, 8), meaning it to be the essence of or the most important element in the Vedas. In both, the imagery used makes it an instrument which with an accessary can be and has to be employed to attain, 'get at', Brahman. In the *Muṇḍaka* passage the syllable is thought of as a bow and its arrow is the individual soul. The target is Brahman and the individual soul can be reached there as an arrow shot from the bow in the form of the sacred syllable. In the *Śvetāśvatara* passage we have a more psycho-ethical setting which involves self-help and self-endeavour of a highly religious order. One's body is conceived as the lower one and the mystic syllable as the upper one of the two pieces of wood, friction effected between which gives the fire in the form of the vision of God. The friction cannot be mechanical and has to take the form of meditation, oft practised.

Lord Kṛṣṇa brought 'om', the symbol of the essence of the Vedas and of

Brahman, into relation with theism, though its close association with the technique of 'yoga' in the process of securing the final release is what is actually mentioned (VIII, 12-13). "Anyone, who, controlling the senses, confining the mind within his heart and pushing the life-breath in the head holds himself in steady concentration, and remembering Lord Kṛṣṇa, the Supreme God, goes on uttering the one-lettered [name of] Brahman, 'Om', at the time of death, attains final beatitude."

The later and current élite practice of using the syllable not as a symbol for Brahman by itself but as an efficacious way of presenting, repeating or performing anything, almost as a sort of a charm-guarantee of the fruitfulness or the success of the activity, religious or not, can be traced to the *BhG* dictum that 'om tat sat' is the three-fold appellation of Brahman and its elaboration (XVIII, 23-6). With the utterance of 'om' it is that all enjoined or ordained and religious or pious activity is begun by religious and wise men.

This mystic significance of 'om' was so far fixed in the time following the age of the *BhG* that, in the normative and till recently extraordinarily authoritative work, *Manusmṛti*, which has governed the moral, social, legal and to a large extent even the religious practice of the Hindus, élite and semi-élite, for fifteen hundred years, lauds its use and enjoins it for specific occasions as an invariable prescription.[29] It went further than the *Upaniṣads* and the *BhG* and boldly propounded the theory that the three letters, 'a', 'u' and 'ma', were 'milked' by the creator-God Prajāpati from the three Vedas (II, 76) and justified its employment as the beginning of every religious activity (II, 74). Emphasizing the identity of the syllable with Brahman and joining on to it other three mystic words it exhorted that by the repetition of the combined formula from day to day for three years one can attain the highest state of beatitude, the state of what is known to all Hindus as that of a 'jīvan-mukta', i.e., a soul liberated even while living and therefore confined in the material body (II, 81-84).

Gods personified receive closer attention as regards their appearance, their physical feature and their sartorial and other equipment. In the *Rgveda* we find a number of descriptions of the leading god's, Indra's, body and equipment. We are also informed indirectly that images of Indra were then made and could be purchased, though they were considered very valuable and not easily parted with.[30] The *ŚvU* does not proceed as far as the *Rgveda* did in the case of such deities as Indra and even Varuṇa in describing the personal god Rudra-Śiva. It refers to the body of Rudra only in general terms as 'auspicious', 'non-terrific' and 'sin-destroying' (III, 4), the last epithet being purely psychological.

The *Bhagavadgītā* takes full strides on the path of visual presentation of the form of the deity. In its XIth chapter the wondrous vision of the Cosmic Form of the Supreme God is presented by Lord Kṛṣṇa before his favourite friend and protégé Arjuna at his express desire. Lord Kṛṣṇa introduces the coming vision with the assertion that Arjuna will be able to see with the help of the divine sight provided by Him many and varied forms of the Lord. He will see most of the Vedic gods, Ādityas, Rudras, Aśvins and Maruts as well as many a miraculous scene. In short, Arjuna is assured that he will find the whole cosmos standing there as a whole in the Cosmic Form. The Form is described by the narrator first, then to some extent by the spectator Arjuna and finally and indirectly by Kṛṣṇa himself.

The description of the Cosmic Form of Lord Kṛṣṇa as the Supreme God by the narrator is particular in mentioning the luminous and divine dress, ornaments, garlands, fragrant unguents and upraised and divine weapons. The lustre of the Form is specially insisted upon with the assertion that it was so bright that it easily equalled the combined lustre of a thousand suns in the sky. Arjuna, though almost stupefied by that marvellous sight, remained composed enough to record his impressions of the Form. This means that in the contemporaneous society, the outlines of the Cosmic Form and of the other major and minor deities were more or less fixed and well known; and the compiler of the *BhG*, the school of Kṛṣṇa-Viṣṇu devotees and worshippers, desired to stereotype the wholly or partly accepted representations of Viṣṇu and some other gods.

Arjuna begins his description of the Cosmic Form naturally with the affirmation that he sees all gods and creatures in it, including the sages and the divine serpents. In his assertion that he sees Brahmā, the lord of all gods, too, there, the qualifying expression that Arjuna uses yields us the important information that Brahmā had come to be represented as seated in a lotus. We cannot definitely conclude that the picture thus conjured up by Arjuna before our mind's eye is that of Viṣṇu-Śeṣaśāyin, Viṣṇu-Nārāyaṇa, whose accepted representation is so beautifully described by Kālidāsa (*Raghuvaṁśa*, X, 7-14; XIII, 5-6). Arjuna's description of the Cosmic Form gives the standard image of Viṣṇu with His crown on the head, the discus in one hand and the mace in another. We cannot be definite if the representation made the image four-armed as in later and current Hinduism. The other features of the form, like extraordinarily bright lustre, firiness and fierceness, are evidently the incidental concomitants of the Cosmic Form. In a chastened mood Arjuna after singing a hymn of praise, which *inter alia* identified the Cosmic Form with a number of Vedic gods including Prajāpati, pays homage with his body bent down and implores and beseeches that the Lord may be pleased to resume His form as Kṛṣṇa. Arjuna's entreaty provides us with the valuable information that Kṛṣṇa by the time of the compilation of the *BhG* had his representation standardized. It had a crown on the head; it is four-armed—the standard number of arms in Hindu iconography for Viṣṇu—, it wields a mace in one hand and the discus in another, the two remaining hands having been left out in the description. The representation of Śiva, though not specified in the *ŚvU*, must have been fixed much before 300 B.C., as is clear from my brief account of the development of the god-head of Śiva given elsewhere.[31] The earliest available representation of that God, the one on the Kushan coins, portrays Him standing leaning against His traditional mount, the bull, dressed in full-length 'dhoti', having two hands in one of which He holds His famous and specific weapon, the trident.

Viṣṇu thus appears from the evidence so far available, to be the first of the three Supreme Gods, Brahmā, Viṣṇu and Śiva, to be thought of and represented with a physical feature, not consonant with human form and evidently designed to emphasize super-human capacity. The four arms of Viṣṇu enabling Him to wield four weapons simultaneously is a feature calculated to portray Him as super-human and extra-ordinarily powerful. Śiva's two hands later got multiplied in iconic representation to eight, though His standard image as 'Naṭarāja' commonly has only four hands, very beautifully poised in the dance-pose making the representation a rhythmic perfection.[32]

Among the polylatrous people of antiquity whose religious consciousness I have reviewed in this study, the Indians since very early in their religion-making endeavour, when postulating anthropomorphic gods, attributed to them physical features, like more heads and faces than one, more eyes than two, and more than two arms or more than two feet, which are beyond the human form. This was a concession to human weakness which for visualizing the figure of the omnipotent and omniscient God needed such extraneous aid, making the form super-human!

The attributes of the Supreme God summarized above give us the view of the people who put up the claims of the Gods who were their special deities, whether actually human or not, of their respective groups. They converge so much that, except for the special features of the man-god Kṛṣṇa-Viṣṇu, they may be accepted to have been the commonly conceived attributes of the Supreme God, whether thought of as Śiva, or as Viṣṇu, about the 2nd century B.C.

I shall now present a brief view of attributes of the Supreme God as they were conceived and believed in élite practice as represented in the poetry of the national poet Kālidāsa about the 4th century of the Christian era. It should be borne in mind that all the well-known philosophical systems of the Vedānta and all the current sectarian religious complexes came to be formulated and presented in texts some centuries afterwards.

The tutelary deity, the patron God of Kālidāsa, was quite clearly Śiva. I have elsewhere[33] presented a brief summary of the description of his favourite deity, Śiva, which Kālidāsa has so lovingly made at the beginning of his five great works and in the body of two of them and of a sixth one. Here I shall confine my observations to Kālidāsa's indirect description of Śiva that we come across in his *Kumārasambhava*. The description is indirect because it is represented as coming either from Pārvatī and in answer to certain queries and doubts about the greatness or the propriety of certain features of Śiva or from the Creator god Brahmā or from the great seven secondary creators of Hindu mythology or from a servant of Śiva.

The portrayal of Śiva through Pārvatī's reply and rejoinders (*Kumārasam-*

bhava, V, 75-81) is quite clearly designed to meet certain objections that must have been common among some sectarians or some sections of the populace. Śiva, though of fierce form, is called Śiva, auspicious, which shows that people do not know Him in his true form and full extent. He may wear on His head a skull or the digit of the moon ; He may have ornaments or only serpents on his body ; He may be dressed in an elephant skin or in a silk garment. His shape and form is Cosmic and is not fully comprehended. He may be besmeared only with ashes from the cremation-ground ; yet the same ashes falling off from his limbs in His great dance are worn on their heads by gods and are known to be capable of effecting purity, physical and mental. He may be poor and may have only a bullock for His mount ; but He is done deep homage to by such gods as Indra riding his mighty elephant and wearing his costly crest-jewels. If His birth is not known that is because He is Himself the source or the cause of the so-called Self-born Brahmā. How can One who is the source of the Self-born have birth ?*

The great sages describe Śiva : "Parameśvara, the Highest Lord, an epithet not applicable to any other god ; Upholder and sustainer of the cosmos ; One sought after by adepts in 'yoga' in their own hearts ; One whose abode is described by the wise as one wherefrom Souls have not to return, i.e., as the abode of eternal bliss and salvation. He is the inner soul of all embodied beings ; He is not to be seen embodied but is felt to be there ; He has three aspects, with one He creates, with another He sustains and with the third he destroys the cosmos (*Kumārasambhava*, VI. 75-77 ; 21-3 ; cf. *Raghuvaṁśa*, II, 44).

Brahmā describes Śiva as dwelling beyond darkness with unlimited lustre, and as not comprehended fully either by Himself or by Viṣṇu (*Kumārasambhava*, II, 58).

It is clear that to Kālidāsa, and presumably to the Indians of Kālidāsa's time, Śiva was not only the Supreme God but also Paramātman or Parameśvara, and as such was not merely the Destroyer-aspect of the Supreme but the Unity of all the three aspects, supposed to be distributed among the three Supreme Gods, Brahmā, Viṣṇu and Śiva. Perception of unity of the Supreme God-head, though named variantly, was thus the central core of the religious consciousness of the Indians of Kālidāsa's time.

Kālidāsa, though a devout worshipper of Śiva as the Supreme God, as Paramātman or Parameśvara or Parabrahman, speaks of Viṣṇu-Śeṣaśāyin, Viṣṇu-Nārāyaṇa, and by implication, of Rāma, whom he considered to be an incarnation of Viṣṇu and spoke of as Hari under the appellation of Rāma (*Raghuvaṁśa*, XIII, 1), in the same or very similar terms and evidently with greater and reverential endearment.

Kālidāsa's portrayal of Viṣṇu-Śeṣaśāyin or Viṣṇu-Nārāyaṇa appears to be

---

* An echo of this ratiocination of Kālidāsa is to be heard in certain Tamil hymns of the great Śaiva saint-poet of Tamilnad, Manikkavasagar (vide Kingsbury and Phillips, *Hymns of the Śaivite Saints*, 102-5, on p. 105), who may be ascribed to the latter half of the 8th century A.D.

the earliest one of that form of Viṣṇu and has been the standard one for later times, whether for artist's material representation or for the devotee-poet's verbal one.

Viṣṇu-Śeṣaśāyin is the Puruṣa *par excellence* or is 'Ādi-Puruṣa', the First Puruṣa (*Raghuvaṁśa*, XIII, 6 ; X, 6). To Hari alone pertains the epithet 'Puruṣottama', Best Puruṣa (III, 9). He is Puruṣa Unborn (VIII, 78) or Purātana, i.e., Ancient (XI, 85). He lies on the body of the serpent Śeṣa with its [seven-pronged] hood lighting up the God's body. Śrī [Viṣṇu's consort] sitting at the foot-end of Viṣṇu, has His feet on her palm placed over her lap. His long expansive four arms are splendidly bedecked with ornaments so that He appears as if He was the heavenly tree 'pārijāta'. He bears on his chest a special mark, ever-known as 'Śrīvatsa', and that extra-ordinary jewel, called 'Kaustubha', which was one of the products of the great churning of the ocean. With His eyes like full-blown lotuses and his light yellow lower garment He appears like an autumnal day pleasing and consoling at the very outset. He is being hymned by Brahmā sitting in the lotus grown out of His navel. His special weapons standing incarnate proclaim His victory, and His mount eagle, forgetting its enmity with serpents, attends on Him with folded palms (X, 7-13, 86 ; XIII, 6).

The glorious and ennobling hymn, which Kālidāsa framed for the gods to laud Viṣṇu, reads : "Bow to You, who first creates, then sustains and then destroys the cosmos, who thus takes three forms [Brahmā, Viṣṇu, Śiva or Maheśa). You are changeless in all states like rain-water which assumes different tastes according to the nature of the soil on which it falls and yet keeps its fundamental nature. You are immeasurable but You have measured the cosmos ; You have no want but You grant entreaties ; You are unconquered, but You are the victor ; You are the cause of all that is manifest though You are unmanifest. You are not seated though You are in the hearts of creatures ; You have no desire yet You perform austerities. You remove the sorrows of others but You are not affected by them. You are ancient yet unageing. You know everything but You are known to others ; You are the creating source of all but You are self-born ; You are overlord of all but You have no master. You are one but You have all forms. You are sung in seven 'sāman'-songs and lie on the surface of seven seas, with the seven-flamed fire for Your mouth. You are the sole resort of the seven worlds. All law, morality, religion, and society have proceeded from You [in the form of] the four-faced [Brahmā].

"Adepts in 'yoga' controlling their minds by practice seek You, the pure lustre, in their own hearts, thereby to attain liberation. In reality who knows You who though unborn takes births, though without desires kills enemies, though sleeping keeps awake ? You are able to enjoy all the objects of sense like sounds and yet to practise hard penance, to protect Your subjects, the people, and yet to keep completely unattached. Though they are many different sects and systems of pursuing the highest ends of human existence all of them converge in You as do the different streams of the Gaṅgā [Ganges] in the ocean. Your greatness like earth and other objects though manifest is unlimited ; what to say about Yourself who can be approached only through the Vedas ('the authoritative word') and inference! Like jewels in the ocean and lustre in the sun Your far-fetched activity transcends praiseful enumeration. There is nothing that is not already obtained by You ; nevertheless You take births, having as their sole object the welfare of the world. You are the guarantee for non-return to this mundane existence in the case of those who have subdued their desires, and having concentrated their minds on You, have dedicated all their activity to You. You purify anyone who simply remembers You, i.e., utters Your name. This one fact is enough to specify the fruits of other kinds of devotional worship of You, i.e., like sight or touch." (*Raghuvaṁśa*, X, 16-31).

With the last pronouncement in the Viṣṇu-hymn of Kālidāsa, which reminds us of Kṛṣṇa-Viṣṇu's assurance given to Arjuna in the *BhG* (IX, 14 ; X, 9 ; XIII, 25), we are much further on the road to mediaeval[34] and current atmosphere of purely theistic Hinduism. But there is one additional feature of the Hinduism of Kālidāsa and the Indians of his time, which sadly was more or less lacking, at least in overt mention,—and there is reason to believe in the light of historical evidence that the feature was not merely lacking without consequences, but was responsible for active enmity between the followers of the two major sects of Hinduism, i.e., Śaivism and Vaiṣṇavism—in the religious complex of the Hindus between about 1000 A.D. and the 16th or the 17th century. And to that I shall now turn.

We have seen above how inspite of the clear-cut differentiation of functions ascribed to the three Supreme Gods of the Hindu pantheon, Brahmā, Viṣṇu, Maheśa, Kālidāsa, relegating Brahmā quite logically and naturally to a secondary position, ascribed all the three main functions of the Supreme God, that of creating, that of sustaining, and that of destroying the cosmos, to both Śiva and Viṣṇu, separately as he described the one or the other of them. This fact itself is a sure indication that Śiva and Viṣṇu were conceived as nominal variation of the same Supreme God. But Kālidāsa, seeing more clearly than any of his contemporaries, predecessors, or successors over more than a thousand years, went further in the active endeavour of removing the least possibility of doubt on the matter, and in clear and felicitous terms asserted the identity of Śiva and Viṣṇu. So says Kālidāsa : "That One Form divided Itself into three as Vedhas/Dhātā [Brahmā], Viṣṇu/Hari, and Hara [Maheśa]. Seniority and juniority, priority and posteriority, precedence and deferment among them is conditioned by occasion and is not inherent" (*Kumārasambhava*, VIII, 44). In including Brahmā in his weighty pronouncement Kālidāsa demonstrates the inveterate tendency of Hindus to be merely syncretic in the field of religious consciousness, a trait which is fostered by the pantheistic appreciation of the nature of God-head, so pronouncedly made out in the *Bhagavadgītā*. Elsewhere as already shown, Kālidāsa has left out Brahmā from the strictly supreme God-head, and has dwelt on the similar attributes and equal greatness of the two Gods, Śiva and Viṣṇu, who are but the same Supreme God under different names.

The *Bhagavadgītā*, though enthroning Kṛṣṇa-Viṣṇu as the Supreme God, both as a personal God and also as the Absolute Brahman of the strict Vedāntic monism, did not advance a strictly monotheistic view, did not enthrone Kṛṣṇa-Viṣṇu to the exclusion of all gods or as the Only true God, rejecting all others in that intolerant manner which could denounce other gods as so false as deserving to be cast aside. Lord Kṛṣṇa does refer to those who either did not acknowledge His God-head or opposed it as ignorant men, false men and so on (VII, 25; IX, 11-13); but He is catholic enough to appreciate the significance of faith in all religious consciousness (XVIII, 3-4). It is the faith with which one approaches one's God that matters to a large extent. Secondly, the doctrine of glorious manifestations of God, of Kṛṣṇa-Viṣṇu, are varied; and many of the Vedic gods find their place among them (XI, 21-23); and it would have been, and is, rather illogical to deny that faith in other gods, too, could make for one's religious advancement. Thirdly, there is the further extension and application of this theory, which gives a pantheistic view of the deity and which Lord Kṛṣṇa states in clear terms in IX, 23-4: "Even those who worship other gods with faith worship Me even though without proper rite; because I am the true lord and enjoyer of all worship." Fourthly, it is the differential fruit that makes for the fundamental difference between worship of Kṛṣṇa-Viṣṇu and that of the other Gods. The worshippers and devotees of other deities go to the worlds of those deities—here the reader should note that the Upaniṣadic cosmography is adhered to just as the Upaniṣadic view of the Supreme God as Absolute Brahman persists—which are all of them perishable (VIII, 6; IX, 20-22, 25). For all these reasons not only does Lord Kṛṣṇa not condemn allegiance to other deities as falsehood but He even assures all those, who would like to march on the road of religious consciousness, that He helps to stabilize their faith and devotion to whatever deity one is attached to and finds spiritual solace in (VII, 21). In view of the fact that this is not the last birth for the largest bulk of men, this devotion and devoted life will lead to a next birth with much better endowment of the religious sense and thus push forward on the path of true worship sooner or later.

It is this complex and undogmatic view of truth about God-head, which, as stated more than once, is both the consequence and the source of the pantheistic monolatry of Hinduism, that has not only tolerated but even encouraged ancient polylatry and widened its scope to accommodate other deities and even deity-like spirits.

The basic view of the Supreme God thus adumbrated in the *Bhagavadgītā* and its synthetic enunciation as made by Kālidāsa gives us the Hindu view of the God-head as it obtained before the formulation and promulgation of the various systems of theistic philosophy and sectarian complexes. This is the second phase of the Hindu view of the God-head.

CHAPTER X

HINDU VIEW OF THE GODHEAD (Third Phase)

With the emergence of two major Gods—the literature, as pointed out, mentions three, and current mythological thought, too, assumes them to be so, yet, as I have already pointed out, the third of the triad, viz., Brahmā, having long ago ceased to play a role which can be adjudged as one of equality with the other two and having been represented in standard mythology and cosmology as having been produced from the navel of Viṣṇu-Śeśaśāyin, has to be left out of consideration—Śiva and Viṣṇu, the Hindu view of the God-head shows a change. This changed view may be said to have been established before Kālidāsa's time and that of the composition of the *Bhagavadgītā*. In its purest and august form it appears in the poetry of Kālidāsa, through the hymns which are already referred to or quoted in the previous chapter. It is evident that the view of both the Supreme Gods, Śiva and Viṣṇu, is fully anthropomorphic. Both have consorts, Śiva's being Umā or Pārvatī and Viṣṇu-Śeṣaśāyin's being Lakṣmī.

Kālidāsa's philosophical identification of Śiva and Viṣṇu was an article of working faith and we have sculptural evidence of its embodiment in the figure of Hari-Hara, Viṣṇu and Śiva combined, one side showing all the emblems of Śiva and the other those of Viṣṇu, in a cave in the Deccan of about A.D. 578.[1]

The Tamil saint Appārswami, who must have lived in the early part of the 8th century A.D.[2], has provided a view of God Śiva and his nature which may be taken as representative of undifferentiated Śaivite view of the Supreme God.

Appārswami[3] expresses His joy over the matted hair of Śiva, His garland of white flowers, His crystal earrings, His ash-besmeared body covered over with an elephant skin, which is dripping being freshly peeled off from the elephant's body, and His trident, and declares that with all this paraphernalia, some of which in Hindu ideas are polluting, He remains ever the undefiled. He mentions some of His exploits and declares Him the Supreme Immanent Being who came out as Śiva with Umā as His part. He thus mentions the Ardhanārīnaṭeśvara form of Śiva to be the direct emanation from the subtle form of Śiva as the Supreme Being. In the Ardhanārīnaṭeśvara form, half the side is Śiva and the other bears all the physical and other characters of Umā or Pārvatī. The sacred river Gaṅgā (Ganges) lies concealed in Śiva's matted hair, while the moon shines on His head. Śiva is declared to be the Lord of Scripture and the celestial light of heaven and to be the true mystic. Sambandar and Sundarar, the other two members of the great trio, too, refer to many of these traits and attributes of Śiva.[4]

The saint Manikkavasagar, speaking of Śiva as father as Sambandar does, makes the additional acknowledgment of His consort Umā's sovereignty over the worshippers. His pronouncement that "though men seek Him, none fully knows Him ; none are His kindred ; there is no evil in Him; Perfect and effortless knowledge is His" breathes the austere atmosphere which is characteristic of much of the later Śaivism and justifies Appār's description of Śiva as austere Lord, though he looks upon Him as parents and friends, and Sambandar calls Him father.[5]

The Vaiṣṇava saints, who poured their religious heart in Tamil poetry, came only a little later than some of the earliest of the Śaiva saints whose view of the God-head, I have put in brief above. In their poetry, which is commonly known in the South as the Tamil Veda, showing the authoritative nature of the poetry composed by the Vaiṣṇava saints, and forms part of the complex of ritual and worship in practice at the temples and even in the households, we find a marked difference in imagery which is used to describe the relation between God and the individual worshipper. It foreshadows the difference in the ritual and the complete plan of religious living which characterize the later developments of the two sects, Śaivism being austere and free from a-moral and non-moral content and Vaiṣṇavism immersed in sportive and ecstatic exercises, their a-moral and non-moral features being differentially exhibited in the different sub-sects.

The God described, praised and prayed to by these Vaiṣṇava saints is commonly Kṛṣṇa, along with many of His dalliances, exploits in the cowherd-settlement near Mathurā.[6] Viṣṇu's three other incarnations Vāmana (dwarf), Rāma and Narasiṁha (man-lion) are referred to.[7] Śrīraṅgam temple and its God Viṣṇu-Śeṣaśāyin with Lakṣmī or Śrī, His consort, at His feet, naturally figures prominently. Expressions used in connection with this form of the Supreme God, known also as Nārāyaṇa, are devoid of any sportive and erotic note. His great work for mankind through His incarnations and His being the Supreme Being are quite often the traits that figure through this poetry. Viṣṇu's abode is Vaikuṇṭha and He Himself is called Vaikuṇṭha after it or even Śrīraṅga.[8] His four arms, His conch-shell of specific name and His discus are mentioned as typical of Him. But though He is called the Lord of Lakṣmī, He is given two more consorts, Bhūdevī and Nīlā (Līlā). And what is worse still their jealousy is referred to. Nammalvar, "the greatest, most famous and most voluminous of the Vaiṣṇava saint poets of Tamil land", says[9] : "When slyly, lotus-lipped with rain-cool eyes, Called by dark ocean by its white waves led, Śrī climbed the serpent couch, Bhūdevī wept ! Cried in high heaven 'Cruel Tirumal !' While tears rained rivers on those hills, her breasts."

The Vaiṣṇava notions of the God-head and of religio-philosophy were put into shape and vigorously propounded and expounded by Rāmānuja in the third quarter of the 11th century, which forms the faith and sets the practice of the sect today, which is well represented among the élite, semi-élite and folk elements of South India. The Supreme Soul according to the doctrines of this sect is called Īśvara and the individual soul is called 'Cit', consciousness. Īśvara conceived in five different modes is free from all faults and defects ; pervades all things, living and non-living ; is the inner controller ('antaryāmin') of all; has the auspicious qualities of knowledge, power etc.; is both the creator and the destroyer of the world; and is pure bliss ('ānanda'). He has a celestial, i.e., non-material, body of unsurpassable beauty. Thus He is both bliss and beauty. He has three consorts, Lakṣmī. Bhū and Līlā, the last being perhaps (?) the same as the one who appears as Nīlā in the Tamil poetry of the earlier Vaiṣṇava saints.

The first of the five modes in which Īśvara can be conceived is, the 'Para', the highest, called either as Para-Brahman or Para-Vāsudeva, the latter designation being specifically the heritage of Bhāgavatism of the Vṛṣṇis. He is Nārāyaṇa, i.e., Viṣṇu-Śeṣaśāyin. His abode is Vaikuṇṭha. He sets or reclines on the couch formed by the great serpent Śeṣa, is attended to by His three consorts, and by His servants and all delivered souls. The fourth form is the one in which Īśvara is conceived of as the inner controller, 'antaryāmin', of all, and accompanies the individual souls even when they go to heaven or hell. The fifth form of Īśvara is represented by idols installed for worship, whether in households or in temples. The third form consists in the incarnations, 'avatāras', they being ten of them, the standard ones of Viṣṇu. The second form is the specifically technical one current among strict followers of Bhāgavatism and may be ignored for our purposes.[10] The Supreme God is more commonly addressed as Nārāyaṇa.

In the other and younger sect of Vaiṣṇavism of the South, that of Madhva, appropriately known as the Dualist school, God, who is conceived as a substance and as having innumerable qualities, is the Supreme Soul no doubt but one who has both the individual souls and the inanimate world as His body. Lakṣmī is His only consort and is almost as Supreme and divine as the Supreme Soul, She being concomitant with Him. She has no material body. All the individual souls are distinct from one another as they are from the Supreme Soul. God or Paramātman to be meditated upon as Bhagavat may be conceived as a single spirit or as having four phases as 'sat', existence or being, 'cit', knowledge or consciousness, 'ānanda', joy or bliss, and 'ātman', spirit.[11]

In the Śaiva system and in Śaivism as a whole, God is known as 'Pati', Lord or Master, who is Śiva, and the individual souls as 'Paśus', literally beasts. In the sub-sect, known merely as the Śaiva system, God has a body made up of powers but is thought to be impelled to act owing to the deeds of individual souls. He does everything and is omniscient. The Paśu or the individual soul is both atomic, eternal and all-pervading. It is distinguished or distinct from Śiva because of its fetters, 'pāśas'. In one of its developments this school attaches to God, i.e., Śiva, as His own development, a Śaktī or power, this latter consisting of the individual soul and material world.[12]

In the Kashmirian school of Śaivism, Śiva otherwise called Śūlin, has a mysterious power, through which, it is believed, He is able to appear in the form of the many individual souls that exist. Thus in this way of thinking the individual soul is identical with the Supreme Soul, Śiva. The former is not able to see or realize this identity owing to impurity or 'mala'. It can be appreciated that in this Kashmirian subsect the relation between the Supreme Soul and the individual soul and the cause of non-perception of that relation are more or less the same as in the monistic school of Vedānta, the cause being called 'mala' or taint in the Śaiva school, while it is called 'māyā' in the Vedāntic school. This latter is, however, accommodated in this Śaiva subsect as one of the three kinds of 'malas', taints. When the impurity vanishes, the vision that shines is called Bhairava who causes it. Śiva is thus otherwise known to the subsect as Bhairava.[13]

One subsect of Śaivism, the Vīraśaiva, falls very much apart from the others whose views on the nature of the God-head are presented above. The first distinction it has, gives the alternative name of the subsect, viz., Liṅgāyat, i.e., Liṇga-wearing one. In this subsect it is the phallus-form of Śiva that becomes virtually the operative and presentable God. Liṅga is what is to be worshipped and to be carried on one's person by a Liṅgāyat man or woman.

The Liṅga-Śiva, however, is Himself the result of the division that takes place in the Brahman, the One only, the Highest principle technically called 'Sthala', the 'Place', through Its own 'śakti', power. Sthala is thus the Supreme God, the Absolute Brahman of the *Upaniṣads*, the *BhG*, and of monistic Vedānta. The Vīraśaiva or Liṅgāyat theology asserts It to be the essence of Śiva. That this is an identification in the spirit of the *ŚvU* can be easily perceived. And the characterization of Sthala or Brahman as 'sat' (existence or being), 'cit' (knowledge or consciousness), and 'ānanda' (joy or bliss) brings it in line with the Vedāntic Supreme Soul. It is called Sthala in this system because in It exists and to It returns the cosmos.

When Sthala divides Itself into two through Its own power, one portion is Liṅga, Liṅga-Śiva, the operative and actually worshipped God. It quite logically receives the full designation of Liṅgasthala, and thus retains its connection with the Absolute in the minds of the Liṅgāyat worshippers. The other half, equally cogently called Aṅgasthala, becomes the individual soul. Thus the individual soul is a moiety of the Absolute.

Liṅgasthala, however, does not remain one whole. It presents Itself in six different forms, which really are so many ways of conceiving God in this subsect. One of these is the bodily form, the body being celestial like one attributed in Vaiṣṇava subsects to Nārāyaṇa. Another of these six forms is Śiva as the Redeemer, the instructor and therefore in actual situation is the person of the religious preceptor, who as Guru attains great importance for the followers of this subsect.

The God to be worshipped, Liṅga, being carried on one's person, the followers of this subsect have no concern with attendance at or worship at temples of Śiva even in the form of the phallus.[14]

In the Caitanyite subsect of Vaiṣṇavism, as Bhandarkar[15] pointed out long ago, the view of the God-head is more or less the same as in the Vedāntic system of Nimbārka which propounds that the individual soul, the cosmos and God are both distinct from one another and identical. Kṛṣṇa is the Supreme God,

Paramātman or Parabrahma. The individual soul is a form of one of the three powers, or rather four, He has. The Supreme Soul is boundless and is complete intelligence, while the individual soul is an atom having intelligence, but evidently not complete. The relation between them is that Kṛṣṇa, the Supreme Soul, is the support (āśraya) and 'jīva', the individual soul, rests on Him. The analogy used to illustrate the peculiarly two-faced relation existing between the two is that of a bee and the honey, the latter representing the Supreme Soul. Just as a bee hovers round the honey, the individual soul, too, is ever seeking the Supreme Soul. The bee when it drinks the honey being full of it becomes one with it [?]. The individual soul, too, when through love he is full of the Supreme Soul, becoming unconscious of himself becomes, as it were, absorbed in Him [?].

One of the powers of Kṛṣṇa which creates the dilatation of heart and joy is that of love. When this power is developed to its highest pitch it constitutes itself into Rādhā, who was the object of the highest love of Kṛṣṇa. Nimbārka[16], two centuries earlier, had already placed Rādhā on the pedestal at the left side of Kṛṣṇa as an object of worship. And that pair, Rādhā-Kṛṣṇa, forms the principal object of worship in the Caitanyite as well as the Vallabhite subsects of Vaiṣṇavism.

In the Vallabhite subsect, spread over Rajasthan, Gujarat and parts of western U.P., Kṛṣṇa with Rādhā is the Supreme deity to be worshipped, a special abode above the usual Vaikuṇṭha of Viṣṇu or Nārāyaṇa being the heaven where the God dwells. The God is known as Śrī-Nāthaji just as among the Caitanyites He is more commonly addressed as Hari. This God Śrī-Kṛṣṇa is the highest Brahman. He has a celestial body, consisting of 'sat' (existence or being), 'cit' (knowledge or consciousness), and 'ānanda' (joy or bliss). He has either two or four arms which are always engaged in playing sports with his devotees. As the most excellent of all objects He is called Puruṣottama, an epithet which the *BhG* applied to Kṛṣṇa, and as the constantly sportive one He is Paramānanda, the highest joy. When He overcomes the joy-aspect of himself with His being-aspect He becomes the Immutable Brahman. This form of His exists in two states. In one state, that of Antaryāmin, inner controller, dwelling in the sun, the earth, etc., He controls all. In the other state He presents Himself to His enlightened devotee and worshipper as without qualities, 'nirguṇa', as the qualities are hidden. This state and form of the Supreme God is thus lower than His form as Śrīkṛṣṇa or Śrī-Nāthaji, who is Saguṇa Brahman. From this Brahman emanate individual souls with the 'ānanda' constituent of Brahman in complete concealment in them. Thus the relation between the Supreme Soul and the individual soul is one of identity. Devotion towards God is either to be cultivated by the effort of the individual souls or is generated by God in the mind of a person. It is this latter type of worshipper who seeks and attains the privilege of redemption in the form of perpetual sportive life in the special Vaikuṇṭha.[17]

It is seen that in the sectarian schools, whether Śaiva or Vaiṣṇava, though Śiva or Viṣṇu-Kṛṣṇa is the focus and the Supreme God, who is to be won by devotion as He is gracious and omnipotent, yet the Vedāntic Supreme, the Absolute Brahman, peeps from behind as the Ultimate and that every now and then attempt has to be made and has been made, whether from the strictly logical viewpoint it is successful or not, to integrate It in the system of God-head—I think such a view of the God-head is better called a system than a single theory—put up as its own by any school.

Both in the Śaiva and the Vaiṣṇava sects two forms of the Supreme God figure. In the former, the phallus form of Śiva is one and the other is Śiva or Mahādeva either singly or with His consort Umā or Pārvatī. In the latter, one of the two forms is like that of Śiva the universal non-man one, and that is Viṣṇu simply or Viṣṇu-Śeṣaśāyin or Nārāyaṇa. He has at least one consort, Lakṣmī, paralleling Śiva's consort Umā or Pārvatī. In a subsect or two one or two more consorts are added, making the God's household polygynous. The other form of Viṣṇu—the subsects centred round that form overwhelmingly outnumber those accepting other forms—is Kṛṣṇa, who lived as a man and is identified with Viṣṇu through the promulgation of the theory of God's incarnations. In the subsects so far dealt with a female named Rādhā is associated with Him and receives fervent worship. Rādhā not having been called a consort must be considered to be, in ordinary parlance, a mistress !

Further developments in the view of the God-head in the Hindu society appeared in the works of saints, poets and preachers who may be said to be non-sectarian in the sense that they have no separate philosophical doctrine or creed, nor have they any authoritative text based on the *Upaniṣads* or the *BhG* to uphold their systems or rather their views, though none the less they are not only popular but widely and fervently held and practised. Tulasīdāsa's *Rāmāyaṇa*, though it is only a rendering in Hindi of Rāma's life mostly as represented in the Sanskrit epic of that name going under the authorship of Vālmīki, presents one such and is the newest, widest and the greatest of all. A brief statement of Tulasīdāsa's view of the nature of the God-head is quite necessary to fill out the picture of the third phase of the Hindu view of the God-head.

First development, though it had long been getting on before Tulasīdāsa's time—in fact it is clear from what has been said already that it must have been fully achieved at least sometime before Kālidāsa—is that Rāma, the son of the Ikṣvāku king Daśaratha of Ayodhyā had come to be installed as the Supreme God having been long ago acknowledged as an incarnation of Viṣṇu.[18]

In this process the fervent and sweet poetry of Tulasīdāsa can claim the lion's share of contribution. Tulasīdāsa who was quite clearly—he was in close touch with Madhusūdana Sarasvatī, the greatest of monistic Vedāntins after Śaṅkarācārya—conversant with monistic view of the God-head and was fully imbued with the necessity of a complete set of moral virtues in practice as a soul-purifying component, puts aside the Nirguṇa Brahman, the Absolute

Brahman, in favour of his favourite deity Rāma and exhorts his listeners to cultivate devotion to him as the be all and end all of human life (VII, Dohās 101-114 ; 151-4 ; 168-89 ; V, Dohās 48-51 ; III, Dohās 67-76 ; 22-3 ; II, Dohās 134-5 ; I, Dohās 150-56 ; 57-63 ; 28-9).

The Supreme God is addressed as 'Saccidānanda', i.e., as 'sat', 'cit' and 'ānanda' in combination forming one word. Incarnations and idols of the Supreme God are authoritatively spoken of in the Vedas and must be implicitly believed in. So must a discriminating appreciation of the 'nirguṇa', attributeless, and 'saguṇa', characterized, forms of the Supreme God be cultivated. It must be realised that it is through the 'māyā', mysterious power, of Hari (Viṣṇu or Paramātmā) that the cosmos is going on. One should serve devotedly Rāma's feet, having realized that the particular form of the Supreme God with full attributes capable of being perceived, i.e., Rāma, 'Saccidānanda', has resulted through the God's grace, through His love for His devotees and worshippers. Rāma in essence being the same as the all-comprehensive Brahman (I, Dohā 124 and Soraṭha 16). Rāmabrahma, or Brahman that is Rāma, is without limitations, without form ; is consciousness (cit) and bliss (ānanda) and is described in the Veda as 'not that', 'not that', i.e., only in negative terms, being without attributes. Śiva, Brahmā and Viṣṇu are Its (His) emanations (I, Dohā 151 ; II, Dohā 100 ; Chanda 17 and Soraṭha 12).

The relation between the individual soul (jīva) and the Supreme Soul (Īśa) is one of identity concealed by 'māyā', illusion, which operates at the will of God. Or, in other words, 'jīva', or individual soul, is God (Īśa) who does not realize that he is God. The distinction between the individual soul (jīva) and the Supreme Soul (Īśa) is caused by 'māyā', illusion, so that the former under its influence is ego-conscious. Illusion ('māyā') under the control of the Supreme Soul (Īśa) produces the attributes and qualities. 'Jīva' is dependent, while 'Bhagavān' (Īśa) is free and self-controlled. The former are many, the latter, Śrīkānta (Viṣṇu or Rāma), is only One. This distinction created by 'māyā', illusion, cannot vanish except through the grace of Hari (III, Dohās 22-3 ; VII, Dohās 113, 174, 188).

The *BhG*, about eighteen hundred years before Tulasī's *Rāmāyaṇa*, had established identity between the Absolute Brahman of the Upaniṣadic sages and Kṛṣṇa, as incarnation of Viṣṇu, and had firmly implanted the Gītā-dharma and the Gītā-view of the Godhead, viz., that Lord Kṛṣṇa-Viṣṇu was the Supreme God and that selfless and unattached activity suffused with intense devotion and complete surrender to Him are the proper ends of human endeavour. Tulasīdāsa appears to have been the saint-poet who propounded the same views centering them on Rāma, instead of Kṛṣṇa, who lived before Kṛṣṇa and was therefore an earlier incarnation of Viṣṇu. In establishing the identity of Rāma with the beginningless, endless, changeless Brahman which is both immanent and transcendent, Tulasīdasa by using Rāmabrahma as the appropriate designation could achieve his objective only in part. For long before his time another God, Śiva, with His consort Umā or Pārvatī, had been enthroned as the Supreme God and had enjoyed that vogue for long. We have seen how the national poet Kālidāsa lavished some finely worded poetry on dwelling on the identity in difference of the two Gods, Śiva and Viṣṇu, both of whom had by then, or rather long before then, come to be conceived as the Supreme God. Tulasīdāsa had, to achieve his purpose in entirety, to propound his view regarding the relation between Śiva and Rāma. And he has done this in a manner only somewhat like Kālidāsa's but mostly differing from it.

It is at the request of Pārvatī, the consort of Śiva, that Śiva is made to narrate the essence of Rāma's life and work. In doing this it is acknowledged without any argument that Rāma is the 'saguṇa', personalized, form of the Absolute Brahman. Śiva is said to remember or utter Rāma's name, i.e., show intense devotion to Rāma, because that is the right way of religious living. It is because the story of Rāma's work and life is not only soul-purifying but soul-saving that Śiva asks Pārvatī to listen to it (I, Dohās 114-29; Soraṭhas 16-9; also cf. V, Dohā 48; VI, Chanda, 67; Dohās 273-4; VII, Dohās 76-80, 160-68, 202-06). Alternatively Tulasīdāsa expresses the view that devotion to Śiva is the necessary preliminary to one's devotional surrender to Rāma (VII, Dohā 70). The most common attitude on the relation between the two Gods, Śiva and Viṣṇu, is that of one Brahmin who was one of the most fervent of Śiva-worshippers. Tulasīdāsa approvingly describes him as a devotee of Śambhu (Śiva) without being a detractor of Hari ('Śambhu-upāsaka nahiṁ Harinindaka') (VII, Dohā 155, v, 4).

Tulasīdāsa presents Rāma, the Absolute Brahman personalized as the Supreme God, not by Himself but with His consort Sītā on His left. Rāma Himself is portrayed as cloud-blue in colour and Sītā as fair-hued. Rāma holds His famous bow and arrow in His hand but unlike Viṣṇu or even Kṛṣṇa He is only two-armed and thus fully human. Hence Rāma is Sītārāma, i.e., Sītā's Rāma (I, Dohās 24, 66, 154-5*, 267-8; VII, Dohā 54.8). Tulasīdāsa makes up for this manifestly mere humanness of Rāma by affirming that His human form was as lustrous as the brilliance of ten billion suns and yet as cooling as the coolness of ten billion moons, as expansive as the width of innumerable billions of skies, as beauteous as the beauty of ten billion Cupids, as powerful as the power of ten billion winds, as capable of destroying enemies as innumerable billions of Durgās (Goddess known to have great demon-destroying prowess) and as luxurious as the luxuries of billion Indras (the king of Gods in heaven, known for extra-ordinary pomp and pleasures). Raghuvīra, Rāma the hero of the house of Raghu, is as immutable as ten million Himalayas and as deep as billion Sindhus (oceans?). He is as terrible

* The Vedic heritage of this Great Brahmin saint-poet peeps through even his utterly devotional mood as when describing Rāma, Laṣmī and Umā, the consorts of Viṣṇu and Śiva respectively as emanations from Sītā, as 'Ādi-Śakti', Original Power Principle, he ascribes to Brahmā as his consort Brahmāṇī in the fashion of Vedic Indrāṇī, the consort of Indra. Brahmāṇī is otherwise not traced in mythology.

as ten billion Yamas (God of death) and yet as wish-fulfilling as ten billion 'Kāmadhenus' (the fabulous cow, yielding the satisfaction of all wishes and desires). He is as purifying as innumerable billion sacred places ('tīrtha') and His name destroys entirely whole mountains and sins. He is as great a protector as ten billion Viṣṇus put together and as great a destroyer as ten billion Rudras. In such strain the poet-preacher draws his picture of the Supreme God, Rāma, whose devotion he prescribed as the only true friend of man (VII, Soraṭha 9 and Dohās 133-4).

The significance for religious consciousness of man in general and of the Hindus in particular of the phenomenon, commonly called transfiguration and named in Hindu terminology as vision of the cosmic form, driven home by the *BhG* and repeated in some of the *Purāṇas* in connection with Kṛṣṇa's Godhood, has gone deep in Indian culture. Tulasīdāsa gives a concrete and not very late illustration of it. He introduces an occasion in the childhood of Rāma to demonstrate His Cosmic nature. Rāma in that circumstance opens his mouth before his mother, as Kṛṣṇa is said to have done before his ; and lo, there is the whole cosmos in situ revealed to the mortal eyes of the fortunate mother (I, Dohās 231-33)!

Tukārāma, one of the greatest of religious preachers and also of the devotees who were convinced of and experienced the highest devotional ecstasy in their worship of a thoroughly personalized god, was born in Maharashtra seventyseven years after Tulasīdāsa and died only twentysix years after him. The personal God he adored and whose worship he fully established in Maharashtra is known as Viṭhobā and has one consort by name Rukmiṇī, or Rakhumāī. He is quite clearly a form of Kṛṣṇa with his consort Rukmiṇī, though His form is only two-armed and thus wholly human, unlike that of Kṛṣṇa. Tukārāma composed a large number of poems, many of which were extempore formulations inspired by the mood and the occasion of the contingencies of his extensive religious discourses. In one collection those accepted as undisputedly Tukārāma's work number more than four thousand. R. G. Bhandarkar[19], who appears to have been inclined to doubt Tukārāma's inclination towards monistic Vedānta of Śaṅkarācārya, stated half a century ago, the fact of a controversy existing in Maharashtra over the question whether Tukārāma followed the philosophy of Śaṅkarācārya.

I find that, in the collection of Tukārāma's poems published by the Nirnayasagar Press under the caption of *Tukārāmācī Gāthā*, of the four thousand and seventynine poems accepted in it as genuine three hundred and fifty, i.e., 8.5 per cent, are classed as non-dualistic, i.e., worded in the spirit and terminology of monistic Vedānta.

I am not satisfied that all these classed as non-dualistic are really in the spirit and terminology of monistic Vedānta, nor do I subscribe to the view that that spirit and mood are not to be met with in other compositions of Tukārāma collected in the *Gāthā*. I am convinced that Tukārāma was very well acquainted with the philosophy of Absolute Brahman and further that like Tulasīdāsa he relegated it to a secondary place and considered the 'saguṇa', personalized, form assumed by Brahman, being taken for the sake of the purely religious-minded worshipper, to be the most appropriate form of devotional worship.

Tulasīdāsa, the Brahmin enjoying the highly intellectual and Vedāntic company of the great ascetic philosopher Madhusūdana Sarasvatī, was very thoroughly imbued with monistic philosophy. Some illustrations of this fact, besides the description of the Supreme God and His relation with the individual soul, have been presented in the proper context above. Here I should like to emphasize the Vedāntic atmosphere in which he lived so as to enable the reader to gauge the nature and intensity of that or similar atmosphere in Tukārāma's outpourings.

Tulasīdāsa's use of the Upaniṣadic descriptive formula 'neti, neti' (I, Dohā 151) is one element; another is his use of one of the 'great sentences' of monistic Vedānta each of which is its quintessence, viz., 'sohamasmi', 'that I am', i.e., I am Brahman (VII, Soraṭha 17). This last formula is the way of feeling of a person which is what is known as 'Brahmībhūta', one who has realized his identity with Brahman. Tukārāma for more reasons than one does not harken back to the Upaniṣads and their Vedānta to that extent. But even he expresses his mastery of the Vedānta with the statement that 'om tat sat' is the essence of the Sūtras, i.e., the *Brahmasūtras* of Bādarāyaṇa; and brings in a veiled reference to the Vedic lore regarding 'speech' and its accents (*Gāthā*, 3469; 3612; 3618).

That Nirguṇa Brahman, attributeless and formless, is the nature of the Supreme Soul is a conviction not given up but superseded in favour of the personalized God owing very largely to the nature of the process of worship securing ecstasy, is clearly from such poems as numbers 579 and 584 in the *Gāthā*. There is also I think one additional reason in the case of Tukārāma prompting him to postulate the personalized form of the Supreme Soul as the proper focus of worship and devotion. Tukārāma appears to me to be moving to a forward position in the line of devotional development in relation to the goal to be achieved, the redemption to be sought, by man. As I shall have occasion to mention in the next chapter, perhaps Tukārāma is the first among the great devotional worshippers of the Supreme God among the Hindus to assert boldly that he was not afraid of recurrent births provided they afforded opportunities for serving at the feet of the personalized God and for the company of His saintly worshippers. This positive ideal, though purely religious and moral, with very little social import in it, is what I think to be the other reason for Tukārāma's prefering personalized Supreme God to Absolute Brahman.

Rāmadāsa, the continuator of Tulasīdāsa's work in the cause of Rāma as the personal God and of Madhūsūdana Sarasvatī's work in the organization of ascetics and of its orientation[20], was about fourteen years old at Tulasīdāsa's death and lived to be eighty years old. He is credited with having started more than seventy centres for his disciples and ascetics entrusting to them the work of propagating his religious preaching to the people of Maharashtra. To him goes the distinction, not very common with the mediaeval saint-preachers of India, of having systematized a doctrine in the vernacular and presented it in the form of a book. His treatise is named *Dāsabodha*, i.e., *Instruction of Servant* (of Rāma), the ascetic having taken the name of Rāmadāsa, i.e., the servant of Rāma, choosing to refer to himself as the servant.

As we have seen already, Rāmadāsa is through and through full of the Sāṁkhya-Vedānta doctrines regarding cosmology and cosmography. He is no less saturated with monistic Vedānta in his view of the Supreme God, His relation with the individual soul and also with the cosmos and its creation.

Rāmadāsa roundly affirms that the so-called Supreme Gods, Brahmā, Viṣṇu and Maheśa (Śiva), have no reality. They are the manifestations or emanations in the process of the unfolding of the three primary qualities or dispositions, 'sattva', 'rajas' and 'tamas'. It is the Parabrahma that is the reality, the One that remains when all is naught and the One that was in the beginning (VI, 3, 17-18; 6, 1; IX, 1-3; X, 2; 4, 16-19; 9; 10; XI, 1; 4; XIII, 2; XIV, 9; XVIII, 8; XX, 10). The Vedāntic saturation of the religious philosophy of the *Dāsabodha* can be gauged from the fact that, leaving out about ten to twelve out of the two hundred chapters in the treatise which deal with the Ultimate Principle under various categories not directly named as Brahman, there are at least eight other chapters which directly speak of Brahman, Parabrahma, Paramātmā or either 'śuddha Brahma', or 'vimala Brahma', i.e., Pure Brahman. And the treatise ends with a chapter on Pure Brahman. With such saturation of monistic Vedānta it is that Rāmadāsa fervently proclaimed the Supreme God-hood of Rāma and exhorted the people of Maharashtra to worship Him. The political conditioning of this religious preaching is touched upon by me in my *Gods and Men*. While appraising the religious significance of this phenomenon I should add that we have to bear in mind the fact that Rāmadāsa, laying down a rigorous schedule of individual daily conduct, prescribed regular worship of household deities and even of temple ones. He goes even further and, without feeling the least possible contradiction with his sponsoring of the worship of Rāma, he prescribes the worship of not only Rāma's factotum, the monkey-god Hanumān, but also that of Viṣṇu-Śeṣaśāyin and the Sun and even Śiva (IV, 6; XI, 3), because all these Gods are the manifestations of the Supreme Soul, or as he puts it immediately after this prescription, all worship offered to any deity reaches Keśava, i.e., Viṣṇu-Nārāyaṇa, the Supreme God conceived in a personalized form. The verse in Sanskrit which he quotes forms one component of the complex formula whereby all worship, whether in the household or in the temple, is brought to a close among the Hindus. Another component of the same formula is even more important for establishing the attitude which I have above ascribed to Rāmadāsa. It is that the water which is the final offering, sealing the dedication of any worship, is poured to the accompaniment of the repetition of the sentence, 'Om, Tat sat Brahmārpaṇam astu', let this be an offering to Brahman which is 'Om Tat Sat'. The Hindu view of the God-head is thus properly characterized as monolatrous pantheism.

CHAPTER XI

HINDU RELIGIOUS LIVING AND ITS GOAL

KANT is known to have maintained in his *Religion innerhalb der Greuzen der blossen Vernunft* that redemption is the supreme concern of all religions and that morality, i.e., the struggle against the principle of evil waged by a man intensely conscious of his need of redemption, is the root of all religion.[1] Redemption is thus the end, and morality or struggle against evil the source, of all religion according to the great philosopher. In the light of the history and development of religious consciousness among the Hindus I think it is correct to speak of redemption, of course with a sense and content which is not identical with those of other religions, as its goal ; but it would be wrong to say that morality or struggle against evil is its source. Morality is one aspect of the pattern of living, called here religious living, which is designed and prescribed as a means of achieving the goal, i.e., the redemption, which is the goal of Hindu religious consciousness.

The goal of Hindu religious consciousness has gone through some changes since the Vedic times, when unlimited and eternal enjoyment in a world known as 'svarga', heaven, was the ideal that was sought after through the modes of religious living then current and believed to be efficacious. I have drawn my readers' attention to the fact that that ideal has persisted, though only in the background, throughout ; and I may mention here that it has acted as another support for polylatry among the Hindus. I shall not go into details further as that goal is no longer the avowed end of religious living or the promised redemption in Hinduism, in theory as in actual practice.

I shall begin with the ideals of the Upaniṣadic age, an age for which in the light of fairly rich sources of information I have already presented an account of cosmology and eschatology, of the view of human personality and of the God-head, with which the goal of religious consciousness of any people must be closely bound up.

The cardinal doctrine that forms the source of redemption through religious living is the conviction that this life is but a link in the chain of endless births and deaths, passing through a myriad different stocks, species and genera of creatures. This is the theory known as the doctrine of transmigration. With its inexorable law it keeps the soul in bondage, confined in a shell and condemned to all kinds of sufferings and shortcomings. The God-head conceived was mainly the Impersonal Absolute Brahman, and the relation an individual soul has with Brahman is one of identity in reality, though, the reality being clouded, the individual soul is prevented from sensing it and more so from realizing it.

The redemption sought, the goal of religious living, therefore, envisaged by the bulk of the sages and schools of thought of the age of the older nine Upaniṣads, and with a slight qualification of that of the youngest tenth, *Śvetāśva-*

tara, is the attainment of freedom from the grip of the inexorable law of the eternal cycle of births and deaths, or in other words, of immortality. The first alternative is expressed in such terms, as non-return to this world of mortals (*ChU*, IV, 15, 6 ; VIII, 15, 15 ; *PrU*, I, 10), or as liberation from 'saṁsāra', freedom from birth (*KaU*, I, 3, 7 ; II, 3, 2 ; *ŚvU*, I, 7 ; I, 11 ; VI, 16). The second alternative is specified through such expressions as becoming immortal or attaining immortality (*BrU*, IV, 4, 7 ; V, 14, 8 ; *ChU*, II, 23, 1; VIII, 6, 6 ; *AiU*, III, 5 ; *IU*, 14 ; *KeU*, I, 2 ; II, 5 ; II, 15 ; *MuU*, III, 2, 9 ; *PrU*, III, 12 ; *ŚvU*, IV, 20).

There is also a third way of expressing the goal of religious living adopted by the Upaniṣadic sages, which is perhaps the aptest way of specifying the objective of redemption on the background of the impersonalization of the Godhead by these bold speculative seers. It is that the individual soul 'goes to Brahman' or 'enters Brahman or the World of Brahman' or 'becomes Brahman' (*BrU*, IV, 4, 6-7 ; *ChU*, III, 14, 4 ; V, 10, 2 ; VIII, 3, 4 ; VIII, 15 ; *MuU*, III, 2, 4) or becomes the 'highest Immutable [Principle], (*PrU*, IV, 10). In personalization contexts *Brahman* is replaced by *Ātman* or 'Puruṣa' or 'Para (Highest) Puruṣa' (*MāU* 12 ; *MuU*, I, 2, 11 ; III, 2, 8). In individualizing contexts, of course, the particular individual name of the Supreme God can be, and in at least two of these ten old Upaniṣads is, substituted, as is done in the *Māṇḍūkya* and the *Śvetāśvatara Upaniṣads* which neme the Supreme God as Śiva (*MāU*, 12 ; *ŚvU*, VI, 5-7 ; V, 14 ; III, 11-12 ; I, 10-13).

Desire for immortality and freedom from death, it is interesting to note, was asked for by a Ṛgvedic seer in his prayer to Tryambaka [Śiva] (*RV*, VII, 59, 12). And Sāyaṇa in his comment on the verse interprets it to mean an entreaty for liberation ending in union, which has been almost the sole goal of élite Hinduism for long ages, since the time of the Upaniṣads to the specific formulation of some of the later theistic systems about the middle of the twelfth century. The specific term for this grand goal of religious living, of redemption and the final destiny of man, for union with the Supreme Soul, from Whom the individual soul during its mundane existence has got separated through the operation of clouding factors, called 'māyā' or 'avidyā', illusion or nescience, is 'sāyujya'. The term is derivable from a root which means to unite and literally means 'union together'. In its agential masculine form 'sayujā', the term is known to be applied to the Supreme and the individual soul in the famous hymn of the *RV* (I, 164) repeated both in the *Muṇḍaka Upaniṣad* (II, 3, 1) and the *Śvetāśvatara Upaniṣad* (IV, 6).

The term 'sāyujya' occurs in the *BrU* in two places (I, 3, 22 ; I, 5, 23) ; and in both the places it is accompanied by the term 'salokatā', the expression being 'sayujyam salokatām jayati', 'wins union [and/or] same-world-habitation'. In later theistic systems the latter state, 'salokatā', is one of the four goals of religious living, being considered a good enough redemption, though it is the lowest of the four states conceived as the final destiny. But this state or the two states mentioned in the *BrU* are referred to as goals only in relation to some of the gods of the Vedic pantheon and not in relation to the God-head as postulated by the Upaniṣadic seers. Deussen, speaking of the difference between the Brahman-goal and the goal aimed at by the earlier Vedic sages, brings in three of the four states of later theistic systems in his remarks. He observes : " . . . . union with the gods after death was the supreme wish of the ancient Vedic ṛṣis, in order to attain to fellowship (sāyujyam)[2] companionship ('salokatā'), community of being ('sarūpatā') with Agni, Varuṇa, Indra, Āditya, etc. Later on the (impersonal) Brahman was exalted above the gods . . . . and the gods were only the doors, through whom Brahman might be attained".

Union with Brahman was thus the goal of religious, nay all, living. But in view of the varied possibilities under the law of transmigration and as a consequence of syncretic or synthetic interaction with the old beliefs regarding life after death, the attainment of heaven or other worlds of the Upaniṣadic cosmology and cosmography loomed as a goal, though, as is made clear in the remarks of Deussen, a secondary one, one capable of advancing the individual soul on its path to final destiny.

Once in the cycle of births and deaths, there is a likelihood of one's being born in better stocks or families, with better individual equipment for religious living, as also of being relegated to lower ones in the births to come. It, therefore, happens to be, though not specifically mentioned as such, a secondary goal to so live one's life here as to insure a better next birth, birth in a better family and/or with a better individual endowment. On the same reasoning it becomes a tertiary goal, at least to prevent the possibility of being pushed down into brute or vermin stocks, wherefrom there could be no possibility of escape to higher forms, wherein alone there is the chance for an endeavour to secure salvation. Birth in such a stock is bound, in effect, to be eternal damnation. It is the paramount duty of all, therefore, at least to live so as to preclude the possibility of one's next birth being of a lower order than the present human one.

These two goals, the secondary and the tertiary as I have called them, have continued to be the same throughout the history of Hinduism, though the main goal in its nature and content has changed, and may be slightly or even largely varying in the different systems, sectarian or not.

And it is because of these two goals and in pursuit of them that the structure of morality, of society and of social obligations is largely what it has been in Hindu civilization.

The goal of religious living propounded in the Upaniṣadic thought, that part of it, which was centred round the view of the God-head as Absolute Brahman and not as personal God, was modified to a certain extent in that component which came to enthrone Śiva as the Supreme God. Rudra-Śiva, at that stage having had next to no mythology about Him, was evidently not assigned any world as His special abode in the Upaniṣadic cosmography. And though we cannot be sure as to the age when Mount Kailāsa came to be associated with Him as His special world, we have reason to believe that the association was in the making about the time of the *Kena Upaniṣad*. For Umā, the consort of Rudra-Śiva in later mythology, was already known as 'Haimavatī', i.e., daughter of, or one belonging to, Himavat (*KaU*, III, 12), the mountain of that name, one of whose numerous peaks is 'Kailāsa'. The *ŚvU*, naturally, does not contain any speculation about the nature of the goal a worshipper or a devotee of Rudra-Śiva would reach except in the most general terms deducible from the context as indicated above.

It must have been fairly long before Kālidāsa's time that a particular peak and region of the Himalayas was specifically believed to be the world of Kailāsa, the blissful abode of Śiva. Kālidāsa's reference to a particular cave in the Himalayas under the special watch and ward of one of Śiva's attendants (*Raghuvaṁśa*, II, 26-38), and to Śiva's abode in 'Kuberaśaila', which Mallinātha renders by Kailāsa (*Kumārasambhava*, VII, 30), and his romantic description of the region where the cloud-messenger was to find its destination in the Himalayas (*Meghadūta*, 58-71) leave no doubt that Kailāsa was, for long before Kālidāsa, looked upon as Śiva's abode.

With Kṛṣṇa-Viṣṇu as personal God raised to the status of the Supreme God as the *Bhagavadgītā* does, we come across a more developed and a markedly different situation in the matter of the goal to be achieved by religious living, the redemption, which is the soul of every religion as Kant has stated. It is clear from the whole discourse continued in that great book that for a fairly long time a complex mythology was forming round Viṣṇu-Kṛṣṇa. It is even probable that one of the great aims the composer of the book had, was the focussing of the ennobling part of that mythology. The fact and legend of Buddha, which had grown stupendous during the three centuries or so that elapsed between the composition of the *Śvetāśvatara Upaniṣad* and the birth of Buddha, on the one hand, and the time of the making of the *BhG* on the other, must have acted as a direct incentive. The leaders of the Indian society ground in Vedic and Upaniṣadic thought had before them an object lesson on the superiority of personality over impersonality, of definiteness over speculative freedom, in the life and career of Buddha and the success of his followers. They must have also received a shock to their complacency about the invulnerability of their current religious thought and pattern of living. And the *BhG*, with Kṛṣṇa-Viṣṇu as the Supreme God assuring Hindu humanity of the then India that a new dispensation formulated around the romantic personality of Kṛṣṇa and stated in a particularly momentous context, purporting to help the cause of the Pāṇḍavas, who were by then the heroes of the Ihdian people, put forward a redemption which, in marked contrast to that offered by Buddha and his followers, was a glorious and covetable one.

The main goal to be achieved is stated in two-fold terminology, one set carrying forward the Upaniṣadic tradition and the other setting out the new one in terms of Kṛṣṇa-Viṣṇu and His abode, though for the time unnamed. There is also the third way already adumbrated in the Upaniṣadic religious complex, which here in the *BhG* is stated, in accordance with the advanced conditions of the age in respect of the doctrine of transmigration, which, with the currency of the life stories of Buddha, must have got so thoroughly fixed in the popular mind as to act as a sort of a nightmare, as a great scarecrow for the erring humanity of India, in full and in assuring terms. The lower goals of the Upaniṣadic complex and of other religio-philosophical systems that had flourished in the interval are there ; but they are placed in their proper stations as steps in the total endeavour of securing release for the individual soul from the recurrent cycle of birth and death.

The goal is either being *Brahman*, going to or into Brahman, achieving Brahman, attaining Brahman-bliss (II, 72 ; IV, 24 ; 26 ; 31 ; V, 6 ; 19 ; VI, 27-8 ; XIII, 30 ; XIV, 26 ; XVIII, 53) or achieving 'Para', the Highest, going to 'Para', the Highest, going to the Highest Abode of origin (III, 19 ; XIII, 34 ; VIII, 28) or going to the Immutable place (XV, 5) or attaining the Eternal place (XVIII, 62) or attaining the Eternal and Immutable place (XVIII, 56) or going to the Sorrowless place (II, 51), or enjoying immortality (XIV, 20) or crossing death (XIII, 25) or again going to the Highest state (VI, 45 ; VIII, 13 ; IX, 32 ; XIII, 28). Once at least the personalized Supreme as Puruṣa is put up as the Highest to be achieved (VIII, 8-10).

There are at least twentythree places where the goal of religious endeavour is stated in terms of Kṛṣṇa-Viṣṇu, which, divested of the varying terminology, some of which is quite clearly dictated by metrical needs, can be grouped into four categories : (1) The Lord speaks of His Highest Abode from where there can be no return as in VIII, 21 and XV, 6, which in the latter passage is described as a place "which neither the sun, the moon nor fire can light up", i.e., which is beyond them and is so effulgent that their light pales before its brilliance. (2) He mentions 'going to' or 'reaching Him' as the goal, as redemption which is promised and sure to accrue to His worshippers on certain conditions of religious living, in a number of places as at IV, 9 ; VII, 23 ; VIII, 7, 15-16 ; IX, 3 ; 25 ; 28 ; 34 ; X, 10 ; XI, 55 ; XIV, 19 ; and XVIII, 65. (3) He speaks of His successful worshippers either as "being fit to assume His nature or form" or as "assuming it" as in IV, 10 ; VIII, 5 ; XIII, 18 ; XIV, 2 ; 19. (4) Kṛṣṇa-Viṣṇu speaks of His devotees either as 'entering Him' or as 'residing in Him' or as 'obtaining permanent bliss in Him' (VI, 15 ; 31 ; XII, 8 ; XVIII, 55).

Fairly long before the 5th century A.D., the specific abode of Vāsudeva, Nārāyaṇa or Viṣṇu had come to be known as Vaikuṇṭha. And going to Vāsudeva's Vaikuṇṭha was popularly known as 'vaikuṇṭhīyā gati', state of dwelling in Vaikuṇṭha, evidently the abode of blissful existence after death, from where there was no fear of return (*Pañcatantra*, I, 227).

These categories are separated by me in view of and in relation to the four types of 'salvation' or 'liberation' standardized as goals in the theistic systems, particularly the Vaiṣṇavite ones : (a) 'salokatā' or 'sālokya', 'residence in the same world as that of the Supreme God' ; (b) 'samīpatā' or 'sāmīpya', 'nearness or companionship with Him' ; (c) 'sarūpatā or 'sārūpya', 'similarity of nature with Him', and (d) 'sāyujya', 'union' or oneness with the Supreme God. The last condition is identical with the goal envisaged in the Brahman-philosophy of the Upaniṣads or of the Vedānta. It is a merging of the individual soul with the Supreme, Brahman, or God.

Whether my categorization of the goal as envisaged in the *BhG* is accepted or not, it is clear that in continuation of the cosmographical notions of the Upaniṣadic age the new religious complex centred on Kṛṣṇa-Viṣṇu had put up one abode as specifically that of Kṛṣṇa-Viṣṇu. Entrance to it was the privilege of the worshippers who followed the religious course laid down by the Lord in the *BhG*. And once an individual soul had entered the abode of Kṛṣṇa-Viṣṇu he need not be in any fear of returning to the cycle of birth and death.

In ultimate analysis, therefore, the goal of religious living, the redemption which forms the soul of Hinduism, is to obviate the natural destiny of man, which is an eternal cycle of birth and death. And the *BhG* states that goal over and over again in varied terms. Either it is simply described as 'non-return', whether owing to the soul of the worshipper having merged with, or having merely gone to, the Lord or His abode or otherwise (V, 17 ; VIII, 21 ; 26 ; XI, 4 ; 5) or impliedly as non-return to the path of death and mundane existence, "mṛtyusaṁsāravartman" (IX, 3). In a more pronounced and the standard theistic manner, the Lord assures freedom from death and the worldly existence to his worshippers, using the more telling imagery of the worldly existence as an ocean (XII, 7). Alternatively Kṛṣṇa-Viṣṇu states that persons living according to the system of religious living advocated or prescribed by Him do not get rebirth or rebirth which is both "ephemeral and full of miseries (IV, 9 ; VIII, 15-16) or that they are neither born at the creation of the cosmos nor are they afflicted at the time of the universal deluge (XIV, 2). Negatively the Lord assures that those who do not reach Him get into the cycle of coming and going (IX, 21). The goal, the redemption, is also described as freedom from old age and death or again as freedom from birth, death, old age and misery (VII, 29 ; XIV, 20). Twice at least the goal is stated simply to be 'full release', 'vimokṣa' (IV, 32 ; XVI, 5).

The terms 'vimokṣa', full release, with its prefix dropped out, i.e., as 'mokṣa', has been the standard one for the goal to be achieved by religious living among the Hindus. And it has a venerable antiquity. It occurs in the famous discourse of Yājñavalkya which he once gave to the philosopher-king Janaka of Videha, during the course of which the king, having been extremely pleased by the ennobling and soul-stirring talk of the sage, offered him a large fee for its continuation ; and that, too, not once but thrice (IV, 3, 14-16). Janaka requests the sage to continue his discourse so that he may have the knowledge for securing full release, 'vimokṣa'.

The theistic systems that came to be formulated as presented, after Śaṅkarācārya had stated with great authority, erudition, and elocution the Vedāntic view of the goal to be achieved by religious living to be the realization of the identity of the individual soul with the Supreme Soul, that identity being lost sight of through the operation of illusion, māyā, propounded the goal, the redemption to be secured, in more or less similar terms as those of the *Bhagavadgītā*, some of the Vaiṣṇavite ones postulating the four kinds or stages of liberation, referred to above. They are more or less clearly enunciated and their specific natures described in the late *Muktika Upaniṣad* (14-25).

In the theistic systems of both Rāmānuja, whose followers are known as the school of Qualified Monism as against those of Śaṅkarācārya, who are known as that of Monism, and of Nimbārka, the individual souls as liberated ones are not entirely absorbed in the Supreme God but continue to have their separate identity.[3]

The Maharashtrian saint-poet-philosopher, Jñāneśvara, in his great commentary on the *BhG*, is clearly in favour of complete union, 'sāyujya', with the Supreme Soul, as the goal or redemption to be sought through religious living. In almost all the passages of the *BhG*, which I have referred to above, he interprets the state of complete release in terms of such union alone (*Jñāneśvarī*, IV, 63-5 ; VIII, 62-8 ; 207 ; 224 ; IX, 365-6 ; 467 ; XIII, 46-7 ; XVIII, 1145-63 ; XIV, 52-6 ; 401-3). In the last referred to passage Jñāneśvara is most outspoken on this point, though the text of the original does not call for any such comment. He says that the realization of Brahman is 'sāyujya', merging or union, and forms the fourth end of human existence, i.e., 'mokṣa', 'salvation'. At least in one passage the great spiritual personality shows himself to be more a Vaiṣṇava theist than a Vedāntist. Commenting on *BhG*, IX, 22, where the theme is the purest devotion to the Lord, Kṛṣṇa-Viṣṇu, and does not involve any reference to the nature of the redemption or its promise, he brings in along with 'sāyujya', the possibility of duality, like that maintained by Nimbārka, if the devotee should have desired to serve the Lord even in liberation (IX, 341). That there was some difficulty in postulating the latter possibility, it appears to me, was well appreciated by the great thinker. For at XVIII, 1185 he speaks of some special type of 'bhakti', devotion, called 'ananyasiddhā'[4], practised without another, i.e., a kind of devotion which needs no outside object for its reception. It is like a tribute offered and paid but to no one outside oneself ! In keeping with this the Lord speaks of such 'bhakti' as His lustre, i.e., as His own attribute, rather than an offering from His worshipper who was erstwhile an entity separate from Him (XVIII, 1113; 1117; 1121; 1123).

This only shows that Jñāneśvara, though he has been hailed as the founder of the Vaiṣṇava cult of devotion, known as the 'vārkarī' sect, sect of pilgrimage-makers, in Maharashtra, was a staunch monist, a follower of 'advaita' philosophy in the form of 'māyāvāda' propounded by his glorious predecessor from further south, Śaṅkarācārya. His comment on the *BhG*, XVIII, 55, which is in effect a grand peroration, rivalling in vernacular idiom the sonorous declaration in Sanskrit made by Yājñavalkya, his ancient predecessor of long ago, the original propounder of the nature of the Supreme as Absolute Brahman, is a testimony to his monistic philosophy.

Three preachers, teachers of religio-philosophy, two of whom gave rise to schools of religio-philosophical practice, which between them may be said to dominate eastern and western parts of India north of the Tāpī (Tapti), and the third swayed the minds of the largest bulk of the Hindus not only in North India but had great influence elsewhere too, did their chief work between the first quarter and the end of the 16th century. Of them Vallabhācārya, whose school of thought is known as pure monists, 'śuddha advaita', and whose sect is known as 'Puṣṭimārga', was the first, having been born in A.D. 1479. His school and sect are spread over the western portion of North India. Caitanya, whose school and sect dominate Bengal, Orissa and Assam, too, was only six years younger than Vallabhācārya. Tulasīdāsa, the third, came much later, having been born in A.D. 1532. His rendering of Vālmīki's *Rāmāyaṇa* in Hindi is a book which can be described as the most-read book of India[5], so popular has its appeal been in Hindi-speaking India and so widespread has been its transcripts in other languages of the country.

In the scheme of religious life preached by the sect of Vallabhācārya, deliverance, redemption, secured by the complete performance of the set of religious acts is of three kinds or stages. In two of them, the distinct entity of individual souls remains intact. In the third, which is really the middling variety, it is asserted that by the grace of Lord the souls "attain the condition of pure Brahman". In one the delivered souls not only exist eternally but would appear to be still there incognito. For they are such sages as Sanaka and others. In the other variety, which is clearly the highest, the most covetable and the one which only the followers of the sect can achieve, the delivered souls become the associates of the Lord in all His eternal sports.[6]

In the Caitanyite school, liberation or redemption consists in becoming one with God, almost the same as in monistic Vedānta theory.[7] Tulasīdāsa appears to have been convinced of 'māyāvāda' and of the ultimate unity of the individual soul and the Supreme God[8] and 'mokṣa', or 'apavarga'[9], which is another word for salvation or 'nirvāṇa', the goal of religious living, is expected to be more or less the same in his view as that in the system of Caitanya. The major difference between the redemptions of the two systems is that in Caitanya's view the God is Kṛṣṇa while in Tulasīdāsa's view it is Rāma.[10] Actually Tulasīdāsa speaks of the goal to be achieved by the total complex of religious living, including his great prescription of one-pointed devotion to Rāma, as 'crossing the ocean of worldly existence' or 'undoing the knot of worldly existence' or 'freedom from the bondage of worldly existence' or 'absence of the distress due to worldly existence' or 'freedom from the misery of transmigration (saṁsṛti')' or 'end of transmigration' or again 'destruction of nescience ('avidyā') the cause of transmigration'.[11] More positively he speaks of the achievement of the abode of bliss-giving liberation (VII, Dohā 180) or of the highest state of loneness ('kaivalya') (VII,

Dohā 188, 3) or reaching 'the state' (VII, Chanda 28) or finally as of 'highest rest' and 'nirvāṇa' (VII, Chanda 30).

Rāmadāsa, the dynamic and activist saint-philosopher of Maharashtra, was born almost a century after Tulasīdāsa. Besides organizing centres for activist propaganda he has left a fairly consistent account of the religio-philosophy he believed in and preached. The book in which this teaching of his is enshrined is called *Dāsabodha*, the instruction of the servant. i.e., of Rāmadāsa, the servant of Rāma. He popularized the worship of both Rāma and his great helper-devotee, the monkey-god Hanumān, in Maharashtra.[12]

Rāmadāsa straightforwardly enumerates the four types of salvation referred to above, in their ascending order of importance and finality as: (1) 'svalokatā [salokatā]', 'residence in the same world'; (2) 'samīpatā', 'proximity'; (3) 'svarupatā [sarupatā]', sameness of form; and (4) 'sāyojya [sāyujya]', merging or union. He states further that the first three types are perishable, but the last is eternal, the souls attaining it not being disturbed even at the end of the great time period, 'kalpa', when the cosmos gets dissolved. It is the goal, the real redemption to be secured by religious living.[13] And 'sāyujya' according to Rāmadāsa is not merging with Rāma but with Absolute Brahman.[14]

He has expanded the brief statement of Lord Kṛṣṇa in the *BhG* about polylatry and the perishable result of such worship. The world of heaven in his cosmography is the abode of all gods, different parts of it being the special domain of specific gods. Worshippers of these gods, among whom the two Supreme Gods, Viṣṇu and Śiva, are included, after death dwell in the specific world of the particular god they worshipped. This state of the soul is known as 'salokatā'. Residence in the same world is 'salokatā'; proximity to God is 'samīpatā'; attainment of same form as His is 'sarūpatā'. This condition, the third type of salvation, Rāmadāsa explains in relation to Viṣṇu, whose world is known as 'Vaikuṇṭha'. He says that in that state, in the third type of salvation, in 'sarūpatā', though the liberated soul attains the form of Viṣṇu yet he is devoid of the two specific mark-ornaments of Viṣṇu, 'śrīvatsa' and 'kaustubha'. He has of course no Lakṣmī with him. He lives in that condition for as long as merit can keep him there. Thereafter he returns to the mundane existence. It is quite another matter with those who have attained the 'sāyujya', salvation, through being one with the Absolute. At the destruction of the cosmos though gods are liquidated, these souls, of course in the form of Brahman, keep on undisturbed.[15] Similarly devotees of Śiva attaining any of the first three types of salvation go to His world, Kailāsa. Further specification of the condition of the souls in the third type of salvation in Kailāsa is not made by Rāmadāsa.[16]

In the religious complex, centred round Rudra-Śiva, which will, henceforward, as is the common usage, be called Śaivism, the redemption, 'mokṣa', is more or less like that adumbrated by Jñāneśvara, i.e., union with the Supreme God, though it does not extinguish the individual souls' separate entity.

In Śaivism, God is Śiva whose presence the liberated soul enjoys fully and consciously. In one sect the liberated soul is called Śiva but is declared to be not independent of Him. This view appears to be more current in the Tamilian form of Śaivism. Saint-poets of Tamilnad, who must have lived before the 10th century A.D. and whose religious hymns have been translated, appear to countenance this view of redemption. The great Vīraśaiva or Liṅgāyat sect of Karnataka, too, shares the same view of redemption, i.e., that it is "union in blissful experience with Śiva". It, however, names the condition 'sāmarasya', identity of essence.[17]

The great Tamilian saint-poet Manikkavasagar sang his view of redemption thus : "I had no virtue, penance, knowledge, self-control. A doll to turn At others' will I danced, whirled, fell. He filled in every limb With love's mad longing, and that I might climb *there whence is no return,* He showed His beauty, made me His. Ah me, when shall I go to Him ?"[18]

Mundane living being thus considered to be a bondage, and eternal freedom from the necessity of going through it being the goal to be secured as soon as possible under the working conditions of this human world, the whole pattern of Hindu living came to be organized as a plan for and a system of living calculated sooner or later to lead to that ultimate objective.[19] Accordingly ends of human existence came to be formulated and stated clearly as four.[20] And characteristically the enumeration begins with 'dharma', 'righteous living',—I think that the rendering given here of the term 'dharma' is the most appropriate one, though I cannot justify it here for fear of a long disgression —as the first 'puruṣārtha' or objective of man, i.e., end of human existence. 'Dharma' as already stated in an earlier chapter was taking on the complex connotation which it came to possess as a member of the quartet of 'puruṣārthas', the imperative and compound goal of human living. The quartet significantly is completed by the end called 'mokṣa' as its fourth member. And 'mokṣa' is release from mundane living, once and for all. The two ends which form the middle pair, 'artha' and 'kāma', wealth and sex-life, are the usual stock in trade and appetitive aspects more or less inherent in human life, almost on the purely bio-psychological plane. They, too, however, in their organization and satisfaction, have, in the Hindu view of living, to be prefaced by and shot through with 'dharma', righteous living. And that is why Lord Kṛṣṇa in the *Bhagavadgītā* (VII, 11) identifies himself with 'kāma', or desire in general, which is not opposed to 'dharma', "dharmāviruddho bhuteṣu kāmosmi bharatarṣabha".

Towards the end of the Ṛgvedic age 'dharma' was identified with sacrifice, the sacrifice of the Primordial Being having been declared in the famous Puruṣa hymn to have been the first rites, 'dharma'. In the *Bṛhadāraṇyaka Upaniṣad* (I, 4, 14) 'dharma' is represented as a creation of Brahman and is equated with 'satya', truth. It is very significant for the history of the vitality of the concept of 'dharma' that the story of its creation credits to its regime the important social achievement that weak persons could and can stand their own against even very mighty people. 'Dharma', thus, in the new dispensation of the Upaniṣadic thought marked by moral fervour in an age of social solidarity, is shown in the most favourable light and as a covetable notion. Readers of this book should be able to appreciate why later authors delighted in deriving the word 'dharma' from the root 'dhṛ', stating that 'dharma' is so called because 'it upholds', 'dhāraṇāt'. In the same Upaniṣad (II, 5, 11-12) 'dharmaḥ' happens to be one of the many objects and notions identified with Brahman, and is fully personalized with the attribution of a 'puruṣa', 'person', to it. The *Chāndogya Upaniṣad* speaks of 'dharma' in the imagery of a tree, 'dharma' having three branches (II, 23, 1). They are sacrifice, study and charity. Here we have the earliest categorization of the contents of 'dharma' or of its components. The view that we get from the combined observations in the two oldest Upaniṣads is that the operation and application of the notion of 'dharma' produced moral order and consideration for others less fortunate than the better off members of the society, encouraged the performance of austerities as a new type of and metaphorical sacrifice, and established the custom of preservation of the learned tradition through regular and prolonged study.

It is in keeping with this role and nature of 'dharma' that we find the teacher exhorting his pupil, while giving him leave to return home at the end of his period of study, in the manner he is shown to have done in the *Taittirīya Upaniṣad* (I, 11). He bids: "Speak the truth. Practise 'dharma'. Do not miss your regular study. Pay your teacher sizeable fees and rear progeny. Do not stray away from truth. Do not depart from 'dharma' . . . . Offer with faith. Do not give without faith. Give gracefully, humbly, fearingly and knowingly. If any doubt about any activity or about any conduct arises in your mind, observe how thoughtful, self-controlled but not harsh, and righteously bent Brahmins act, and mould your activity or conduct, as the case may be, in accordance with that observation."

These lineaments of the important notion of 'dharma', of course, cannot exhaust its contents as conceived in the Upaniṣadic age; but we cannot fill in the outline properly for lack of data. We know that some centuries later, the *Bhagavadgītā* made 'dharma' the central plank of its socio-religious platform; and Lord Kṛṣṇa used it as an effective argument. Thrice in the course of the whole disquisition and argument, twice almost at its beginning, II, 31 and III, 35, and again almost at its end in the eighteenth chapter (47), Lord Kṛṣṇa appeals to one's own 'dharma', i.e., the pattern of duties and living which are more or less the ordained ones for one's station in life. In two of these contexts he asserts that one's own 'dharma', though appearing defective, is better than the one of another person or group. Intellect, 'buddhi', of the first or the purest variety enables one to distinguish the nature of salvation but one requires at least the second order of intellect to discriminate between what is 'dharma', and 'non-dharma' (*BhG,* XVIII, 30-1). This juxtaposition of the two notions 'mokṣa' and 'dharma', and their appreciation by two kinds of intellect which are closely akin, raises a presumption that 'dharma' is the instrument of 'mokṣa', that the final goal may be achieved through it or that it is a help towards that end. To impress that this is not a pure conjecture I shall refer here again to the Lord's announcement, which I have already quoted in its other context, that of God's incarnations. It is for the upholding of 'dharma' that God incarnates Himself whenever He finds the opposite of 'dharma' flourishing (*BhG*, IV, 7-8). The Lord further declares Himself to be the source and stay of 'dharma' that is eternal (XIV, 27).

Arjuna himself puts forth at the very outset a sort of rationalization to cover up his defeatist mentality, in terms of 'dharma', particularly that aspect of it which is centred in the family, 'kuladharma' (*BhG*, I, 40-41 ; 43-44), and in class.

In II, 40, Lord Kṛṣṇa definitely equates 'dharma' with His special system of religious living called 'karmayoga', or selfless activity of an ordained nature to be dutifully, and without attachment conscientiously, carried out. And later (XII, 20) He characterizes the doctrine and practice of devotion to Kṛṣṇa-Viṣṇu which He preaches as nectarine 'dharma', i.e., the unfailing and completely satisfying pattern of religious living. The final exhortation of the Lord, too, is couched in the 'dharma'-terminology as He asks Arjuna to seek refuge in Him abandoning all other 'dharmas' (XVIII, 66).

In the *Manusmṛti*, about a century or two later, 'dharma' is called 'Bhagavān Vṛṣa', Lord Bull (VIII, 16), and is consequently described as having four feet, meaning the four main components of 'dharma' according to that authoritative text (I, 81). 'Dharma' is praised as the only friend of man that persists after the destruction of one's body and accompanies the soul (VIII, 17 ; IV, 238-43). In relation to the scheme of the four ages of the world the components of 'dharma' are stated in a schematic manner, to decrease from four to one. Whereas all the four components, austerity, knowledge, sacrifice and charity, formed the 'dharma' of the first, i.e., 'krita', age, charity is said to remain the most important one for the current, i.e., 'kali', age, the other three remaining subsidiary ones (I, 81 ; 85). 'Dharma' in the view of the *Manusmṛti* represents the totality of practice and faith, including the domestic and other rites and observances along with strictly philosophico-religious and ethical ideals of practices. Leaving out the first part, which may be said to be in effect an expansion or perhaps an epitomization of the third of the four components, with a little of the first and the last, i.e., austerity and charity, added, I shall briefly indicate the other contents of 'dharma'.

Before passing on to the topic of the contents of 'dharma' I should like to refer to an observation of the national poet, Kālidāsa, about 'dharma', indicating his view and also to some remarks about 'dharma' in the popular epic, *Rāmāyaṇa* of Vālmīki, as evidence of the then current notions of 'dharma' as the liberator, or as the mode of achieving the goal of religious living.

It is in an extraordinary context that Vālmīki has acquainted us with the then current view of 'dharma', the occasion being a homily by the self-effacing and genteel wife Sītā to her husband and the eve of their starting off for the Daṇḍaka-forest to extirpate the demons. She is said to have admonished or warned Rāma about the proper 'dharma' of a Kṣatriya, i.e., that it is the protection of the distressed, though her admonition consists in pointing out to Rāma the possibility, or even the probability, of his indulging in killing demons who had shown no enmity towards him. Killing anyone who had not done any offensive act against oneself was 'a-dharma', non-'dharma', and Rāma was starting on an endeavour which was very likely to land him into perpetrating it. Sītā, therefore, exhorts (III, 9, 30-1): "From 'dharma' proceeds wealth; from 'dharma' flows happiness; by 'dharma' anything is obtained; this world is established in 'dharma'. And 'dharma' consists in observing rules and subjecting oneself to their disciplinary process but not in following one's instincts for pleasure." Kālidāsa has put in the mouths of the gods, addressing Brahmā, the following sentiment which felcitiously portrays the role of 'dharma': "Dharma is what is sought as their leader by those who strive for salvation ('mokṣa'), as it leads to cutting off of the bondage of activity and to the cessation of worldly existence" (*Kumārasambhava*, II, 51).

In the 3rd century B.C., i.e., during about a century before the compilation the *Bhagavadgītā*, according to the date accepted as the correct one for its composition, the word 'dharma' and the notion too were so rife in India that it may be said to have been dinned into the ears of the people. The large number of edicts issued by emperor Aśoka, promulgated and inscribed on large rocks or pillars in many places over the length and breadth of the whole country, some of which at least were prefaced as 'dhammalipi', i.e., writing on 'dharma', using the term 'dhamma' in various combinations and aspects, must have familiarized the term to such an extent that it must have behaved as what is called today a stereotype. Aśoka's special officers entrusted with the task of carrying the message through oral communication, called 'dharmamahāmātras', high officers of 'dharma', must have further acted as a stabilizer and an interpreter, so that India can be said to have been very receptive in about 250 B.C. to the notion called 'dharma'.

The 'dharma' preached by Aśoka, though a selective and synthetic amalgam of the then accepted Buddhist doctrines and of the main Hindu principles not directly opposed to Buddhist ideas, cannot be considered as a true representative of the content of 'dharma' as conceived in Hinduism. For, first of all, as is clear from my observations in a previous chapter, the goal of religious living in Aśoka's scheme of living did not reach beyond the attainment of heaven. Second, when Aśoka does clearly define 'dharma', as in the second pillar-edict (Delhi-Topra version)[21], he specifies only four of the ten attributes of 'dharma' as Manu[22] lays it down, or of the nine as Yājñavalkya[23] in his *Smṛti* enumerates them, or of the thirteen as the *Viṣṇusmṛti*[24] has them. He lists compassion, charity, truth and purity as the main positive attributes of his 'dharma'. In the third pillar-edict Aśoka adds the negative attributes, the states and actions to be avoided as not being 'dharma', irascibility, cruelty, wrath, arrogance and jealousy[25]; and in the seventh pillar-edict he enlarges the group of positive attributes with the addition of softness, and goodness.[27] With all this it will be seen, from what follows, that much of the content of the Hindu notion of 'dharma' was not represented in Aśoka's selective synthesis in his 'dhamma'.

For the Hindu notion of 'dharma' and its contents, excluding, of course, as already stated, the routine rites and daily or seasonal or occasional rituals, we have to turn to the *Bhagavadgītā* which in its present compilation was ready by the time Aśoka's glory was coming to an end. The *Gītā* idea of 'dharma' is in other respects, i.e., strictly religio-philosophical and ethical, not only comprehensive and almost complete but carries in it a continuation of the main contribution of the Upaniṣadic age to the religious consciousness and practice of the Hindus.

Summing up the discourse on His special mode of religious striving, consisting of devotion to Kṛṣṇa-Viṣṇu, i.e., Bhakti, combined with 'karmayoga', i.e., the new philosophy of activity, Lord Kṛṣṇa affirms quite positively that activity comprising of sacrifice, charity, and austerity must never be abandoned. For sacrifice, charity, and austerity purify the mind. This purificatory action of the three types of activity mentioned is further enhanced, if, in accordance with the new philosophy of work, this threefold activity is pursued without any attachment and expectation of returns (*BhG*, XVIII, 3-6). From this statement of the Lord we conclude quite inevitably that the *Gītā* notion of the 'dharma', conducive to the achievement of redemption, the goal to be secured through religious living, envisages five constituents of that 'dharma'. They are: sacrifice ('yajña'), charity ('dāna'), austerity ('tapas'), devotion ('bhakti') and knowledge ('jñāna').

Knowledge (jñāna) must be considered to have formed a constituent, though not the central core, of the *Gītā* notion of 'dharma'. The fire of knowledge ('jñānāgni') burns the binding consequences of activity (IV, 37). There is therefore nothing as sacred as knowledge (jñāna) (IV, 38). Because 'jñāna' or knowledge is an important constituent of the 'dharma' that guarantees redemption, the Lord expounds the whole system of knowledge in the VIIth chapter, assuring *inter alia* (17-18) the immense superiority of a 'jñānī'-devotee, i.e., a devotee who has cultivated devotion after having mastered the knowledge about the nature of God and the cosmos, of God and the individual soul and of their interrelations. Not having fully exhausted the system of knowledge so essential to His notion of 'dharma', Lord Kṛṣṇa follows up the topic in the IXth chapter placing Himself, as the Supreme Soul, at the centre or at the culminating point (27-34). Even the grace of the Lord leading the worshipper on to the path of salvation is guaranteed through the "brilliant light of knowledge ('jñāna')" (X, 10-11). Knowledge, 'jñāna', therefore, finds a place in the group of traits that form the 'divine wealth' of human personality and facilitates the attainment of the ultimate goal through an appropriate mode of religious living (XVI, 1-5). In the total complex of 'dharma' laid down in the *Bhagavadgītā,* knowledge (jñāna), of course, plays a subsidiary role as it is declared to be not only second best, as a mode calculated to gain redemption, to the new theory and practice of non-attachment to work and non-expectation of its fruits, but also to the old Yogic method of concentration (XII, 12). All the same it is absolutely necessary as a step to or an adjunct of the other component of the *Gītā*'-'dharma' (IV, 10; XIII, 34; XIV, 2; XVI, 1).

The development of knowledge (jñāna) is both a function of 'buddhi', reason, and its source, which being an important constituent of human personality, is quite often referred to as 'buddhi'. Specially this is the case when the Lord wants to emphasize the role of knowledge in enabling a person to achieve equanimity and non-attachment-attitude (II, 48-53). Such is the significance of 'jñāna' that in one mood Lord Kṛṣṇa has identified it with almost the whole complex of mental make-up and active behaviour which is as near as possible the same as the *Gītā*-'dharma'. In XIII, 7-11 knowledge is described as not only the discriminating appraisal of defects like birth, death, old age, disease and sorrow, not only the clear understanding of the eternity of the knowledge of 'ātman', but also as non-attachment to one's wife, children and home, as absence of pride, absence of hypocrisy, non-injury, forbearance, rectitude, purity, steadfastness, self-control, absence of ego-sense, indifference to objects of sense, and as perfect and allround equanimity, and even as attendance on one's teacher. Most of these qualities are further found listed in the 'divine wealth' of a person while the opposites of the good ones are grouped in the class of 'demoniac wealth' (XVI, 1-16). Some of the categories in appropriate forms are mentioned later, the good ones as 'sāttvika', i.e., due to the disposition of 'sattva', and the bad ones either as 'rājasa', or more often as 'tāmasa', i.e., as due to the disposition of 'rajas', or 'tamas', darkness (XVIII, 20-43).

With this very wide net of mostly moral traits spread over the field of knowledge the *Bhagavadgītā* made its mode of God-seeking a high moral endeavour, adding to this the negative or the denunciatory complement of the moral complex which is very elaborately, though intermittently, made in other contexts. One cannot fail to realise that the purely ethical component of the *Gītā*-'dharma' for redemption is almost two parts, out of five, a moral endeavour. I shall briefly, therefore, summarize that negative complement.

To Arjuna's query regarding sin and its perpetration by a person, Lord Kṛṣṇa answers by affirming that the devils of the piece, the great mischief-makers of man, the forces that impel him to commit sinful acts, are the lower ingredients or components of his own personality, which are generated in his mind as a result of the disposition of 'rajas'. They are desire ('kāma'), anger ('krodha'), and greed ('lobha'), and are described as the gate to hell (XVI, 21). One is enjoined to avoid the triad. Of these the first two, and the need to conquer them, especially the first, the second being a derivative condition resulting from the non-fulfilment of the first (III, 37 ; II, 62), are repeatedly mentioned (II, 62 ; III, 37 ; V, 23 ; 26 ; XVI, 12 ; XVIII, 53 ; VI, 24 ; VII, 20 ; XVIII, 24). With desire operating in the more or less normal manner ego-sense is heightened (II, 71) ; for it is insatiable and as such envelops not only the senses but also the mind and the reason (III, 38-40). It is therefore imperative to kill that enemy, viz., desire, which is difficult to catch hold of (III, 43).

In a system of religious living, a philosophy of life, which prizes most highly non-attachment to work and is centred on non-expectation of fruits of one's action, on utter indifference as to the result of one's activity, it is but natural that desire in any form should be countered as an evil to be banished once for all. In two other forms, desire, as love and wish, too, is mentioned as an evil to be fought against. And to this list along with anger ('krodha') are added both fear and hate (IV, 10 ; V, 28).

This ethical viewpoint of the *Gītā* is further brought out by the clear distinction it makes, even in the domain of the older triad of purifying activity, i.e., that of sacrifice, charity and austerity, with whose mention we started on our journey through the domain of spiritual enterprise prescribed for redemption in the *Bhagavadgītā*, and which forms the soul of most Vaiṣṇavite sectarian prescriptions and infuses and suffuses also most Śaivite ones. It is laid down, of course, that these activities must, as every one else, be performed in the most disinterested manner. But that is not all. Each one of the triad is distinguished in three varieties (XVII, 5-7 ; 11-22).

Yajña, sacrifice, performed or offered with full faith and without any desire for any gain from it is called 'sāttvika', i.e., best ; so, too, is charity which is made to one who cannot return the obligation and who is a fit person (XVII, 11-13 ; 20-22). 'Tapas' or austerity is eventually distinguished into nine varieties, of which the one which is both mental and 'sāttvika' is the best. It consists in cultivating mental serenity, mildness, silence, self-control, purity of temper, being undertaken with full faith without the slightest desire for any return (XVII, 14-19).

The list of qualities and patterns of behaviour included in the 'divine wealth', 'daivī sampad', of a person, which is conducive to his final absolution, redemption, is a convincing proof of the moral earnestness characteristic of the *Gītā*-'dharma'. They are : "Absence of fear, purity of temper, appreciation of knowledge, charity, self-control, sacrifice, regular study, austerity, rectitude, non-injury, truthfulness, absence of anger, renunciation, peacefulness, absence of back-biting, compassion, absence of greed, softness, modesty, steadiness, vigour, forgiveness, fortitude, purity, and absence of malice and pride." This list includes double the number of qualities and types of behaviour recommended in the much later *Viṣṇusmṛti* referred to above.

Thus all in all the *Gītā*-'dharma' may be said to be a moral endeavour and rendered a spiritual enterprise with the addition of devotion, 'bhakti', to Kṛṣṇa-Viṣṇu.

The crystallization of the ethical aspect of the complex notion of 'dharma' made by Lord Kṛṣṇa got thoroughly infused in the pattern of religious living of Hinduism since then. The normative literature of later time, so fully surcharged with ritualistic details as to give the idea of its Hinduism being a religion of only rituals, rites and vows, incorporated, as already mentioned, a number of moral virtues in its notion of 'dharma' enjoined on the people for practice. The *Manusmṛti* (VII, 92), the most authoritative text among such, specifies the following ten qualities and pursuits as 'marks' of the 'dharma' it enjoins the people to practise : (1) Fortitude ; (2) forgiveness ; (3) self-control ; (4) non-stealing ; (5) purity ; (6) control over senses ; (7) reasoning ; (8) learning ; (9) truthfulness ; and (10) freedom from anger.

To help the cause of this moral endeavour and the whole spiritual enterprise, which the *Gītā* advocates and prescribes for redemption, and which I should like to name 'naiṣkarmyabhaktiyoga', i.e., devotion buttressed by selfless and disinterested activity, using the very words which Lord Kṛṣṇa has employed from time to time to characterize the new way, 'dharma', He has promulgated in the *Bhagavadgītā*, He prescribes a short course of Yogic practice, control of breath and such other techniques. Their practice, without going far as the confirmed and sectarian Yogins do, carried out day to day, enables one to control one's senses and to bring one's mind to a steady condition. It is also calculated to stabilize one's 'buddhi', reason. The chapter (VI) in which this prescription is detailed is called 'dhyānayoga', the way of meditation. The possibility of achieving redemption through the complete and constant practice of 'yoga' combined with the final achievement of concentrating "life-breath between the eyebrows at the time of death" is fully subscribed to. But what is prescribed is quite clearly not such complete and constant practice of 'yoga' but only a limited use of it for steadying the mind and bringing the senses under its control (VIII, 10-14). For, all those who run after the Absolute tread a difficult path full of trouble and pitfalls ; on the other hand, those who are devoted to Kṛṣṇa-Viṣṇu, dedicating all their actions to the Lord are easily saved (XI, 55 ; XII, 2 ; 5-10 ; XIV, 26 ; XVIII, 46 ; 53-57 ; 65-66).

Subordination of the practice of the 'yoga'-technique made in the *Bhagavadgītā* stands out clearly when the role assigned to it in the *Śvetāśvatara Upaniṣad*, which is, as made clear earlier, a theistic and devotional text centred round Rudra-Śiva, is compared. In it the mysterious powers believed by 'yoga' experts to ensue from the constant practice of its full technique are mentioned and the attendant wondrous condition of the individual soul, too, is more than hinted at (*ŚvU*, II, 11-14).

Even more important as an indication of the development of religious consciousness is the turn given to the newer doctrine of 'bhakti', devotion, by Lord Kṛṣṇa. In the *ŚvU* supreme devotion, 'parā bhakti', to Rudra-Śiva and also to one's teacher is declared to be the basic requirement for a person to understand and realize the religio-philosophical doctrines stated in it. It is also asserted that the sage, after whom the Upaniṣad is named, received enlightenment through both the prowess of his austerity and the grace of the God (Rudra-Śiva). A person desirous of redemption is said to have sought, and is asked to seek, refuge in God (Rudra-Śiva) (*ŚvU*, VI, 18-23).

Kṛṣṇa not only details some at least of the features, which taken together form the complex attitude and sentiment known as 'bhakti', devotion, but also extends its connotation and evidently simplifies it. His endeavour in this line reached so far that the complex called 'bhakti' may be said to have been stereotyped by him. Later religious development took it as the standard and is patterned more or less on it.

At the end of the 14th chapter, after having described in highly eulogistic terms the attainment of superiority over and insensivity to the operation of the three dispositions of 'sattva', 'rajas' and 'tamas', Lord Kṛṣṇa suddenly, and therefore purposely to stress His emphatic affirmation, asserts that one who serves Him with one-pointed devotion attains such a condition and gets ready to realize Brahman in himself. And here it is that for the first and the last time in the *BhG* the term 'bhaktiyoga' occurs (XIV, 26). 'Bhakti', devotion, is thus given the same prestige-position as other and older systems of God-seeking, 'Jñānayoga' or 'Sāṁkhyayoga', and 'Yoga' proper. 'Bhakti' thus was formed into a systematized mode of God-seeking. It is, however, the XIIth chapter of the *Gītā* which is described in its colophon as the chapter on 'Bhaktiyoga'. The subject-matter of the chapter, starts with the question of Arjuna requesting a relative estimate of the worth of those who are devoted to Kṛṣṇa-Viṣṇu and those who seek the unmanifest and immutable Brahman. In the very short chapter comprising only twenty verses, the word 'bhakti' as such does not occur. Instead of devotion it is the person who has this devotion, the devotee, either in the form of 'bhakta' or 'bhaktimān', that is mentioned five times, and is declared to be dear or very dear to the Lord (14, 16, 17, 18, 20). The intervening verses having to be taken to refer to a devotee again, altogether eight, beginning with the thirteenth, are thus concerned with the Lord's affirmation of His endearment of His devotees. In three verses (3-5) meditation on Brahman is declared to lead the worshipper to the Lord and is adjudged to be a much more difficult way of approach to the goal, which is identical with that of 'bhakti'. Four verses (9-12) are entirely devoted to the statement and praise of the special contribution, an important development in the Indian religious field and a unique one in the history of man, of Lord Kṛṣṇa to the pattern of religious living, to 'dharma'. The remaining three verses (6-8)—one verse which is only a prelude to the Lord's reply need not be counted—though the word 'bhakti' does not occur in them, form a clear but general statement of what constitutes 'bhakti' and an emphatic assertion of the grand end it assures to its practitioner. The act, however, of worshipping the God is spoken of in the Upaniṣadic terminology and Brahman-ideology as 'upāsanā', meditation, and contemplation. And the system is called 'one-pointed system', 'ananyayoga', which corresponds to 'avyabhicāra', steadfast, which is an adjectival amplification of 'bhaktiyoga' in the penultimate verse of the 14th chapter. That 'bhakti', devotion, has to be one-pointed, 'ananya', is stressed in many contexts (VIII, 22 ; IX, 22 ; XI, 54 ; XVIII, 62 ; 66).

The contents of the notion of 'bhakti' as revealed in these verses are rather limited and couched in terms which are redolent of the Upaniṣadic 'upāsanā' than of 'bhakti' proper. Arjuna is asked to fix his mind in Kṛṣṇa-Viṣṇu and to direct his 'buddhi', reason, upon Him. Arjuna is further informed that those who worship Him with meditation, dedicating all their activity to Him, and are intent on Him are swiftly saved by Him from the ocean of worldly existence. Thus, while the contents of the notion of 'bhakti' as laid out here are not specifically of the new pattern of religious living, they are, on the other hand, mixed up with the very original notion of 'naiṣkarmya' or 'niṣkāmakarmayoga', philosophy of conscientious and disinterested activity, which is the special contribution of the *Bhagavadgītā* to the pattern of religious living designed to meet the requirements of a work-a-day world and the accepted theory of transmigration having its cause and source in mundane activity.

The contents of the new pattern of 'bhakti', devotion, which can be gathered from other verses are : (1) Remembering Kṛṣṇa-Viṣṇu, which is so potent a power for the spiritual good of a person that even if he does so only at the time of death he not only reaches Kṛṣṇa-Viṣṇu but attains His form, i.e., the third, and the highest stage, for a pure theist of the Vaiṣṇava sect, of salvation. And it is because remembering a particular object at the time of death is not feasible unless one is most commonly and incessantly accustomed to remember it during the whole of life that Arjuna is asked to remember Kṛṣṇa-Viṣṇu in all circumstances and at all times. He is further assured that if he goes on fighting while remembering Kṛṣṇa-Viṣṇu all the while he will reach Him after death. Lord Kṛṣṇa further emphasizes the significance of this feature of the notion of 'bhakti' by affirming that He is easy of access to one who always and in all circumstances remembers Him (VIII, 5-7 ; 14). This feature is known as 'smaraṇa', remembering, of Viṣṇu and forms one of the nine items, specified as forming the notion and practice of nine-itemed 'bhakti' as laid down some centuries later in the *Bhāgavata-Purāṇa* (VII, 5, 23)[27].

There is clear evidence of the great importance attached to remembering the name of God, Viṣṇu in this case, as a mode of working for one's salvation some centuries before the *Bhāgavata-Purāṇa* or even *Hārītasmṛti*, another work, which is perhaps earlier than the *Bhāgavata-Purāṇa*, but mentions the fact of 'bhakti' being a nine-itemed complex. Kālidāsa in his hymn addressed to Viṣṇu, Śeṣaśāyin, in *Raghuvaṁsa* (X, 29) says : "You purify a person even if he merely remembers You", and thus affirms the faith he and his contemporary India had that mere remembering God, Viṣṇu in this case, was enough to purify a person.

That Kṛṣṇa meant by 'smaraṇa', remembering, only remembrance of Kṛṣṇa-Viṣṇu, either His form or His name, but not the muttering or the uttering of the name follows from His affirmation (VIII, 13) that persons on their death-bed who, "remembering Me and muttering Om, which is one-lettered Brahman", leave their bodies, attain the highest state of salvation. In later history, however, 'nāmasmaraṇa', remembering the name of God, which has come to occupy so significant a pclae in the pattern of religious living prescribed by any one of the many theistic sects, connotes and subsumes nothing but the muttering or uttering of God's name. And whether Śiva or Viṣṇu, God has been given one thousand or one thousand and eight different names, out of which at least twenty-four in the case of Viṣṇu and one hundred and eight in the case of Śiva must be uttered or muttered by a devout or pious person daily, to acquire merit and to guarantee that one of the God's names will be on his lips at the time of death.

In the complex nine-itemed notion of 'bhakti' one item is named 'kīrtana', which literally means telling but is quite competently said to be the same as utterance of God's name and His glory.[28]

Different epithets and names given to one and the same God, evidently stemming from mythological details, is an ancient phenomenon in India. There is a hymn known as Śatarudrīya in the *Yajurveda*, which is famous as a formula ; for it is more or less a string of Śiva's epithets and is current even today for certain religious purposes as a potent formula.[29]

Among the modes of approach to the deity taking the name, whether as mere remembering, 'smaraṇa', or in its later form of muttering, i.e., 'japa', does not figure in the approaches prescribed by the Upaniṣadic teachers. We find in the *Bṛhadāraṇyaka Upaniṣad* (II, 5), seeing ('darśana'), listening ('śravana'), thinking ('manana') and contemplation ('nididhyāsana') as the prescribed modes of approach to the deity but neither remembering ('smaraṇa'), nor muttering ('japa').

The muttering of certain formulae or uttering, i.e., recitation, of certain hymns, must have become a highly respected mode of religious living even before the time of the *Bhagavadgītā*. In X, 25 the Lord not only mentions 'japayajña' as the foremost among sacrifices but also identifies Himself with it as it is the best of its class, viz., sacrifices. We discover in the *Manusmṛti*, too, a high status assigned to muttering either of mystic words or names or of sacred texts, it being called a sacrifice, and being as such placed far above the four food-sacrifices, out of the five daily ones universally and consistently known as the 'five great sacrifices'. Further a distinction in utterance or recitation is made which bespeaks influence of the ethical attitude of the *Bhagavadgītā*. Distinct and audible utterance is the lowest and the least valuable of the three grades into which utterance of words or texts is classified.[30] Muttering without making it audible is declared to be hundred times better than audible muttering ; and mere mental 'utterance' (?), i.e., mere remembering without the aid of vocal organs, is assessed as thousandfold important.

'Kīrtana', telling and praising, which includes also muttering or utterance of God's name, though principally it is concerned with the praise of God, making full reference to all the great and many things He has done for men, is another item mentioned as a component of the notion and practice of 'bhakti' in *BhG* (IX, 14) and forms one of the nine items of the standard complex. It is otherwise referred to as 'kaṭhā' (X, 9), a term which is colloquially most common in vernaculars as 'Ḥarikathā'. In IX, 14 and IX, 34 'namana', obeisance or bowing down, is mentioned. In the standard formula it figures as 'vandana', another word for obeisance, and in the tautologically another item, 'pādasevana'. This last item etymologically means to serve the feet, i.e., make very reverential obeisance.

The item 'archana', worship, of the standard formula must be taken to be covered by *BhG*, IX, 25. In covering the item of worship in the manner the *Bhagavadgītā* did it quite clearly struck a new path, simplifying the procedure of worship. Worship must have included an offering and must have involved an elaborate procedure during three or four centuries before the compilation of the *BhG*.[31] Lord Kṛṣṇa liberalizing His mode of religious living and throwing it open to all classes of society and all kinds of persons, irrespective of caste, sex or previous conduct, laid down a very simple form of worshipping Him, and thus enhanced the value and significance of spirit over form and its content. He says (IX, 26) : "Whatever, either a leaf, a flower, a fruit or even water, a person offers Me with devout spirit I accept [with delight]."

The devout spirit mentioned here is suggested or implied in other places either as 'śraddhā', faith in Kṛṣṇa-Viṣṇu (VI, 47 ; XII, 2 ; XII, 20) or as 'dṛḍhavrata', confirmed rule (VII, 28 ; IX, 14), or as 'ananya-cetas', single-pointed mind (VIII, 14 ; IX, 22 ; XII, 7 ; XVIII, 66).

Another item of the standard formula is 'śravaṇa', listening to, which is one of the Upaniṣadic modes of approaching the deity. It finds its place in 'bhakti' of the *Gītā* with a highly intellectual and emotional accent. The Lord (*BhG*, X, 9-10) speaks of those worshippers who "being intent on Him with their life-breath fixed on Him speak of Him among themselves enlightening [on His nature and work] one another by their talk, feel blissfully happy and sportively engaged" as the dear ones on whom He showers His grace by providing them with adequate knowledge enabling them to attain to Him, i.e., achieve the highest salvation. The importance of 'śravaṇa', listening to, is so great that even the listening of the dialogue of Kṛṣṇa and Arjuna in the *Bhagavadgītā*, i.e., the text of the *Gītā*, would secure salvation and attainment of the appropriate world to one who is trusting and faithful (XVIII, 71). This newly appreciated and appraised potentiality of 'śravaṇa', listening to, is so firmly and highly praised that it led Kṛṣṇa to raise it to the position of the sole mode of approach to the deity, complete and adequate by itself for the purpose of the attainment of redemption, even when the deity is conceived in the Upaniṣadic way or in the way of Brahman-seekers (XIII, 25)!

It is seen that the 'bhakti' complex preached in the *Bhagavadgītā* comprised six of the nine items of the standard complex as laid down in the *Bhāgavata-Purāṇa*, and mostly followed by Vaiṣṇavite sects later. The three items not finding a place in it are 'dāsya', servitude, 'sakhya', companionship, and 'ātmanivedana', self-surrender.

As against this, the 'bhakti' complex of the *Gītā*, which is strong both on thinking and considering (IX, 22 ; X, 11 ; XII 8 ; 20), on enlightening and knowing (X, 9-10; XII, 20 ; XVIII, 54-55), remains both a moral and intellectual endeavour, though securing ecstatic delight to the worshippers, who are participants in the common enterprise of God-seeking. The late 'bhakti' complex even when it is pure and strictly within moral bounds tends to become a-moral and almost non-intellectual rising into a purely ecstatic exercise!

The unique contribution of the *Bhagavadgītā*, as mentioned earlier, to the pattern of religious living designed to guarantee the desired goal, the redemption, may now be stated. Activity, having been considered to have a binding consequence leading to transmigration, must either be renounced and thus its transmigratory consequence nullified or the grace of God must be invoked as powerful enough to counteract it or some other method and plan must be formulated which will secure release from the bondage of activity. For activity is quite essential, and activity which is ordained and proper is a purifying agency. It must, therefore, be carried on. Even in the case of highly evolved and liberated souls there is social reason for their carrying on their usual activity. As Lord Kṛṣṇa declares (III, 20-6) about Himself and such persons as the venerable and model king Janaka, and the reason for his engaging Himself in routine activity, the social reason is social welfare, carrying the common people with oneself, preventing any possible misconception on their part that they may avoid routine and usual activity which is so necessary not only for the upkeep of an individual but also for society.

Lord Kṛṣṇa found out a way to avoid the transmigratory consequences of activity without violating His insistence on moral endeavour and using the power of God's grace inherent in any religious theory of devotion to God. He found scope for moral endeavour in an individual's non-attachment to and selfness about all activity that he engages in. And as much of the mental and moral ill of activity is a direct result of the expectation of its fruits, a person who engages in all activity without any thought of its fruit may be said to have risen superior to the common evil of activity. In effect in a way he may be said to be not 'really' acting (IV, 20). With this view firmly held Lord Kṛṣṇa told Arjuna that man has a right only to activity, asked him and other men not to expect any fruits of their activity, and forbade him and others to indulge in non-active life in a verse (II, 47) which is a bye-word with many élite Hindus even today when the study of Sanskrit language has dwindled so much. He exhorted Arjuna and others to do their work without any attachment, and with perfect indifference about success or failure in it. Finally working on the key of indifference Kṛṣṇa made an important declaration equating the equanimity-attitude towards activity and its consequences with the then standard philosophy and practice of equanimity-'Yoga' (II, 48).

This, Lord Kṛṣṇa affirming 'samatva' as 'Yoga' equated 'Yoga' with indifference towards the result of one's active work, disposed of satisfactorily the subjective side of work, the consideration of it from the viewpoint of the agent. Viewing work or activity from the side of work or activity itself Kṛṣṇa equally firmly, perhaps even more patently, identified 'Yoga' with skill in one's work or activity, asserting in the next but one verse (II, 50) 'yogaḥ karmasu kauśalam'.

The philosophy of work or activity presented as an entirely new doctrine in the *Bhagavadgītā* may be stated to be : "The habit of doing every piece of work well and conscientiously, without any expectation of results, as an end in itself and for its sake, is as good as the practice of full Yoga-technique and the consequent spiritual upliftment."[32] This is a grand philosophy of work propounded at a time when such or analogous ideas were rare. It stood India well as a working faith and a social philosophy, reaping her in the next ten centuries or so a rich harvest of splendid artistic, literary and academic achievements. And it is the products of this harvest that have immortalized her !

Consistent with the theistic philosophy centred in Kṛṣṇa-Viṣṇu as personal God, the practitioner of this philosophy of work is enjoined and exhorted to cultivate the habit of dedicating all work to God, Kṛṣṇa-Viṣṇu, as an offering and in token of his complete surrender to the will of God. God's grace is then promised as a help towards liberation from the usual binding consequences of activity, either directly or through the medium of correct knowledge which God's grace can bestow (III, 30 ; IV, 24 ; V, 10 ; X, 10-11 ; XII, 6-7 ; 10-11 ; XVIII, 56-7).

Sacrifice of the standard variety, Vedic proper, or more properly of the kind of daily ones, called the five great sacrifices[33] have been enjoined since about the end of the Vedic period to be offered by the twice-born castes as a purificatory procedure. Purification of body and mind to make them both receptive to religious consciousness and piety, being only an extension of the idea of ceremonial purity, an adjunct of the sacrificial religion of the Vedas, may be said to have been a routine item in the pattern of Hindu religious living from before 500 B.C. When, therefore, the *BhG* spoke of the triad of sacrifice, charity, and penance or austerity, it only stated the current view, and by its acceptance of it emphasized it.

The lower octave of austerity in the form of penance for divesting oneself from impurity or sin, too, has been in evidence from very early times. Either as 'prāyaścitta' or as 'kṛcchra', penance is known from the later Vedas.[34] In the *Gautama-dharmasūtra* (26, 10-12 ; 19, 12) muttering, 'japa', of some of the hymns of the *RV* is prescribed as purificatory rites or as 'prāyascittas', penances. All of them and many more in connection with expiation of certain offences and sins, with the prescribed number of mutterings in each case, are found in the *Manusmṛti* (XI, 248-60), with the same objective. This fact shows continuity of tradition in Hinduism and its syncretic nature, making the Vedic past serve the Hindu present, in a way appropriate in the changed circumstances of the view of God-head and of the goal of religious living. The morning and evening prayers known as 'sandhyā-vandana', 'sandhyā'-adoration, since long prescribed for the twice-born is an epitome and a complex illustrating this statement. A complete account of it, with translations of important Vedic verses to be quoted during its performance, is available in Monier William's *Religious Thought and Life in India* (pp. 401-8). Fruits of Vedic religious consciousness are used generally as purificatory, valedictory and benedictory technique.

Taking one's food is a kind of sacrifice in Hinduism, though since when it came to be so treated we have no knowledge at present. The kind of food taken by a person and the spirit and temperament he shows have been considered to be related as cause and effect at least since the time of the *Chāndogya Upaniṣad* (VII, 26, 2). For it is stated in the text referred to in the brackets that a person's spirit and temperament are purified if he takes pure food, whatever might have been the food or foods which were then considered as pure. And as early as the *Śatapatha Brāhmaṇa* (I, 1, 1)[35] there was a curiosity about food and fasting. Perhaps fasting—food-taking being such an essential and routine affair—had a particular value as a vow, being an abstention (?). We are told in the above-mentioned text that there was one sage who observed fasting as a vow. Discussing his practice the text points out that taking nothing at all would land one into a particular religious anomaly, while eating one's food on a particular day, the day to be observed as a fast, would lead to the perpetration of sin against gods. The conclusion, which is very interesting as testifying to the tenacious continuity of tradition in Hinduism, is reached that one should eat on such a day, a fasting day, only roots and fruits which are the products of forests. Strict fast-observers of even to-day would take only such fare on a fast day! It goes without saying that fast thus observed was considered to be a meritorious act even since before the time of the *Śatapatha Brāhmaṇa*, i.e., from at least about 900 B.C.

Fasting, in the foregoing work, is referred to as 'anaśana', non-eating. Not long after the work must have come the material which forms the *Bṛdāraṇyaka Upaniṣad* and the *Chāndogya Upaniṣad*. In the former, complete fasting is called 'anāśaka' (IV, 5, 21) and in the latter 'anāśakāyana' (VIII, 5, 3). In the former it is a qualifying adjunct of 'tapas', austerity, thus giving us the valuable information that fasting, by the time of the *Bṛhadāraṇyaka Upaniṣad*, i.e., by the 8th century B.C., had come to be regarded as a variety of austerity. In the *ChU* passage it is equated with celibacy. In the *BhG* there is a reference to terrific austerity contrary to the injunctions of the sacred law which is condemned by Lord Kṛṣṇa as distressing to the five elemental constituents of human personality (XVII, 5-6). While distinguishing three varieties and grades of austerity, Lord Kṛṣṇa favours mental and disinterested austerity as the best, and instances austerity distressing oneself or intended to harm others, as the worst (XVII, 16-19) and therefore to be avoided. Perhaps limited and moderate fasting for purification was contemplated to be recommended. For moderate and controlled eating, 'yuktāhāra', is praised by the Lord (*BhG*, VI, 17). Jñāneśvara commenting on the earlier verses mentions (XVII, 257) along with such acts as keeping oneself enclosed in live coal or carrying burning resins on one's head, purposeless [unordained] fasting as an instance of the condemned variety of austerity.

The *Manusmṛti* (XI, 194-5), carrying on the tradition of the earlier age, continued in a developed form in the normative literature of the last few centuries before the Christian era, fully established fasting under the title of 'kṛcchra', penance, as a respectable and accredited mode of self-purification (XI, 208-221).

Fasting at regular intervals on stated days has continued to be an ordained item in the complex of religious living among all sects, significant differences pertaining only to specific days and less so to the total number of fasts. Fasting is a regular mode of both self-purification and of propitiation of the deity in whose name the fast is undertaken.

Now I may mention the grand finale of the *Gītā*-'dharma', the specific exhortation or rather injunction of Lord Kṛṣṇa regarding the carrying out of the regimen as a self-enterprise to turn it into a spiritual endeavour designed to achieve the desired-for redemption. In *BhG*, VI, 5 the Lord asks mortals to raise themselves by themselves giving His reason for His injunction in the next verse. And it is that unless one's self is conquered and befriended all effort and all so-called spiritual benefit remains shaky. The *Gītā* asks (IV, 34) Arjuna and us mortals to take knowledge from those who know, by supplicating and, be it remembered, by asking searching questions ('paripraśna'). Having done that, during which process the act of questioning has convinced one's reason and not stupefied it, one has to put in one's own further endeavour to perfect the 'dharma'-complex for oneself, trusting only to God, to whom one has surrendered as a worshipper and a devotee, to help one in achieving the self-realization for which one is endeavouring. There can be no middleman, no intercessor, except one's own moral and spiritual endeavour, in the spiritual process advocated in the *Bhagavadgītā*.

The emphasis laid by the *Gītā* on its 'dharma' being practised as a self-endeavour and which was implicit in the earlier theory of religious living in the form of the fourth stage of life, 'āśrama', wherein one had to seek salvation by oneself living as an ascetic in a solitary condition, established the pre-eminence of inner direction of religious life. Even the *Manusmṛti*, which is a book full of ritualistic rules and regulations and is embedded in the purely authoritarian spirit, makes allowance for inner direction in its definition of 'dharma' and the specification of its sources. The Vedas are the infallible source of sacred law, 'dharma', no doubt ; but not only is the conduct of well-behaved men of character, another source, but so, too, is the inner voice of the person concerned still another. Such in effect is the full connotation of the first and the sixth verses of the second chapter of the book. In the words of the *Manusmṛti* the satisfaction of oneself and the concurrence of one's heart[36] are relevant considerations and factors of the 'dharma' an individual has to practise. It is noticeable that this inner reference is also present in the appeal to character, 'śīla', of the learned and well-behaved persons whose conduct and memory are mentioned as another source of 'dharma'. And Hārīta, another but later writer on sacred law, lists the following thirteen qualities and traits as constituting character ('śīla')[37] : "Brahminhood, devotion towards gods and manes, meekness, non-disturbance of others, absence of malice, softness, absence of harshness, friendliness, endearing talk, gracefulness, helpfulness, compassion and tranquillity."

It is in keeping with this that, in the midst of meticulous regulations about physical mortifications and ritualistic acts, and in the atmosphere fully saturated with externalist approach to offences and sins, the *Manusmṛti* (XI, 227) should find an honourable place for remorse or repentance, 'anutāpa', as a restorer of the moral and spiritual balance in human personality which is upset by the commission of an offence or a sin. "A man who has committed sin gets free from it by performing penance but he is purified only by his affirmation of his resolve not to do it again." (*Manusmṛti*, XI, 230).

The nine-itemed complex of devotion was enlarged by most of the Vaiṣṇavite sects under the preaching of the principal propounders of the sectarian doctrines, like Rāmānuja, Madhva, Vallabha and Caitanya. The extension observed in the school of Rāmānuja-thought and practice, is the repetition of the twelve-lettered formula, 'om namo bhagavate Vāsudevāya', 'Om, bow to Lord Vāsudeva', or the eight-lettered formula, which is more common in the Rāmānuja sect, 'Om, namo Nārāyaṇāya', 'Om, bow to Nārāyaṇa'. The 'sakhya' or companionship-item out of the earlier nine is, however, dropped. The other extensions including imprinting of Vaiṣṇava emblems on one's body, and observing fasts, placing 'tulasī'-leaves on the idol of the deity, drinking the water with which God's feet are washed, and eating the food first offered to God etc. are common to both the Rāmānuja and the Madhva sects. The former sect has many of the moral virtues mentioned in the *BhG* in its code of purifying behaviour. The latter sect, however, counting the extensions among its eighteen enjoined observances, has some which harken back to the *Gītā* and the *Upaniṣads*, both selfless and unattached activity and meditation figuring in them. Love of God is one of the items, which is not found in the nine-itemed complex of the *Bhāgavata-Purāṇa*. But it is the noblest form of love "consequent on the knowledge of God's greatness and his being the best of all".[38] The extravagance of the sectarian practice lay in branding the Vaiṣṇava emblems on the body, which has now fallen into disuse and may fortunately be said to be extinct.

The two North-Indian sects of Vallabha and Caitanya have laid down a ten-itemed complex of devotion, the tenth item being their special extension. It is known in the former school as 'Premabhakti',[39] or devotion through love. It is alternatively known as 'vātsalya', tenderness. But this tenderness is of the type which is said to have existed between the cowherdesses of Vṛndāvan-Mathurā and youthful Kṛṣṇa. The item therefore is more properly characterized as 'madhurabhāva', sweet sentiment of love, which is an alternative term used in the sectarian literature to describe the tenth item of the 'bhakti'-complex of the sect.[40]

In the Caitanyite sect this 'madhurabhāva' or 'madhurā bhakti' is much more prominent and is spoken of as 'madhura rasa', sweet flavour. The sweetness further is centred round Rādhā as the lady-love of Kṛṣṇa. It is therefore a tender feeling like that of a girl for her lover.[41]

The mode of approach to the deity in the Vallabhite sect may be said to be of elaborate worship of God, and perhaps even more of the head of the sect as preceptor and virtual representative of the deity. The worship procedure of the deity will be described a little later. It must be mentioned here that the exaggerated importance the sect-head has received in this sect is contrary to the preaching of Lord Kṛṣṇa in the matter. In the two South-Indian sects water drunk by worshippers as holy water is that with which the deity's feet are washed but in the Vallabhite sect, 'caraṇāmṛta' means water in which the Guru's feet are washed.

The mode of approach in the Caitanyite school is that of extreme ecstasy, brought about through incessant muttering and uttering of the names of God, Hari, singing his praises, playing music which is devotional and emotional, as well as making bodily contortions and a kind of dance, almost frenzied.[42] The type of religious living may be said to be a state of ecstasy procured through varied extra-rational procedure. Frenzied ecstasy cannot be trusted to respect rules of morality. To that extent this school, too, has strayed away far from the ennobling path laid out in the *Bhagavadgītā*.

Tulasīdāsa, the next important saint-poet-preacher, and one whose influence must be counted as more than equal to that of any three of the other saint-poet-preachers of India, adheres to the complex of nine-itemed 'bhakti' as the appropriate pattern of religious living, calculated to take the practitioner to the desired goal. He has, however, changed the content of the items and has dwelt on the cultivation of moral virtues even perhaps more prominently and incessantly than the *Bhagavadgītā*. His complex of 'bhakti', as already mentioned, is directed to Rāma.

Rāma himself—the device used by Tulasīdāsa to put his ideas on the nine-itemed complex in the mouth of Rāma as expounding them to the great archetype of Rāma-devotees, the Śabara lady known as Śabarī, is suggestive of his intent to put his complex against that of the *Bhāgavata-Purāṇa* and also of the *Bhagavadgītā*, 'bhakti' in the latter work having been expounded by Lord Kṛṣṇa himself—describes 'navadhā bhakti', ninefold devotion (*Tulasīkṛta Rāmāyaṇa*, III, dohās 58 and 59).

The first item in this complex of 'bhakti' is association with saints ('santa-saṅga'). This mode of mediate approach through one's association with and company of saints assumed such significance with Tulasīdāsa that he describes the third item of devotion again as referring to it, it being a deeper appreciation of such saints, though it is described as the service of one's 'guru', spiritual preceptor. The other items and modes of the complex are : (2) To take delight in listening to stories of Rāma's life, the fourth and fifth and the seventh being higher octaves of this ; (4) To sing the praises of Rāma ; (5) To mutter or utter the sacred chant based on Rāma's name, which Tulasīdāsa asserts is proclaimed as a mode of devotion in the Vedas [?] the seventh mode being an intensification of this. (6) The so-called sixth item is a compound one, consisting of the most essential of moral qualities and activities. It prescribes the cultivation of self-control of the senses and of moral character as well as indifference towards the worldly goods and engrossment in good deeds, the eighth adding contentment and absence of faultfinding. The seventh item of the complex prescribes that Rāma should be understood to be everywhere and saints should be valued even more than Rāma. The ninth mode is really speaking an epitome of the whole complex consisting as it does of the cultivation of the absence of malice and the practice of simplicity together with an intense and fervent faith in Rāma, accompanied by perfect equanimity rising superior to the emotions of joy and sorrow.

It can be seen that Tulasīdāsa's ninefold 'bhakti' complex is essentially an amalgam of three principal constituents, viz., (1) Fervent devotion to and intense faith in Rāma, which naturally shows itself in overt behaviour, other than that of worship, in the form of repeating his name, listening to and singing his praises and the great deeds of his life;[43] (2) Great respect for saints, and more particularly for one's spiritual preceptor, and close associations with them for constant enlightenment ;[44] and (3) Cultivation of most of the desirable moral qualities and of good conduct culminating in perfect equanimity in routine behaviour.[45] His mention of the standard formula of nine-itemed 'bhakti' as 'śravaṇādika navabhakti',[46] the nine modes of devotion beginning with remembrance of name, is conclusive evidence of his faith in the complex he evidently formulated as against the standard one. The relationship between God and the devotee worshipper, however, remains that of the master and the servant.[47]

About sixty to seventy years later in Maharashtra, Rāmadāsa, an activistic ascetic who galvanized the people for political action in defence of their religion, wrote his *Dāsabodha*, which is perhaps the most systematic of all, as it is one of the rarest of independent treatises on it, in a vernacular language produced between the end of the thirteenth century and the beginning of the eighteenth. In it Rāmadāsa devotes a whole section (IVth) out of the twenty comprising the treatise to explain in detail the nine-itemed 'bhakti'-complex of the Vaiṣṇava sect as laid down in the *Bhāgavata-Purāṇa*, each item having a chapter to itself. The item of 'śravaṇa', the first in the list, as it is expounded by Rāmadāsa appears expanded and more comprehensive both in desirable and also in undesirable ways due to the inveterately persisting habit of syncretism. The desirable extension includes in 'śravaṇa' the whole of theology and philosophy, and the undesirable one consists in many different types of 'incantations', 'miracle-formulae', 'yantras' or mystic figures, and meditation on mystic forms (IV, 1, 22 ; 32). The impress of the *Gītā*-'dharma' is reflected in the fact that 'manana' or thinking over what is listened to is further included in it (VII, 8 ; VII, 9 ; XVII, 3).

The second item is 'kīrtana' or narration or telling stories about God's, Viṣṇu's, great deeds done for the sake of sorrow-immersed and frail humanity. By the time Rāmadāsa appeared on the Indian scene of Maharashtrian variety this type of religious activity was very highly developed, especially in Maharashtra and Bengal. It had also come to have a new appellation side by side with the old one, the new one specifying the narrative activity as stories regarding Hari ('Harikathā' or 'Harikīrtana'). The technique developed by the early leaders of this activity—they appear to have been intuitive experts in what is modernly called the theory of group-communication—to create ecstasy among the participants was the periodic chant in chorus of certain names of God and of very short formulae to the accompaniment of rhythmic and periodic jingling instrumental music. This whole set was designated 'bhajana', which etymologically means worship or adoration but must be rendered as 'chanting names of God or/and short or long hymns on Him in chorus to the accompaniment of appropriately jingling and periodic instrumental music'. The increased importance of this mode of religious living, making attainment of ecstatic delight an essential and certain component of it, is shown by Rāmadāsa's devoting three additional chapters in other sections of his treatise (VI, 7 ; XIV, 4 and 5). The preacher who conducts this type of devotional meet had, by then, been given the designation of 'haridāsa', servant of Hari. The influence of the *Gītā*-teaching is reflected even in an extension of the nature of this mode of religious living. In a separate chapter (X, 7) Rāmadāsa emphasizes the great significance of hymn-singing activity being conducted without any desire and in a perfectly disinterested manner.

In describing the mode of 'bhakti' called 'pādasevana' in the Purāṇa-text, which is really tautology as pointed out already, Rāmadāsa obviates its criticism as tautology by falling in line with the new religious set up of the post-classical age and lauding reverential attitude and approach to one's 'Guru' or spiritual preceptor (IV, 4). In the invocatory chapters of the book, after invocations to deity, Rāmadāsa has devoted one to invocatory praise of what he has rightly named 'sadguru', true preceptor (I, 4). He has further dilated on the great value of a true preceptor for one's religious endeavour in many other places (V, 1, 34-46 ; VII, 10, 38-44 and IV, 5-10). He has, however, not only insisted on appropriate qualifications of a true preceptor (V, 2) but has asked the disciple to be on his guard and to some extent at least to make an intellectual endeavour. Such warning and circumspection, even though it is a fall from the *Gītā*-position on this matter, is a distinct gain over the utterly servile attitude and practice laid down by Rāmadāsa's greater predecessor, Jñāneśvara (*Jñānesvarī*, XIII, 369-459).

Rāmadāsa's description of the seventh mode of 'bhakti' known as 'dāsya', servitude, gives us the picture of a religious living which is more active than perhaps any before its time. Institutions, endowments and services calculated to help people in distress and to increase aesthetic and intellectual pleasure among all, in short, conducive to the all-round increase of happiness, as well as those leading to better and richer ritual services to the deities—all are to be covered by this activity of a worshipper, and therefore are the visual effects of the mode of 'bhakti' called 'dāsya', servitude. Service to man is in effect service to God (IV, 7).

The eighth mode of 'bhakti', viz., companionship or friendship, is in effect to live in the presence of the will of God for His kindness is like the love of one's mother. One should therefore converse with Him through confession to oneself and seek refuge in His will and mercy.

The ninth and the highest and the most developed mode of 'bhakti' in Rāmadāsa's view is nothing short of realization of the oneness of God and his ubiquity and also of the unity of self and God (IV, 9). Later in the treatise in one whole chapter (XII, 5) he again reverts to this aspect and asserts even more unequivocally that 'ātmanivedana', dedication of self, so-called, is nothing but the realization by oneself of the unity of oneself with Absolute Brahman.

The grand notion of Absolute Brahman as the one Reality in the cosmos and of the identity of the individual soul with that Absolute, which is missed through 'illusion', 'māyā', or nescience, 'avidyā', as adumbrated by the Upaniṣadic sages and freely propounded by Śaṅkarācārya has ever afterwards stood at the background of most of the religious thought of India!

The exposition of the activity of the three dispositions of 'sattva', 'rajas' and 'tamas' brought into the complex of religious living by the *Bhagavadgītā* is followed up and appropriately expanded by Rāmadāsa, expressing *inter alia* the requirements of the more dynamic type of it which had come to be formulated by him. Thus among the many activities, attitudes and practices typical of the higher disposition 'sattva', and therefore tacitly recommended, and even enjoined on the religiously striving people, figure eagerness to lead people on the right path by teaching them, to feel sorrow at the distress of others and joy at their happiness to look upon others' faults as one's own, and in short to do active service for the betterment of the lot of one's fellowmen, and such other modern-looking attitudes and activities (II, 7-8; XIX, 4). Most of the religious-looking practices, which are really speaking magic and degrading superstition, torturing and mortifying rituals, on the other hand, are credited to the preponderance of the 'ṭamas' disposition (II, 6).

Rāmadāsa has gone further than other writers on religion in outlining a daily routine for one who desires to live a life of striving for redemption (XI,3). The items begin with one's early rising in the morning and end with the exhortation that not only knowledge, not even meditation along with it, but also activity combined with them both is the way to redemption. Among the morning duties besides the strictly religious ones, like worshipping the deities, figure regular study and both thought over it and discussion with others on the topics of one's reading.

The philosophy of work, that aspect of it particularly which lauded skilful and conscientious performance of any work as 'Yoga', as a valuable religious instrument, found special favour with this activistic ascetic, who did his part in energizing the people of Maharashtra in the cause of the preservation of their religion and culture. He has devoted two chapters (XIX, 1-2) to impress upon the class of people whose occupation and duty were to write, and to expound the great need, almost as a religious requisite, to cultivate excellent hand-writing to be admired both for its beauty and its legibility, and to write the books accordingly in a beautiful format and appearance as well as to keep them in equally good condition.

In Rāmadāsa's teaching combined with Tukārāma's devotional activity Vaiṣṇava scheme of religious living may be said to have reached its culmination. It became a compassionate humanism suffused by ecstatic worship.*

This humanistic and organizational development which was so late in Vaiṣṇavism occurred very early within the Śaiva sect, whose scheme of religious living for the desired redemption has been both simpler, more ethically accented and, incongruously enough, cruder and more mechanistically oriented.

In a number of Upaniṣads of rather late date, the earliest of which is perhaps the *Atharvaśiras*, some of the practices forming the later and current Śaiva scheme of religious living have been prescribed with such strong and fervent exhortation that one can understand the tenacity with which they have persisted in one or other of the subsects of Śaivism.

R. G. Bhandarkar's[48] résumé of the scheme of religious living as interpreted by an old commentator on the *Atharvaśiras Upaniṣad* is so succinct that I cannot do better than quote the following relevant portion of it: "For the knowledge of Rudra [which of course effects the desired redemption] one should use moderate food, devote himself to listening ('śravaṇa'), thinking ('manana'), etc., become a Paramahaṁsa or a single-minded devotee, and spend his time thus . . . One should undertake a vow . . . [and] Greed and anger should be given up. Forgiveness should be realised. The muttering of Om should be practised, and meditation resulting in [true] perception, should be resorted to."

And now I come to the more mechanical oriented prescription laid down in the same work. Its precept to the worshipper or follower to besmear this his body with (sacred) ashes is accompanied by a behest to repeat a formula, while carrying out the precept daily, which equates the ashes with the twenty-four or all the cosmic elemental constituents including the senses and the mind.[49] The *Bṛhajjābāla Upaniṣad* is so full of the praise and prescription of the sacred ashes as a redemption instrument that it speaks of ashes, which in Sanskrit

* It is not suggested that these two saints were the sole or even the greatest of the contributors to this development which has a long line of illustrious preachers, saints, poets and philosophers from Rāmānanda, through Kabīra, Narasiṁha Mehta and Ekanātha. They are the latest ones and as brilliant in their fields as any of their great predecessors.

is 'bhasma', burnt thing or residue, as 'vibhūti', majesty, which is the more current later term for sacred ashes, and may be called 'Vibhūtiyoga', a treatise on redemption through the use of 'vibhūti'. The text suggests the etymology of the latter term and in effect gives its justification when it describes it as the bringer in or producer of great majesty ('mahāvibhūti').[50] Another item which is much insisted on is the wearing of beads known as 'rudrākṣa' (Elaeocarpus ganitrus). And a whole Upaniṣad[51] deals with their varieties and significance.

In the subsection, which is known merely as the Śaiva system, one of the components of the whole complex of religious living, that called the 'Yoga' part, consists very largely of 'yoga' practice and meditation, concentration and such other intensely psycho-moral practices. And in the Vīraśaiva or Liṅgāyat subsect the highest of the God-seekers is one who, going through the whole discipline of observing all the vows and restraints, practises truth, morality and cleanliness etc. with a firm belief in the unity of God.[52] The importance attached to the preceptor and to the grace of God in the *Śvetāśvatara Upaniṣad* continue in most of the subsects of the Śaivas in a more developed form and particularly is this so in the last mentioned subsect.

'Japa' or muttering of God's name and/or of some formula embodying one's surrender to God, in this case Śiva, is, as pointed out above, a constituent of the complex of religious living conducive to redemption. Śaivism, in the present state of our knowledge, is clearly the first sect to have devised a formula and prescribed its muttering. At least it is the Śaiva formula that is recorded in literature as having been in use by religious-minded people in the popular Sanskrit book called *Pañcatantra*[53], which must have been composed in the fifth century or perhaps earlier but not later. We learn from the use of that formula that its pronouncement was a prelude to an appropriate gesture of obeisance to a Śaiva ascetic. The formula, characterized in the work as 'Śivamantra', Śiva-chant, and as six-lettered, is 'Om namaḥ Śivāya', Om, bow to Śiva. Apparswami, one of the famous trio of Tamilian Śaiva saints, who must have lived before 9th century A.D., composed a whole hymn of three verses in praise of that formula, with the Vedic Brahmanic 'Om' dropped out. The formula is, therefore, rightly known, as the five-lettered one as Apparswami himself spoke of it, in Tamil country.[54]

Private worship, i.e., worship of the idol of a deity in the household has been a very old practice as already pointed out. It is enjoined as a help in the religious enterprise, to be performed daily by an individual, whether he be a Vaiṣṇava or a Śaiva. We know[55] that by the 7th century A.D. the complex of Śiva-worship as performed by an individual had come to be known as 'pañcopacāra pūjā', five-itemed worship, i.e., a worship in which five different items were to be gone through as offering of service to the deity. We know, on the other hand, that for ages the whole complex of worship as practised by Vaiṣṇavas, whether in the individual household form or in the public temple form, has comprised sixteen items of service and has been appropriately known as 'ṣodaśopacāra pūja', sixteen-itemed worship. R. G. Bhandarkar[56] accepted its earliest mention in this form to be the same as a Rāmānuja-follower contended, and that is in the *Padma-Purāṇa*. The household form of worship current even among the Śaivites is known to be identically styled.[57] The main difference between domestic worship and temple ritual has lain in royal richness of items and the paraphernalia of the latter in contrast with the simpler objects and things, with a number of substitutes for actual things and objects and some make-believe arrangements in the domestic worship. I shall have to deal with temple worship for more reasons than one in the chapter on Hindu shrines. To avoid unnecessary repetition I shall desist from describing the household worship. Prayer, too, being an organic part of the complex of worship will have to be dealt with in the last chapter.

Ascetic element, too, manifested itself the earliest within Śaivism.[58] Asceticism centred round Śiva temples evidently quite early. The large number of ascetics reported by the Chinese traveller Hiuen Tsang of the 7th century testify to this feature of Śaivism in the North. But even earlier, as stated by me elsewhere[59], Śaivism had reached the South, almost the extreme South-east. And the testimony of the popular Sanskrit book of stories, *Pañcatantra*, which pushes back the date of Śaiva currency in the South by two to three centuries, is quite conclusive for the prevalence not only of Śaiva asceticism there but also for its organised work in the cause of the cultivation of learning and of propagation of religious doctrines. We are told of an ascetic and his troubles in his monastery—the Sanskrit word used is the regular technical term for such an institution, viz., 'maṭha'—which was also a temple of Mahādeva, i.e., Śiva. We also learn from the account that it was a big institution with many workers. Further it was a most difficult task in those days to maintain and manage an institution of that kind. And what is intriguingly interesting is the fact that it was situated in what is modern Mylapore near Madras, its Sanskrit name having been Mahilāropya. It is from this place that the great Southern centre of the Ramakrishna Mission founded by Swami Vivekananda has been carrying on its varied work of a religious and social nature since 1897. I have already brought together in my *Indian Sadhus* (pp. 55-6) some epigraphical evidence establishing not only the currency of such institutions in the South in the 10th and 11th centuries but also showing that their work was of a social welfare nature. That it must have been a fairly developed form of compassionate humanism is further supported by epigraphical evidence about the activities of the Golaki 'maṭha' in Andhra Pradesh[60], which included even the running of a maternity home, in the 13th century.

Hindu view of the goal of religious life thus has been freedom from the necessity of recurrent birth and death. The plan of religious living is meant to achieve that goal, the redemption, in one's present birth or, in the alternative, through a number of successive ones. As it is a rare phenomenon for anyone to achieve the redemption in one particular existence, it is incumbent on any God-seeking or religious-minded person to live one's present life in an ethically correct and socially useful pattern, exercising one's potentialities to the best, so as to guarantee a better next birth. In this process compassionate humanism has found an appropriate place in the ideology and practice of both the main sects of Hinduism, viz., Śaivism and Vaiṣṇavism.

In the chorus of deprecation of mundane existence, in the concert of praise of striving to break away from the so-called chained wheel of recurrent birth it is a portent that one of the most ecstatic of Vaiṣṇava preachers and devotees, the Maharashtrian saint-poet Tukārāma, in the second quarter of the 17th century—I think Caitanya, Mirābāi and Tukārāma are the trio that carries the palm for ecstatic preaching and devotion—should have strayed away in moments of rare vision from the usual path of God-seeking chants and expressed the goal of his God-seeking, in a more modern idiom. There are at least four or five verses among his famous chants, outpourings of his yearning—for-God-heart, which express the fervent desire to serve saints and God in birth after birth. They form such a tiny fraction of the whole outpouring, which is nothing but a chorus and a concert harping on the dire need of immediate release from mundane existence, that I should have desisted from mentioning their sentiment as in any way significant. But the established practice of the great Maharashtrian tradition of preaching through 'kīrtana', of which Tukārāma was the unequalled master, of repeating the most emphatic and outspoken of these verses, the one which is numbered 962 in the current collection of his chants known as the '*Gāthā*', is a good enough ground and justification for my singling them out as a fresh and original contribution of this prince of God-seeking men to Vaiṣṇavism in particular and generally to Hinduism. The verse mentioned above is usually repeated at the end of many types of worship, especially those which entail group-participation. It reads : "Oh God ! grant me this gift that I may never forget you, that I should sing your virtues with great delight and as the be-all and end-all of my life. I want neither salvation nor wealth but grant me the uninterrupted company of saints. If you will do this You may with the greatest pleasure decree another [and still another] birth for me". The purifying company of religious-minded God-seekers and one's inclination towards and persistence in God-seeking are enough to counterbalance the usual disadvantages and demerits of mundane existence. Opportunity to be engaged in the process of self-purification tends to become the new goal of religious living rather than cessation of birth and death.

This sentiment of a fervent Vaiṣṇava God-seeker of the 17th century proved a veritable prevision of the development that was to occur in Hinduism about two hundred and fifty years thereafter. For Swami Vivekananda, who founded the Ramakrishna Mission in 1897 for active humanistic work, proclaimed this new faith in a more pronouncedly active and intensely social idiom : He says : "May I be born and reborn again and suffer a thousand miseries if only I am able to worship the only God in whom I believe, the sum total of all souls, and above all my God, the wicked, my God, the afflicted, my God, the poor of all the races."[61]

CHAPTER XII

THE MESOPOTAMIAN SHRINE

THE material embodiment of religious consciousness is the shrine, which houses some kind of representation, or has something which reminds those present, of the "holy", and is quite distinctive of every one of them. In the past, in the case of the extinct religious complexes, the same was the situation. The sacred structure, the shrine, the temple, of no two of them was alike.

The main shrine of Mesopotamians since the chalcolithic period had throughout their history been built on a high built-up platform. The Ziggurat, or the 'high place', the stage-tower as it was called, is a peculiar feature of the Mesopotamian architecture.[1] One of the very early temples, the one at Eridu, which was rebuilt and enlarged no less than six times, in its last form stood on a platform 26.5 m. long and more than 16 m. wide, and the temple on it measured 23.5 m. long by 12.5 m. It consisted of a long cella with an altar at one end and a podium or offerings-table near the other and was flanked by chambers arranged laterally on either side. And that form remained more or less the standard for most temples of Mesopotamia.[2]

The next landmark, which so far remains unique among the temple-structures even of Mesopotamia, is formed by the picturesque temple, standing almost on one edge of a high platform and approached by a flight of stone-steps, constructed as an integral part of the platform, at al 'Ubaid dedicated by King Aannipadda of the 1st dynasty of Ur about 2700 B.C. It bore against the temple wall—like those of the White Temple at Erech they were white, it should be carefully noted—copper statues of bulls, with a copper-frieze of reclining cattle worked in relief coming higher up. Above these there was a mosaic frieze of a milking scene. Higher up still a bird-frieze decorated the outside of the temple wall. The porch of the temple stood so on the edge that the steps provided led direct into it. The beams and supporting columns of the porch were of wood overlaid with polished copper. The lintel was supported on mosaic columns, above which was set into the wall a huge copper relief plaque, 7 ft. 9 inches long and 3 feet 6 inches high, showing the mythical bird, Imgig or Imdugud.[3] Well can one appreciate Woolley, the brilliant restorer, waxing eloquent about it as it must have appeared originally. He says : "We can picture the whole building as something very gay and fanciful, the gold and colour of its decoration vivid against the white walls, and we can admire the skill with which elements of the decoration are graded according to their height from ground . . . and the knowledge of perspective which prefers simpler and broader effects for the top row of all."

This 1st dynasty Ubaid temple so far stands unique among all the temples known in the Mesopotamian past in having the symbolic adornment and also in the decorative use of both metals and shell and other materials for mosaic. All this disappears in the development of temple architecture, a feature very much in need of explanation, which followed. The later adornment, excepting that of the most famous Ziggurat, that of Babylon, that too of the later period, consisted in the blue colour of the bricks and in sculptures representing the receipt of the divine order or prompting by the king or the governor for the building of the temple, and depicting its actual execution by the king or the governor, leading the labour force engaged in it. The white colour of the walls which disappeared about 2500 B.C. reappeared in the Semitic religious complex about the 7th century A.D. when Islamic shrines, the mosques, began to be built.

In the development, the first feature, it appears, that received aggrandisement was the number of stages by which the tower rose so that it began to have three to seven stages, rearing its temple-head as high as fifty yards according to Saggs. Woolley having reconstructed the second famous Ziggurat temple of Mesopotamia, the ziggurat of Ur, tells us that the tower, as reconstructed by Nebuchadnezzar and Nabonidus in the early part of the 6th century B.C., held the Holy of Holies of the moon-god Nannar "just over a hundred and sixty feet" high.[4] Evidently Mesopotamians were soaring higher and higher in the implementation of their ideas about gods and their heaven. Heaven was already in Sumerian times named Dilmun and was conceived of as a "land of immortality where there is neither sickness nor death", but strangely devoid of fresh water. But according to Sumerian theologians it was meant for gods alone and not for mortal man. A saying current among them ran : "Who is tall enough to reach up to heaven". Only one mortal man named Zinsudra, a pious king, by zealous worship of gods saved through their special favour from the Deluge, is said to have been admitted there.[5] The Mesopotamians, therefore, could not have thought of reaching the adorants there as they seem never to have aspired to be with their gods in eternal bliss after death. As a matter of fact no adorant, except the priest and perhaps the king, could ever have been permitted to reach the Holy of Holies. The tower-temple was thus only symbolic of the abode of gods as the high heaven. Its prestige value as impressive structure and as showing the builder's mastery over all kinds of material resources was the incentive that determined its aggrandisement.

In the meanwhile there was going on diversification of priestly functions and increase of magical incantations as well as the number of women of all types to be attached to the temple. Theologians' systematization of the pantheon and the assignment of consorts and attendant or subordinate gods to the major ones, too, necessitated erection of shrines, independent though perhaps small, to more than one god in the vicinity of the temple of the principal one. The development of the seasonal festivals and the needs of the processions accompanying their celebration was another call on space within the precincts of the temple. The temple properties, their management and the domestic industries organized in that connection requiring numerous manual workers, and clerks for keeping check and accounts, were another source of the extension of the temple area. Add to this the functional need of keeping numerous tablets, bearing appropriate incantational texts for the use of the priests, and also of the very laudable, though perhaps a byeproduct of the procedure, institution of the school conducted by the priests. One can realize the forces working in favour of extension of the temple area, the increase in the number of temples within it and of the rooms and courts required to be provided for therein. The rise in the height of the stage-tower might have received additional impetus from the Mesopotamians' appreciation of the relation between horizontal spread and vertical expansion, needed to make the whole temple area, temenos as it is called, an organic whole.

The temple precincts constituted a very large area. At the foot of the ziggurat was generally located the 'lower' temple, the temple proper of the principal god to whom the whole was consecrated, and there were in the adjacent areas the smaller chapels for various associated gods. It must be noted that even the god's consort was not placed by his side or within his temple but had a separate temple of her own. Thus in the temple area of the ziggurat of Ur, a small shrine of Ningal, the consort of Nannar, the moon-god, who was the lord and sovereign of that area, was accommodated at one end on what became the "first floor platform" of the ziggurat as finally reconstructed by Nabonidus in the sixth century B.C.[6]

The ziggurat of Ur as built by Ur-Nammu about 2100 B.C. which as Gadd says "has never been lost nor even much obscured" since, had only three stages for the tower, with the lowest stage measuring at the ground level "a little more than 200 feet in length by 150 feet in width and about 50 feet in height"[7]. On the topmost stage stood "the little one-roomed shrine" of Nannar, the moon-god, the God of Ur. A stela commemorating the receipt of divine direction of Ur-Nammu for building the temple and Ur Nammu's actual manual activity in that direction, and summing up, as Woolley describes it, "the whole duty of kingship", adorned the structure. The great temple of Nannar at the base of this ziggurat platform lay on a raised terrace and by its south-east side was another temple, wherein both Nannar and his consort Ningal appear to have their chambers.

The Neo-Babylonian ziggurat as it emerged after the great reconstruction carried out in the 6th century B.C. by Nebuchadnezzar and Nabonidus came to have seven stages for the tower. The three ancient stairways, one in front and two at the two sides, converged on to the domed gate-tower on the lowest of the stages. Above it stood the six stages, diminishing in size and in height, with a staircase which looked like a spiral, as each led to the higher one only after going round the plane of the stage reached by the previous one. On the topmost stage stood the shrine of Nannar, "a small square building of bright blue-glazed bricks surmounted by a golden dome". Each stage of the tower was painted in a different colour, the lowest being black with bituminous coating. About its appearance and effect Woolley observes: "Viewed from the front the effect was dramatic in the extreme."[8]

The vastness of the expanse giving a good idea of the increase in spread of the sacred and priestly establishments, is vividly brought to one's notice by the great wall put up by Nebuchadnezzar II round the whole "sacred area" covering a space of 400 yards by 200 yards. The great wall was 30 feet high and equally broad. Its whole face was "decorated with the double vertical grooves which were traditional for the external walls of temples", and had six fortified gateways, "the main gate having a high tower set back in a deep recess". The whole must have presented the appearance of a huge and impregnable fortress. Towering high above all, stood the ziggurat almost at one corner of the sacred area rearing its top over a hundred and sixty feet high on which stood the Holy of Holies with its golden dome. Woolley[9], who in his first appraisal spoke of this temple, or rather of a Mesopotamian temple at its zenith, as a monastery rather than as a Christian church, goes one better in his later description of it as "at once temple and palace, government offices and stores and factories".

By far, however, the most famous Mesopotamian temple is the ziggurat of Babylon[10], known to history as the Tower of Babel. An old inscription found in the ruins ascribes the structure the enormous height of 300 feet covered in its seven stages. The wall enclosing the whole sacred area was about 330 metres long. The chamber of Marduk, the god of the house, the city, and the state, known as the "bed house", i.e., the bed room, which also formed the treasury of the establishment, measured 62.5 m. by 15.0 m. The floor of the main chamber was covered with alabaster, the ceiling had the cedar beams covered with gold and precious stones. The wall of the Holy of Holies on the top, as Nebuchadnezzar II, the renovator proclaims, was covered with "sparkling gold". The outside was covered with bright blue enamelled tiles, and the enclosing wall of the whole area, too, was faced with blue enamel. The ship used for the celebration of the annual *akitu* festival was decorated by the same monarch with gold and precious stones. The street by which the procession was to pass by the palace was paved with huge limestone pieces, with red and also white-striped stones by the sides, making the pavement picturesquely gorgeous. Mass, form, colour, precious metal and stones combined with height-all were used in profusion to create majesty and splendour that should stupefy or benumb the spectators or the passive participants. Brilliance rather than solemnity, loudness rather than serenity, sensuous pleasure rather than inward elevation of spirit, thus, were likely to be the achievement of the external manifestation of the complex, if they were the ends actually not sought after by the state, the theologians and the other élite.

The Assyrian monarch Tiglathpileser I in the last quarter of the 12th century B.C. boasts of his temple-renovating activity in these terms: "Its interior I made brilliant like the vault of heaven, decorated its walls like the brilliancy of the rising stars and made it superb with shining brilliance." Morris Jastrow[11] has drawn the conclusion regarding traditional and cultural continuity shown in "the fondness for brilliant colouring" in Oriental arts by tracing it to this Mesopotamian trait. Only he has failed to note that the Mesopotamian fondness for brilliance was not confined to secular art, it having been manifested perhaps even more prominently and even egregiously in sacred and hence spiritual buildings. And in use of that feature it is the mosque of the Islamic people and the Church of the Christians that figure prominently, Hindu temples having very little colour introduced in the interior. It is the Semitic temperament and its manifestation which have been passed on to others along with the two religions of Semitic origin. It is not a matter of contrast between the orient and the occident but of Semitic religious complex and non-Semitic ones, more specifically Aryan.

Nearly half a century ago Morris Jastrow commented on the development of the Babylonian ziggurat tower as preserved on a Babylonian monument, the picture of the temple of Anu-Adad at Ashur occurring on a "Boundary stone, recording the grant of a certain piece of property through a ruler of the thirteenth century B.C." There are two towers flanking the temple on its back which rise in three stages above the stage on which the temple stands at its backside corners, bulging that stage on three sides. The ascent to these towers was evidently independent of the frontal steps of the temple tower. He has reproduced also a Muslim tower of the 9th century A.D. existing at Samara, "some ninety miles above Bagdad". It is a stage-tower of seven stories on the top of which is a rotunda from which the *muezzin* calls the faithful to prayer. He states that many mosques follow the standard Babylo-Assyrian tradition making the minarets independent adjuncts of mosques.[12] J. H. Breasted[13], too, derived the minarets of the mosques from the same source and illustrated the evolution of the one from the other with pictures.

K. A. C. Creswell[14], a recent authority on Muslim architecture, accepts the fact of Mesopotamian influence on early Muslim minarets and mentions the spiral minaret at Samara, "built between 849 and 852 A.D.", which is still standing, as directly based on the ziggurat.

CHAPTER XIII

THE EGYPTIAN SHRINE

In the outward manifestations of beliefs, it has been well-known, Egypt has monopolized the attention of the world for a long time. And that is in the fitness of things as the Egyptians were the one people who required, and, since almost the beginnings of their civilization, had, structures to enshrine or protect the practices of their beliefs. One type of such structures, the earlier of the two principal types, has been so peculiar and so impressive that it has deservedly been regarded as the symbol of the Egyptian civilization. And that is the structure raised over the mummified dead king to preserve his remains etc. intact and known as the pyramid.

The three great pyramids at Gizeh which rivet the attention of a traveller are the tombs of the three Pharaohs, Chiofs or Kufu, Chefren or Khafra and Mycerinus or Menkaura of the IVth dynasty. And they are the biggest of all the pyramids that stretch for more than forty miles north to south. So striking are they that a historian of the calibre of H. R. Hall[1] is led to remark : "They are the mark which the king Khufu, Khafra, and Menkaura have for ever placed upon the land which they ruled about six [?] thousand years ago." To appraise the kind of endeavour needed for such achievement of sepulchral immortality it is necessary to remember that each of the three kings reigned for about sixty years.[2] The biggest of the three structures, that of Khufu, has, at its base, sides about 750 feet long and a height of 446 feet, which originally was 475 feet. It covers an area of about 13 acres. The pyramid of Chefren or Khapra had its sides 700 feet long, being at present only 684 feet, and a height of 466 feet, which at present is only 443 feet. Compared with these giants raised by father and son, the pyramid of Mycerinus is but a baby with about 258 long sides and a height of 201 feet at present.[3]

The speciality of Egypt in the matter of erecting stupendous or impressive structures over the dead, as we know from later cultural history of man, has not remained its unique feature, other civilizations, particularly the Islamic one, abounding in these mortuary structures.

There was another peculiarity of Ancient Egyptian civilization intimately connected with it which had resulted from the Egyptian belief in the godly status of the king. The king, the Pharaoh, the living god, when dead was provided with a shrine where he could be worshipped by himself. The structure to house the statue of the dead king for the purpose of worship was an elaborate structure and was a sort of an organic part of the mortuary structure. Such structures are known as the funerary or mortuary temples. They may be said to have remained a unique feature so far.

The temple, where gods were worshipped, was a structure distinct from this and showed itself much later. It is known as the valley temple and may be called god-temple to distinguish it from the mortuary temple wherein only the dead kind's statue was worshipped.

The earliest valley-temple extant in some shape is that of Chefren or Khafra. Lange and Hirmer describe it as a "magnificently simple building". It is in shape almost a perfect square. "It is distinguished by the beauty of its proportions and the brilliance of the materials, which even today is still striking." Its main structure is in the form of an inverted 'T', the top-bar being on the east and the stand or stem lying east-west from the western side of the top-bar hall. The east-west hall has three aisles formed by two rows of monolithic granite pillars, 13 feet 6 inches high. Here is the earliest evidence of the clerestory principle of lighting in its beginning. The extant oblique openings at the top make it clear that light entered this "long hall", as it is called by Lange and Hirmer, sideways from above. This "long hall" was so to say a gallery of royal statues, there being evidence of accommodation for twentythree such statues. A passage about five hundred yards long from the north-western corner of the top hall connected it with the very much larger and more elaborate funerary temple abutting on the eastern side of the pyramid-tomb.[4]

The earliest extinct god-temple, on the other hand, hails from the Vth Dynasty and that, too, one built by the fifth Pharaoh, Ne-userra, out of the eight belonging to this Dynasty,[5] i.e., more than about one hundred and fifty years after Chefren or Khafra. It is the Sun-temple of Abu Gurab, between Gizeh and Abusir. Wallis Budge's[6] description of the sun-temples built by "the later kings" of the Vth Dynasty applies to this temple. He states that it was about 325 feet long and 245 feet broad at the west end of which stood a truncated pyramid surmounted by a stone obelisk. In front, on the east side, there was an altar of alabaster. Cyril Aldred[7] adds the information that this court was on an upper level. That the ritual of sacrificing the offered animals was practised here is made clear by Budge and also Aldred. On the east and south sides of this walled enclosure there were passages decorated with reliefs. From the east-side gateway a passage led down to another gate which gave access to the enclosure at the lower level. Budge states that it was "about 1000 feet square" and that it accommodated the priests and also housed the sacred objects required in processions on festival days.

The internal dimensions of a processional temple*, which is only slightly later, having been put up by Pepi I of the VIth Dynasty, at Abydos, are forty and fifty feet. Senusret or Senusert I, about four and a half centuries after, rebuilt it increasing its size to three times. Thothmes III, as many centuries after Senusret I, enlarged the whole making the temple itself a big structure measuring 130 feet by 200 feet.[8]

As for the god-statue temples, that of Seti I at Abydos, with whose mention

* A processional temple was a squarish structure with open gateways and was meant to hold the barge in which the image of the deity was to be carried in the festival processions (Petrie, op. cit., p. 57 ; *E.B.* I, p. 69).

our study of the Egyptian religious complex began, though much later than the great national complex known as the Amen-temple at Karnak, Thebes, may be briefly alluded to here before describing the great structure at Karnak which is cherished by the world as a wonder even in its ruins. Seti's temple was peculiar in that it was designed to house the six major gods and goddesses of Egypt among whom Seti was to figure as the seventh god. Another peculiar feature of it was that it was designed to meet the needs of the Osiris cult practices. Another departure from the standard plan of an Egyptian temple was that the rooms connected with the temple services were attached to the temple itself as an integral part and not separately arranged in the sacred area, as we noted to be the case in the earliest extant god-temple at Abu Gurab near Abusir. Seti's temple was originally 550 ft. long and 350 ft. wide, but the fore-courts having been in ruins, the present length is only about 250 ft.

The standard plan of an Ancient Egyptian temple may be described as under : The approach to the temple premises lay through a paved road lined with sphinxes on both sides. The entrance was marked by one or more gateways called pylons. A pylon was a tripartite construction in appearance, with two towers on two sides and a door in the middle. High flag-staves were planted on two sides of the door in front of the pylons. Two obelisks stood, on two sides of the door, a little distance in front, and two others at the head of the sphinx-lined pavement, more or less in line with those at the door but within a small and low open enclosure. Immediately beyond the pylon was the peristylar court, an open court surrounded by a covered colonnade of pillars, in the further wall of which was the entrance, again a pylon with flag-staves and two obelisks, to the hypostyle hall. The obelisks range from 60 to 100 feet in height. This gigantic hall, whose roof was supported by massive pillars, commonly arrayed in six rows, the two central rows having higher ones than those in the side rows, is the most distinguishing feature of an Ancient Egyptian temple and was the highest feature in the whole complex structure. Immediately behind the obelisks standing in front of a pylon were placed colossal statues, varying from four to six, of the Pharaoh who built the pylon, ranging from 20 to 45 feet in height. Beyond this was the Holy of Holies, a rather small and dark chapel or chapels, generally three in number. In the central one of these stood the barge with the image of the god in it. It was generally a deep and dark recess. A pond or a lake somewhere inside was an invariable feature of any great temple. The Holy of Holies was the lowest portion of the temple, every structure beyond the first hypostyle hall progressively diminishing in height. The whole complex excepting the paved and sphinx-lined passage, was enclosed by a very high and thick wall, having in appropriate cases gates and entrances in the sides. It was in the back or side wall at the chapel end of the temple that some rooms for storing articles of worship and festival-use were provided.[9]

The girdle-wall of the main temple at Medinet Habu[10] which was built by the last of the great Pharaohs Rameses III, is nearly sixty feet high. There is also an outer wall some distance from the girdle-wall which stands thirteen feet high with a crenellated top. The towers flanking the entrance-gate in the inner wall rose 70 feet high.

This temple complex, which dates back to Amen-hotep I and may be said to end with the work of Rameses III, is much ruined and the great temple whose girdle-wall was so high was only a funerary temple. I have mentioned it here as illustrative of the measurement of the height of the girdle-wall of a great Egyptian temple. It is clear from this height that all ceremonies performed in the temple premises were securely guarded from public view. There are one or two other features associated with this temple which are commonly not met with in any of the other great temples and which, it appears to me, are likely to be interesting and even instructive to Indians or to students of Indian social and religious history; and I shall mention them here, as there will be no occasion for them to be mentioned elsewhere.

The first feature, which is paralleled by and of which the prototype is the Ramessum or the funerary temple of Rameses II, is that the palace of the king adjoined the first court of the great temple. From the projecting balcony, which was supported on the heads of the statues of many of the kings and chiefs the king had defeated in his campaigns, the king and his harem could see all the religious processions and enjoy the sight. For daily enjoyment the scenes, sculptured or painted in the courts and on the pylons, dealing with the king's battles with the Sudanese, the Lybians and the Syrians, his mighty and heavily manned ships destroying the enemy barges, the king's triumphal presentation of all the rich spoils to Amen, the pitiable condition of the defeated and miserable chiefs begging "Breath! O great Ruler, strong-armed, great in might! Give us breath that we may bow the knee to thy double serpent crown, that we may speak of thy might to our son's sons", were not the only means, though exciting enough. There were others who bespeak not only the faults of the individual king, who is adjudged "an incomparable general" in so many words or in other terms, a creditable general, a great organizer and a peaceful governor, but also the approaching decadence of the nation over which he ruled.

The towers of the entrance with guard-rooms on the ground floor were used as living rooms for the ladies of the Pharaoh's harem. The walls of these towers bear on their outside the sculptured scenes of the warlike and hunting exploits of the king. But in the inside are portrayed the beautiful ladies so that this Pharaoh, "who more than any other prided himself on his licentiousness", is shown "as a king of the harem".[11]

It is to the temple of Karnak at Thebes, however, that one must turn to study the material embodiment of ancient Egyptian religion, to appraise man's endeavour to concretize his religious consciousness and the role it played in ancient times. The great student of comparative architecture, J. Fergusson, writing almost a century ago, who was equally interested and proficient in anthropo-archaeological topics, observed about it: "St. Peter's with its colonnades and the Vatican make up an immense mass but as insignificant in extent as in style compared with this glory of ancient Thebes and its surrounding temples."[12]

The temple of Amen serves to focus the history and life of Ancient Egypt for almost fifteen hundred years out of the total of about 2500 years. In the thousand years before the beginning or coming into existence of this temple, the two temples, one at Heliopolis for Ra and the other and more important one at Memphis for Ptah, played that role. But the structures, neither then nor later, attained anything like the extent and magnificence that the temple of Amen at Karnak did. The result has been that even in its ruins the temple has not only excited the ungrudging admiration of the world but has figured as a marvel and as an inspirer of some features of the religious structures of other nations. Unlike the two above-mentioned temples, this again became at least since the XVIIIth Dynasty a complex comprising a sacred area, and included within its precincts at least by 1000 B.C. fourteen or fifteen distinct units, of which eleven are separate shrines of five gods and two goddesses. As religious architecture the temple embodies the best that Egypt devised, both from the point of view of the inwardness of religious consciousness and of that of outward majesty and impressiveness. Lastly, as Breasted[13] has put it : " . . . the vast temple complex discloses the growth of ritual and sacredotalism which resulted in the decadence of late Egyptian religion."

Perrot and Chipiez who have characterized the temple as "the most colossal assemblage of ruins which the world has to show" tell us that the longest axis from north to south measures 1560 yards and the transverse 620 yards. The whole perimeter of the walls is nearly two miles and a half.[14] The area of the precincts amounts to, in round figures, 0.97 million square yards or about 0.31 sq. miles. The Egyptian temple was not specifically oriented. In this complex the Great Temple, that of Amen, is turned to the west, that of his son Khonsu to the south, that of his consort Mut, to the north.

The Great Temple, that of Amen, oriented to the west, from its first pylon on the west to its eastern extremity measures 1215 feet long. Its greatest width, which it has at the first pylon on the west, is 376 feet. The enclosure round this temple is approximately a square of 1500 feet.

The first pylon—I shall not enter into the details of the chronology of these structures which make up the Great Temple but shall pass on to the description of the complex as it emerged at the end of the reign of Sheshonko I and was found by modern explorers—belongs to Ptolemaic times and is perhaps the biggest ever put up. It is 376 feet wide at the base and 50 ft. thick. Its two chief masses are 146 ft. high, almost equalling the Vendome column in Paris. The pylon of the Luxor temple built by Rameses II, which appears to be the second biggest, is 76 ft. high with the gate only 56 ft. high. Beginning with the pylon at the entrance there are three of them beyond which there is a small open court of much less width, on the eastern side of the 3rd pylon.

This is known as the Central Court for it connects the structure to its west, which appears as a unit, with the one to its east which, too, appears to be a unit by itself, even more so, having double enclosing wall on three sides. This eastern unit contains the shrine of Amen. Access to the shrine from the Central Court is given through three successive pylon-entrances, marked in plans and known in descriptions as the IVth, Vth and VIth pylons. The VIth pylon which is the entrance proper of the shrine itself is the smallest of all the pylons, both in height, width and thickness, the first being the largest, every successive one being smaller than the preceding one.

Crossing the first pylon one enters a peristylar hall of huge dimensions, known as the Fore Court. Immediately on crossing the inner side of the entrance to one's left there are three chapels facing south. They were dedicated to the Theban Triad, Amen, his consort Mut and their son Khonsu. They are believed to have been put up by Seti II. Proceeding further straight eastwards towards the 2nd pylon one comes across ruins of a hall in the centre which being later than 900 B.C. is not our concern here. From this site one sees to one's right a structural projection from the southern side of the peristylar court, breaking the peristylar feature on that side. It should, however, be borne in mind that in history the court came to be formed much later than the time of Rameses III. The projection has a well-marked entrance and marks the front of the temple which was raised by Rameses III lying athwart and projecting beyond the southern wall of the main temple-structure, thrice or four times as long as its projection into the peristylar court. It was dedicated to the Theban Triad or is believed to have been built to commemorate the victory of the Pharaoh over the Sea-peoples. In the same side just a little to the east of the eastern end of the temple of Rameses III stood a portico with a side entrance into Rameses' temple. This was the work of the last Pharaoh with whose end I have proposed to date the end of this great temple complex, Sheshonko I.

Return to the centre of the Fore Court and proceeding straight east, on passing through the entrance guarded formerly by statues of Rameses II, one on either side, of the 2nd pylon, one finds oneself in that pillared hall, to which, as Lange and Hirmer have put it, "Karnak owes its fame" and which ever since ancient times has been proclaimed one of the "wonders of the world", and which as architect Fyfe has put it. "is one of the architectural achievements of the world". It was put up by Seti I and Rameses II. It was thus long a-building. The magnificent structure is a hypostyle hall covering "an area of roughly 5800 square yards, that is to say more than a third of St. Peter's in Rome". Its dimensions are variously put down between 335 to 340 for length and 169 to 177 for width. Its internal dimensions are specified to be 329/330 ft. by 170 ft. It is nearly as large as the largest of the North European cathedrals, that of Cologne.[15] The number of pillars supporting the roof, too, are stated to be either 134 or 140. The whole structure comprises three sections, the central nave being flanked by two aisles on the two sides of the central nave.

I shall take the number of pillars to be 134,* represented on the ground plan presented by the latest authority as in Lange and Hirmer's illustration. Perrot and Chipiez's older estimate of the same number was based on a very much older authority.

Perrot and Chipiez have correctly stated the number of the gigantic pillars supporting the central nave as 12, remarking that these pillars, more than 33 feet in circumference and "equal to the column of Trajan", are "without a doubt, the most massive pillars ever employed within a building". Breasted[16] has more concretely conveyed the size of the pillars by pointing out that on the top of any one of these twelve as many as one hundred men can stand together.

The twelve pillars are set in two rows of six each. As regards their height, too, there are variations. Perrot and Chipiez have probably correctly stated the dimension as 70 feet from the ground to the summit which supports the architrave ; but when Lange and Hirmer speak of "the two middle rows of the 78 feet high centre aisle" they have included the height of the architrave, too. Margaret Murray is even more indefinite when she says that "the pillars of the two central rows are nearly eighty feet high". The other pillars are disposed in seven rows on each side of the central nave, the row on each side nearest to the central pillars having seven each and the other six nine each. Thus the total of the round pillars whose measurements alone are given, amount to one hundred and thirtyfour. There are too more pillars one each in the row next to the row of the central nave at the 3rd pylon end of the hall which are square and are not measured or counted in the total of the round ones. But if we include them, and I think as they are organically connected with the roof of the hall they must be counted, the total number of pillars supporting the great roof of this huge hall comes to be one hundred and thirtysix. I have not been able to account for the number 140 adopted by Lange and Hirmer. The capitals of the higher pillars are of the palm-leaf type and those of the shorter ones lotus-bud form.

The height of the central nave as given by Perrot and Chipiez is 76 feet and that of the side aisles 43 feet. Margaret Murray informs us that the smaller pillars in the side rows are fortytwo feet in height. I cannot believe that the architrave resting on their tops can be only 1 foot high when the architrave of the central aisle is known to be six feet high !

The central aisle, its tripartite frontal division, giving the whole structure a pentafrontal appearance and the system devised for lighting the central aisle by means of light coming from both its sides from above the top of the side-aisles make the hypostyle hall the prototype of the Christian church frontage and of its lighting system for the deep central nave. It is known as the clerestory window lighting. To secure these windows through which light was to be let into the central nave a wall was raised over the rows of

---

* This is the number specified in the *E.B.*, VIII, too.

smaller pillars, which is the nearest to the row of the large central pillars on both its sides, and lattice-work windows pierced in it along the whole length of the central nave. The roofing of the nave was carried on the two side walls raised over the two rows of the smaller pillars. Thus was not only ample light provided in the long nave, which would otherwise have been too dark, but because of the slanting light coming from over the sides and the lattice-work of the windows curious light effects were secured.

It may be stressed here that in sacred architecture there is observed a persistent effort at securing weird light effects or colour effects with internal decoration. The former method so typical of the Egyptian sacred architecture is not altogether unknown in Hindu temples. The latter method also present in the Egyptian temples is abundantly demonstrated in the Christian Churches and also in Islamic mosques in a modified form.

The pillars, which are believed to have been plain when originally set up, bear inscriptions either incised or painted. The effect of the lighting system on the paintings on the pillars and the arrangement of the pillars prompted Margaret Murray to observe: "When the eye became accustomed to the dimness of the Hall the colours must have taken on a brilliancy which is never seen in the full glare of the sunlight. The arrangement of the hall gives vistas in every direction, the rows of columns melting into the darkness, while shafts of sunshine from the clerestory windows cut the gloom with startling suddenness. The restorations, which have been recently carried out, have revived some of the ancient beauty of the hall, and its solemn grandeur remains as a lasting memorial of a splendid past." This is almost an echo of the earlier appraisal by James Fergusson,[17] the great student of comparative architecture.

Proceeding east through the IIIrd pylon, which was put up by Amenhotep III, there were four obelisks, two on each side of the visitor, one of them being close to the eastern side of the pylon and the other a little to its east in a straight line. Perhaps they were set up by Thothmes I, the one standing there till the experts' inspection of the place being his, and marked the entrance to the temple, which then was only the structure lying to the east of them. The standing obelisk is over 70 feet high and 6 feet square at the base. It bears inscriptions not only of Thothmes I but also of Rameses IV and Rameses VI[18]. The IVth pylon at the eastern end of this Central Court, built by Thothmes I opens into a smaller hypostyle hall, much smaller than the one already described, also built by Thothmes I. It is decorated with statues of Thothmes I in the form of Osiris. It was as a hall originally roofed but Hatshepsut appears to have removed the roof to accommodate the pair of tall obelisks she set up there, the one still standing being the highest of all obelisks in Egypt. This monolithic obelisk measures 96 feet high.* All the obelisks, those of Thothmes and of Hatshepsut, were originally topped with caps of pale gold.

---

* The note on Obelisk in the *E.B.* specifies the height as 97 ft. 6 inches and states that the highest one was that of Thothmes III measuring 105 ft. at present lodged in Italy.

The Vth pylon was perhaps constructed by Hatshepsut but is claimed for Thothmes I.

The VIth pylon, the last on the eastern side of the complex and the structures between the Vth pylon and it were put up by Thothmes III. Beyond the VIth pylon the structures, excepting the present sanctuary, were also put up by Thothmes III. The present sanctuary or shrine of granite is a late work. The walls of the ambulatory surrounding the shrine bear very important and interesting inscriptions, which as documents are unique in antiquity and redolent of greatness and modernity. This portion of the temple is otherwise known as the second hall of annals of that king. In the centre of this stands the chapel for the barge of Amen. The peristylar court between the VIth pylon and the shrine complex is known as the first hall of annals. To the east of the eastern wall of the sanctuary complex there are ruins of the oldest shrine at this place dating from the XIIth Dynasty occupying a space larger than that filled by the court, hall and sanctuary complex to the east of the VIth pylon.

Beyond the ruins and some vacant space, stands the Festival Hall built by Thothmes III. It is in the form of a pavilion and is also known as the ceremonial temple of Thothmes III. Adjoining it there are a number of rooms and halls on the southern, eastern sides and on a part of the northern side. The Hall which is five-aisled lies south and north. Entrance to it is provided in the western wall towards its southern end and is accessible directly straight from the small hypostyle hall between the IVth and the Vth pylons. The three chapels in the hall-temple face south. They were dedicated to the Theban Triad and the figure of Mut is still visible. The total south to north length is 143 feet and the west-east width is 52 feet, so that the area of the hypostyle hall in front of the chapels is about 7000 sq. feet. It is supported on twentyfour round pillars disposed in two rows to form the central nave and twentyeight square pillars distributed on the four sides spaced appropriately fiom the wall. The round pillars have bell-capitals and are believed to represent tent poles, the intention of the martial Pharaoh having been to make the structure resemble his war-camp tent. The nave was lighted in more or less the same way as that of the great hypostyle hall of the temple complex already described. But for lighting the side aisles, two on each side of the nave, an ingenious system of clerestory windows had to be devised which being in complete ruins can be only partially visualized. In one of the rooms was discovered what is known as the "Karnak Table of Kings", which is a list of his predecessors set up by Thothmes III. The riches borne by the walls of the rooms and halls of this structure, however, are unique in another field of activity than that generally comprised under the historical category. They proclaim Thothmes III to be the first "founder of zoological and botanical gardens" in the world. A very brief description of the contents will be given in the last portion of this chapter.

Outside the temple-walls, a little away to the south side there is a lake which is almost as big as the area covered by the section of the complex enclosed by the walls beginning with that of the sanctuary on the west and ending with the outer wall of the complex on the east. It was also built by Thothmes III. The barge of Amen floated on it during solemn festivals, a usual ritual and show. Perhaps it also served another purpose, that of ritual cleanliness of the visitors, who might have washed their feet with its water, before going into the sanctuary or the hall for view. At its north-west corner lies the giant stone scarab, the symbol of heart, set up by Amenhotep III.

Apropos of this lake I may mention that Flinders Petrie has traced the existence of a tank within sacred precincts to much earlier times, those of the XIIth Dynasty. At Kahun he found "a tank, and paved area for cleanliness" adjoining what seemed to him "to have been a place of devotion". As for the XVIIIth Dynasty, he is quite definite, and specifies the temple of Hathor in Sinai, where were found "a large court with circular basin in the middle, and a lesser court with a tank", while "a third tank, for washing, stood at the side of the entrance". It is Petrie's comment, establishing the long continuity of the ritual practice and the underlying religious mentality, that illumines these old relics which could easily be missed and their significance completely ignored. Observes Petrie : "The custom of washing the feet when going into a sanctuary is usual in the East . . . a great circular tank for washing is to this day to be seen in every mosque of Islam."[19] The presence of a tank or a pond in the enclosure of the great South Indian temple complexes may also be borne in mind.

There are a number of structures adjoining the Central Court on its south side ; and they deserve our attention now, as the structures are the work of Hatshepsut, Thothmes III, Amenhotep II and Haremhab, and the continuation of the modern numbering of the pylons leads one that way. From the Central Court a small doorway opens into a court which bears the inscription of Merenptah, the successor of Rameses II, recording his victories over the enemies of Egypt, among whom the Etruscans and the Achaens figure. On the site two shrines, one of the Middle Kingdom period and another of the time of Amenhotep I, are known to have stood previously. The South wall and end of this court is formed by the VII pylon which was built by Thothmes III. The entrance of the pylon both at the southern and the northern sides is flanked on its two sides "by statues chiefly of Thothmes III". From the fact of the existence of a broken obelisk on the southern side it is inferred that two obelisks standing in front of the statues on the southern side indicated, in the time of Thothmes III, that the entrance to the temple of Amen from that of Mut, very much further out to the south, lay through the VIIth pylon. In the eastern wall of the second court, rather towards its northern end, there is a doorway which opens into a small chapel, again built by Thothmes III. Its dedication has not been apparently ascertained. The southern wall of the court is formed by a pylon, known to have been put up by Queen Hatshepsut and numbered now as the VIIIth. It leads one to the third court which is much bigger than the earlier ones but is open and quite bare. The IXth pylon which forms its southern wall was put up by Haremhab out of the material recovered by demolishing the temple, which the reformist king Ikhnaten had erected for Aten there. On the east side of the court, which is bigger than the third and open and uncolonnaded, almost in the middle of the wall, is the temple of Amenhotep II which is entered by a sloping way from the court. It was complete with one sanctuary on the north side and another on the south side of a hypostyle hall which was directly entered by the sloping way. It was dedicated to Amen. It is believed, on the strength of the ruins and an opening in the western wall of the court, that a sanctuary or a temple also lay on that side of the court. In the south side of the court, Haremhab built another pylon, the Xth in the current reckoning, and is the one which is more commonly mentioned as his pylon. The Xth pylon is the entrance-gate from the temple of Mut and is thus on the processional way from that temple to that of Amen.

There are two temples within the walled precincts of this huge temple-complex. The temple of the Memphite god Ptah lies just by the side of the northern wall, a little to the east of the opening in it which is about its middle. It is oriented to west. Perhaps coming from the XIIth Dynasty it was rebuilt by Hatshepsut and Thothmes. The entrance curiously enough is formed by six successive gateways. The temple thus rivals or copies the Great Temple of Amen. Most of them are later in date than the time of the XVIIIth Dynasty. The sixth pylon, which is the gateway nearest to the temple, is considered to have been put up by Hatshepsut or Thothmes III. It is the smallest of all and between it and the Vth gateway is a small court with four pillars. The temple itself is a hall, the roof of which is supported by two pillars which are sixteen-sided. There are three altars in the hall, one of which has an inscription by Amenemhat I of the XIIth Dynasty and another by Thothmes III. The santuary proper lies in the main axis in the middle of the eastern side and is directly approached from the hall. In it stands a damaged statue of Ptah. There are two chapels, one on each side of the sanctuary of Ptah, which are approached through it. One of them is known to be a shrine of the goddess Sekhmet who is treated in mythology as the consort of Ptah. Margaret Murray[20] thus describes the representation placed there : "The statue represents a young woman with a lioness's head ; the human part of the figure is a beautiful example of Egyptian work, the youth and symmetry of the rounded limbs is above the average of divine statues." The other chapel, I may surmise on the analogy of the The baid triad, held a statue of Ptah's so-called son, whose place, by then, must have been acquired by Imhotep, the great architect-physician of the IVth Dynasty.

A little to the north of the southern, almost in the north-west, corner of the walled precincts of the temple-complex there are two temples. The temple of Khonsu lies south-north approached from outside through an opening on the southern side in a straight line with the temple-gateways. It forms so to say the terminal of the processional way from Luxor, a village or town to the south-west of Karnak having another great temple of the Theban Triad, to Karnak. It was begun by Rameses III, but was completed in the reign of Rameses XI, about 1125 B.C. It is surmised that, as it was in the axis of the sphinx-lined road from Luxor to Karnak, it "may have served as a gate-chapel to those coming on foot from the south". The shrine has a passage at the back, i.e., on the northern side enabling processions to pass out that way towards the great Temple of Amen. The reproduction of Khonsu occurring in such books as Lange and Hirmer's is from the statue found in this temple. A stela with an important inscription found in the temple is another remarkable fact about it.

The inscription on the stela in the temple of Khonsu narrates the story of the demoniacal possession of a Syrian princess, a sister of the Queen of Rameses II, and the services of Khonsu and his image, sent to Syria on special request, in curing the princess of it.[21] It is the earliest mention of demoniacal possession in man's cultural history, having to be dated about 1200 B.C. India furnishes, perhaps, chronologically the second specimen of such phenomenon. It is recorded in the oldest of the *Upaniṣads*. It states that the wife of one Pātañjala Kāpya of the Madra country—it ceased to be a part of India in 1947 having been incorporated in the Country of Pakistan—was "possessed by a 'gandharva' ", that being the Sanskritic equivalent of what is known in English language as "demoniacal possession".[22] It is about four centuries later than the Egyptian story. There is a strong contrast in the sequel of the two episodes, which underscores the fundamental difference between the religious consciousness of the Ancient Egyptians and of the Ancient Indo-Aryans.

At right angles to the temple of Khonsu stands at the southern end of it the temple of Ypet, the hippopotamus-goddess of birth. But it is non-Egyptian. It was built by Ptolemy IX and is a standing monument to the Hellenistic policy of pandering to the common people's preferences in religious matters. The goddess we are told had no shrine exclusively for her worship till then; and she was one of the goddesses approached by the common folk, and not attended upon by priests.[23]

At this stage I should like to draw the attention of my readers to the phenomenon, which is observable in the construction of the main temple and even more so in the later erection of halls and pylons and courts. It is that there is a persistent tendency to increase in size, massiveness and grandeur seen here, which is more or less parallel to the similar increase, including wherever permissible or possible rise in height too, which we noted in the outward manifestation of the religious consciousness and practice of the Ancient Mesopotamians.

This phenomenon of increase in extent, size, mass and height of the shrine, in the place of worship is very pointedly brought to one's notice when one compares one single shrine with another removed in time by a long gap. Pepi I of the VIth Dynasty erected a ceremonial temple at Abydos whose inside dimensions were 40 feet by 50 feet. The processional temple of Thothmes III of the XVIIIth Dynasty, on the other hand, measured 130 feet by 200 feet![24]

The Xth pylon of the great Temple is connected with the temple of the goddess Mut, who with the rise of Amen came to be treated as his consort, by an avenue of sphinxes, which is as long as the distance between the Xth pylon and the southern wall of the Central Court of the great Temple. The standing temple of the goddess is believed to be the work of the XVIIIth Dynasty and is enclosed by a wall, going around its precincts like that of the Amen temple-complex. Outside the principal gate are two statues of Amenhotep III, who thus appears to have been the chief Pharaoh concerned in the construction or completion of the temple. The girdle-wall leaves a large ambulatory round the temple, with a large horseshoe-shaped sacred lake intervening on the western, southern and eastern sides of the temple. To the south-west of the bend of the lake in the south-west corner of the walled area there is a small temple put up by Rameses III which was dedicated to the Theban Triad.

This completes the description of the greatest temple-complex of antiquity and one of the biggest of sacred complexes of all time and places. It is also, as we shall find on comparison with the biggest of India's temples later, the largest with a polylatrous pantheon. Here I shall note a feature or two of special interest to the student of the sociology of religion. The principal temple is quite clearly of the One God of the Imperial Age, Amen. Later kings, however, have put up small shrines or fair-sized temples within the walls of the great Temple, which emphasize the triune deity, Amen, his consort Mut and their son Khonsu. In this feature of a nuclear family being the One Divinity, Ancient Egypt appears as the prototype of the Tamilian concretization of the Śaivite mythology of India in keeping the bronze images of Śiva, his consort Pārvatī, and their son Skanda, for worship and pomp at the processional festivities.[25] The fact of an independent shrine for Khonsu is also intriguingly tantalizing. It invites closer comparison with the Indian religious phenomenon in view of the fact that there are temples dedicated to Skanda in South India which are very famous.

The fact that the temple of the consort goddess is not only brought into connection with the temple of the male god but also lies outside the walls of the temple complex of the male deity is unlike the common Indian practice, wherever there is an independent shrine to the consort-goddess. The fact that Mut was originally an independent goddess, and later came to be subordinated to Amen to be associated with him as his consort may explain the difference (?).

Another pantheonic aspect revealed by this temple-complex dedicated to the One God, who had become the one national god, is worth noting as a characteristic feature of a polylatrous society. Amen or Amenra, the national god, as we have seen in the earlier chapters is the God who was made the focus for rallying the frontier peoples to the banner of Egypt. In short Amen was the God of colonialism and imperialism. Amen, too, was the God, who was prayed to for success in expeditions and victory in war by a number of great Pharaohs, the most prominent amongst whom were Thothmes II, the great empire-builder, and Rameses II, another imperial Pharaoh, a great warrior, who enriched the treasury of Egypt and spent vast wealth on self-glorification and on the advancement of Amen. Yet within the great precincts of the temple of Amen at Karnak one finds a temple, albeit small, dedicated to another God, Ptah of Memphis, who was really speaking the only other god, quite distinct from Amen, to form the triad or rather the three-in-one-God of the Imperial theologians. For Ra, the third deity, was already so far assimilated with Amen that one can hardly recognise him separately.

The Egyptian performance at the height of Egypt's glory, a performance which continued to be her religious destiny till almost the time when her native religion was overshadowed and supplanted, in pantheonic contraction towards monolatry is an achievement of which Ancient Egypt could justly be proud. That Jewish and Christian humanity profited by it has been amply demonstrated by such an authoritative yet persuasive writer as J. H. Breasted. Half a century ago he emphasized the debt of Christianity to the sacred-architecture of Ancient Egypt in regard to the external manifestation of religion, the temple, the shrine, the church.

Finally, I shall briefly dwell on the kind of nonarchitectural adornment of the great Egyptian temple described above, a feature common to both Indian (Hindu) temples, especially South Indian and to some extent to the Christian churches.[26]

To begin from the east end of the temple-complex, I shall mention here, again, the great biological representations and description on the walls which have been together described as the earliest botanical and zoological gardens. The birds and plants illustrated were brought by the great campaigner Pharaoh, Thothmes III, himself from the many lands which he had traversed in his martial exploits, "as a memorial before my father Amen for ever". On a number of columns here as elsewhere in the complex, particular Pharaohs, the ones who specifically were the erectors of these particular structures, are generally painted or sculptured in the act of offering sacrifice to or merely as in the presence of the chief God, Amen or the whole Triad.

On the walls of the ambulatory of the shrine, further west, there are the famous inscriptions of the Syrian campaigns of Thothmes III. The account of the battle of Megiddo, "evidently copied from a diary kept by the King's own secretary", is the earliest account of a military action from a military point of view, in short the earliest, by far, study of a battle, the plan, strategy, tactics and actual attack all revealed very clearly. Incidentally the intrepid and leader-like character of the King, too, is revealed in the document. Of the quality of the writing itself Hall[27] writes : "This is the largest and most important historical inscription in Egypt, and it is at the same time one of the most graphic, often rising to the highest level of descriptive writing, and showing considerable literary power." A stela in the temple bears what is an address by the God Amen himself to "his glorious son", i.e., the King, Thothmes III, on his victorious return, which according to Hall, is "in some ways the finest example of Egyptian poetry". Hall quotes in fittingly fine translation 59 lines as "the most fitting epilogue to [his] account of the deeds of the great king".

I transcribe below a few of the lines, which appear to me to have a significant bearing for comparison and contrast on what Lord Kṛṣṇa said to Arjuna when he got dejected on the battle-field, on what the great Gupta monarch, Samudragupta, and his court-poet, or two other great Gupta monarchs, or what Kalhaṇa, the poet-historian of Kashmir on one or two occasions in Kashmirian history or again what Allauddin Khalji on occasion, or Shivaji on one or two occasions, in our history, is recorded to have written, said or done in a similar situation :

"Saith Amen-Ra, lord of Karnak :
My two hands make thy limbs to have protection and life.
Doubly sweet is thy might to my bodily form.
I have set thy will and the fear of thee in all countries.
The chiefs of all lands are gathered in thy grasp ;
I myself have stretched forth my two hands and bound them for thee.
I have struck down thine enemies beneath thy sandals,
The Earth in its length and breadth, Westerners and Easterners are subject to thee.
I have caused them to see thy Majesty as a lord of radiance,
Thou hast shone in their faces like my image . . . ."

Without going into the details of the sculptures and/or inscriptions of Amenhotep II and of Merenptah and the innumerable scenes on the gigantic pillars of the stupendous hypostyle hall and also the very late exploit records of Sheshonko I, one may conclude that generally speaking the decoration of the temple corresponded with the sacred character of the structure. Representations of Gods, brilliantly painted or sculptured, quite often in the situation of blessing the thing and assuring him of "millions of festivals in life, duration, and purity", and of festivals are the commonest. Representations of the king's smiting his enemies, are not infrequent. While the inscriptions and many of the sculptured or painted scenes are mere glorifications of the Kings they are proved to be more decorations than real homages, as they are used to fill in the blank spaces wherever necessary, being "all turned in the opposite direction for the sake of symmetry".[28]

There are historical reliefs, however, on the walls of the hypostyle wall, one of which at least depicting and describing the campaign of Rameses II against the Hittites, both because of its similarity with some of the incidents of the campaigns of Thothmes III and also of the pathos of the situation and the courage of the young King demonstrated in the dangerous situation and also of the difference in tone, which deserves to be recorded appropriately as the finale of the section on external manifestations of religion. The inscription on the other wall to the east of the south gate of the great hall contains the text of the great treaty, one of the most significant ones in man's cultural history. It is well-known among students of the history of the Ancient East that the vaunts in which Rameses II indulged in his inscription were not wholly justified. There was no victory as such in the campaign. It is from that portion of his inscription that posterity has received the interesting information that the horses of his war-chariot bore not romantic but "magic" names, calculated to inspire confidence and courage in its occupier and his army. Named mounts of great personalities and generals thus are so old a practice ! One of the two horses of Rameses II, and they appear to have been mares, was "Victory-in-Thebes" and the other "Mut-is-content". Thebes must typify Amenra or Month, the war-god. Mut is the Theban goddess, also identified with the lioness-headed war-goddess Sekhmet, and the consort of Amen. The particular occasion at the battle of Kadesh in the valley of the Orontes in Syria, when Rameses II was cut off from his main army and was completely surrounded by the large enemy forces and the situation was quite desperate, is described in great detail in the inscription. And posterity is assured that the King found succour in his horses only and that he was so grateful to them for this invaluable succour that he avowed to feed them daily himself when he returned to his palace in Egypt.[29]

At the critical moment he prayed and appealed to Amen on the field and then struck at his enemies. The fervent prose poem enshrining his prayer runs : "What then, my father Amen ? Can it be that a father has forgotten his son ? I call to thee, my father Amen. I am in the midst of strangers whom I know not. All the nations have banded together against me. And I am alone and no other is with me. My soldiers have abandoned me and not one of charioteers turned his head to seek me. If I cry after them, no one of them hears me. But I call and see that Amen is better for me than millions of foot-soldiers and hundreds of thousands of charioteers, better than ten thousand brothers and children who stand together as one man. The work of many men is nothing, Amen is better than they. I have come here obedient to the thoughts of thy mouth. [It was the convention with the Imperial Egyptian Pharaohs that they carried out invasions at the dictate of Amenra.] Amen ! And I have not departed from thy thoughts."[30] The King placed the responsibility on Amen and began to fight back. One can realize the echoes of this in the words of Lord Kṛṣṇa believed to have been addressed to Arjuna, on the battle-field near Delhi about two centuries later "Remember Me and fight on !"

CHAPTER XIV

THE HINDU SHRINE

THE history of religious consciousness in India is such that for a long time it did not necessitate a more or less permanent abode as an external manifestation of it and as a necessary aid to its fulfilment. In the prehistoric Indus-valley civilization, whose most telling remains stand in Western Pakistan and which flourished between about 2500 B.C. to about 2000 B.C., there have been discovered no indisputable traces of any structure or artefact which can be called a shrine.

The Vedic religion being one of sacrifice would be and was practised with the help of an altar and a temporarily put-up shed for a hall, though both these appurtenances of the religious complex were occasionally at least personified. Many of the deities were wholly anthropomorphized, their personal appearances being fully and even lovingly and admiringly described. Yet students of Vedic religion are quite unanimous that there was no shrine raised in the Vedic age for their worship.

As made out in an earlier chapter, a change in the mode of approach to the deity must have been completed before the 6th century B.C., when also the beginnings of the new pantheon became manifest. Worship of a deity of more or less the same form as its later one, though not at all in anything like the same elaboration, is mentioned as early as the 5th century B.C. if not earlier.[1] The two Gods, Śiva and Viṣṇu, with their personal attributes almost fully formulated, were clearly conceived of before the 3rd century B.C. And there is clear indication in literature of the existence of some kind of shrines from the 5th century B.C. We thus see that the nature of the God-head and the mode of approach to the deity are intimately connected with the existence of a shrine or its absence. Shrines being structures largely conditioned by the nature of the approach to the deity, or in other words by the kind of worship to be offered, it is best to begin our brief account of Hindu shrines with a short description of the fully developed ritual of temple-worship current among the Hindus, tracing back its history as far as possible in the briefest manner, and then to go on to match the sacred structures known to be existing at particular dates.

The Śiva temple at Rāmeśvaram in the extreme south is one of the most sacred and famous shrines of India. The ritual of worship current at that religious centre was described in minute detail, along with the sacred texts in Sanskrit and also some in Tamil recited therein, by the great epigraphist and antiquarian J. Burgess eighty years ago.[2] It may be summarised thus: (1) At about 4.30 or 5.00 a.m. an officiant known as 'pādaśaiva' in Sanskrit and as 'osan' in Tamil, with a small [flat] gong hanging on his right wrist and a small stick held in the fingers of the same hand and a conch shell, 'śaṅkha', in the other, blows the conch thrice, plying his stick on the gong, which is known as 'jayaghaṇṭā' in Sanskrit and as 'sekandi' in Tamil and 'jhaṅgaṭa' in dialectal Marathi, at the east porch, and proceeding south repeats the performance at other gates. This is the summons, the call. He is followed by a troupe of regular musicians, three of them being drummers, two pipers, one a castanet player and one a trumpeteer; (2) Officials with their keys, priests purified by a bath, and a dancing girl[3] in charge of the services for the days dressed as a Brahmin lady bathed over the head, her hair hanging loose behind and wearing no jewellery but only the sacred beads, 'rudrākṣa', come up to the great 'maṇḍapa' along with menial servants and get the doors unlocked and opened upto those of the great hall of the temple and all the lights lighted. Thus it is the first enclosure that is entered. Provisions are given into the charge of the cooks to prepare the meals for worship. There are about a dozen other officiants present, one of whom has the duty of bringing the meal-offering along with water for the deity on the back of an elephant, and another who repeats the Vedic and other formulae at the completion of the total worship requesting the deity to accept it. Unfortunately Burgess has not given the text repeated by this officiant. The fact that he is stated to have been called 'mantrapuṣpa'—this must be a solecism for one who performs the 'mantrapuṣpa'-rite, that is how, at least in Maharashtra, it would be expressed. I take it that the text must be the standard one, which is current in Maharashtra for group and such other special occasion worships; (3) By the time all the paraphernalia of worship including the food to be offered to the deity get ready it is about 5.30 a.m. and the doors of the 'mahāmaṇḍapa', the great hall of the shrine of Rāmalingeśvarasvāmin—that is the name by which Śiva is known in the Rāmeśvaram temple complex—are opened. All the appropriate officiants then proceed to the Amman shrine, the shrine of the God's consort, known here as Parvatavardhinī, the musicians playing their music, and opening the doors of the great hall reverentially awaken Śiva, addressing the image in Sanskrit with a text which runs thus: "Awake, Lord of the Universe, Author of good to this whole world! and *for the world's benefit be pleased to accept my daily worship.*"*

The golden image of Śiva, which has been lying in a bed by the side of Pārvatī, is then placed in the palanquin. A procession, with all the marks of royalty in attendance, the musicians playing their music and the dancing girls performing on the way, starts out from the south door of the great hall of the Pārvatī shrine and going round the second enclosure by west enters the Swami-shrine by its east-gate. The image is then placed in the 'ardhamaṇḍapa', the vestibule, of the Swami-shrine. At this stage the appropriate priest entering the cella, the 'garbhagṛha', of the shrine, removes the old flowers from the phallus-emblem. (4) The priest then starts with the regular programme of the ritual beginning with declaration, 'saṁkalpa'; (5) An appropriate officiant brings water from a well [tank ?] situated in the outermost, the third,

* Italics mine,

enclosure, and fills with it a large vessel standing in the shrine ; (6) The officiant bathes the phallus-emblem with this water, repeating during the process the following verse preceded by another: "May the Sindhu, Sarasvatī, Yamunā, Godāvarī, Narmadā, Kāverī, Kapilā, Prayāganiyatā, Vetrāvatī, Kṛṣṇā, Bhīmarathī, Phalgu, Gaṇḍakī, Gomatī—may these rivers that take their source from the feet of Hari [Viṣṇu] ever give prosperity." Curiously the Gaṅgā does not figure in the galaxy of the rivers. The 'Gaṅgā-tīrtha' is mentioned in the text recited before this verse.

An appropriate officiant at this stage draws the curtain across the vestibule so that the priest in the cella should be able to dry the phallus-emblem with the piece of cloth to be used as bath towel, the idea being to cover the deity from the profane eyes while going through the routine of receiving the services. After the bath the phallus-emblem is dressed in two clothes, one for the lower part and the other as the scarf. Sandal paste is applied in the standard fashion, garlands of flowers and leaves of 'bilva' tree, so dear to Śiva, and the specific sacred offering to Him are placed on it and the meal brought on the back of an elephant is offered with the famous 'Gāyatrī' verse, the Vedic and the standard invocation to Sūrya, the Sun-god, being recited over it. Camphor is lighted, incense is burnt and light is waved. The whole ritual comes to an end with the recitation of an ordinary request to the deity to accept the food-offering. Curiously there is no mention of any bell-ringing during the waving rites ; but I have no doubt the bells at the door of the cella or in the vestibule must be ringing all the while, some specific officiant attending to them.

This first worship, we may justly call it the 'prabhāta-pūjā', the dawn-worship, comes to an end at about 6 a.m. ; and at about 7 the second service of the day's routine of worship starts. After one or two items, including that of sprinkling a little water over the phallus-emblem in token of its bath, are gone through, the curtain drawn in the vestibule at the earlier service is removed. The deity is offered the service of light-waving and camphor and incense burning before it. This done, the door of the cella is locked and the priest leaves the shrine.

The third service begins at about 9 a.m. At this service the pot of water from the well in the outer enclosure is carried in a procession on the back of an elephant round the shrine enclosure, the procession being headed by another elephant. This last makes a bow at the east gate to the elephant carrying the water pot and leaves. The officiant in charge of the water pot gets down with it and places it in the vestibule. The priest carrying out the ritual of actual worship at this stage goes through what are known as five purities and the whole standard complex of worship proceeds. After a number of items have been gone through and the 'pañcāmṛta'* five-nectars-offering is made, the priest enters the cella and removes the flowers of the morning service from the phallus-emblem and takes them to the chapel of another subsidiary deity.

* This is a mixture of curds, honey, milk, clarified butter and sugar in certain proportions.

Now he offers to the image of Gaṇapati, gracing one side of the vestibule, worship to guarantee freedom from obstacles in his task of performing the worship of Śiva. It is time now also to remove the flowers of earlier services, previous day's, on the bodies of Śiva's bull, Nandī, and other deities and their consorts. At this stage the curtain in the vestibule is again drawn. The bath given to the phallus-emblem at this service contains some soap-nut-powder. There is a second bath with water in which powdered cinnamon and tumeric is mixed, followed by another with water of a fresh tender cocoanut. Next comes three successive baths with curds, clarified butter, and honey respectively, followed each time by a pure water bath. Another bath, this time with a mixture of the five exuents from a cow, known as the 'pañcagavya', is given and the whole bath process is brought to an end by a pure water ablution. Then the sandalwood paste is applied and the phallus is dressed up in two pieces of cloth as at the earlier service. The 'naivedya', the food-offering, that follows is a specific one known as 'mudgānnam', a savoury rice-and-green-gram-pulse preparation, known in Marathi as 'mugācī khicaḍī'. With the waving of burning incense in a five-bowled pan to the accompaniment of the ringing of the bell, the waving of a lamp and the burning of camphor, the esoteric part of the procedure comes to an end and the curtain in the vestibule is withdrawn only to be drawn once again immediately. After further ablutions, dressing and sandalpaste application, the silver eyes are brought in and stuck at the proper places on the phallus-emblem. A garland is then put on the emblem. After other subsidiary deities are treated with some sandal paste, etc. again a food-offering is brought to the accompaniment of music; and the priest offers it at the base of the phallus-emblem. All the while, when the offering is made with the recitation of appropriate texts, music goes on. When the formal offering is over all the food is removed to a room to the south-east of the Amman, Pārvatī shrine. The priest in the Swāmi temple, ringing the bell in his left hand all the while, waves to the phallus-emblem a number of lights, one after another, specifically called by names showing their special form or their fancied resemblance or their purpose. The manner of waving is particular. He first moves the light in a wavy motion from above downwards and then thrice in a round motion going up on the left and down on the right side. Lastly he brings it straight downwards. After further services like besmearing the phallus-emblem with ashes, 'bhasma', presenting a looking glass, holding a small umbrella over it, and waving a small chowrie, whisk, and a fan made up of peacock-feathers, the priest offers flowers and 'bilva'-leaves to it and recites the following formula which is important as indicative of the attitude the worshipper has in his worship and his prayer: "For the atonement of any mistakes that I may have committed in my worship, I have now performed the worship. May it give you pleasure."

After recitation of the one thousand and eight names of Śiva by an appropriate officiant standing in the vestibule, and offering of some items of service by the priest in the cella, another offering of food is made and is taken to be offered to other subsidiary deities in the temple. In between, holy ashes, 'bhasma' or 'vibhūti', 'bilva'-leaves and holy water are distributed to those participants who have been attending through this ritual, standing and praying in the great hall. Offerings are then made to the doors of the great hall and the offerings-altars in the middle enclosure, while carrying in a palanquin a copper trident fixed in a hemispherical base. Finally the palanquin is brought out to the great altar that stands behind the banner-post at the outermost east entrance and a food offering is made there. The palanquin is carried back to the great hall, where, it appears, it rests. The priest then locks the door of the vestibule and this brings the third service to an end ; and it is about noon then.

The fourth service of the day, however, begins very soon thereafter and lasts for about an hour and a half. It is exactly like the first service, the only difference being that, the image of the deity being already in the shrine, the part concerned with bringing it from the shrine of the consort is absent.

At the completion of the fourth service, it appears, the doors of the great hall, too, are locked and all officials and officiants go for their meals. It is only about half-past five that ritual activity shows signs of beginning. The usual troupe-music begins to be played. At sunset the conch is blown in the porch, doors of the shrine are opened and lights are lit up. The appropriate priest, having bathed, offers worship which is a replica of the third service and is witnessed and participated in by many, including pilgrims, who visit this temple by hundreds and sometimes by thousands. It comes to an end about 9 or 10 p.m.

The sixth service which follows soon is a repetition of the morning service, which done the priest removes the golden image of Śiva to the palanquin. With the usual paraphernalia, identical with that of the dawn service, the palanquin is taken in procession passing, in its path by the statues of Tirumalai Setupati and his son which stand by the side of the south entrance, through the innermost enclosure (?) to the shrine of the consort. On every Friday at this occasion the statues of these donors and builders of the southern portion of the second enclosure are honoured by being garlanded and offered betelnut and flowers. The image is taken out by the priest at the south entrance of the shrine of the consort and placed in the bed beside Amman, Parvatavardhinī. A camphor light is waved and a milk offering is made, whereafter the priest comes out of the shrine. At this stage the dancing girl in attendance used to sing a Tamil song and another reciter another Tamil song, both suggesting Śiva's superiority to Viṣṇu. The images during the recitation are sung, the beds being arranged on a swing, and fanned so that the deities, the royal personages, may have comfortable sleep. People present at this service there are then given sacred ashes. It is now about midnight and all the doors are locked and everything at the temple is quiet.

The ritual of worship observed at a Śiva temple, not famous but one of the better known and richer ones, at an older centre only six years before Burgess gave the above account of the one current at the Rāmeśvaram temple, is described by Monier Williams[4], having taken it from Dr. Rajendralal Mitra's book on the Antiquities of Orissa[5]. The ritual observed at Bhuvaneśvara in the Śiva temples is listed in twentytwo items, many of which are identical with those of the ritual at Rāmeśvaram, being less ostentatious, less royal and less elaborate. The afternoon service begins with the rousing of the deity at 4 p.m. In the evening instead of the offerings to several phallus-emblems in the enclosures of Rāmeśvaram, at Bhuvaneśvara, five masks representing the well-known five faces of Śiva—Śiva is 'pañcamukhī' or five-faced—and Śiva's favourite musical implement, the two-sided small-drum, are given the particular honour. Apparently there is no palanquin procession nor are there any enclosures to the temple to be traversed. Presumably there is neither a shrine of the consort nor even perhaps her image nearby in the temple. There are only three services a day instead of the six at Rāmeśvaram. The items of the morning and the evening services make them out to be what the texts and sectarian worshippers describe as sixteen-itemed worships, 'ṣoḍaśopacārapūjā'. The midday service is ten-itemed. Any other worship offered, as commonly the domestic worship of Śiva, is known as 'pañcopacārapūjā', five-itemed worship.

Mrs. Sinclair Stevenson[6], about fortyfive years after Monier Williams, account of Orissan Śiva worship as seen by Rajendralal Mitra, describes the ritual as observed in an ordinary town or village temple of Śiva in Saurashtra. There are said to be four services per day. There is four-handed image of Pārvatī somewhere in the temple and it gets its worship too. The afternoon service is not worship proper but reading of some sacred text which is listened to by many, mostly women. So in reality the worship service is offered only three times a day. There is neither the Śiva-image, nor the palanquin procession, nor even the putting-to-bed rite here. Here is Śiva worship, as it is expected to be from the theological and other literature of the sect, fairly simple and austere.

Still later C. G. Diehl[7] describing the Śaiva ritual of worship from South Indian (Tamilian) Agamic sources, affirms that six services a day is the prescribed number in the literature, adding, however, that full ritual has to be gone through only three times a day. He has followed his account with a brief description of the actual ritual as observed in the great temple at Madurā which is known to the world as Mīnākṣī temple but is actually a double-temple, the two shrines making it up being dedicated to Sundareśvara and Mīnākṣī respectively. The timings of the various services more or less coincide with those observed for the ritual at Rāmeśvaram described above, except that the temple remains closed between 12.30 p.m. and 4.00 p.m. and that the evening service starts at 7 p.m. and not earlier. On Fridays the last item, the palanquin procession and its accompanying service, takes place a little later, about an hour, so that the services of the day terminate only with its end at 12 midnight.

The ritual of worship followed in the temples dedicated to Viṣṇu is more or less the same, the variation mainly pertaining to the differences in the mythological incidents and attendants and marks. Rajendralal Mitra[8] describing the ritual as observed at the great Viṣṇu-Kṛṣṇa temple at Puri, known to all as Jagannātha, almost as sacred as and perhaps more famous than the Rāmeśvaram temple, remarked ninety years ago that the daily round of ritual there was very much the same as what obtained in the Liṅgarāja temple at Bhuvaneśvara.

R. G. Bhandarkar[9] listed fourteen items composing the full ritual of worship offered in the large Vallabhite subsect of Vaiṣṇavism. Mrs. Sinclair Stevenson[10], writing of Vaiṣṇavite temple worship of that part of India where Vallabha School of Vaiṣṇavism predominates, informs us that the number of services offered per day in Kṛṣṇa temples is commonly counted as seven. But one of them, the one known as "afternoon nap" for three hours, being another way of saying that the temple remains closed during that period, the services proper are only six. Thus the ritual of Kṛṣṇa-temple-worship is not very much different from that of the Śiva temples. The two differences that deserve mention are : First, in the Vaiṣṇava temples there is no separate temple for the consort of the deity and that part of the ritual which is concerned with the bringing and returning of the image of the deity to another shrine is absent ; secondly, in the Vaiṣṇava ritual, at least in the North Indian one, one of the services is known as 'śriṅgāra', dressing and adorning of the deity being named that way, and another is called 'rājabhoga', royal repast. The principal offering of food is so named ; and we shall find later that in the North Indian, especially Vallabhite and Caitanyite, Vaiṣṇava temples, there came to be put up an additional structure, as a continuation of the shrine, known as 'bhogamaṇḍapa', repast hall.

The difference in the matter of the service item of food-offering to the deity between the Śaiva and Vaiṣṇava sects stems from the fundamentally different treatment in theological speculation given to the food offering made to the two Gods. The food-offering of Śiva must not be eaten by ordinary worshippers while that of Viṣṇu is prized as an auspicious gift of a sacred nature and is called 'prasāda' to be shared by all.

In the South Indian ritual there appears to be a variation which replaces this second difference between the two rituals. The food-offering there is not specially marked out ; nor does there appear to be a special 'maṇḍapa', known as 'bhoga-maṇḍapa' in the Vaiṣṇava temples of South India. However,—at least it is so in the famous Vaiṣṇava shrine of Tirupati—the hall commonly called the 'mahāmaṇḍapa' is known as 'ārtamaṇḍapa', the hall for the distressed ; and the fourth item in the ritual of worship there is known as Durbar when the deity is seated in that hall to receive light refreshments.[11]

In the foregoing accounts of services and worship no mention is made of the act of bowing or making obeisance to the deity at any stage of the procedure but it is well understood that there must be more than one occasion during it when the worshipper has to do and does his obeisance. In the list of the sixteen items which form the compound whole called the 'ṣoḍaśopacārapūjā', the sixteen-itemed, i.e., full-fledged worship, however, the two penultimate items certainly and the one previous to them very construably, constitute obeisance.

A brief view of this compound worship is necessary at this stage in order to make the later account of the shrine-structure and its development intelligible and also to enable the reader to realize how the growth of mechanical and ritualistic approach has attended on the elaboration of worship, or how both elaboration of worship and increase in ritualism have gone hand in hand in the history of Hinduism.

Years ago, R. G. Bhandarkar[12] accepted the statement of sixteen-itemed worship in the *Padma-Purāṇa* as perhaps the earliest mention of it. And these are the items accepted as correct and put into practice in the Rāmānuja subsect of Vaiṣṇavism. The items listed as composing it, however, are not identical with the later standard complex of worship, such as the one in practice at the great temples already described. Nor are they all of them items of worship as such. Many of them are modes of approach to the deity, eight items out of the sixteen being the same as those that constitute, with the addition of one more, the nine-fold devotion, 'navavidhā bhakti'. Among these eight figures the item of constant worship with devotion which is quite clearly a pure tautology, if compounded in the complex described as modes of approach to the deity, though three of them can be included in the worship-complex as personal preliminaries, like making of the sectarian marks on one's body reciting the appropriate formulae. There is only one item, that of laying the 'tulasī'-leaves on the image of Hari, Viṣṇu, corresponding to the item of laying the 'bilva' leaves on the phallus-emblem in Śaiva worship, which is an item of worship, pure and simple.

The items in the ritual of worship as observed in the Vallabhite subsect are :[13] (1) the ringing of the bell, (2) the blowing of the conch, (3) waving of lamps, (4) offering of morning refreshments, (5) bathing the image, (6) awakening of the Lord, (7) dressing it, (8) offering of special food, (9) leading the cows out for grazing, (10) the midday dinner and (11) waving of lamps. After this the screen or curtain is drawn and the deity rests. It is no time for any one to have sight of God. Thereafter there is what is called (12) finishing up, (13) the evening meal and (14) putting to bed. As can be easily appreciated the ritual categorized thus gives a day's routine for the service of the deity by the worshipper. It does not detail the compound of various services, actions and offerings which taken together are called the sixteen-itemed worship.

Worship at a temple can be and is performed three times a day but domestic worship is generally performed only once a day, the evening worship being epitomised in putting up a light or at best waving it in front of the household deity.

Fifteen of the sixteen items of the worship-complex, making the latter a sixteen-itemed worship, are detailed in the poems of the Vallabhite group of saint poets of Northern India known as 'Aṣṭachāpa'.[14] They are : (1) Invoking the deity to be present, (2) offering a seat, (3) water for washing the feet, or washing the feet, (4) pouring of water as a respectful offering, (5) offering water for sipping, (6) offering of five-itemed mixture as reverential reception, (7) bathing the image, commonly with water but with the mixture called 'pañcāmṛta', five nectars (curds, milk, clarified butter, honey and sugar), on special occasions followed by bathing with ordinary water*, (8) putting on or offering dress and ornament, (9) putting the sacred thread or scarf, (10) applying or giving fragrant unguent, (11) putting on flowers, (12) some eatable offering, (13) betel leaf and nut offering, (14) circumambulation, (15) salutation by itself or after offering a handful of flowers which is called either as 'flower handful' (puṣpāñjali) or on group, formal or special occasions as 'mantrapuṣpa'† 'consecrated flowers' and (16) sending off or rather taking leave of the deity.

Items numbered 6 and 13 are unusual and their inclusion in the list has ousted incense and light, which are to be waved one after another in a burning state before any eatable-offering is made. Ringing of bell is not mentioned for it is an accompaniment of a number of items like that of bathing and is not an independent one.

That the ritualistic and mechanistic attitude, increasing in its intensity, volume and extent, was leading to elaboration in externals like the items of service in worship is further supported by the exhortation in the 'tantras' of making it an eighteen-itemed one by the addition of garlands and unguents as distinct from the earlier items of fragrant unguent ('gandha') and flowers ('puṣpa').[15]

As regards the probable date of the first elaboration of worship, whether into eight-itemed or sixteen-itemed, we have to infer from Lord Kṛṣṇa's affirmation of His worship as a simple affair (*BhG*, IX, 26) that it had taken place at least some time before 200 B.C.

It is no plan of this work to give a complete or even a brief history of the growth of the modes of approach to the deity or their nature in particular items. The main concern is with the ritual in its relation to the plan of the shrine and secondarily with treating such other items as are interesting and instructive from the comparative point of view. Before going on with the consideration of the shrine, for which enough about the ritual has been said, I should dwell on the nature and development of the mode of obeisance current among the Hindus, an aspect of the ritual of worship having close connection with the plan of the shrine, and on some history of the paraphernalia of worship in a temple for identical reason. The nature of obeisance, in the light of what has been said in the early chapters regarding the mode of obeisance among the Mesopotamians and Egyptians, claims our attention first.

* These items are mentioned as they are known in current practice.

† 'Mantrapuspa' is mentioned in Rāmadāsa's *Dāsabodha*, XIX, 5, 11.

Salutation is denoted in Sanskrit by the words, among others, 'namas' and 'vandana', the latter of which appears in the above list of sixteen items of worship as envisaged in Northern India about the 15th and 16th centuries. 'Namas' as a more ancient attested word having been used very many times in the *Rgveda*, both in the singular and the plural. It is rendered by the commentator Sāyaṇa sometimes by 'praise', sometimes by 'salutation', and sometimes even by 'worship' if it is in the verbal form.[16] Griffith has most often translated it by homage, following Sāyaṇa in translating by worship if the form is verbal. Vedic 'namas' many mean adoration, salutation or obeisance. Yet the question remains what was the form of that salutation which 'namas' meant. At least in one of the passages in an explicit reference to what must be considered to be one of the forms of obeisance there is clear indication of the limbs of the body that were brought into play and of the manner of doing it. In *RV*, 72, 5, the first part of the verse is thus rendered : "Nigh they approached, kneeling they paid worship." 'Paid worship' is the translation of 'namas' in the verbal form, while 'kneeling' is that of the word 'abhijñu', which is a contraction or technical formation or 'abhi' and 'jānu', the latter word meaning knee. In the Ṛgvedic age we may take it that one of the forms of salutation was by kneeling, i.e., resting one's knees on the ground. And if we can take it, as I think we may, that the word 'namas' applied to some form of joining the palms, then we may further infer that a particularly reverential mode of salutation consisted in kneeling before the object to be shown reverence to and joining one's palms in supplication.

By 500 B.C. reverence shown to a deity had already come to be the standard of reverence, and one's preceptor was enjoined to be shown the same reverence as a deity. More specifically the disciple was enjoined to touch his preceptor's feet with his hands as common salutation, which involved of course the bending of one's body from above the waist.[17] The *Bhagavadgītā* (IV, 34 ; XI, 14 ; 35 ; 44) leaves not the least doubt that before its compilation the standard mode of reverential salutation had come to be fixed, that the palms were to be joined, that the head was to be bowed low, and that the person had to prostrate himself before the object to be shown reverence to. In some of the scenes of Buddhist worship[18] we find the mode of reverential salutation to have consisted in joining the palms of the hands placing the joined unit over one's head and also kneeling down before the object reverenced. This latter feature, Ṛgvedic in antiquity and origin, does not figure in later Hinduism. The *Manusmṛti*[19] acquaints us with a further elaboration in name and also in the manner of making obeisance. The disciple had, according to that text, to fold his hands together at the beginning of his day's study, such folding of the palms being named 'brahmāñjali'. He had to bow down to the preceptor no doubt by touching or grasping his feet with his hands but he had to manage it so that his right palm catches his preceptor's right foot and the left the other ; in short, he had to cross his hands, of course the right going over the left.

In later times and currently the mode of reverential obeisance consists in falling prostrate at the feet of the object to be reverenced, though it can be modified, in the case of human beings to be reverenced, so that one kneels down and touches the feet of the person reverenced with one's head. The full and prostrate bow is known as 'sāṣṭāṅga praṇipāta' or 'sāṣṭāṅga namaskāra', salutation with eight limbs. It is noteworthy that the limbs that can touch the ground or the feet of the person reverenced are not eight; and the total is made up by the inclusion among them of non-physical items of human personality. The limbs actually enumerated are: the head, the chest, the hands, the knees and the feet. The non-physical elements added to these to make up the number of eight are: intellect, sight and speech.

The earliest reference to the use of this mode of obeisance, that too by this name, is the one, or rather two, that we have in the popular Sanskrit book of the 5th century A.D. by name *Pañcatantra*. We know that one used to show one's reverence for a Śaiva ascetic, then, by first pronouncing the Śaiva sacred formula, 'Om, adoration to Śiva', and then by prostrating oneself before him.[20] From the same work we learn that the Vedic practice of kneeling for obeisance had by then been completely appropriated by and was common among the Jainas. One greedy person is described as having gone to a Jaina temple ('vihāra') and to have shown his reverence for Jina by circumambulating the image thrice and by kneeling before it.[21]

Mention of three circumambulations in connection with reverential salutation of Jina leads one to the consideration of circumbulation as an item in Hindu worship already listed. It may be mentioned at once that circumambulation ('pradakṣiṇā')* as a component of reverential salutation is a peculiarity of Hinduism, its occurrence in the only other great religion, viz., Buddhism, having to be regarded as derivative. In a Christian church or cathedral a particular part of it is known as ambulatory and it surrounds the altar no doubt; but circumambulation as a component of reverential adoration is not the purpose served by it, such a feature not being a component of Christian adoration.

Since when circumambulation has been an established mode of reverential adoration I have not been able to ascertain; but it appears to me to be a very ancient one. In the ritual of marriage three circumambulations round the fire by the bride and bridegroom together are a necessary rite, which is so ancient that three circumambulations of fire guaranteeing the witness of Fire to the union may be taken to be a Vedic heritage. Kālidāsa has drawn upon this feature in his *Kumārasaṁbhava* (VII, 79) at the marriage of Śiva and Pārvatī as well as in his *Raghuvaṁśa* (VII, 24) at the marriage of Aja and Indumatī. Sage Kāśyapa arranging for an auspicious send-off to Śakuntalā asks her to circumambulate the fire enkindled by him while pronouncing his protective benediction (*Śākuntala*, IV, 6-7). In describing the daily

* In this act of obeisance the performer moving round the object of reverence has to keep it to his right side throughout the round.

worship which the queen of king Dilīpa used to offer to the calf of the heavenly cow of sage Vasiṣṭha, Kālidāsa makes it clear that the actual salutation, the bow, followed circumambulation and that red-coloured rice, 'akṣatā' as it is called, was to be used for such worship (*Raghuvaṁśa*, II, 21).

Circumambulation is such a necessary item of adoration and of worship that when circumstances make it impossible to circumambulate the object of worship the worshipper rotates round himself, turning from right to left and then folds his palms in obeisance. When the Sun is the object of worship this is the only, and therefore the standard, manner of adoration.

Worship at a temple and its paraphernalia are rather rare to get at in the literary sources; and temples themselves which can give indication of the paraphernalia are very late in date. I shall mention here one or two indications which I have come across. The oldest such indication is I think the one we get in Hāla's '*Saptaśatī*', an anthology of Prakrit poems dated not later than the 2nd century A.D. From II, 72 we know that the then existing temples of Goddess Chaṇḍikā used to have big bells, tied, perhaps, at the front door. From II, 94 we know that fresh garland of flowers were an item in daily worship of the town-deity in the temple dedicated to it.

Kālidāsa's brief but appealing description of the great temple of Śiva at Ujjayinī, known as Mahākāla, makes it clear that in a Śiva temple there used to be a big drum, perhaps like what are found today in Hindu temples, particularly Śiva ones, a kettle-drum, its hide-side being beaten with two small sticks to make the necessary rather sonorous sound—whose sound when beaten must have resembled the deep rumbling of clouds. It is also clear from Kālidāsa's tabloid description that worship was offered there twice a day, morning and evening, and that the beating of the drum or drums was one of the accompaniments of each worship. The word used for specifying the time of worship being 'sandhyā', it follows that there were two worships. The commentator Sthiradeva makes them to be three, taking noon as included in 'sandhyā', a doubtful interpretation. Actually, however, Kālidāsa specifically refers only to the evening dusk worship offered at the temple of Mahākāla, as is quite clear from a perusal of the four verses, 34-37, of his lyric *Meghadūta*. Another even more interesting item, accompanying the dusk worship of Śiva mentioned by Kālidāsa in this connection is the 'chowrie'-dance executed by dancing girls evidently attached to the temple. The girls are described as dancing so long and so vigorously that they would be mightily pleased with the cloud for a few drops of very covetable rain at that time. This item of dancing girls and their dance, as we have seen, was a regular feature of Śiva-worship at Rāmeśvaram till recently and must be presumed to have been a common feature of Śiva-worship all over India. It appears to have dropped out from North India, probably with the advent of the Muslims, and was preserved in South India for a few hundred years, till, under new ideas of propriety and public morality, it has come to be very properly discontinued.

Kālidāsa next uses the mythological information about Śiva's dancing, His evening 'tāṇḍava'-dance, which He is said to have executed after killing the dreaded demon Gajāsura[22], using its wet skin as a covering for himself thus adding weirdness to the vigorous intricacy of His movements.

With this knowledge of the ritual of worship in its development and in its current practice we are fairly well equipped for a proper understanding and appraisal of Hindu shrines as the material and outward manifestations of the religious consciousness of the Hindus. The earliest known, reconstructed though, structure that is indubitably a Hindu shrine cannot be dated earlier than A.D. 400.[23] On the other hand, shrines must have existed from before the 5th century B.C.[24] The earliest shrine, extant or reconstructed, is, further, a very small, an almost poor, affair. It is just a cella and a porch, the cella having a flat top like that of the porch and just a little taller than the latter. The real distinction between the porch and the cella is that the latter is a closed structure except for its front door, while the porch is open on three sides and is supported on columns, thus presenting a columnar appearance contrasting with the solid walls of the cella behind.

The earliest reference in an authentic record that is almost certainly datable is the one we have in the inscription of King Khāravela of Kaliṅga in the Hāthīgumphā cave of the Udayagiri Hills near Bhuvaneśvara in Puri district. It is ascribed to the end of the 1st century B.C. at the latest. In it Khāravela informs us that he repaired all temples belonging to the different sects in the land, that some of these structures had their courts, 'prākāra', and their towers, 'gopura', blown by winds; and also that he built new temples, 'śikhara', provided with strong and beautiful entrance arcades, 'gopura'.[25]

The few literary references I have been able to gather pertaining to the appearance and structural parts of a Hindu temple, dating from before the 2nd century A.D., to before A.D. 400, the date of the earliest reconstructed temple, presume a tall and a relatively magnificent structure. In Hāla's *Saptaśatī* (I, 64) we have a reference to the condition of a village, or at best a town, temple whose top portion had some special part partially broken. The portion of the top partially revealed owing to its superstructure having been broken is rendered by the word 'śaṅku' in Sanskrit; and the commentators' explanation envisages the breaking away of the top portion known in Hindu temple architecture as 'kalaśa' or bellied pot. The side-opening affording birds the chance to enter from the top and to have their nests inside in the recesses of the superstructure, the temple was full of birds humming their sexual and parental energy and creating a peculiarly murmuring sound. The poet fancies the temple in that condition as a being suffering from an attack of stomach-ache. Leaving the poetic fancies and the suggested use of the precincts, one can quite well realize that the kind of structure presumed, when intact, must have resembled more a structure like that of the temple at Deogarh near Sanchi (A.D. 500), if not like that of Paraśurāmeśvara temple (A.D. 700) or of Mukteśvara temple (A.D. 990) at Bhuvaneśvara in Orissa.

The dramatist Bhāsa, 2nd century A.D. or a little earlier, in his play named 'Pratimā', through the indirect information supplied in Bharata's description of approaching Ayodhyā, has clearly presented the fact of temples of his time in North India having been rather high, so that they were the objects first sighted by a visitor to a city or a town from afar. In the description of Ayodhyā, as it appeared very early in the morning of the day when Rāma's coronation was intended to be effected, occurring in the *Rāmāyaṇa* (II, 6, 11-13), among the many places, spots and buildings which carried on high fluttering banners, flags and buntings, figure not only terraces of tall mansions, not only the 'caitya'-trees, which must necessarily have been tall, but also temples of gods with pinnacles having the splendour of white clouds. And these banners being hoisted on such tall objects could be seen from everywhere. The temples of Ayodhyā had 'śikharas', the technical name of the spire of a Hindu temple, rising over the cella or the shrine, which were both white and very high.

An inscription from Mandasor in Gwalior district dated about A.D. 460 records the construction of a temple dedicated to the Sun-god by various craftsmen, who having left their own region of Gujarat had settled in modern Mandasor and had flourished in various occupations. The temple that they built was unparalleled or incomparable, 'atula', and expansive, and had a high spire, 'śikhara', which was as white as the bunch of the rays of the rising moon and as easily seen as a mountain. In the same inscription some of the mansions of the city are described as having tops like the high peaks of Kailāsa mountain.[26]

In a slightly earlier inscription[27], one from Bilsad in Etah district, U.P. and dated about A.D. 415, the construction of an entrance gate, called there 'pratoli', and neither 'gopura' nor 'toraṇa', in front of a temple of Skanda-Mahāsena, which is described as extremely white-looking like a piece of crystal, is mentioned.

These references, both in records and in literature, though few and rather laconic, justify us in maintaining that temples, both expansive and magnificent, having spires which rose very high into the air, and not infrequently either gilded white or constructed out of white marble, were a fairly common occurrence in the cities of India at least from about 200 B.C. to about A.D. 460. Under these circumstances to begin an account of Hindu temples with the kind of simple structures, which conceivably can be their distant predecessor or even ancestor, as if they began to be made about A.D. 410 for the first time, as Percy Brown has done appears to me to be wrong. My purpose, however, not being to trace the origin and growth of temples but only to study the outstanding specimens in relation to the type of religious living and the mode of ritual worship I shall not enter into that question.

The ritual of worship, which, as indicated, could not have been very simple, required a kind of temple which was more than a mere cella or a shrine. Though the few references to certain parts of a temple that I have been able to trace in records, literary or historical, do not expressly mention a structural component of a temple, later known as 'sabhā-maṇḍapa' or 'mahāmaṇḍapa', the general description of temples being expansive and beautiful can be interpreted to suggest the existence of such an adjunct. With their towers or spires rising high and even being very white, either because they were gilded or were made of marble, specifically described as objects seen from afar, temples must have been objects of attraction and reverence, awe-inspiring and soul-lifting. The ritual with its accompaniment of the kind of music that large kettle drums and bells could make was evidently calculated to inspire the feeling of not only awe but also mystery. And the high tower, presumably hollow from below, going over the cella, the recitation of formulae accompanying the ritual worship below it would immensely strengthen the feeling of mystery, any sound within such a cella having a sort of reverberation and rumbling complementing it.

Now that we have had an introduction to what is perhaps the most notable and noticeable feature of a Hindu temple throughout its known history, viz., 'śikhara', and also to another, which is less specific and more restricted, viz., 'gopura' or the entrance-gate, it is opportune for us to mention the other parts and alternative terms for such of them as have them and to trace them in history if possible.

A temple is either 'devālaya' or 'devāyatana', house of God.* The former word, which is by far the commonest now, is contracted dialectically into 'devul', 'deval' or 'deul'. It consists of a cella, wherein the image of the deity stands, and is generally known as the 'garbha-gṛha', the embryo-house, i.e., the innermost house. The term as the designation of the sanctum or the innermost part of a temple, the apartment where evidently the image was placed, is found used in that sense by Bhavabhūti, in the 8th century A.D., in his play *Mālatī-Mādhava* (I, 20, 7 ; VI, 2, 10). It is closed on three sides by solid walls. On its eastern side adjoining the door and as a narrower continuation of the cella structure it has a passage-like projection. It is generally known as 'antarāla', the intervening space, though sometimes it is known also as 'ardha-maṇḍapa', half-pavilion, having breadth and depth both much less than those of the structure, which adjoins it on the east known as 'maṇḍapa' or 'sabhāmaṇḍapa', assembly hall. Over the cella, including the ambulatory, if it is provided round the cella, rises as its covering and top a pyramidal or curvilinear structure which resembles a spire. It is called 'śikhara', top. This unit of the temple is known as either 'prāsāda' or 'vimāna'. The former word means a mansion and is used also to designate great civil buildings, royal palaces etc. The latter word means an air-vehicle, aeroplane in modern terminology, a car in which gods in Hindu mythology are described as travelling through air, that of God Indra being considered the most majestic, commodious

* The learned poet-dramatist Bhavabhūti, who lived about the first quarter of the eighth century, in his play *Mālatī-Mādhava* (III, lines 13, 21 ; VI, 2, 2 ; VI, 7, 26; IX, 1) speaks of Śaṅkara's, i.e., Śiva's, temple as the "house of Śaṅkara", of a temple of another god as the "house of so and so" and of a temple as the "house of God".

and speedy. Sometimes this word is used to denote the spire of the shrine.

What is perhaps more interesting is the fact that the word 'vimāna', like the other term for a temple, 'prāsāda', first appears in literature as a word signifying a mansion, a big house. In his description of the city of Alakā, Kālidāsa (*Meghadūta*, 63 and 68) has at least twice used the word to denote a very high building, high enough to have clouds resting on its top. It is in the same sense that he uses the word in his description of Śiva's marriage (*Kumārasambhava*, VII, 40), combining with it in a compound another, the whole meaning tops of high mansions. It is, however, noteworthy that the same great poet and master of Sanskrit expression uses the word 'vimāna' to denote a pavilion, 'maṇḍapa' (*Raghuvaṁśa*, XVII, 9). It is curious that in an earlier record a great celled structure on the top of a mountain is described as being similar to the best of aeroplanes, viz., Puṣpaka, owned by god Indra.[28] Having used the word 'vimāna' to signify a tall mansion in his description of Alakā, Kālidāsa in the very next verse speaks of its high mansions as 'prāsāda' and describes them as having tops high enough to kiss the clouds (*Meghadūta*, 64). In a popular work of the 5th century A.D., the *Pañcatantra* (I, 221), 'prāsāda' is qualified as 'saptabhūmika', i.e., seven-storied, but a four-storeyed building is referred to as a house, 'gṛha' (IV, 65), and not as a 'prāsāda'. It is to be noted that in lexicons we have a compound word 'pañcaprāsāda' which denotes a temple of a particular size with four pinnacles and a steeple.[29]

Apropos of 'gopura' as a part of a temple mentioned in the Orissan inscription of King Khāravela of the first century B.C. I should point out that literary sources mention 'toraṇa', gateway-arch, permanent and therefore like 'pratoli' already mentioned, equivalent to 'gopura' meaning either the outer gate or the ornamental arch on it. In the latter case (*Meghadūta*, 72) Kālidāsa has used the feature, not only because it is rainbow-coloured but also because it is very high and therefore sightable from afar, to characterize the Yakṣa's house to enable the cloud messenger to find it without difficulty. But there is no indication in the use of this word that it is a building, much less a storeyed one. The most famous structures known by this appellation are the gateways in the railing around the 'stūpa' of Sanchi, though that of Bharhut[30] is the oldest. But that is a Buddhist relic and not a Hindu one. A number of such structures in various stages of development and form are known to have existed in Northern India. A number of them, one of which is figured, are recorded as from Gujarat and dated in the 11th century A.D. in Fergusson's great work.[31] Others, again one of them being given as an illustration from Warangal down south, which have to be ascribed to the 13th century, are reported in the same book. The earliest of so far known structures of this designation, however, is the 'toraṇa', 'archway', in front of the Mukteśvara temple at Bhuvaneśvara in Orissa. It is ascribable to the last quarter of the 10th century, according to Percy Brown.[32] Some of these were quite evidently, at least according to these experts, intended to serve as gateways of temples. The same expert[33] gives us the positive information that there are four gateways in the outer enclosure wall of Jagannātha temple at Puri. But Brown the latest of them adds about them: "These gateways, although substantial structures with pyramidal roofs, bear no resemblance to the gopuram type of the southern style." We cannot necessarily equate them with 'gopuras' of Khāravela's inscription which does not mention any 'toraṇa'.

A Hindu shrine, before the end of the 9th century A.D., may be taken to have consisted of a cell, with an ambulatory round it and a pavilion in front of it, the two being joined through a part often known specifically as 'antarāla', intermediate room. The outward mark of a shrine was a spire or tower-like projection up into the air crowning that part of it which housed the cella and its ambulatory. For the surviving examples of shrines, which indubitably are ascribed to a time before A.D. 1000, this type of a Hindu shrine, whether for Śiva or for Viṣṇu, can be shown to have been widespread in the country.

Shrines of such date whose pictures or plans or both are easily available in such works as those of James Fergusson or Percy Brown may be listed as follows: (1) Pāpanātha temple at Pattadakal in Dharwar; (2) Malegitti Śiva temple at Badami in Bijapur district; (3) Shore Temple at Mamallapuram near Madras; (4) Kailāsanātha temple at Kāñcī (Conjeevaram); (5) San-(gameśvara temple at Pattadakal; (6) Virūpākṣa temple at Pattadakal; 7) Kailāsa at Verula (Ellora); (8) Vaitāl deul at Bhuvaneśvara in Orissa; (9) Mukteśvara temple at Bhuvaneśvara; (10) Koraṅganātha temple at Śrīnivāsanalur in Tiruchirapally district; (11) Śītaleśvara temple at Candrāvatī, near Jhālārapatan in Rajasthan; (12) Śiva temple at Baroli near the falls of the Chambal; (13) Liṅgarāja temple at Bhuvaneśvara and (14) Bṛhadiśvara temple at Tanjore.

All these temples, except perhaps the one at Candrāvatī, have spires over the cella unit, their forms dividing them into two groups. The spires of the southern temples, except of some of them in Dharwar, take the form of a stepped pyramid, while those of the north assume a more flowing and unitary type, curvilinear in outline. The height of the 'śikhara' or 'vimāna', i.e., the spire or tower-like projection of the roof over the cella unit, naturally makes out a shrine, whether it is of the bigger and grander variety or of the smaller and ordinary one. Though the heights of all the 'śikharas' or 'vimānas' are not available, those that are given in the works of the experts, considered on the background of the pictures of others, lead to the conclusion that generally the later the shrine the taller is its spire or tower. The height data available in the sources give us the following heights of the three earlier Orissan temples: Vaitāl and Mukteśvara, 35 feet each, and Paraśurāmeśvara 44 feet. The great Liṅgarāja temple, the latest in the series so far, rises 160 feet high.[34] While the base of the spire of Paraśurāmeśvara is only about 23 feet square that of the great tower of Liṅgarāja is very massive, being 56 feet square.

Of the Madras, i.e., South India, mainly Tamilian, specimens, height is not given either for the tower of the Shore temple or for that of Kailāsanātha temple. In the latter case Brown has observed that its pyramidal tower dominates the scene.[35] And he has given the height of the tower of Vaikuṇṭha Perumal temple nearby it in Kāñcī, which is only a little later than Kailāsanātha temple, as 60 feet.[36] We may not be very wrong if we take the height of the tower of Kailāsanātha temple as about 65 feet. Its base can be made out from the plan in Fergusson's work to be about 30 feet square. The tower of Koraṅganātha temple in Tiruchirapally district rises 50 feet high with a base which is 25 feet square. The great tower of Bṛhadīśvara temple, almost the gem of South Indian or Tamilian temple architecture, rises much higher than that of its contemporary Orissan specimen, Liṅgarāja, standing majestically 190 ft. high. Its massive base measures 82 feet square. About it Fergusson remarked, "... *the tower dominates over the gopurams* and surrounding objects in a manner that imparts great dignity to the whole composition".[37] Writing much later and appropriately drawing upon British Christian Church parallels Brown observes : "As a measure of its size the vimāna [spire] is equal in height to the central tower of Worcester cathedral, but the temple as a whole is only two-thirds the area of this Gothic example."[38]

The unique piece of architecture—unique not only in India but in the world for it happens to be perhaps the only structure cut out free standing from hillrock and not into the hill-rock—known as Kailāsa, because being Śiva's abode, i.e., a temple dedicated to Śiva, it is like His mythological abode mount Kailāsa, at Verula (Ellora) has its spire tower—it is not a proper spire of the Orissan type nor completely a tower of the Southern Tamilian variety—standing 96 feet above the level of its court. Fergusson observes about it : "... the outline of the vimāna or śikhara is at first sight very similar to that of the raths at Mamallapuram, but on closer inspection we find everything so modified at Elura as to make up a perfect and well-understood design."[39] P. Brown has rightly gone a step or two forward in summing up his judgment on this unique piece of what I should call sculptural architecture. He says : "The temple of Kailāsa at Ellora is not only the most stupendous single work of art executed in India, but as an example of rock-architecture it is unrivalled ... The Kailāsa is an illustration of one of those rare occasions when men's minds, hearts, and hands work in unison towards the consummation of a supreme ideal."[40] The base of the spire-tower is 40 by 45 feet, not being a perfect square.

The sanctum, call it 'garbhagṛha' or 'vimāna', over which the spire or the tower rises majestically leading the eye of the visitor or worshipper up into the atmosphere, i.e., in the traditional direction of heaven, is further marked off in its elevation and outline from the other component unit or units so as to stand out before the visitor or the worshipper as the abode of God going up heavenward as it, mythologically speaking, should.

The sanctum, with or without its ambulatory, is further marked out in the elevational outline of the shrine. When the other component unit, or units as the case may be, has almost the same breadth as that of the sanctum-unit, the two or more units forming the shrine present a unified outline. The sanctum unit, in such cases, having quite often a different basic plan stands out distinguished from the other unit or units. Thus the sanctum of Pāpanātha of Pattadakal, as of Paraśurāmeśvara shrine at Bhuvaneśvara, is distinguished in outline from its 'sabhā-maṇḍapa' by the two balcony projections at the two sides and that of the great Kailāsanātha shrine at Kāñcī by the seven small sanctuaries jutting out on three sides of the sanctum, giving it a broader appearance. Much more often as in Kailāsa of Verula, Mukteśvara of Bhuvaneśvara, and even Virūpākṣa of Paṭṭadakal, the sanctum unit is distinguished by its being narrower and thus recessed sideways in outline. This side-ways recessing of the sanctum is commonly observed in those shrines which have an 'antarāla', intervening room, connecting the 'maṇḍapa' with the sanctum, as is the case with the graceful temple of Liṅgarāja at Bhuvaneśvara. In the Shore temple of Mahābalipuram and Koraṅganātha temple of Śrīnivāsanalur the sanctum unit is broader than the front component unit and stands out sideways.

Provision of an ambulatory within the shrine is made in all the three Dharwar shrines, viz., Pāpanātha, Saṅgameśvara and Virūpākṣa. Equally clearly no such provision is seen in any of the Orissan shrines. Of the South Indian shrines Kailāsanātha of Kāñcī belongs to this class, with its alround ambulatory running well outside the phallus-emblem cella. Both Kailāsa of Verula and Bṛhadīśvara of Tanjore belong to the class of temples which expect the worshippers to circumambulate round the sanctum from outside, either on the platform provided or in the enclosure put up round the temple.

All these shrines except Pāpanātha of Pattadakal, are two-units-structures, the third unit seen in Kailāsanātha temple of Kāñcī being a very late addition, which effected a slight modification in its plan. The entrance to the original second unit came to be provided at its side. The additional two units of Liṅgarāja shrine of Bhuvaneśvara are similarly later additions, of which more later on.

The size of this two-units-shrine, wherever the breadths of the two units are not markedly different, may now be mentioned to give the reader an idea of the size of the place of worship in the pre-mediaeval expression of Hindu religious consciousness. Of the Orissan shrines whereas Paraśurāmeśvara has an area of only 960 sq. ft., the great Liṅgarāja shrine began with an area of more than 6100 sq. ft. for its like two units. Virūpākṣa shrine of Pattadakal, Pāpanātha shrine of the place having to be left out for the present as it is a three-units-structure, similarly has an area of more than 6000 sq. feet. Whereas Kailāsanātha temple of Kāñcī has covered only about 3000 sq. feet with two of its component units, which are its original possession, the ponderously majestic Bṛhadīśvara shrine of Tanjore measures more than 6700 sq. feet in its area. The mystery-creating rock-cut Kailāsa stands between Kailāsanātha of Kāñcī on the one hand, and Virūpākṣa, Liṅgarāja and Bṛhadīśvara on the other, having an area of over 4300 sq. feet. It must be remembered that

Kailāsa was excavated out of rock at a place which is not known to have been a capital city. It therefore represents the material embodiment of religious consciousness in its purest form, devoid of any adventitious consideration of socio-political prestige lending its support for its size, grandeur, grace or magnificence.

We may describe these shrines, with only two component units, 'antarāla', vestibule, either not existing or not being counted as a unit, as the first phase of Hindu temple structuring embodying their religious consciousness. The great importance accorded to the sanctum unit, the care taken to have it clearly marked out in outline from its adjunct of the hall, is noticeable. This feature along with the height of the spire soaring high over it, combined with the darkness in the cella and many times also in the 'maṇḍapa', pavilion-unit, outside, mark the Hindu shrine as a place of mystery designed to enable the worshipper to have soul-lifting experience of awe and mystery. Inviting attention to the sanctum, by making it the most noticeable structural element of the shrine from outside, this treatment of it is in marked contrast to that of the ancient Egyptians. These great people, as made out in the previous chapter, made their sanctuary the lowest of the structural units in a long succession of such. This architectural difference, as will be appreciated on a reading of the relevant chapters of this book, is in consonance with the differential nature of the functions the shrine fulfilled in the two societies. Sight of God or the deity is a regular feature of religious living of the Hindus but apparently was not so with the ancient Egyptians.

The upward soaring of the spire or tower over the sanctum or the Holy of Holies in the very early Hindu shrines, as adumbrated above from before the 2nd century A.D., foreshadows the more or less similar placement of a spire or a tower later in Christian churches.

Another feature of the shrine, later known through Greek use of it as temenos, is the enclosure round it, or round it and its accessories and subsidiary shrines, which we have encountered in both the Mesopotamian and Egyptian shrine construction and placement, and which we know to have been such a prominent aspect of Christian sacred architecture, particularly of Christian cathedrals. The sacred area is marked off by an enclosure under this arrangement. And an enclosure means at least a wall, high or low, and one entrance gate. These effectively shut off the shrine and the Holy of Holies within from all possible stray gaze. This feature is both logical and necessary in a society where the shrine is a place of worship only at stated times and/or occasions. But in a society and in a system of religious consciousness wherein the individual is not restricted to specific times for his adoration of the deity, in fact wherein he is expected to offer it whenever he feels like it or passes by a shrine, such an arrangement argues a development in religious living and in mode of approach to the deity which has deviated from the standard laid down by the society or the authoritative text on the subject.

Among the shrines of the first phase enumerated above, the Orissan shrines lack such an enclosure ; most of the Dharwar specimens, excepting Virūpākṣa shrine, too, do the same. On the other hand, Kailāsa of Verula and the Shore temple at Madras, Kailāsanātha of Kāñcī and Bṛhadīśvara of Tanjore have the enclosure. Enclosure may be said to be a South Indian feature, not infrequent in practice from rather early times.

After about A.D. 1000, the Hindu Temple plan appears to have entered, what I should call, its second phase. Though the sectarian schools of Hinduism had not by then made their appearance or at least had not put up any doctrinal scheme, the poly-itemed devotion and mode of worship had come to be formulated in the developed form of Viṣṇu worship as represented in the *Bhāgavata-Purāṇa.* The extension of various aspects of worship and devotion could not fail to be reflected in the temple plans of the age after A.D. 1000. But unfortunately in Northern India the age coincided with the iconoclastic activity ushered in by the Muslim invaders and conquerors, leaving very few traces of the temple structures of the age till about the reign of Akbar. Inspite, however, of all the destruction wrought by the Muslims, who despoiled the temples to build their mosques out of them, there are a number of ruins adequate even in their ruined condition to indicate that their plans could not have materially differed from those of the few sheltered temples in the old country of the Chandelas, later known as Bundelkhand, like the justly famous and infamous shrine at Khajurāho, about 150 miles south-east of Gwalior, which is dedicated to Śiva and is known as Kandārya Mahādeva temple.

This series of temples of the second phase in Northern India, extending through Western India to Mysore region in a modified form, may be said to begin with the temple at Osia about 30 miles north-west of Jodhpur, which though assigned to the 9th century appears to me from its high plinth, low side walls with curved seats and low pillars to be of a later date, and to end with the two Viṣṇu temples which the famous Kṛṣṇa-devotee Mirābāi, wife of far-famed Kumbha Rāṇā of Mewar, built about the middle of the 15th century. In the Deccan and in Mysore region the series ends about A.D. 1320, when the Muslims overrunning South India carried everything before them and struck terror into the hearts of the Hindu inhabitants. In eastern India, i.e., in Orissa, the end came about seventy years earlier, with the Sun temple at Konarak near Puri which is dated about A.D. 1250. The Orissan second phase shows the widest variation from the second phase of Hindu temple structures of the other areas. It appears to have been entirely tuned to the highly developed ritualism of the newer Vaiṣṇavism adumbrated in Jayadeva's literary work and later formulated in practice by Caitanya.

In Northern India the representatives of this second phase are : (1) Temple at Osia, mentioned above ; (2) Sāsbahū temple at Nagda ; (3) Viṣṇu temples built by Mirābaī and Kumbha at Chitor ; (4) Navalākhā temple at Sejakpur in Saurashtra ; (5) Udayeśvara temple at Udayapur, about 30 miles north-north-east of Bhilsa and about 120 miles south-east of Khajurāho ; and (6) the great temple of Śiva at Khajurāho, the glory of the Chandelas typifying the stubborn stand of the Hindu faith.[41]

The combination of high plinth, low wall and low pillar with an eaves, or 'chajjā' as it is known, provide eminence to the structure and induce humility in the visitor, enhancing much more the sense of mystery, which is the aim of the central cella placement, by cutting off and shading light coming through the small open space between the roof of the pavilion and its low wall over high plinth. The seats, inclined backwards, provided at the top of this low wall bespeak intensified use of the pavilion for religious discourses or/and contemplative sojourn of the worshippers. The temple is not only a place to visit for sight of the deity but is also a place to rest a while and imbibe the sacred atmosphere. From Fergusson's[42] remarks about Mirābāi's Viṣṇu temple at Chitor that its one distinction in the plan is the non-provision of the ambulatory within the shrines, the same having been arranged on the platform outside, bring out two other common characteristics of this series of temple, viz., (1) they provide an ambulatory within the shrine as in the Kandārya Mahādeva temple at Khajurāho and (2) they stand, at least some of them, on raised platform, another method of enhancing the eminence of a shrine. As distinguished from the temples of the Deccan and of Mysore region these do not have enclosure walls and do not have any gateways apart from their own porches. These porches have tended to be made more artistically impressive and much deeper than early ones. This best comes out in the Kandārya Mahādeva temple of Khajurāho.

In dimensions the Khajurāho temple approaches very nearly the Liṅgarāja temple of Orissa with its first two components, the area of Khajurāho specimen being a little over 6500 sq. ft. as against the sixtyone hundred and odd square feet of Liṅgarāja. The component units are : (1) the cella which is a rectangle about 12.5 by 10 feet ; (2) the 'antarāla' ; (3) the 'sabhā-maṇḍapa' and (4) the porch or the 'ardhamaṇḍapa' ; (5) projecting balconies round the sanctum-unit on three sides ; and (6) 2 such balconies on the two sides of the 'sabhā-maṇḍapa'. The ambulatory within goes round the sanctum and the 'antarāla' as one unit. The plinth height deducible from the dimensions of height given by Fergusson is great, being 28 feet. The top of the 'śikhara', spire, from the floor of the temple is stated to stand 88 feet high. From the ground level its height is 116 feet which gives the height of the plinth to be 28 feet.

The spire of the Kandārya Mahādeva temple thus ranks fourth among the extant spire-towers of the sanctum unit of any Hindu temple. The spire-tower of the world-renowned temple of Jagannātha at Puri as will be noted later is the highest soaring nearly 200 feet high.[43] As already stated the heights of the spire towers of Bṛhadīśvara temple at Tanjore and of Liṅgarāja temple at Bhuvaneśvara are 190 and 160 feet high respectively. Experts are agreed that inspite of its height the tower-spire of Jagannātha temple is disappointing in comparison with the graceful one of Liṅgarāja temple. To me the tower-spire of the Khajurāho temple appears to be the most graceful and not being in lonely eminence to be more satisfying as a part of a whole complex of sanctity.

Fergusson[44], with his keen eyes and his competence resulting from comparative study of a vast area of the world, not at all convinced that the amount of skill and labour spent on the tower-spires was well spent, comparing the tower spire of Liṅgarāja temple with that of its near contemporary from the South, Bṛhadīśvara temple of Tanjore, unhesitatingly declared it to be "by far the finer design", and added : "Besides, however, greater beauty in form, the northern example excels the other immeasurably in the fact that it is wholly in stone from the base to the apex, and every inch of the surface is covered with carving in the most elaborate manner." On the tower spire or 'vimāna' of the Khajurāho masterpiece Fergusson makes a comment, which, coming from one who had all the three or five great tower-spires of Hindu temples in view, must be considered to be decisive. He says : "The vimāna or tower . . . is built up of smaller repetitions of itself, which became at this age one of the favourite modes—it may not be said unjustly that it was this temple that must have made this type of śikhara a prestige symbol of Hindu sacred or religious architecture—of decoration, and afterwards an essential feature of the style. Here it is managed with singular grace, giving great variety and play of light and shade, without unnecessarily breaking up the outline."[45] Percy Brown[46], too, with all the later valuations at his disposal, has no other view but that the Khajurāho 'śikhara' with its "more taut and tenuous contour" and "flowing profile" is more beautiful than the Orissan ones.

I should like to add to this considered aesthetic valuation of the experts my own appreciation of the total composition of the roofs of the temple. The temple has four roofs for its four component units ; and the 'śikhara , which is aesthetically so highly valued, is the roof of the last and the principal unit, the sanctum. The roofs of the three units in front coming one after another in continuation are so arranged that from the roof of the porch, which is the lowest, there is a regular but gentle gradation of height and form in the roofs, only the roof of the sanctum projecting above a little more than any of the others over its predecessor. The total effect is that the four roofs take the form of a composition making it a unity. The observer's eye, first falling on the top of the porch as he comes near, gently and imperceptibly glides over the next two roofs only to be taken straight up to the top of the graceful 'śikhara', giving it the picture of a unified whole, massed grace in stone. That the temple as a whole is the sacred object and the 'śikhara' must not be allowed to monopolize that honour and attention for itself, appears to have been the view of the great king who built it, an idealist who stood for the integrity of his, of his family's and of his country's faith with such defiance and determination that he and his family have become immortal in the annals of India !

The second phase of temple structuring in the eastern, i.e., Orissan, region is represented by the famous temple of Jagannātha at Puri. That this phase was inspired by the Vaiṣṇavite development of the mode of approach to the deity, which in a highly appealing literary composition was voiced and dramatised later by the Bengali poet Jayadeva[47], is stressed by the fact of its being dedicated to Kṛṣṇa with Rādhā. The temple when it was consecrated in A.D. 1118 had only the two first component units, the sanctum with the 'antarāla' and the 'jagamohan' or the 'sabhā-maṇḍapa', the first pavilion. The other two units making up the whole temple known as 'naṭa-mandira', dance-hall or pavilion, and 'bhoga-mandira', the food-offering hall or pavilion are believed to have been the additions of later centuries. 'Bhoga' literally means 'enjoyment' and connotes in the Caitanyite-Vallabhite Vaiṣṇavism the food-offering, which must be a sumptuous and exceedingly large one, to be offered to the deity and then to be distributed to the various dignitaries and others.[48] These two adjuncts or extensions of the Orissan temple plan became necessary after the 12th or the 13th century, these units in the Liṅgarāja temple at Bhuvaneśvara being assigned to the 12th or the 13th century. Another temple with these four component units extant ascribed to about A.D. 1200 is that of Ananta Vāsudeva a form of Viṣṇu.[49] This fully developed temple plan of the Orissan temples of the second phase of temple structuring in Northern or Eastern India with four component elements occurs only sporadically in the temple plans of the other parts, one particularly noteworthy example from the Mysore region, as will be made clear later, being known to occur in the second phase of temple structuring in the South.

The length of the first two units, the sanctum or 'vimāna' and 'jagamohan' the hall, is 155 feet and the breadth is 800 feet. The area covered by them, i.e., by the temple as it must have been when it was consecrated a century after Liṅgarāja temple of Bhuvaneśvara, is thus 12400 sq. feet. Contrasted with the area of the parallel two units of Liṅgarāja, which is a little over 6000 sq. feet, that of Jagannātha illustrates my observation about temple plans and sizes that they became bigger and more elaborate with time which among other reasons has prompted me to speak of three phases of temple structuring. The total area covered by the four units, i.e., by the fully developed temples, is a little over 13 thousand square feet for Liṅgarāja and 24800 for Jagannātha. What an increase in size ! The increase in the height of the tower-spire has already been commented upon.

I shall pass on to another trait of the second phase of temple structuring, which is very important, as it establishes much closer affinity between the east and the south of the country than is possible through the universal characteristic of a Hindu temple, the 'śikhara' or the 'vimāna' over the sanctum, which is always a kind of tower or spire but is never a flat floor or a dome in any of the notable specimens. And that is the existence of an enclosure round the temple, the creation of temenos in place of an individual temple, with its gateways which, however small in the case of the Orissan examples, establish a closer affinity between the Orissan notions of designing a temple as an instrument of religion and the South Indian ones. As we shall see later the enclosure and the gateway, known as 'gopuram' in the South tends to become common in the South only with the second phase of temple designing. It may be emphasized at this very juncture that the Orissan temple-designer, unlike his South Indian compeer, kept the principal objective of making the temple itself the object of attention intact, subordinating the gateways to their proper places, as mere accessories which must not obtrude on the visitor to the sacred precincts and their treasure, the temple.

It is further noteworthy that whereas Liṅgarāja temple has only one enclosure, 'prākāra' as it is called in Sanskrit and Tamilian temple terminology, the later and the bigger temple of Jagannātha has two enclosures, i.e., an enclosure for the temple within the larger enclosure accommodating other shrines and establishments. Yet it should be borne in mind that there is no evidence of a shrine for the consort of the deity, which will be met with in the South Indian temples of the second or perhaps the third phase.

Just as the size of temple increased with time so did the size of the enclosure too; and, as we shall see in the case of South Indian ones, even the number of enclosures registered the same tendency. Whereas the area covered by the enclosure, 'prākāra', of Liṅgarāja temple is about 240 thousand sq. feet, the area encompassed by the outer enclosure of Jagannātha temple is nearly 429 thousand sq. feet. What an increase in size! What an effort to accommodate the increase in the number of worshippers on occasions of public worship on festival days which under the newly developed complex of Vaiṣṇava worship must have become memorable and coveted occasions of religious gatherings! The enclosure of the great Bṛhadīśvara temple of Tanjore, more or less contemporary with Liṅgarāja shrine and only about a century and a quarter or a half earlier than Jagannātha shrine, measures only 125 thousand square feet.

In the Deccan and the Mysore regions the second phase of temple structuring replacement is represented by the following temples, which are selected for being listed, as their plans or photos or both are available in the works referred to. Many of the others which could have perhaps further enlightened us on the relation between mode of worship and its ritual on the one hand, and the temple of plan on the other, are in ruins. (1) Gondeśvara temple at Sinnar in Nasik District, (2) the combined temple at Hannamkonda near Warangal; (3) Chenna Keśava temple at Belur in Hassan district; (4) Hoysaleśvara temple at Halebid, ancient Dvārasamudra, the capital of the Hoysala kings of Mysore region, about 50 miles to the north of Belur; and (5) Somanāthapura temple near Seringpattam. All these, and many others more or less like them, some of them very much bigger than the first of this series, were built between A.D. 1100 and 1300.

The principal characteristics of this series of temples are: (1) they stand on a raised platform; (2) their plinths are high and the open space between the wall and the roof of the front pavilion and others too, is small; (3) generally this space is filled up by perforated lattice-work-like walls; (4) they have only three component units and not four as in the Orissan examples. They are: (*a*) the sanctum and the 'antarāla' which is common and known as 'sukhāsani', (*b*) the 'sabhā-maṇḍapa' known as 'navaraṅga' and (*c*) the porch known as 'mukhamaṇḍapa' which may or may not be open-sided; (5) they stand within an enclosure. At least the Nasik specimen as also the Somanāthapur one show such an enclosure, with one or more gateways, the modest predecessor of the Tamilian 'gopuram' gateway; (6) internally they have no provision for an ambulatory but the platform is so arranged in its width that ample room for an ambulatory is provided for.

Another feature of many of the Mysore region temples of this phase is so important that it must be separately mentioned. And that is the existence among them of not only double-shrined but also of triple-shrined and even quadruple- and quintuple-shrined temples.[50] The number of 'śikharas', spires on one temple, thus, unlike the generality of Hindu temples, is more than one,—a feature which looking to the theory and practice of pantheonic and other aspects of Hindu religious consciousness appears to be un-Hindu.

It is a very interesting development which appears to me to have been due to the urge of unification that was felt, and particularly so by the great Hoysala dynasty, which stood forth as the advance-guard of resurgent Hinduism in South India. The dynasty of the Hoysalas successfully brought under its sway a large part of South India; and it appears it kept it in a fairly prosperous condition for about a century and a half. To that extent its step at unification through this religious stratagem may be said to have succeeded. But its power, though so far away from the Muslim-dominated North and so well sheltered, crumbled before the first onslaught of the Northern Muslim power. The gains of the unification step, if any, in the political field were thus short-lived. From the purely religious point of view the unification-step was retrograde. A type of pantheonic unification was in working order in North India about A.D. 1000. As I have elsewhere[51] pointed out, in temple-designing it had taken the more appropriate form of grouped temple-complex. In it the main temple, in the centre of the group and a prominent one, was dedicated to the principal deity in whose name the particular pentad was to be known. The other four deities of the complex were accommodated either in smaller shrines spread round the principal temple or in niches specially made to receive them. In the Mysorian experiment the three, four or five deities, whose shrines together form a single temple, receive equal prominence and attention. The worship thus tends to be polytheistic. The compound-temple rises as one unit with three, four or five 'śikharas' in one group. They proclaim many gods as against the one God typified by a single 'śikhara' of a temple.

The Mysore experiment was however not altogether a unique or an entirely novel one. A three-shrined temple from Amva in Kotah district and another from Balsane in Khandesh are known.[52] I am not in a position to state if they have or had three spires. In the case of Mysore ones there is reason to believe that the number of 'śikharas', spires, corresponded to the number of shrines which together formed the temple. At least the three spires of the Keśava temple of Somanāthapura stand out in the pictures of that temple; and its plan leaves no doubt about them. And Fergusson specifically mentions the three 'vimānas' or 'śikharas', spires, of the Hannamkonda temple listed above and also of the Kedāreśvara temple at Balagami.[53]

This type of development, plurality of spires over a Hindu temple as a trait, is seen in the third phase of Eastern Indian temple designing which flowered in Bengal towards the end of the 17th or the beginning of the 18th century. A well reproduced specimen of it from Kantanagar near Dinajpur which was completed in A.D. 1722 is known. It has nine spires or towers. P. Brown's observations on the Bengal temples include a statement that "according to the number of these [towers] the temple is classified as *pañca-ratna*, of five gems, meaning towers, or *nava-ratna*, nine-towered, and so forth".[54] Whether this classification is a purely Bengali one or is derived from older and Sanskritic sources is not clear. The derivation of this development from more or less purely Islamic practice is to my mind not tenable. If its spread was due to Islamic influence the feature in its inception appears to be Jaina.

Thirteenth century Jaina temples present a skyline of a cluster of tapering spires, just as the Islamic mosque presents one of a spread of domes. Fergusson[55] commenting on the large number of small 'śikharas' seen on the Jaina temple of the early part of the 13th century at Mt. Abu drew attention to the doctrines of the Jaina creed, which, in its faithful carrying out, necessitated them, everyone of the important 'tīrthaṁkaras' requiring independent reverential treatment. He has further obliged us by stating the actual number of 'śikharas' and recounting the main domes occurring on the Jaina temple at Ranpur near Jodhpur built during the reign of the great king Rāṇā Kumbha about the middle of the 15th century. He points out that of the twenty domes four are big and double, one over the other; and that there are twelve "larger" 'śikharas', spires, and eightysix cell-shrines with their smaller ones. The picture of the temple as it appears on plate XXII of his book (vol. II)[56] reveals a veritable forest of 'śikharas' and domes.

The way Jainism had prospered and was making great headway in the South, I think, must partially at least account for this multiple-shrining with a plurality of 'śikharas' on top in the Mysorean temple-planning and structuring of the 13th century. The great kings of the Hoysala dynasty, their able ministers and their great superintendents of religious architecture, had got so much enamoured of their experiment in providing multi-spired temples, though not in strict conformity with the Hindu ideas of Godhead, that they planned towards the abrupt end of their sway after about A.D. 1300 or so—the temple had to be left in an utterly incomplete stage when the Muslims overpowered the dynasty in A.D. 1311—a temple which is a double one, both the shrines evidently having the phallus-emblem as the deity purposely, it would appear, to create a sacred edifice with a plurality of 'śikharas', spires. The temple I have in view is that of Hoysaleśvara at the then capital of the kingdom, Halebid. The Hoysaleśvara temple at Halebid in its conception and design is almost an anathema of the Hindu view of Godhead and of God's earthly abode, the temple, however architecturally and aesthetically grand it might be.

Fergusson wrote about it as the one piece of architecture on which the Hindus can stake their reputation as architects, a judgment even more favourable to it than the much more modern one of Percy Brown. And what is even more important, Fergusson did not stop with the above-mentioned judgment. He instituted a comparison with the all-time masterpiece not only of Greek architecture but also of all European architecture, the Parthenon at Athens. He says : "All the pillars of the Parthenon are identical, while no two facets of the Indian temple are the same ; every convolution of every scroll is different. No two canopies in the whole building are alike, and every part exhibits a joyous exuberance of fancy scorning every mechanical restraint. All that is wild in human faith or warm in human feeling is found portrayed on these walls ; but of pure intellect there is little-less than there is of human feeling in the Parthenon."[57]

As stated earlier Hoysaleśvara temple is a double one, i.e., there are two shrines side by side, joined with each other at the western ends of their pavilions. Like other temples this double-temple stands on a platform wider than the temple, leaving an ambulatory round it but not round either of the shrines separately. The structure according to Fergusson would undoubtedly have had eight 'śikharas', spires, showing two great pyramidal spires over the [two] sanctuaries, four lower ones in front of these, and two more, as roofs—one over each of the two central pavilions. I feel sure from the plan that there would have been one more spire of the smaller variety over the juncture of the two pavilions on the eastern front. The nine spires of this double temple of Hoysaleśvara would thus have forestalled the Bengali 'navaratna' temple of Kantanagar of the first quarter of the 18th century by more than four centuries. Nine spires of this temple intriguingly invite a comparison of this temple with the great cathedrals of Western Europe, particularly the French ones at Chartres and Rheimes, the former having had eight and the latter seven towers originally designed all of which evidently did not materialize. In actual fact the cathedral of St. Basil near the Kremlin in Moscow with its cupola-like dome-towers is the closest in appearance.[58]

My contention that the multi-shrined and multi-spired temple attempted by the Hoysalas and their religious architects was a flamboyance, which went against the inwardness of Hinduism, and was, therefore, against its grain, is upheld by the subsequent history of temple-planning and structuring in the country as a whole and in that part of it, in particular, where the Mysore political and cultural influence ruled the strongest for about three centuries, with only a short break of about fifty years during its entire period. The well-known temples of the Vijayanagar dynasty, the successor power to the Hoysalas, and the temples of Tamilnad during the later three centuries and more, marked by exuberance, extravagance and even blatant flamboyance in certain respects, did not care or dare to repeat the experiment of the Hoysala temple-planning and structuring!

The second phase of temple-planning and structuring, so well represented by the Hoysala temples of the Mysore region, evidently did not reach south-east into Tamilnad. The North Indian and Eastern second phase, of course, remained so confined to the respective regions that it is rarely represented south of Nasik district. And from the available data the temple-designs of Tamilnad cannot be traced through about two centuries from about A.D. 1025 to about A.D. 1250, when the definitely dated 'gopura' of the famous Nateśa temple at Chidambaram in South Arkot district proclaims the established new phase of temple-design in that region. The 'gopura', the gateway, which stands 135 feet high in the eastern wall of the single enclosure, 'prākāra', of the temple is ascribed to king Sundara Pāṇḍya of the Pāṇḍya dynasty.[59]

The shrines of this temple are known to be much older than the reign of the Pāṇḍyas. The Chidambaram temple-complex even in the eleventh century measured about 320 feet square[60], i.e., it covered an area of more than 102 thousand square feet. One of its halls, later known as 'kanaka-sabhā', golden hall, was covered with gold by Parāntaka I, of the Chola dynasty. The temple of Pārvatī, which stands on one side of the Nateśa temple but much behind it, is believed to have been erected in the 14th or the 15th century. And the 'gopura' in the north wall of the enclosure, which being 140 feet high is the highest of the four 'gopuras' of this temple-complex, is ascribed to King Kṛṣṇa-deva of Vijayanagar, c. A.D. 1520. The thousand-pillared pavilion of the complex is a 17th century structure. Between the hall and the front of the Pārvatī temple lies the holy pond called Śivagaṅgā, measuring 175 by 100 feet, with a colonnade round it.[61] According to Fergusson it was between 1595 and 1685 that the temple received many donations, the thousand-pillared hall was built, and the outermost enclosure begun which remained incomplete. The dimensions of this 'prākāra' wall being 1040 by 780 feet it covers an area of over 811 thousand square feet.[62] The four gopuras, of the two of which heights are given above, are gateways in this wall. The gopuras on the east and the west are famous for the representations of the hundred and eight postures in dancing mentioned in *Bhārata-Nāṭyaśāstra*.[63]

The temple complex of Nateśa at Chidambaram is representative of a typical Tamilian full-fledgod temple-complex in essentials, though it does not appear to possess what in some of the other temple-complexes of this phase is called 'kalyāṇa-maṇḍapa' or marriage-pavilion. Temple complexes, which are known to have been full-fledged and completed even before this Chidambaram complex, are known to have a 'kalyāṇa-maṇḍapa', while in some others completed in the 17th century it appears to be lacking, though the temple-complex concerned is a double-temple, i.e., one which has one shrine for the male deity and another for the consort of the deity. The early 16th century temple of Viṭhṭhal at Vijayanagara and the temple at Vellore of about the same time and of the same inspiration have each a 'kalyāṇa-maṇḍapa'.[64] The slightly later temple at Rāmeśvaram, though from the outset planned in totality, does not appear to have one.[65] It appears that in these cases any pavilion, and there are colonnades and colonnades in these great temple-complexes, is used for the celebration of the marriage of the deity and the consort.

The idea of celebrating the marriage of the principal deity with the consort appears to have been formulated after Rāmānuja, about the third quarter of the 11th century, promulgated his way of looking at the Godhead, whom he ascribed three consorts.

Rāmānuja is known to have had great influence at the court of the contemporary Hoysala king whom he weaned away from Jainism to Vaiṣṇavism. One of the earliest of the great temples which the Hoysalas built is that of Keśava or Chenna Keśava at Belur. The deity to whom it was dedicated is Vijaya Nārāyaṇa by Himself. The image is a big one being about 6 feet in height. Tradition later got busy explaining why the consort of the deity was not placed with the deity.[66] This is admission enough, in tradition, that the male deity was expected to be accompanied by the consort, if the male deity was Viṣṇu.

The Vijayanagar dynasties carrying on the Vaiṣṇava tradition of the Hoysalas put up many magnificent Vaiṣṇava temples at Hampi, their capital. Four of them are well-known and highly prized. Of these one was dedicated to Rāma, another to Viṭhṭhala and the third to Viṣṇu Anantaśayana, and the fourth was known as Acyuta Rāya's temple. All of them expecting the third have an Amman shrine as an independent unit in each of the temple-complexes. But the third which is dedicated to Anantaśayana has no such shrine. The image of the deity in the well-known lying pose has the two consorts Śrī and Bhū sculptured behind the lower parts of the legs of the reclining form.[67]

In the Anantapadmanābha, Anantaśayana, Śeṣaśāyin or Raṅganātha, as the famous Vaiṣṇava centre at Śrīraṅgam in Tamil region has it, forms of Viṣṇu and His consorts, i.e., Śrī and Bhū, are portrayed as at His feet in the total image of the deity. And it should be noted that the greatest temple-complex of India, the Raṅganātha temple at Śrīraṅgam in Tiruchirapally district, does not have a separate Amman shrine.[68]

In this connection it should be borne in mind, as I have pointed out elsewhere[69], the concept of Śiva as a family man, i.e., not only with His consort, Umā or Pārvatī, but also with their son Subrahmaṇya, as the deity to be worshipped came to be developed in the Tamil region. And that development, too, must have taken place about the 11th century when new spirit was infused in the Śaivism of South India by great ascetic preachers coming from the North and establishing monasteries in the South.

The number of occasions every year when worship on a grand scale was to be conducted, festivals to be celebrated and large concourse of visitors and pilgrims to be expected had also grown by the 12th or the 13th century. Many of the shrines which were already in existence came to be extended to meet the demands of the newer rituals, which again the wealth and splendorous pomp of the Cholas, of the Hoysalas and later of the Vijayanagar dynasty had made not only more elaborate but had approximated them in majesty and splendour to a super-royal norm. The newer ritual and the larger clientele required much larger room than the pavilion of a shrine and it appears the managers of the time hit on the idea of roofing more or less the whole of the enclosure of the shrine in as easy and simple a manner as could be done, with a colonnade or cells running round the walls of the enclosure. Already a well-known feature of earlier temples, as in Kailāsa of Verula[70] or in Kailāsanātha at Kañcī[71], the idea could come to be executed by putting up colonnades round the shrine and covering them with flat slabs. This is what appears to have been actually done so much so that P. Brown[72] was led away a step or two ahead of the actuality to characterize these temple-complexes as having the central portion "of two flat-roofed courts, one enclosed within the other", within the inner of which "is the sanctum, the cupola of which, often richly gilt, may be seen thrusting itself through the flat roofs, thus denoting the focal centre of the entire scheme".

To evaluate the observation of P. Brown at its correct extent I must bring together into one perspective the characteristics of the Hoysala, of the Madurā class as Brown calls them, and of the Vijayanagara temples in regard to their plan and elevation.

Leaving out the special features of the Hoysala temples, which I have dealt with at fair length, I should point out that the spires or towers of their sanctums are not only not particularly high but are rather dwarf. Fergusson[73] states the height of the spires of the Keśava temple at Somanāthapura as 30 feet. P. Brown[74] mentions the existence of a 'gopura', gateway, at the Somanāthapura temple but not that of the two 'gopuras'[75] in the eastern front of the enclosure in which its great predecessor, the Chenna Keśava temple of Belur, stands. Brown's relevant comment on the Somanāthapura temple sanctuary that "these moderate dimensions enable one, on entering the courtyard through its eastern gateway, to see the building in its entirety at a single glance", though correct, bypasses the main issue in the comparative evaluation of the temple plans and elevations, that being the relative appearance of the 'gopura' or 'gopuras' and the sanctum spire. His omission to take into account the existence of gopuras in one front of the Belur temple enclosure further militates against the scientific balance of his judgment on the Madurā class sanctum spires partially quoted above.

The tower of the sanctum, the vimāna, of Sundareśvara shrine in the temple-complex Mīnākṣī of Madurā, the so-called cupola is not the crude cupola of an earlier stage, not even that of the great Bṛhadīśvara temple of Tanjore but has the form of a regular crown with spreading hood-like facets. It, far from merely 'jutting' out of the surrounding flat roof of the enclosure, stands well above and in the beautiful colour-photograph of the temple-complex by Albert B. Franklin, U.S. Consul General at Madras, published in *Span* (December, 1963), shows it standing elegantly above the flat roof, beaconing attention to its gilded dignity. The description given by the highly educated and cultured diplomat, too, leaves no doubt about the special prominence of the 'vimāna' and its top. He says, describing the great occasion of the Kumbhābhiṣekam that took place in May 1963 : "A stir in the central portion of the temple yard, before the gilded Vimānam under which the goddess Mīnākṣī is henceforth to stay, attracted our attention ... He [Śaṅkarācārya] approached the ladder leading to the top of the Vimānam .... With a vigour surprising in so old a man, he [seized] the railing of the ladder in a long-fingered, bony hand, and rapidly climbed seven or eight rungs to a point from which he [could] reach the top of the Vimānam with his stick." Of course the height of the 'vimāna', the tower over the sanctum is not 'dizzy' as that of a gopura of the temple but it is not so short as to fit the description Brown has given in the quotation made above.

Jagadisa Ayyar[76] has obliged us by giving the pictures of the "vimāna-finials of two of the most famous temples of this class, Rāmeśvaram and Śrīraṅgam. Both of them conform to the form mentioned above and answer the description truly. On both of them we see very fine sculpture. In the top-crown of the Śrīraṅgam specimen in the frontal hoodlike frame-arch a beautiful image of four-armed Viṣṇu is so finely sculptured that it appears to stand out. On its top and top-end there are standing two fine wiry tall men, fully answering the description which more than forty years later a highly cultured and highly placed American Christian was destined to give !*

Thus the 'vimānas', the tower-spires, of the Madurā class temples were, inspite of the great care, skill and manpower drafted on to the construction of the accessories the tall 'gopura' towers, structures far from being relegated to a seconday place or from being in the position of jutting out cupolas ! Nor does it appear that the 'gopura's of Hoysala temples, of three to four centuries before the full-fledged Madurā class temple-complex, were very meagre or ordinary structures or that they did not number more than one or so per temple. That is not to say that they were much like the 'gopuras' of these later temples ; but it only means that relative to the size of the 'śikhara', sanctum tower, which in most Hoysala temples was of very moderate size, the 'gopuras' were fairly attractive. P. V. Jagadisa Ayyar's[77] reproduction of one of the 'gopuras' engenders this conviction in me. Ayyar describes it as a "lofty" 'gopura'.

The relative sizes of a 'vimāna' and a 'gopura' considered on the background, however, of that seen in the Bṛhadīśvara temple at Tanjore and that existing

---

* Albert D. Franklin in *Span* (December 1963).

in the temple-complexes grouped under one class as Madurā class by P. Brown and characterized as of the final phase of the Dravidian style, establishes the fact of the 'vimāna' having ceased to domineer over the whole scene and the 'gopura' having completely usurped it. And that is because a temple by A.D. 1200 had, owing to the development in the ritual and technique of approach to the deity, become a complex of many parts and had not remained a mere shrine. It had also become not only the super-royal mansion of God but was coming to be looked upon as the image of the cosmos over which God presided.

A separate shrine of God's consort, which, as earlier pointed out, was not a feature even of the Hoysala temples, had, by the fourteenth century, come to be looked upon as a 'must' for a temple. This fact is demonstrated by the existence of what is called an 'Amman' shrine, in almost all temples of the Madurā class. That this feature had become a general one and one of the essentials of a great temple by the 15th century is proved by the existence of such shrines in most of the large temples of Vijayanagara period at Hampi. The fact, however, that temples like that Mīnākṣī at Madurā, which were constructed most probably in the thirteenth century, have shrines for the consorts of the deity is testimony for an earlier date of the origin of this feature of the South Indian temple-complex. For these temples, which are small compared with their surrounding enclosures, could not have been modified or added to, in later ages when the outer enclosures with their buildings for the multifarious items of a super-royal household and the super-royal splendour and pomp of the ritual attending the visits of the consorts to the deities and vice versa or the even grander occasions of periodic festivals were formed.

The ground-plans of the temples of this group, the Hoysala, the Madurā class and the Vijayanagara ones, are most of them—all in fact, except the peculiar double-temple of Hoysaleśvara at Halebid and the Raṅganātha temple at Śrīraṅgam—three-units-ones, i.e., the sanctum, with or without the vestibule, and two pavilions one in front of and attached to another. They register a clear departure from the ground plans of the earlier temples of Tanjore and Kāñcī. We have seen that in the eastern, Orissan, pattern of temple planning in its second phase, there are three pavilions. In these South Indian temples the distinction of this phase gets marked out between the Hoysala temples on the one hand, and the other two groups, viz., the Vijayanagara ones and the Madurā class ones, on the other. The former group does not have a third pavilion at all. On the other hand, the other two groups generally have a third pavilion, though it is a detached structure. It is significantly called 'kalyāṇa' maṇḍapa, 'kalyāṇa' meaning, particularly† in Kerala, 'marriage', as in the common expression 'taliketṭu kalyāṇam'. Both the developments in Orissan as well as South Indian, announce the

† 'Kalyāṇa' is a good Sanskrit word, used in the sense of 'festival', 'rite' or 'ceremony' in *Manusmṛti* (VIII, 392).

growth of ritualism and greater anthropomorphism in practice, almost turning deification into humanization!

Gateways, 'gopuras', are a characteristic not only of all these temples but also of the earlier ones like Virūpākṣa of Pattadakal and the Orissan specimens of the 11th and later centuries. The great difference that exists in this matter separates the Tamilian temples of the Madurā class from all others. The gopuras of temples other than those of the Madurā class are fairly short and small, in comparison to those of the Madurā class temples which are generally big and high. The height of the gopura of a Tamilian temple, it appears to me, was once for all more or less conditioned by the size and height of the ponderously majestic 'vimāna', sanctum-tower, of the Bṛhadīśvara temple. According to Percy Brown[78] 'gopuras' of the first class or grade rise generally to a height of between 150 feet and 200 feet in as many as 16 storeys. All the four 'gopuras' in the outermost enclosure wall of the Mīnākṣī-Sundareśvara temple-complex of Madurā are 150 feet high. The 'gopura' put up by Sundara Pāṇḍya about A.D. 1250 at Nateśa temple of Chidambaram in South Arkot is only about 135 feet high.[79] The principal 'gopura' of the Varadarājasvāmi temple, a Vaiṣṇava institution at Kāñcī, rises in its seven storeys to a height of about 100 ft., while that of the Valmīkeśvara temple at Tiruvalur in Tanjore is 118 feet, its western 'gopura' being only 101 feet, high.[80] The famous temple at Rāmeśvaram, which stands apart from the Madurā class of temples in not having a thousand-pillared hall and which is the latest of them to be constructed and one of the few to be planned and built as one whole plan, stands apart from all these temples in the matter of its 'gopuras'. Two of the three 'gopuras' of its outermost enclosure-wall are believed to have been, when in good standing state, much higher than at present they are in their ruined condition. However, the smaller 'gopura', which is standing complete on the western side, is only 78 feet high. Of the two gopuras provided in the second enclosure wall, the smaller one is complete and though its actual height cannot be gathered from the observations of Fergusson or Brown, it is clear from the plan in Fergusson's book that it must be much shorter than the one in the western side. The incomplete 'gopura', which is very much bigger and would have been higher than the western 'gopura', was begun in A.D. 1640.[81]

The size and height of the gopuras of the Tamilian temples, temples of the Madurā class in Brown's terminology, though not their number, which was much more determined by the number and dimensions of enclosures ('prākāra'), were conditioned or at least greatly influenced by the Bṛhadīśvara temple at Tanjore, proclaiming the wealth, ability and majesty of the great Chola king Rājarāja. The first big gopura, imitating the grandeur and adding to the glamour through sculptural representations, which in some cases at least as at Madurā were painted[82], was put up by the Pāṇḍyas. The Pāṇḍyas followed the Cholas in their dominion over the Tamilian region and it was one of the greatest of them, Sundara Pāṇḍya[83], that constructed the first 'gopura'[84] that is reliably dated and that too at the famous religious centre of Chidambaram lying only about 60 miles to the north-east of Tanjore. The height of the 'gopura' built by this Pāṇḍya king, who was thereby attempting to raise his structure by rivalling the much greater Chola king of about two and a half centuries earlier. Some corroboration of my suggestion that competition of the royal personages coming in historical succession as the preeminent rulers of their time over that part of India which comprised the region, south of the Tuṅgabhadrā, the homeland of the Cholas, Pāṇḍyas and Cheras, is provided but the fact that in the very same temple, Kṛṣṇadevarāya of Vijayanagara, the greatest king of the Vijayanagara dynasty, constructed another gopura in about A.D. 1520 and that it actually rises 5 feet higher[85] than the 'gopura' which Sundara Pāṇḍya erected about two hundred seventy years before ! I should further ask the reader to bear in mind the fact that a 'gopura' at Kumbhakonam, perhaps of Pāṇḍyan inspiration, which is dated about A.D. 1350, is only 130 feet in height.[86]

Kṛṣṇadevarāya of Vijayanagara was evidently emulating his great South Indian predecessor, the Chola King Rājarāja. For in the Ekāmbaranātha temple at Kāñcī he erected the biggest of the 'gopuras' of that temple which stands 188 feet high[87], thus vying with the majestic 'vimāna', sanctum-tower, of the Bṛhadīśvara temple at Tanjore built by the illustrious Rājarāja.

The Nāyak Kings came on the scene immediately after the eclipse of the Vijayanagara dynasty, and though none of them could compare either with Rājarāja Chola or Kṛṣṇadevarāya of Vijayanagara, held sway over the southern end of the country for about two centuries. Their great building activity and their temple-construction of note, however, is mostly confined to the period A.D. 1623-1659, when Tirumal Nāyak was reigning. The grandeur and expanse of both the Mīnākṣī temple at Madurā and the Raṅganātha temple at Śrīraṅgam may be said to be the gifts of this great builder. At Madurā the great builder was evidently satisfied with putting up a 'gopura' only 150 feet high.

By his time the demand, nay the craze, for stylar structures, whether thousand-pillared pavilions or pillared colonnades was so strong and insistent and the Nāyak kings satisfied it to such an extent that the mediocre size of the gopuras can well be understood as the consequence of their great efforts having been directed towards putting up the stylar structures. The popular usage, recorded by W. Taylor[88] years and years ago, of calling these lofty towers, gopuras, as 'Rayer gobaram' emphasizes the fact of the 'gopuras' put up by the Vijayanagara king Kṛṣṇadevarāya being the tallest or near tallest.

Apropos of the unfinished 'gopura' of the Rāmeśvara temple, begun about A.D. 1640 by Sadayaka Tevar Dalvaya, the Setupati chief of Ramnad, Fergusson observed[89] : "Had it been finished, it would have been one of the largest of its class, and being wholly in stone [all 'gopuras' have their superstructure above the door lintel, from a little above, in brick], and consequently without its outline being broken by sculpture, it would have reproduced more nearly the effect of an Egyptian propylon than any other example of its class in India." While stating his considered conclusions on his survey of "the great Dravidian temples" Fergusson widened his field of comparison with the Egyptian sacred architecture and keeping in view specially the 'vimānas' of temples like that at Tanjore and the columnar colonnades of temples like that at Rāmeśvaram, remarked : "Taken altogether, they certainly do form as extensive, and in some respects as remarkable, a group of buildings as are to be found in provinces of similar extent in any part of the world—Egypt, perhaps alone excepted; but they equal even the Egyptian in extent, and, though at first so different, in some respects present similarities which are startling. Without attempting to enumerate the whole, it may be mentioned that the gopurams both in form and purpose, resemble the pylons of the Egyptian temples. The courts with pillars and cloisters are common to both, and very similar in arrangement and extent. The great mantapams and halls of 1000 columns reproduce the hypostyle halls, both in purpose and effect, with almost minute accuracy . . . There are besides, many similarities that will occur to any one familiar with both styles." He, however, did not ignore or forget the difference, though it appears he failed to give due weight to it in his final and summing up judgment, between the two structures. He stated that in the Egyptian temples "the absence of any central tower or 'vimāna' over the sanctuary is universal" but in the Indian ones its presence is almost universal.[90]

Pondering over these similarities and giving whatever consideration to the dissimilarities he thought proper, and keeping in view the fact of the possibility or even perhaps the ease of tracing the Indian developed features as a growth from rudimentary beginnings on the Indian soil, Fergusson stated his conclusion about affinities positively, though guardedly, in these words[91]: "The interval of time is so great, and the mode in which we fancy we can trace the native growth of most of the features in India seem to negative the idea of an importation; but there certainly was intercourse between Egypt and India in remote ages, and seed may then have been sown which possibly had fructified long afterwards."

Percy Brown, writing his compendium on Indian Architecture more than seventy years after the first edition of Fergusson's book and more than thirty years after its second edition, has devoted a whole large paragraph to a discussion of the Egyptian affinities of some of the larger temples of this [Madurā phase] period. He[92] admits that "the likeness" of these to the temples of the ancient Egyptians is easily "noticed" and adds "but any such analogy is more apparent than real" inspite of his further admission that "a comparison brings into relief certain interesting facts". He states that the apparent similarity is "produced by two causes", i.e., by the presence of two features which are: (1) the entrance pylon, and (2) the form of the layout. As regards the first feature he is convinced that the Dravidian gopuram and the Egyptian propylon are "two different structural conceptions". This structural difference consists in the fact that whereas the Egyptian pylon is "a double composition with the doorway produced by an opening between the two sloping towers", the Indian 'gopura' is a "single edifice", an "opening" through the centre of which produces the doorway. As to the form of the layout Brown finds much greater similarity between that of the Egyptian temple and the one of the Indian temple. In both, as he points out, high and imposing structures, forming the entrance, begin the component units and "the courts comprising the interior progress by diminishing stages, each compartment leading to a lesser, until the whole scheme terminates in one relatively small and inconspicuous cell in the centre".

Brown finds such a layout to be contrary to the fundamental principles of rational architecture and therefore is forced to seek some explanation which will plausibly account for the similarity or the convergence in plan. He thinks it "possible" that in both the Egyptian and Indian instances "the underlying concept was primarily not architectural but spiritual", i.e., "they were planned with the object of engendering religious emotion in the mind of the devotee". And this objective in both cases was sought to be achieved, i.e., religious emotion was sought to be engendered, by confronting the worshipper with the majestic entrance tower, filling him with awe, and leading him "by a process of progressive abasement from one hall to another each smaller and dimmer than the last, until, he finds himself, reduced to infinitesimal nothingness, as in a dream before the mystery of the darkened shrine, into the holy of holies and in the presence of the god himself".

Brown's firm conviction that the Egyptian aim in temple-planning and structuring was of the kind mentioned above, it is clear from his further remark, was strengthened by his view that "each of the great temples of the Pharaohs was a unity definitely established from the first". Brown has, however, not mentioned in support of his view any Egyptologist's opinion or statement and expects it to be taken on his authority. Readers of the previous chapter of this book will appreciate my disinclination to do so. I have given there enough expert opinion to show that, for example, the great temple of Karnak was a growth of not only three to four centuries but also of a much longer period. The temples planned as unity, on the other hand, do not answer fully the description of the plan believed by Brown to have been the standard one.

Turning to the appraisal of the plan of the actual temple it must be pointed out that it is the hypostyle hall that has excited admiration of the world and earned encomiums for the Egyptian architects of old. And that hall is a part and parcel of the shrine ; because the other component units are so to say a prolongation of it. The main distinction of the hall is that it is very much broader and higher than the other units which abut on it on its inner side. From that end, the structure including the actual cellas—it must be borne in mind that there could hardly be any great temple in Ancient Egypt which had only one cella, there must have been at least two, and in many cases as that of Seti's temple or that of Karnak, there were as many as five or even seven side by side—was one, there being only the cross walls and doorway, or doors in the case of the cellas to demarcate the units. The cella structure was the lowest no doubt, so that the whole temple can rightly be described as one of units of diminishing heights, that of the cella structure being the lowest, indeed so low as to make it perfectly inconspicuous. As regards the provision of light, no doubt the cella was the darkest part of the structure. As against its darkness, the play of light and shade and the brilliance of the colours of the sculptured columns of the hypostyle hall are remarkably contrasting. The glow and the glamour created before the entrants' eyes would have very materially increased the mysterious darkness pervading the inside of the cella. But in the Egyptian ritual, as known through the study of Egyptologists, the ordinary citizen worshipper, or even devotee, had nothing to do with the part which required the opening of the doors of the cella-structure. In fact the view of his temple-God the Ancient Egyptian got was only when the image was brought into the great hall or was taken in procession within the temenos. In daily practice the priest alone was concerned with the ritual. And the priest in theory, and not infrequently in practice, was the Pharaoh himself, who too, was a god or god in the making. It is neither the ritual of worship nor the mode of approach to the deity that could have mainly settled the form of the shrines of Ancient Egypt.

On the other hand in the Indian temples, and it should be borne in mind not only in the Madurā class or the Dravidian temple whose similarities with the Egyptian temples form the subject-matter of Brown's comment, the mysterious dark inside of the sanctum is a deliberate attempt in fulfilment of the needs of the ritual and in pursuance of the view of Godhead. Perhaps the inside darkness secured in some other types of Indian temples than the Madurā class ones is even more intense. The purpose served by the vestibule between outer closed pavilion, generally dark itself, and the very dark sanctum with its darkened narrowness heightens the inside darkness and enables the entrant to have what may be called a vision of the deity as in a flash because the eyes of the image are of some bright metal.

The cella or the sanctum of the Indian shrines though dark within is always prominent from outside. Even in the temples of the Madurā class, the tower or the spire over the sanctum with its brilliant golden top-cover, its fine sculptures and the inviting shape stands out beaconing the entrant as soon as he gets within the enclosure. This contrast, which should have been particularly remembered by Brown while comparing the two layouts and which was specifically mentioned by Fergusson in similar context, is somehow missed or ignored by him. The sanctum of a Hindu temple including even the Madurā-class Dravidian ones cannot be described as inconspicuous.

It ought to be thus clear to an impartial reader that whatever similarities appear between the Ancient Egyptian temples on the one hand, and the Madurā-class temples of Tamilian region on the other, are not due to similarity of notions, either of ritual and worship or of the nature of Godhead. The so-called similarities in the layout which Brown supposed to exist are not all there. To add to this there are two other items in the layout of the temenos in which as will be evident a little later, the Indian specimens differ from the Egyptian ones.

The similarity which appears and impresses is due mainly to the existence of (1) huge and ponderous entrance or gateway or gateways, (2) peristylar court or courts, and (3) columnar or hypostyle hall or halls and court or courts. Before taking these seriatum for discussion I should like to draw the reader's attention to the great contrast that marks the two groups in the matter of the approach or the avenue. In the Madurā class temple it is commonly a covered colonnade that provides this. In the Egyptian temple of Karnak, for example, the avenue is formed by dignified-looking and mysterious sphinxes in a row.

Peristylar court appears to me to be a purely functional structure ; it is a natural solution of a particular problem which confronted not only the religious architects of these two peoples but is known in history also to have done so in the case of the Greeks, the Romans and later the Christians.

Huge and ponderous gateways in the wall of the temenos or at the entrance-end of a temple or as an egress from one shrine precinct to another within the same temenos is a peculiarity of Ancient Egyptian temple planning and structuring, that of the great complex at Karnak having in all eight or twelve such gateways, small or big. In the number of gateways the temple-precincts of Śrīraṅgam, with its 21 gateways altogether, surpasses any other known temenos in the world. The other great temple-complexes of the Madurā-class, too, have a plurality of these structures, the Mīnākṣī temple-complex of Madurā having ten of them, the Valmīkeśvara at Tiruvalur having eight, the Tinnevelly double-temple having seven, the great Rāmeśvaram complex having five and the Nateśa temple of Chidambaram having only four. As we have seen, the tallest of these structures extant today is 200 feet high. The tallest of the Egyptian gateways, propylons as they are called in the more technical language, that at Karnak is only 146 feet high.

Brown is perfectly right in emphasizing—nay, even pointing it out as the difference, which is very material and has almost always been overlooked or ignored in all such comparisons—the essential difference between the two structures, the Egyptian pylon or propylon and the Indian 'gopura'. As a matter of fact in the Egyptian example the feature, called in its totality a portal, is described as consisting of "two towers . . . . connected by a smaller gateway".[93] These towers again have sloping walls. Each of the tower is a whole without any upper stages and not like the Indian 'gopura' an edifice of stages of diminishing sizes.

The exact counterpart of the Indian gateway structure is known to have been a feature of Cambodian temples. That it should be known there by the same term as the Indian one, i.e., 'gopura', only highlights the cultural debt of Cambodia to India in the late centuries before and the early centuries after Christ. The one gopura which is actually recorded in Fergusson's great work is a gateway to the enclosure of the sanctuary of the temple, which is one of the smaller ones and not the great and famous ones of Ankor Vat or Ankor Thom. The description[94] of the ruined tower that its "two upper stages are gone" clearly establishes its close affinity with the Indian 'gopura'. Its height is not given. The height of the tower over the sanctuary of the great temple at Ankor Thom consecrated by King Yaśovarman about A.D. 900, is said to be 130 feet above the floor of the temple. As the temple stands on a platform which is 34 feet high, the sanctuary tower—we are not informed how it is named in Cambodia—of the Vayon temple stands 164 feet high.[95] It compares well with the Indian sanctuary towers, being almost equal in height to the graceful one of the Liṅgarāja temple at Bhuvaneśvara in Orissa. The date of the temple to which the ruined gopura mentioned above was attached is not given; but from the political history given it becomes probable that it was earlier than the great and magnificent temple of Bayon at Ankor Thom.[96] What is still more significant from our present point of view is that the city wall of Ankor Thom, a city founded by the king, who might have built the above referred to temple, and was fully occupied by about A.D. 900 in the time of Yaśovarman, had five gates. Two of them on the east were like gopuras, their central gateway being 52 ft. square.[97]

Another feature of the great Cambodian temples at Ankor Vat and at Ankor Thom is even more significant for our quest of the affinities and origins of the Madurā-class temple-planning and structuring. And it is their having literally vast lengths of colonnades. The Bayon temple at Ankor Thom is stated to have 36000 feet of colonnades, the more famous one at Ankor Vat having only about half that. The pillars and the sculptures on the walls both received eloquent encomium from the pen of Fergusson, who comparing Indian parallel performances gave the palm unreservedly to the Cambodian achievement, remarking that "no such piers occur anywhere in India" and that "there is not a single bracket capital nor an Indian base".[98]

Hypostyle halls of Egyptian temples, even the most imposing one of Karnak, so magnificent as to be considered as one of the wonders of the world, though big by any measure had their roofs carried on a fairly small number of columns. The famous hall at Karnak had only 134 columns. The so-called 1000 pillared halls of the Madurā class temples of India have as near as possible 1000 pillars each. In at least two of the three greatest temples of Cambodia, Ankor Vat and Beng Mealea, we are told of the existence of a "series of magnificent halls" within the enclosures. They appear, however, to have been rather small and rather elongated. Only one dimension, that of length, is specifically mentioned, which being 1800 feet, the so-called halls must be considered to be like the colonnades of some of the Indian specimens rather than halls. The number of columns supporting their roofs is not available.[99]

In size the 1000 pillared halls of the great temples of the Madurā-class compare well with the grand hypostyle hall of Karnak. The two halls of the Mīnākṣī temple of Madurā, the Pudumaṇḍapa, the Vasanta maṇḍapa or Tirumal Nāyak's Chowdi just outside the temple-complex, and the Mīnākṣī

Nāyak Maṇḍapa in the outermost enclosure measure respectively 333 feet by 105 feet and 250 feet by 240 feet. The latter is known to be a thousand-pillared hall. Its area is 60000 square feet. The thousand-pillared hall of the Nateśa temple at Chidambaram is slightly bigger and better-proportioned, its length being 338 feet and breadth 197 feet. In area it is about 6500 sq. feet larger than the Mīnākṣī hall. The hall of the Śrīraṅgam temple, the biggest of its kind, and that of the Tinnevelly temple, perhaps the smallest of its kind, are ill-proportioned, that of the latter being fit to be described as a covered corridor rather than a pavilion or a hall. The Śrīraṅgam hall is 500 feet in length and 138 feet in breadth, while the Tinnevelly one is even longer, being 520 feet long and very narrow being only 63 feet in breadth. The area of the latter is less than 33000 square feet but of the former is 69000 square feet. The grand Karnak hall with a breadth of 329 feet and a length or depth of 170 feet had an area of 55930 square feet. Thus three of the four Indian temple-halls, whose dimensions are known, are bigger than the grand hypostyle hall of Karnak. The hall of the Nateśa temple at Chidambaram is even better-proportioned. Perhaps it is also a hall proper, being walled on three sides. The others appear to be walled on either two sides or one but not on three. The heights of these halls are not known in all cases. Fergusson[100] has given the height of the Śrīraṅgam hall which makes it out to be quite clearly an ill-shaped and ugly structure. At one end it is hardly over 10 feet high and in the highest spot it is only 20 feet high. Brown[101] has remarked on the architectural insignificance of both this and the Mīnākṣī halls. The only claim for consideration these halls have is the fact of the columns being many times monolithic and of the grotesque sculptures on them. Thus it is seen that the so-called hypostyle halls, the 1000 pillared halls, of the Mīnākṣī-class temples are very poor structures not deserving to be spoken of in terms of the grand Karnak hall or even in its context as some kind of its peers, which they do not resemble in the least.

The hypostyle hall of an Ancient Egyptian temple was an organic part of the shrine. The hall, the 1000 pillared one, of the Madurā-class temples of India is an appendage which often stands in the third enclosure in its north-east corner but also is known to be located in the south or south-west corner. The feature common to both is that they are connected with the ritual of worship.

The above discussion of the various features of affinity and dissimilarity between the temple-planning and structuring of the Madurā class temples of India on the one hand, and of the Ancient Egyptian temples of about 2000 B.C. to 800 B.C. and of Cambodian ones of about A.D. 900 on the other, leads one to detect a closer affinity of the Indian specimens with the Cambodian temples. It is known that there was much and prolonged intercourse between India and Cambodia from about 200 B.C. onwards to about the time Islam made its debut in South-East Asia. The great nobility and the wealthy merchants of India who must have been impressed by the great temples of

Ankor Vat and Ankor Thom might have brought with them a desire to emulate them and also perhaps some technical help to achieve their purpose.

Fergusson recognised certain Egyptian influence in Cambodian temples both in the stepped pyramid form of the platform on which the temples stood and in the great sphinx-like size, appearance and technique of the great Brahmā faces of the towers of the Bayon. He was impressed by the depiction of a scene of religious procession on one of these temples so much as to be "startling".[102] The apparent similarities of the Indian with the Ancient Egyptian temples can be explained as being due to their Cambodian models having preserved them in their adaptation. It appears to me that some such deferred and mediate influence alone is what is indicated by the nature of affinities and dissimilarities detailed above.

Another feature associated with the Madurā-class temple complexes marks them out as distinct from not only Orissan and the first and second phase temples of South India but also from the 15th and 16th century temples of Vijayanagar, is the large tank, pond or lake within their enclosures, generally second but sometimes third. This feature invites comparison of these temple-complexes much more with the grand temple-complex of Karnak in Egypt of about three thousand years earlier than with the enclosure of Islamic mosques recent and contemporary. The pool of water within the enclosure of an Islamic mosque only emphasizes the common trait of ablution or lavation being looked upon as a necessary preliminary to making an approach to the deity or to offering prayers within sacred precincts. Generally it is not big enough to receive a canoe to be rowed round. The ancient Egyptian pond or lake on the other hand is almost an exact prototype of the Tamilian temple pond in extent.

The pond or lake as an appurtenance of the Hindu (Tamilian) temenos, however, is a great improvement over that of its ancient Egyptian counterpart. It has become one of the most charming components of the Hindu temple-complex. It carries in the great temple-complexes invariably a colonnade round it on its banks, a colonnade whose columns quite often are a thing of beauty being an attractive feature. Added to this attraction is the charm of the temple tower and/or the 'gopura' tower reflected in the water of the pond, which is often conveniently situated for such a scene to occur.

Another speciality of these Tamilian temple-complexes is the fact of a plurality of enclosures which stand more or less in concentric configuration. The huge Egyptian temple-complex of Karnak even cannot parallel either the Chidambaram, the Madurā or the Rāmeśvaram one and is very far behind the Śrīraṅgam complex in this aspect. Upto the time of the Madurā-class temple-complex no temple is known to have had more than two enclosure walls, more or less concentric as in the Jagannātha temple at Puri.[103] All the temples mentioned above, on the other hand, have three or more enclosures, three, it appears, being considered the minimum. The Chidambaram complex has four and the vast conglomeration of Śrīraṅgam seven, almost a sacrosanct and magic number in Hindu cosmology and cosmography.

The fact that Śrīraṅgam temple-complex has seven enclosures which are concentric, with the shrine placed in the central or the first enclosure, inclines me to the view that the seven 'prākāras' or enclosures represent the seven coverings, 'kañcukas' or 'āvaraṇas', referred to in cosmological and cosmographical accounts and mentioned in the appropriate chapter. The deity of this temple-complex being Viṣṇu-Śeṣaśāyin appropriately represents Nārāyaṇa, the Eternal source of the cosmos. The shrine being the abode of this Eternal Nārāyaṇa, and His cosmos having seven coverings or sheaths, provision of seven 'prākāras' alone can adequately represent Nārāyaṇa's earthly abode as the sovereign ruler of the cosmos. The seven-enclosured temple-complex is the cosmos materially represented, over which God presides and rules from His abode in the innermost enclosure, i.e., at the centre of the cosmos.

For whatever support it may be taken to offer to my above view regarding seven enclosures of the temple-complex of Śrīraṅgam, I may mention the popular belief putting forward a claim for such perfection in temple-planning on behalf of the Airāvateśvara temple, a Śaiva one, at Darasuram near Kumbhakonam recorded by P. V. Jagadisa Ayyar.[104] The temple well-known for its pavilion has at present only one enclosure but it is believed that formerly it had seven courts.

The earthly cosmos of Raṅganātha of Śrīraṅgam with its seven coverings spreads over the huge area of 7.1 million square feet. Even the area covered by only the first four enclosures, 'prākāras', which may be said to define the limits of the temple-complex proper, is larger than that of the Chidambaram complex, being nearly 1.05 million square feet. The complex of Mīnākṣī-Sundareśvara temple occupies only about 0.61 million of square feet, thus ranking third as regards the area of the temenos, Nateśa of Chidambaram having 0·81 million of square feet. The temple at Rāmeśvaram which appears to be the fourth in extent occupies only 0.59 million square feet. And this area is not much bigger than that covered by the Jagannātha temple of Puri which is about 0.43 million square feet.

To appreciate the growth in the size of the temenos, the temple-precincts, one has to bear in mind that the area covered by Bṛhadīśvara temple-enclosure measured only about 125 thousand square feet, while even the extent of the enclosure of the great Viṭhṭhalasvāmī temple, built by a wealthy and zealous Vijayanagara king in about A.D. 1520, i.e., only about a century and a half or so before these great Tamilian complexes attained their maximum limits, did not measure more than 165 thousand square feet. The area covered by the temple-precincts proper, i.e., even by the first four enclosures of the stupendous complex of Śrīraṅgam is thus more than six times that covered by the Viṭhṭhalasvāmī temple at Hampi. What a growth! It upholds the thesis propounded here in respect of shrines of the peoples and religions dealt with in this book, specifically of the Mesopotamians, the Ancient Egyptians, and the Hindus, that upto a certain stage and size they have tended to grow bigger, higher, brighter or more sculptured so as to capture the imagination of the people concerned with impressive and awe-inspiring exterior and externals.

That a temple of the Madurā class, whatever its component parts and their artistic or religious content, is adequate to fulfil its central purpose, the one end for which a shrine is made, in full measure is abundantly clear from the eloquent and recent testimony of a highly cultured American Christian diplomat, some of whose reactions to the scene at the Madurā temple at the time of a special dedication ceremony which he witnessed I have quoted above. I shall quote here some pregnant observations directly coming from his trained mind, surcharged with religious emotion at the sight of the temple and its ritual. About the temple he says: "It is so huge, and so constructed that neither the eye nor the mind comprehend it all at once. From the distance it is a cluster of great and small towers, but on closer approach it becomes many things and it has many faces. It is a cool forest of granite pillars. It is a series of decorated galleries around a large and welcoming rectangular pool. *It is the very odour and mystery of worship. It is a replica of the hidden places of the mind.* And even in its most secret depths, the surrounding presence of the greater and lesser towers, the gopurams and maṇḍapams is always felt, for a startling perspective of one or more of the towers is never far to seek." Of the atmosphere during the actual conduct of the ceremony he says: "Glancing up at familiar towers, I had a sense of vertigo and shock. The figures had come alive! They were moving! . . . But I looked back again and again, and never, at first glance, did I fail to receive the breath-taking impression, aided by the life-like colouring of the gods and goddesses, animals and mythological figures, that they were all alive, there, watching, waiting, participating in the ceremony along with the rest of us." About the special ritual itself he remarks: "I cannot recall any ceremony I have ever attended matching it in wonder."[105]

REFERENCES

CHAPTER I

1. Gordon Childe, *New Light on The Most Ancient East*, pp. 11, 114, 117; Leonard Woolley, *Excavations at Ur*, p. 125 ; H.W.F. Saggs, *The Greatness That was Babylon*, pp. 24-25.
2. Variously spelled as Ninhursaga or Ninkhursaga or Ninkharsaga.
3. H. Frankfort, *Before Philosophy*, pp. 150, 158-9 ; S. N. Kramer, *History Begins at Sumer*, 1958, p. 147.
4. Frankfort, op. cit., p. 150.
5. Morris Jastrow, *Civilization of Babylonia and Assyria*, p. 209 ; *E.B.* (14th Ed.), Vol. 2, pp. 857-8 ; Saggs, op. cit., pp. 328-31, 340, 411.
6. *E.B.* 2, p. 89 ; Saggs, op. cit., pp. 329, 331.
7. *E.B.* 2, p. 857 ; Frankfort, op. cit., pp. 158-9.
8. C. J. Gadd, *History and Monuments of Ur*, p. 63 ; Woolley, *Excavations at Ur*, p. 95.
9. *E.B.* 2, p. 858.
10. H. Frankfort, op. cit., pp. 170-9 ; Saggs, op. cit., pp. 418-9.
11. Gadd, op. cit., p. 62 ; Saggs, op. cit., pp. 416-8.
12. Frankfort, op. cit., pp. 158 ; Woolley, *Excavations at Ur*, p. 95.
13. Woolley, *Excavations*, p. 117 ; Jastrow, op. cit., pp. 232-6, pl. XXIX, 3 ; S.A. Pallis, *The Antiquity of Iraq*, pp. 573-74, 694; Saggs, op. cit., pp. 79, 332-3.
14. Saggs, ibid., p. 334.
15. *Sumerians*, pp. 107, 121.
16. *E.B.*, vide "Ishtar".
17. Gadd, op. cit., p. 128 ; M. Jastrow, op. cit., pp. 232-3.
18. *E.B.* 17, p. 570; A. Stein as quoted by Eduard Meyer in *E.B.* 17, p. 577.
19. Saggs, op. cit., p. 327.
20. Frankfort, op. cit., pp. 161, 198 ; Saggs, op. cit., pp. 329-31, 338-42 ; *E.B.* 2, p. 858.
21. Morris Jastrow, pl. XXXIV ; Saggs, pl. 21B.
22. Morris Jastrow, *Civilization of Babylonia and Assyria*, pp. 203, 207, 211-2 ; L. Woolley, *Sumerians*, pp. 17, 116-119, 121 ; Frankfort, op. cit., pp. 183, 192-4, 198, 222-3, 237 ; Saggs, op. cit., pp. 72, 145-7, 267, 277-98, 332, 338-42, 413, and pl. 21B ; *E.B.*, II, pp. 853, 863 ; XIV, p. 872.
23. Frankfort, op. cit., p. 223.
24. Ibid., pp. 152-3 ; Saggs, pp. 329, 343 and pl. 49 opposite p. 444.
25. Frankfort, pp. 157, 161 ; Jastrow, pp. 194-200, 209-11, 217-19 ; Saggs, p. 330.
26. Frankfort, pp. 145-6 ; Saggs, pp. 241-2.
27. *Religion and Philosophy of the Veda and the Upaniṣads*, pp. 88-9.
28. Op. cit., pp. 203-5, 215, 216.
29. *E.B.* 2, p. 859 ; Frankfort, pp. 157, 161 ; Saggs, p. 327.
30. *The Antiquity of Iraq*, pp. 691-2, 695-97 ; Saggs, p. 329 ; *E.B.* 17, p. 568.
31. *E.B.* 17, p. 568.
32. *E.R.E.* 6, p. 283.
33. Frankfort, op. cit., pp. 17, 75-6.
34. Wilson in Frankfort, op. cit., p. 73 ; *E.B.* 8, p. 58.
35. *R.V.* I, 164, 46. Full comments on the significance of this passage and the attitude enshrined in it will be made in the Indian section. Cf. A. Bouquet, *Comparative Religion*, p. 63.
36. Frankfort, op. cit., p. 145.
37. *E.B.* XIV, p. 872.
38. Frankfort, p. 151.
39. *Sumerians*, p. 129.
40. Jastrow, op. cit., p. 271; C. J. Gadd, pp. 232, 234-43 ; Woolley, *Excavations*, pp. 192, 228 ; S. A. Pallis, op. cit., pp. 693, 697, 700, 705-6; Saggs, op. cit., pp. 357-8.
41. Jastrow, pp. 239-68, 276-8 ; Langdon

in *E.B.* II, pp. 859-61 ; Woolley, *Sumerians*, pp. 125-8 ; Pallis, op. cit., pp. 697-99 ; Frankfort, pp. 214-6 ; Saggs, op. cit., pp. 345-54.

42. Pallis, p. 698 ; Jastrow, p. 277.
43. Saggs, p. 347.
44. Langdon in *E.B.* 2, p. 859 ; Langdon in *E.R.E.* 12, p. 758.
45. Pallis, pp. 706-711.
46. Woolley, *Sumerians*, pp. 119, 128, p. 89, pl. 21A ; Jastrow, p. 422 Pl. LXXVII(2) ; *E.B.* 2, p. 845 (pl. II, 2) ; Saggs, p. 44 (pl. 49).
47. Jastrow, pp. 270-2 ; Frankfort, op. cit., pp. 218-19 ; Pallis, p. 705 ; S. N. Kramer, *History Begins at Sumer*, p. 168 ; Woolley, *Sumerians*, pp. 119, 129, 139 ; *Excavations*, p. 192 ; The Discovery of Woolley effectively disposes of the conjecture of S. Langdon about the Sumerians having been "incapable of individualism in worship" stated at p. 165 in *E.R.E.* 10.
48. Woolley, *Sumerians*, p. 71 ; Gadd, op. cit., p. 82 ; Pallis, p.705.
49. Frankfort, pp. 220-22, S. Langdon in *E.R.E.* 10, p. 164.
50. Ibid., pp. 222-3, 227-8 ; Pallis, pp. 705-6.
51. Woolley, *Excavations*, pp. 190-2.
52. See my *Gods and Men*, 1962.
53. Jastrow, pp. 208-9, 280, 428, 456-7 ; Langdon in *E.B.* 2, p. 858 ; Woolley *Sumerians*, p. 121 ; Frankfort, pp. 196, 198, 208, 211, 224, 233, 239 ; Saggs, pp. 329, 426.
54. Jastrow, p. 279-82, 453 ; Woolley, *Sumerians*, pp. 120-1 ; S. N. Kramer, pp. 153-6 ; S. G. Brandon, *Man and his Destiny in the Great Religions* (1962), pp. 73-79.
55. On this see Elwood Whitney : *Symbology*, pp. 169-82.
56. Op. cit., p. 422.
57. *E.B.* 2, p. 861.
58. Op. cit., p. 328.
59. *Sumerians*, p. 89, pl. 21A.
60. Woolley, *Sumerians*, frontispiece. A better reproduction in pl. 49 of S. Piggott's *The Dawn of Civilization* (1961), shows the heads from which it is clear that the figure is that of a goddess.
61. Op. cit., pl. 49 opp. p. 444.
62. Saggs, p. 367 ; Frankfort, p. 221.
63. *E.R.E.* 12, p. 758 ; Frankfort, 230 ; Saggs, pp. 71, 334, 438.
64. *J.R.A.S.*, 1919, pp. 553-4.
65. Saggs, op. cit., pp. 357-8.
66. C. J. Gadd, pp. 231-2; Woolley, *Excavations*, pp. 224-8, 232.

CHAPTER II

1. *E.B.* VIII, p. 108.
2. H. R. Hall, *The Ancient History of the Near East* (fifth ed.), p. 314.
3. Ibid., p. 102 ; Erman, *Life etc.*, p. 320.
4. Frankfort, *Birth etc.*, p. 112 ; K. Lange and M. Hirmer, *Egypt*, 1956, p. 296.
5. Hall, p. 314.
6. J. H. Breasted, *Development of Religion and Thought in Ancient Egypt*, 1912, p. 42 ; Margaret A. Murray ; *Egyptian Temples*, pp. 36-44 ; E.A.W. Budge, *From Fetish to God in Ancient Egypt*, 1934, p. 128 ; Wilson in Frankfort's *Before Philosophy*, pp. 61, 66, 77.
7. Wallis Budge, *Tutankhamen*, 1923, pp. 1-12 ; Frankfort, *Ancient Egyptian Religion*, p. 54 ; *Birth etc.*, p. 27.
8. H. R. Hall, pp. 168, 255 ; Wallis Budge, *Tutankhamen*, pp. 34-45 ; W. M. Flinders Petrie, *Religious Life in Ancient Egypt*, 1924, p. 97 ; Breasted, *The Dawn of Conscience*, 1935, p. 270, 275-6.
9. Adolf Erman, *Life in Ancient Egypt* (trans. by H. M. Tirard), pp. 44-5, 56-7 ; Hall in *E.B.* VIII, p. 59 ; Wallis Budge, *From Fetish etc.*, p. 208.
10. Hall in *E.B.* VIII, 58 ; Wallis Budge, *From Fetish etc.*, pp. 205-10.

11. Budge, ibid., pp. 159, 269.
12. Ibid., pp. 159-62.
13. Hall in *E.B.* VIII, p. 59; Wallis Budge, *From Fetish etc.*, pp. 159-61.
14. Op. cit., pl. 210 ; Erman, *Life etc.*, p. 271 ; Lange and Hirmer, *Egypt*, pls. 208, 210, 212.
15. See my *Gods and Men*, 1962.
16. *Rgveda*, I, 139, 11.
17. Erman, pp. 45, 259 ; Flinders Petrie, op. cit., p. 97 ; Hall, *The Ancient History of the Near East*, pp. 133, 149, 152, 168 ; Wallis Budge, *Tutankhamen*, pp. 17-30, 34 ; *From Fetish etc.*, pp. 166-170 ; Margaret Murray, *The Splendour that was Egypt*, 1949, pp. 125-7, 212.
18. Breasted, *Dawn etc.*, pp. 34-42 ; Wilson in Frankfort, *Before etc.*, pp. 65-9 ; Lange and Hirmer, p. 312.
19. Wallis Budge, *From Fetish*, pp. 273-7, 286-8; Breasted, *Dawn etc.*, pp. 106-114 ; Margaret Murray, *The Splendour etc.*, pp. 164, 212.
20. Erman, p. 386 ; Breasted, *Dev. of R.*, pp. 142-3, 285 ; *E.B. VIII*, pp. 58, 60 ; Hall, p. 169 ; Wallis Budge, *From Fetish*, pp. 273, 286-9, 340-1 ; Breasted *Dawn*, pp. 55-61, 253-65 ; Frankfort, *An. Eg. Re.*, pp. 103-10, Wilson in Frankfort, *Before etc.*, pp. 115 ; Margaret Murray, *The Splendour*, pp. 209-12.
21. Erman, pp. 265-71 ; Wallis Budge, *From Fetish*, pp. 122-3, 150, 199-200, 459-62 ; Murray, *Splendour*, pp. 169-70.
22. Wallis Budge, *Tutankhamen*, pp. 15-24, 27, 33, 40-2 ; *From Fetish etc.*, pp. 17-8, 62-5, 75, 91, 101, 152, 164-6, 168, 172, 409-14 ; Erman, *Life etc.*, pp. 283, 302-3 ; Murray, *Egyptian Temples*, pp. 77, 96, 102-3, 114 ; *The Splendour etc.*, p. 178 ; Lange and Hirmer, Egypt, pls. 95, 122, 123, and pp. 310-2, 321-22, 324, 327, 344 ; Hall, *Ancient History etc.*, 139-140, 146-7, 150, 165, 224 ; Breasted, *Development etc.*, pp. 346-8.
23. Erman, pp. 23, 66, 245, 432, 473 ; Hall, *Ancient History, etc.*, p. 94, f.n. 2; Murray, *Egyptian Temples*, pp. 49-52 ; Wallis Budge, *From Fetish etc.*, pp. 62-5, 75, 160.
24. Erman and Blackman, *Literature etc.*, pp. 187-8
25. Pritchard, *The Ancient Near East*, Fig. 134.
26. Erman, p. 473.
27. Erman and Blackman, *The Literature etc.*, pp. 282, 284.
28. *Kingship and the Gods*, pp. 188-9.
29. H. Frankfort, *Kingship and the Gods*, p. 180 ; Budge, *Egyptian Tales etc.*, p. 144 ; *From Fetish etc.*, p. 165.
30. H. R. Hall, *Ancient History etc.*, p. 22.
31. Erman and Blackman, p. 293 f.n.
32. Erman and Blackman, *The Literature etc.*, pp. 282-88, 293-302.
33. Loc. cit., vol. I, p. 332, pl. 3.
34. Perrot and Chipiez, I, p. 22 (Fig. 13).
35. *E.B. VIII*, p. 58, pl. VIII ; Pritchard, *The Ancient Near East*, illustration 159.
36. Pritchard, illustration 99.
37. H. Frankfort, *Kingship and the Gods*, Figs. 12 and 15 ; Perrot & Chipiez, I, pp. 300, 436, Figs. 225, 254.
38. Wilson in Pritchard, pp. 175-82 ; *Ancient History etc.*, pp. 250-2. Italics mine.
39. Hall, *Ancient History etc.*, pp. 252-5.
40. Op. cit., p. 335 and pls. 196-99.
41. Erman and Blackman, *The Literature, etc.*, pp. 18, 48, 85, 134, 168, 207, 258-9, 261, 263-4, 267-9, 271 ; Pritchard, pp. 4, 179, 182, 183 ; Murray, *Egyptian Temples*, pp. 146, 148, 232.
42. Erman and Blackman, *The Literature etc.*, p. 296, f.n. 5.
43. Murray, *The Splendour etc.*, p. 214.
44. Erman and Blackman, *The Literature etc.*, p. 276.
45. *Gods and Men*, 1962.
46. Erman, pp. 56-65. The illustration, a line-drawing from the original, shows the 'fans' to be almost identical with "abdāgirs" as the high-poled lustrous

fan-shaped objects which accompany palanquin processions of Hindu deities are called in Marathi; Breasted, *Dev. of R.*, pp. 15-6; Perrot & Chipiez, *History of Ancient Egyptian Art*, Vol. I, pp. 189-94; Wilson in Frankfort, pp. 80-88; Murray, *The Splendour*, pp. 174-7.

47. Erman, *The Literature of the Ancient Egyptians* (Blackman's translation), p. 107.

48. Erman, pp. 26-7, 101, 307-14, 317; Hall, pp. 123, 152; F. Lt. Griffith, in *E.B. VIII*, p. 70; Wallis Budge, *From Fetish etc.*, pp. 331, 340-4; Breasted, *Dev. of R.*, pp. 64-69; 135-9; *Dawn*, pp. 56-63, 224-7; Frankfort, *Ancient etc.*, pp. 61, 92; Murray, pp. 185-6.

49. F. Ll. Griffith in *E.B. VIII*, pp. 70-1; A. M. Blackman, op. cit., pp. 75-83, 93-108, 108-110, 110-15; Lange and Hirmer, pp. 15, 307; Breasted, *Dawn etc.*, pp. 178-90, 197-8, 200-205.

50. Erman, *The Literature etc.* (Blackman's translation, pp. 93-107. The statement about embalming occurs twice and the last one about sarcophagus occurs thrice.

51. Wallis Budge, *From Fetish etc.*, pp. 340-1; Breasted, *Dawn etc.*, pp. 223-6, 238-42; Murray, pp. 185-7; Wilson in Frankfort, *Before etc.*, pp. 118-9; Frankfort, *Birth etc.*, p. 93; Lange and Hirmer, pp. 308-12.

52. Perrot and Chipiez, *History of Ancient Egyptian Art*, I, 1883, pp. 135-150; Hall in *E.B. VIII*, pp. 60-1; Erman, *Life etc.*, pp. 312-7; *E.B. XV*, pp. 954-5; Frankfort, *Ancient Egy. etc.*, p. 93.

53. Petrie, *Religious Life in Ancient Egypt*, 1924, p. 116; Hall, *Ancient History etc.*, p. 169; Erman, *The Literature of the Ancient Egyptians* (trans. by Blackman), 1927, p. 217.

54. J. A. Wilson in Pritchard, *The Ancient Near East*, pp. 1-2; J. H. Breasted, *Develop. etc.*, pp. 43-7, 146; *Dawn etc.*, pp. 19-21, 33-4, 116 f.n. Breasted mentions the fact of his not having realized the early date of another document when he wrote what is in effect the very first and for long the only connected account of the development of religious thought in Egypt, in 1912. That document is the Maxims of Ptahhotep. It was since recognized as a document of the Old Kingdom. And he duly noted it and treated it as such in his *Dawn etc.*, p. 129 and f.n.; Wallis Budge, *From Fetish etc.*, pp. 16, 44, 46, 284, 323-4.

55. *Ancient Egyptian Religion*, pp. 63, 100-2, 106, 121.

56. *Before Philosophy*, pp. 57, 108, 118.

57. *From Fetish etc.*, pp. 327-8, 335-6, 347.

58. *Rgveda*, X, 15; 56; 90.

59. Wallis Budge, *From Fetish*, pp. 328-30; Breasted, *Development etc.*, pp. 53-5; *Dawn*, pp. 49-50; Frankfort, *Anc. E. R.*, pp. 91, 96; Wilson in Frankfort, *Before etc.*, pp. 65, 95, 107; Erman, *Life etc.*, pp. 307-12, 322; Murray, *Splendour etc.*, pp. 189-92.

60. Erman, *Life etc.*, p. 315.

61. Perrot & Chipiez, I, 129, 187, 193, 230, 259-60, 263-305; Erman, *Life etc.*, p. 326; Lange & Hirmer, pp. 297, 298-301, 315-19, 321; *E.B. VIII*, p. 58, pl. VIII; Pritchard, *The Ancient Near East*, picture 159.

62. Wallis Budge, *From Fetish etc.*, pp. 304-5, 327-8, 330-334, 336; Breasted, *Dawn etc.*, pp. 47-9; Frankfort, *Ancient etc.*, pp. 96-9; Murray, *Splendour etc.*, p. 210.

63. Frankfort, ibid., p. 96; Wallis Budge, *From Fetish etc.*, p. 308; Breasted, *Development etc.*, pp. 65, 59, 61.

64. Frankfort, *Ancient etc.*, pp. 86-7, 141-4; Breasted, *Dawn etc.*, pp. 168-78.

65. Erman, *The Literature etc.*, pp. 78, 83.

66. Pritchard, op. cit., pp. 184, 186.

67. Erman and Blackman, p. 205.

68. Breasted, *Development etc.*, p. 55.

69. Erman and Blackman, pp. 173-4.

There is a curious parallel to this in the speculative literature of India which cannot be dated later than 700 B.C. A similar but a much longer disputation between half a dozen or more elements of the human body with the final triumph of 'prāṇa', 'vital breath', is recorded in the two oldest Upaniṣads, *Bṛhadāraṇyaka* (VI, 1, 7-14) and *Chāndogya* (V, 1, 7-15.)

70. Erman and Blackman, pp. 57-9; Wilson in Pritchard, pp. 234-5.
71. *The Dawn of Conscience*, pp. 254-5, 262-3, 324.
72. Wallis Budge, *Egyptian Romances and Tales*, pp. 95-110.
73. Breasted, *Dawn etc.*, fig. 2 opp. p. 26.
74. Erman, *Life etc.*, pp. 322-4, 326; Breasted, *Development*, pp. 62-9; 259-70, 362; *Dawn etc.*, pp. 53-6, 225-36; Murray, *Splendour etc.*, p. 190.
75. Erman and Blackman, pp. 15, 77, 115, 236; Wilson in Pritchard, *The Ancient Near East*, p. 6.

CHAPTER III

1. *The Dawn of Conscience*, pp. 242-6; *Development etc.*, pp. 144-50.
2. Wallis Budge, *From Fetish etc.*, pp. 191-6.
3. Frankfort, *Ancient etc.*, p. 10.
4. Lange and Hirmer, pl. 210.
5. Budge, *From Fetish*, pp. 503-16.
6. *Egyptian Tales*, pp. 96, 176.
7. *From Fetish etc.*, pp. 6, 85, 197, 211 (fig.), 345.
8. Budge, ibid., p. 282; Breasted, *Dawn etc.*, p. 260.
9. Budge, *Egyptian Tales etc.*, pl. opp. p. 96; In the papyrus of Anhai, too, Matt is shown as standing. (Budge, *Egyptian Tales etc.*, pl. opp. p. 76.)
10. Budge, *From Fetish etc.*, pp. 285-6, 289; Erman and Blackman, pp. 77-8; Breasted, *Dawn etc.*, pp. 21-2, 250-1, 255-61; Wilson in Frankfort, *Before etc.*, p. 119.
11. Budge, *From Fetish etc.*, pp. 211-4; 287-307.
12. *From Fetish etc.*, p. 296.
13. Erman, p. 278; Budge, *From Fetish etc.*, pp. 274-6, 287; Breasted, *Dawn etc.*, pp. 245-6.
14. M. Murray, *Egyptian Temples*, pp. 40-1.
15. Budge, *Tutankhamen*, pp. 31, 41, 64, 95-6; *Egyptian Tales*, pp. 172-3; *From Fetish etc.*, pp. 95-6, 133-4, 351-79; Breasted, *Development etc.*, pp. 123, 144; *The Dawn etc.*, pp. 112-3, 241-2, 267-71 (Nether world); M. Murray, *The Splendour etc.*, pp. 192. 209.
16. Wilson in Frankfort, *Before etc.*, p. 57; Budge, *From Fetish etc.*, pp. 352-3.
17. Budge, *From Fetish etc.*, pp. 353-79.
18. Ibid., pp. 356-7, 379.
19. Budge, *Egyptian Tales etc.*, pp. 138, 172-6; *From Fetish etc.*, pp. 365-7; Murray, *The Splendour etc.*, pp. 209; Erman and Blackman, *Literature etc.*, p. 315.
20. Budge, *From Fetish etc.*, pp. 106-11, 173, 229; Murray, *The Splendour etc.*, pp. 127-8; Hall, *Ancient History etc.*, p. 152.
21. Murray, *Egyptian Temples*, p. 15; Erman, p. 327; Budge, *From Fetish etc.*, pp. 253-4.
22. Erman, p. 272; Flinders Petrie, *Religious Life etc.*, pp. 198-9.
23. Frankfort, *Before Philosophy*, pp. 107-8.
24. *From Fetish etc.*, p. 279.
25. *Ancient History etc.*, p. 324.
26. Erman and Blackman, *The Literature etc.*, p. 306.
27. Op. cit., p. 199.
28. *History of Ancient Egyptian Art*, I, pp. 53-4, 60.
29. Erman, *Life in Ancient etc.*, p. 275; Perrot &. Chipiez, I, p. 318; Petrie, *Religious Life etc.*, pp. 20, 57.

30. Erman and Blackman, *The Literature*. p. 82.
31. Wallis Budger, *Tutankhamen*, pp. 6-7.
32. M. Murray, *The Splendour etc.*, p. 212 ; Wallis Budge, *Tutankhamen*, p. 34.
33. Wallis Budge, *Tutankhamen*, p. 34.
34. Lange and Hirmer, *Egypt*, pls. 44-47 and p. 302.
35. Op. cit., pls. 92, 94, 95, 98 and p. 312,
36. Hall, *The Ancient History etc.*, pp. 131-2 and f.n. ; Budge, *From Fetish etc.*, pp. 322-5.
37. Op. cit., pls. 36-9 and p. 301, pl. 78 and p. 306 ; pl. 85 and p. 312 ; pls. 108-09 and p. 313.
38. Op. cit., pp. 162, 164.
39. Murray, *The Splendour*, p. 259.
40. Erman, p. 477 ; Lange and Hirmer, pl. 176 and p. 332, pl. 182 and p. 332; pl. 229 and p. 353 ; *E.B.* I, p. 68.
41. Perrot and Chipiez, vol. II, p. 277. N.B.—For partial and late analogy in India one has to read descriptions of the Madurā and Rāmeśvaram temples.
42. Erman, pl. 503 ; Wallis Budge, *Tutankhamen*, pp. 24-5, 66-7; Hall, *Ancient History etc.*, pp. 160-1, 272-4 ; Murray, *The Splendour etc.*, pp. 213-4. The installation of Senusret is affirmed by Erman; and I have followed him, though Hall writing later states that it was Thothmes III who rededicated the temple along with Khnum "also to the deified Senusert, who thus became the tutelary deity of the reconquered land".
43. *Egyptian Temples*, p. 78.
44. *Ibid.*, p. 147.
45. Wallis Budge, *From Fetish etc.*, p. 267.
46. *Tutankhamen*, p. 62.
47. Budge, *From Fetish etc.*, p. 267 ; Wilson in Pritchard, *The Ancient Near East*, p. 2.
48. Murray, *The Splendour etc.*, p. 182.
49. Petrie, *Religious Life in Ancient Egypt*, p. 207 ; Breasted, *The Dawn of Conscience etc.*, p. 330.
50. Erman, pp. 284-5; Murray, *The Egyptian Temples*, p. 92 ; Hall, *The Ancient History etc.*, pp. 152-3.
51. Erman and Blackman, *The Literature etc.*, p. 51. Italics are mine. The last sentence cannot fail to bring to the intelligent reader's mind, particularly that of an Indian, similar declaration of Emperor Aśoka more than 1500 years later.
52. Wallis Budge, *Tutankhamen*, pp. 34-5 ; Erman, *Life etc.*, pp. 271, 273-5, 277, 279, 291, 295-6, 301, 395.
53. Erman, *Life etc.*, pp. 46, 47, 51, 260, 296 ; Perrot and Chipiez I, pp. 26(15), 126, 246(165); W. Budge, *Tutankhamen*, pl. V ; *Egyptian Tales*, pp. 96, 172 ; Lange and Hirmer, *Egypt*, pls. 153, 174, 204; Pritchard, *The Ancient etc.*, illustration 158.
54. Budge, *Egyptian Tales etc.*, p. 91.
55. Erman, *Life etc.*, pp. 271, 283 ; Perrot and Chipiez, I, p. 45, pl. opp. p. 124 ; Pritchard, illustrations 158, 162; Lange and Hirmer, pl. 128.
56. Erman, p. 283; Budge, *From Fetish etc.*, p. 306; Pritchard, illustration 158 ; Lange and Hirmer, pp. 131.
57. Perrot and Chipiez, I, p. 45(33).
58. Perrot and Chipiez I, p. 26(15).
59. Erman and Blackman, pp. 33, 34.
60. Erman and Blackman, p. 142.
61. Ibid., pp. 48, 170, 288.
62. Erman, p. 275. N. B. : Falling on the face is the same as the "eight-limbed bow" (sāṣṭāṅganamaskāra) of the Hindus.
63. Wallis Budge, *Tutankhamen*, pp. 17, 34-5 ; A. M. Blackman in *E.R.E. XII*, 777-780 ; Flinders Petrie, *Religious Life etc.*, pp. 28-31, 51-2, 189-92 ; Erman, *Life etc.* pp. 65, 273-5, 278, 283, 291-9 ; Murray, *Splendour etc.*, pp. 183-5.
64. Erman, pp. 268, 288, 301 ; Lange and Hirmer, pl. 212.
65. Erman, pp. 278-9, 295-6 ; Murray, *The Splendour etc.*, pp. 222-3, 249.
66. See my *Gods and Men*, 1962.
67. Erman, pp. 65-7, 278-9 ; Flinders

Petrie, *Religious etc.*, *pp.* 28-31, 39, 189-92 ; Murray, *The Splendour etc.*, pp. 184-5, 212-3.

68. Erman and Blackman, *The Literature etc.*, p. 82.

69. Budge, *Tutankhamen*, p. 97 ; Erman, p. 65 ; Perror and Chipiez I, p. 260 (fig. 172).

70. See my *Gods and Men*, 1962.

71. Hall, *The Ancient etc.*, pp. 285-6, f.n. ; Erman and Blackman, *The Literature etc.*, p. 282.

CHAPTER IV

1. *The Birth of Civilization in the Near East*, 1951, p. 68.

2. A. M. Blackman in *E.R.E.* 12, p. 780 ; Flinders Petrie, *Religious Life etc.*, p. 209 ; Erman, *Life etc.*, p. 283 ; Illustration and note.

3. Erman and Blackman, *The Literature etc.*, p. 83.

4. Ibid., pp. 235, 239.

5. Erman and Blackman, *The Literature etc.*, pp. 24, 153, 240, 302-3, 310-1.

6. *Development of Religion and Thought in Ancient Egypt*, 1912.

7. *The Dawn of Conscience*, pp. 33-42.

8. *From Fetish to God etc.*, p. 16.

9. Frankfort, *Before Philosophy*, pp. 64-9.

10. Wilson in Frankfort, *Before etc.*, p. 68, in Pritchard, p. 2.

11. Budge, op. cit., p. 267 ; Breasted, *The Dawn etc.*, pp. 97-8.

12. Frankfort, *Ancient Egyptian etc.*, pp. 20, 24.

13. Budge, op. cit., p. 159.

14. Budge, *From Fetish*, pp. 8, 101, 146-7, 152-6 ; Frankfort, *Ancient Egyptian etc.*, pp. 10-11.

15. Breasted, *The Dawn etc.*, p. 40.

16. *Development etc.*, p. 11.

17. Budge, *From Fetish etc.*, p. 10-11, 144 ; Breasted, *Dawn etc.*, p. 258.

18. Wilson in Frankfort, *Before etc.*, *p.* 105.

19. *The Dawn of Conscience*, pp. 141, 394-5.

20. Erman and Blackman, *The Literature etc.*, pp. 63-4. These passages are not excerpted by Wilson in his excerpts from this document given in Pritchard, *The Ancient Near etc.*, pp. 234-7.

21. *Ancient Egyptian Religion*, p. 24.

22. *From Fetish etc.*, pp. 15, 266; Breasted, *The Dawn etc.*, p. 35 ; Wilson in Frankfort, *Before Philosophy*, p. 67.

23. *R.V.*, X, 90. This hymn is known as the "Puruṣasūkta", the Hymn of the Primaeval Being ; X, 81, 3 ; X, 82, 3-6 ; I, 164, 2, 13, 14.

24. *R.V.*, X, 82, 3.

25. *R.V.*, X, 125, 1-4. The rendering within quotation marks is Griffith's translation of the text.

26. Griffith's translation of the text.

27. Hall, *The Ancient History etc.*, p. 214 ; Murray, *The Splendour etc.*, p. 28.

28. Hall, *The Ancient etc.*, pp. 220-2.

29. Murray, *Egyptian Temples*, p. 67.

30. Lange and Hirmer, Pls. 92, 94, 116, 117, 120, 312, 319.

31. Budge, *From Fetish etc.*, pp. 411-12 ; Erman and Blackman, *The Literature etc.*, pp. 282-4.

32. Wallis Budge, pp. 87-9, 107, 109, 139-40, 207-11; Murray, *Egyptian Temples*, pp. 43, 125, 146, 163, 166, 170-1 ; *The Splendour etc.*, pp. 170-3, 300-03 ; Hall, *The Ancient History etc.*, pp. 219, 314-5.

33. Hall, *The Ancient History etc.*, p. 112.

34. Budge, *From Fetish etc.*, pp. 16-7, 263, 270 ; Frankfort, *Ancient Egyptian Religion*, pp. 24-5.

35. Erman and Blackman, *The Literature etc.*, pp. 54-67.

36. Budge, *From Fetish etc.*, pp. 259-60.

37. Erman and Blackman, *The Literature etc.*, p. 82.

38. Hall, *The Ancient History etc.*, pp. 110-2, 122, 129 ; Murray, *Egyptian Temples*, pp. 108-110 ; Frankfort, *Ancient Egyptian etc.*, p. 10 ; Wallis

Budge, *From Fetish etc.*, pp. 73-4, 194.

39. *The Ancient History etc.*, p. 129; Wallis Budge, *Tutankhamen*, pp. 61-4.
40. Erman and Blackman, *The Literature etc.*, p. 44; Hall, op. cit., pp. 129-30.
41. Lange and Hirmer, pls. 94, 95.
42. Murray, *Egyptian Temples*, pp. 92-3; Lange and Hirmer, p. 346.
43. Lange and Hirmer, pp. 344-6; Budge, *Tutankhamen*, pp. 34-5.
44. Erman and Blackman, p. 282, f.n. 2.
45. Erman and Blackman, *The Literature etc.*, pp. 305-6.
46. Ibid., pp. 137-9, 140-1.
47. *Gods and Men*, 1962.
48. *Raghuvaṁśa*, X, 7-14, 16-32.
49. *The Literature etc.*, p. 283.
50. Hrozny in *E.B. XI*, pp. 599-600, 602-06.
51. Hall, *The Ancient History etc.*, pp. 196, 254, 257-8, 261, 270.
52. Hall, ibid., pp. 264-8, 297-303, 307, 345-53; Wallis Budge, *Tutankhamen*, pp. 75-114; Breasted, *The Dawn etc.*, pp. 280-99; Frankfort, *Ancient Egyptian etc.*, pp. 24-5, 135; Wilson in Frankfort, *Before Philosophy*, p. 98; Lange and Hirmer, p. 331; Murray, *The Splendour etc.*, pp. 54-5; Wilson in Pritchard, *The Ancient etc.*, pp. 226-7; Erman, *Life etc.*, pp. 45-6.
53. *Śvetāśvatara Up.* II, 1-7; *Gods and Men*, pp. 5-10.
54. Wallis Budge, *Tutankhamen*, pp. 4-7.
55. Ibid., pp. 4, 7.
56. Erman and Blackman, *The Literature etc.*, pp. 293-304.
57. Erman and Blackman, *The Literature etc.*, p. 263.
58. Flinders Petrie, *Religious Life etc., etc.*, p. 105.
59. Gurney, *The Hittites*.
60. Hrozny, in *E.B. XI*, pp. 599-606.
61. Erman, *Life etc.*, pp. 261-3, 273.
62. *Development of Religion etc.*, pp. 349-62, 364-5.
63. *From Fetish etc.*, pp. 45-6. I have put in the italics to draw the attention of the reader to the fact that *mutatis mutandis* the expressions italicized can be applied to the Hindus and Hinduism.
64. *Development of Thought etc.*, pp. 306-11.
65. *Before Philosophy*, p. 100.
66. Ibid., pp. 126-7; Pritchard, *The Ancient Near East*, p. 239.
67. Erman and Blackman, *The Literature etc.*, p. 301.

CHAPTER V

1. *Māhārāṣṭrīya Jñānakośa* (in Marathi) Vol. II, pp. 235, 392; P. V. Kane, *History of Dharmaśāstra*, Vol. IV, p. 162.
2. On this see my *Family and Kin in Indo-European Culture*.
3. The Girnar version of the Fourth Rock-edict reads in the original 'saṁvaṭakapā' which is rendered in Sanskrit as 'saṁvartakalpa' and translated as 'āpralayam' i.e. upto the deluge; and the sixth rock edict has 'yāvatsaṁvartakalpam' (D. S. Sircar, pp. 22-4).
4. D. C. Sircar, *Select Inscriptions*, p. 170.
5. *Raghuvaṁśa*, XIII, 6 (cp. Mallinātha's comment.)
6. *Raghuvaṁśa*, X, 21; VII, 56.
7. *Rājataraṅgiṇī*, VIII, 3405.
8. Vide, pp. 42-43 of Jwalaprasad Mishra's preface to his edition of *Tulasīdāsa Rāmāyaṇa*.
9. *Dāsabodha* (in Marathi), VI, 4.
10. *Dāsabodha*, XIII, 4; VI, 4, 22; VI, 6, 9; XVI, 9, 16.
11. VII, dohās 119-22; X, 5, 3-28.
12. *Dāsabodha*, VIII, 4, 40-2; X, 3, 2 X, 4, 9; XI, 1, 5-7; XII, 7, 10-11; XII, 8, 1; XIII, 3, 4-5; XIII, 3, 16; XVI, 10, 1-4; XVII, 4, 7.
13. *Dāsabodha*, IV, 9, 24; IV, 10, 1-2; VII, 4, 28-9; VIII, 4, 12-42; IX, 8, 4-5; IX, 8, 15-24; IX, 9, 14-22;

X, 3, 1-15 ; X, 4, 10 ; X, 5, 11 ; XIII, 3, 7 ; XIII, 6, 10 ; XIII, 7, 1 ; XV, 9, 15-17 ; XVI, 10, 1-6.

14. Op. cit., VIII, 4, 48 ; XV, 8, 29 ; XVI, 7, 15.
15. Op. cit., VII, dohā 116.
16. Kālidāsa's *Raghuvamśa*, XIII, 41.
17. S. Chitrav, *Prācīnacaritrakośa*, Appendix 2.
18. Ibid.
19. *Dāsabodha*, VIII, 4, 49-52 ; VIII, 5, 14-17; X, 10, 21; XIII, 4, 5; XV, 8, 15.
20. Ibid., IV, 10, 4-6, 10.
21. Ibid., IV, 2, 24 ; III, 8, 19-27.
22. *Dāsabodha*, XI, 1 ; XII, 6, XIII, 3 ; XIII, 4 ; VIII, 8, 1-15 and 17 ; IX, 1 and 2 ; IX, 6, 32 ; IX, 9, 4 ; X, 10, 11 ; XI, 10, 20-27 ; XIV, 9, 19-20 ; XVIII, 8, 18-9 ; XX, 2, 7-11.
23. Op. cit., VI, 5 ; VII, 2, 55-9 ; VII, 3, 64 ; VIII, 4 ; IX, 5, 4 ; IX, 6, 4-14 ; 6, 26, 6, 33 ; X, 4, 16 ; X, 5, 25-7 ; X, 9, 1-3 ; X, 10, 13-14 ; XI, 1, 9 ; XII, 6, 6 ; 8, 1 ; XIII, 3, 4 ; XIII, 4, 22-3 ; XV, 7, 9 ; XX, 3, 12.
24. Ibid., X, 10, 12-3 ; XI, 1, 5-9 ; XII, 6, 4 ; XIII, 3, 3 ; XX, 5, 4-5.
25. Ibid., VIII, 1, 20 ; VIII, 5, 7 ; VIII, 7, 24 ; IX, 5, 32; IX, 7, 43 ; XII, 7, 16 ; XIII, 3, 15 ; XVII, 2, 33; XX, 3, 2 ; XX, 6, 3.
26. Ibid., XIII, 3, 3.
27. *Jñāneśvarī*, VII, 24 ; XIV, 107 ; XV, 149.
28. *Kumārasambhava*, II, 4-13; V, 77-8; VI, 18, 21-6; 75-80; VII, 44 ; *Raghuvamśa*, III, 45 and 49 ; X, 14-32 ; XIII, 6.

CHAPTER VI

1. *Vedic Mythology*, p. 166.
2. Ibid.
3. *The Principal Upaniṣads* (Eng. trans.), (1921) p. 663.
4. *Mahārāṣṭrīya Jñānakośa*, Vol. II (1921) (in Marathi), p. 390.
5. "Egyptian Affinities of Indian Funerary Practices" in my *Anthropo-Sociological Papers* (1963).
6. V. M. Apte, *Brahma-Sūtra-Śāṅkara-Bhāṣya*, 1960, pp. 499-528.

CHAPTER VII

1. *R.V.*, I, 36, 18 ; I, 125, 5 ; V, 63, 2 ; V, 55, 4 ; IX, 113, 7-11 ; X, 14-2; X, 14, 8-14 ; X, 15, 14 ; X, 16, 2-5 ; X, 17, 21 ; X, 56, 1 ; X, 135, 7 ; Deussen, *Philosophy of the Upaniṣads*, pp. 319-21, 323 ; *Atharvaveda*, IV, 34, 2-6 ; VI, 120, 3 ; XVIII, 2, 26 ; Cf. S. V. Ketkar, *Mahārāṣṭrīya Jñānakośa*, II, pp. 390-1.
2. S. V. Ketkar, ibid.
3. Deussen, op. cit., p. 309.
4. *R.V.*, X, 14, 2-6 ; X, 15, 1-13 ; X, 56 ; A. A. Macdonell, *Vedic Mythology*, p. 170 ; Deussen, op. cit., p. 321 ; P. V. Kane, *History of Dharmaśāstra*, IV, pp. 346-7.
5. S. V. Ketkar, op. cit., pp. 393-4.
6. Elliot : *Hinduism and Buddhism*, I, pp. 233-4 ; E. J. Thomas, *The Life of Buddha*, pp. 189, 207.
7. *Select Inscriptions*, p. 30, f.n.
8. Op. cit., pp. 26, 30, 33, 40, 44, 48, 56, 59.
9. Ibid., pp. 26, 31, 32, 33, 40, 44, 48, 56, 59, 61.
10. D. C. Sircar, op. cit., p. 181.
11. Siddheshvarshastri Chitrav, *Prācīnacaritrakośa*, pp. 327-8.
12. Cf. *Tait. Upaniṣad*, II. 8. A. B. Keith, *Religion and Philosophy of the Veda*, pp. 71, 82.
13. S. Chitrav, *Prācīnacaritrakośa*, pp. 3, 294-5.
14. S. V. Ketkar, op. cit., p. 392 ; *Tait. Sam.*, VI, 6, 9.

15. *Śākuntala,* II, Vidūṣaka's remark before verse 17.
16. Jwalaprasad Mishra's edition of Tulasīdāsa's *Rāmāyaṇa*, pp. 1263-6.
17. S. V. Ketkar, op. cit., p. 391.
18. Ibid., pp. 235, 292 ; *Vājasaneyī Samhitā*, XXX, 5 ; *A.V.*, II, 14, 3 ; V, 19, 3.
19. *History of Dharmaśāstra*, Vol. IV, pp. 349-52.
20. Op. cit., pp. 353-8.
21. *Bṛh. Up.*, II, 1, 1.
22. D. C. Sircar, op. cit., pp. 189-90 and f.n. p. 158.
23. III, 94, 11-15.
24. In my *Family and Kin in Indo-European Culture* (2nd ed.), pp. 45-6, I had put this about three or four centuries earlier basing my conclusions on the data presented by P. V. Kane and others. Following my own line of research in more recent years I have come to the above conclusion. The material and argument placed before the readers through three chapters, this and the two previous ones, are sufficient to justify this change.
25. P. V. Kane, op. cit., IV, p. 352.
26. My *Family and Kin in Indo-European Culture* (2nd ed.), pp. 55-61; *Manusmṛti*, III, 80-2; III, 122-3; III, 259 ; III, 273-4 ; III, 281-4 ; IV, 150 ; P. V. Kane, op. cit., IV, p. 518.
27. *Family and Kin in Indo-European Culture.*
28. *Manusmṛti*, III, 146.
29. Ibid., III, 272, 30 ; ibid., III, 273, 31; ibid., 275.
30. D. C. Sircar, op. cit., pp. 165-6.
31. Kaṭha Up., I, 3, 7 ; *Śvet. Up.*, VI, 16 ; *Māṇḍūkya Up.*, 12; *BhG.* IX, 3; XII, 7.
32. *BhG.* V, 17 ; VIII, 15-16 ; XV, 4 and 6 ; *ChU.* IV, 15, 5; V, 3, 2 ; *Pr. Up.* I, 10.
33. *Bṛh. Up.*, IV, 3, 16 ; *Māṇḍūkya Up.*, 12 ; *Śvet. Up.* VI, 16; *Ch. Up.* VIII, 7, 26.
34. *Raghuvamśa*, X, 27.
35. *Vedic Mythology*, p. 166 ; *Philosophy of the Upaniṣads*, p. 323.
36. Op. cit., pp. 190, 192.
37. *Ś. Br.*, X, 4, 3, 10; X, 5, 6, 9 ; I, 5, 3, 14.
38. Op. cit., p. 169.
39. Op. cit., p. 392. Both Macdonell and Ketkar assert that the idea of the weighing of the deeds and of getting appropriate reward or punishment is also found in Iranian literature ; but they have not quoted appropriate references. I have therefore not taken that observation into consideration.
40. Op. cit., IV, p. 265.
41. D. C. Sircar, op. cit., pp. 184, 189.
42. S. V. Ketkar, op. cit., p. 392.
43. P. V. Jagadisa Ayyar, *South Indian Shrines*, 1922, p. 75.
44. See my *Family and Kin in Indo-European Culture* (2nd ed.) and *Anthropo-Sociological papers* (1913).
45. P. V. Kane, op. cit., IV, p. 487, f.n. 1094.

CHAPTER VIII

1. *Vedic Mythology*, 1897, p. 88.
2. Ibid., p. 96.
3. Ibid., p. 103.
4. Ibid., p. 102.
5. Ibid., pp. 101-03.
6. Ibid., p. 37 ; Keith, op. cit., pp. 106-7.
7. Ibid., p. 51.
8. Ibid., pp. 49, 51.
9. Ibid., pp. 49, 54.
10. *E.B.*, 23, p. 988. A. B. Keith, op. cit. I, pp. 114, 232.
11. *E.B.*, 12, pp. 604, 606 ; Hall, op. cit. pp. 201, 331.
12. Keith's statement at p. 117 that the evidence of the Boghaz-koi tablets for the early attestation of Nāsatyas (p. 5) "makes it most probable that the

Avesta knew them" and that "before the reform of Zoroaster the Naonhaithya must have been great gods" is without any basis in fact and is very dubious in logic.

13. Macdonell, op. cit., p. 54 ; Keith, op. cit., p. 124.
14. Macdonell, op. cit., pp. 18, 55, 79, 81.
15. Ibid., p. 64.
16. Op. cit., p. 132.
17. Macdonell, op. cit., pp. 56, 65 ; Keith, p. 34.
18. Ibid., p. 110.
19. Op. cit., pp. 124, 166, 168. Italics mine.
20. Op. cit., pp. 64-5.
21. Macdonell, p. 39.
22. Ibid., pp. 58, 62.
23. *The Ancient History of the New East*, pp. 190-202.
24. *E.B.*, 11, p. 604.
25. Macdonell, pp. 74, 77, 81.
26. Ibid.
27. Macdonell, pp. 30-4.
28. Macdonell, p. 33 ; Keith, p. 105.
29. Macdonell, p. 39.
30. Macdonell, pp. 43-5.
31. Hall, op. cit., p. 201.
32. Macdonell, p. 45.
33. Keith, p. 106 ; Macdonell, p. 33.
34. Keith, p. 107.
35. Macdonell, p. 45.
36. *R.V.*, X, 12, 8. Griffith's translation.
37. *R.V.*, VII, 81, 10, repeated as VII, 83, 10. Griffith's translation.
38. Op. cit., p. 20.
39. Macdonell, op. cit., pp. 20, 54, 77, 88, 104.
40. Macdonell, p. 20.
41. Keith, p. 75.
42. Ketkar, op. cit., pp. 228-36 ; Keith, pp. 75-6, 233-6.
43. Macdonell, p. 103.
44. Keith, p. 231.
45. Keith, pp. 96-7 ; Macdonell, pp. 24-5.
46. Op. cit., p. 34.
47. Op. cit., pp. 32-3.
48. O. R. Gurney, *The Hittites*, (1952), p. 139.
49. *E.B.*, 11, pp. 604-5 ; Gurney, loc. cit., pp. 17-8, 68, 104-05, 128-9.
50. Keith, op. cit., p. 106.
51. Keith, op. cit., pp. 35, 83-5 ; Hall, op. cit., pp. 260 ff ; Hrozny in *E.B.*, 11, p. 604.
52. Op. cit., pp. 20, 22-3.
53. Keith, pp. 101-4 ; 96-8.
54. Ibid., p. 90.
55. Macdonell, pp. 24, 58, 98.
56. *R.V.*, X, 125.
57. Macdonell, pp. 26-7.
58. *R.V.*, VII, 86, 2-6.
59. Ibid., p. 11 ; Keith, pp. 83-5, 249.
60. Macdonell, p. 26 ; *R.V.*, V, 67, 4 ; VII, 66, 12 ; VIII, 25, 4.
61. Op. cit., p. 246, f.n. 1.
62. Op. cit., p. 58.
63. Griffith's rendering.
64. Op. cit., pp. 84, 248-9, 479.
65. *R.V.*, I, 18 ; Macdonell, pp. 104, 109 ; Keith, p. 258.
66. Griffith's rendering.
67. Macdonell, pp. 119-20 ; Keith, p. 211.
68. D. C. Sircar, *Select Inscriptions*, pp. 466-7.
69. Keith, pp. 24, 70. Ketkar, pp. 152, 223.
71. Keith, pp. 258-61, 310.
72. Op. cit., pp. 253-6.
73. Macdonell, pp. 124, 142, 148-150.
74. See my *Gods and Men*, 1962.
75. Macdonell, p. 125 ; Keith, pp. 218-9.
76. Macdonell, p. 118-9.
77. Macdonell, pp. 5, 14, 130 ; also Keith, p. 86 ; *RV.*, VII, 35, 6.
78. *RV.*, I, 139, 11.
79. Op. cit., p. 86.
80. Op. cit., p. 16.

CHAPTER IX

1. Op. cit., p. 323.
2. See Keith, op. cit., pp. 450, 581.
3. Op. cit., pp. 394, 396.
4. Op. cit., p. 441.
5. Op. cit., p. 358.
6. On this see my *Anthropo-Sociological Papers.*
7. *Bṛh. Up.*, I, 4, 10 ; I, 6 ; II, 3, 1-2 ; II, 4 ; IV, 3, 7 ; IV, 5, 15 ; *Ch. Up.*, III, 14 ; VI, 15, 3 ; VIII, 1, 1-3 ; *Tait. Up.*, II, 1 ; II, 9 ; III, 1 ; *Kena Up.*, I, 3-8 ; *Kaṭha Up.*, I, 3, 15 ; II, 2, 14-15 ; II, 3, 1-3 ; *Muṇḍ. Up.*, I, 1, 6-7 ; II, 2, 11 ; III, 1, 7 ; *Bṛh. Up.*, II, 4, 5 ; III, 7, 2 ; III, 9, 26 ; IV, 2, 4 ; IV, 4, 2 ; IV, 5, 15 ; *Ch. Up.*, III, 14, 2 ; VIII, 1, 5 ; VIII, 7, 1 ; VIII, 12, 2-3 ; *Tait. Up.*, II, 4 ; *Kaṭha Up.*, I, 3, 10-2 ; II, 2, 12-5 ; II, 3, 7-9 ; *Muṇḍ. Up.*, III, 1, 1-5 ; *Muṇḍ. Up.*, VI, XII ; *Śvet. Up.*, III, 8-9, 12-17 and 18-21 ; VI, 1-2 ; VI, 9-13.
8. Op. cit., pp. 14-26, 106-12.
9. *Jñāneśvarī* (in Marathi), XVIII, 1390-1485 ; XV, 571-93.
10. *Gods and Men.*
11. III, 254.
12. The specific verses will be noted in a later context where a free rendering of the verse will be presented.
13. *Kumārasambhava*, II, 58.
14. VIII, 9.
15. *BhG*, VII, 23 ; VIII, 16 ; IX, 20-1 ; IX, 23 and 25 ; XI, 22, 37-9.
16. Ibid., II, 14, 45-6; III, 10-17 ; IV, 23-33 ; IX, 15, 20 ; X, 25 ; XVII, 4 and 11 ; XVIII, 2-6.
17. This is repeated at *Kaṭha Up.*, II, 3, 1.
18. *Bṛh. Up.*, III, 4 ; IV, 4, 13-21 ; *Kena Up.*, I ; *Iśa Up.* 4-8 ; *Praśna Up.*, IV, 7-11 ; *Kaṭha Up.*, II, 1-3 ; II, 2, 8-13 ; *Śvet. Up.*, VI, 10-13.
19. The paraphrase which forms the verse 16 is itself a rendering of a verse from the *Rgveda* (X, 81, 3) already embodied in the *Upaniṣad* as III, 3.
20. *The Principal Upaniṣads*, p. 69. Surendranath Dasagupta, too, (*A History of Indian Philosophy*, I, p. 75) makes a more or less similar observation without furnishing a reference to any authoritative text.
21. P. 134. The earliest occurrence as known from this work is of course that in the dualistic philosophy of Madhva ; but therein we have the addition of a fourth element to the trio (p. 61) and Madhva's activity dates not earlier than 1150 A.D.
22. P. 159.
23. Bhandarkar, op. cit., pp. 33-4 ; 102-7 ; Ketkar, op. cit., pp. 313-4, 323-4 ; Keith, op. cit., 110-2 ; 143-9.
24. R. G. Bhandarkar, p. 107.
25. Macdonell, pp. 39-41 ; Bhandarkar, p. 34 ; Ketkar, pp. 228-30, 241 ; Keith, pp. 110-112.
26. Macdonell, p. 39 ; Ketkar, p. 228.
27. Cf. *Chāndogya Upaniṣad*, VIII, 12, 2.
28. *Māṇḍūkya Upaniṣad*, I, 1; *Taittirīya Upaniṣad*, I, 8.
29. Cf. Kālidāsa in *Kumārasambhava*, II, 12. Mallinātha in his comment quotes a statement from the Appendix to Yāska's *Nirukta* which, if the Appendix is Yāska's, would date the enthronement of 'om' at the beginning of all religious endeavour at least three centuries earlier, i.e., before 500 B.C.
30. Ketkar, op. cit., p. 284.
31. See *Gods and Men*, 1962.
32. Brahmā's representation in later and current Hinduism having passed out of general use is not dealt with here.
33. *Gods and Men.*
34. Monier Williams, *Religious Thought and Life in India*, 1883, p. 66-8 ; Bhandarkar, pp. 50 ; 75-84 ; P. V. Jagadisa Ayyar, *South Indian Shrines*, 1922, pp. 227-8.

CHAPTER X

1. Bhandarkar, p. 44.
2. See my *Gods and Men.*
3. Kingsbury and Philips, pp. 41, 51, 59, 61, 63.
4. Ibid., pp. 17, 19, 23, 73, 75, 81.
5. Ibid., pp. 25, 49, 77, 93.
6. J. S. M. Hooper, *Hymns of the Alvars*, 1929, pp. 34, 37-9, 43-5, 48, 50-7, 61-8, 70, 72, 76-8, 81, 85, 87.
7. Ibid., pp. 35, 38, 50, 53-4, 71-4, 77-9, 86.
8. Ibid., pp. 34-7, 40-46, 50, 52, 53, 58, 61, 75.
9. Ibid., pp. 75-6.
10. Bhandarkar, pp. 52-3.
11. Ibid., pp. 57, 59-60.
12. Ibid., pp. 121-2, 124, 127.
13. Ibid., pp. 129-30.
14. Bhandarkar, pp. 134-9.
15. Ibid., pp. 63, 85.
16. Bhandarkar, pp. 65, 81.
17. Bhandarkar, pp. 78-81.
18. On this see my *Gods and Men.*
19. Op. cit., p. 98.
20. See my *Indian Sadhus* (2nd ed.) 1964,

CHAPTER XI

1. A. Jeremias in *ERE*, III, pp. 745, 746.
2. Op. cit., p. 342.
3. I think with the utmost deference to Deussen that 'union' is the more correct rendering of the Sanskrit term 'sāyujya'.

   Monier Williams, op. cit., pp. 122-3; Bhandarkar, op. cit., pp. 54, 64.
4. *Jñāneśvarī*, XVIII, 1200 ('advaya-bhakti'); also cf. XVIII, 1151.
5. Bhandarkar, pp. 74, 77-9, 80, 83; N. Macnicol, pp. 116-20, 128-32.
6. Bhandarkar, p. 78.
7. Bhandarkar, p. 85
8. *Rāmāyaṇa*, I, D. 31, 1-2; III, D. 22; VII, D. 127, 7-8; D. 128; VII, Dohās, 85-7; D. 190, 5; D. 192, 10.
9. Ibid., I, D. 357, 6; VII, D. 67, 8; D. 70, 7; D. 186, 6; D. 192, 10; D. 205; Chanda, 30.
10. Ibid., VII, D. 66, 7-8; D. 67; D. 73, 1-4; D. 79, 1-8; D. 125; D. 178, 9-14; D. 183; D. 188, 6-7; Chanda 29.
11. Ibid., III, So. 7, 14; VII, D. 69; D. 84; D. 180, 13; D. 183, 5-7; D. 188, 7; D. 189.
12. See my *Gods and Men.*
13. *Dāsabodha*, IV, 5, 26-30; I, 10, 16; II, 7, 3; IV, 10, 16; II, 7, 3; IV, 10, 27; VI, 2, 1; VII, 1, 13; VII, 6, 44-46; XX, 6, 12.
14. Ibid., XI, 1, 42; IV, 10, 30.
15. IV, 10, 22-31.
16. I, 10, 14.
17. Bhandarkar, pp. 125, 137. N. Macnicol, pp. 169-70; Cf. S. C. Nandimath, *A Handbook of Vīraśaivism*, p. 175.
18. F. Kingsbury and G. E. Phillips, *Hymns of the Tamil Śaivite Saints* (1921), p. 127 (136).
19. See my *Anthropo-Sociological Papers* (1963).
20. *Bhagavadgītā*, XVIII, 30 and 34; *Manusmṛti*, II, 224; VI, 35 and 36.
21. D. C. Sircar, *Select Inscriptions*, p. 57.
22. VII, 92.
23. *Yājñavalkyasmṛti*, I, 122.
24. *Viṣṇusmṛti*, II, 7-8.
25. Sircar, p. 59.
26. Sircar, p. 69.
27. Bhandarkar, pp. 41-55.
28. Bhandarkar, p. 41.
29. Monier Williams, op. cit., pp. 76, 78, 81, 105; Bhandarkar, pp. 103-5.
30. *Manusmṛti*, II, 85-7.
31. On this see my *Gods and Men* (1962).
32. Cf. *BhG*, IV, 19-21; V, 11; 13; VI, 1; XII, 6-12; XVIII, 49.

33. Ketkar, p. 181 ; *Śat. Br.* XI, 5, 6 ; *Manusmṛti*, III, 78.

34. *Tait. Saṃhitā*, VI, 2, 8, 5.

35. Ketkar, p. 155.

36. Cf. *Manusmṛti*, II, 12.

37. Quoted by Kullūka in his comment on *Manusmṛti*, II, 6.

38. Bhandarkar, pp. 55, 61.

39. Mayarani Tandon, *Aṣṭachāpakāvyakā Sāmskṛtic Mūlyāṅkana* (in Hindi), 1960, pp. 501-21.

40. Monier Williams, pp. 135-7 ; Bhandarkar, pp. 79-82.

41. Monier Williams, pp. 140-1 ; S. K. De.

42. Monier Williams, p. 141; Bhandarkar, p. 84.

43. *Tulasīkṛta Rāmāyaṇa*, I, dohās, 28-31 ; dohās 57-66 ; d. 123-7 ; III, dohās, 23-4 ; VII, dohās 59, 61; dohās 65-69 ; dohās 71-2.

44. *T.R.*, I, dohās, 5-13 ; dohās 2-5 ; III, dohā 23 ; VII, dohās 37-8 ; dohā 61, 5-8 ; dohā 63 ; dohā 70, 7-8 etc. dohās 185-8.

45. *T.R.* III, dohā 23, 12; VII, dohās 623-4 ; dohā 73 ; dohā 99 ; dohā 151.

46. *T.R.* III, dohā 23-8.

47. *T.R.* VII, dohā 189.

48. Op. cit., p. 112.

49. Cf. The description of this part of a Brahmin's daily routine given by Mrs. Sinclair Stevenson, *The Rites of the Twice-Born*, 1920, pp. 216-7, 348.

50. *Bṛhājjābāla Upaniṣad*, VI, 7. The Chinese traveller Hiuen Tsang in the 7th century refers to one subsection of the Śaivas by this characteristic (see my *Indian Sadhus*).

51. *Rudrākṣa-Jābālopaniṣad ; Pañcatantra*, I, 178 ; Mrs. Stevenson, p. 388 ; *Indian Sadhus*, pp. 102-4.

52. Bhandarkar, pp. 121, 136-7.

53. I, 174-9.

54. Kingsbury and Phillips, pp. 57, 67 ; P. V. Jagadisa Ayyar, *South Indian Shrines*, p. 205.

55. See my *Gods and Men*.

56. Op. cit., p. 55.

57. Mrs. Stevenson, p. 232.

58. See my *Gods and Men*.

59. *Indian Sadhus*.

60. *Journal of the Andhra Historical Research Society*, Vol. 4, p. 147.

61. R. Rolland, *Prophets of the New India*, p. 250.

CHAPTER XII

1. Woolley, *Excavations at Ur*, p. 125 ; Jastrow, p. 376.

2. Gordon Childe, *New Light on the Most Ancient East*, pp. 119-20.

3. C. J. Gadd, pp. 51-2 ; *E.B.*, 2, pt. II opp. p. 845 ; Childe, op. cit., pp. 125-6 ; Saggs, pl. 10 p. 108 and 364; Woolley, *Excavations*, pp. 91-7.

4. Jastrow, p. 375; Saggs, p. 355; Woolley, *Excavations*, p. 220.

5. Frankfort, *Birth of Civilization*, p. 233 ; S. N. Kramer, pp. 194-205.

6. Woolley, *Excavations*, p. 134 ; *Sumerians*, p. 151 ; Pallis, pp. 699-700 ; Gadd, op. cit., p. 129.

7. Woolley, *Excavations*, pp. 130, 159-61, 219.

8. Woolley, *Excavations*, p. 219.

9. Woolley, *Excavations*, pp. 144, 220, 222 ; *Sumerians*, p. 150.

10. Jastrow, pp. 372-5, 376 ; Pallis, pp. 701, 703, 704.

11. Op. cit., p. 374.

12. Op. cit., pp. 376-78.

13. *Ancient Times*, p. 704.

14. *Early Muslim Architecture*, II, p. 261 ; Saggs, pp. 499-500.

CHAPTER XIII

1. *The Ancient History of the Near East*, p. 121.
2. Perrot and Chipiez, *A History of Art etc.*, I, pp. 198-200.
3. Perrot and Chipiez, I, p. 198, have recorded the heights of the three pyramids as 482, 454 and 218 feet respectively. They have given in f.n. on p. 225, earlier measurements of the pyramid of Khufu. Breasted quoted by Wilson in Frankfort's *Before Philosophy* (p. 105) gives the base sides as 755 feet long and the height as 481 feet.
4. Lange and Hirmer, 297, 300-1 ; M. A. Murray, *Egyptian Temples*, pp. 19-23. She gives the height of a pillar as 18 feet.
5. Lange and Hirmer, p. 303 ; Hall, *The Ancient etc.*, pp. 130-1.
6. *Tutankhamen*, pp. 61-2.
7. Piggott, *Dawn of Civilization*, p. 119. Aldred gives the dimension as 330 ft. by 250 ft.
8. *E.B.* I, p. 69.
9. Perrot and Chipiez, I, fig. 207, view opp. p. 307, fig. 213 ; pp. 334-60 ; Erman, pp. 280-2, and plans A. H. Gardiner in *E.B.* (11th ed.), Vol. XI, pp. 48-52, 54.
10. Murray, *Egyptian Temples*, pp. 144-52 ; Lange and Hirmer, pp. 350-52 ; pls. 232-33.
11. Murray, *Egyptian Temples*, pp. 77, 145, 148 ; Hall, *The Ancient History*, pp. 379-83.
12. J. Fergusson, *A History of Architecture in All Countries*, 3rd revd. ed., Vol. I, p. 123.
13. *The Dawn of Conscience*, p. 327, fig. 17 and f.n.
14. Perrot and Chipiez : *History of Ancient Egyptian Art*, vol. I, pp. 362-66, figs. 214-5 and pl. ; Murray, *Egyptian Temples*, pls. XV(2), XVII(2) ; Lange and Hirmer, pp. 343-8, figs. 30-32 and pls. 118, 128-9, 136-9, 198-9, 216-9 ; *E.B.*, VIII, p. 107, sectional view and plan.
15. J. Fergusson, op. cit., p. 122.
16. *Ancient Times*, p. 87 and fig. 66 with its letterpress.
17. Op. cit., pp. 123-4.
18. Lange and Hirmer, op. cit., p. 319.
19. Flinders Petrie, *Religious Life etc.*, p. 200.
20. *Egyptian Temples*, pp. 92-5.
21. Wallis Budge, *Egyptian Tales etc.*, pp. 142-9.
22. *Br. Up.*, III, 7.
23. Murray, *Egyptian Temples*, pp. 100-01 ; Hippopotamus-hunting was actually a sport well indulged in and represented in the artistic remains (Erman, *Life in Ancient Egypt*, pp. 239-40).
24. *E.B.* I, p. 69.
25. See my *Gods and Men*, 1962.
26. Breasted, *Ancient Times*, pp. 611, 688, 703.
27. *The Ancient History etc.*, pp. 233-40, 250-2; Murray, *Egyptian Temples*, pp. 71-3. Wilson Pritchard, *The Ancient Near East*, pp. 175-83.
28. Erman, *Life in Ancient etc.*, pp. 282-4; Murray, *Egyptian Temples*, pp. 46-8, 81-4, 117, 125, 135, 166 ; Hall, op. cit., pp. 131, 290, 381-2, 438-9.
29. Erman and Blackman, *The Literature etc.*, p. 268.
30. Ibid., p. 264 ; Lange and Hirmer, op. cit., p. 347.

CHAPTER XIV

1. See my *Gods and Men*, 1962.
2. *Indian Antiquary*, 1883, pp. 315-26.
3. The dancing girls are not in evidence; see Carl Gustav Diehl, *Instrument and Purpose*, 1956, p. 106.

4. *Religious Thought and Life in India*, pp. 93-94.
5. Vol. II, pp. 76-7.
6. *The Rites of the Twice-born*, 1920, pp. 370-95.
7. *Instrument and Purpose*, pp. 138, 148-52.
8. Op. cit., vol. II, p. 128.
9. Op. cit., p. 81.
10. Op. cit., pp. 401-3.
11. Diehl, op. cit., pp. 152-3.
12. Op. cit., p. 55.
13. Bhandarkar, op. cit., p. 81 : I have counted 'offering of morning refreshment' as a separate item. It is too important to be included in that of 'awakening' as one with it.
14. Mayarani Tandon, *Aṣṭachāpa-Kāvyakā Sāmskṛtic Mūlyāṅkana*, 1960, pp. 505-6.
15. V. S. Apte's *Skt. English Dictionary*, under 'aṣṭan'.
16. *R.V.*, I, 27, 13 ; 72, 5; 114, 2, 4, 11 ; 136, 1 ; 189, 1 ; IV, 50, 6 ; 58, 2 ; VI, 51, 8-9 ; X, 69, 12 ; 85, 17.
17. *Āpastambadharmasūtra* (*Sacred Laws of the Aryas*, vol. I, p. 23), I, 2,6, 13 ff; I, 5, 21 ; I, 14, 7 ; *Baudhāyana*, I, 3, 25 ff.
18. F. C. Maisey, *Sanchi and its Remains* (1892), Pl. IX ; Ananda K. Coomaraswamy (1935), Pls. LI and LX.
19. II, 70-2.
20. *Pañcatantra*, I, 175.
21. Ibid., V, 11-15.
22. See my *Gods and Men*, 1962.
23. Percy Brown, *Indian Architecture*, 1942, p. 56.
24. See my *Gods and Men*.
25. D. C. Sircar, *Select Inscriptions*, pp. 211-3.
26. Ibid., pp. 288-94.
27. Ibid., p. 279.
28. Nasik Cave Inscription of Vāsiṣṭhīputra : D. C. Sircar, op. cit., pp. 198-200.
29. V. S. Apte, *Sanskrit-English Dictionary*, under 'pañcan'. As no literary reference is given I have taken it to be from a lexicon.
30. P. Brown, op. cit., p. 17.
31. *History of Indian & Eastern Architecture*, II, 136 ;
32. Op. cit., pp. 120-3.
33. Fergusson, II, pp. 108-9 ; Brown, p. 124.
34. P. Brown, op. cit., pp. 99, 120, 121, 122 ; Fergusson, II, p. 101. The height of the spire of Liṅgarāja is taken from Brown's book. Fergusson states the heights of both this and that of Bṛhadīśvara to be nearly the same being 180 feet.
35. Ibid., p. 96.
36. P. Brown, op. cit., p. 98.
37. Op. cit., I, p. 363. Italics mine.
38. Op. cit., p. 99.
39. Op. cit., I, pp. 343-4. Brown (p. 87) states the height to be 95 feet.
40. Op. cit., p. 87.
41. Fergusson, II, pp. 141-3, 146-7, 148-51 ; Brown, pp. 129, 131, 135, 137, 140-1, 143.
42. II, p. 150.
43. Brown, p. 123. Fergusson, however, (II, p. 109) gives the height as only 192 feet.
44. II, p. 101.
45. Ibid., p. 143.
46. Op. cit., p. 130.
47. See *Gods and Men*, p. 175.
48. For Caitanyite mode of worship see Monier Williams, op. cit., pp. 144-5. For Vallabhite mode see Bhandarkar, op. cit., p. 81 ; Fergusson, II, pp. 108-10 ; Brown, pp. 118, 122-3.
49. P. Brown, pl. LXX, p. 124.
50. P. Brown, op. cit., pp. 164, 166.
51. *Gods and Men*.
52. Fergusson, II, p. 56 ; Brown, pp. 136, 150.
53. Fergusson, I, pp. 437, 442.
54. Op. cit., pp. 187-8.
55. Op. cit., pp. 38-43, 45-7.

56. Opp. p. 47.
57. Fergusson, I, pp. 444, 449 ; Brow,n op. cit., p. 169.
58. *E.B.* (14th ed.) Vol. XXII, p. 331(a) ; Vol. V, p. 34 ; Vol. XIX, p. 746.
59. Fergusson, op. cit., I, 374 ; Brown, op. cit., pp. 103-4, 115.
60. Fergusson, I, p. 374. Brown (p. 115) says it is 325 ft. square.
61. P. V. Jagadiśa Ayyar, *South Indian Shrines*, p. 206.
62. Brown, p. 115 ; Fergusson, I, p. 374.
63. Ayyar, op. cit., p. 207.
64. Fergusson, I, pp. 396, 401-02 ; Brown pp. 107-8.
65. Fergusson, I, pp. 381-5 ; Brown, p. 115.
66. P. V. J. Ayyar, op. cit., pp. 617-8.
67. A. H. Longhurst, *Hampi Ruins*, pp. 72-3, 107, 112-3, 120.
68. Fergusson, op. cit., I, plan on p. 369.
69. *Gods and Men.*
70. Fergusson, I, p. 343 (199).
71. Ibid., p. 358.
72. Op. cit., pp. 110, 112.
73. Op. cit., I, p. 437.
74. Op. cit., p. 166.
75. Op. cit., I, p. 439.
76. Op. cit., pp. 494, 450-1.
77. Op. cit., p. 615-16.
78. Op. cit., p. 112.
79. Fergusson, I, p. 374 ; Brown, pp. 103-4.
80. Fergusson, I, pp. 361, 367.
81. Ibid., pp. 380-3.
82. *Span*, Dec., 1963, p. 49.
83. *The Cambridge Shorter History of India*, p. 185.
84. Brown, pp. 103-4, 115.
85. Fergusson, I, p. 374 ; Brown, p. 115.
86. Ibid., p. 396 ; Brown, p. 104.
87. Fergusson, I, p. 360 ; Brown, p. 113.
88. Fergusson, I, p. 360, f.n. 2.
89. Op. cit., I, p. 383.
90. Ibid., pp. 407-08.
91. Fergusson, op. cit., I, p. 408.
92. Op. cit., p. 111.
93. *E.B.* (14th ed.) VIII, p. 108.
94. Fergusson, II, pp. 379, 401.
95. Ibid., pp. 379, 392.
96. Ibid., p. 374.
97. Ibid., p. 401.
98. Ibid., pp. 383-89, 394.
99. Ibid., p. 400.
100. Op. cit., I, p. 368.
101. Op. cit., pp. 113-4.
102. Fergusson, op. cit., II, pp. 378, 382, 386, 390, 392.
103. Fergusson, II, p. 103, Plan.
104. Op. cit., p. 350.
105. Albert B. Franklin, U.S. Consul General, Madras, *Span* (Dec. 1963), pp. 46, 49, 50. Italics mine.

INDEX

A

Aah : 27
Aahmes : 27
Aannipadda : 291
Absolute Brahman : 133, 229, 235, 248, 250, 253, 254, 264, 265, 280
Absolute Principle : 145
Abu Gurab : 297, 298
Abu Simbel : 29
Abydos : 20, 52, 60, 66, 74, 297, 307
Ādi Nārāyaṇa : 126
Aditi : 216
Ādityahṛdaya : 167
Ādityas : 79, 164, 185, 197, 198
Agastya : 167, 174
Agni : 103, 162, 171, 172, 191, 192, 193, 195, 202
Agnidagdhas : 164
Agniṣvāttas : 163, 164, 167
Ahaṁkāra : 11, 118, 122, 132, 136, 146, 149, 150, 153, 155, 156, 158
Ahura Mazda : 197, 199, 207
Airammadīya : 107
Airāvateśvara Temple : 354
Aitareya Upaniṣad : 98, 112, 134, 135, 137, 139, 143, 186, 219
Ājyapās : 164
Ākāśa : 118, 120, 122, 125, 126, 133, 134
Akṣara : 224
Aldred, Cyril : 297
Amen : 25-30, 32, 54-57, 61, 62, 63, 65, 70, 77, 80, 81, 83, 86, 87, 88, 91, 93, 94, 97, 298, 300, 301, 305, 306, 307, 308
Amenemhat I : 25, 28, 48, 63
Amenemhat II : 59, 306
Amenemhat III : 59
Amenemopet : 96
Amenhotep I : 27, 31, 61, 81
Amenhotep II : 82
Amenhotep III : 22, 25, 28, 63, 65, 299, 303, 305, 308
Amenophis III : 61
Amenophis IV : 60
Amen-Ra : 21, 23, 27, 28, 29, 30, 31, 53, 54, 57, 65, 80-84, 86, 87, 88, 90, 92, 311
Amman shrine : 313, 315, 316
Amon : 24
Ānanda : 132, 149
Ananta Vāsudeva : 335
Aṅgasthala : 248
Āṅgirasas : 163, 164
Ani : 94, 96
Ankor Tham : 351, 353
Ankor Vat : 351, 353
Annunaki : 12
Anṛta : 149
Antaḥkaraṇa : 148, 152, 158, 159
Antaḥkaraṇa-catuṣṭaya : 155
Antaryāmin : 148
Antum : 2
Anu Adad : 295
Anu (An) : 1-6
Ap : 118
Āpaḥ : 120
Apiladad : 11, 15
Appar : 246
Appārswami : 288
Ara : 107, 108
Aralu : 12
Arcirādi : 110, 115
Ardha-maṇḍapa : 326, 333
Arjuna : 93, 114, 170, 174, 186, 232, 239, 281, 311
Artaxerxes II : 4
Aruru : 2
Aṣat : 149
Aśmā : 141
Aśoka : 17, 120, 165, 166, 269, 270
Aṣṭadhā Prakṛti : 117, 126
Astarte : 65
Aśvin : 79, 164, 167, 193
Aten : 91, 95, 200
Atharvaveda : 101, 104, 162, 200, 215
Ātman : 99, 132, 134, 137, 143, 146, 148
Atum : 58, 63, 65, 73-76, 78, 80, 81, 84, 86, 87, 94
Atum-Khepre : 87
Aum : 104, 151
Āvāntara pralaya : 120
Āvaraṇa : 122, 354
Avyakta : 103, 136, 149, 150
Ayyar, P. V. Jagadisa : 343, 354

B

Bādarāyaṇa : 115, 147, 154, 156-58, 171, 179, 181, 183, 254
Badrikedāra : 128
Badrinārāyaṇa : 128
Barhiṣadas : 175
Bast : 54, 56

Bayon Temple : 351
Benben : 88
Bethshan : 29
Bhagavadgītā : 94, 101, 103, 114, 115, 117, 119, 122, 123, 125, 127, 144, 146, 148, 149, 151-53, 168, 174, 180, 184, 186, 187, 216, 222, 224, 234, 235, 238, 244, 263, 281
Bhāgavata-Purāṇa : 284
Bhāgvatism : 247
Bhairava : 248
Bhakti : 272, 274, 276, 277, 284, 286
Bhandarkar, R. G. : 222, 227, 228, 231, 248, 288, 318, 319
Bhārata-Nātyaśāstra : 340
Bhogadeha : 179
Bhṛgus : 163
Bhuvaneśvara temple : 317, 327
Bilva leaves : 315, 316
Blackman : 28, 43, 45, 49, 51, 56, 86, 90
Book of the Dead : 76, 88
Brahma 118-121, 125-127, 146, 160, 167, 169, 170, 208
Brahmabhuvana : 117
Brahmacarya : 149
Brahmā Hiraṇyagarbha : 119
Brahma-hole : 158
Brahmaloka : 122
Brahman : 78, 98-104, 106, 107, 110, 111, 115, 134, 140, 143, 144, 177, 205
Brahmāñjali : 321
Brahman-knowledge : 172, 219, 220
Brahmapatha : 106, 113
Brahmarandhra : 141
Brahma-realization : 112, 115, 116
Brahmasūtra : 115, 147, 154, 158, 171, 181, 254
Brahmā-Svayambhu : 125
Brahmībhūta : 254
Brahminic Hinduism : 172
Breasted, J. H. : 38, 45, 49, 52, 63, 72, 73, 76, 77, 95-97, 302, 309
Bṛhardāraṇyaka Upaniṣad : 98, 102-104, 106, 109, 111-114, 130, 132, 133, 135, 137, 138, 140, 142, 143, 146, 149, 167, 174, 177, 179, 182, 204, 205, 218, 219, 221, 228
Bṛhadīśvara Shrine : 330, 332, 334, 336
Brother-sister marriage : 27
Brown, Percy : 325, 327-329, 334, 338, 339, 342, 344, 345, 347, 349, 352
Bubastis : 54
Buddha : 165, 173, 229, 261
Buddhi : 117, 118, 120, 122, 132, 136, 137, 146, 148, 149, 151-53, 155, 157, 160
Buddhism : 166
Budge, Wallis : 24, 28, 29, 38, 40, 47, 50, 52, 53, 55, 57, 62, 72, 73, 75, 78, 83, 91, 96, 97, 198, 200
Burgess, J. : 312, 313, 316

C

Caitanya : 149
Cambodian temples : 350, 352
Cetas : 131
Chāndogya : 99, 102, 104-14, 130-35, 137, 140-43, 147, 168, 182-83, 205, 219, 221
Chartres cathedral : 339
Chenna Keśava temple : 336, 341, 342
Chepren : 58, 59
Chidambaram temple : 340
Chipiez : 56, 60, 300, 302
Cidākāśa : 156
Cit : 246
Citta : 131, 156
Cittavṛtti : 155
Citragupta : 181
Conjeevaram : 181
Cosmography : 11, 117
Cremation : 141

D

Dāsabodha : 113, 122, 124, 125, 127, 128, 158, 234, 255, 265
Der-el-Bahri : 27, 60, 82
Deussen : 162, 176, 220, 259
Devālaya : 326
Devaloka : 111
Devapatha : 113
Devayāna: 109-111, 113, 114, 206
Dharma : 98, 149, 267, 270
Dhyāna : 131
Diehl, C. G. : 317
Dilmun : 292

E

Ea (Enki) : 1, 4, 14
Ego-sense : 132, 136
Egyptian shrine : 296
Ekāmbaranātha temple : 346
Ellora : 329
En-Engur : 14
Enki (Ea) : 1, 2, 3, 10

Enlil (Bel) : 1, 3, 5, 6, 7, 58
Ennead : 21, 23, 46, 73, 79
Erech : 1, 2, 3
Eridu : 1
Erman : 29, 38, 43, 45, 49, 51, 55, 56, 86, 90, 94

F

Fergusson, James : 299, 303, 327, 328, 333, 339, 340, 345, 347, 350
Fire-kindling : 151
Frankfort : 39, 41, 42, 49, 69, 78, 83
Franklin, Albert B. : 343
Fyfe, D. T. : 20

G

Gadd, C. J. : 20
Gaṅgā (Ganges) : 243, 245
Gardiner, A. H. : 34
Gāthā : 89, 253, 290
Gilgamesh : 12, 69
Gizeh : 58, 296
Golaki maṭha : 289
Golden embryo : 134
Gondeśvara temple : 336
Gopura : 325, 326, 336, 348
Griffith : 204, 210, 212, 321
Gudea : 11, 14-16, 18, 19, 58
Guṇas : 117, 122, 152

H

Hall, H. R. : 20, 30, 38, 59, 61, 85, 309, 310
Hampi : 341
Hammurabi : 15, 16
Hannamkonda temple : 336
Harakhti : 87, 94
Hathor : 21, 54, 58, 86, 87, 305
Hatshepsut : 26, 27, 82, 92, 303, 305, 306
Heliopolis : 300
Heremhab : 56, 68, 306
Hermonthis : 25
Himālaya : 114, 128, 252, 260
Himavat : 260
Hindu-resurgence : 175
Hiraṇyagarbha : 79, 101, 118, 125, 126, 164, 191, 214
Hirmer : 31, 59, 297
Hittites : 90, 94, 193, 194, 196, 198, 199
Hiuen Tsang : 289
Horus : 21-24, 26, 50, 57, 71, 74-76, 78, 85
Hoysaleśvara temple : 336, 339
Hoysala : 339, 340
Hṛd : 129, 150, 153
Hṛdākāśa : 156
Hṛdaya : 137, 143, 144
Hṛdaya-ākāśa : 156
Hyksos : 28, 81

I

Ikhnaten : 17, 21, 31, 57, 60, 68, 91-93, 198, 200
Ila : 208
Ilya : 108
Im-Hotep : 22, 77, 306
Imgig : 291
Impersonal Brahman : 224, 225, 229, 257
Impersonal Principle : 224
Indra : 79, 95, 102-104, 108, 167-169, 180, 181, 186, 192-194, 203
Indrāgnī : 79
Innini : 1, 2
Ipuwer : 33-35
Ishtar : 2, 3, 14, 16, 90
Isis : 21, 24, 49, 90
Iśvara : 121
Izezi : 45

J

Jacobsen, Thorkild : 5, 10, 11
Jagannātha temple : 328, 333, 336, 353
Japa : 279
Jastrow, Morris : 3, 6, 13, 14, 18, 19, 294, 295
Jīva : 148, 156
Jīvaghana : 147
Jīva-Śiva : 157, 159
Jīvātman : 147, 158, 159
Jñānayoga : 274
Jñāneśvara : 119, 126, 127, 154, 155, 156, 158, 168, 189, 223, 233, 263, 265, 281, 285
Jñāneśvarī : 127, 154, 159
Jūti : 137, 149
Jyoti : 155

K

Kadesh : 311
Kagemni, instruction for : 83
Kahun : 305
Kailāsa : 128, 259, 260, 265, 325

Kailāsanatha temple : 328, 329, 330, 332
Kālidāsa : 89, 120, 121, 123, 124, 125, 126, 127, 153, 167, 169, 170, 171, 173, 209, 223, 224, 232, 233, 234, 239, 240, 241, 242, 243, 245, 250, 252, 260, 268, 322
Kalpa : 117, 119, 120, 121, 122, 123
Kalpānta : 121
Kalpa-periods : 122, 170
Kalyāṇa-maṇḍapa : 341
Kañcukas : 354
Kandārya Mahādeva : 332
Kane, P. V. : 171, 179
Karma : 178, 183
Karmadevas : 103, 167
Karmavipāka : 186
Karnak : 21, 27, 28, 29, 30, 31, 54, 57, 60, 61, 63, 81, 86, 88, 298, 299, 300, 301, 307, 309
Kāśī (Vārāṇaśī) : 142
Kassites : 196, 197, 198
Kaṭha Upaniṣad : 103, 104, 107, 132, 136, 138, 142, 143, 144, 146, 151, 171, 177, 184, 222, 224
Kauśītakībrāhmaṇa Upaniṣad : 102, 103, 106, 107, 109, 110, 135, 142, 170
Keith, A. B. : 5, 113, 167, 193, 194, 195, 202, 203, 206, 208, 209, 210, 214, 231
Kena Upaniṣad : 107, 146, 205, 260
Ketkar : 105, 135, 163, 172, 176, 177
Khafra : 59, 296, 297
Khemenu : 75
Khamuas : 54
Khāravela : 324, 327, 328
Khnemu : 55
Khonsu (chous) : 24, 27, 28, 300, 301, 306, 307, 308
Khufu : 85, 296
Kīrtana : 276
Konarak (Sun temple) : 332, 333
Koptos : 26, 31, 55
Koranganātha temple : 328, 329, 330
Kramer, S. N. : 1, 9, 18
Kremlin : 339
Krodha : 154, 159
Kṛṣṇa : 89, 93, 101, 103, 114, 117, 119, 120, 121, 128, 164, 170, 174, 186, 216, 223, 228, 232, 234, 238, 244, 248
Kṛṣṇaism : 235
Kṛṣṇadevaraja : 346
Kṛṣṇa-Viṣṇu : 260, 261, 262
Kulaparvatas : 123
Kumbhābhiṣekam : 343
Kuṇḍalinī : 156, 157
Kurukṣetra : 93

L

Lagash : 14
Lange and Hirmer : 31, 59, 297, 301, 302, 307
Laṅkā : 170
Libation : 8, 15
Life after death : 49, 64, 69
Liṅgarāja temple : 318, 328, 329, 333, 336
Liṅgāyat sect : 228, 248, 266
Logos : 202
Lokapālas : 181
Lokatraya : 117, 127
Ludlul bel Nemeqi : 16
Lugal-zaggisi : 11
Luxor : 300, 307

M

Maat : 50, 51, 52, 61, 66
Macdonell : 113, 129, 176, 192, 193, 194, 195, 199, 200, 201, 202, 203, 215, 231
Mahābhārata : 115, 116, 169, 174
Mahābhūtas : 10, 103, 108, 129, 134, 140
Mahākāla : 323
Mahān ātmā : 103, 118
Mahāpralaya : 123
Mahāviṣṇu : 157
Mahat : 122, 136
Mahat brahma : 125
Maheśa : 126, 127
Malegitti Śiva temple : 328
Mammalapuram : 329
Manas : 117, 118, 122, 123, 129, 136, 137, 138, 139, 140, 143, 144, 148, 149, 150, 151, 152, 156, 158, 178
Maṇḍapa : 327
Manikkavasagar : 245, 266
Mantrapuṣpa : 320
Manu : 118, 119, 120, 123, 164, 172, 173, 185, 269
Manu-period : 123
Manusmṛti : 116, 117, 118, 119, 120, 121, 124, 125, 126, 148, 163, 164, 166, 167, 175, 178, 181, 185, 187, 189, 238, 273, 281, 321
Manu Vaivasvata : 119
Manvantara : 119, 120
Marduk : 5, 6, 7, 8, 11, 16, 294
Mārīcas : 164

Mārtaṇḍa : 197
Maruttash : 196
Maṭha : 289
Mātrā : 130
Māyā : 121, 286
Medhā : 149, 152
Medinet Habu : 62, 68, 298
Megiddo : 30, 309
Memphis : 20, 54, 73, 74, 85, 86, 93, 300, 309
Memphite Theology : 72, 73, 74, 78, 83, 84, 85
Mena : 20
Menkaura : 58, 59, 296
Mentu : 25, 26, 28, 29, 31, 80
Mentu-hotep : 26
Merenptah : 305
Merodach-baladin : 15
Meru : 128
Mesopotamia : 129
Metempsychosis : 104
Meyer, Eduard : 3, 7
Min : 24, 25, 26, 28, 55, 80, 81, 87
Mīnākṣī temple : 317, 350
Mitannis : 196, 201
Mitra : 95, 197, 198
Mitrashshil : 196
Mitrāvaruṇau : 79
Moscow : 328, 339
Mother-goddess : 3
Mṛtyu : 101, 127, 177, 218
Mṛtyuloka : 117, 128
Mukha-maṇḍapa : 337
Mukteśvara temple : 324, 327
Mūlamāyā : 126
Mūlaprakṛti : 125
Müller, Max : 5
Mummification : 36
Muṇḍaka Up. : 104, 109, 114, 131, 138, 142, 144, 147, 205, 222, 224, 258
Murray, Margaret : 53, 61, 302, 303, 306
Mut : 24, 27, 31, 54, 80, 300, 301, 304, 306, 308, 311
Mylapore : 289
Mycerinus : 58, 296

N

Nabonidus : 17, 18, 293
Nabu : 16
Naciketas : 144, 151, 177, 222
Nammalvar : 246
Nana : 3, 4, 18
Nandimukha : 185
Nannar : 15, 58, 292, 293
Nara : 118
Nārāḥ : 118
Naraka : 105, 111, 117, 124, 128, 165, 176, 180
Nārāyaṇa : 118, 125, 126
Nāsadīya Sūkta : 204
Nāsatya : 95, 193, 196
Naṭeśa temple : 340
Nātha seet : 157
Navagvas : 163
Navalākhā temple : 332
Navavidhā bhakti : 319
Neb-matt-Ra : 22
Nebre : 71
Nebseni : 50
Nebuchadnezzar II : 17, 293, 294
Nefer-Tem : 21, 22
Neferohu : 48
Nekhebt : 27
Nephthys : 52
Nineveh : 3
Ningal : 293
Nin-gish-zida : 12
Ninkhursag : 1, 2
Ninkil : 1
Ninkurra : 2
Ninlil : 2
Nintud : 2, 3
Nippur : 2
Nirayapuri : 128
Nirguṇa Brahman : 250
Nirvāṇa : 161
Nubia : 28, 60, 61

O

Om : 238
Osiris : 21, 22, 23, 24, 26, 29, 32, 42, 44, 47, 49, 50, 51, 52, 53, 54, 55, 65, 70, 74, 88, 303

P

Pañcamahābhūtas : 122, 125, 126, 132, 149
Pañcāmṛta : 314, 320
Pāñcāyatana : 23
Pañcopacārapūjā : 317
Pantheism : 78
Pāpanātha temple : 328
Pāpman : 149
Parabrahma : 121, 125, 126

Pāralaukika : 166
Paraloka : 166
Paramātmā : 121, 125, 126
Paraśurāmeśvara temple : 324
Paratra : 166
Pāratrika : 166
Pārvatī : 240, 251
Pa-sag : 12, 16
Pātāla : 124, 127
Pepi I : 297, 307
Perrot : 56, 60, 300, 302
Petrie, Flinders : 55, 56, 57, 63, 68, 305
Phiops : 59
Pitṛloka : 105, 111
Pitṛs : 110, 111, 117
Pitṛyajña : 171
Pitṛyāṇa, 109, 110, 114
Prabhāta-pūjā : 314
Prajāpati : 100, 101, 102, 103, 104, 117, 119, 125, 143, 202, 207, 214, 215, 219, 238, 239
Prajñā : 149, 152
Prajñāna : 137
Prakṛti : 101, 117, 122, 126, 136, 149, 229
Pralaya : 117, 121
Premabhakti : 282
Prāṇa : 130, 131, 132, 133, 135, 138, 139, 140, 141, 150, 154, 155, 156
Prapañca : 176
Prasāda : 326
Praśna Up. : 104, 105, 109, 114, 130, 131, 135, 136, 138, 139, 140, 141, 142, 147, 205, 225
Primordial Being : 118, 135, 163, 207, 266
Ptah : 21, 22, 23, 24, 28, 30, 31, 54, 57, 59, 70, 73, 74, 76, 77, 79, 80, 83, 84, 86, 90, 92, 93, 300, 306, 309
Ptah-soker : 21, 22, 66
Ptolemy IX : 307
Purītat : 142
Puruṣa : 103, 134, 136, 144, 145, 146, 147, 191, 222, 226, 229
Puruṣottama : 216, 242, 249
Puryaṣṭaka : 178
Pūṣan : 162, 171, 192, 193, 195
Pyramid : 32, 40

Q

Qualified monism : 263

R

Ra : 24, 25, 30, 31, 32, 54, 55, 65, 70, 72, 73, 75, 86, 87, 92, 94, 300, 309
Rādhā : 249, 250
Radhakrishnan, S. : 130, 131, 221
Rājarāja : 345
Rajas : 127, 187
Rāma : 119, 157, 167, 168, 169, 170, 188, 253, 269, 284
Rāmadāsa : 113, 116, 121, 122, 124, 125, 126, 127, 154, 155, 158, 159, 160, 189, 234, 254, 255, 256
Rāmānuja : 147, 246, 263, 282
Rāmāyaṇa : 119, 122, 124, 127, 157, 167, 169, 188, 198, 209, 250, 251, 264, 341
Rameses II : 20, 28, 29, 31, 32, 57, 60, 65, 66, 71, 82, 93, 94, 299, 300, 309
Rameses III : 44, 61, 66, 68, 298, 299, 301, 307, 308
Rameses IV : 303
Rameses VI : 303
Rameses IX : 71
Rameses XI : 303
Rāmeśvaram (temple) : 312, 313, 317, 323
Ramkrishna Mission : 289, 294
Rāṇā Kumbha : 338
Raṅganātha temple : 346
Rayed Disc : 21
Ṛbhus : 210
Rebirth : 185, 186
Re-Harakhte : 21, 22, 71, 92
Reisner : 58
Religion, spiritualisation : 2, 71, 78, 85
Religious Consciousness, need for : 69, 70
Rene nut : 96
Renutet : 55
Ṛgveda : 7, 41, 50, 78, 91, 95, 101, 105, 109, 113, 114, 118, 125, 135, 145, 161, 191, 192, 199, 202, 215
Rheimes cathedral : 339
Rituals : 8, 13, 65-67, 96
Ṛta : 149
Rudra : 79, 90, 101, 164, 185, 195
Rudra-Śiva : 101, 117, 230, 236, 260, 265

S

Sabhā-maṇḍapa : 326, 337, 383
Saccidānanda : 251
Śacī : 195
Sadāśiva : 127
Sādhyas : 106, 164, 167
Saggs : 14, 15, 16, 18, 19, 292
Saguṇa-Brahman : 249
Śaivism : 49, 243, 265

Sakkarah : 22
Śakti : 49, 121
Sālajya : 108
Salvation : 128
Samara : 295
Sambandar : 245, 246
Saṁkalpa : 131, 132, 136, 138, 146, 149
Saṁkhya : 115, 122, 130, 274
Saṁsāra : 128, 176
Saṁyamana : 171
Sanatkumāra : 109, 131, 221, 222
Sandhyā-vandana : 280
Saṅgameśvara temple : 328
Śaṅkara : 147
Śaṅkarācārya : 115, 125, 150, 152, 153, 155, 181, 183, 223, 227, 250, 253, 262, 263, 286
Santāna : 169
Santānika : 167
Śānti : 116, 149
Sapiṇḍīkaraṇa : 179
Saptadvīpa : 123
Saptakañcuka : 122
Saptaraśmi : 123
Saptarṣi : 123
Saptaśatī : 323, 324
Sapta-sindhus : 123
Sarasvatī : 208
Śarayū : 169, 170, 209
Sargonid era : 3
Sāsbahū temple : 312
Sāṣṭāṅga praṇipāta : 322
Sat : 101
Śatarudrīya : 276
Sattva : 127
Sāttvika : 187
Satya : 98, 100, 107, 111
Satyaloka : 128
Sāvitrī : 90
Sāyaṇa : 204, 207, 321
Sekhmet : 22, 26, 31, 66, 306
Self-born Brahmā : 241
Self-sense 131
Senusret I : 21, 28, 48, 58, 61, 63, 71, 80, 81, 86, 297
Senusret III, 60, 63, 80, 81
Set : 82
Seti : 20, 21, 22, 23, 24, 29, 31, 52, 66, 297, 298, 301
Shamash, 3, 4, 5, 7, 9, 15, 201
Shay : 97
Shedit : 63
Sheshenk I : 61
Sheshonko I : 300, 301
Śhore temple : 328, 330
Shivaji : 234, 310
Shu : 74, 76, 79
Siddha 157
Śikhara : 326
Sinuhe : 71
Śītaleśvara temple 328
Śiva : 122, 126, 127
Śivagaṅgā : 340
Śoka : 149, 159
Solomon : 16
Soma : 79, 107, 191, 204
Somapās : 164
Śomnāthpura temple, 336
Śraddhā : 138, 149
Śrāddha : 171, 172, 174, 175, 185, 208
Śrīraṅgam temples : 354
Sṛti : 110, 114, 115
St. Basil : 339
Stella : 15
Stevenson, (Mrs.) Sinclair : 317, 318
Sthala-devatā : 12
Sthiradeva temple : 323
St. Peters : 301
Sudarśana : 90, 120
Sukha : 149, 153, 154
Sūkṣma : 178
Sundara Pāṇḍya, 345
Sundarar : 245
Supreme Being : 120
Supreme Creator : 120
Supreme Soul : 133, 136, 137, 145, 146 149, 157, 179, 180, 181, 185, 249, 255, 263
Surendraloka : 117
Sūrya : 91, 92
Suryash : 197
Suṣumṇā : 135, 136
Sutek : 82
Sutekh : 94
Svaḥ : 101
Svarga : 116, 117, 124, 127, 128, 165, 166, 167, 168, 169, 170, 180, 184, 189
Svargaloka : 107
Svargārohaṇa : 169
Svayambhu : 118
Śvetaketu Āruṇeya : 109, 110
Śvetāśvatara Upaniṣad : 90, 92, 101, 107, 133, 136, 138, 144, 146, 147, 151, 184, 218, 220, 222, 227, 230, 231, 258
Śvetavārāha : 120

T

Taittirīya Āraṇyaka : 105, 112, 113, 145
Taittirīya Upaniṣad, 104, 132, 138, 183, 205
Tamas : 127, 187
Tamilnad : 266
Tapas : 101, 111, 149
Ta-urt : 55
Tefnut : 74, 76, 79
Tejas : 130, 157
Temenos : 331
Temu : 73, 74
Teren : 93
Thanksgiving (Christian) : 140
Theban Triad : 301, 304, 307, 308
Thebes : 91, 298, 299
Thoth : 21, 23, 27, 28, 51, 55, 70, 73, 74, 75, 76, 78, 80, 87, 92
Thothmes I : 23, 26, 27, 303
Thothmes II : 309
Thothmes III : 27, 29, 30, 31, 42, 60, 61, 66, 86, 87, 304, 305, 306, 308
Thothmes IV : 29, 90, 91
Tiglathpileser I : 294
Tirqa : 16
Tirumalai Setupati : 316
Tirumal Nayak : 346
Tirupati : 318
Toraṇa : 325
Tower of Babel : 294
Trailokya : 127
Transmigration : 104, 126, 185, 186, 189
Tretā : 119
Triguṇa : 118
Triśanku : 113, 145, 169
Tryambaka : 258
Tuat : 53
Tukārāma : 89, 112, 253, 254, 290
Tulasīdāsa : 122, 124, 127, 156, 157, 169, 170, 189, 250, 252, 253, 254, 264, 283, 284
Tutankhamen : 21, 26, 29, 31, 47, 57, 60
Tvaṣṭṛ : 79

U

Ubaid : 1, 2, 291
Udāna : 134, 135, 141
Udayagiri Hills : 324
Udayeśvara temple : 332
Uddālaka Āruṇi : 109, 110, 226
Ultimate Reality : 226
Ummer : 11
Unas : 59
Universal Being : 145
Universal Self : 141
Upaniṣadic Cosmology : 133, 135
Upaniṣads : 129, 139, 152
Ur : 1, 4, 8, 10, 13, 15, 16, 291
Ur Nammu : 15, 293
Ursa : 123
Urukogina : 11
Uttararāmacarita : 127
Uttarāyaṇa : 114, 115, 116
Uttu : 2, 4

V

Vaikharī : 158
Vaikuṇṭha : 117, 128, 261, 265
Vaikuṇṭha Perumal : 329
Vairūpa : 163
Vaiṣṇava : 101, 117, 223
Vaiṣṇavism : 235, 243
Vaiśya : 118, 183, 187
Vaitāl Deul : 328
Vāk : 140 : 208
Vallabha : 147, 282
Vallabhācārya : 264
Valmīkeśvara temple : 350
Vālmīki : 119, 250, 268
Vāmadeva : 8, 107, 112, 113, 145, 168, 186, 229
Vāmana : 233
Vandana : 321
Vanaspati : 213
Vāṇī : 158
Varadarājasvāmi temple : 345
Vārāṇaśī : 122
Varṇa : 118
Varuṇa : 91, 92, 95, 103, 161, 162, 195, 196, 198, 200, 201, 202, 203
Vāsanā : 150
Vasiṣṭha : 153, 163, 164
Vāsudeva : 261
Vasus : 167, 185
Vatican : 300
Vāyu : 100, 103, 120, 126, 134, 155
Vedānta : 78, 113
Vedic Cosmology : 145
Vendome : 300
Vibhu : 108
Vibhūti : 316
Vibhūtiyoga : 288
Vicakṣaṇa : 108

Vicikitsā : 138, 149
Videha : 262
Vidṛti 9 141
Vidyādharas : 168
Vijñāna : 131, 132, 137, 138, 146, 149
Vijñānamaya : 138
Vijñātā : 138
Vimāna : 326, 327, 335
Virajā : 108
Vīrāsana : 65
Virāṭ (Virāj) : 118, 125, 126
Virgin Wife Cult : 3
Virūpākṣa temple : 328, 332
Viśākhadatta : 181
Viṣṇu : 89, 90, 117, 121, 122, 123, 126, 127, 128, 161, 195, 196, 232
Viṣṇusmṛti : 269, 272
Viśvakarman : 207, 214, 216
Viśvāmitra : 169, 192
Viśvedevas : 79
Viṭhoba : 89
Viṭhṭhal : 341
Vivasvat : 93
Viveka : 160
Vivekānanda : 289, 290
Vṛndāvan-Mathurā : 282-83
Vṛṣṇi : 93, 247
Vṛtta : 149
Vyāna : 135, 141
Vyavasāyātmikā : 152

W

White Temple : 1
Williams, Monier : 280, 317
Wilson, J. A. : 30, 39, 43, 45, 53, 55, 96
Woolley : 10, 13, 14, 16, 17, 19, 293
Worcester Cathedral : 329

X

Xerxes : 6, 207

Y

Yajña : 218
Yājñavalkya : 102, 109, 132, 135, 145, 172, 225, 226, 262, 263, 269
Yajurveda : 92, 101, 209, 276
Yakṣas : 118
Yama : 105, 114, 161, 162, 163, 180, 181, 208, 218
Yamas : 253
Yaśas : 149
Yāska : 105
Yaśovarman : 351
Yeṣṭiha movements : 108
Yoga : 115, 131, 139, 278, 279
Yoga-attitudes : 151
Yoga-vāsiṣṭha : 153
Yogín : 115
Yoni : 126
Ypet : 307
Yudhiṣṭhira : 169
Yuga : 117, 120, 121
Yuktāhāra : 281

Z

Zagros : 3
Zend-Avesta : 193, 197
Ziggurat : 291, 292, 293, 294, 295
Zinsudra : 292
Zoroaster : 199